Fifty Years of *Rhetoric*

Fifty Years of Rhetoric Society Quarterly: *Selected Readings, 1968–2018* celebrates the semicentennial of *Rhetoric Society Quarterly*, bringing together the most influential essays included in the journal over the past fifty years. Assessed by members of the Rhetoric Society of America, this collection provides advanced undergraduate and graduate students with a balanced perspective on rhetorical theory and practice from scholars in both communication studies and rhetoric and writing studies. The volume covers a range of themes, from the history of rhetorical studies, writing and speaking pedagogy, and feminism, to the work of Kenneth Burke, the rhetoric of science, and rhetorical agency.

Joshua Gunn is Associate Professor of Communication Studies and Affiliate Faculty with the Department of Rhetoric and Writing at the University of Texas at Austin, USA. He has published a scholarly monograph, a public speaking textbook, and over seventy-five essays and chapters on the topics of rhetoric, media, and cultural studies.

Diane Davis is Professor and Chair of the Department of Rhetoric and Writing and Affiliate Faculty with Communication Studies at the University of Texas at Austin, USA. Her work is situated at the intersection of rhetorical theory and continental philosophy.

Fifty Years of *Rhetoric Society Quarterly*

Selected Readings, 1968–2018

Edited by
Joshua Gunn and Diane Davis

Routledge
Taylor & Francis Group

NEW YORK AND LONDON

First published 2018
by Routledge
711 Third Avenue, New York, NY 10017

and by Routledge
2 Park Square, Milton Park, Abingdon, Oxon, OX14 4RN

Routledge is an imprint of the Taylor & Francis Group, an informa business

Library of Congress Cataloging-in-Publication Data
Names: Gunn, Joshua, 1973– editor. | Davis, D. Diane (Debra Diane),
    1963– editor. | Rhetoric Society of America History.
Title: Fifty years of Rhetoric Society Quarterly : selected readings,
    1968–2018 / [edited by] Joshua Gunn, Diane Davis.
Description: New York, NY : Routledge, 2018.
Identifiers: LCCN 2017055886 | ISBN 9781138086708 (hardcover) |
    ISBN 9781138086715 (softcover) | ISBN 9781315108889 (ebook)
Subjects: LCSH: Communication—Research. | Rhetoric—Research. |
    Discourse analysis—Research.
Classification: LCC P87 .F43 2018 | DDC 302.2/0721—dc23
LC record available at https://lccn.loc.gov/2017055886

ISBN: 978-1-138-08670-8 (hbk)
ISBN: 978-1-138-08671-5 (pbk)
ISBN: 978-1-315-10888-9 (ebk)

Typeset in Minion Pro
by Apex CoVantage, LLC

This volume is dedicated, with much gratitude, to the past, present, and future editors of RSQ. If we continue to hear and see better, it is by clinging to the ears and standing on the shoulders of giants.

Contents

Contributors   xi

Acknowledgments   xv

1   Introduction: *RSQ's* Greatest Hits!   1
    JOSHUA GUNN AND DIANE DAVIS

I   The Early Years (1968–1989)   **11**

2   Rules, Conventions, Constraints, and Rhetorical Action   15
    GEORGE E. YOOS

3   Composition Then and Now   24
    HANS P. GUTH

4   General Specialists: Fifty Years Later   32
    EVERETT LEE HUNT

II   The Nineties (1990–1999)   **41**

5   Re/Dressing Histories; Or, on Re/Covering Figures Who Have
    Been Laid Bare by Our Gaze   45
    MICHELLE BALLIF

6   Kenneth Burke Among the Moderns: *Counter-Statement* as
    Counter Statement   54
    JACK SELZER

7   Rhetorical Criticism of Public Discourse on the Internet:
    Theoretical Implications   82
    BARBARA WARNICK

8   Aristotle on Epideictic: The Formation of Public Morality   94
    GERARD A. HAUSER

III   The Naughts (2000–2009)   **113**

9   Feminist Methods of Research in the History of Rhetoric:
    What Difference Do They Make?   119
    PATRICIA BIZZELL

10 Forum Discussion on Agency   131
CHERYL GEISLER, CHRISTIAN LUNDBERG AND JOSHUA GUNN

*How Ought We to Understand the Concept of Rhetorical
Agency? Report From the ARS   131*
CHERYL GEISLER

*"Ouija Board, Are There Any Communications?" Agency,
Ontotheology, and the Death of the Humanist Subject, or,
Continuing the ARS Conversation   139*
CHRISTIAN LUNDBERG AND JOSHUA GUNN

*Teaching the Postmodern Rhetor: Continuing the Conversation
on Rhetorical Agency   158*
CHERYL GEISLER

11 Unframing Models of Public Distribution: From Rhetorical
Situation to Rhetorical Ecologies   165
JENNY EDBAUER (RICE)

12 What Can Automation Tell Us About Agency?   183
CAROLYN R. MILLER

13 Between Archive and Participation: Public Memory in a
Digital Age   201
EKATERINA HASKINS

14 Identification: Burke and Freud on Who You Are   221
DIANE DAVIS

IV   *RSQ Lately (2010–Present)*   243

15 "This Is Your Brain on Rhetoric": Research Directions
for Neurorhetorics   247
JORDYNN JACK AND L. GREGORY APPELBAUM

16 The Mock Rock *Topos*   276
MICHELE KENNERLY

17 *Parrēsia*, Foucault, and the Classical Rhetorical Tradition   301
ARTHUR E. WALZER

18 Deep Ambivalence and Wild Objects: Toward a Strange
Environmental Rhetoric   322
NATHANIEL A. RIVERS

19 Exigencies for *RSQ*: An Afterword   343
    RYAN SKINNELL AND MAUREEN DALY GOGGIN

    Index   357

Contributors

Greg Appelbaum is an Assistant Professor in the Department of Psychiatry at the Duke University School of Medicine, USA. He is director of the Brain Stimulation Center and head of the OptiLab where his research addresses neuroplasticity and human performance optimization that can be achieved through behavioral, neurofeedback, and neuromodulation interventions.

Michelle Ballif, Professor of English at the University of Georgia, USA, Associate Editor of *Rhetoric Society Quarterly* for Special Issues, and most recently, editor of *Theorizing Histories of Rhetoric* (SIUP), investigates rhetorical theory and historiography as complicated by the distinctions between the living and the dead, the timely from the untimely.

Patricia Bizzell is Distinguished Professor of English at Holy Cross, USA. Recent publications include a history of Jesuit rhetoric in *Traditions of Eloquence* (Fordham, 2016) and a study of English language instruction in South Korea in *Crossing Divides* (U.P. of Colorado, forthcoming). Recent honors include the 2016–2017 Cardin Chair, Loyola University-Maryland.

Diane Davis is Professor and Chair of the Department of Rhetoric and Writing and Affiliate Faculty with Communication Studies at the University of Texas at Austin, USA. Her work is situated at the intersection of rhetorical theory and continental philosophy.

Cheryl Geisler is Professor of Interactive Arts and Technology at Simon Fraser University, USA, is a recognized expert on verbal data coding. She recently edited a special section of the *Journal of Writing Research* on Current and Emerging Methods in the Rhetorical Analysis of Texts. In 2014, Rhetoric Society of America created the Cheryl Geisler Mentorship Award in recognition of her work on Career Retreats for Associate Professors.

Maureen Daly Goggin, Professor of Rhetoric at Arizona State University, USA, is author, editor, and co-editor of nine scholarly books and a textbook. Her latest forthcoming work titled *Serendipity in Rhetoric, Writing, and Literacy Research* is co-edited with Peter N. Goggin. She is also co-editing with Shirley Rose *Women's Ways of Making*.

Joshua Gunn is Associate Professor of Communication Studies and Affiliate Faculty with the Department of Rhetoric and Writing at the University of Texas at Austin, USA. He's published a scholarly monograph, a public speaking textbook, and over seventy-five essays and chapters on the topics of rhetoric, media, and cultural studies.

Hans P. Guth is Professor Emeritus of the Department of English and Comparative Literature at San Jose State University in California, USA.

Ekaterina Haskins is Professor of Rhetoric at Rensselaer Polytechnic Institute, USA. She is the author of *Logos and Power in Isocrates and Aristotle* (2004) and *Popular Memories: Commemoration, Participatory Culture, and Democratic Citizenship* (2015). She has published numerous essays on the history of rhetoric, public memory, and visual culture.

Gerard A. Hauser is Professor Emeritus of Communication at the University of Colorado Boulder, USA. He has received NCA's Nichols Book Award and Winans-Wichelns Book Award, and RSA's Distinguished Book Award. He is an NCA Distinguished Scholar and RSA Fellow, Editor Emeritus of *Philosophy and Rhetoric*, and a past President of RSA.

Everett Lee Hunt was a major voice in the field of Speech, a Professor of English and Public Speaking, and Dean Emeritus at Swarthmore College, USA.

Jordynn Jack is Professor of English and Comparative Literature at the University of North Carolina, Chapel Hill, USA, where she teaches rhetorical theory, rhetoric of science, and women's rhetorics. She is former Director of the Writing Program at UNC and currently co-directs a Health Humanities lab and Master's degree program. Her books include *Science on the Home Front: American Women Scientists in World War II* (University of Illinois Press, 2009), *Autism and Gender: From Refrigerator Mothers to Computer Geeks* (University of Illinois Press, 2015; winner of the Rhetoric Society of America Book Award in 2016). Her articles have appeared in journals such as *College English*, *College Composition and Communication*, *Quarterly Journal of Speech*, *Rhetoric Society Quarterly*, and *Rhetoric Review*.

Michele Kennerly is an Assistant Professor of Communication Arts and Sciences at Penn State University, USA. She is the author of *Editorial Bodies: Perfection and Rejection in Ancient Rhetoric and Poetics* (2018) and co-editor with Damien Smith Pfister of *Ancient Rhetorics and Digital Networks* (2018).

Christian Lundberg is an Associate Professor of Rhetoric and Cultural Studies at the University of North Carolina at Chapel Hill, USA. His research engages the intersection of public culture, rhetorical theory, and contemporary critical theory, with a specific focus on questions of enjoyment in public life.

Carolyn R. Miller is SAS Institute Distinguished Professor of Rhetoric and Technical Communication, Emerita, at North Carolina State University, USA. She is a Fellow and former President of the Rhetoric Society of America and former editor of *Rhetoric Society Quarterly*. Her interests include genre studies, rhetorical theory, and rhetoric of science and technology.

Jenny Edbauer (Rice) is an Associate Professor of Writing, Rhetoric, and Digital Studies at the University of Kentucky in Lexington, USA. Her work had been published in such journals as *Philosophy and Rhetoric*, *College English*, *Quarterly Journal of Speech*, and *College Composition and Communication*.

Nathaniel A. Rivers is Associate Professor of English at Saint Louis University, USA. His current research addresses topics such as environmentalism, locative media, and accessibility. He co-edited *Thinking with Bruno Latour in Rhetoric and Composition* (SIUP, 2015). His recent work has appeared in journals such as *RSQ*, *enculturation*, and *QJS*.

Jack Selzer is retiring in 2018 as Paterno Family Liberal Arts Professor at Penn State, USA. In addition to collaborating with his colleagues over the years on respected graduate and undergraduate programs, he served RSA as president from 2008–2009. His recent publications have mainly been devoted to Kenneth Burke.

Ryan Skinnell is an Assistant Professor of Rhetoric and Composition at San Jose State University, USA, where he teaches rhetoric and writing. He is the author of *Conceding Composition: A Crooked History of Composition's Institutional Fortunes* (USUP, 2016) and co-editor of *What We Wish We'd Known: Negotiating Graduate School* (Fountainhead, 2015).

Arthur E. Walzer, Professor Emeritus, Communication Studies, University of Minnesota, USA, has published a monograph on George Campbell and co-edited collections on the rhetorical tradition and on Aristotle's *Rhetoric*. His critical edition of works on counsel by Thomas Elyot will be published by Brill. He is editor of *Advances in the History of Rhetoric*.

Barbara Warnick is Chair Emeritus of the Department of Communication at the University of Pittsburgh, USA.

George E. Yoos was the first editor of *Rhetoric Society Quarterly*. He is Professor Emeritus of the Philosophy Department at State Cloud State University in Minnesota, USA.

Acknowledgments

The idea for this anniversary volume grew out of RSA board meeting discussions about how we might celebrate the fiftieth anniversary of our society and journal. It was decided that a special issue of *Rhetoric Society Quarterly*, edited by Michelle Ballif, would re-investigate major concepts and themes in a series of commissioned essays penned by RSA members, and that yours truly would edit a companion volume—a little ditty by Josh and Diane—of *RSQ*'s "Greatest Hits." The seventeen essays collected here should give readers a sense of the teaching and research interests of the membership over time, as well as index those essays that members believe have had a significant impact or helped to advance a particular agenda.

Special thanks to Dave Tell for advocating the project and keeping us on track. Essays selected for the volume were chosen using four different measures (further elaborated in the Introduction). One of those measures consisted of interviews and with past leaders of the society, *RSQ* editors, and a number of field historians. These include: Michelle Ballif; Karlyn Kohrs Campbell; Greg Clark; Sharon Crowley; Rosa Eberly; Richard Enos; Eugene Garver; Maureen Daly Goggin; Jerry Hauser; David Henry; Susan Jarratt, Jim Jasinski; Philip Keith; Joan Faber McAlister; Carolyn R. Miller; Kendall R. Phillips; Ryan Skinnell; Dave Tell; Jeff Walker; James D. Williams; Victor Vitanza; and David Zarefsky. We reserve an extra-special shout-out to Ryan and Maureen for agreeing to write the Afterword and for keeping our own writing in check (that is, they ate and rated the whole enchilada). Mad props are owed to Brian Sharkey Vaught for the excellent cover art and design, and to Michelle Kennerly and Carly S. Woods for inspiring the cover conception by moving *Rhetorica* farther and further. Finally, we appreciate the good cheer and careful guidance of Laura Briskman and Nicole Salazar at Routledge for helping us to better row the quackers.

1
Introduction
RSQ's *Greatest Hits!*

JOSHUA GUNN AND DIANE DAVIS

Lobbying, Minneapolis, 1968

The silver-haired Nelson J. Smith was apparently a dapper fellow. On a chilly April day in 1968, the well-spoken, mustachioed man worked the lobby to make more than an acquaintance; he hunted bedfellows. Spying Ross Winterowd, who was waiting in a line to check into the conference hotel, Smith approached with aplomb, jovially introduced himself, and thereby wrangled a roommate.[1] The meeting of these two pedagogues would result in the creation of the scholarly journal we know today as *Rhetoric Society Quarterly*—but not for a decade, not without booze, and certainly not without the dedicated support of many lovers of rhetoric, especially the guiding hand of a Minnesota philosopher named Yoos.

English professors Smith and Winterowd were attending the 19th Annual Conference on College Composition and Communication in Minneapolis (the 4Cs or simply, "the Cs"), which originally began as a joint meeting between members of the Speech Association of America (SAA) and the National Council of Teachers of English (NCTE) in 1947.[2] Ennobled by Harvard University's endorsement of a civically minded commitment to general education in the postwar period,[3] a hybrid of public speaking and writing instruction dubbed the "communications course" was rapidly incorporated into general education curricula across the country, thus promising to reunite speech and writing teachers with a renewed, pastoral purpose.[4] Although intended to ally and coordinate teachers of the emergent hybrid course, unfortunately the '47 fellowship fizzled.[5] Nor would the interdepartmental dream of a hybrid skills course endure, at least in part because of institutional pressures to achieve scholarly legitimacy through "specialization."[6] Regardless, two years later an annual conference on basic *writing* instruction was catalyzed by discussions at the '47 postwar revival, which is why the 4Cs retains "communication" in name even though an attention to speaking and listening skills in English departments would be muted by century's end.[7]

The institutional imperative for legitimacy through specialization and the identification of some object domain—often in tandem with a sanctioned methodology—was and remains hegemonic in higher education.[8] Disciplines emerge, expand, and collapse in struggles and debates over their titular objects and methods, but first comes the provision of an object domain and the cultivation of a common interest, and then an assembly of these into canons and organs (and sometimes departments). And so it was with "rhetorical studies" and between the brand-new, bosom bunkies Smith and Winterowd, whose burgeoning interest in a formal academic society was likely catalyzed, either directly or indirectly, by Wayne Booth's now-canonical clarion call to English teachers just four years prior.

Evangelizing Rhetoric

Three years after the publication of his profoundly influential tome *The Rhetoric of Fiction*, at the 1964 meeting of the Modern Language Association in New York, Wayne Booth proclaimed that

> in a rhetorical age[,] rhetorical studies should have a major, respected place in the training of all teachers at all levels; . . . specialization in rhetorical studies of all kinds, narrow and broad, should carry at least as much professional respectability as literary history or as literary criticism in non-rhetorical modes.[9]

Of course, Booth's admonition was designed to challenge a perceived hierarchy of souls within English departments that would swap out Plato's reigning philosopher with the professor of literature, and that of the lowly sophist with the service course instructor. Around the same time of Booth's rhetorical studies manifesto, comedian Rodney Dangerfield was busy establishing his self-depreciating catchphrase on television talk shows: "I get no respect!"[10] Dangerfield's lament is an apt rap for the *perceived* climate for writing and speech instruction in the early twentieth century, a perception that led many teachers of "oral English," public speaking, or simply "speech," to leave the NCTE in 1914 to establish their own association, journals, and departments,[11] many in pursuit of the esteem and resources with which the social sciences were and are rewarded.[12]

Regardless, over the course of the '68 Cs, Winterowd and Smith "talked almost interminably (and drank almost as interminably)" about rhetoric and formally organizing the congeries of instructors who professed similar interests into a society.[13] Winterowd and Smith were not alone in their ambition; they were in Minneapolis at the behest of John Carter Rowland of New York State University at Fredonia, who invited them and more than a dozen others from English and Speech departments—including Wayne Booth, the philosopher Henry Johnstone, Jr., and public address pioneer Donald C. Bryant—to a workshop dedicated to working-through the "revival" of rhetoric Booth had been trumpeting, variously termed the "new rhetoric" or "modern rhetoric" at the time.[14] The workshop helped to mix the batter for a tasty cake of US rhetoricians, but it didn't really set until the dashing Nelson, who "had a flair for organizing and, in the best sense, promotion," whipped up a newsletter and started demanding dues.[15] The *Newsletter of the Rhetoric Society of America* helped to conjure, at least in the minds of interested parties, the presence of a society with the rhetorical magic of simply asserting there was such a thing on paper: Abracadabra! Cake![16]

Although the actual date of publication is unclear,[17] Smith opened the first mimeographed newsletter, dated December 1968, with an invitation: "With the arrival of this newsletter the organization of the Rhetoric Society of America is announced to you. Your name has come to our mailing list from lists submitted by members of our board of directors"—the attendees of the '68 workshop, of course. "You are herewith invited to full membership in the Rhetoric Society," the name of which, Smith notes parenthetically, "is merely provisional."[18] In the two page document Smith explains that the new society "consists of scholars from many different disciplines and sub-disciplines, all of whom are interested in the use of language, and the nature of language in use." Smith then outlines the principles and purposes of the new society, which include the "dissemination" of knowledge about rhetoric, the sponsoring of programs at MLA and the 4Cs, and the encouragement of "direct implementations of, experiments in, and research into the implementations of rhetoric in composition, speech, and communication courses."[19] In this rather informal and low-tech manner, what we know today as the Rhetoric Society of America and its chief organ, *Rhetoric Society Quarterly*, came to be.

The fledgling fraternity—and the academy in general—proved a bit too low tech for Nelson, who "appeared like a comet in the sky of the discipline and vanished just as rapidly," reports Winterowd.[20] After briefly chairing an English department in Connecticut, expressing a bitter disenchantment with unmotivated students and educational politics, Nelson traded his typewriter for a tape recorder and started a "tutor cassette" company (Mediasmith),[21] as if to leave the society scribeless for an affair with microphones.

Then provisional RSA president Rowland called the group together again at the 1969 Cs in Miami for a publisher-sponsored cocktail party, ostensibly to ruminate on the lead essay of Johnstone's new journal, *Philosophy & Rhetoric* (it was a modest essay by Speech professor Lloyd F. Bitzer titled, "The Rhetorical Situation").[22] Winterowd recalls, however, that those attending mostly discussed the "future of our group, for at that point, there was little organization, just a bunch of eager, interested rhetoricians wanting to maintain contact."[23] In an effort to keep the gang going, Winterowd began drafting a constitution for the society—a project taken up later by Richard L. Larson—and managed to eke out an issue of the newsletter in September 1971. Even so, during these years the society languished.[24] Larson published the only newsletter in 1972, wherein RSA "Board Chair" Edward P. J. Corbett of Ohio State "reactivated" the organ and declared "The Rhetoric Society of America (RSA) is alive and kicking once again."[25] By most accounts, however, the newsletter did not mature until a recently minted philosophy professor at St. Cloud State University in Minnesota was appointed editor in 1971. His name was and remains George E. Yoos.

As rhetorical historian Maureen Daly Goggin explains, during its infancy the Rhetoric Society of America "might have well expired by 1970" were it not for the "intense commitment of the original members to keep the organization alive."[26] She explains that what "ultimately saved the RSA and its journal" in the 1970s was the constitution and the editorship of Yoos at *RSQ*. Yoos used *RSQ* somewhat like Mina Harker used her typewriter in Bram Stoker's *Dracula*: it functioned as the beating heart or central organ that kept rhetorical information in circulation, making the society stronger primarily through the cultivation of a deeper sense of self-awareness and common commitment. Gradually the newsletter would transform from a repository for announcements, musings, bibliographies, and book reviews into a full-fledged, peer-reviewed research journal.

The early pages of our society's central organ make for fascinating insights into the formative psyche of an interdisciplinary field that deliberately tried to exist outside of departmental and disciplinary constraints. For reasons that have more to do with space and cost, however, most of the essays collected in this volume reflect the post-1980, peer-reviewed era after the newsletter had completely metamorphosed from mimeographed pages to a bound and typeset journal.

In celebration of the society's anniversary, then, *Fifty Years of* Rhetoric Society Quarterly: *Selected Readings, 1968–2018* presents seventeen choice cuts from the archived record. We have three primary objectives with the collection: (1) to gather the best or most influential scholarship published in the journal in one volume, (2) to provide an indirect history of field of rhetorical studies through its scholarship, and (3) to create a collection that can be used as an introduction to the journal, the society, and the field that has decidedly eschewed any one departmental home.

The short introductions to each of the four, chronologically arranged sections of the collection will provide additional but brief historical context for the essays they organize. For the remainder of our general introduction to the book, we explain the rationale of the collection, how the essays were selected, and the reason for their present configuration.

The Title That Almost Was: A Rationale for Cultivation

At the behest of the governing board of RSA, Dave Tell of the University of Kansas approached the editors in the spring of 2016 and asked us to cultivate a collection of the "best" essays that have been published in *Rhetoric Society*

Quarterly. He explained that this book collection complements a sister volume in the form of a special, anniversary issue of the journal edited by Michelle Ballif of the University of Georgia (volume 48, third issue). *Fifty Years* is thus intended to showcase the journal's primary, prized essays, while the special issue features a number of rhetorical scholars enjoined to investigate, survey, and re-imagine concepts that have been central to the journal's scholarship. For us, then, the challenge of cultivating a "best of" companion collection is more historical and reputational than conceptual, balancing the demands of an inevitably revisionist historical imperative with something like a useful map. Our charge is not to provide a history of the association vis-à-vis the journal; Goggin has already done this.[27] Nor is our *primary* task to detail the scholarly agendas of the past or to advance some for the future; Ballif's edited special issue of *RSQ* does this. Our goal, rather, is classically epideictic and functionally pragmatic: to provide some semblance of the contours of the rhetorical studies community by looking at our labor and noticing what kind of interdisciplinary tunes we have been repeatedly reading and citing—or dancing to!

Contrary to collections of its kind, however, we were less interested in producing something like a Whitman Zeitgeist Sampler, if only because of the inevitable, tiresome truffles and tedious treacle that no one enjoys but has to eat to be polite (except, perhaps, your beloved and cultured Auntie Quarian). Outside of the consensus of the membership over what essays should be included, we exercised some veto power to eliminate essays on redundant topics, and tried to craft a volume without by-products or empty calories.

Owing its chronicled and cultivated character, while completing this volume we had music collections in mind, something more akin to a K-tel compilation record album, the "as seen on TV" LPs that were a common feature in K-Mart music departments in the '70s and '80s (which also happens to be the formative years of *RSQ*!). Outside of film soundtracks, the K-tel company was among the first to devise records comprised of music artists from different record labels, somewhat unwittingly inspiring the practice of teens perched at cassette decks waiting to record favored songs on the radio in pursuit of the perfect mixtape.[28] Our working title for *Fifty Years* was actually "*RSQ's* Greatest Hits!" in part to suggest Communication, English, Philosophy, and Speech are akin to record labels that may economically and institutionally enable and constrain scholars, but which have not and cannot contain the pursuit and study of rhetoric, broadly construed. Still, some of our reviewers and the publisher worried such a title lacked class.

Yet, the proletarian connotation of "*RSQ's* Greatest Hits!" was also partly the reason for the working title, as even the most cursory review of the journal tracks an early anxiety of legitimacy gradually giving way to increasingly insightful, well-researched scholarship, no doubt reflecting the growing, robust membership of RSA. In the end we developed a more straightforward title for a sense of inclusion and as an invitation to those readers new to rhetorical studies and the society.

The Nitty Gritty Dirt Plan: Selection and Organization

With the exception of Part 1, most of *Fifty Years of* Rhetoric Society Quarterly collects essays from the quasi-peer-reviewed era to the full-blown peer-reviewed status of the journal beginning roughly in 1981. Limiting the selection to thirty-seven years of scholarship still proved daunting, however, as the pool still consisted of hundreds of essays. To help narrow and cultivate our selection, we devised a survey for the RSA membership using the Qualtrics data collection software licensed by our university, which was distributed to the participants, on a voluntary basis, using the society's email list, website, and Facebook page in the spring and summer of 2016. Participants were asked to identify essays that were influential in establishing or changing research agendas in the field, essays that were important to their own scholarship, and essays that they routinely assigned to their undergraduate and graduate courses. The results of our survey identified sixteen top essays, with four receiving almost overwhelming support.[29]

Unfortunately, the survey results had a marked recency effect and neglected almost any mention of essays, articles, or bibliographies published in the 1968–2000 period. Consequently, we elected to poll all (living) previous editors of the journal and presidents of RSA, as well as interview a number of well-known, disciplinary historians (the names of whom are mentioned in the Acknowledgments). This approach yielded a robust list of sixty-five "important" essays prior to 2000, which we reduced to ten based on those most frequently mentioned. It is at this juncture where our editorial judgment most actively intervened: we combined the "newer" surveyed list of sixteen with the older, poll- and interview-based list *and then* cross-referenced them with Taylor & Francis's "most cited" and "most read" records, which thankfully provided a remarkable consistency across all four measures. The result was a twenty-essay list of top essays, which unfortunately was still too long given the space constraints specified by the publisher. Our most pointed intervention as editors, then, was to eliminate three of these essays on the basis of thematic redundancy. For example, two of the top twenty essays concerned the rhetorical theory of Kenneth Burke; we eliminated one of them because the other seemed more synoptic and useful to the readership than the other. Admittedly, the selection process was far from scientific; our editorial labor is perhaps better compared to that of disc jockeys, like Daft Punk surveying the dance floor, noticing what seems to be getting butts and mouths moving, and then trying to throw down choice beats.

We should mention that the selection process, however, presented the editors with one final, tricky pickle: three of the essays that the membership selected in our primary survey were authored or co-authored by us. Eliminating one of these editor-authored essays was relatively easy because of the redundancy criterion we had used to eliminate other essays. But what of the remaining two, one by each of us? We asked a number of board members and colleagues in the field about whether or not we should eliminate our own essays from the collection because of a perceived conflict of interest. The consensus was that we should include our own essays in the collection because they were, in fact, determined by the membership and among the top four in the survey. Even so, we remain ambivalent about their inclusion and leave it to readers to decide whether our decision to include them was sound.

The organization of the essays was overdetermined by the epideictic and anniversarial spirit of the collection: a chronological pattern, instead of a thematic one, seemed the better route because it allows readers to glean a sense of how the mission and scholarship of the journal gradually evolved over the past five decades. We considered adding an alternative table of contents that would suggest a thematic arrangement of essays, but in the end we determined that the essays were so varied in interest, scope, and specialization that whatever alternative organization we developed could be met with objection, depending on one's scholarly vantage and institutional affiliation. In lieu of an alternative table of contents, we note that over the course of fifty years a number of conceptual interest-clusters emerged:

- What constitutes a discipline or field of "rhetoric?" The relationship between rhetoric in Speech, English, and Philosophy.
- The history of speech and writing pedagogy and composition.
- An investment in ancient rhetorical theory, especially Aristotle.
- An obsession with the theories of Kenneth Burke.
- A pioneering and robust commitment to feminism and feminist scholarship.
- A confrontation with poststructuralism and posthumanism.
- A sustained engagement with electronic and digital rhetorics.
- Rhetorics of science, health, and health campaigns.
- And more recently, an interest in public memory and environmental rhetoric.

Of course, these themes do not exhaust all of those encountered in our review of the hundreds of essays that were published in *Rhetoric Society Quarterly*, but barring a sustained content analysis, these are the ones that we observed recurring.

Readers will notice the themes above are represented in the four sections that comprise the collection. Organized roughly chronologically, "Part 1: The Early Years (1968–1989)," collects three, non-peer reviewed, solicited essays that reflect the concerns and interests of the membership moving from self-consciousness as an interest group and quasi-social society toward an increasingly scholarly one; during this period *RSQ* was predominately— although not exclusively—identified with rhetoricians affiliated with English departments. "Part II: The '90s (1990–1999)" collects four essays that showcase the emergence of a dedicated, scholarly pursuit of rhetorical studies that actively intones a cross-disciplinary commitment, bringing scholars together from across the English, Speech, and Communication disciplines. Notably, this period also marks a moment in which feminist scholarship became a conspicuously dominant and welcome theme for the journal. "Part III: The Naughts (2000–2009)" collects the largest number of essays in the collection, indexing a robust engagement with *theory*, as well as a renewed commitment to interdisciplinarity invigorated by the largest agenda-setting meeting of US rhetoricians to date, the Alliance of Rhetorical Societies meeting at Northwestern University in the fall of 2003. The introduction to this section will more fully detail the profound import of this conference to RSA and *RSQ* and how both reinforced and changed the mission and scholarship of RSA members. Finally, "Part IV: *RSQ* lately (2010–Present)" collects a four notable essays of recent interest, three of which attest to an investment in "new" materialisms.

Because the editors of *Fifty Years* work predominantly in the areas of rhetorical theory and criticism, we recognize our limitations as skilled archivists and historians. To help us provide a more accurate and robust historical and institutional context for the essays collected here, we note that we relied heavily on the archival work of a number of field historians, especially James Berlin, Herman Cohen, Pat Gehrke, and William Keith. To this end, we sought to add balance to the volume by approaching two rhetorical historians active in our society, Ryan Skinnell and Maureen Daly Goggin, who graciously agreed to pen the epilogue.

Notes

1 W. Ross Winterowd, "Fragments of History, Personal and Institutional," *Visions and Revisions: Continuity and Change in Rhetoric and Composition*, ed. James Dale Williams (Carbondale: Southern Illinois UP, 2002), 36.

2 James A. Berlin, *Rhetoric and Reality: Writing Instruction in American Colleges, 1900–1985* (Carbondale: Southern Illinois UP, 1987), 105.

3 A similar mission was well underway in speech departments after the First World War; see William M. Keith, *Democracy as Discussion: Civic Education and the American Forum Movement* (New York: Lexington Books, 2007).

4 We say "reunited" because teachers of "Oral English" formally left the NCTE in 1914 to form the National Association of the Academic Teachers of Public Speaking, leading to the rapid formation of "Speech" departments. See Pat J. Gehrke and William M. Keith, *A Century of Communication Studies: The Unfinished Conversation* (New York: Routledge, 2015), 3–6; Herman Cohen, *The History of Speech Communication: The Emergence of a Discipline, 1914–1945* (Annandale: Speech Communication Association, 1994), 29–84; also see Berlin, *Rhetoric and Reality*, 93–94. For insightful accounts of the emergence of the communications course, see Berlin, *Rhetoric and Reality*, 92–119; and Sharon Crowley, *Composition in the University: Historical and Polemical Essays* (Pittsburgh: U of Pittsburgh P, 1998), 155–86. For an astute discussion of the function of pastoral power in the speech classroom, see Darrin Hicks, "The New Citizen," *Quarterly Journal of Speech* 93 (2007): 358–60; and Ronald Walter Greene and Darrin Hicks, "Lost Convictions: Debating Both Sides and the Ethical Self-Fashioning of Liberal Citizens," *Cultural Studies* 19 (2005): 100–26.

5 Berlin, *Rhetoric and Reality*, 105.

6 The push toward specialization—often in the name of knowledge-production—was particularly pronounced in the formation of the field of speech in the 1910s and 1920s, most conspicuously in debates between Charles H. Woolbert (who championed scientism) and Everett Lee Hunt (who championed "general specialism" and pragmatic curiosity). See Everett Lee Hunt, "General Specialists," *Quarterly Journal of Public Speaking* 2 (1916): 252–63; Theodore Otto Windt, Jr., "Everett Lee Hunt and the Humanistic Spirit of Rhetoric," *Twentieth-Century Roots of Rhetorical Studies*, ed. Jim A. Kuypers and Andrew King (Westport: Praeger, 2001), 1–30; and Charles H. Woolbert, "A Problem in Pragmatism," *Quarterly Journal of Public Speaking* 2 (1916): 265–74.

7 Perhaps encouraged by the success of the deferred dream realized by RSA, there have been more recent calls to hasten hybridity once again; see William Keith and Roxanne Mountford, "The Mt. Oread Manifesto on Rhetorical Education 2013," *Rhetoric Society Quarterly* 44 (2014): 1–5.

8 For the example of the field of "speech," see Joshua Gunn and Frank E. X. Dance, "The Silencing of Speech in the Late Twentieth Century," *A Century of Communication Studies: The Unfinished Conversation*, ed. Pat J. Gehrke and William M. Keith (New York: Routledge, 2015), 64–81.

9 Wayne C. Booth, "The Revival of Rhetoric," *PMLA* 80 (1965): 8–12.

10 Gregory Kirschling, "Everybody Loves Rodney!" *Entertainment Weekly* 67 (28 May 2004): 86–93.

11 Cohen, *The History of Speech*, 29–84.

12 Responding to the general sentiment of MLA in the early 60s, Richard Young observes that for English scholars interested in rhetoric, there were, of course,

> rhetoric scholars in speech departments who might have been helpful, but the balkanization of universities tended to discourage contact with one of the few sources of rhetorical expertise at that time. And for the most part people in English didn't talk to people in speech, another blind spot among the many that plague English studies.

Consequently, there was a need for the Rhetoric Society of America. Richard Young, "Working on the Margin: Rhetorical Studies and the New Self-Consciousness," *Rhetoric Society Quarterly* 20 (1990): 326.

13 Winterowd, "Fragments of History," 36.

14 See Berlin, *Rhetoric and Reality*, 92–138.

15 Winterowd, "Fragments of History," 36.

16 The association of magic with rhetoric is as old as Gorgias's comparison of oratory to spellbinding and witchcraft; see William A. Covino, *Magic, Rhetoric, and Literacy: An Eccentric History of the Composing Imagination* (Albany: SUNY P, 1994); and Jacqueline de Romilly, *Magic and Rhetoric in Ancient Greece* (Cambridge: Harvard UP, 1975).

17 Nelson notes that a discussion of the society name would take place at the NCTE meeting in Milwaukee of that year, which was actually in November, and which probably means Nelson composed the newsletter earlier than December. Yoos reports the first newsletter was July, 1969. See Winterowd, "Fragments of History," 36.

18 *Newsletter: Rhetoric Society of America* 1 (December 1968): 1.

19 Ibid., 2.

20 Winterowd, "Fragments of History," 36.

21 Ann V. Masters, "Educator Sheds College Life for 'Tutor Cassette' Field," *The Bridgeport Post* (29 July 1973): 49.

22 Lloyd F. Bitzer, "The Rhetorical Situation," *Philosophy & Rhetoric* 1 (1968): 1–14.

23 Winterowd, "Fragments of History," 40.

24 Maureen Daly Goggin, *Authoring a Discipline: Scholarly Journals and the Post World War II Emergence of Rhetoric and Composition* (New York: Routledge, 2000), 75; Winterowd, "Fragments of History," 37; Young, "Working on the Margin," 326–27.

25 *Newsletter: Rhetoric Society of America* 2 (1972): 2.

26 Goggin, *Authoring a Discipline*, 75.

27 Ibid.

28 "K-Tel: The Secret History!" *The Independent* (9 January 2005). www.independent.co.uk/arts-entertainment/music/features/k-tel-the-secret-history-14334.html.

29 The number one, most frequently mentioned essay among participants was Jenny Edbauer (Rice), "Unframing Models of Public Distribution: From Rhetorical Situation to Rhetorical Ecologies," *Rhetoric Society Quarterly* 35 (2005): 5–24.

I
The Early Years (1968–1989)

Now, baby we can do it/Take the time, do it right
We can do it, baby/Do it tonight
                    —S.O.S. Band, "Take Your Time (Do It Right)"

To a remarkable degree, the story of the emergence of the Rhetoric Society of America (RSA) parallels the story of the National Communication Association (NCA), particularly in their similar responses to a commonly held self-perception that those who taught and researched rhetoric were neither recognized nor rewarded as handsomely as their colleagues in literary studies and the social sciences. Given the strong, well-sourced, and widely researched material published in the journal today, it is perhaps somewhat indecorous to note that the published content of *RSQ* from 1968 until the late 1980s is repeatedly sweat-spotted by such hand-wringing. But there it is. A lot of it. Yet, we should not react to the inscribed insecurities with embarrassment as much as we should a sense of wonderment and achievement; now with the robust growth of RSA from a dozen to over a thousand members—not to mention the spread of rhetorical studies across Europe and Asia today—what started as mimeographed newsletter has assuredly super-sized.

Although the impulse to create an anchoring, archival organ as a corrective to perceptions of disrespect among scholars in communication and English is some fifty years apart, in either case the result eventually proved successful: for speech rhetoricians this would be the *Quarterly Journal of Speech*, the first volume appearing in 1915.[1] For RSA this organ would first appear as the

Newsletter of the Rhetoric Society of America, which, as we noted in the introduction, Nelson Smith feverishly banged out on his typewriter in the late 1960s. The newsletter would later metamorphose into a journal of researched scholarship in the mid-1970s under the guidance and leadership of George E. Yoos.[2]

In his published notes on the meeting of the RSA Board of Directors in 1975, Richard L. Larson reported that six of the eleven members present voted to change the name of the newsletter to *Rhetoric Society Quarterly*, which would "be bound with a spiral binding and placed within light cardboard covers."[3] From that moment forward the journal took on an increasingly scholarly character; however, Yoos actively discouraged unsolicited essays because he "simply did not have the resources or staff" to handle it.[4] In part, Yoos also wished for the journal to primarily focus on book reviews, bibliographies, comments about conferences, and papers he admired in an effort to avoid simply mimicking "what other academic journals were doing at the time."[5] With the gradual addition of more editorial staff and the institution of a small editorial board, however, the policy changed, and by the early '80s *RSQ* began featuring scholarly essays in each issue; by 1981 scholarly essays were actively solicited. At the end of the '80s the journal would still feature bibliographies and book reviews, but these gradually recede until, by the early '90s, the journal would consist primarily of peer-reviewed research.

The three essays chosen to represent the second decade of the journal—but the first decade of *RSQ*'s scholarly era—were not peer-reviewed, and perhaps best reflect the transition from a society newsletter into a research journal. The first essay by George E. Yoos is especially demonstrative of his initial but rapidly transforming vision for the journal as a meeting place for rhetoricians to think aloud about their shared interests and directions for future research and pedagogy. Like a number of the more "scholarly" essays published in the previous decade, Yoos's essay weaves between personal reminisces and a citational imperative, foreshadowing the scholarly norms that would become entrenched in the 1980s. One can also glean a sub-rosa distinction between speech and writing through his engagement of speech act theory and the written "monologue," underscoring how the primary readership of the journal was predominately on the English-side of rhetorical studies.

The second essay by Hans P. Guth, "Composition Then and Now," extends Yoos's focus on written rhetoric with an attention to writing pedagogy—a dominant theme in the essays published in *RSQ* throughout its history. Notably, Guth frames the goal of his piece as the achievement of "respectability" in the academy for compositionists through sound teaching practice. He advocates what was an increasingly popular approach to writing instruction in the 1970s and '80s: positive reinforcement and encouraging students to make personal experience a component of writing, which Guth presents as an alternative to a more perfunctory and adversarial mode of instruction.

Admittedly somewhat anachronistically, Everett Lee Hunt's 1965 speech, "General Specialists: Fifty Years Later" rounds out our selection of publications for the early years of the journal for a number of reasons. First, we note Hunt's remarks are *not* necessarily representative of this period of the journal's history, which skews toward the publication of work from rhetoricians in English departments. Its reprinted inclusion in *RSQ* some twenty years later, however, represents the interest and presence of communication- or speech-side rhetoricians in the society, as well as a marked investment—at least on the part of Yoos and his co-editor at the time, Eugene Garver of St. John's University in Minnesota—in recultivating the interdisciplinary membership established in the RSA constitution. Second, Hunt reflects on his decades-long teaching of rhetoric and the debates and tensions in speech between the humanists and social scientists, ultimately to conclude that rhetorical scholars "need not be as much disturbed" by a lack of recognition in the wider academy. "The laments of our so-called humanistic scholars over their neglect, as the money goes to the scientists, seems rather pathetic," he quips, arguing that we "must take refuge in a sense of humor" and continue to teach the humanities for the goods internal to the practice.[6] As we shall see in succeeding decades, the pages of *RSQ* will begin to reflect precisely such an attitude, as anxieties about rhetoric's proletarian status in the academy give way, gradually, to well-researched, careful but somewhat conservative, peer-reviewed scholarship.

Chapters in Part I

George E. Yoos, "Rules, Conventions, Constraints, and Rhetorical Action."
Hans P. Guth, "Composition Then and Now."
Everett Lee Hunt, "General Specialists: Fifty Years Later."

Notes

1 See Pat J. Gehrke and William M. Keith, "Introduction: A Brief History of the National Communication Association," *A Century of Communication Studies: The Unfinished Conversation* (New York: Routledge, 2015), 1–25.

2 See Ross W. Winterowd, "Fragments of History, Personal and Institutional," *Visions and Revisions: Continuity and Change in Rhetoric and Composition*, ed. James Dale Williams (Carbondale: Southern Illinois UP, 2002), 33–47.

3 Richard L. Larson, "Notes on the Meeting of the Board of Directors of the Rhetoric Society of America, 28 November 1975, in San Diego, California," *Newsletter: Rhetoric Society of America* 5 (1975): 19–20.

4 Goggin, *Authoring a Discipline*, 77.

5 Ibid.

6 Everett Lee Hunt, "General Specialists: Fifty Years Later," *Rhetoric Society Quarterly* 17 (1987): 175.

2

Rules, Conventions, Constraints, and Rhetorical Action

GEORGE E. YOOS

As a boy I lived with uncles who were farmers. Every fall they butchered hogs for food. I used to wonder why there were no pork chops. Finally they explained to me that when they split the hog along the backbone, the loins were cut out and put into the sausage. I think an analogous process happens in logical analysis. When we make distinctions in our concepts along certain lines, we fail to see or conceptualize adequately certain phenomena. To see certain phenomena properly we need sometimes to make our cuts differently. I propose to make a somewhat new cut to the phenomena of rhetoric. I want to draw distinctions somewhat unorthodox in discussing terms such as "rules," "conventions," and "constraints" with respect to rhetorical action. What I wish to show by analysis is that the rules and conventions of linguistics and speech act theory are inadequate for a complete account of rhetorical phenomena.

What I am specifically interested in is the difference between the rules, conventions, and constraints that operate in conversation, dialogue, or dialectic and those that function in public speaking and extended prose. I want to argue that the rules, conventions, and constraints of rhetorical action differ from those operating in conversation or dialogue. Not only is the difference a quantitative mix but a qualitative one as well. Moreover, I want to argue that in view of the fact that rhetorical action and strategies are in large part determined by constraints generated by aim, media, audience, and situation, rhetorical action is in large part not constrained by rules and conventions that are universal to human action or the language used. Thus, my argument is to the effect that although linguistic conventions and rules, including speech act theory, are incidental to defining the "felicity" of certain rhetorical genre and modes, the main thrust of the art of rhetoric and rhetorical strategy deals with constraints not grounded in conventions and rules.

- 1 -

As a first step we need to make a clear cut between dialogue and monologue. Such a distinction is perplexing to make, for there are monologues within dialogues and dialogues within monologues. Plato's *Dialogues* display a fascinating interplay between dialogue and monologue form. Many of the issues over rhetoric, written text, and dialogue are dramatized and discussed in the *Dialogues*. Several facts about Plato's *Dialogues* are worthy of note. One is that the *Dialogues* themselves are written texts in dialogue form containing set speeches and myths. Another is that Socrates is constantly refusing to engage in fixed speeches, and he argues at length for the supremacy of dialogue (or dialectic) over written texts and the rhetoric of lengthy speeches. Yet, paradoxically Plato's reader is much in the same place as Socrates complaining about lengthy speeches and the meaning of written texts, for we cannot interrupt Plato's *Dialogues* to have Plato explain Socrates's meaning, nor can we have Socrates answer an objection to his arguments. As Socrates complains in the *Phaedrus*, we cannot talk back to the written text. As literary fictions Plato's *Dialogues* are then not real dialogues. Plato's *Dialogues* are, we might say, Platonic monologues displaying fictive dialogue. Much in the manner of Keats and his Grecian urn, Socrates exists in the *Dialogues* in the mode of eternity, eternally fixed in Plato's terms and argument in a written text.

I propose then by my cut to call attention to the noninterruptable feature of monologue both as written text and public address. One can stop reading a piece of prose, but one cannot question its author. And public address is noninterruptable, not because of an absent author, but by social conventions or procedural rules. Sometimes it is the situation that permits the speaker to speak at length without interruption. On other occasions it is the speaker's position or authority that commands silence. Either way what is important rhetorically about noninterruptability is the freedom that the rhetor has to control his presentation.

One of my old professors had a rule in his lectures that he was not to be interrupted on a point of objection. He would admit questions on points of clarification, for clarification of meaning did not violate his wish to avoid digression. He wished to stick to his outline that gave structure and integrity to his presentation. I maintain that my old professor was right. Interruptions mar continuity and timing. The lecturer loses control of his argument and material. Like with narratives breaks and intrusions can be disastrous to dramatic effect.

If discourse is going to move along deliberately controlled lines, it must be free from interruptions and derailment. Monologue can thus be defined by the right of the rhetor to pursue complex aims, to say what he wishes to say without intrusion, diversion, or interruption. Obviously this right exists within a framework of constraints. But these constraints merely mark a negative side to rhetoric. Rhetoric has on the contrary a positive side, and monologue permits the rhetor to fully exploit the positive side. Monologue gives the rhetor an opportunity to exercise his inventive ingenuity. It frees him to dispose in a manner and style appropriate to his aims. Monologue and rhetoric are best viewed in terms of liberty. But as with liberties in general we need to view rhetorical freedom on a background of rules, conventions, and constraints.

Recently I heard James J. Murphy in discussing the meeting of the International Society for the History of Rhetoric at Zurich last year compare the European conference to American ones. He pointed out that the European conference planners did not put time limits on the presentations as in American conferences. Speakers took as much time as necessary to make their presentation. Obviously such a convention is not designed to please conference planners. But it is a convention nevertheless designed to give scholars an opportunity to make their case fully, which after all is the purpose of monologue. Thus, we see at least in this case the conventions grow in part out of the need to give a speaker an opportunity to present himself or his case fully. The noninterruptable feature of extended discourse outlines the rhetor's freedom, but yet at the same time it creates new constraints and new demands that he needs to meet if he is to discourse at length. Not only does monologue introduce new problems of securing and maintaining audience attention, but it has special problems of securing uptake and audience comprehension. Moreover as monologue enables rhetors to present complex semantic and pragmatic intentions, the added complexity creates a greater demand for clarity and perspicuity in saying what is said. We know all too well the limitations of presenting complex material to audiences through a discussion method. Certain types of communication require silent and lengthily attentive audiences. It is thus the value of monologue to present complex statements.

Finally, it is worthy of note pedagogically that occasions for extended speech and extended prose are not ordinary transactions. Public speaking is not something we all have need of. Nor do many people need to write polished literary essays. Extended speech or prose is again not something we learn to do in dialogue at mama's knee. It is an educated piece of behavior. As with literacy the competency to engage in monologue is not something we acquire with linguistic competence or socialization in the family unit. Monologues including story telling are very unnatural conventional acts that need to be learned in special circumstances. Importantly for the argument of this paper monologue is an act that is learned apart from the mastery of ordinary language and speech acts in conversational situations.

- 2 -

What part then do rules, conventions, and constraints have in the mastery of monologue? "Rules," "conventions," and "constraints" are not parallel terms as the grammar of my title reflects. "Rules" and "conventions" are frequently overlapping, if not synonymous terms. But "constraints" in contrast is frequently defined in opposition to rules and conventions. Yet we often speak of constraints without reference to rules and conventions. What seems to limit action and freedom are not just rules and conventions but our aims and the facts about the social situations in which we are involved. Thus, if we are to see how rhetorical strategies differ from the "felicity" making conditions of speech act theory, we need to distinguish carefully these overlapping and contrasting uses of these three terms. We need to see how the different notions of rules, conventions, and constraints cut into rhetorical phenomena.

Although the terms "rule" and "convention" are often interchangeable in discussions of speech acts, differences in uses of the two terms reflect theoretical differences. As an interesting illustration of this point, J. L. Austin discusses speech acts in terms of "conventions" while John Searle does so in terms of "rules."[1] P. F. Strawson in his essay "Intention and Convention in Speech Acts," in *Philosophical Review* (1964) calls attention to the shifts in the use of the term "conventions" that mark Austin's discussion of speech acts.[2] Interestingly Strawson speaks of illocutionary acts as conventional only in an unconventional sense of conventional. He is thus thereby able to draw a line between illocutionary acts and performatives. Performatives are based upon social conventions. Illocutionary acts are not. Christening, for example, is a conventional ritual procedure. Promising is not. But explicit performatives as distinguished from performatives are for Austin illocutionary acts. Their illocutionary force follows from linguistic conventional meaning. Thus, the explicit performative, "I hereby promise that p," secures uptake from the conventional meaning of the illocutionary force indicator "hereby" and not from the uptake generated by a conventional ritual procedure. But what does Strawson gain by speaking of conventions as strictly customary conventions and ruling out as conventions the more universally applied conventions of language and human action? Similar problems about terms apply to rules. Most rules are thought to be conventional, so therefore in what sense can rules although conventions be unconventional?

We need therefore to be careful about terms, for they are fraught with traps. A good place to start pursuing these weaseling terms is with Searle's definitions of constitutive and regulative rules. As he defines, "Regulative rules regulate a pre-existing activity, the existence of which is logically independent of rules. Constitutive rules constitute (and also regulate) an activity the existence of which is logically dependent on the rules."[3] Constitutive rules for Searle define new forms of behavior. Regulative rules regulate old forms of behavior. But interestingly as Searle defines rules, they are always regulative. But isn't saying that rules are regulative nothing more than a redundant piece of etymology? Should not Searle be speaking of "auxiliary rules" instead of "regulative rules?"

Another difficulty that I have with Searle's discussion of rules, especially constitutive rules, is that the rules of a game, such as chess, although conventionally closed, are theoretically open to reconvention. Obviously games, such as football, basketball, and baseball, are open to reconvention. But Searle's discussion of promising argues that there are logical criteria for promising, and the criteria are specified by the rules for promising much in the same way that the rules of chess define chess. Searle thus seems to be arguing that there are a priori nonconventional rules for speech acts existing in the social institution of promising. Searle seems not to want to think of promising as conventional and arbitrary, subject to reconvention. If otherwise, promising would no longer be promising. It would be much the same as removing knights and replacing them with different pieces with different movements. The game would no longer be chess. But why not knightless chess? Can we ever close the rules of any game of any convention? I take it that these issues are involved in Searle's argument that threats are not promises. As Searle argues a promise is not strictly a promise if the promisee does not welcome it. But, to say that a threat is a kind of promise in a loose sense seems to be a matter of lexical convention. Why can't we think and talk of threats as promises if we find such talk promising?

Similar difficulties about loose and strict senses occur in discussions of conventions. The fact that many conventions are adopted by rule, law, or prescription leads many to think of conventions strictly as prescriptive or as rules. But many conventions are independent of legislation and decree. Consequently we have conventions that are thought of as rules or maxims, and we have conventions that are merely customary or traditional. The latter sort of conventions are freely adopted as preferred modes, sometimes out of loyalty and sometimes as convenient and efficient modes of action. We have thus the liberty to choose whether or not to conform to many customary or traditional conventions. Such customary conventions are not only comfortable and familiar but they are useful in generating mutual expectations and understandings. They are simply the adopted modes of action sufficiently familiar that others can fully anticipate and follow and appreciate what we are doing. As customary modes of action they convey conventional meaning to those familiar with the traditions that we conform to. For example, many genre and forms of the fine arts are conventional in this sense. They are customary. They can be flouted.

To flout constitutive rules and conventions however following Searle is to make certain rhetorical actions impossible. It is to render language and speech acts inconsistent, invalid, and confusing. But on the other hand many conventions can be flouted with meaning and effect. The decisive issue for rhetoric is not so much what rules and conventions can or cannot be flouted with impunity, but what sorts of flouting generate rhetorical opportunities. I take it that this is the program of H. P. Grice in his now famous article "Logic and Conversation."[4] For Grice the flouting of rules for informing is communicative, not by convention, but by conversational implicature. For Grice we communicate literally by deliberately "flaunting" our "flouting." What seems important for rhetoric from Grice's analysis is not so much speech act conventions themselves but how by improvisation and imagination we use them to communicate in innovative ways.

Finally, constraints too break down along lines parallel to those discussed in rules and conventions, for constraints are generated by conventions and rules. But again importantly for rhetoric there are two sorts of constraints that develop apart from rules and conventions. First, there is the sort that emerge from audience and situational demands. Second, there are constraints generated by the rhetor's commitment to his aim or purpose in saying what he says. Interestingly oral rhetoric is intimately tied to concerns generated by situational constraints. Written rhetoric in contrast is more intimately connected with the writer's aims and commitment. Rhetorical theory therefore needs, I suggest, to focus on the major differences in constraints between those in speech situations and those in the writing of manuscripts. It is largely, I maintain, because of these basic differences in constraints that oral rhetoric differs from written rhetoric. If linguistic rules and speech act conventions were the chief constraints operating in oral and written rhetoric, we should expect rhetoric to be a single art. But the academic division of rhetoric into rhetorics suggests that the division is based upon distinct sets of problems generating separate rhetorics. Much like the fine arts the division of rhetorics is based upon media differences, each art or rhetoric having its own peculiar genre, limitations, capabilities, and problems.

- 3 -

To what extent then do rhetorical strategies deal with constraints generated by speech situations and speaker's [sic] commitments and aims? If we consider oral rhetoric first, we find that many genres of public address, evidenced by genre labels, conform to rules or conventions of speech acts. Speakers operate in situations and audience contexts that constrain their aims and limit their strategies in fulfilling their aims. Modes or genres of speeches are thus usually classified along lines situationally defined. They break down into elemental speech acts such as eulogies, encomium, apologies, installations, christenings, inaugurals, welcomings, farewells, sermons, lectures, thanksgivings, and declarations. Speakers need to conform to these elemental speech act conventions so far as the situation and occasion demands the conventions. Yet, despite the fact that a welcoming speech, for example, must meet certain logical criteria for the speech to be a welcoming speech, welcoming someone simply does not require an elaborate or extended monologue. To enlarge upon a greeting is to complicate and alter the rhetorical aim of the speech. The genres of public address, although nominally simple speech acts, serve larger functions. They are opportunities for speakers and audiences to have complex demands and expectations satisfied. Thus, given opportunities to engage in extensive monologue, speakers accept them both to pursue their own interests and to satisfy larger demands of rhetorical situations. Constraints are thus not simply those specified by the conventions of the speech act genre. Rather the constraints that are important are those that emerge from the complex situation of audience and occasion.

The foremost constraint in the context of oral rhetoric is the difficulty in dealing with actual audiences and situations. In contrast with written rhetoric speakers face audiences. In so far as a speaker's act is simultaneous with his audience's perception of him, the speaker, as with pen and ink drawings, cannot modify his act of expression. A speaker is constrained by his own visage, voice, and actions in his presentation. Nor can he define his aim freely apart from his audience context. He cannot pretend to be someone other than what he appears to his audience. He is captive to his situation.

Yet despite the fact that speakers are severely situationally constrained, there is an opposite or liberating constraint in public address. There is an expectation, if not a demand, to defy expectations, to be innovative, enterprising, and delightfully surprising. The speaker is expected to find, discover, and invent words for the occasion. The speaker is not just being called upon to conform to the conventions of a greeting. He is expected to utilize the convention of greeting to transcend it. Rhetorical situations are, so to speak, conventionally rhetorical. Speakers are expected to be inventive, to be thoughtful, and to be capable of improvisation. Speakers are constrained to avoid dullness and conventional formity.

Writers on the other hand are usually free from particular contexts, occasions, audiences, and situations. Writers simply do not have an audience present in physical terms. They address one in the present within their text, but writers in that sense are imaginatively projecting their audience. Their real audience is in the future. Not only are writers free to elect their audience and situation, they are also free to construct their own style and tone. They control the presentation of themselves in writing in idealized ways that speakers cannot. In speaking there is a need to harmonize one's personal display of character, expression, and action with words. The writer, however, since his sole medium is within his written text, can control fictively all the dramatic aspects of his rhetoric. Walter Ong argues that writers create imaginary audiences.[5] But writers can also create imaginatively *ethos*, voice, tone, style, and attitudes towards audience. Writers are thus situationally free to choose their aim, voice, occasion, audience, and situation. They create these elements within their text. Is it, I ask, an historical accident that teachers of composition have been hired from students of literary fiction?

In one sense speakers choose aims by choosing the occasion. But writers choose first and foremost to express themselves by putting what they have to say on paper. The writer is able thus to divorce expression from communication. He is able rhetorically to hide behind a script in dealing with his audience. The writer is able to separate his expression from his rhetoric and in turn transfer and filter one into the other. He controls what he says in ways not possible in speech. While a speaker in his expression gropes for precision in his response, the writer can choose his words to fit his expression. His rhetoric creates his meaning prior to communication.

A major difference between speech and writing is that to edit and revise a speech is not to produce a speech. To revise a written script is simply to produce a written text. Another way of looking at the difference is that editing frees the writer from the major constraints operating against speakers. But although the writer has his advantages, his liberty incurs costs. Readers too have certain natural advantages over listeners. The very permanence of a text that makes revision and editing possible increases the critical capabilities of readers. Not only does a written text give a writer increased opportunities to be logical and precise, it imposes an increased demand on the writer to be logical and precise. Readers can scrutinize texts, interpret, logically evaluate, examine hidden agenda, explicate contextual implications, detect implicit suggestion and connotation in ways not possible in listening. Thus, written rhetoric operates in the face of a long list of constraints introduced by the analytic and critical skills of readers.

In the final analysis what is important in written rhetoric are the constraints introduced across all levels of reading by critical and uncritical readers. Written rhetorical strategy thus has a whole set of problems in securing quick and efficient reader uptake. Rhetorical strategy in writing needs to anticipate and allay the apprehensions and misapprehensions of both critical and uncritical readers. An important part of rhetorical strategy in written rhetoric is in facilitating reading comprehension. Since writing makes possible the communication of complex semantic intent, writing calls for additional and different rhetorical strategies to communicate increased complexity. In the last analysis written extended discourse needs to make its complex aims and intent clear and perspicuous to readers *not* listeners.

I have thus argued that the major thrust of rhetorical strategy is to peculiar constraints that develop as a writer or speaker engages in monologue. It is the nature of monologue on account of time, length, and complexity to present problems different from those found in dialogue. The speaker needs to define himself and his relationship towards his audience in monologue situationally. The writer in contrast needs to focus primarily on his expressive aim. The literacy of readers adds a completely new set of problems to written rhetoric. Writing is not basically an action, but primarily an artifact for reading. Speech is like the snow that "falls in the river, a moment white then melts forever." Writing however is "a foster child of silence and slow time."

Notes

1   J. L. Austin, *How to Do Things with Words* (Oxford: Clarendon Press, 1962).
    John R. Searle, *Speech Acts: An Essay in the Philosophy of Language* (Cambridge: Cambridge UP, 1969).

2 P. F. Strawson, "Intention and Convention in Speech Acts," *The Philosophical Review* LXXIII, no. 4 (1964): 439–60.

3 Searle, ibid., 33–42.

4 H. P. Grice, "Logic and Conversation," *Syntax and Semantics*, Vol. III, *Speech Acts*, ed. Peter Cole and Jerry L. Morgan (New York: Academic Press): 41–58.

5 Walter J. Ong, S.J., "The Writer's Audience Is Always a Fiction," *PMLA* XC, no. 1 (January 1975): 9–21.

3
Composition Then and Now*

HANS P. GUTH

In recent years, the teaching of composition as a major responsibility and a major commitment of English departments has come into its own. In the minds of legislators, administrators, and the general public, the teaching of literacy and effective communication has come to loom large as a major inadequately filled need. University and college English departments have come to recognize officially what was always true even in days of condescension and neglect: the teaching of written communication is a major and central contribution of English departments to the general education of young Americans. It has to be based on something more than dreary old habits and unexamined assumptions. It needs adequate recognition and support if it is to be what at its best it can be: a reputable scholarly and humanistic enterprise of great potential educational and practical value for the student.

Composition is an ancient Latin word that means "putting it together"—getting it together, getting something into shape. A successful student composition is a piece of writing that has purpose, substance, structure, and style, and that uses language that is right for the job. What progress there has been in the teaching of the composition in the last twenty years has been generally in two major directions: First of all, we have learned to attend to these major dimensions of student writing in a more balanced way. We are no longer spending most of our time perpetuating a few simplistic and often misguided rulings on style. We are no longer spending most of our time revising sentences that were not worth writing in the first place. Second, we have come to approach the teaching of writing generally in a more positive and productive way. We have learned much about showing our students how to do things right—rather than constantly taking inventory of everything they did wrong. We have learned how to make our students experience some of the rewards and satisfactions of worthwhile writing, honestly done.

---

* [This article is based on talks given at the University of Iowa and Ohio State University in the spring of 1980. The written version was prepared for publication in the *Rhetoric Society Quarterly*.]

More specifically, the following developments have during the last ten years or so helped make the teaching of composition a more reputable, more productive, and less frustrating task:

(1) *Teachers of composition have changed their basic attitude toward student writing.* We have come to take the student's writing seriously—insisting on real writing, something that the writer wanted to say and that gives the reader something worth reading. In the days of yore, the real purpose of a writing assignment was more or less frankly to elicit from the student a "writing sample." This sample could then be subjected to an error count; it could be marked up and corrected. No matter what the surface plausibility of this procedure as a way of correcting deficiencies, it tends to distort two basic relationships—that between the writer and the subject, and that between the writer and the reader. Students know that ostensibly they are asked for an opinion, for an interpretation, or an argument, but the real purpose of the exercise is to make them go out on a limb so that their mistakes can be counted and exposed—after the fact. The result is a pervading sense of unreality (read: dishonesty) in much old-style, conventional student writing. Nothing is drearier, and ultimately more opposite to what English teachers stand for, than writing that no one wanted to write and that no one really wants to read. Much conventional student writing was vapid, and cliché-ridden because its basic impulse was defensive—to anticipate and sidestep criticism.

The basic requirement for success in a composition course is that a different kind of respect for writing be created very early in the course. Students must sense that if they write seriously and honestly, their writing will be read seriously and honestly. Many composition programs now include a strong component of writing drawing on the students' personal experience: the basic reason is that in this kind of writing we can most directly and persuasively demonstrate to our students the difference between verbiage and the truly written word. A topic like "Is prejudice on the decline?" can be treated in dreary second-hand generalities. But if approached with the right kind of expectations, it can also generate responses like the following[1]:

> Discrimination toward Asian-Americans today is usually so unobvious that people of Asian ancestry may not be able to recognize the prejudices against them. I, personally, am very sensitive to verbal reactions. There is always the question, "What are you?" The mere fact of being questioned makes me stiffen with resentment at the ignorance of those who felt that they had to ask. There have been times when I have been completely at a loss for words on how to reply. I could answer, "American," "Japanese," and "Japanese-American," but somehow I feel unnatural and placed in an awkward situation. I do not consider myself totally American, because of obvious visible differences, nor do I think of myself as Japanese, since I was not brought up with the strict traditions and culture. Being thought of as a member of a minority makes me slightly uncomfortable, and responding to

that question has made me sometimes regret my existence. I am a person, just like everyone else.

We can tell this is real writing: our first impulse is *not* to write in the margin symbols for vague reference, dangling modifier, or mixed metaphor. If we write anything, we are likely to write: "I see what you mean. You have a point there. That is worth thinking about. On this we don't have all the answers." When students have something to say, questions of usage and mechanics become a matter of communicating effectively with the reader. They become a matter of meeting the expectations of the audience as concerns language and form. Correction and revision cease to be viewed in the context of an adversary relationship between teacher and student. Part of the teacher's task becomes to help students make a worthwhile piece of writing as viable and as little vulnerable as possible, to teach the editing skills that help communications survive in the marketplace of ideas.

(2) *Teachers of composition have come to stress the process of composition rather than the finished product.* Old-style materials stressed the end result: The student was asked for a paper with a clear outline, a thesis sentence, a topic sentence in every paragraph, and the like. But traditional textbooks furnished few clues as to how these results were to be produced. Where would students find material for a paper? How would they marshal it, working out a structure fit for the subject? How would they learn to funnel their observations into a good topic sentence, or how would a defensible thesis emerge from their thinking through of an issue? On these and similar questions, traditional textbooks had little or nothing to say.

Modern writing programs and textbooks typically start farther back. They ask where good writing comes from, and how it is produced. They recognize, for instance, that good writing is rooted in observation and experience. They try to do justice to the important preliminary stage where we take things in. We learn to notice things; we learn to use our own eyes and ears. Students learn much from writing assignments that ask them simply for a faithful accounting of "what was there." Student responses like the following show that the student writers are learning something essential about the relation between words and reality:

> From the tops of tall buildings that block out much of the sunlight, pigeons watch the street. Occasionally, one will spring out in flight, as if pushed by one of its comrades; there is a desperate flutter of its wings as it returns to its home base.
>
> A man pauses in front of half a dozen rusty old newspaper stands, debating where to drop his coins. He carefully studies each box, apparently reading each exposed page; then, fumbling, his fingers too thick to handle the coins, he finally drops them in, lifts up the cover of the box, retrieves his paper, and departs.

> There is a huge mass of rubble on one corner. Thick and heavy blocks of cement are scattered and piled in a place where a building once stood. A crane extends upward into the sky, like a giraffe reaching for green leaves on the small branches at the top of the tree.

Modern approaches to composition label the major phases of the writing process in somewhat different ways, and they differ considerably in the emphasis or priority they assign to each. But they each in their own way pay some honest attention to four major stages or dimensions of the process of composition:

—PURPOSE: Teachers have become more concerned with what it takes to activate good writing. What brings it on? What kind of assignment, and what kind of preparation or groundwork, makes students say things like the following?

> "I would like to speak to that."
> "On that I have something to say."
> "I agree with you up to a point; however, in all fairness I must point out that...."
> "This is indeed something that is often said, but on closer examination it turns out to be merely a stereotype."

A major part of the task of a successful composition teacher is the search for writing assignments that will make students *want* to write. It is the search for assignments that will make students want to talk back, to take a stand, to fill a gap in their information, or to weigh the pros and cons.

—SUBSTANCE: A key requirement for successful writing is knowing how to work up a subject, learning how to become involved in a topic. No one can write a substantial paper from an empty mind. Students have to learn how to mobilize their resources. They have to learn how to draw on their memory, their observation, and their reading for relevant material. Modern composition programs recognize an indispensable preliminary phase that was often slighted with a traditional approach—that of immersing oneself in a subject, following up false leads, and slowly working up a rich fund of material that gives substance to a paper.

—STRUCTURE: The crucial stage of the composition process is reached when writers begin to do the sorting and organizing that will get their materials into shape. This is the phase where writers have to show their ability to get a subject under control. They have to take the crucial step from substance to structure, from observation to meaning. As teachers of composition, we have always had a pressing need for

	exercises and practice runs that develop the organizing abilities of our students. In a variety of situations and with different kinds of tasks, they have to practice essential organizing and structuring skills: funneling related details into a generalization, tracing the common thread in a series of incidents, sorting things out into major categories, weighing the pros and cons in order to reach a balanced conclusion.
—AUDIENCE:	Sooner or later, writers ask themselves: is anybody listening? When we present information, how much of it do our readers take in, and how much of it do they consider relevant? If we argue a point, how many readers agree or disagree with us, and why? If we fail to get any kind of fair hearing, what interfered—was it a matter of basic assumptions, of an ill-chosen approach, or of outward form? Such questions bring us face to face with basic matters of strategy and style. They make us ask ourselves: How do we make a dent? How do we overcome resistance or obstacles? What does it take to get attention? What does it take to mobilize a consensus? What conventions of language and form do writers ignore at their peril? Much final editing and revision is aimed at protecting ourselves against criticism, at honoring the standards and expectations of educated readers.

(3) *Teachers of composition have learned to do positive, constructive work with language, and especially with the English sentence.* In recent years, we have seen a flourishing of sentence writing and sentence practice. In many classrooms, the emphasis has shifted from negative, remedial work with grammar to a positive concern with sentence resources and sentence craft. In days gone by, a favorite teaching tool was the "horrible example." Students early came to feel that the English sentence was prone to every kind of disaster. In constructive sentence work, our first task is to show students that the English sentence is alive and well, and that it is in fact a magnificent and eloquent instrument when well constructed. We read to our students, and we write on the board, sentences that make readers want to say, "Well put! Well said":

> Nature made ferns for pure leaves, to show what she could do in that line. (Henry David Thoreau)
> Rage cannot be hidden; it can only be dissembled. (James Baldwin)
> The quality of strength lined with tenderness is an unbeatable combination, as are intelligence and necessity when unblunted by formal education. (Maya Angelou)

Much work with sentence style today uses the sentence imitation approach to help give students greater confidence and a greater range in drawing on the linguistic repertory and the stylistic resources of the English sentence. Model sentences for imitation can cover the whole range from fairly simple structures to more elaborate ones:

MODEL:	Time is a dressmaker specializing in alterations.
IMITATION:	A jail is an institution relying heavily on return business.
MODEL:	I always go to sea as a sailor because they make a point of paying me for my trouble, whereas they never pay passengers a single penny that I ever heard of. (Herman Melville)
IMITATION:	I always ride my bicycle everywhere, because it asks absolutely no questions, whereas I have to give full details about reasons, time, and place whenever I take the car.

Sentence imitation can be used as a means of teaching specific stylistic effects, such as parallelism, or simple inversion:

MODEL:	Studies serve for delight, for ornament, and for ability. (Sir Francis Bacon)
IMITATION:	Cars serve for transportation, for recreation, and for ostentation.
MODEL:	Stronger than the mighty sea Is Almighty God.
IMITATION:	Bleaker than a misspent youth Is life without experience.

Especially valuable to the composition teacher is sentence work that provides the bridge from the sentence to the larger units. The following "details-first" sentences help teach, in the more limited context of the single sentence, one of the most basic or pervasive of rhetorical principles: the relationship between specific and general, between concrete and abstract. Students are asked to fill in several concrete details *before* they present the general label that concludes the sentence. They thus learn something about what we mean by an *earned* generalization, or a *legitimate* label:

MODEL:	Red, white, and blue banners; crowds of people cheering, booing; candidates with tired eyes, smiling and shaking hand after hand: *this is a political rally*.
RESPONSES:	Crowds of people, machines clanging, bells ringing, lights flashing, kids running to one then another: *this is an arcade*.
	The peeling paint, the squawking gulls, the pungent odors, the creaking sounds of the water-logged hulls: *a wharf*.
	A long dirt road running endlessly toward a large house unseen through a forest of trees miles from civilization: *land of paradise*.

If sentence work of this kind is used in close conjunction with full-length writing assignments, it can provide the kind of preparation and limbering-up for the whole theme that was usually missing in traditional programs. The sentences written by students as part of this kind of activity are already mini-compositions: they require the ability to bring a topic into focus, to select and arrange details, to funnel specifics into a general conclusion. Creative sentence practice of this kind is therefore more organically related to the main purposes of the composition course than the kind of sentence combining whose merits have recently been widely debated in our professional journals. As described by experimenters like James W. Ney, orthodox sentence combining furnishes the building blocks for a larger sentence ready-made. These elements are then combined in the larger sentence according to a set formula. Often, students are required to combine material from simpler source sentences in such a way "that there is only one correct form for the combined sentences."[2] Whatever the gains in fluency and confidence that such sentence combining may produce, more open-ended or more truly generative kinds of sentence work seem better suited to hold the attention and challenge the abilities of beginning college students.

(4) *Teachers of composition are witnessing a major redefinition of preparatory or "remedial" work.* In the teaching of literacy and basic skills, much truly dedicated (and little recognized) work has long been done in writing clinics and communication labs, in special courses for minority students, as part of open admissions programs, and in similar situations. Whatever our official euphemisms, alibis, and evasions, large numbers of college students have always required more elementary assistance with the forms and conventions of edited written English than the standard first-year course in composition provides. In the past, students with special needs were often subjected to traditional rules and drills that, with dumbfounding unimaginativeness and insensitivity to the students' needs, merely repeated methods of teaching that had failed these same students in the past. In recent years, teachers around the country have developed new and more positive teaching patterns for such students. They have offered such students, at their level of readiness and need, bona-fide positive instruction in language and composition designed to appeal to their latent intelligence and their buried gift for language. Publications of student writing inspired by such teaching, such as the publications from the English 100 program at Purdue, have gone far toward dispelling the smug assumption that the students in such programs are any less gifted, articulate, or eloquent than the pundits who deplore "mass illiteracy" in the public press.

An early leader in the movement to redefine "remedial" instruction was Mina P. Shaughnessy, whose widely read and quoted *Errors and Expectations* (1977) offered a guide to the teacher of "basic writing." Her work inspired many teachers to go beyond the simplistic and obsolescent traditional rules in order to take a new and more helpful look at the gropings of the beginner. She assumed that many student problems, rather than being the result of ignorance or carelessness, are the result of earnest attempts to navigate in the new and unfamiliar waters of academic discourse. As one of her associates said,

> The very term "basic writing," now in general use, was her term initially and grew out of her refusal to see the students who studied that subject as remedial, or handicapped, or deprived except in the sense that their previous education had failed to serve them.

Many teachers who have put in their time in areas of true need have come to share the

> conviction that faculty, not students, need to be remediated if writing is to be taught well, that the overwhelming majority of semi-literate students that populate basic writing classes can become articulate writers if their teachers can only discover sufficiently effective ways of leading them to that goal.[3]

Successful work with students with special needs requires a paradoxical combination of attitudes. On the one hand, we must preserve a patient respect for the elementary needs of the student who asks us to explain one more time the difference between *its* and *it's*. We must be willing to write on the board one more time a list of "unforgivables" that includes *believe, definite, separate*, and *perform*. On the other hand, we must keep alive our faith in our students' native gift for language. We have to find ways to foster and recognize and promote the writing of ordinary students. We have to find ways to make them participate in the patterns of challenge and rebuttal, of grievance and boast, of testimony and inquiry, that are part of the true dynamics of living language. Certainly, we will encounter in such endeavors a fair portion of what is trivial or juvenile. But we will also encounter often enough a piece of writing that lifts the pall from our dark spirits and makes our humanistic enterprise seem worthwhile.

Notes

1 The quoted material here is indented in the typewritten original.
2 James W. Ney, "A Short History of Sentence Combining: Its Limitations and Use," *English Education* 11 (February 1980): 171.
3 Barbara Quint Gray, "Introduction," in *Journal of Basic Writing* 2 (Spring/Summer 79): 3–4.

4

General Specialists
Fifty Years Later

EVERETT LEE HUNT

[An Editorial Note: In July 1965, Everett Lee Hunt (1890–1984) gave the key-note address at the Bowling Green State University Conference on Rhetoric and the Modern World. He had spent a term teaching a graduate seminar at Cornell University and trying unsuccessfully to save the Department of Speech at that university where he had made such a mark in his early career. For the occasion at the Bowling Green Conference, he chose to reflect both on his recent brief return to university teaching and upon the fifty years of the speech profession. His prepared remarks are printed here with the permission of Theodore Otto Windt, Jr., the executor of his papers, and Mrs. Marjorie Hunt, his widow.]

In the spring of 1965 I asked some of my students in a graduate seminar [at Cornell] why they had chosen rhetoric as a field for advanced study. Several of them had come from smaller colleges not widely known for their academic standing, and they had aroused my curiosity by their keen interest, their intel-ligence, and their creative capacity. All of them said they had been active as undergraduates in debate groups or in dramatic performances, and had been influenced by the breadth of interest and the personalities of their teachers. Several of them, on coming to the university, had chosen to associate their stud-ies in rhetoric and public address with work in literature, history, psychology, political science or philosophy. Nearly all of them reported that their work in rhetoric had been frowned upon. They had been told that it was not an estab-lished discipline, but was associated with several related fields in a causal way, and had no territory of its very own which could be enclosed with a "no tres-pass" sign. One of them thought he would take up literary criticism because he had been stimulated by contemporary critical essays. He had been told that he should concentrate upon Shakespearean critical essays from 1690 to 1700 so that he could become known as an authority in his field. Another wanted to write on how presidents get elected; but he had been told that this was the work of a journalist, and that he should concentrate on something that could be proved. What interested me in all this was that the students should be some-what appalled and rebellious.

If, some of them said, the study of rhetoric is no less confining than other disciplines, then we might as well turn to a field where early reward for the sacrifice of human interest seems assured. We have been hoping, they said, that rhetoric would somehow tolerate wandering, that one could explore paths from rhetoric to ethics, to politics, to poetry, to philosophy, and still find some unity in all these adventures. Some of them said they had a vague desire to be "intellectual," even if they could not exactly define the term. They felt that an "intellectual" was not an expert, not a lawyer, not a doctor, not a scientist, but a man who could turn a trained intellect on any human problem that did not seem soluble by experts. Intellectuals, they admitted, had their weaknesses; they were detached, sometimes alienated, a bit irresponsible, perfectly willing to denounce the Vietnam war without proposing a way out. "Intellectuals," as they read them in *Daedalus*, or the *Journal of the History of Ideas*, or *The American Scholar*, came from such a variety of backgrounds that the only thing they had in common was a certain rhetorical skill. But had they any rhetorical training? Or had it come naturally?

Such questions kept disturbing the orderly progress of our discussion of the topics of Greek, Roman, English and American orators, and added some hours of indecisive talk to our sessions.

All this was a revelation to me. I had left the university atmosphere forty years ago. My administrative duties had brought me in contact with young instructors fresh from the graduate schools who were delighted to be authoritative specialists. Many of them did not want to teach anything in which they were not unique authorities. And they were largely successful in attracting an undergraduate following. I talked with sophomores who told me not only what graduate school they were aiming for, but what professor they wanted to direct their Ph.D. thesis. The university, it had seemed to me, was transforming the college into a center for pre-graduate school training. Junior and senior courses were elected after consulting graduate school requirements. Of course there were some rebels; some of them were the brilliant dropouts, others were the ambitious young writers who wanted to find their own subject matter, and others stayed in college to be eligible to join the Peace Corps. There were still many professors who were highly esteemed for personal warmth and human interest, but this was not accepted as a substitute for being an authority in the field. College students are a different breed from those of my day, I reflected. Perhaps, for better or worse, one of the major causes is the pressure to get from high school to college to graduate school. But what surprised me most in my belated return to instruction in a university, was to find graduate students who still rebelled at what they called the confinements of over-specialization. A free and creative mind may need discipline, but it rebels against the loss of meaning in its work.

The nostalgic reminiscences of an emeritus professor probably should not be taken seriously, if listened to at all, but I can't help recalling the situation which led me into the teaching of "rhetoric and oratory." As an undergraduate in a very small college, which I entered in 1909, I majored in Greek and Latin because my father had done so in his preparation for the ministry, but I had not the least expectation that it was a specialized training for a career. My real enthusiasm was for debating, and especially debating both sides of a question. This did lead to my appointment as an instructor with a minimum of anything like technical training. I rejoiced in the freedom to argue about almost anything that interested me, especially if it had a touch of philosophy about it. I was enthusiastic about the "field" I had entered, although it did not really occur to me to call it a field. Then the next year came the *Quarterly Journal of Speech Education* with its aim to establish its claim to the field of speech, and to show that studies in that field could be as scholarly and scientific and specialized as any academic pursuit. O'Neill and Woolbert outlined the procedures in masterly fashion, and I want to pay tribute to their work and its lasting effects. But to me, in my innocence of the meaning of graduate studies, their program seemed to center attention on matters that interested me very little. It now seems that I was inconceivably brash in 1916 to write an essay called "General Specialists," and it was very kind of editor O'Neill to publish it, after sending it to Professor Woolbert with a request to write a rebuttal to be published in the same number. Let me repeat my thesis as it was stated in three points:

(1) Neither speech science nor speech art can be confined to a particular field of knowledge.
(2) Any general acceptance of the idea that speech art or speech science possesses a distinctive and individual field for specialization will prevent the instruction in public speaking from reaching its highest effectiveness.
(3) The Professor of Public Speaking in a college finds his greatest work in stimulating, as a means of effective expression, a wide range of general reading and a keen interest in contemporary thought and action. In other words, the Professor of Public Speaking must be a specialist in versatility.[1]

It was a kindly reply to such an insufferable heresy for Professor Woolbert to say:

Mr. Hunt and I differ so widely as to fundamentals that it cannot be said we are arguing. We are merely stating personal preferences. . . .[2]

And he was always kindly and tolerant toward me, if not to my unprofessional ideas. He even tried to educate me by securing a university fellowship in philosophy for me. But he went on to say in his reply:

I stand for a search for the facts, the facts of how speaking is done, of what its effects are under specific conditions, how these facts may be made into laws and principles; and how other people may be taught to apply them.

Mr. Hunt and I are of different epochs and countries. He is of a romantic, golden age, I, of the common, ignoble now. He is from Greece, I am from Germany (!)—he probably by choice, I per force.

He cries out for the glory that was Greece and the grandeur that was Rome; I am surrounded by laboratories and card catalogues.

I am a university professor. My circumstances compel me to accept the university's definition of a professor as "one who finds and teaches truth." They do not have to "find" truth. The college likes the general specialist.

Hunt is a sort of lay pastor, an intellectual and spiritual knight-errant, an educational court physician.[3]

Professor Woolbert's description of the inevitable results of my approach to my subject is an astonishingly accurate prediction of my subsequent career, and for good or ill I have to accept it. I do confess to a considerable satisfaction in it for its human relationships, even if I have made no scientific contributions.

I am not trying to revive this ancient debate. I think there has been much development on both sides. The research that Woolbert called for has produced an impressive body of knowledge upon which many of us base our hopes for professional recognition. And the relatively unscientific studies of rhetoric and public address are building up a literature that may eventually have some significance for the historian, the political scientist, the philosopher, and the general public. There has been a great growth in both directions.

But what are some of the results of the fifty years of educational progress since the contrast between these two points of view was so sharply drawn?

In the early period of splitting off from departments of English, we had a feeling that we were establishing a new profession, and many of us were inclined to feel that our own individual interests were fundamental, and should be the guiding forces in our professional development. When some of us turned to the past we felt that we had rediscovered a great tradition, which only needed to be revived. Others turned to contemporary science and found there the hope for the future. Now we can see more clearly that both are relevant, and that in following our own interests and developing creatively our own temperaments we can each in our own way contribute to the development of the whole field of speech, which shortly may be known as the field of communication, with speech as one province.

The field of rhetoric and public address has been developing a unity and traditions of its own. It is becoming clearer that we have to attend to both form and substance, and that while form may be increasingly stated in scientific terms, the substance of public address is essentially unscientific. The orators of the past dealt with probabilities, and they still do today, even after they consult with their scientific advisers. Their subject matter may be determined by their quest for power, but when the wisdom of the orator produces an aphorism, a proverb, a phrase that becomes famous, we do not know scientifically whence it comes, nor to what it owes its influence.

There may be endless dispute as to whether our orators have merely interpreted impersonal social and economic forces, whether they have created or directed such forces. At the time of the deaths of such figures as Churchill and Stevenson we recall our quotations from their eloquence as we give thanks for their leadership. We do not dismiss as mere eulogy the tribute of Governor Kerner that Stevenson had "a greatness which somehow seemed to bring to each of us a special feeling, a particular kind of pride, a sense of satisfaction that we lived in the world of Adlai Stevenson."

We agree with James Reston as we read his column in *The New York Times*:

> The tragedy of Adlai Stevenson is not that the U.S. has lost a representative in the United Nations, but that the western world has lost another of its few eloquent men.
>
> Language is power, and in the last few years the West has lost most of the men who could define its purposes—Churchill, and Gaitskell in Britain, Kennedy in the United States, Hammarskjold at the United Nations, Nehru in India, not to mention those spokesmen of the western literary world, Frost, Faulkner, and T. S. Eliot.

Here we have the statement that the great function of eloquence, or oratory, or rhetoric is to define the purpose of society, and Reston's apprehension about our lack of powerful voices is shared by such a contemporary historian as Henry Steele Commager, and such a poet-spokesman as Archibald MacLeish:

> Our political morality has suffered in the past from the belief that America is somehow outside the workings of history, about the processes of history, exempt from such laws as may govern history. This attitude is noted in the long popular notion of Old War corruption and New World innocence. And for generations it has blinded us to our shortcomings, which we could hope to conceal from the world at large. But now this is no longer possible, and we must take seriously the reasons which moved the First Continental Congress to acknowledge "a decent respect for the opinions of mankind." We must not now fall a victim to the rhetoric of power.[4]

MacLeish asks

> Do Vietnam and the Dominican Republic mean that we are no longer that idealistic nation of the first World War—no longer a people attached to those enormous phrases, those almost irrepressible aspirations which impose their own sometimes quixotic laws of self-restraint? Have our ways of thinking and feeling altered? Are we "realistic" now? "Hardheaded"? Indifferent to those opinions of mankind put in the first sentence of their first communication to the world?

Is it possible we have changed, MacLeish asks, and then answers his own questions.

> Nations, like men, grow harder headed as they grow older, more skeptical of their earlier aspirations, and we have lived a long time in the climate of a high and noble rhetoric.[5]

But McGeorge Bundy also has a high and noble rhetoric for the policy he espouses. In his extemporaneous reply to Archibald MacLeish he says that Franklin Roosevelt (surely a noble rhetorician) first articulated the three primary elements of a continuing American attitude toward world affairs:

> . . . an acceptance by the United States of the responsibility of holding and using power, a permanent and passionate commitment to the ideal of peace, and a readiness to judge ourselves to be judged in terms of the effect of our behavior on others. . . . (These) continue to be the main strands of our policy today.
>
> We do not expect there will always be agreement. We used to. We no longer suppose that because there is cheering for Woodrow Wilson in the aftermath of our armistice, there is whole hearted concurrence with his desire to arrange the map of Europe as he thinks best.
>
> We do not suppose . . . there will be unanimous approval of our decisions in those difficult and dangerous areas of Vietnam and the Dominican Republic. We do, however, expect to be able to defend them, to explain them, to act responsibly in carrying them out, and we expect to be judged in the end . . . in terms of the true interests of those with whom we come in contact.[6]

It is interesting to note that what is feared as a fundamental change in our national policy is attacked in terms of being untrue to our traditional rhetoric; and that the reply is that the old rhetoric still holds; it merely needs to be understood in the light of new conditions. Perhaps this is a dialogue characteristic of many debates, but it does confirm the belief that if the great debates of history are to be understood, there must be an arduous study of the history of the times in conjunction with the study of the style and personality of a particular speaker. The two complementary aspects of this are that the rhetorician must know more about history, and the historian must know more about rhetoric. Marie Hochmuth Nicols in her epoch marking book, *Rhetoric and Criticism*, has made one aspect of this clear in her report on what historians have said about our National Association's volumes *The History and Criticism of American Public Address*. I need not repeat here the detailed criticism that historians wrote to her when she asked them how to make rhetorical studies more acceptable to them. Most of you have read this in her book.

It takes considerably more courage, perhaps, to attempt to point out to some historians their shortcomings resulting from a belief that speeches do not matter. But I have an example. Professor John Bakke of Cornell is completing a thesis with Professor Donald Bryant of Iowa on the parliamentary debates on the Fox and Pitt East India bills. He discusses the belief of such historians as Lewis Namier and his school that since the vote on the bill would have been much the same if the debates had not been held, the historian can well ignore them. Bakke points out the errors in historical judgment due to the failure to understand the speeches of Fox. Since this study is not yet available, let me offer a very inadequate summary of his conclusions:

> It took the government of England almost twenty years to do what it wanted to do; to control India. To accomplish this, three things had to happen:
>
> (1) The company had obviously to make a shambles of its own affairs—historical dynamic.
> (2) The political situation in England had to go through some machinations by which both the majority and minority had committed themselves to a reform—political dynamic.
> (3) A policy had to be presented that disassociated the public from the company, and that changed public sympathy for the company—this was the rhetorical dynamic.
>
> Fox and Burke showed how the problem could be solved; Pitt made the solution publicly acceptable, and Fox and Burke publicly acceptable.
>
> I feel that the more we know about the functions of rhetoric in a free society, the more clear will become the rhetorical dynamic of our society.

These citations are merely to confirm our long-established belief that rhetoric is an important dynamic in all the great decisions of society, but also to emphasize the belief that the study of rhetoric must be supported by a more extensive study of the history, politics, ethics and philosophy involved. In making these studies I think we should address ourselves less to our own professional colleagues, and more to the writers in various fields whose purpose is to disseminate knowledge, yes, even popularize it, and to influence public opinion. We may need to attack some of their oversights, but we also need to show that we understand what they are saying. In carrying this out we shall not be writing scientifically. That is, the "truth" we discover may still arouse controversy. In spite of the advance of science we shall be chiefly concerned with human problems that remain in the realm of probability.

The statement inviting us to this conference called our attention to areas in which discussion should be acute and extensive. And we shall have to make more use of the "dialogue" which Martin Buber has called for in reaching an understanding in religious matters. But we have in this company of scholars who have in various ways long been interested in the association of rhetoric with its principal subject-matter fields—history, politics, ethics, philosophy. I am hoping merely to introduce the discussion in this conference.

May I say in closing that I am quite optimistic about our field, or rather fields—wherever we may roam, we will eventually come home. First, I believe that we are and long have been in a special position to do an effective job of undergraduate teaching, where human relations are especially significant, and that the importance of this is being more widely recognized as our more specialized experts have neglected it. Second, I believe that the contribution of both scientific specialists and general specialists in the past half century has created a substantial discipline. Third, I think we need not be as much disturbed as some of us have apparently been by what is called a lack of recognition. The laments of our so-called humanistic scholars over their neglect, as the money goes to the scientists, seem rather pathetic, and sometimes seems to lead to making their own studies less human in the attempt to imitate the scientists. An acquaintance with scientists leads an administrator to become conscious of the many levels of condescension that exist among them. They are far from being the happy, prestigeful fraternity that our lonely humanists imagine them to be. And an administrator also lives with the very thinly disguised contempt showered upon him by those who feel that an administrator has no excuse for existence on a campus of intellectuals. I have just finished reading a scholarly analysis of novels about college life entitled *Fiction and the American College*. Of course our fiction writers are mostly satirists these days, but even making allowance for this, the pictures of both students and professors are so disenchanting that one who expects to live it out on the campus must take refuge in a sense of humor, the saving humor that we need to cultivate when we feel that we are not being adequately recognized.

Such conferences as we are here attending should convince us that we have work of significance beyond the confines of the campus, and should encourage us in doing it, without worrying too much about status.

Notes

1 Everett Lee Hunt, "General Specialists," *Quarterly Journal of Speech Education* (July 1916): 253–63.
2 Charles H. Woolbert, "A Problem in Pragmatism," *Ibid.*: 264.
3 Ibid., 265.
4 Henry Steel Commager, "A Historian Looks at Our Political Morality," *Saturday Review* (10 July 1965).
5 Archibald MacLeish, "What Is 'Realism' Doing to American History?" *Saturday Review* (3 July 1965).
6 McGeorge Bundy, "The Uses of Responsibility," A Reply to Archibald MacLeish, *Saturday Review* (3 July 1965).

II
The Nineties (1990–1999)

I'm a bitch, I'm a lover/I'm a child, I'm a mother
I'm a sinner, I'm a saint/I do not feel ashamed

—Meredith Brooks, "Bitch"

In the '90s *RSQ* emerges as a serious scholarly publication outlet for rhetoricians in English and Communication Studies; open to rhetoricians in any field (philosophy, economics, anthropology), it nonetheless remains a mostly bi-departmental organ that flexes out of hiding in the rallied hoopla of an increasingly popular biennial conference. An examination of the scholarship published in *RSQ* from 1991–1995, under the guidance of co-editors Eugene Garver (1987–1995), Philip Keith (1991–1995), and Rex Veeder (1993–1995), indicates an almost complete transition to the dominance of peer-reviewed work and a shift from an entrenched interest in the ancients and pedagogy toward more contemporary ethical, theoretical, and political concerns, trends that would continue under the editorship of Jeffrey Walker from 1996–1999. What was once a straight, Yoos-driven enterprise arrived in the '90s as a polymorphous, rhetorical jubilee.

The progressive professionalization of *RSQ*'s content called for the professionalization of its form, as well. The final issue of 1990, 20.4, curated and introduced by Philip Keith, is a collection of essays in honor of George Yoos; it's also the last issue of *RSQ* to "be bound with a spiral binding and placed within light cardboard covers," to quote Richard L. Larson's 1975 directive.[1] In his introduction, Keith declares that "after this final issue of 1990, *RSQ* will change its format to a printed 9x6 journal that will, fortunately or unfortunately, look somewhat similar to other professional journals on your shelves and in your libraries."[2] The first volume of 1991 does look more like a journal, but it was still produced in Word, photocopied, stapled, and mailed to addresses compiled somewhat haphazardly into an RSA mailing list. The responsibility for keeping the mailing list, producing the journal, and mailing it out still fell mainly to Veeder and his colleagues at St. Cloud State, all without remuneration. The mailing list had grown to more than 1,000 by then, but there was still no method of determining if recipients had moved, left the discipline, or died. According to Walker, an investigation revealed "that we were mailing 1,000 copies to less than 300 who were actually dues-paying members of RSA."[3]

By 1994, the production process was running about two years behind, as well, and issues were published whenever it seemed there was enough material to fill one.[4] Veeder therefore implemented a catch-up strategy in preparation for the transition to Walker's editorship, emptying his submission drawer: volume 24 has only two issues; volume 25 has only one. In the months before taking over in 1996, Walker began writing to scholars and soliciting articles. He opens volume 26.1 with the announcement of an array of updates designed to bring *RSQ*'s form, function, and content up to professional standards.[5] With the full support of Penn State University and its large community of rhetoricians in the departments of English and Communication Arts and Sciences, Walker created a graduate student position to maintain the membership directory, had the cover and layout of the journal redesigned again, this time professionally, and instituted infrastructural changes, including a double-blind review process for "each credible submission," an 8–12 week deadline for acceptance decisions to be communicated to authors, and "a journal that appears on schedule" four times per year.[6]

Walker calls for content shifts, as well. According to Garver, Yoos believed *RSQ* should take its inspiration from journalism and write for an audience with a short attention span looking to read brief pieces that intersect with their daily lives and interests of the moment;[7] Walker, on the other hand, believed *RSQ* should devote itself to more enduring questions and scholarly modes of thought, calling for more symposia ("article-sets") and special issues, as well as longer individual pieces.

> To be consistent with the goal of publishing significant, high-quality work, *RSQ* will make space—when appropriate—for longer, more substantial articles, by which I mean texts ranging up to 30 pages in print. Particularly noteworthy contributions of even greater length will also be considered. . . . *RSQ* may also devote an issue to a short monograph that advances an especially significant argument or that presents original research findings of major importance. . . . *RSQ* will also make space, when appropriate, for editions, translations and "recoveries" of texts that have importance for the rhetorical tradition but that have not been widely available.[8]

By the end of the 1990s, for all intents and purposes, *RSQ* has completed its transition from an aspiring society newsletter to a highly selective and professional scholarly journal in rhetorical studies.

During this decade, three of the most influential themes to appear between *RSQ*'s covers were feminist history/historiography, Kenneth Burke, and online communication; three of the four essays reprinted here reflect those themes. In 1992, Susan Jarratt guest edited an enormously generative special issue, volume 22.1, devoted to "Feminist History and Academic Practice." The first essay reprinted in this section is Michelle Ballif's poststructuralist contribution to that issue.[9] Already in the *Newsletter* in 1973, W. Ross Winterowd lists Kenneth Burke's *Language as Symbolic Action* as one of the top five essential works in modern rhetorical theory and practice.[10] However, a flurry of rhetorical scholarship explicitly focused on Burke emerged in *RSQ* in the mid to late '90s. In 1996, volume 26.2 devoted all four essays to this thinker, and Jack Selzer's contribution to it is the second essay reprinted in this section.[11] In 1994, Netscape Navigator became the first free-of-charge graphical web browser for noncommercial uses, and computer-mediated communication exploded. The third essay reprinted in this section is Barbara Warnick's much-cited 1998 study on the implications, for rhetorical theory and criticism, of anonymous, nonlinear, nonsynchronous online public discourse.[12] The final essay reprinted in this section, originally published in 1999, is Gerald Hauser's return to ancient rhetoric with a contemporary aim: he teases through Aristotle's theory of epideictic rhetoric for the purpose of contemplating its constitutive possibilities for modern ethics and politics.[13]

Chapters in Part II

Michelle Ballif, "Re/Dressing Histories; Or, on Re/Covering Figures Who Have Been Laid Bare by Our Gaze."

Jack Selzer, "Kenneth Burke Among the Moderns: *Counter-Statement* as Counter Statement."

Barbara Warnick, "Rhetorical Criticism of Public Discourse on the Internet: Theoretical Implications."

Gerard A. Hauser, "Aristotle on Epideictic: The Formation of Public Morality."

Notes

1 Richard L. Larson, "Notes on the Meeting of the Board of Directors of the Rhetoric Society of America," 28.

2 Philip Keith, "Essays in Honor of George Yoos: Introduction," *Rhetoric Society Quarterly* 20, no. 4 (1990): 323.

3 Jeffrey Walker, email message to authors, 29 September 2017.

4 Ibid.

5 Jeffrey Walker, "A New Start Toward the Next Millennium: A Note from the Editor," *Rhetoric Society Quarterly* 26, no. 1 (1996): 5–7.

6 Ibid., 6.

7 Eugene Garver. In discussion with Diane Davis, 27 September 2017.

8 Walker, 6.

9 This special issue comes on the heels of two significant bibliographies published in 20 no. 4: "Women and the History of Rhetorical Theory to 1900" was compiled by Jane Donawerth, and "Gender and Writing" was collaboratively produced by Kelly Belanger, Heather Brodie Graves, Andrea Lunsford, Melanie Boyd, Diane Chambers, Marcia Dickson, Patricia Kedzerski, Carrie Shively Leverenz, Veronica Lopez, Margaret Gentry Neff, Kari Schneider, Sarah Sloane, Tracy Vezdos.

10 W. Ross Winterowd, "Essential Materials," *Newsletter: Rhetoric Society of America* 3, no. 3 (1973): 4.

11 Jack Selzer, "Kenneth Burke among the Moderns: *Counter-Statement* as Counter Statement," *Rhetoric Society Quarterly* 26, no. 2 (1996): 19–49.

12 Barbara Warnick, "Rhetorical Criticism of Public Discourse on the Internet: Theoretical Implications," *Rhetoric Society Quarterly* 28, no. 4 (1998): 73–84.

13 Gerald Hauser, "Aristotle on Epideictic: The Formation of Public Morality," *Rhetoric Society Quarterly* 29, no. 1 (1999): 5–23.

5

Re/Dressing Histories; Or, on Re/Covering Figures Who Have Been Laid Bare by Our Gaze

MICHELLE BALLIF

"Women! This coin which men find counterfeit!" laments Euripedes's Hippoly-tus.[1] "Why, why, Lord Zeus, did you put them in the world, in the light of the sun? If you were so determined to breed the race of man, the source of it should not have been women" (II.616–20). Phaedra is, as all women, the counterfeit coin. Her exchange rate is never quite legitimate. *She* is never quite legitimate. As the gold standard is Man, is Truth, Woman never measures up. She is always found lacking Truth—the Truth that is man—and is thus, like Phaedra, a coun-terfeit coin. But she is a coin imprinted with His signature, bearing His name, nevertheless. With his imprint, Woman's exchange rate is secured. Like a coin, she changes hands—from father to husband.[2]

Woman, the counterfeit coin, the site of false words and deeds, is inscribed with guilt; indicted with deception, penned as the Unspeakable and Undiscern-ible Lie, sentenced to silence. Woman is the text that paradoxically cannot speak but nevertheless speaks in its silence. Her silence *is* the message; it desires to be read. And now we—as historiographers of male-authored texts concerning women, as "feminists," as proponents of the "Discourses of the Other"—desire to (re)cover and (re)read Phaedra's, Diotima's, Aspasia's silent message.[3]

But why? What motivates our desire to read these women? What propels our desire to make these women readable? Are we not, perhaps, attempting to reinvest these women with value? Are we not trying to redeem them from charges of counterfeit? Are we not, then, merely making Woman into a *legit-imate* coin, a *proper* currency, a *respectable* asset? Are we not, then, merely increasing her exchange rate, but without questioning the very standard—the phallogocentric standard of Truth—that finds her lacking, that is responsible for her devaluation?

It is my argument that our attempts to (re)read women, to (re)cover women, to (re)present women, and to therefore (re)cast history, are insidious acts of (re)appropriation.

Everyone knows that the exchange rate of a dog of papered lineage—of legitimate birth—is exponentially greater than that of a mongrel. To provide Woman with a history is to increase her value by making her legitimate, by giving her a proper name, by locating her within a proper family, by situating her in a proper narrative. This act of confirmation is nothing less than the ideological exercise of what Gayatri Spivak calls the "tyranny of the 'proper'— in the sense of that which produces both property and the proper name of the patronymic" ("Feminism" 91). To make woman proper by providing her with a history *is* the patronymic, phallogocentric enterprise par excellence. Derrida terms this enterprise the "*metaphysics of the proper [le propre]*— self-possession, propriety, property, cleanliness" (*Grammatology* 26; emphasis in original). This making proper—and thus making present—is achieved through the violence of naming. Working out of Derrida, Spivak reminds us of the tyranny and violence of any given episteme ("Subaltern?" 287)— any paradigmatic system of truth and presence. By implication, an important question to ask of our "standard" and "justified" narrative paradigms is: what violence has occurred in order to tell these stories this way, and more importantly, what violence has occurred in order to establish these stories (common sensically) as the way they should or ought to be told.[4] Wherein, then, I ask, lies Woman-with-a-history's value, if her value is granted only in terms of the Name-of-the-Father?

It is my argument that the traditional narrative paradigms—namely the Aristotelian Narrative of Linearity and the Freudian Narrative of Triangularity— are used to construct histories which are essentially patronymic and phallogocentric. These narrative paradigms are discourse strategies used to construct a reasonable, well-ordered, whole subject with a proper name and, thus, an essential and responsible identity to be then appropriated and bartered by the *polis* all in accordance with a phallo-libidinal economy. Legitimate histories construct legitimate subjects.

Not all stories, Socrates tells us, are good, true, and acceptable (see, for example, *Phaedrus* ¶260–65). Aristotle, as one of our first acknowledged "legislators of the wor(l)d," defines in his *Poetics* the conditions of a legitimate narrative. One of the most important, if not the single most important, condition is a unified, coherent, and reasonable plot (*Poetics* 1450.a.23–4). The stories we tell, Aristotle suggests, should make our experience *reasonable*: this happened because of this, if A then B. His poetics is an aesthetic syllogism. He writes: "the poet's function is to describe . . . what is possible as being probable or necessary" (1450.a.35). Good plots arrange events according to a logic—a logic of cause and effect. The worst plots, according to Aristotle, are "episodic"; he writes, "I call a Plot episodic when there is neither probability nor necessity in the sequence of its episodes" (1451.b.30).

And hence, another—and yet related—condition of a narrative: it must be sequenced, it must be *ordered*. According to Aristotle:

We maintain. . . [who is We?] that the first essential, the life and the soul, so to speak, of Tragedy is the Plot; and the Characters come second—compare the parallel in painting, where the most beautiful colours laid on without *order* will not give one the same pleasure as a simple black-and-white sketch of a portrait.

(1450.a.38–1450.b.3)

According to Aristotle's aesthetics, a narrative must be arranged according to some organizing principle. And, lucky us, he provides us with this organizing principle: He states,

"Now a whole is that which has beginning, middle, and end. . . . Again: to be beautiful, a living creature, and every whole made up of parts, must not only present a certain order in its arrangement of parts, but also be of a certain definite magnitude" (1450.b.25, 35). Aristotle also offers us the classificatory system of binaries to help us *order* our stories, to order our experiences, to order ourselves.

This order of the plot can be described as hypotactical. Hypotaxis is a grammatical structure based on the notion of hierarchies, of subordination. Elements in a sentence are assigned positions of value. Likewise, for Aristotle, elements in a plot are ranked: the position of supreme value is the end. The beginning and middle—although indispensable—are nevertheless subordinate to the denouement. Thus, the linear structure of plot development is based on a developmental model, on a progressive scheme, that moves irresistibly—like the syllogism—to the conclusion, to closure—indeed, to death. Aristotle writes: "and the end is everywhere the chief thing" (1450.1.20).

Another condition which Aristotle prescribes is that the narrative must deal with a single issue, "and not (as some tell us) a double issue" (1453.a.10). And that the narrative must avoid "incongruities" (1455.a.25). This "single issue" is the single self—the hero and the truth of his psyche, the progression of his soul (1454a.15–40).

Freudian psychoanalytical theory tells an analogous and overlapping narrative. Claiming to speak from the "neutral viewpoint of a science" (Foucault, *Sexuality* 53), Freud tells the tale that One's *normal* sexuality and *normal* Self is repressed—entrapped in the dark spaces beneath the conscious mind.[5] The "dark twins" of torture and confession are thus employed in psychoanalysis in order to produce "true discourses" concerning sex and, hence the Self.[6] But to dredge up "true" discourses, to grasp at the "fragments of darkness," to mine this "deeply buried truth" is a taxing pick and shovel job. Hence the "truth" exists within us, unbeknownst to us; the "truth" "lies" within Dora, unbeknownst to her. And hence the "truth" of Dora is the "truth" of Dora's sexuality. Freud writes: "sexuality is the key to the problem of psychoneuroses and of neuroses in general. No one who disdains this key will ever be able to unlock the door" (*Dora* 136). And how *convenient* it is that Freud is the key master, "the master of truth" (Foucault, *Sexuality* 67), the one equipped to decipher Dora's

48 • Michelle Ballif

latent truths. The pattern from which Freud's key is cut is fashioned according to these two claims, these two narrative conditions: (1) "that the causes of hysterical disorders are to be found in the intimacies of the patients' psycho-sexual life," and (2) "that hysterical symptoms are the expression of their most secret and repressed wishes" (*Dora* 22)—both of which are functions of a triangular Oedipal economy.

And, according to Freud's key, Dora's most "secret and repressed" objects of desire are Herr K and her father. Therefore the "true" explanation for Dora's hysterical symptoms is repression. But it is not enough that Freud unlock Dora's harbored secrets; it is necessary for Dora to face the "ah!" which lies behind the door. It is necessary, in order to "cure" Dora's hysterical symptoms, that Dora articulate the repressed, that Dora "translate into conscious ideas what was already known in the unconscious" (66), that Dora state the "truth" of her sexuality, of her Self, according to a "logic of concupiscence and desire" (Foucault, *Sexuality* 78), contain it within an acceptable, Oedipal narrative, and therefore be healed and whole.

Hence, Dora is liberated, is cured, is normalized, is *created* as a "mirage" reflecting in "the dark shimmer of sex" (*Sexuality* 157). The "cure" is a part of the disease of Freud's narrative. According to Freud's narrative, the hysteric, like Dora, suffers from reminiscences; that is, she is unable to maintain the correct distance from her memories. The hysteric suffers from the past—presently—on her body. Hence, for Freud, the hysteric is cured once she tells her story straight—that is, once she subjects her reminiscences to a linear and Oedipal narrative, and therefore comes into *possession* of her own story and into *possession* of her Self (Bernheimer and Kahane 11, 21, 70, 71, 185, 187).

The Oedipal narrative is the history of the proper Self appropriating itself appropriately. And according to Irigaray, this is the project of phallogocentrism, the work of the Father: "Property, ownership, and self-definition are the attributes of the father's production. They define the work of the father 'as such.' To be. To own. To be one's own. Properties" (300). The cure and the disease are a tandem creation of the repressive myth which is itself a construct[7]—which in turn constructs a diseased self that must be inscribed in the discourses of pleasure in order to be cured via the discourses of pleasure in order to be created as a Self—normal and nonhysterical—in order to be *used*, to be appropriated, by the system in order to guarantee the perpetual spirals of power and Truth (Butler 99, 116).

These narrative conditions prescribed by Aristotle and implied by Freudian psychoanalytic theory have been embraced and re-prescribed over and over again with few amendments. A "good" and "satisfying" story is the story that cures the subject by making him/her whole, and thus legitimate. The cure is the history, is the ordered, linear story, the ordered, triangular story. It is a story with a beginning, a middle, and an end. A story with "a mommy, a daddy, and a Me" (Deleuze and Guattari, *Anti-Oedipus*). A story based on hypotactical construction and a cause/effect logic. It is a story of progression and a story of the progression of a hero toward the final goal which, more often than not, is the state of Manhood—of autonomy, courage, maturation, selfhood.

The traditional conception of the *Bildungsroman* is built on this model: young neophyte begins journey, undergoes series of initiation rites, overcomes relationships with others, faces ultimate challenge, proves himself, and then gains a Self—an autonomous and mature identity. Joseph Campbell's mono-myth traces the same model: young man walks the road of trials, crosses the threshold, receives a call to adventure, becomes a "master of two worlds," encounters woman as temptress, overcomes challenges, receives ultimate boon, achieves apotheosis, and, again, gains a Self.

These traditional narrative paradigms are the twin tales told by idiots which pump out reasonable and ordered selves—mature humans. The Aristotelian Linear Narrative and the Freudian Triangular Narrative tell basically the same story; it is the story of liberal humanism: "the possibility of a unified self and an integrated consciousness that can transcend material circumstance is repre-sented as the fulfillment of desire, the happy closure at the end of the [develop-mental] story" (Kaplan 152). The so-called happy closure comes when Oedipus finds his identity, when Dora masters her hysteria, when Indiana Jones finds the Holy Grail, when the neophyte finds a unified Self, an individuated Self. The happy closure comes when the cheese stands alone. The linear and triangular epic narrative is a well-choreographed funeral march. A march to the end, to closure, to death.

That Aristotelian poetics and Freudian psychoanalytics have been labeled "masculine," "logocentric," and "phallocentric" is not unjustified. The stories that have been told have been told overwhelmingly by men. The narratives that have been constructed have focused almost exclusively on male heroes. You do the math. Although Aristotle claims that his poetics is an accurate reflection of "the way things are" and that his aesthetics represent the "natural fitness of things," I am arguing that his narrative conditions as well as Freud's love trian-gle, encode not a natural reality, but a socially constructed ideology of patron-ymy and hierarchy.

And herein lies my argument with attempts to construct the history of women. Efforts to make women legitimate by situating them in patronymic narratives does nothing to enfranchise them—because it does nothing to the phallogocentric economy which disenfranchised them.[8] Women do not need to think such a history. Helene Cixous writes, "Phallocentrism. History has never produced or recorded anything else. . . . And it is time to change. To invent the other history" ("Sorties" 96). But this "other" history of which she writes is the history which is *not* one, which is not One. Page duBois argues: "fem-inists need to . . . observe not sameness but difference—historical difference (new narratives, not the same story at every historical moment)" (*Sowing* 10). Again, the call is for a history which is not One, which is not a story of the Same, of the Selfsame.[9] It is, rather, a story of difference, a story told—in Fou-cault's words—"genealogically," that is, a "history" told of "local, discontinuous, and illegitimate knowledges" (*Power/Knowledge* 83, 117, 190).[10] It is a sophistic history—a tale of differing local *nomoi* and kairotic happenings—which displaces the Grand Narrative of a philosophic history.[11] Spivak writes, "We must strive moment by moment to practice a taxonomy of different forms of understanding, different forms of change, dependent perhaps upon resemblance and seeming substitutability—figuration—rather than on the self-identical category of truth" ("Feminism and Critical Theory" 88).[12]

Such little narratives constructed moment by kairotic moment serve not merely to rethink history but—most importantly—to *unthink* the Aristotelian and Freudian Grand Narratives of history. Cixous in her "Laugh of the Medusa" wants the phallological economy of patronymic narratives to be *depense* (252).[13] Paul Smith explains the neologism: "*depense* as in unthought, de-thought; and also *depense* in the sense of spent, and spent by the production of new feminine discourse" (Smith 146). Thus Cixous, here, echoes Sophocles's Jocasta who pleads with Oedipus to unthink his history, to unthink his Identity. According to Deleuze and Guattari, Man (as exemplified by Oedipus) constitutes himself as a gigantic memory. "Becoming Woman," in contradistinction, is anti-Oedipal, anti-memory, anti-history, anti-*chronos* (*A Thousand Plateaus* 293).[14] For "Woman," time is experienced *kairotically* not chronologically, and, thus, is not subject to the "logic of identification" (Kristeva 37) nor to the "economy of rationality" (Gorz 109) nor to their attendant and constitutive discourses and narratives.[15]

What is at stake, then, in re/dressing histories is the production of new narratives, new discourses, new idioms. The task *is not* to add women to the already existing history. Adding women to history is not synonymous with adding women's history (Fox-Genovese 6). Filling in the gaps is definitively not the answer (Fox-Genovese 12), for it is most certainly the impetus of phallogocentrism. If Phaedra is plugged into a patronymic narrative, she will be as mute as ever. Spivak tells us that there is "no space from which the sexed subaltern subject can speak" ("Subaltern?" 307) because she has no *proper* identity. But again, the task is *not* to endow the subaltern with identity, for to do so would be to situate her in a proper patronymic narrative with a proper and thus legitimate relationship (i.e. one of dominance, control, and mastery over) with language.[16]

But perhaps Woman can (un)speak in the unthought, not-yet-thought, nonspaces produced by alternative paradigms, by new idioms, by paralogical and paratactical and, thus, illegitimate discourses.[17] What "hitherto unrecognized possibilities" could we explore if our narratives had no syllogistic, metonymic, linear, or triangular structure? If we broke the sequence (and the sentence)? If the subject wasn't coherent, unified, and whole? If there was no hero? If there was no developmental model? If there were no binaries, no either/or alternatives? If there was no cure?

What if there were no conditions of a narrative, no universal criteria for judging the Truth or legitimacy of a narrative (Lyotard, *Postmodern Condition*

61; Lyotard and Thebaud, *Just Gaming* 14, 28)?[18] What if Truth were a Woman (Nietzsche)—that is, a counterfeit coin—what then?

Cixous replies,

> Then all stories would have to be told differently, the future would be incalculable, the historical forces would, will, change hands, bodies, another thinking, as yet not thinkable, will transform the functioning of all society.

("Sorties" 93)

Notes

1 I would like to acknowledge the silent yet omnivociferous influence of Victor Vitanza in the following ruminations and to note that his article "'Notes' Towards Historiographies of Rhetorics" served as the seedbed for my positions set forth here. I would also like to thank Jan Swearingen for providing the conditions of possibility for this paper. And, finally, I would like to thank Lisa Ede and Susan Jarratt for their many thought-provoking responses to this paper.

2 I am invoking here a well-documented history of Woman as exchange object (cf. Levi-Strauss; Mauss; Irigaray 122; Butler 38) and as semiotic object (cf. Silverman, de Lauretis, Brooke-Rose).

3 The work of Waithe, duBois, and Pomeroy, for example, is demonstrative of feminist historiography.

4 On the insidious violence of "common sense" see Victor J. Vitanza's "'Notes' Towards" (64–66).

5 See also Kaja Silverman's reading of Freud (*The Subject of Semiotics* 132–49).

6 Cf. Deleuze and Guattari's polemical counter in *Anti-Oedipus* to Freud's territorialization of the unconscious.

7 See also Jean Baudrillard's *Seduction*.

8 Cf. Spivak ("Can the Subaltern Speak?" 307 and "Discourse of Woman" 174).

9 According to Butler, this is the critical task of feminism: "to locate strategies of subversive repetition enabled by those constructions, to affirm the local possibilities of intervention through participating in precisely those practices of repetition that constitute identity and, therefore, present the immanent possibility of contesting them" (147; see also 148).

10 See also Foucault's "Nietzsche, Genealogy, and History" (162; Butler 129).

11 Cf. the work of Victor J. Vitanza (especially "'Some More' Notes, Toward a 'Third' Sophistic"), Jean Francois Lyotard (*The Differend*), and Susan Jarratt (especially "The First Sophists"). Although Jarratt proposes sophistic notions of history and subjectivity, she stands in contradistinction to Vitanza, Lyotard, and myself in that she seeks to found a politics, albeit via *nomoi*.

12 Or in the terms of Deleuze and Guattari, different forms of "becoming." Alice Jardine states: "With 'becoming' there is no past or future, and certainly no present—there is no linear history. . . . 'Becoming' is topological, geological, geographical, not historical" (215). Cf. Deleuze and Guattari's *A Thousand Plateaus*, especially 186, 188, 292, 311.

13 Spivak calls for a similar kind of *depense* when she advocates that we "unlearn our privilege as our loss" ("Can the Subaltern Speak?" 295).

14 Nietzsche was in the process of becoming woman when he forgot his umbrella—that is, when he unthought the metaphysics of presence (see Derrida, *Spurs* 123).

15 According to Andre Gorz, linear time is demonstrative of economic rationality, wherein "counting and calculating is . . . the quintessential form of reifying rationalization" (109).

16 Although this is precisely what many—mostly American—feminists posit as *the* guarantee of liberation and empowerment. For example, see Scott's *Gender and the Politics of History* and Smith's *Discerning the Subject*.

17 See Deleuze and Guattari (*A Thousand Plateaus* 189); Lyotard (*The Postmodern Condition* 82 and *The Differend* 13, 68); Derrida ("Choreographies" 171).
18 Lyotard makes a call similar to Cixous's in—as elsewhere—*The Differend* (13, 68).

Works Cited

Aristotle. *The Poetics*. Trans. Ingram Bywater. New York: Modern Library, 1984.

Baudrillard, Jean. *Seduction*. Trans. Brian Singer. New York: St. Martin's P, 1990.

Bernheimer, Charles and Claire Kahane, eds. *In Dora's Case: Freud, Hysteria, Feminism*. New York: Columbia UP, 1985.

Brooke-Rose, Christine. "Woman as a Semiotic Object." *Poetics Today* 6.1–2 (1985): 9–20.

Butler, Judith. *Gender Trouble: Feminism and the Subversion of Identity*. New York: Routledge, 1990.

Campbell, Joseph. *The Hero with a Thousand Faces*. 1949. 2nd ed. Princeton: Princeton UP, 1968.

Cixous, Helene. "The Laugh of the Medusa." Trans. Keith Cohen and Paula Cohen. *New French Feminisms*. Ed. Elaine Marks and Isabelle de Courtivron. New York: Schocken, 1980a. 245–64.

———. "Sorties." Trans. Ann Liddle. *New French Feminisms*. Ed. Elaine Marks and Isabelle de Courtivron. New York: Schocken, 1980b. 90–98.

de Lauretis, Teresa. *Technologies of Gender*. Bloomington: Indiana UP, 1987.

Deleuze, Gilles and Felix Guattari. *Anti-Oedipus*. Trans. Robert Hurley, Mark Seem, and Helen R. Lane. Minneapolis: U of Minnesota P, 1983.

———. *A Thousand Plateaus: Capitalism and Schizophrenia*. Trans. Brian Massumi. Minneapolis: U of Minnesota P, 1987.

Derrida, Jacques. "Choreographies." *The Ear of the Other*. Trans. Peggy Kamuf. Lincoln: U of Nebraska P, 1985. 163–85.

———. *Of Grammatology*. Trans. Gayatri Chakravorty Spivak. Baltimore: Johns Hopkins UP, 1976.

———. *Spurs: Nietzsche's Styles*. Trans. Barbara Harlow. Chicago: U of Chicago P, 1978.

duBois, Page. *Centaurs and Amazons: Women and the Pre-history of the Great Chain of Being*. Ann Arbor: U of Michigan P, 1982.

———. *Sowing the Body: Psychoanalysis and Ancient Representations of Women*. Chicago: U of Chicago P, 1988.

Euripides. *Hippolytus*. Trans. Kenneth Cavander. San Francisco: Chandler, 1962.

Foucault, Michel. *History of Sexuality. Vol. 1: An Introduction*. Trans. Robert Hurley. 1978. New York: Vintage, 1980. 3 vols. 1980–1984.

———. "Nietzsche, Genealogy, and History." *Language, Counter-Memory, Practice*. Trans. Donald F. Bouchard and Sherry Simon. Ithaca: Cornell UP, 1977.

———. *Power/Knowledge*. Trans. Colin Gordon. Brighton, Sussex: Harvester, 1980.

Fox-Genovese, Elizabeth. "Placing Women's History in History." *New Left Review* 133 (1982): 5–29.

Freud, Sigmund. *Dora: An Analysis of a Case of Hysteria*. Ed. Philip Rieff. New York: Collier, 1963.

Gorz, Andre. *Critique of Economic Reason*. Trans. Gillian Handyside and Chris Turner. London: Verso, 1989.

Irigaray, Luce. *Speculum of the Other Woman*. Trans. Gillian C. Gill. Ithaca: Cornell UP, 1985.

Jardine, Alice. *Gynesis: Configurations of Woman and Modernity*. Ithaca: Cornell UP, 1985.

Jarratt, Susan C. "The First Sophists and Feminism: Discourses of the 'Other.'" *Hypatia* 5 (1990): 27–41.

Kaplan, Cora. "Pandora's Box: Subjectivity, Class and Sexuality in Socialist Feminist Criticism." *Making a Difference: Feminist Literary Criticism*. Ed. Gayle Greene and Coppelia Kahn. New York: Methuen, 1985. 146–76.

Kristeva, Julia. "Women's Time." Trans. Alice Jardine and Harry Blake. *Feminist Theory: A Critique of Ideology*. Ed. Nannerl O. Keohane, Michelle Z. Rosaldo, and Barbara C. Gelpi. 1981. Chicago: U of Chicago P, 1982. 31–53.

Levi-Strauss, Claude. *The Elementary Structures of Kinship*. Trans. James Harle Bell and John Richard Von Sturmer. Boston: Beacon, 1969.

Lyotard, Jean Francois. *The Differend: Phrases in Dispute*. Trans. Georges Van Den Abbeele. Minneapolis: U of Minnesota P, 1988.

———. *The Postmodern Condition: A Report on Knowledge*. Trans. Geoff Bennington and Brian Massumi. Minneapolis: U of Minnesota P, 1984.

Lyotard, Jean Francois and Jean Loup Thebaud. *Just Gaming*. Trans. Wlad Godzich. Minneapolis: U of Minnesota P, 1985.

Mauss, Marcel. *The Gift: Forms and Functions of Exchange in Archaic Societies*. Trans. Ian Cunnison. Clencoe: Free P, 1954.

Plato. *The Phaedrus*. Trans. W. C. Helmbold and W. G. Rabinowitz. Indianapolis: Bobbs-Merrill, 1956.

Pomeroy, Sarah B. *Goddesses, Whores, Wives, and Slaves: Women in Classical Antiquity*. New York: Schocken, 1975.

———. *Women in Hellenistic Egypt: From Alexander to Cleopatra*. New York: Schoken, 1984.

Scott, Joan. *Gender and the Politics of History*. New York: Columbia UP, 1988.

Silverman, Kaja. *The Subject of Semiotics*. New York: Oxford UP, 1983.

Smith, Paul. *Discerning the Subject*. Minneapolis: U of Minnesota P, 1988.

Spivak, Gayatri Chakravorty. "Can the Subaltern Speak?" *Marxism and the Interpretation of Culture*. Ed. Cary Nelson and Lawrence Grossberg. Urbana: U of Illinois P, 1988. 271–313.

———. "Displacement and the Discourse of Woman." *Displacement: Derrida and After*. Ed. Mark Krupnick Bloomington: Indiana UP, 1983. 169–95.

———. "Feminism and Critical Theory." *In Other Worlds: Essays in Cultural Politics*. New York: Methuen, 1987. 77–92.

Vitanza, Victor J. "'Notes' Towards Historiographies of Rhetorics; or the Rhetorics of the Histories of Rhetorics: Traditional, Revisionary, and Sub/Versive." *Pre/Text* 8 (1987): 64–125.

———. "'Some More' Notes, Toward a 'Third' Sophistic." Forthcoming in *Argumentation*.

Waithe, Mary Ellen, ed. *A History of Women Philosophers*. Vol. I. Boston: Martinus Nijhoff, 1987.

6

Kenneth Burke Among the Moderns
Counter-Statement *as Counter Statement*[1]

JACK SELZER

It is no overstatement to claim that Kenneth Burke was weaned on modernism, that indeed he was a pivotal figure among the remarkable moderns who gathered in Greenwich Village in the years just before and after World War I. Yet the observation bears repeating nonetheless. Born in 1897 in Pittsburgh and educated there through high school, Burke moved with his parents in 1915 to an apartment in Weehawken, New Jersey, just across the Hudson River from 42nd Street in New York City. Though he studied at Ohio State during the spring semester of 1916 (with his thoroughly modernist friend James Light) and though he commuted from Weehawken to Columbia University throughout 1917, Burke gradually determined to take his instruction from Greenwich Village rather than from the university; having insinuated himself into the literary and intellectual scene, he moved to Greenwich Village early in 1918. There he met, associated with, befriended, and/or worked with a host of Village writers, artists, and critics, including (to mention only the ones that seem most prominent today) William Carlos Williams, Malcolm Cowley, Hart Crane, Marianne Moore, Eugene O'Neill, Alfred Stieglitz, Georgia O'Keeffe, Van Wyck Brooks, Edmund Wilson, Allen Tate, Jean Toomer, and Katherine Anne Porter. Burke was on hand for the most experimental and successful period of the Provincetown Players, and he followed political and artistic developments in *The Masses*. While spending much of his time after 1922 writing, reading, editing, and translating at his Andover, New Jersey farm, Burke remained very much a physical and verbal presence in the Greenwich Village modernist scene, contributing poetry, fiction, criticism, and translations to modernist magazines. As an editorial assistant at *The Dial*, the most prominent such magazine of the era, he provided editorial services on behalf of Williams, Crane, Ezra Pound, Thomas Mann, T. S. Eliot, Arthur Schnitzler, and Wallace Stevens. And he maintained his social and artistic relations through extensive, occasionally spectacular correspondences with Williams, Crane, Cowley, Light, Moore, Tate, Stieglitz, Matthew Josephson, Gorham Munson, Waldo Frank, Margaret Anderson and

Jane Heap, Harold Loeb, R. P. Blackmur, Austin Warren, Ivor Winters, and any number of others.

Burke as a writer did much more than keep up a vigorous correspondence. He published a number of poems in modernist magazines. He wrote and published a couple of dozen short stories for those same magazines, collecting most of them in *The White Oxen, and Other Stories* in 1924. He translated the Modern Library edition of *Death in Venice* still in print today. He published reviews, criticism, and essays on literary topics in *The Dial, Vanity Fair, Hound and Horn, The Bookman, The Freeman, 1924, The Saturday Review, The Little Review, The New Republic,* and elsewhere; in 1931 he collected a number of these articles into *Counter-Statement,* his first book of criticism and theory. So promising and influential was Burke's earliest writing that he was recognized as one of a half dozen members of "this youngest generation" for whom Gorham Munson founded the experimental magazine *Secession* in 1922. Burke also published a modernist novel, *Towards a Better Life,* in 1931. For his contributions to literary modernism, Burke was awarded The Dial Award for 1928, an honor previously extended in the 1920s to Sherwood Anderson, T. S. Eliot, Van Wyck Brooks, Marianne Moore, E. E. Cummings, William Carlos Williams, and Ezra Pound.

One good way, then, to understand Kenneth Burke—at least the early work of Kenneth Burke—is against the backdrop of modernism in general and the culture of Greenwich Village, 1915–1931, in particular. But despite a notable exception here and there (e.g., Warren; Warnock), scholarship on Burke has mostly discounted the early Burke, the modernist Burke. That's neither surprising nor blameworthy: Burke's tremendous contributions to literary and rhetorical theory after 1930 have, for good reason, attracted tremendous interest to that part of his life and work; and so scholars have understandably attended mostly to the theoretical and critical works in Burke's canon, most of them published after 1931, rather than to the critical and literary works that Burke produced before that time. In addition, Burke has customarily been considered as an "individual," as a solitary genius and a gadfly, as someone apart from movements and schools; because of the originality of his insights, Burke is often admired, with some justice, as an unaffiliated scholar and autodidact who was somewhat immune from social and intellectual movements, somehow free to pursue in his own strange way his own personal and idiosyncratic agenda—an unaffiliated scholar and maverick genius (sometimes infuriatingly so) not only in the sense that he remained remote from and critical of intellectual fashions current on university campuses but in the sense that his ideas remained eccentric from and independent of other recognizable intellectual schools. One of the best recent overviews of Burke's criticism, for example, begins by stressing

his irregular career. Without a college degree, with minimal formal training in literature, philosophy, psychology, or political science, with no permanent full-time academic appointment, and with no conventional area of specialization, Burke . . . has [produced] a body of work whose breadth, rigor, and theoretical grounding is unmatched by the work of any other American critic.

(Paul Jay, "Kenneth Burke" 68)

Another notes "the free play of private idiosyncrasies" in Burke's work (Jameson, "Symbolic Inference" 508). If they have not stressed Burke's independence and his later work, then scholars have understood Burke in relation to a variety of contexts and isms rather different from literary modernism—New Criticism, for example, or pragmatism or poststructuralism or one or another version of neo-classicism.[2] It has always been difficult, then, to "place" Burke; he is famous for his independence and his uneasy relation to any number of schools and movements. Nor is it the aim of this study to "correct" these legitimate ways of understanding Burke or to smooth out Burke's thought or his prose, for it is largely his independence and iconoclasm that make his work so intriguing. Still, Burke's independence has been overstated, and it has been too easy to excuse him from membership in formative cultural groups that gave Burke his intellectual lifeblood—and that drew lifeblood from him. My argument is that Burke was a key point of articulation for modernist ideology—that Burke defined his early self and his early work both with and against several key strains in the modernist conversation.

Counter-Statement (1931) is a notable case in point. Like many things Burke wrote before the Great Depression, *Counter-Statement* developed out of Burke's relationships to *The Dial* and to the other modernist groups and individuals that he encountered in New York. A document with clear links to the Symbolists as well as to other modernist groups and doctrines, it takes up standard modernist artists, texts, topics, and controversies—Cézanne and Gide and Baudelaire and Verhaeren; *Death in Venice, R. U. R.*, and *The Waste Land*; psychology, aesthetics, form; the artist's confrontation with industrialism; the grounds of artistic merit and appeal; and the relations between art and society, artists and observers. But the book is not easily or simply modernist, for if Burke in *Counter-Statement* incorporates some doctrinaire esthete and modernist notions into his understanding of art, he also counters some others. To put it another way, in *Counter-Statement* Burke, from a position squarely within the modernist conversation, nevertheless destabilizes certain key modernist assumptions—and in the process destabilizes his book as well.

The general aim of *Counter-Statement*, to delineate the essential character of art and the relationships that exist between art and society, is certainly a modernist staple. As such, the collection of essays, arranged generally in the order in which they were composed and revised for the occasion of book publication, participates in one way or another in the tradition of analogous collections such as the multi-authored *Criticism in America: Its Function and Status* (1924), Norman Foerster's *Humanism in America* (1930), Hartley Grattan's *A Critique of Humanism* (1930), Benedetto Croce's *Aesthetic* (1902), Joel

Spingarn's *Creative Criticism* (1917, 1925, 1931), Irving Babbitt's *Rousseau and Romanticism* (1919), Clive Bell's *Art* (1913), I. A. Richards's *Principles of Literary Criticism* (1924), V. F. Calverton's *The Newer Spirit* (1925), Van Wyck Brooks's *Emerson and Others* (1927) and *Sketches in Criticism* (1932), T. S. Eliot's *Sacred Wood* (1928), and Edmund Wilson's *Axel's Castle* (1931), as well as in the tradition of critical statements and reviews by Spingarn, Ezra Pound, Wilson, H. L. Mencken, Brooks, Gorham Munson, Ivor Winters, Malcolm Cowley, Joseph Wood Krutch, Granville Hicks, and others in periodicals like *Seven Arts, The Dial, Contact, The Bookman, Secession,* and *The New Republic.* As its title suggests, *Counter-Statement* is in a complex dialogue with these and other modernist critical texts, and, since it is a revision of a number of earlier essays and since one of its essays ("Lexicon Rhetoricae") is subtitled in part a "correction" of two earlier essays in the book, in a kind of dialogue with itself. The result is a book which promotes a unique, if sometimes elusive and even contradictory, modernist account of the place of the artist and art in the early twentieth century.

Burke begins *Counter-Statement* by dealing with established modernist topics essentially as a turn-of-the-century esthete or Symbolist would, that is, in a way that positions the modern artist as radically alienated and aloof from society, working in a realm of pure art that is insulated against the philistine masses. The "Three Adepts of 'Pure' Literature" from a departed generation, whom Burke describes to open the volume, were all modernist heroes, and Burke had originally written about all three Europeans in the early 1920s while in the midst of his most committed rendezvous with aestheticism.[3] Flaubert "had always looked upon art as an existence-in-itself" (1); Walter Pater, whom Burke admired for his "superior adjustment of technique to aesthetic interests" (9), was of course the most notable of the British esthetes; and Remy de Gourmont, who "made one think of literature as a risk, a kind of outlawry" (64), was the Symbolist critic who was perhaps most admired by the most influential modernist imagemakers during the first few years after World War I.

Burke's Flaubert is truly an esthete at heart, withdrawn from the world, adopting early in life (and never renouncing) a decadent interest in things illicit, striving monomaniacally after beauty rather than after the personal status or wealth pursued by Balzac, trying to conceal his art in pure form though ultimately failing in that because of his commitment to the novel, a form ill-suited to the concealment of art. It would be an exaggeration to say that in its description of Flaubert the essay paints an uncritical portrait of the ideal life as something akin to the ones dramatized in Wilson's *Axel's Castle* or Huysmans's *A Rebours*—the ideal life as a purposeful retreat in the course of which an estranged solitary tries to give himself or herself as many pure moments of individual artistic satisfaction as possible. But the pronounced tendency toward that stance is certainly there, for Burke does not reprove Flaubert's residence in "the *tour d'ivoire* school of writers" (1) or his single-minded devotion to his art. For Flaubert, according to Burke, the good life amounted to the deliberate multiplication of private and sublime emotional experiences that are produced mostly by contact with art; the ideal is something akin to the "poundings of the heart" Flaubert once "felt on beholding a bare wall of the Acropolis" (6), an intensity of feeling that he hoped to evoke through and in his writing. And good art for Flaubert was just as radically separated from public, civic action and from utilitarian ends:

> What seems beautiful to me, what I should most like to do, would be a book about nothing, a book without any exterior tie, but sustained by the internal force of its style, a book which would have no subject, or at least in which the subject would be almost invisible, if that is possible. The most beautiful books are those with the least matter.
>
> (6)

Far from reproving this attitude, Burke was identifying strongly and personally with it and with Flaubert, whom he admired greatly for his artistic innovations and achievements, as well as for his attitudes. Not only did Burke exclaim the identification in his letter to Cowley of January 6, 1918—"I shall get a room in New York and begin my existence as a Flaubert. Flaubert is to be my Talmud, my Homer, my beacon"—but he also betrayed it in a revealingly personal sentence in the version of the Flaubert essay published in *The Dial* in February 1922 (a sentence deleted from *Counter-Statement*): rather like Burke himself or like some of his closest friends Crane and Cowley, "Flaubert at eighteen had all the earmarks of a promising young genius in revolt against Ohio, destined to come to New York and get a job with some advertising agency" ("Correspondence of Flaubert" 148).

Burke's words on Pater reveal just how thoroughly aestheticized is Burke's account of Flaubert, for Burke's Pater is indeed the prototypical esthete. Locked away in an artistic "cloister" so restricted that "he derived the characters and environments of his fiction by research" (10) rather than through experience, Pater is appreciated for the innovation of placing style and artistic technique above everything. "Art to Pater was 'not the conveyance of an abstract body of truths' but 'the critical tracing of . . . conscious artistic structure.' He thought of a sentence as a happening, [and] . . . his preference for artifice was consistent" (12). Residing in "the Immutable, the Absolute" world of Beauty, placing aesthetics above ethics, Pater "proclaim[ed] the dignity of man in art" (15). For Pater art was its own reward, and artists first and foremost should seek Beauty rather than private virtue (let alone civic amelioration, except insofar as aesthetic refinement itself serves as a benign and constructive force in society). "Ideology in Pater was used for its flavor of beauty, rather than of argument. He treated ideas not for their value as statements, but as horizons, situations, developments of plot, in short, as any other element of fiction" (14).[4] Burke's tone here is reportorial rather than explicitly laudatory, but the patience and sympathy in his account still essentially mirror his sympathy for Pater's project.

Moreover, Burke's sympathy for Pater shows up further when his account is seen as in general opposition to the New Humanists' disapproval of Pater, on the grounds that Pater's criticism was impressionistic, based only on shifting and emotional sensations rather than on firm aesthetic foundations.[5] By crediting Pater with residing in that "Immutable and Absolute" world of Beauty rather than in a lower world of impermanent flux and by emphasizing Pater's fiction rather than his criticism, Burke countered the New Humanists' demonizing of Pater's alleged subjectivism. Burke's approval of Pater's reverence for The Beautiful thus allies him with the Symbolists as well as with Croce and Spingarn, whose own aestheticism may well have influenced Burke's views before 1925.[6]

But it is Burke's portrait of Gourmont that is the most revealing one among the "Three Adepts." Though Gourmont is barely remembered today, he was greatly admired by influential early moderns for his broad and deep learning, for his many plays, poems, stories, novels, and works of criticism, for his Symbolist literary values, for his editorial efforts on behalf of the Symbolists in connection with the periodical *Mercure de France* (which he founded and edited), and for leading a radically cloistered personal life that seemed committed to art above everything. *The Little Review* devoted a special hagiographic number to Gourmont in February/March 1919. T. S. Eliot considered Gourmont a formative influence on his life and art, as references and ideas in *The Sacred Wood* and *Selected Essays* attest. Amy Lowell and Richard Aldington considered Gourmont a pioneer in vers libre and imagism, Aldington publishing a lavish, two-volume, illustrated edition and translation of selected works by Gourmont in 1928. And Ezra Pound not only contributed a cranky review of Aldington's edition to *The Dial* while Burke was working there as music critic—it was cranky towards Aldington's work but not Gourmont's—but he also translated for *The Dial* all the epigrammatical quasi-poetry in Gourmont's previously unpublished *Dust for Sparrows* in eight consecutive issues of *The Dial* in 1920–1921, issues that also contained reviews and fiction by Burke. Pound was indeed a great admirer of Gourmont as early as 1912; he communicated with Gourmont until Gourmont's death in 1915 (at the age of 57), touted Gourmont's innovative genius and mourned at his passing, appropriated Gourmont's ideas into his own views of poetry and criticism, and included several essays on Gourmont in *Pavannes and Divisions* (1918).[7]

Burke's fascination with Gourmont is not unusual, therefore, particularly given his early enthusiasms for Continental writers in general and for the Symbolists in particular. Like Gourmont's other admirers, Burke personally appreciated Gourmont's disgust for social and artistic convention and his reclusive lifestyle—one spent in devoted service to art. In that Gourmont served as a role model, then, he was "almost a 'traumatic' experience in my development," Burke later recalled (Fogarty 59). He also appreciated Gourmont's advocacy for a refined aristocracy of art and for an equally refined style. Burke's letters reveal that as early as 1916 he was reading Gourmont and that the enthusiasm continued for some time. Three years later he was still discussing Gourmont with Josephson (Josephson to Burke, March 27, 1919), and quoting him in his fiction ("Mrs. Maecenas," published in *The Dial* in March, 1920). And in the early 1920s he was sending Gourmont's books to William Carlos Williams to study. Accordingly, then, Burke devotes half of "Three Adepts" to this one figure, and he describes Gourmont in keeping with received wisdom on him—as a prototypical Symbolist and modern.

Gourmont, that is, like Pater and Flaubert "remained until his death a man closed in his study, seen by a few intimates, living almost exclusively with books" (18); like Burke's Flaubert and Pater, Gourmont "had much too strong a detestation of democratic standards to be anything but a disciple of Art for Art's Sake" (16). A follower of Mallarmé, like Mallarmé a "leading apologist of symbolism" (21), a person who pursued throughout his life the intensely felt "exclusively personal experiences which are important so long as sensation endures" (20), an agnostic who was interested in the Catholic Church as an artistic pageant, Gourmont also had a Symbolist weakness for illicit subjects and a modernist "fever for innovation" and originality (16):

> This attitude manifested itself in the experimental nature of both his critical and imaginative writings. His one imperative was to be venturesome. Since art, by becoming an end to itself, became a matter of the individual—or by becoming a matter of the individual, became as end in itself—he was theoretically without external obligations, at liberty to develop his medium as he preferred.
>
> (17)

This radical individualism, a staple of Symbolist decadence, was at the center of Gourmont's work.

Burke's overview of that work, an overview that shows the detail in Burke's knowledge of Gourmont, underscores Gourmont's enthusiasm for pure style, for the "complete lubrication of phrase" (17) that insulated Gourmont, as it had Pater, from philistine society: Gourmont had "little time for those perfect systems of government wherein the aggregate of humanity is to be made happy at the expense of each individual" (20). And Gourmont's innovation in thought was, appropriately, his "dissociative method," a "companion discovery to symbolism" (23)—that is, a suitably modernist method of invention designed to liberate words and beliefs from the conventional associations that have through time fossilized around them. An effort to rejuvenate knowledge, the dissociative method was designed to free thinkers from inherited dogma by offering a critique of inherited commonplaces and by generating for inquirers new associations for words and concepts. Burke illustrated the dissociation of ideas in *Counter-Statement* by quoting Gourmont's own examples—the associations between Byzantium and decadence and the associations that the English and French have held for Joan of Arc—both of which Gourmont had dissociated productively. With obvious enthusiasm, then, Burke concludes one segment of "Three Adepts" by crediting the concept of dissociation of ideas with influencing modernist prose experiments by Stein and Joyce and by speculating on possible extensions of the concept to literary criticism: "Any technical criticism of our methodological authors of today must concern itself with the further development and schematization of such ideas as De Gourmont was considering" (24).[8]

While the artistic heroes cited and discussed in *Counter-Statement*—Flaubert, Pater, and Gourmont in the opening chapter, Mann and Gide in a later one, and Cézanne, Shakespeare, Goethe, Eliot,[9] Joyce, Dostoevsky, Baudelaire, and assorted others elsewhere in the book—tie *Counter-Statement* intimately to the discourse of modernism, an even closer tie is forged by the book's preoccupation with a central modernist topic, the nature of form. From the beginning readers have noticed the centrality of this issue in *Counter-Statement*, and Burke himself emphasized the importance of form to *Counter-Statement*, for instance in the Preface to the second edition, where he describes his theory of form as "the gist" of his book. *Counter-Statement* in general—and "Psychology and Form," "The Poetic Process," and "Lexicon Rhetoricae" in particular—presents Burke's fullest elaboration of thoughts about form that he would continue to develop throughout his career and that he had begun to formulate at least as early as 1921, when Cowley was identifying Burke and the other members of his generation as writers obsessed with form.

"Psychology and Form," the best-known essay in *Counter-Statement*, does contain of course Burke's most quotable contribution to a theory of form: "Form is the creation of an appetite in the mind of the auditor, and the adequate satisfying of that appetite" (31). As I will indicate soon enough, Burke deserves enormous credit for this formulation because in it he reconceives form such that it is far less a static textual feature and far more a dynamic act of cooperation among writer, reader, and text that is more broadly rhetorical and social than purely aesthetic. In establishing "so perfectly the relationship between psychology and form, and so aptly illustrat[ing] how the one is to be defined in terms of the other" (30), Burke's theory of form is a tremendous innovation.

Nevertheless, it would be wrong to overstate the extent of Burke's innovation, to exaggerate his distance in "Psychology and Form" from modernist dogma. First, Burke's very use of psychology as a grounding for aesthetic form is consequent upon the modernist appreciation for the new science; considering the Symbolists' and the other moderns' powerful interest in Freudian and Jungian systems and explanations, and considering his own experiments with psychological arrangements in his short stories, Burke's interest in psychology and form in *Counter-Statement* in some ways seems less startling, almost inevitable. Indeed, in his 1932 review of *Counter-Statement*, Harold Rosenberg noted explicit parallels between Burke's views and ones propounded in Paul Valery's Symbolist *Introduction to the Method of Leonardo da Vinci* (1894): "Poe has clearly established his appeal to the reader on the basis of psychology and probable effects. From this angle . . . the work of art becomes a machine designed to arouse and combine the individual formulation of these minds" (120). Second, as you would expect of someone who described himself as "completely in the aesthete tradition" (Woodcock 708) until his composition of "Psychology and Form," Burke confines his account of form in that essay almost completely to form in art. Nonartistic discourse is regarded as a lower species, as mere "information" that trades in "facts," the kind of form deriving from mere surprise and suspense that one perceives in the daily newspaper (37).[10] Burke's examples in the chapter are accordingly drawn from drama, from Goethe's rather rarified prose, from Shakespeare's *Hamlet, Much Ado About Nothing*, and *Julius Caesar*, and from that purest, most autonomous of art forms, music, which "is by its very nature least suited to the psychology of information. . . . Here form cannot atrophy" (34).

In addition, Burke intimately involves in his discussion of psychology and form the terms "intensity" and "eloquence," two staples drawn from the esthetes. The modernist desire for intensity, for those moments of ecstasy when the artist and his audience might burn alike with something akin to a hard, gemlike flame, derives from form when form is somehow created by eloquence, which

> is the minimizing of this interest in fact, per se . . . until in all its smallest details the work bristles with disclosures, contrasts, restatements with a difference, ellipses, images, aphorism, volume, sound-values, in short all that wealth of minutiae which in their line-for-line aspect we call style and in their broader outlines we call form.
>
> (37–38)

In other words, if Burke's theory of form is innovative in incorporating audience psychology, it also backs away at certain points from too profound a move from the text by collapsing text, audience, and author once more and "mak[ing] three terms synonymous: form, psychology, and eloquence. And eloquence thereby becomes the essence of art" (40). The rest of "Psychology and Form" enlarges not so much on psychology as on eloquence, on "the exercise of propriety, the formulation of symbols which rigidify our sense of poise and rhythm" (42). Much of that remainder is in close keeping indeed with the assumptions of the Symbolists and particularly with the rarified and refined attitudes toward style that are associated with Gourmont.

Burke's theory of form is also developed elsewhere in *Counter-Statement*, in "The Poetic Process" and in "Lexicon Rhetoricae." "The Poetic Process" was in fact first composed as a companion piece to "Psychology and Form." After *The Dial* accepted "Psychology and Form" in December, 1924 (Gregory to Burke, December 15 and 19, 1924; Burke to Gregory, November 20 and December 23, 1924), for publication in July of 1925, Burke in February offered *The Dial* "The Poetic Process" as well because he had designed the latter as the second of three projected essays on the laws of artistic effectiveness, the nature of audiences, and the problem of artistic permanence. When "The Poetic Process" was nonetheless quickly and summarily rejected by *The Dial* (Gregory to Burke, also February 4, 1925), Burke published it in *The Guardian* (a monthly magazine of modernist criticism in literature published in Philadelphia) in May 1925. He apparently abandoned the notion of completing the third essay until he could incorporate his ideas into his "Program" and his "Lexicon" in *Counter-State-ment*—"Lexicon," after all, is Burke's "codification, amplification, and correc-tion" of "Psychology and Form" and "The Poetic Process" (123)—and, in very different terms, into his later essay "The Philosophy of Literary Form."[11] "The Poetic Process" appropriately is restored therefore right after "Psychology and Form" in *Counter-Statement* as part of a coherent core statement about exactly how form is psychological in nature, how form in a work of art derives from an artist's need to express his or her inner emotions in a way—that is, in a symbol—that appeals to the predisposition for perceiving form that inheres in every human brain.[12]

For if "Psychology and Form" gives the impression that form is somehow relative, inhering not on the page but in the apparently ephemeral raising and satisfying of variable audience expectations, in "The Poetic Process" Burke is emphatic in giving form an anything-but-relative foundation: the psychologi-cal processes that operate within people to permit an apprehension of form are eternal and universal. "Certain psychic and physical processes . . . in the human brain" make it possible to perceive formal patterns "which are at the roots of our experience"; thus, certain recurrent patterns in nature—"the accelerated motion of a falling body, the cycle of a storm, the procedure of the sexual act, the ripening of crops," and so forth—strike humans as having formal resonance "because the human brain has a pronounced potentiality for being arrested, or entertained, by such . . . arrangement[s]" (45). An artist (like Thomas Mann) can offer a crescendo (like the progress of a cholera epidemic in *Death in Ven-ice*) in order to produce form because the pattern of a crescendo is inherent in nature and in the wiring of the brain:

> Throughout the permutations of history, art has always appealed, by the changing individuations of changing subject-matter, to certain potential-ities of appreciation which would seem to be inherent in the very germ-plasm of man, and which, since they are constant, we might call innate forms of the mind.
>
> (46)[13]

The forms of the mind, "the potentiality for being interested by certain pro-cesses or arrangements," make possible the apprehension of eloquent patterns such as crescendo, contrast, comparison, balance, repetition, disclosure, rever-sal, contraction, expansion, magnification, series, and so on, all of them subdi-visions of the major forms, unity and diversity. Analogous to Plato's sense of "certain archetypes, or pure ideas, existing in heaven" (47), Burke's archetypal "psychological universals" are thus the root source of form: "for we need but take his [Plato's] universals out of heaven and situate them in the human mind" (48) in order to have a grounds for artistic form that is as observable as gravity, the cycle of a storm, or the maturation of crops (45).

In this way the opening pages of "The Poetic Process" offer Burke's solution to a dilemma that he and other modernist critics had been wrestling with during the early 1920s. Are the foundations of aesthetic form and aesthetic judgment relative and in flux, as Bergson had offered? Are they radically personal, as in the impressionistic criticism of Croce, Anatole France, and Paul Rosenfeld? Are they therefore influenced inevitably (as Freudians held) by the variable drives and predispositions of the critic? Or are there fixed and eternal grounds for form and critical judgment, as the New Humanists insisted? Burke proposes his own compromise in "The Poetic Process" and, in greater detail, in sections 11 through 18 of "Lexicon Rhetoricae," detail which he again summarized in section 18:

> The various kinds of moods, feelings, emotions, perceptions, sensations, and attitudes discussed in the manuals of psychology and exemplified in works of art, we consider universal experiences. . . . The[se] universal experiences are implicated in specific modes of experience. . . . The range of universal experiences may be lived on a mountain top, at sea, among a primitive tribe, in a salon—the modes of experience so differing in each instance that people in two different schemes of living can derive very different universal experiences from an identical event. The hypochondriac facing a soiled glove may experience a deep fear of death to which the trained soldier facing a cannon is insensitive. The same universal experience could invariably accompany the same mode of experience only if all men's modes of experience were identical.
>
> (149–50)

Literature, then, as a "verbal parallel to the pattern of experience" (152), as a symbol, is in one sense permanent, transcendent, ahistorical; "the formal aspects of art appeal in that they exercise formal potentialities of the reader" (142), potentialities that are as tangible as universal biological processes like systole and diastole, inhalation and exhalation (140). In so stating, Burke sides with those moderns who saw literature as offering a fixed foundation against contemporary flux and confusion. But in recognizing that different people experience art from differing modes of experience, that "each work re-embodies the [universal] formal principles in different subject matter" (142), he also acknowledges the perspectives of the Bergsonians, impressionists, Freudians, and Dadaists who were more skeptical about the universality and timelessness of art.

If Burke's meditation on form in "Psychology and Form," "The Poetic Process," and certain parts of "Lexicon Rhetoricae" ties him to the Symbolists, to the Freudians, and to other moderns, then so does his emphasis on symbol itself—on the link between the artist's inner emotions and the audience's emotions that is supplied by what Burke here calls Symbol. In "Psychology and Form," "The Poetic Process," and "Lexicon Rhetoricae," Burke does shift interest from the emotions of the writer to the emotions of audience. But he does not discard the emotion of the author as a source of "the poetic process." Far from it. As the rest of "The Poetic Process" makes clear, and as Burke further clarified in the sections of his "Lexicon" which garnish "The Poetic Process" (i.e., 150–66), while the apprehension of form does indeed depend on the psychology of the perceiver and on the characteristics of the object being perceived, form in art also derives ultimately from the artist's emotional need to articulate emotional states. For instance, some "psychic depression" within a person might "translate itself into the invention of details which will more or less adequately symbolize this depression" in the same way that a sleeper depressed for some reason might (as Freud offered) through a dream invent details that symbolize that depression; "the poet's moods dictate the selection of details and thus individuate themselves into one specific work of art" (49–51; see also the amplification of "The Poetic Process" in section 19–24 of "Lexicon Rhetoricae"). Thus while the poetic process might end with audience, it certainly begins, as modernists in the tradition of Bergson and Croce and Bell and the Symbolists would have it, with the artist's deeply emotional need for self-expression, for a means of articulating symbolically his or her inner emotional world. True, Burke differs from the Symbolists and Freudians in contending that artists do not stop with expressing their emotions but also seek a form through which to evoke emotion in their audiences; the artist "discovers himself not only with a message but also with a desire to produce effects upon his audience" (54).[14] But in arguing that "the poet steps forth, and his first step is the translation of his original mood into a symbol" (56), that "the artist begins with his emotion, he translates this emotion into a mechanism [or symbol] for arousing this emotion in others, and thus his interest in his own emotion transcends into his interest in the treatment" (55), Burke in "Psychology and Form" and "The Poetic Process" does associate himself both with Symbolism and with "the purest aestheticism," as Gorham Munson contended in quoting from those essays even before their *Counter-Statement* versions were published (*Destinations* 153). That is particularly so, given that Burke at the end of "The Poetic Process" goes to some lengths to explain how artists painstakingly refine their symbols through style and technique until they attain the status of The Beautiful (58). Granville Hicks therefore agreed with Munson's assessment of Burke's aestheticism when he reviewed *Counter-Statement* late in 1931. The editor of the leftist *New Masses* and biographer of John Reed objected in *The New Republic* that Burke was too "principally concerned with eloquence" and with technique at the expense of the social aspects of art; Burke was keeping writers and their work "as far removed as possible from the controversial and important issues of the day" (75–76). In this judgment Hicks was joined by Malcolm Cowley, who also complained from a Marxist perspective that Burke was giving too much emphasis to technique.

In a very real sense, then, Burke developed central chapters in *Counter-Statement* by working from orthodox modernist premises. After presenting as models Flaubert, Pater, and Gourmont, after introducing them as heroes who maintained a sympathy for the illicit, a stomach for analysis, an exuberance toward excess, and an attachment toward the odd and insane (2–3) and who lived for art in an elite opposition to mainstream society, Burke offered innovation and form and stylistic refinement as the defining concerns of critics and artists alike. Understanding "eloquence" and "intensity" as central terms in aesthetics, and self-expression as implicated "in all human activities" (52), Burke sought to account for all the sources of form. Convinced with the Symbolists that the emotion of the artist is the generating force behind the poetic process, Burke also offered that form is the result of the artist's desire to produce effects on an audience: "he attain[s] articulacy by linking his emotion to a technical form," to a symbol (56) refined into eloquence through stylistic technique. *Counter-Statement* depicts The Good Life as a multiplication of private emotional experiences that are produced by aesthetic retreat with art. The opening chapters in most respects take up "matters of purely aesthetic judgment" (31) or identify art and aesthetics or wall off aesthetics from morality and truth as thoroughly as had Croce and his American disciple Spingarn and the artists who enacted their views.

And yet *Counter-Statement* truly articulates "the purest aestheticism" only if one ignores the qualifications on pure aestheticism that Burke placed in "Psychology and Form," "The Poetic Process," and "Lexicon Rhetoricae" (where Burke is at pains to stress that "the self-expression of the artist, *qua* artist, is not distinguished by the uttering of emotion but by the evocation of emotion in others" [53], only if one ignores the essays written for the book after 1925, which Munson had not read when he made his comment), and only if one ignores the changes Burke made even in essays originally published before then. Indeed, particularly in the latest-composed chapters of *Counter-Statement*, Burke is offering his own original and rather socio-rhetorical contribution to modernism, one that is in fact very different from what Munson and Hicks saw in *Counter-Statement*. For *Counter-Statement* ultimately upholds art not as self-expression but as communication, not as self-contained and autonomous object but as moral and civic force. Even as early as the latter years of the 1920s Burke was staking out his position on literature as "equipment for living"—as social and rhetorical action.

The "Mann and Gide" chapter expresses Burke's growing alienation from the radical esthetes. Originally published in *The Bookman* in June, 1930, after being turned down by Marianne Moore and *The Dial* in its final months (Moore to Burke, October 1, 1931), "Mann and Gide" revisits two writers whom Burke had considered many times before.[15] Thomas Mann and Andre Gide, probably the most famous living Continental moderns, Burke understood as drawing certain traits directly from the esthetes, particularly an appetite for the repellent, the sick, the illicit, an identification with "outsiders," and a fascination with "the non-conforming mind's constant preoccupation with conformity" (93). Gide's earlier work, including *The Immoralist*, displayed "the same rotten elegance as characterizes Wilde's *The Portrait of Dorian Gray*" as well as a "Baudelarean tendency to invoke Satan as redeemer" (93–94), while Mann aggrandized dissolutes like Aschenbach and articulated the "notion that the artist faces by profession alternatives which are contrary to society" (95). Original and experimental and innovative, Mann and Gide belong in these senses with the "Three Adepts" who open the book.

But unlike the esthetes of the previous generation, Mann and Gide were fundamentally moralists and rhetoricians, Burke now argues. As the second half of the essay emphasizes, instead of living with art and pursuing beauty inside an Axel's castle, Mann and Gide devised in their fiction a rhetoric that was fundamentally moral in its thrust. "One need not read far in the writings of Gide to discover the strong ethical trait which dominates his thinking"; even when it contains the weird sex and violence of *Lafcadio's Adventures*, his art is full of "categorical imperatives," "scruples," "moral sensitiveness," and the like (100–01). Mann too considered moral problems to be the subject of his work— "moral chaos" and "moral vacillation" (101–02). Misunderstood as morally bankrupt when actually his subject is moral uncertainty and his technique irony, Mann to Burke in 1930 was socially responsive and responsible:

> Society might well be benefitted by the corrective of a disintegrating art, which converts each simplicity into a complexity, which ruins the possibility of ready hierarchies, which concerns itself with the problematical, the experimental, and thus by implication works corrosively upon those expansionistic certainties preparing the way for our social cataclysms.
>
> (105)

Mann and Gide were to Burke (as to everyone else) anything but conventional, but they maintained as well the role of "praeceptor patriae" (106), haranguing people in their own way toward virtues of their own defining.

The social effects of literature on "the reader" and "society" are easy enough to discern in "Mann and Gide." But even "Three Adepts of 'Pure' Literature" itself, in retrospect, can be seen as setting up Burke's social and moral views on the effects of art. For by the end of the 1920s Burke had gained a healthy moral distance on all three objects of his undeniable respect. The quotation marks around the "pure" in his title indicate his knowing irony, his cool awareness of the impossibility of such as thing as purely asocial art. From the perspective of 1930, it is easy to see that not even Burke's Flaubert is fully and completely an esthete, for although he certainly longed for refinement and withdrawal, he "never succeeded in arriving at an aesthetic amenable to his temperament" (5), particularly in that he chose a medium (the realistic novel, as opposed to criticism or poetry) whose social outlook was at odds with his aesthetic tendencies. Flaubert wished to write with attention to pure form, to compose "a book about nothing, a book without any exterior [i.e., social] tie, but sustained by the internal force of its style, . . . a book which would have almost no subject" (6); but he in fact worked in a medium that wouldn't permit such a thing. He ultimately "suppress[ed] the verbalistic side of his interests" in favor of expressing concrete experience (9). By the time he came to prepare a reprint of the Flaubert essay for *Counter-Statement*, Burke understood the social nature of art well enough to delete a paragraph meditating on Flaubert's "art-for-art's sake doctrine" (153–54) as well as his original concluding paragraph, which indicated his earlier strong appetite for "pure technique," for technique as "the profoundest element of art" (155). Instead of that original conclusion (which would have given Hicks far more cause to complain of Burke's emphasis on technique), Burke for *Counter-Statement* composed four new paragraphs (7–9) which disclose the difficulty of pursuing a pure aestheticism in fiction. "A distinction between 'pure form' and 'pure matter,'" he now wrote, "may enable one to speculate about books which talk beautifully about nothing, but it provides no hints at all about specific matters of methodology" (8–9). The revisions in the Flaubert essay show Burke backing off his earlier aestheticism—even though he was still sympathetic with Flaubert's effort at an art so artistic that it concealed its art. And he made similar revisions to the Gourmont portion of "Three Adepts," too. The 1922 admiration for Gourmont remains, but by 1931 Burke could leaven his admiration for Symbolist aestheticism by inserting three new paragraphs (16–19) which place aestheticism itself in a social and rhetorical context.

Burke elsewhere in *Counter-Statement* critiques Flaubert's wish (one he shared with other moderns, of course) that some sort of pure form might be possible in art, that "a book which would have no subject" might be somehow producible. As I have already indicated with respect to "The Poetic Process" and the corresponding glosses of "The Poetic Process" in "Lexicon Rhetoricae," Burke by 1931 held that subject matter is impossible to divorce from artistic form. Indeed, it is only through subject matter that an artist can achieve form, can embody form for the apprehension of the reader or observer. Universal form on the page ultimately corresponds to and derives from the variable capacity to perceive form that exists in an audience whose circumstances change from time to time and place to place; "there are no forms of art which are not forms of expression outside art" (143). In arguing that variable content as well as permanent form determine the reaction of an audience, Burke was challenging not just a Flaubertian ideal but Clive Bell's more immediate—and certainly no less aesthetic—view that form alone creates aesthetic response. Bell's *Art* (1914), an avant-garde treatise on the modern visual arts, depicted the artist as radically detached from life, pursuing a "significant form" that is divorced from content, a pure form "behind which we catch a sense of ultimate reality. . . . In the moment of aesthetic vision, [the artist] sees objects not as means shrouded in associations, but as pure form" (45–46). Burke had disputed Bell on the relation between form and content in literature as early as his June 1923 review of Gertrude Stein's *Geography and Plays*, a work which attempts (Burke felt) a pure formalism in literature but which inevitably fails to achieve it; and that critique of Bell reappears in section 10 of "Lexicon Rhetoricae"—the tip-off is the use of Bell's phrase "significant form" as a header—a section which initiates a lengthy technical argument on the relation between form and content in literature.[16]

Burke began rethinking Flaubert and Gourmont's aestheticism early in the 1920s, then, and began adding audience to his aesthetic at least as early as the winter of 1924–1925. True, since "Psychology and Form" and "The Poetic Process" were both published rather early in Burke's career, Burke's sense of "the audience" in those essays is rather uncomplicated. His "audience" is still the stable and perceptive and rather passive individual reader or observer, still a qualified and predictable "we" (30)—someone rather like The Critic, who, if informed and sensitive, will respond as others do to the same artistic experiences. The psychology of the audience becomes the trained, coherent psychology of individual experts from roughly homogeneous backgrounds who are sensitive, accomplished, and experienced enough to perceive the subtleties of form and the distinctions between art and mere information. Note for instance how often audience in "Psychology and Form" and "The Poetic Process" is described in singular terms or as an unproblematical, homogeneous "we": in the 1925 essays, artists write in order to move elite individuals and not heterogeneous groups. Cultures may change—"The Poetic Process" emphasizes that—but within cultures audiences are stable and coherent and passive and unproblematical.

But Burke's view of form in these early essays is still a major advance over most modernist conceptions of form for at least three reasons. First, during a period when new interest in psychology was generating new psychological analyses into literary characters and their creators (e.g., Brooks's *The Ordeal of Mark Twain* and Charles Baudouin's *Psychoanalysis and Aesthetics*, both mentioned in "Psychology and Form"), Burke was instead pushing towards a consideration of the psychology of readers and how their perceptions are manipulated by artists to achieve certain effects: "Modern criticism, and psychoanalysis in particular, is too prone to define the essence of art in terms of the artist's weaknesses. It is, rather, the audience which dreams, while the artist oversees the conditions which determine his dream" (36). Second, Burke thereby shifts emphasis from art as mere self-expression of personal emotions to art as inducing emotions in an audience. Where Bell could offer that artists "do not create works of art in order to provoke our aesthetic emotions, but because only thus can they materialize a particular kind of feeling" (44), Burke was to emphasize the reverse:

> If it is a form of self-expression to utter our emotions, it is just as truly a form of self-expression to provoke emotions in others. . . . [T]he self-expression of the artist, *qua* artist, is not distinguished by the uttering of an emotion but by the evocation of emotion. . . . We will suppose [in opposition to

> other critics] that the artist . . . discovers himself not only with a message, but also with a wish to produce effects upon his audience.
>
> (53–54)

Third, in doing both of these things Burke was laying the groundwork for the even more expansive notion of audience and the even more rhetorical conception of art that he would express in "Lexicon Rhetoricae" and "Program." Rather than confining form to structural features, as Bell had, Burke in those essays in *Counter-Statement* was adding a rhetorical dimension to form; he was indeed in the midst of "shifting from self-expression to communication" as a way of viewing art.

"Lexicon," then, is a major contribution not so much in acknowledging audience (for Richards was doing the same at about the same time) but in pointing to new conceptions of audience and art. In keeping with its subtitle—remember, it is billed not just as a codification and amplification of "Psychology and Form" and "The Poetic Process," but also as a "correction" (123)—"Lexicon" emends those earlier chapters in a number of ways. For instance, audience in "Lexicon" is conceived not as the simple, passive, relatively monolithic, and unproblematical collection of individuals of "Psychology and Form," but as complex and heterogeneous. There is no such thing as the "perfect reader": "Aristotle points out in his *Rhetoric* that there are friendly readers, hostile readers, and simply curious audiences" (179); some real readers may even have "contrary patterns of experience" (177); and "the actual reader is obviously an indeterminate and fluctuant mixture of the [hysterical and connoisseur]" (180)—though the artist still remains "expert" enough to "reduce the recalcitrant reader to acquiescence," even to "overwhelm the reader and thus compel the reader to accept his interpretations" (176). The reader, less than self-contained now, is (like the writer and the art object) part and parcel of a culture. As sections 15 and 25 make clear, anything-but-autonomous readers are situated in a cultural setting or "ideology" that directs their experience—"Othello's conduct would hardly seem 'syllogistic' in polyandrous Tibet" (146)—and audience expectations, similarly shaped by culture, are anything but purely personal and idiosyncratic. Indeed, "an ideology is the nodus of beliefs and judgments which the artist can exploit for his effects . . . [and] in so far as its general acceptance and its stability are more stressed than its particular variations from person to person and from age to age, an ideology is a 'culture'" (161). The artist, in other words, manipulates ideological assumptions for persuasive purposes, and thereby "persuades" and "moves" and "contributes to the formation of attitudes, and thus to the determining of conduct" (163). Art is political and moral. A Symbol not only "interprets a situation" (154), but it serves as "the corrective of a situation"—as "an emancipator" that persuades active readers in search of transformation to alter their values and attitudes and conduct (155–56). Already in 1931 literature for Burke is "equipment for living": the phrase later made famous in *The Philosophy of Literary Form* is a foreshortening of an important sentence from the penultimate paragraph in "Lexicon Rhetoricae": Art, far from being walled off from life in the manner of the esthetes, is "an equipment, like any vocabulary, for handling the complexities of living" (183). In keeping with Burke's essay in the 1930 *Critique of Humanism*, Burke's "Lexicon" involves art indelibly in life, conduct, ethics, morality. In the final pages of *Counter-Statement*, Burke, by way of summary, concludes with a call for the rehabilitation of rhetoric. For "effective literature could be nothing else but rhetoric, . . . [which is] the use of language in such a way as to produce a desired impression on the hearer or reader" (210).

Building, then, on the same assumptions he had formulated for "Lexicon," "Psychology and Form," and "The Poetic Process"—art is eternal in that "it deals with the constants of humanity," while it is also social and situated in that it is "a particular mode of adjustment to a particular cluster of conditions"—Burke in "Program" turned to the attitudes and material conditions which he felt ought to be addressed by artists in the midst of the crisis of the Great Depression (*Counter-Statement* 107). In 1931 Burke wanted artists and critics to address the fundamental tensions of American society: the stresses between the "new" industrial ethos and traditional agrarian values, the inevitable conflict between the "bourgeois" practical and the "bohemian" aesthetic worldviews, the emerging collision between decentralized democracy and statist fascism, the problems of unemployment. That Burke offers just such a list should not be surprising, for a major and perennial problem for modernist artists was and is what to do with and about new technology, industrialism, and urban life—witness, for instance, the Futurists and the Dadas. And that this list of Burke's is increasingly political and social is surely by design: in proposing these concerns, Burke was placing art and artists and critics in close relation to society, resisting any temptation toward aesthetic remove or elitism. In juxtaposing art and politics, art and non-art (the chapter is unique in *Counter-Statement* in its avoidance of now-canonical modernist works), Burke was now seeking to heal the modernist alienation between artist and society in a way that the Dadas and the leftists of *Seven Arts* (and, for that matter, the New Humanists) would have appreciated. The urgent cadences of "Program" articulate an aesthetic position very different from the one proposed by the earliest-written chapters of *Counter-Statement*. Here, in the chapter he wrote last for his book, Burke opts for an absolutely committed position for art and the artist. For good reason he could say in his preface to the second edition that "Program" is an "attempt to translate aestheticism into its corresponding political equivalents" (xiii). Art and criticism for Burke have now become part of a political attitude, "part of an intervention into history" (Jay, "Kenneth Burke" 72), part of an understanding of aesthetics that hearkens back to the reformers at *The Masses* and that anticipates the Marxist aesthetics so powerful during the 1930s.

At the same time that he was being criticized by Hicks (from the left) for being excessively aesthetic and insufficiently concerned with social amelioration, then, Burke was voicing opinions about the social value of literature that were leaving him vulnerable to attack (from the right) for just the opposite reasons. Burke in "Program" puts certain tendencies of the moderns—to regard art as autonomous and autotelic and to understand art as the product of a sensitive elite divorced from the rough and tumble of impermanent daily life (tendencies visible in Burke's thinking in the early 1920s)—into juxtaposition with a different modernist view, one that looks back to the attitudes towards art of Randolph Bourne, John Reed, and John Dos Passos and forward to the socially committed artists and critics of the 1930s. While remaining respectful of canonical writers and skeptical of Dada hyperbole, Burke nevertheless retained an appreciation for the Dadas' overt rhetoricality—of their intuition that the Enlightenment distrust of rhetoric and belief in the transparency of language in the face of right reason could not be sustained in a period professing a Nietzschean skepticism toward Western conceptual systems. The experience of reading *Counter-Statement* recalls Calinescu's and Poggioli's measured observations that a central tension within modernism is the one between two kinds of avant-garde, the esthetes and the social activists—one repelled by the philistinism of the masses into ascetic withdrawal, the other stressing the artist as committed forerunner and prophet. Within Burke's revisionist modernism, neither the doctrine of the autonomy of art nor the view of the artist as prophetic leader is precluded; Burke in *Counter-Statement* represents and juxtaposes both positions in a manner that both recognizes and denies extremes. *Counter-Statement* begins by assuming an esthete stance, by aestheticizing morals, by declaring the existence of "matters of purely aesthetic judgment," and by emphasizing music as a prototype for ideal art; but by the time it closes, Burke, without discarding his respect for technique and eloquence and form, has ceased to organize ethics and morals under aesthetics and has begun to consider drama as the central terrain of modernism—a drama that quickly brings to mind "roles" and "play" and "audience" and rhetoric, a drama that Burke encountered in his first days in Greenwich Village with the Provincetown Players and the leaders of *The Masses*, and of course a drama that Burke would later develop into his most famous explanatory metaphor.[17]

The same tension (perhaps I should say complementarity) between the aesthetic and the social animates "The Status of Art" and "Applications of the Terminology," two of the other latest-composed essays in *Counter-Statement*.[18] "The Status of Art" intrudes on a tempest involving the esthete critics among the moderns (who in anticipation of the New Critics wished to attend to works of art "from within," "on their own terms," as a form of self-expression) and the geneticists (who approached art from the perspective of one or another theory of causation). Thus the chapter on one hand defends the inutility of art in a way that the esthetes would have approved, offers a measured but sympathetic further commentary on Flaubert and Gourmont, and critiques Freudians (like Brooks) and Spenglerians who were understanding literature as *merely* the reflection of internal drives or "contemporary political and economic issues" (79) or irresistible historical cycles. On the other hand, the chapter emphasizes once again Burke's insistence that literature be considered "as a means of communication" with social utility. For all their protests that "ethics should be a subdivision of esthetics" (68), Pater, Baudelaire, Wilde and other esthetes were also social critics attempting to amend mainstream society through shock tactics and radical critique; while constituting a distinct minority, even experimental *tour d'ivoire* writers can nevertheless influence millions (70–72). "Far from being 'in retreat,' [the artist] must master ways of exerting influence on the minds and emotions of others" (74). "Applications of the Terminology" also steers between aesthetic and ideological positions vis-à-vis the relation of art to society. Like "Lexicon Rhetoricae," which it names or echoes at several points, the chapter traces several implications of the points Burke had made in "Psychology and Form"; it too should be read as a "codification, amplification, and correction" of earlier chapters in *Counter-Statement*. In drawing those implications—for classic and romantic, objectivity and subjectivity, art and life, convention and originality—Burke insisted once more that artists should never forget to seek aesthetic beauty. Artists should never become so excessively "proletarian" in seeking "to eradicate certain forms of social injustice" (189) that they forget to appeal to the universal components of form detailed in "Psychology and Form": "The most 'unreal' book in the world [even Lyly's *Euphues*] can properly be said to 'deal with life' if it can engross a reader" (192). However, Burke in "Applications" is equally insistent that "effective literature [is] nothing else but rhetoric" (210) in that it seeks to move audiences and change attitudes. Literature as a form of action resists removal from life.

In short, Burke in *Counter-Statement* both borrows from and critiques modernists of every stripe. He could appreciate Spengler's critique of the myth of progress as much as the author of *The Waste Land* did, while simultaneously being critical of "genetic" criticism inspired by *The Decline of the West*. He could capitalize on the Symbolist enthusiasm for Freud while tempering extravagant psychological explanations for the appeal and genesis of art. He could appreciate the New Humanists' insistence on fixed standards while criticizing their inflexibility and their demonization of Pater. He could remain apart from the Dadas while still understanding that their appreciation of the radically new and mechanical and urban could be the basis of a new American literature. He could agree with Hicks and other leftists that art must have a social agenda while reminding them that art has a commitment to aesthetic form as well. And so on. Burke, in sum, could state that he "stands for nothing" (91) except the integrity of his own responses to and formulations about modernist concerns, responses and formulations that try to remain faithful to both the aesthetic and social wings of modernist thought.

Thus, I disagree with Robert Heath's statement that "not until the mid-1930s did Burke incorporate political philosophy into his aesthetic" (11) and with Rueckert's recent assessment that *Counter-Statement* "remains . . . a work by a literary critic who has not yet developed a real sense of the larger social context" that is found in his later work (Rueckert, "Field Guide" 10). That social context is indeed present in an emphatic way in the dramatic internal dialogues of *Counter-Statement*. True, Burke would go even further in associating art with culture and politics in his next critical book (e.g., "The Rout of the Esthetes" is one of the subtitles of *Auscultation, Creation, and Revision*) and in later works. But *Counter-Statement* already shows Burke's substantial movement in that direction—as well as the desire (which he never lost) not to rout the esthetes entirely. Therefore I appreciate Greig Henderson's argument that "Burke's aestheticism [in *Counter-Statement*] is a strategy for encompassing a sociohistorical situation; moreover, it aims to have a corrective or corrosive effect upon that situation and is thus practical; art, for Burke, is anything but useless" (175). And I prefer Rueckert's earlier conclusion about *Counter-Statement*: the book is a "both/and" document that "is equally concerned with two seemingly contradictory areas of investigation: the purely aesthetic and the sociological" (*Drama* 32):

> *Counter-Statement* is actually a kind of dialogue, with three speakers apparently contradicting each other. One of the speakers defends pure art by arguing that the end of poetry is eloquence . . . the second speaker defends art as revelation by arguing that the end of poetry is wisdom; and the third speaker defends art as catharsis. . . . The dialogue is resolved by transcending the contradictions; all three attitudes can be accepted if one adopts an attitude of critical openness which permits many angles of vision.
>
> (*Drama* 10)

That *Counter-Statement* is meant as a dialogue, as an exploratory discourse calculated to stimulate the active reader's thinking, not to resolve it, that, unlike most critical tracts, it is meant not to close off debate but to generate further dialogue, accounts for the book's difficulty as well as its continuing interest. And that *Counter-Statement* is an internally conflicted, even contradictory document, self-reflective and critical of its own codifications, marks it as modernist, too, of course, for the hybrid, polyphonous text is a modernist staple—witness Toomer's *Cane* and Faulkner's *The Sound and the Fury* and Cage's *Empty Words*. Like other such documents, *Counter-Statement* is itself an instance of "perspective by incongruity," an experiment itself in form. Rather than raising and fulfilling expectations in any conventional way, its chapters make coherent arguments that tend to parody or correct or undermine the arguments contained in previous chapters; containing chapters linked by emotional and intellectual associations, it is an instance of "qualitative form" (Warnock 66). Rather like *In Our Time* or *Go Down, Moses* or *Dubliners* or *Winesburg, Ohio* or even Burke's own *White Oxen* and *Towards a Better Life*, *Counter-Statement* is something of a collage, a collection of more-or-less self-contained items that nonetheless cohere uneasily, experimentally, yet undeniably and invigoratingly, into a whole book.[19] Instead of scorning Burke for "fail[ing] to advance a coherent and sustained critical standard" (Heath 10–11), instead of expecting internal consistency and conventional form from a book with chapters that were written over a period of nearly a decade, instead of growing impatient with Burke's decision not to smooth out inconsistencies, a reader of *Counter-Statement* is better advised to make the inconsistencies a virtue, to gain perspective by the incongruities Burke offers, to read the book as the record of the Growth of the Critic's Mind, and to understand it as an instance of Burke's "debunking" attitude—of his characteristic skepticism toward and resistance to just about everything, including systems of his own making. Deeply serious and yet playful and theatrical, *Counter-Statement*, in modernist fashion, calls attention to itself as form.

Kenneth Burke's *Counter-Statement*, then, is a "counter" statement in at least three overlapping ways. Most obviously it counters the genteel poetics and cultural practices that all the moderns were combatting: in championing new modern writers, in advocating experimentation, in anatomizing form, in understanding art as "naturally antinomian" (Preface), Burke was placing himself and his ideas counter to the writers and critics of genteel, mainstream culture. Then again, *Counter-Statement* also counters certain prevailing notions within the modernist community: "each principle it [the book] advocates is matched by an opposite principle flourishing and triumphant today," Burke noted in the Preface. That does not mean that the book is an explicit, tract-like counter-attack or systematic refutation of a set of dogmas. As Burke notes in the Preface, *Counter-Statement* "deals only secondarily and sporadically with refutation," except for the chapter on "The Status of Art." "My solution is to attempt a more constructive type of criticism," he wrote to Cowley on his twenty-fifth birthday, "not merely to attack the existing but to build up a counter-structure." If the book is not a systematic refutation, it is nevertheless directed to fellow members of the modernist community—a community that is able to sponsor and contain and accommodate a surprising range of views about the nature of art and the relationships between art and society.

Finally, *Counter-Statement* is internally conflicted; it "counters" itself. The sentiments in "Three Adepts" are subtly countered by another chapter on literary adepts, "Mann and Gide." "Psychology and Form" and "The Poetic Process" (which work together) are both supplemented and corrected by "Lexicon Rhetoricae" and "Applications of the Terminology." And all of these are countered to a greater or lesser degree in "Program." Operating as a "counter-statement" in all three ways, then, *Counter-Statement* amounts to a particularly interesting and internally conflicted instance of modernist criticism; it is a characteristically Burkean statement within modernism of what its values, and what its range and possibilities, might be.

Notes

1 This essay is excerpted from Chapter 7 of *Conversing with the Moderns: Kenneth Burke, 1915–1931* (U of Wisconsin P, in press); some of my many debts are acknowledged in the Preface to that work. References here to Burke's correspondence with Malcolm Cowley are to Paul Jay's edition; references to *Counter-Statement*, indicated by page numbers in parentheses, are to the second edition (U of California P, 1968).

2 Vincent Leitch, for instance, discusses Burke in relation to the New Critics, who were certainly modernist enough. But Leitch also concludes, correctly, that Burke remained separate from the formalists because he fashioned his "complex machine for textual analysis" out of various other-than-formalist hermeneutical approaches, biographical, psychological, sociological, philosophical, political, ethical, religious, and anthropological (41–43). Henry Bamford Parkes (209), Giles Gunn, and Paul Jay (*American Literary Criticism*) have noted Burke's relationship to the pragmatists. Fredric Jameson understands Burke not as a modernist but as a poststructuralist ideological critic ("Ideology" and "Symbolic Inference"), Cary Nelson similarly regards Burke as a poststructuralist (171), and Frank Lentricchia has lately studied Burke as "a man of the 1930s" (56) in order to recapture both the political Burke (*Criticism and Social Change*) and the historical thinker ("Reading History with Kenneth Burke"). Other poststructuralist critics have understood Burke as a proto-deconstructionist (e.g., Harris; Lentricchia, "Reading History," 136). But see also Denis Donoghue's *Ferocious Alphabets*, which treats Burke as an anti-deconstructionist, and Lentricchia's *Criticism and Social Change*, which poises Burke against Paul DeMan. A recent volume of essays edited by Bernard L. Brock, *Kenneth Burke and Contemporary European Thought*, places Burke in relation to the thought of Habermas, Grassi, Foucault, and Derrida. And cultural studies critics of the past decade have embraced Burke as one of themselves.

Scholars in rhetoric, who also emphasize Burke's independence and mostly attend to his work after 1940, have also understood Burke apart from modernism. Burke's invention of "dramatism" and "identification" have of course captured particular attention since the publication of *A Grammar of Motives* in 1945 and *A Rhetoric of Motives* in 1950; the two notions, especially dramatism, have often been understood as keys to his interpretive system (e.g., Rueckert, *Drama*; Fogarty; Foss, Foss, and Trapp). Burke has been interpreted as a neo-Aristotelian by Virginia Holland and associated with neo-Aristotelians of the Chicago school by Booth (*Critical Understanding*) and Donald Jammerman; and Cynthia Sheard, Michael Hassett, and others have emphasized his ties to the Sophists. In the past decade, as rhetoricians have turned their attention to setting and context, Burke has been seen as a prescient social constructivist.

3 Come to think of it, American writers are conspicuously absent from consideration in *Counter-Statement*, unless you want to count Eliot as an American and unless you count vague allusions to Twain (in "Program") and to American theater (156). In this way Burke distances himself and his book from the American literary nationalists, still active late in the 1920s (as attested by Burke's reviews of the American Caravan books for *The New York Herald* in 1927 and 1928).

4 This is the first use of the term "ideology" in *Counter-Statement*; it's a key term in the book, for, as Paul Jay has noted ("Kenneth Burke" 71), the relationship between ideology and form is a major issue in Burke's book. Indeed the two words *ideology* and *form* are central to the major tension in the book, the conflict between an artist's strivings for aesthetic achievement and his or her drive for social impact, between the artist as esthetician and the artist as rhetor, between the artist as segregated from society into a domain of art and the artist as emerging from and contributing to a localized social circumstance.

5 See Paul Elmer More, *The Drift of Romanticism: Shelbourne Essays* (1909; rpt. New York: G. P. Putnam, 1967), 114; and Burke's former associate Gorham Munson, writing as a New Humanist in his essay "Our Critical Spokesman," *Humanism in America*, ed. Norman Foerster (New York: Brewer and Warren, 1930), 350. Burke responded (temperately) to the Foerster volume and its New Humanist readers in his essay "The Allies of Humanism Abroad" in Grattan's *Critique of Humanism*. For a summary of the New Humanists, those original twentieth-century conservative culture critics, see Hoeveler; Hoeveler's account of the New Humanists' attitude toward Pater is on pages 56–59.

6 Croce's *Aesthetic* (1902) posits both art and criticism as the expression of an individual's intuitions, rather than as the product of historical or social forces. A handbook on aestheticism, the book describes art as autotelic, as uninvolved with morality or practicality. Burke knew Croce's

work well enough to work on an essay on Croce's views (never published; see Burke to Waldo Frank, June 13, 1922—Waldo Frank Papers, Van Pelt Library, University of Pennsylvania) and to recommend Croce's *Aesthetic* to Cowley in a letter of March 18, 1923. Spingarn's famous essay "The New Criticism," first delivered as a lecture in 1910, frequently reprinted, and later of course influential to the New Critics, defended Croce's positions on the autonomy of art.

7 The connection between Pound and Gourmont is the subject of Sieburth's *Instigations*. To learn more about Gourmont, the reader may also consult Schwartz (79–85), Burne, Pondrom, and Burke's longer, *Dial* version of his *Counter-Statement* essay published in February, 1921 (it was Burke's first published essay). Gourmont is also a leading figure in Wilson's *Axel's Castle*, the early analysis of the moderns that associates Joyce, Yeats, Eliot, Proust, and Stein with the Symbolist tradition.

8 Armin Paul Frank contends that Burke himself made precisely this "development and schematization" of the ideas of Gourmont (52). For a very complete description of "the dissociation of ideas," see Burke's own exposition in *A Rhetoric of Motives*, 149–54.

9 In "Psychology and Form," Burke refers at some length to Eliot's *The Waste Land* (39). It is worth remembering that "Psychology and Form" originally appeared in the July 1925, issue of *The Dial*, less than three years after the spectacular first appearance of *The Waste Land*, also in *The Dial*, in November 1922 (a major modernist event dramatically recalled in Williams's *Autobiography*, 174). As an editorial assistant at *The Dial*, Burke helped to set *The Waste Land* into type for the first time in the summer of 1922.

10 Burke's distinction here between art and information, one that recurs in the preface to *Towards a Better Life*, repeats the terminology of Clive Bell's 1914 *Art*.

11 Burke's recollection of the chronology and circumstances of the composition of "Psychology and Form" and "The Poetic Process" is also contained in his letter to Cowley of December 1, 1940. There Burke traces the germ of "Psychology and Form" to a review he wrote on J. Middleton Murry for the December, 1922, issue of *The Dial* (a review that distinguishes "the psychology of form and the psychology of subject-matter"); recalls that the never-completed third essay would have been entitled "On the Sublime"; dates "Psychology and Form" to 1924 and "The Poetic Process" to the winter of 1924–1925; and protests Cowley's claim that Burke's formula tying form to audience expectations derived from I. A. Richards's *Principles of Literary Criticism* (published in 1924) or *Science and Poetry* (published in 1926) or Richards's and Ogden's *The Meaning of Meaning* (published in 1923). Burke says that he encountered *The Meaning of Meaning* only after completing "Psychology and Form" and "The Poetic Process" (and in fact Richards's book was reviewed in *The Dial* by Bertrand Russell as late as the August 1926, issue of *The Dial*) and that he

> was so knocked over by it that I was unable to write the third essay. And it was not until the "Philosophy of Literary Form" item . . . that I was able to treat of the material for the third essay, though it is there in a much altered state, affected by all that has intervened.

I am persuaded to take Burke as his word that he encountered Richards only after completing "Psychology and Form" and "The Poetic Process," but it is easy to see how Cowley made the connection. (Isidor Schneider also noted a link between Richards and Burke in his 1932 review of *Counter-Statement*, though on strictly chronological grounds Schneider is surely wrong in attributing a debt to Richards's *Practical Criticism* [1929], which offers a demonstration of the reading behaviors of actual readers in the act of encountering poetry.) The *Principles of Literary Criticism*, like "Psychology and Form," ties interpretation to the psychology of the audience; like the later essays in *Counter-Statement*, it also counters the art-for-art's sake community and conceives of poetry as "in no qualitative way different from actual experience." That phrase comes from Burke's brief review of *Principles of Literary Criticism* as "A New Poetics" in the September 1925, *Saturday Review*: Burke commended Richards for distancing himself from a too-strictly-aesthetic position and for understanding art as "incipient action" and as influencing the attitudes of an audience. ("Attitude," of course, would become an important word for Burke.) *The Meaning of Meaning*, meanwhile, argues from the work of C. S. Peirce that the interpretation of signs depends on context and that meaning is ultimately rhetorical and contextual in nature, notions that are certainly generally in line with Burke's views in the later-written essays of *Counter-Statement*. My own conclusion, based on a study of Burke's correspondence through the 1930s as well as his and Richards' writing, is that Richards' impact on Burke's thinking is felt mostly on later works, such as *Permanence and Change* and *Philosophy of Literary Form*, and I plan to develop more completely the relationships among Richards's and Burke's works in a subsequent study of Burke in the 1930s.

12 The idea that art derives from the artist's need to express emotion is a Romantic notion that was fundamental to the Symbolists and many of their modernist successors. Clive Bell's emphasis on emotion in his 1914 *Art* is representative: e.g., "The starting point for all systems of aesthetics must be the personal experience of a particular emotion" (17); artists "need a problem that will become the focus of their vast emotions" (52).

13 As Armin Frank has noted, Gourmont also tied aesthetic sensitivity to physiology (52). Gourmont, however, favored a highly impressionistic criticism according to which the only reliable grounds for literary judgment was the individually cultivated sensibility.

14 On pages 53–54, Burke distinguishes his position particularly from the Freudian approach of Van Wyck Brooks. Brooks in his *The Ordeal of Mark Twain* (1920) had explained Twain's fiction as an externalization of Twain's innermost drives, conflicts, and emotions, but stopped short of explaining how those emotions were then "formalized" in Twain's fiction. Burke had also criticized Brooks's brand of Freudian criticism in his essay on Brooks's book, "Art and the Hope Chest" (*Vanity Fair*, December 1922), because it emphasized Freudian explanations of the author to the exclusion of considerations of "the work as it is" (59). That article, as well as the emphasis in *Counter-Statement* on a work's formal properties, helps to explain why the early Burke has at times been identified with the New Criticism.

15 Burke had translated *Death in Venice* and other stories and essays by Mann, reviewed his *Buddenbrooks*, translated other Mann contributions to *The Dial*, and modeled his own fiction in many ways after Mann; and he wrote "Andre Gide, Bookman" for *The Freeman* in April 1922.

16 Burke's 1923 critique of Stein and Bell appeared in "Engineering with Words." The reference to *The Waste Land* which closes section 10 of "Lexicon" is lifted directly from the conclusion of that review, which Burke published in *The Dial*. Incidentally, it should be clear from what I have already said that I both agree and disagree with Gabin's assessment that Burke in *Counter-Statement* counters the intuitionism and aestheticism of Croce in its American (i.e., Spingarnian) form. Not one to set art above life, Burke both counters and reasserts the aestheticism of Croce and Spingarn.

17 Conceptually Burke hit upon dramatism not simply from his immersion in modern drama but also from his exposure to "the schoolmen's subdivisions of a topic: *quis, quid, ubi, quibus auxiliis, cur, quo modo, quando*" (*Counter-Statement*, 141). Aristotle's exposition of the Four Causes also contributed to the formulation of dramatism. Burke understood Aristotle's theories, like his own, as based "upon *action*. His whole system is a *dramatistic* mode of analysis. His formula for God was 'pure act,' which of course, Aquinas could take over" (Skodnick 22).

18 "The Status of Art" was written for the occasion of *Counter-Statement*, with the exception of the section on Spengler, which appeared in large part in Burke's brilliant long review of *The Decline of the West* (*The Dial*, September 1926; Burke also translated the long excerpts from *Decline of the West*—about sixty pages in all—that appeared in *The Dial* from November 1924 to January 1925). Since "The Status of Art" was written well into the 1930s, no wonder "its true subject . . . is the relation of aesthetics to politics" (Lentricchia, *Criticism* 95); Lentricchia's discussion of "The Status of Art," 96–102, is by far the best one that I know of. "Applications of the Terminology" is a slight revision of an essay called "Redefinitions" which appeared in three installments in *The New Republic* from July to September, 1931, even as *Counter-Statement* was being published. *Counter-Statement* includes everything in "Redefinitions" (albeit not always in the same order), but Burke also added to "Applications" the passages on Racine and Hamlet, as well as the final segments on "conventional form" and "rhetoric."

19 I am certainly not the first to note the internally contradictory character of *Counter-Statement*. In 1933, Austin Warren noted that *Counter-Statement* is "not a systematic treatise." In merging "essays of . . . quite different sorts . . . it damages if not destroys any impression of unity" (354–55). I have also quoted Rueckert's opinion in *Kenneth Burke and the Drama of Human Relations* (32) that *Counter-Statement* expresses a tension in Burke between "two seemingly contradictory areas of investigation: the purely aesthetic and the sociological. In fact, Burke actually seems to contradict himself in the book." Jay has also said that "there is something of a split in the book . . . as he moves . . . away from conceptualizing art in aesthetic terms as self-expression and toward viewing it as a socially symbolic act" ("Kenneth Burke," 70). Henderson concludes that "the conflict between the aesthetic and the practical remains unresolved in *Counter-Statement*" (179). And Burke himself noted in *"Permanence and Change*: In Retrospective Prospect" that in *Counter-Statement*, under the tutelage of Flaubert, who on the one hand proclaimed aestheticism but on the other tweaked social norms, he developed a theory of literary form designed to discuss the work of art *in itself*, as a set of *internal relationships* to be analyzed and appreciated in their own right. But in the course of considering how such pure principles of form and style become "individuated" in terms of the details proper to each individual case, this line of thought ended with the recognition that the artist ultimately appeals to an audience's attitudes, which are ultimately grounded in natural susceptibilities quite outside their role in any one specific artistic tradition (302).

Works Cited

Babbitt, Irving. *Rousseau and Romanticism*. Boston: Houghton-Mifflin, 1919.

Bell, Clive. *Art*. London: Chatto and Windus, 1913; rpt. New York: Capricorn Books, 1958.

Booth, Wayne. *Critical Understanding: The Powers and Limits of Pluralism*. Chicago: U of Chicago P, 1979.

Brock, Bernard, ed. *Kenneth Burke and Contemporary European Thought*. Tuscaloosa: U of Alabama P, 1995.

Brooks, Van Wyck. *Emerson and Others*. New York: E.P. Dutton & Company, 1927.

———. *The Ordeal of Mark Twain*. Intro. James R. Vitelli. New York: E.P. Dutton & Company, 1920.

———. *Sketches in Criticism*. New York: E.P. Dutton & Company, Inc., 1932.

Burke, Kenneth. "The Allies of Humanism Abroad." *A Critique of Humanism*. Ed. Hartley Grattan. New York: Brewer and Warren, 1930. 169–92.

———. "Art and the Hope Chest." *Vanity Fair* 19 (December 1922): 59, 102.

———. "The Correspondence of Flaubert." *The Dial* 72 (February 1922): 147–55.

———. *Counter-Statement*. New York: Harcourt, Brace and Company, 1931; Berkeley: U of California P, 1968.

———. "The Critic of Dostoevsky" [Review of J. Middleton Murry's *Still Life* and *The Things We Are*]. *The Dial* 73 (December 1922): 671–74.

———. "Engineering with Words" [Gertrude Stein's *Geography and Plays*]. *The Dial* 74 (April 1923): 408–12.

———. *A Grammar of Motives*. Berkeley: U of California P. 1969.

———. *Kenneth Burke Papers*. Pattee Library. Pennsylvania State U.

———. "A 'Logic' of History" [Review-Essay of Spengler's *The Decline of the West*]. *The Dial* 81 (September 1926): 242–48.

———. "A New Poetics" [Review of I. A. Richards's *Principles of Literary Criticism*]. *The Saturday Review of Literature* 2 (September 1925): 154–55.

———. *"Permanence and Change*: Retrospective Prospect." Foreword to *Permanence and Change*. 3rd ed. (original publication 1935). Berkeley: U of California P, 1984.

———. *The Philosophy of Literary Form*. 1941. Berkeley: U of California P, 1967.

———. *A Rhetoric of Motives*. Berkeley: U of California P. 1969.

———. *The White Oxen, and Other Stories*. New York: Albert and Charles Boni, 1924.

Burne, Glenn S. *Remy de Gourmont: His Ideas and Influence in England and America*. Carbondale: Southern Illinois UP, 1963.

Calinescu, Matei. *Five Faces of Modernity*. Durham: Duke UP, 1987.

Calverton, V. F. *The Newer Spirit: A Sociological Criticism of Literature*. New York: Boni and Liveright, 1925.

Donoghue, Denis. *Ferocious Alphabets*. Boston: Little, Brown, 1981.

Eliot, T. S. *The Sacred Wood*. London: Methuen, 1928.

———. *Selected Essays 1917-1932*. London: Faber and Faber, 1932.

Foerster, Norman, ed. *Humanism in America*. New York: Brewer and Warren, 1930.

Fogarty, Daniel S.J. "Kenneth Burke's Theory." *Roots for a New Rhetoric*. New York: Columbia UP, 1959. 56–87.

Foss, Sonja K., Karen Foss, and Robert Trapp. "Kenneth Burke." *Contemporary Perspectives on Rhetoric*. Prospect Heights: Waveland P, 1955. 153–88.

Frank, Armin Paul. *Kenneth Burke*. New York: Twayne, 1969.

Gabin, Rosalind. "Entitling Kenneth Burke." *Rhetoric Review* 5 (1987): 196–210.

Gunn, Giles. *The Culture of Criticism and the Criticism of Culture*. Chicago: U of Chicago P, 1987.

Harris, Wendell. "Critics Who Made Us: Kenneth Burke." *Sewanee Review* 96 (1988): 452–63.

Hassett, Michael. "Sophisticated Burke: Kenneth Burke as a Neosophistic Rhetorician." *Rhetoric Review* 13 (1995): 371–90.

Heath, Robert. *Realism and Relativism: A Perspective on Kenneth Burke*. Macon: Mercer UP, 1986.

Henderson, Greig. "Aesthetic and Practical Frames of Reference." *Extensions of the Burkeian System*. Ed. James Chesebro. Tuscaloosa: U of Alabama P, 1993. 173–85.

Hicks, Granville. "In Defense of Eloquence" [Review of *Counter-Statement*]. *New Republic* 69 (2 December 1931): 75–76.

Hoeveler, J. David, Jr. *The New Humanism: A Critique of Modern America, 1900-1940*. Charlottesville: U of Virginia P, 1977.

Holland, Virginia. *Counterpoint: Kenneth Burke and Aristotle's Theories of Rhetoric*. New York: Philosophical Library, 1959.

Jameson, Fredric. "Ideology and Symbolic Action." *Critical Inquiry* 5 (1978–79): 417–22.

———. "The Symbolic Inference; or, Kenneth Burke and Ideological Analysis." *Critical Inquiry* 4 (1977–78): 507–23.

Jammerman, Donald. "Kenneth Burke's Poetics of Catharsis." *Representing Kenneth Burke*. Ed. Hayden White and Margaret Brose. Baltimore: Johns Hopkins UP, 1982. 31–51.

Jay, Paul. *American Literary and Cultural Criticism and the Problem of Modernity*. Unpublished manuscript.

———. "Kenneth Burke." *Dictionary of Literary Biography. Volume 63: Modern American Critics, 1920-55*. Ed. Gregory S. Jay. Detroit: Gale Research, 1987. 67–86.

———, ed. *The Selected Correspondence of Kenneth Burke and Malcolm Cowley 1915-1981*. New York: Viking, 1988.

Leitch, Vincent. *American Literary Criticism from the 1930s to the 1980s*. Columbia: Columbia UP, 1988.

Lentricchia, Frank. *Criticism and Social Change*. Chicago: U of Chicago P, 1983.

———. "Reading History with Kenneth Burke." *Representing Kenneth Burke*. Ed. Hayden White and Margaret Brose. Baltimore: Johns Hopkins UP, 1982. 119–49.

More, Paul Elmer. *The Drift of Romanticism: Shelbourne Essays*. New York: G. P. Putnam, 1909; rpt. New York, 1967.

Munson, Gorham. "In and About the Workshop of Kenneth Burke." *Destinations: A Canvass of American Literature Since 1900*. New York: J. H. Sears and Company, 1928. 139–59.

———. "Our Critical Spokesman." *Humanism in America*. Ed. Norman Foerster. New York: Brewer and Warren, 1930. 342–69.

Nelson, Cary. "Writing As an Accomplice of Language: Kenneth Burke and Post-Structuralism." *The Legacy of Kenneth Burke.* Ed. Herbert W. Simons and Trevor Melia. Madison: U of Wisconsin P, 1989. 156–73.

[Nichols], Marie Hochmuth. "I. A. Richards and the 'New Rhetoric.'" *Quarterly Journal of Speech* 44 (1958): 1–16.

Parkes, Henry Bamford. *The Pragmatic Test.* San Francisco: Colt P, 1941.

Poggioli, Renato. *The Theory of the Avant-Garde.* Cambridge: Harvard UP, 1968.

Pondrom, Cyrena N. *The Road from Paris: French Influence on English Poetry 1900–1920.* Cambridge: Cambridge UP, 1974.

Pound, Ezra. "Mr Aldington's Views on Gourmont." *The Dial* 86 (January 1929): 68–71.

———. *Pavannes and Divisions.* New York: Knopf, 1918.

Richards, I. A. *Principles of Literary Criticism.* London: Routledge & Kegan, 1926.

———. *Science and Poetry.* New York: W. W. Norton, 1926.

Richards, I. A. and C. K. Ogden. *The Meaning of Meaning.* London, 1927; rpt. New York: Harcourt, Brace and Company, 1927.

Rosenberg, Harold. Review of *Counter-Statement. The Symposium* 3 (1932): 116–20.

Rueckert, William H. "A Field Guide to Kenneth Burke—1990." *Extensions of the Burkeian System.* Ed. James Chesebro. Tuscaloosa: U of Alabama P, 1993. 3–34.

———. *Kenneth Burke and the Drama of Human Relations.* Berkeley: U of California P, 1963.

Schneider, Isidor. "A New View of Rhetoric" [Review of *Counter-Statement*]. *New York Herald Tribune Books* (13 December 1931): 4.

Schwartz, Sanford. *The Matrix of Modernism: Pound, Eliot, and Early Twentieth-Century Thought.* Princeton: Princeton UP, 1985.

Sheard, Cynthia M. "Kairos and Kenneth Burke's Psychology of Political and Social Communication." *College English* 55 (1993): 291–310.

Sieburth, Richard. *Instigations: Ezra Pound and Remy de Gourmont.* Cambridge: Harvard UP, 1978.

Skodnick, Roy. "Counter-Gridlock: An Interview with Kenneth Burke." *All-Area #2* (Spring 1983): 4–32.

Spingarn, Joel. *Creative Criticism.* 1917; 1925; rptd. and expanded. New York: Harcourt, Brace and Company, 1931.

Warnock, Tilly. "Reading Kenneth Burke: Ways In, Ways Out, Ways Roundabout." *College English* 48 (1986): 62–75.

Warren, Austin. "Kenneth Burke: His Mind and Art." *Sewanee Review* 41 (1933): 225–36; 344–64.

Williams, William Carlos. *The Autobiography of William Carlos Williams.* New York: Random House, 1948.

Wilson, Edmund. *Axel's Castle: A Study in the Imaginative Literature of 1870–1930.* New York: Charles Scribner's Sons, 1931.

Woodcock, John. "Interview with Kenneth Burke." *Sewanee Review* 85 (1977): 704–18.

7

Rhetorical Criticism of Public Discourse on the Internet
Theoretical Implications

BARBARA WARNICK

The Internet and access to it have grown exponentially in the past three years. Georgia Tech's Graphic, Visualization, and Usability Center reports that, since January 1994 when its first survey of Internet users was conducted, the Internet has grown from 1250 servers to over one million servers. There are over thirty million users of the Internet in the United States alone (Graphic, Visualization, and Usability Center). The versatility of the medium has increased along with its size, as the addition of Java technology and other features has increased the dynamism and interactivity of websites and as conveyance via television has increased access.

Mass communications scholars and our colleagues in interpersonal, organizational, and small group communication have been studying computer-mediated communication [CMC] for some time. Mass communications researchers have been concerned with a number of questions—how First Amendment protections and intellectual and property rights transfer from print to CMC; what factors play a role in attracting audiences to Internet sites; what strategies can be used to determine accuracy of information on the Internet; and so forth (McChesney; Morris and Ogan; Reeves and Nass). Interpersonal communication researchers have studied the development and maintenance of relationships online (Walther; Parks and Floyd), while small group researchers have examined the dynamics of group process in computer-mediated environments (Savicki, Lingenfelter, and Kelley; Rafaeli and Sudweeks). In addition to these, there have been many other forms of communication research studying Internet discourse and interaction. But rhetorical critics and theorists are latecomers to the scene.

There are many possible reasons for this. Many humanists have been slow to take up interest in discourse in electronic environments, perhaps because they suspect that critical work and critical theory will need to be changed to suit the new communication environments, and this is true because in a hypertext environment, author, audience, and text are dispersed. While such dispersion can and does occur in other modalities, computer-mediated discourse is particularly prone to it. The function of the author as originator of a message can be suppressed in group-authored, disguised, or anonymous Internet postings. As I will show later, identifying the nature and reactions of audiences is made more difficult in computer-mediated environments. And when text becomes hypertext, the text itself is dispersed and assimilated and loses its stability. As Ted Friedman (73) noted,

> few [critics in the humanities] have paid much attention to the emergence of new media that call into question the very categories of author, reader, and text. . . . Interactive software—computer games, hypertext, and even "desktop" programs and databases—connect oppositions of "reader" and "text," of "reading" and "writing," together in feedback loops that make it impossible to distinguish precisely where one begins and the other ends. Recognizing a reader's changing expectations and reactions as a linear text unfolds is one thing, but how do we talk about interactions in which every response provokes instantaneous changes in the text itself, leading to a new response, and so on?

The malleability of the text, the indeterminacy of authorship, and the changing natures of community, audience, and public in new communication environments surely complicate the critic's task.

There is nonetheless a point of entry for study of public discourse in computer-mediated environments. It is the same point of entry rhetorical critics have always had—the study of specific communication practices. Despite the altered state of authorship, audience, message, and text in cyberspace, communicators nonetheless support values and ideologies, influence one another, and shape beliefs and attitudes. They do this, as they always have, in situated acts of persuasion and communication. As Laura Gurak (ix) argued in her recent study of advocacy in the Lotus MarketPlace and Clipper Chip controversies,

> it is important to move away from generalizations about life in cyberspace and begin to analyze specific instances of computer-mediated communication, not only as a way of understanding patterns of current discourse but also as a method of building theory.

As this essay will show, the theory that emerges from critical study of computer-mediated rhetorical activity will need to be adapted to the modality and environment of new communication technologies. The various forms of Internet communication are discontinuous, fragmented, interactive, increasingly multi-mediated, and they lack the cues of face to face interaction and the seeming transparency of print. To study them, we will need to rethink many of our critical constructs and categories—for example, style, in light of the new graphical interfaces and digitized images, and credibility in light of the dispersion of authorship. Furthermore, critics need to be sensitive to the extent to which the medium shapes our consciousness even as our use of it shapes the medium. As Giuseppi Mantovani observed, "new communication environments do not only represent an important background for interpretation of messages which pass through them, but are themselves metamessages" (p. 69).

An important task for rhetorical critics studying Internet communication will be to answer what Richard Lanham (175) has called "the Q question"—how to connect discursive practices with moral judgment. Rhetoricians who have considered how computer mediation has affected messages produced in the medium have found such phenomena as overcompliance with group norms, unnecessarily aggressive behavior, a decline in the quality of deliberation, gender marginalization, and technological elitism. The considerable potential benefits to society of new media should be weighed against their negative dimensions, and rhetoricians as humanistic scholars are well positioned to join in this conversation. In this essay, I will consider how alterations in new media affect the practice of rhetorical criticism, survey some work completed by rhetorical critics studying CMC, and suggest possible directions for future research.

From Print to Hypertext: Rhetorical Criticism of CMC

Many traditional forms of rhetorical criticism are suited to print and spoken texts that unfold in time and in idea sequence. Practices such as neoclassical criticism and close textual reading assume a text that is relatively stable and finite, although it may be subject to a range of interpretations. While the text may be appropriated in various ways, it nonetheless provides a matrix or score to circumscribe the various readings. Part of the artistry of close textual reading is to plumb the intricate and subtle nuances of a speaker or writer's style. Style is viewed as a means of penetrating the text, of exposing the workings of its author's consciousness and its resonance with larger themes. George Landow (*Hyper/Text/Theory* 34–35) contrasts this state of affairs with the situation confronting the rhetorical critic of hypertext:

> Critics can never read *all* the text and then represent themselves as masters of the text as do critics in print text. True, one can never fully exhaust or master a particular printed text, to be sure, but one can accurately claim to have read all through it or even to have read it so many times as to claim credibly to know it well. Large hypertexts and cybertexts simply offer too many lexias for critics ever to read. Quantity removes mastery and authority, for one can only sample, not master, a text.

Hypertext as we experience it on the Web, for example, is, when compared to print, monologic speech and, unlike certain other media texts, an unstable and rather limitless text. Web hypertexts are disorderly and often disorienting.

The browser reading hypertext chooses his or her own path through a set of possibilities and creates the text s/he reads. The interactivity of many forms of Internet communication leads to a malleable text where one can clip someone else's discourse and paste it indiscriminately into one's own, where digitized images can be altered and reposted, where one can instantaneously move from a website advocating a position to one in total opposition, where windows can be opened over other windows until one forgets where one is. Even though the instability of hypertext may destroy certain notions presently associated with text, it need not necessarily destroy text (Landow, *Hypertext* 53). Instead, we may have to change our expectations of what texts are and how they function.

What can the rhetorical critic say of the discontinuous, malleable, fugitive texts of public discourse on the Web, in newsgroups, listservs, bulletin boards, and other Internet venues? Regardless of their comparative instability, such texts construct identities, hold readers' attention, influence attitudes, appeal to values, shape opinions, and hail their readers as subjects. They also represent viewpoints, take positions on public issues, and attempt to influence reader behavior. They are thus rhetorical texts and can be fruitfully studied by the rhetorical critic, but the critical theory used to study them may have to be adapted to suit the new communication environment in which these texts are produced.

My own experience and that of other critics who have studied computer-mediated text and hypertext indicates that such texts might best be studied as a system of circulating signifiers in a larger discursive environment. Critics can read a large number of texts that are sampled in an orderly fashion to discover what patterns and regularities are discernable. Critics will have to take some care to sample a range of sites or postings, but this problem is not unique to study of electronic texts; some justification for the selection of a text/texts is a standard *topos* with which critics must deal. In CMC, where one often cannot tell where one text ends and another begins and in which the text is indeterminate, the study of a large number of texts to understand and describe their operation seems to be a viable strategy. Studying texts as a system also works well in a communication environment in which website postings are continuously revised, where postings are periodically removed and updated, and where many sites and postings are becoming increasingly interactive. The critic's task is even further complicated by the fact that, by removing a text from its environment and studying it in "freeze frame," one brackets out its dynamism which may be an important part of its message. Also complicating the critic's task is an idea well expressed by Stephen Doheny-Farina that the World Wide Web, for example, is "primarily a graphics delivery system, a presentation medium masked as an interactive network. Deliberative rhetoric is defeated every time by image" (78). Mere attention to the words on a web page will not suffice, since the images are so important to textual meaning. Even in texts without images, the way that the text is displayed on the screen has rhetorical impact.

Let me provide some examples of how this might work. In her studies of the Lotus MarketPlace and Clipper Chip controversies, Gurak looked for patterns and regularities in the texts she studied and found that certain styles of communication seemed to be differentiated along gender lines. Male posters to certain newsgroups and lists tended, among other things, to make very strong assertions, engage in *ad hominem* attacks on posters who disagreed with them, use humor or sarcasm, and engage in self promotion. Women, on the other hand, tended toward use of "attenuated assertions, apologies, explicit justifications, questions, a personal orientation, and the supporting of others" (109). My study of parodic political websites in the 1996 presidential campaign indicated that much of the activity on websites designed for parody was self-fulfilling. This included undelivered petitions, polls with results posted only to the site in question, political computer games, and online chat (Warnick, "Appearance"). Critics seeking patterns and regularities in Internet discourse might ask questions such as the following: what sorts of roles are being enacted? What kind of participation or response is being sought? How are value orderings implied or reinforced? What sort of online community is assumed, and what are its conventions and values? What are the significant absences—who is excluded; what values are suppressed; what is not said? Since such questions can be asked and answered on a systems level, the indeterminacy of text becomes less of a problem.

A second factor complicating rhetorical critical study of public discourse in electronic contexts is what happens to the notion of audience. This is a very real problem for any critic seeking corroboration for his or her textual reading or claim about the effects of discourse. In the first place, the identity of the audience as distinct from the rhetor in many forms of CMC is quite difficult to place. In an age where messages can be forwarded like chain letters, so that messages are "fanned out," mailed and remailed, and where hierarchies are flattened as the gatekeeping function is suppressed in an open and freewheeling environment, the audience is often not readily identifiable. Everyone is a rhetor, and everyone an audience. It is true that devices known as "cookies" can be used to track who visits a site and how often. But such devices can only measure "attendance," not audience reaction, and "cookies" can be blocked. Furthermore, people can register at websites, but many prefer not to. A recent survey of Web users also reported that 30% acknowledged that they falsified information when they did respond (Graphic, Visualization, and Usability Center). Many rhetorical critics studying print or spoken texts now turn to the intertext—the texts produced in the environment in which a message has appeared—to discuss the text's impact. The Internet, however, is, more than many other communication environments, one in which so many texts are being produced, consumed, duplicated, forwarded, and altered that the notion of a discrete audience for a discrete message has become quite problematic.

This is not to say that rhetorical critics cannot provide support for readings of texts. They can, but the support would have to come from probable readings of the texts they have studied, and they would have to be enacted in such a way that the evaluator of the critic's work is positioned to make an independent judgment of the critic's reading. There are many critical resources available to support the critic in his or her reading of texts, even when those texts are dispersed and data about audience effects is unavailable. For example, in my recent study of discourse intended to invite women online (Warnick, "Masculinizing"), I argued that the dissociations, metaphors, and narrative constructions in the discourse operated to marginalize its readers, so that women were being invited to participate in an excluding way. For example, women who were resourceful, assertive, and active were dissociated from and valued over those who were under resourced, hesitant, or passive. Metaphors in the discourse connected women who had been on the net to pioneer women, to the vanguard who cleared the way for recently arrived "latecomers." And narratives in the discourse welcomed the newcomers while still expressing a concern that, by their participation, they would somehow diminish the stature of Internet participation or bring an end to the "rough and ready" nature of online environments. Since these argument forms and narrative constructions were produced and reproduced in the discourse itself, I could provide support for my account of invitational discourse that excludes even while it invites.

Another consideration germane to the question of audience has to do with the nature of computer-mediated environments as contexts for communication. Some critics of CMC have argued that it is a solipsistic environment, one whose activity is often essentially self fulfilling. Sherry Turkle, for example, has spent over a decade ethnographically studying the ways in which people talk and think about their use of computers. Her interviews and observations lead her to conclude that "we are moving from a modernist culture of calculation toward a postmodernist culture of simulation" (20). On the Internet, identities are assumed, genders reversed, anonymous messages forwarded, digitized images altered, computer games played, and pseudo events and pseudo messages constructed for the sake of user entertainment. The Internet is one environment where the Derridean observation that "there is nothing outside of the text" may be quite true in many respects (Derrida 158). In my study of parodic websites in the 1996 campaign, I found pseudo sites designed to mimic genuine sites, pseudo candidates who were composites of actual candidates, fabricated allegations, altered photographs, and unsubstantiated charges of conspiracy. In short, I found in these parodies and accusations a postmodern environment such as that described by Turkle. Here is an environment where "rhetors" assume opposing positions, speak patched-together nonsense, and utter with impunity charges that in any other environment would make them subject to libel suits. In such an environment where "no reference exists for the world on the computer screen" (Friedman 85), is not the whole question of audience misplaced? Should the question of whether the discourse had the "effects" intended by the "author" (what author?) make sense? In light of this consideration, my best advice to the rhetorical critic is to describe what s/he finds and to critique it, but to be very circumspect when making claims about audience "effects."

Much that I have said here about rhetoric on the Internet has been negative, but it is also worth considering the other side. Researchers and students who use the Web and other Internet resources advisedly have a great deal to gain. Because of its capacity for storage, search, and retrieval of information, the Internet is a very rich resource for anyone interested in rhetorical communication. Full texts of speeches, until recently difficult to obtain, are much more readily available and indeed, for the teacher of public address, invaluable. Public debates, discussion groups, issues forums, and many other forms of public discourse have been widely disseminated in the new venue. Research can be done more quickly, efficiently, and effectively due to the presence of online resources, in particular, searchable databases. Nonetheless, rhetorical critics are obligated to study the quality and nature of public discourse in electronic forms and to ask, among other things, what impact the new modalities have, both on what is communicated and how it is communicated.

The Question of Authorship

Many forms of neoclassical rhetorical theory and traditional public address criticism view the message as legitimated and formed by an identifiable author. Critics using these approaches view texts at least partially in terms of the author's experience, education, values, and purpose. Recourse to such a framework in studying computer-mediated discourse often is made problematic by various difficulties that grow out of the nature of the medium. As Landow (*Hypertext* 23) observed, "electronic linking reconfigures our experience of both author and authorial property, and this reconception of these ideas promises to affect our conceptions of both the authors (and authority) of texts we study and of ourselves as authors." What is it about the medium that problematizes agent-centered criticism?

First, the question of authorship is no more easily answered than the question of audience. Many websites are posted by groups or individuals who do not choose to reveal their identities. Most of the parodic websites attacking political candidates in the 1996 presidential campaign had no identifiable author (Warnick, "Appearance"). Gurak noted (82) that in her case studies, "postings did not even need an author's name to inspire . . . trust and be reposted. Anonymous postings were also provided as a kind of community service." Second, in the Internet environment, anyone's message can be clipped, altered, forwarded, and reposted. Gurak (72) reports that the process of cutting, pasting, and reframing others' messages "represents one way online rhetorical discourse functions, because the technology promotes rapid reposting and because the Internet does not have many gatekeeping functions in place." One result of this is, of course, widespread use of inaccurate information. (As one observer [Dowe 55] pointed out, "the net is terrible for propaganda but it's wonderful at conspiracy.") Hypertext appears to be particularly amenable to authorlessness. Third, as is well known, authors of electronic texts often disguise their identities. Participants in MUDs, MOOs, chat rooms, and other Internet venues often swap genders or construct personae that are purely virtual (Turkle 16, 228–30). Frequently, then, one cannot tell who the author is, nor does it make any sense to ask this question in the traditional way. As Mark Poster (6) observed, "in the . . . electronic stage the self is decentered, dispersed, and multiplied in continuous instability."

The absence of an identifiable author in many Internet venues leads to the problem of credibility. If Mantovani (126) is right that "we act in a world in which it is important to respond promptly to situations," in which people's tendency is "to treat all representations as true," then aspects of the medium itself may confer credibility on a message even when its author and origin are unknown.

Indeed, this is just what some recent studies of Internet discourse have found to be the case. Again returning to the "systems" view of a group of texts, Gurak found in her study of the Lotus MarketPlace and Clipper Chip controversies that ethos was an artifact of a group or set of interests, that it was based on posters' stated professional affiliations and contributions. Furthermore, she found that communities were self selecting and sustained their own ethos. Gurak concluded that, in the online communities she studied, "consensus was the norm" and that, whenever a poster did not believe MarketPlace or the Clipper Chip to be a problem (thus deviating from the group norm), "their opinions were quickly dismissed by others" (94). The community ethos in these online groups was quite powerful, since the postings of dissenting individuals were often ignored or sanctioned either by disagreement or *ad hominem* attacks. My recent study of discourse inviting women online also revealed a group *ethos*—that of the "cybergrrls"—successful women in the avant-garde of computer technology (programmers, media executives, software developers, webzine editors, and authors). These women touted the advantages of online participation, their promises and claims of wealth and career advancement being manifest in their own personal histories and situations. The persona they projected was a group persona, one marked by "in your face" assertion, personal resourcefulness, an "in the know" understanding of technology, and general fearlessness. These attributes, as a composite, set up many opportunities for persuasive appeal based on argument from model to get offline women online. Ethos as a critical construct may need to be reformulated by rhetorical critics to determine how texts whose origin is of secondary importance and whose authorship is undetermined nevertheless project an ethos by dismissing opposing views, by perpetuating and confirming the dominant values of a group, or by associating themselves with ostensibly desirable traits and accomplishments.

Some Rhetorical Patterns in Internet Discourse

Research on Internet communication by rhetoricians has suggested a number of features and trends in computer-mediated public discourse. First, the nature of the medium itself seems to discourage users from distinguishing between what is virtual and what is "real." As Friedman (82) noted, "technology may mask the constructedness of any simulation." One potential implication is that browsers may take simulated participation in the public sphere for real participation. But there is a difference between voting on a website and voting in an election, between a "community forum" on the Web and a town meeting, and between playing political computer games and volunteering in a real campaign (Lakoff; Warnick, "Appearance"). In all three cases, the first may be personally gratifying, but only the second affects the political process. In their 1996 edition of *Habits of the Heart*, Bellah and colleagues argued that "one of the keys to survival of free institutions is the relationship between private and public life, the way in which citizens do, or do not, participate in the public sphere" (xlii). Furthermore, they observed that "the Internet, the electronic town meeting, and other much ballyhooed new technological devices are probably civically vacuous because they do not sustain civic engagement" (xvii). The question of how and whether computer-simulated political participation affects the public sphere can be fruitfully addressed by rhetoricians.

Second, there appears to be something about computer mediation that fosters pressure to conform to group norms, values, and ideology and that discourages deviation and disagreement. Steven E. Miller observed that "online discussion [*sic*] have a high 'noise-to-signal ratio.' Virtual groups do not handle controversial topics very well, often degenerating into 'flame wars' that are as likely to kill the group as to lead to any relevant insights" (336). Gurak's study of online discussion groups in the Lotus MarketPlace and Clipper Chip controversies led to a pessimistic diagnosis of group deliberation. She concluded that such communities of interest were self selecting. Drawn together by their own like-mindedness, they penalized participants who disagreed with the group. As Gurak concluded, "in some of these discussions there was no 'other side' to be weighed, because individuals who held the minority position were not comfortable challenging the dominant ethos of the . . . community" (103). Similar conclusions have been reached by other researchers who have studied usenets and discussion lists (Herring; Anderson).

A third pattern emergent in discourse on and about new technologies is technological elitism. In my study of discourse inviting women online (Warnick, "Masculinizing"), I found that technophiles and people knowledgeable about technology were constructed as savvy, "in the vanguard," resourceful, innovative, and in control, while their technophobic counterparts were viewed by implication as fearful, ill-informed, regressive, and hesitant. This contrast is intimated through hierarchies and distinctions made in metaphors, dissociations, and arguments from models used in public discourse. It is pervasive in publications touting technology such as *Wired* and other computer periodicals (Borsook). Technological elitism discursively produces and reproduces a distinct mode of domination in a society in which the technologically well endowed benefit while the technologically bereft are relegated to the underclass.

The resources and skills required by technology systematically favor dominant ethnic groups, the highly educated, the developed world, and the affluent. The ways in which technological domination is rhetorically established and reproduced should be of interest to critics.

Other patterns in CMC have been noted that are potentially of interest. These include a decline in the quality of deliberation (Doheny-Farina), marginalization and harassment of females (Herring; Anderson), proclivity for parody and entertainment (Friedman), and a tendency to treat computers as social entities (Reeves and Nass). It could be that concerns raised about the impact of CMC on society—on maintenance of the public sphere, on sustenance of community, and on consciousness—could be focused through case studies of the rhetorical dimensions of computer-mediated discourse.

Conclusion

In light of the indeterminacy of text, author, and audience in computer-mediated environments, many of the more traditional approaches that have been used by rhetorical critics will need to be jettisoned or conceived differently when CMC discourse is studied. This essay has argued that studying Internet texts as systems of texts rather than as discrete texts may prove fruitful. Rhetorical critics can read texts produced on the Web, and in bulletin boards, lists, and newsgroups. By studying the micro practices of posters to these sites, critics can identify regularities and patterns of communication behavior which will assist them in better understanding how public discourse in electronic environments functions to construct identities and influence public opinion.

The websites and other venues I have studied have used a number of rhetorical strategies to influence recipients. The composite narratives that emerged embedded specific plots whose structures could be described. Argument schemes such as person/act relations, dissociations, and metaphors promoted value hierarchies and gave presence to some elements over others. The ways in which texts co-opted or appropriated positions that opposed or promoted their own were examined. The visual presentation of these sites—their layout, use of images, graphics, and photos—supported or replaced their verbal messages. As the interactivity of sites increases, the ways in which browsers collaborate in the construction of meaning and experience can also be studied by rhetoricians.

Rhetorical criticism of Internet discourse will probably be increasingly influenced by the "agent-lessness" of the phenomenon itself. Discourses will be viewed by critics as produced by some interest, not authored by some agent; as intertwined with their larger discursive environment rather than as discrete; and as of interest as much for their absences as for what they have to say. Nonetheless, the task of the rhetorical critic will be, as it has been, to make the forces and functions embedded in the discourse visible and nontransparent.

Works Cited

Anderson, Judy. "Not for the Faint of Heart: Contemplations on the Usenet." *Wired_Women: Gender and New Realities in Cyberspace*. Ed. Lynn Cherny and Elizabeth Reba Weise. Seattle: Seal P, 1996.

Bellah, Robert N., Richard Madsen, William M. Sullivan, Ann Swidler, and Steven M. Tipton. *Habits of the Heart: Individualism and Commitment in American Life*. 1985. Berkeley: U of California P, 1996.

Borsook, Paulina. "The Memoirs of a Token: An Aging Berkeley Feminist Examines *Wired*." *Wired_Women: Gender and New Realities in Cyberspace*. Ed. Lynn Cherny and Elizabeth Reba Weise. Seattle: Seal P, 1996.

Derrida, Jacques. *Of Grammatology*. Trans. Gayatri Chakravorty Spivak. 1974. Baltimore: Johns Hopkins UP, 1976.

Doheny-Farina, Stephen. *The Wired Neighborhood*. New Haven: Yale UP, 1996.

Dowe, T. "News You Can Abuse." *Wired* (January 1997): 53–56.

Friedman, Ted. "Making Sense of Software: Computer Games and Interactive Textuality." *Cybersociety: Computer-Mediated Communication and Community*. Ed. Steven G. Jones. Thousand Oaks, CA: SAGE, 1995. 73–89.

Graphic, Visualization, and Usability Center. *GVU's 7th WWW User Survey* (1977). Online. www.gvu.gatech.edu/user-surveys-1977-04; accessed 18 August 1997.

Gurak, Laura J. *Persuasion and Privacy in Cyberspace: The Online Protests over Lotus MarketPlace and the Clipper Chip*. New Haven, CT: Yale UP, 1997.

Herring, Susan. "Gender Differences in Computer-Mediated Communication: Bringing Familiar Baggage to the New Frontier." American Library Association Annual Convention, Miami, 27 June 1994. Online. Internet. www.cpsr.org; accessed 7 August 1997.

Lakoff, George. "Body, Brain and Communication." *Resisting the Virtual Life: The Culture and Politics of Information*. Ed. James Brook and Iain A. Boal. San Francisco: City Lights, 1995.

Landow, George P. *Hypertext: The Convergence of Contemporary Critical Theory and Technology*. Baltimore: Johns Hopkins UP, 1992.

———. "What's a Critic to Do?: Critical Theory in the Age of Hypertext." *Hyper/Text/Theory*. Ed. George P. Landow. Baltimore: Johns Hopkins UP, 1994.

Lanham, Richard A. *The Electronic Word: Democracy, Technology, and the Arts*. Chicago: U of Chicago P, 1993.

Mantovani, Giuseppi. *New Communication Environments: From Everyday to Virtual*. London: Taylor & Francis, 1996.

McChesney, Robert W. "The Internet and U. S. Communication Policy-Making in Historical and Critical Perspective." *Journal of Communication* 46 (1996): 98–124.

Miller, Steven E. *Civilizing Cyberspace: Policy, Power, and the Information Superhighway*. Reading: Addison-Wesley, 1996.

Morris, Merrill and Christine Ogan. "The Internet as Mass Medium." *Journal of Communication* 46 (1996): 39–50.

Parks, Malcolm R. and Kory Floyd. "Making Friends in Cyberspace." *Journal of Computer-Mediated Communication* 1.4 (1996). www.ascusc.org/jcmc/vol1/issue4/cover.html; accessed 25 July 1998.

Poster, Mark. *The Mode of Information: Poststructuralism and Social Context*. Chicago: U of Chicago P, 1990.

Rafaeli, Sheizal and Fay Sudweeks. "Networked Interactivity." *Journal of Computer-Mediated Communication* 2.4 (1997). www.ascusc.org/jcmc/vol2/issue4/index.html; accessed 25 July 1998.

Reeves, Byron and Clifford Nass. *The Media Equation: How People Treat Computers, Television, and New Media Like Real People and Places*. Cambridge: Cambridge UP, 1996.

Savicki, Victor, Dawn Lingenfelter, and Merle Kelley. "Gender Language Style and Group Composition in Internet Discussion Groups." *Journal of Computer-Mediated Communication* 2.3 (1996). www.ascusc.org/jcmc/vol2/issue3/index.html; accessed 25 July 1998.

Turkle, Sherry. *Life on the Screen: Identity in the Age of the Internet.* New York: Simon and Schuster, 1995.

Walther, Joseph B. "Interpersonal Effects in Computer-Mediated Interaction: A Relational Perspective." *Communication Research* 19 (1992): 52–90.

Warnick, Barbara. "Appearance or Reality? Political Parody on the Web in Campaign '96." *Critical Studies in Mass Communication* (In press).

———. "Masculinizing the Feminine: Inviting Women on Line Ca. 1997." *Critical Studies in Mass Communication* (In press).

8

Aristotle on Epideictic
The Formation of Public Morality

GERARD A. HAUSER

Recent scholarship on epideictic has provided important insights into the inventional character of rhetoric as it was practiced by the sophists and rhetoricians of Greek antiquity.[1] Works such as Nicole Loraux's study of funeral orations as inventing the Athenians' understanding of their city, John Poulakos's examination of the differences between Gorgian and Isocratean conceptions of encomia, and Takis Poulakos's explorations of the relationship Isocratean epideictic bore to moral action and the character of classical funeral orations move beyond the definitional concerns that were at the center of scholarly discussion for at least the first half of the twentieth century (see Chase). Collectively they suggest epideictic discourse was understood to play an important role in the public realm beyond simple commemoration.[2] In important ways, the occasion for praising or blaming significant public acts and actors also afforded the opportunity to address fundamental values and beliefs that made collective political action within the democracy more than a theoretical possibility. This scholarship, which examines the performance of epideictic, demonstrates how rhetorical choices of inclusion and omission inscribed contrasting visions of the polis. Insofar as political relations are still formed by the character of public discourse, these explorations into epideictic's premodern constitutive possibilities alert us to the news an originary understanding of epideictic can convey about the possibilities of rhetoric for late- or postmodernity.

At first glance the constitutive possibilities of epideictic may seem misaligned with recent discussions of rhetoric's political character. Analyses of the contemporary public realm[3] typically depict it as a debilitated arena, in line with the informative and informing work of Jürgen Habermas. Habermas himself leaves little room for a rhetoric with inventive possibilities. He depicts the bourgeois public sphere as the arena of middle class political opinion which shapes public policy, as corrupted by an invidious instrumental rationality. He argues that the ideological commitments of capitalism and the internal contradictions of the welfare state result in a systematically distorted political discourse in which public opinion is treated in terms of group psychology, and public policies are legitimated by a manufactured public opinion. Given his explicit neo-Kantian distrust of instrumental rhetoric as strategic communication, he holds little hope for it to instigate vital and redeemable political relations. For him, rhetoric is the cause of, not the solution to the current disintegrated state of political discourse. His critique would seem to hold especially for epideictic, whose inherent conservative tendencies run counter to critical theory's emancipatory project.

Habermas is not alone is his assessment of the possibilities for public discourse. In addition to his analysis of the bourgeois public sphere, culture critics (Robbins 1993), historians (Ryan), philosophers (Arendt; Taylor), political scientists (Calhoun; Fraser), rhetoricians (Eberly; Farrell; Goodnight; Hauser), and media scholars (Forester; Herbst), among others, have found the concept of the public sphere both central to understanding the role of discourse in political relations and disturbing for the political consequences of rhetorical practices, to borrow Nancy Fraser's (1990, 57) felicitous phrase, in "actually existing democracy." Most of these analyses bemoan contemporary public discourse as distorted by its dominant preoccupation with advancing the objectives of instrumental reason. There is no gainsaying that political discourse often leaves much to lament. Yet a good deal of this criticism springs from a priori standards of argument grounded in philosophical conceptions of rationality rather than the working standards of reasonableness that provide a political community with its ongoing frame of reference,[4] and betrays abandoned hope that rhetorical enactments of civic virtue might include inventive possibilities with liberatory consequences. Although the work of rhetoricians has advanced a more positive understanding of rhetoric and its inventive possibilities, it has focused almost exclusively on the deliberative arenas in which public issues are open to discussion and debate, giving scant, if any attention to the relationship between epideictic and the quality of political discussion. Yet, as the work of Robert Bellah and his associates during the early 1980s reminds us, before citizens can imagine the possibility of a vibrant public realm, they require a vocabulary capable of expressing public issues and experiences of publicness, which are civic needs, I will argue, that epideictic addresses.

In this paper I wish to explore a dimension of Aristotle's discussion of epideictic that adds to the recently emerging literature focused on this genre's political ramifications. My concerns are to extrapolate from his discussion a relationship between epideictic and *phronêsis* that suggests how it was possible for an enlightened rhetoric to overcome the emotion of prejudice in framing public issues and in realizing rhetoric's *telos* of *krisis*. I then wish to suggest the implications of his rhetorical vision for a modern day public sphere.

I

A pessimistic analysis of "actually existing democracy" is not new to our times. From its inception, democracy's emphasis on public deliberation and the importance of rhetoric for arriving at communal decisions has forged an uneasy balance between the reign of the majority and the rule of elites. On one side are concerns of the educated and powerful over the general citizenry's susceptibility to the demagoguery of unscrupulous rhetorical practices.[5] On the other, democracy continually asserts its principal value of majority rule, which assumes a trustworthy neighbor who can be relied upon to participate responsibly in resolving public issues. This tension was managed best by a strong leader, such as Solon early on or Pericles later, who understood that competing interests could produce powerful and destabilizing factions fully capable of imposing their will on the minority. Thus Solon, for example, was as sensitive as Madison to the need for compromise to maintain order and preserve political freedom for all citizens of the polis. When he was elected Archon in 594 his challenge was to heal the rift between rich and poor and restore a sense of solidarity to Athens. His compromise sought to ameliorate economic divisions by abolishing debt slavery, which was particularly odious to the poor, and returning from foreign slavery as many Athenians as possible. He also revoked the monopoly of the aristocracy by establishing three classes based on the annual harvest of a land owner's property. This meant that wealth rather than birth became a fundamental measure of an Athenian male. Still, Solon remained distrustful of the common person's capacity to govern; he believed "The *demos* will best follow its leaders when it is neither driven by violence nor given too free a rein" (Sagan, 58–65).

Pessimism was encouraged equally by the realities of daily life in Athens, which remained somewhat more perilous than sanitized idealizations sometimes portray. For example, after combing through the legal and the rhetorical artifacts of the fourth century, Barrington Moore reports that public life was still unsettled by acts of violence and threats to life and limb. He offers these telling remarks on the importance of the death penalty in this context:

> Major threats to public order feared by the Athenians were treason, deception and failure to keep promises made to public bodies, sacrilege, and felonious assault. Probably they resorted to the death penalty for this wide variety of crimes because public authority lacked other means to cope with them. There was only a very primitive form of police, and imprisonment seems to have been a method of holding the accused—and by no means all accused—for trial rather than a form of punishment. In that sense public authority was still rudimentary. Furthermore, as present-day experience makes plain, public systems for catching and punishing criminals are not very effective in the absence of generalized acceptance of public authority and respect for it. The death penalty was one way of insuring such respect.
>
> (111)

Moore's depiction emphasizes the difficulty facing rhetors of this period. Although in theory the Athenian democracy suggested that disputes among citizens were resolved through rhetorically induced consensus, the moral integrity of those who were party to public disputes was not completely reliable. Athenian political relations remained strained by class differences and the distorting influences of power-lust. The well-born and wealthy placed considerable value on the political utility of *philoi*, or friendship bonds. Political opportunists, such as Kleon and Alcibiades, placed equal value on the power of oratory to organize the *phouloi* or common men.[6] Their countervailing import in Athens during the fifth and fourth centuries BCE produced constant tension between the right of the people to reign and the privilege of the well positioned to rule. In addition to the dangers of factions and demagogues, these competing interests also made it extremely difficult for the scrupulous leader to satisfy all sides (Connor; Sagan).

Xenophon's *Hellenika* offers a concrete example of the problem of trustworthy speech brought to the fore of Athenian political consciousness by the newly emergent rhetorical practices. Athenian commanders had directed their fleet to a significant naval victory in the battle at Arginoussai, in 406 BCE. However, a small contingent of the fleet became separated from the rest, and some sailors had been left behind. When the leaders realized what had happened, they directed a small number of ships to return and rescue their compatriots. Bad weather ensued, the rescue attempts failed, and the stranded sailors were left to drown. Upon return to Athens, instead of receiving glory for their victory, the generals were charged with cowardice. The ensuing trial is particularly illustrative of the problematic consequences of passions aroused through rhetoric, perhaps still alive in public memory when Aristotle cautioned against their use at the beginning of the *Rhetoric*. Amidst the onslaught of emotional appeals, the citizens lurched back and forth for two days over how the commanders should be tried, then whether they were innocent or guilty, and finally over remorse at having rendered a guilty verdict. After the generals were executed, the dikasts changed their minds, and sought retribution against the accusers, whom they charged with deception for having persuaded them to return the guilty verdict.

Two decades later, when Aristotle was in residence at Plato's Academy, the Athenian democracy was in decline and the responsible officers of state were no longer the leading figures in the Assembly nor military commanders in the field. Kitto (160–69) notes that professional orators like Aeschines and Demosthenes were the voices of influence in the Assembly but held no office or field command. Prudent administrators like Eubulus were otherwise unnotable, while generals like Iphicrates and Chabrias were the equivalent of professional soldiers who also served foreign powers and lived abroad. The force of shared understanding that had informed the rhetoric of Pericles had given way to oratorical cleverness then in vogue.

Aristotle's observations at the beginning of his *Rhetoric* reinforce the picture of instability within Athenian political relations that accompanied public deliberation. After denouncing the uneven rhetorical practices of the day he pointedly observed that currently prevalent theories and practices were over-emphasizing emotionality. He depicted such appeals as non-essential to the *technê* of rhetoric, which consisted of the *pisteis*; verbal attacks and emotional appeals disconnected from the facts were speech outside the subject of rhetoric. They frustrated rhetoric's *telos* of *krisis* and he condemned this practice and the rhetorical handbooks of his day that offered instruction in such techniques as "warp[ing] the jury by leading them into anger or pity: that is the same as if someone made a straightedge rule crooked before using it" (1354ª12–35).

In response to the uncertain civic conditions of the day, Aristotle proposed that a rhetorical practice adhering to artistic precepts would improve the quality of public life. His rhetorical vision advanced an idealized notion of a true art practiced by a person who was skilled at making enthymemes in the service of true opinion. This, of course, was his *phronimos* who was skilled at practical reasoning that led to sound judgment and conduct. The *phronimos* was coveted as a leader because he was a skillful observer of the best course to follow when confronted by choices of right and wrong, of utility and impracticality, and of virtue and vice and, consequently, could offer insightful and valuable advice on practical matters.[7] Significantly, there is nothing in the *Rhetoric* to suggest that Aristotle regarded his vision of artistic rhetoric as an exclusively theoretical ideal. As he asserts in its opening passages, he believed that rhetoric's precepts could be abstracted from successful practices of the day.

Aristotle's *Rhetoric* was composed to deal with the practical necessities and uncertainties of governance in a free society. It posed an alternative to the reign of force imposed by a tyrant and the rule of authority imposed by those deemed superior in moral and intellectual virtue. Rhetoric makes most sense in a world where peers govern themselves. As Aristotle saw the matter, these were free humans who desired neither to experience any form of subjugation nor to impose subjugation upon their fellow citizens. For this reason, Aristotle maintained that rhetoric came under the architectonic of the ethical branch of politics. Mastering its precepts empowered the citizen to participate in weighing alternatives and shaping policies that constituted communal realities.

The uneven ethical commitments of Athenian public life raise a question about the conditions of possibility for a politics of persuasive arguments among citizens sometimes lacking in moral rectitude. Aristotle advocated rhetorical means for resolving public issues because he envisioned the artistic practice of persuasion in concert with the person of his ideal rhetor and the teaching function such a person exercised (Hauser 1985). This teaching function is nowhere more evident than in Aristotle's treatment of epideictic.

II

Of the three genres set forth in the *Rhetoric*, the deliberative and forensic clearly are concerned with the civic requirements of establishing and upholding the laws. Epideictic has had a murkier relationship to the necessities of political life.

Some, such as Cope, have interpreted it as a speech of display, an entertainment not to be taken as seriously as its counterparts in the affairs of the polis. In Cope's view:

> The third branch is inferior to the two preceding in extent, importance, and interest. It is the . . . demonstrative, showy, ostentatious, declamatory kind: so called because speeches of this sort are composed for "show" or "exhibition," *epideixis,* and their object is to display the orator's powers, and to amuse an audience . . . who are therefore *theoroi* rather than *kritai,* like spectators at a theater, or a contest for a prize . . . rather than any serious interest or real issue at stake.
>
> (121)

Others have emphasized the different functions of the audience as crucial, the political and judicial speeches calling for a judge, the ceremonial address calling for a witness. Embellishing this point, Rosenfield, for example, claims that the essence of epideictic is in commemorating the luminosity of a person or an event. For him, the heart of the matter

> may be more accurately thought of as "acknowledgment" and "disparagement," the recognition of what *is* (goodness, grace, intrinsic excellence) or the refusal to so recognize in a moment of social inspiration. In either case the experience afforded to participants is the opportunity of beholding reality impartially as witnesses of being.
>
> (1980, 133)

Rosenfield's claim, of course, denies privilege to Aristotle's apparent emphasis on praise and blame as the fundamental tactics of epideictic. And it also treats Ch. Perelman and L. Olbrechts-Tyteca's contention that the epideictic speaker is an educator as a distinctly modern notion out of keeping with the thinking of Aristotle.[8]

Perelman and Olbrechts-Tyteca actually introduce the didactic function of epideictic with a witty comment by Isocrates to underscore their contention that the values emphasized by this genre must be ones already deemed worthy of providing guidance. Otherwise, Isocrates wonders, "Is it right to compose speeches such that they will do the most good if they succeed in convincing no one among those who hear them?" (52). This reference to an ancient source indicates that for these Belgian scholars the educative function they emphasize for epideictic spans from the present to the period when its theory originated.

Perelman and Olbrechts-Tyteca's point leaves us to question why Rosenfield's distinction between judging and witnessing necessarily excludes a didactic function from an Aristotelian conception of epideictic. Although speeches of display were common at that time, the contents of the epideictic address were not necessarily frivolous. When juxtaposed with the requirements for an audience competent to understand Aristotle's model rhetor, epideictic subject matter suggests that this genre served an important educative function.

Evidently Aristotle thought that humans were unequally endowed with insights into the truth. In a variety of epistemological discussions, he holds to the view that we learn from a teacher who has insight into the truth and is able to lead the less knowledgeable to insight. For example, at the end of the *Posterior Analytics*, he is intent on explaining the process whereby we pass from sense perception, which affords knowledge of particulars, to knowledge of the principle that underlies the particular case (100^a14–$^b5$). Aristotle's concern is not with a justification of knowledge claims, but with how we come to grasp the truth of an initial premise, what D. W. Hamlyn (1976, 182) refers to as a genetic account of knowledge. Aristotle's view is that humans are capable of seeing or grasping through direct awareness that such and such elements of experience must go together. But this awareness requires appeal to specific cases, so that Aristotle assumes, as an epistemological necessity, that we are capable of putting like with like. Most significantly, this potential does not become actualized by itself. It requires a proper selection of particulars in the first place for the epistemological process to eventuate. In this regard, it is of some importance that the *Posterior Analytics* opens by acknowledging its concern with giving instruction and its presupposition that the instructor has knowledge. In such a context, its concluding discussion of intellectual insight is significantly modified because the use of *epagôgê* there, as in all that preceded it, assumes that not everyone can perform the act of recognition without the aid of a teacher to bring the cases to mind. Just as in ethics, *hexis* alone is insufficient.

The place of the teacher is no less important in rhetoric than in scientific thought. Aristotle maintains that only a few have the ability to see the universal unaided and the requisite skill to help others to recognize it: the teacher in technical subjects, the *phronimos* in matters of practical conduct.

From its outset, Aristotle's *Rhetoric* is consistent with his view of exclusivity about the few whose advice is worthy. He makes clear that although many engage in attempts to persuade, not all who speak with persuasive intent do so artistically. Rhetoric is presented as both a *technê* and a *dynamis*, which means it is a principled activity whose precepts can be articulated, taught and learned, and mastered. But rhetoric is more than this, it is also discussed as *dynamis*, a power of observing the available means of persuasion in the given case. The *technê* of rhetoric can be set down in objective fashion. But knowing the rules is insufficient to make one a rhetor; a rhetor must be able to actualize these principles, must translate knowledge into practice through the crafting of persuasive arguments. The subjective actualization of this *dynamis* allows the rhetor to engage in the artful practice of rhetoric and to extend its practice to any subject whatsoever. As William Grimaldi puts it, "Thus the one who has mastered the *technê* of rhetoric acquires a *dynamis* which enables him not only to actualize the elements which constitute the art of rhetoric but also to apply those elements to any subject so as to discern the possibly suasive in that subject" (6).

Acquiring this *dynamis* is rare in Aristotle's view. Only skilled arguers—those who understand syllogisms and induction and who are knowledgeable in relevant subject matters—can frame such proofs. Moreover, they have to frame them in a way that shows discernment and good judgment on matters of practical conduct. For Aristotle, the rhetorically potent person possesses both the capacity to make—a productive capacity—and also *phronêsis*, since affairs of rhetorical interest are ones determining right conduct in practical life. Such a person teaches the right course of action in the given case. This is the rhetor of whom Aristotle speaks.[9]

III

The ancient Greeks considered the ability to engage in public deliberation a virtue. Aristotle argues that *phronêsis*—practical wisdom or prudence—emerges through thoughtful assessment of the consequences that might flow from proposed actions. Understanding the implications of actions for oneself and the community is of little value without a corresponding capacity to make this understanding known through words and deeds sufficiently powerful to gain assent. In Books II and VI of the *Nichomachean Ethics*, Aristotle is intent on distinguishing the philosopher's wisdom, *sophia*, from the practical wisdom that he considers our best guide amidst the contingencies of prudential conduct. Whereas *sophia* offers insight into truth, the preserve of *phronêsis* is insight into what to think and do when confronted by conflicting alternatives. Its end is not theoretical knowledge but responsible action to resolve the differences of divergent perspectives that surface when we address concrete problems (Graham and Havard). In short, it is the type of reasoning peculiar to public life.

The goal of rhetoric and the function of the audience, in Aristotle's view, are one and the same, *krisis* or judgment. Aristotle's discussion implies an audience that is led to the point of judgment by engaging in practical reasoning. *Krisis* implies judgment informed by a disposition to act and feel in a particular way. As he makes clear in the *Nichomachean Ethics* (1144^a11-36), the starting point of action is virtuous insofar as it emerges from considering the phenomena of prudential conduct in terms that exceed one's personal interests and apply generally. Unlike instrumental reasoning exercised as a calculus of consequences, Aristotelian *krisis* eventuates from thoughtful consideration of contingent affairs in order to achieve the common good of *eudaimonia* or happiness.

Practical reasoning is concerned with making specific choices about the preferable and the good relative to the situation at hand. There is no god's-eye view that offers a single account of what these may be (Nussbaum, 290–317). We locate them through deliberation tempered by the fortunes of our particular way of life. The good life is not achieved by *technê* (*Nich. Ethics* 1140^b1), since what counts as "good" for Macedonians was not necessarily so for Athenians. Rather than a scientific enterprise, Aristotle maintains we achieve *eudaimonia* through "a true and reasoned state of capacity to act with respect to the things that are good or bad for a man" (*Nich. Ethics* 1140^{b}4–6).

Aristotle's ethical works, including his *Rhetoric*, position *eudaimonia* so that it is inclusive of a variety of constituents that may co-exist but are nevertheless independent of one another. Good health, respectful children, wealth, friends, love, and so forth are incommensurable and desired for themselves. They cannot be weighed against one another in terms of a foreordained understanding of the good life. We estimate their relevance and importance amidst a sea of changing circumstances, since they are the elements that contribute to the good life as it is gauged by the non-scientific calculus of deliberation.

We display deliberative virtuosity by knowing how to resolve a problem in line with the views of those being addressed, and the choices of wise men and women reflect their experience at dealing with human problems subject to deliberation. Since the elements of *eudaimonia* are incommensurable, in Aristotle's view, their meaning and relative value depend on one's view of the good life. Even though practical reasoning is not a *technê*, it is more than brute impulse or caprice. Aristotle regards it as an intellectual virtue, prudence, on which practical wisdom rests (*Nich. Ethics* 1106^{b}36–7^{a}2; 1140^{b}24–5). Prudence is an excellence, *aretê*, made visible in a person's capacity to locate the golden mean between the vices of excess and defect. Practical reasoning involves an ability to project the consequences of actions in line with an understanding of other commitments.

Obviously, an Athenian citizen had to posses an understanding of these values to participate effectively in the *ekklêsia*. Making and judging public arguments presupposed then, as now, literacy in the community's political and moral values as an a priori condition to assessing their relative importance to collective judgment on a particular issue. Aristotle's commonplace observation that we will get much further praising Athens before Athenians than we will before Spartans reflects the more fundamental assumption that questions of preference are always framed by the contingencies of values and ambitions held by those whose judgment counts.

In a democracy, those whose judgment matters includes individuals who lack experience in making public policy decisions and are absent the intellectual virtue of practical wisdom, but Aristotle maintains nevertheless that everyone who wishes to partake in public life must understand *phronêsis*.

> Practical wisdom issues commands, since its end is what ought to be done or not to be done; but understanding only judges. . . . Now understanding is neither the having nor the acquiring of practical wisdom; but when learning is called understanding when it means the exercise of the faculty of knowledge, so "understanding" is applicable to the exercise of the faculty of opinion for the purpose of judging of what some one else says about matters with which practical wisdom is concerned.
>
> (*Nich. Ethics* 1143^{a}8–14)

Aristotle's distinction implies that participation in public life requires a rhetorical competence of understanding in order to render competent judgments on issues of contingent choice, issues open to discussion and deliberation. Publicness requires both individuals who are able to summarize wise thoughts of others and apply their insights with flexibility in the given case, and individuals who are able to distinguish wise advice from that which is merely clever. The former requires *phronêsis* to offer sound advice; the latter requires recognition to form a sound judgment.

Aristotle's analysis of practical reasoning and of the ideal rhetor as *phronimos* poses no inherent impediment to regarding the rhetor's epideictic function as didactic and, in fact, there may be good reason to underscore this point. *Phronêsis* in the political and judicial domains leads to actions that are products of sound judgment. Deliberative rhetoric contributes to the ongoing political education of the polis. Similarly, forensic rhetoric contributes a parallel education on legal matters. In both cases, virtuosity emerges through rhetorical transactions. Esteemed attributes speak eloquently about the polis and the person of the statesman-rhetor, since the prevailing rhetoric is a statement of communal beliefs and commitments as well as a demonstration of the rhetor's practical wisdom.

IV

Aristotle's notion of a properly ordered rhetoric assumes that responsible persuasion translates the theoretical contents of politics and ethics into the praxis of statescraft and citizenship. But such action requires a quieting of the more partisan impulses Moore found in the hurley-burley of Athenian public life and that Aristotle cautioned against at the outset of the *Rhetoric*. Otherwise, how is virtue to make its appearance in city life? In this respect, then, epideictic occupies a unique place in celebrating the deeds of exemplars who set the tone for civic community and the encomiast serves an equally unique role as a teacher of civic virtue.

The contention that Aristotle assigned epideictic the important duty of teaching public morality admittedly seems to cut across the grain of his text. Cope, for example, correctly notes that Aristotle thought epideictic was a form given to the excesses of display. The frivolous oratorical flights of such stock performances doubtless were less intent on the welfare of the community than on applause, a fact Aristotle could hardly be expected to abide. But Aristotle was not single minded in regarding encomiasts as rhetoric's low lives. He also provided epideictic with a serious purpose by assigning nobility and baseness as its fundamental subject matter.

Aristotle regards nobility as intrinsically worthy, which makes it both inherently desirable and worthy of praise (1366ª33–34). The noble qualities to be presented in an epideictic address are those that benefit the community since, "If virtue is a faculty of beneficence, the highest kinds of it must be those which are most useful to others" (1366^b3). For this reason, acts of courage and justice are the most laudatory, since they embody virtues that aid the whole community.

Aristotle also enhances the role of epideictic by assigning its practitioners the responsibility for telling the story of lived virtue. Other modes of presentation might tell the community what a great person has done: the works performed or the offices held or the honors won. But the rhetorical version, along with the *mythos* of poetic, must concretize these virtues by displaying their manifestations in a distinguished life. The epideictic speech does not seek to *tell* what a person did, but to *display* nobility at the level of praxis. "Praise," says Aristotle, "is the expression in words of the eminence of a man's good qualities, and therefore we must display his actions as the product of such qualities." He then continues to link the display-like quality of the ceremonial speech with the storyteller's craft, saying, "Encomium refers to what he has actually done; the mention of accessories, such as good birth and education, merely helps make our story credible" ($1367^b27–29$).

The subjects of epideictic rhetoric are not themselves the teachers of society. Heroes caught up in the forward press of their actions resort to the means appropriate to resolve conflict. The moral of their acts emerges not in what they did but in the storyteller's province of how their deeds are narrated. The encomiast's gaze, like the storyteller's, is backward to the lives of important public individuals and to consequential events that provide building blocks for the community's story. Just as Lincoln at Gettysburg or presidents at their inaugurations or Isocrates in his *Evagoras*, Aristotle recognizes the ceremonial occasion as a time for celebrating deeds that transcend partisan factions and selfish interests. By valorizing heroes who are emblematic of a society's best qualities, encomia provide concrete guidance on how to live in harmony with noble ideals. For this reason, Aristotle holds that "to praise a man is in one respect akin to urging a course of action" (1367^b35). If the poet makes a mark through discourse mimetic of life, the encomiast makes one by encouraging a life mimetic of a public morality constituted through discourse.

In addition to aligning epideictic's purpose with *aretê*, Aristotle assigns a special function to the genre's audience. Unlike deliberative and forensic speeches, which require an audience to sit in judgment on concrete and problematic cases, epideictic does not address a problematic situation requiring a decision. It displays honorable deeds and asks its audience to witness what appears before it. Although Aristotle indicates at I.3 that the object of observation is the oratorical display itself, later, at I.9, where he expounds on the special topics of such speeches, he invests epideictic with a less trivial mission. The rhetor assumes the facts of the case are known; "our business," he says, "is . . . to invest these (facts) with dignity and nobility" (1368^a29), since "any superiority is held to *reveal* excellence" (1368^a25; italics mine). In addition to observing rhetorical skill, the auditors also are *observing* or bearing witness to virtuosity as it is revealed in the lives of exemplary citizens. They testify to its reality in the world and as a manifestation of their communal aspirations, a point Rosenfield develops at some length in his insightful analyses.

Noting the special function of the epideictic audience to witness, we are left to ask what excellence it observes. Surely it is not just the individual deeds of political and military actors. Aristotle believes that virtue transcends the individual, finding its place in the life of the city. Indeed, for Aristotle the individual is intelligible only as *zôon politikon*. To be virtuous in the community, one must know how to apply the laws and live within them. The lauded hero's life is exemplary of a larger commitment to ethical bonds and moral rectitude. Importantly, this message requires rhetorical forging; civic virtue is not cast in the logical terms of philosophical statement but in the episodic terms of events. To follow the story and, more importantly, to testify to its truth requires the ability to grasp it as a statement of communal ethos; it requires understanding the golden mean. Indeed, it would be odd not to extend Aristotle's view that the golden mean provided relief from the excesses of vice to those excesses that likely characterized Athenian factions.

In this respect, Aristotle's ideal rhetor occupies a special place. The *phronimos* rises above the corruptions and brutish self-interestedness that forms the perilous crucible of public affairs. Aristotle's exemplars of epideictic, such as Isocrates, Pericles, and Sappho, illustrate how we may exhibit knowledge about "virtue (*aretê*) and vice (*kakia*) and honorable (*kalon*) and shameful (*aiskhron*); for these are the points of reference for one praising or blaming" (1366ª23–24). They illustrate how we may offer the city images of civic virtue through comparison with traits of known actors and rival ways of life. When Sappho counsels Alcaeus, who claims shame restrains him from speaking openly, with:

> If you had a longing for noble or honorable things
> And your tongue had not stirred up some evil to speak,
> Shame would not have filled your eyes,
> But you would have been speaking about what is just.
> (qtd. in *Rhet.* 1367ª11–15)

her poem becomes emblematic of the encomiast's function of offering counsel against vice; she offers the advice of the golden mean. But her poem is more than an exhortation to action consonant with the good. Aristotle cites it in a context delimiting the particularity of the good to each situation. In a speech whose text is *aretê*, offering praise of virtues teaches the meaning of civilized action in a city of free citizens and encourages virtuous civic conduct.

And now we return to the audience of epideictic, depicted by Aristotle as spectators. By observing an epideictic performance, citizens experience the story of the golden mean as it is lived in their community. The mimetic function of the encomiast provides the moral story of the community; it provides models for overcoming the city's partisan imbroglios. Epideictic offers instruction on recognizing virtue and thereby on retaining persuasion as an alternative to authority or force in the public domain. By encouraging the golden mean in the community, Aristotle's *phronimos* practices a rhetoric calculated to cool the intemperate passions he decries at the *Rhetoric*'s opening, encouraging *mimesis* of a nobler ideal than individual advantage. The audience's collective recognition affirms virtue's worldly appearance. Absent this recognition whereby they realize their *telos* as witnesses to civic virtue, it is difficult to imagine how citizens might participate responsibly in a deliberative and forensic rhetoric whose very proofs require shared assumptions of civic norms on which enthymemes ultimately rest. A political and judicial rhetoric relying on enthymemes of argument, emotion, and character requires an audience attuned to a more temperate norm of shaping society's course by weighing alternatives. Epideictic teaches a new, less volatile means for managing the irrational eruptions that seem always to threaten public life.

V

Thus far I have argued that Aristotle's ideal rhetor, the *phronimos*, functioned as a teacher as well as a persuader. In the less than idyllic conditions of Athenian public life, this mediating influence was essential to bringing its sometimes cantankerous citizens to a common sense of the virtuous path. This teaching function is especially highlighted in epideictic oratory, in which the rhetor celebrates public virtue while the audience acts as its witness. The encomiast presents the story of individuals and deeds worth imitating. Memorials of their acts stand as themes on the golden mean, whose understanding is essential for the *phronimos* to have sway over the minds of citizens neither completely freed from the passions of the moment nor the guiding spirit of self-interest.

In this account, I have subordinated the characteristics of display to those of community instruction. There is no gainsaying the abuses of epideictic in the hands of rhetors disposed to exhibit their theatrical skills in search for applause. On the other hand, epideictic is not alone in this vulnerability, as over two millennia of verbally facile excesses have managed to demonstrate. By exploring an alternative tendency in Aristotle's remarks, I have attempted to highlight an additional and serious contribution epideictic makes to life in the city, a contribution that is suggestive of epideictic's role in shaping the Athenian public realm and also for the multiple arenas of the modern public sphere.

Contemporary social theory typically models the public sphere in terms of formal structural features that make it possible for industrially developed societies to conduct public business in ways that involve the masses. Typically these accounts are scientized by overattention to the technology of public opinion polls (Hauser 1998a) and, as I noted earlier, pessimistic, since the possibility of a responsible public forming and having an impact on the business of the state is regarded as a counterfactual ideal. In Aristotle's more rhetorically tuned public realm, where citizens interact in ways that join theory and praxis in political action (MacIntyre), an alternative set of assumptions is operative.

Epideictic was essential for acclimating the Athenian public realm to the activities it had to accommodate. This public realm was an active domain for political participation. Epideictic encouraged the constitutive activity pro-paedeutic to action: reflecting on public norms for proper political conduct. Aristotle's discussion italicizes an essential didactic element necessary for a smoothly functioning public sphere to exist.

More specifically, elsewhere (Hauser 1998a) I have conceptualized the pub-lic sphere as a discursive realm with a reticulate structure in which citizens can engage freely in communication about matters of mutual interest, invent their common sense of what appears before them, and assert their common views in ways that identify them as a public. Open discussion, in the manner of deliberative rhetoric, is emphasized in spirit, if not in fact, by this formulation. However, Aristotle's account of epideictic adds a dimension not readily appar-ent in an understanding of public spheres as exclusively deliberative arenas: the importance of these arenas in establishing the very traditions that make delib-erative rhetoric possible. Deliberative discourse is definitively factional, with the engaged parties each attempting to appropriate historicity. But historicity, as contemporary scholars such as postmodernist Jean-Francois Lyotard and hermeneutist Paul Ricoeur suggest, can only be brought to discourse through narrative. One must be cautious not to turn Aristotle *himself* into a postmod-ernist or a hermeneutist. However, his suggestion that epideictic constructs accounts of nobility worthy of *mimesis* emphasizes how its narrative character sets the conditions for a viable public sphere in which a people may engage in politics.

Examining epideictic provides insight into how a public sphere may serve as the crucible in which a people constitute and validate their tradition. For exam-ple, when President Clinton eulogized the Americans who died in the Croatian air crash in 1996, he pointed to their lives of dedicated service as a lesson to the entire nation. In an era of special prosecutors and seemingly endless scan-dal associated with government officials, it is easy to become cynical about the conduct of civil servants. But this speech is not cynical. In fact, by valorizing the dead Americans, many of whom were not much older than the typical under-graduate student, for their commitment to public service, for the high ideals that called them to service, and for their optimism toward making a differ-ence in the world, it acts as cynicism's anti-matter. Those on that ill-fated flight had embarked on a mission of hope to overcome the tragedy of the Balkans. Eulogized, these mostly average Americans become concrete representatives of renewed hope for a country and a future in which citizens seem disillusioned by politics and government. Clinton offers us hope with tomorrow's sunrise, fittingly Easter's sunrise, of redemption through continuing their dedication to an America that pursues the public good. Against the pervasive aura of debil-itating cynicism, his remarks offer instruction in a more noble and rewarding alternative.

Equally, epideictic may serve more polemical ends and raise controversy, such as Philipp Jenninger's 10 November 1988 commemorative address on the fiftieth anniversary of the event known as "Kristallnacht" that marked the onset of Nazi Germany's pogroms against the Jews (Farrell, 308–321), or Charles Althorp, Earl of Spencer's funeral eulogy to his sister, Lady Diana Spencer Althorp. Althorp attracted international attention when he interjected this pledge to his dead sister to look after the spiritual well-being of her sons, William and Harry:

> And beyond that, on behalf of your mother and sisters, I pledge that we, your blood family, will do all we can to continue the imaginative and loving way in which you were steering these two exceptional young men. So that their souls are not simply amassed by duty and tradition but can sing openly, as you'd planned. We fully respect and encourage them to their royal role. But we, like you, recognize the need for them to experience as many different aspects of life as possible, to arm them spiritually and emotionally for years ahead. I know you would have expected nothing less from us.

This remark, understood as an indirect address to the British royal family, asserted alternative values to those of the British crown. As such it played into the continuing British controversy over the role of the monarchy and England's changing place in the international community.

In addition to teaching, a rhetoric that commemorates noble deeds also can inculcate a common vocabulary of excellence among its witnesses. The Greeks could speak to one another about civic virtue because they shared a common language of virtue. By implication, a public sphere populated by factions is reduced to babel without a common language with which they may articulate acts of excellence. This does not mean factions must agree with one another nor use the same vocabulary to frame their experiences, as the provocative work of M. Bakhtin in this era has taught us. But it does mean they must be able to call one another to a sense of conscience and duty because in some fundamental sense they live in the same reference world.

Epideictic celebration contributes another unique aspect to a public sphere. Commemorating a specific excellence makes its virtuosity intelligible to the community. The shared testimony of audience members both certifies the reality of this excellence as a civic virtue while joining community members with bonds of affiliation to the celebrated values and deeds. Political actors cannot unite out of common interest without first recognizing shared bonds of community that transcend individual differences. A rhetoric celebrating the golden mean encourages tolerance and makes common action conceivable. It makes a public sphere a rhetorical space where community is invented and shared in performances of virtue through stories of significant individuals and momentous events. These rhetorical enactments of civic virtues are worth imitating because they teach lessons for making society itself more noble. Epideictic exhibits public morality; we learn it through *mimesis* of deeds unfathomable were they not publicly exhibited and validated.

Conversely, the didactic function of epideictic suggests that as a public sphere ceases to celebrate public morality and, instead, substitutes a scientistic or a bureaucratic model of public relations for political relations, the public that inhabits this sphere is denied the very instruction on which its survival as a politically relevant body depends. We can see this occurring, for example, in political campaign films that often display the candidate as an object for public consumption rather than the candidate's actions as a source of possibility for political invention. A public illiterate in models of proper conduct and inarticulate in expressing the moral bases for its beliefs soon becomes moribund and relinquishes the discursive basis for its political actions to authority or force.

To Aristotle's way of thinking, virtue had no rules; it was the product of sound judgment. One knew sound judgment because it could withstand the scrutiny of partisan perspectives. Such a rhetoric commemorated the importance of the public realm itself. At a time when privileges of wealth, power, and technological expertise have rendered politics suspect, this reading of epideictic accentuates the perils inherent when that realm becomes distorted. But it also provides a significant clue to the possibilities for thoughtful epideictic to reinvigorate enlightened discussion based on something more than the emotions of self-interest or vengeance. It can educate us in the vocabulary of civic virtues that may constitute citizens as an active public, and communicate principles on which responsible citizenship may be based and a vibrant public sphere can thrive.

Notes

1　An earlier version of this paper was presented at Fordham University in 1988 as part of a symposium on Aristotle's *Rhetoric* to commemorate the retirement of William M. A. Grimaldi, S.J., and is dedicated to his memory. I wish to acknowledge the critical comments and helpful suggestions of Rosa Eberly for revising that earlier draft. I bear sole responsibility for this paper's contents and final form.

2　In this regard, see also Beale; Condit; Duffy; Sullivan; and Walker.

3　For the purposes of this discussion I use the terms "public realm" and "public sphere" interchangeably, although when referring to classical Athens, I use "public realm" exclusively. I am mindful that the concept of the public sphere has historical meaning which grows from the rise of civil society during the enlightenment and that, strictly speaking, ancient Athens lacked a public sphere as we know it today, since those who were interacting outside official fora were the same individuals who were voting in the *ekklesia*. I have addressed this point elsewhere in some detail (Hauser, 1998). However, for purposes of this discussion, which is concerned with the larger issue of attuning citizens to civic virtues that may guide public judgment, the considerations relevant to epideictic intersect with those of theorists and commentators currently discussing the role and function of the public sphere.

4　See Edwin Black (1965, 1970) for a discussion of frame of reference in rhetoric.

5　See, for example, George Boas's discussion of *vox populi* as a central concept in Western forms of governance.

6　I use masculine references in this and subsequent sections that discuss classical antiquity to preserve with accuracy their understanding of a public domain of politics that was exclusively male.

7 For a discussion of the ways in which women might occupy a public leadership role in the ancient Athenian polis, see Christine Sourvinou-Inwood.

8 A contrary view is advanced in Christine Oravec.

9 See Christopher Lyle Johnstone for a detailed account of the role of the *phronimos* in Aristotle's conception of rhetoric and the rhetor's relationship to politics and truth. Martha Nussbaum (Ch. 10) develops an insightful account of how Aristotle thought *phronêsis* functioned to arrive at morally rectitudinous and practically wise choices. Thomas Farrell (72–83) offers a provocative extension of practical wisdom to include the reasoning audiences.

Works Cited

Arendt, Hannah. *The Human Condition*. Chicago: Chicago UP, 1958.

Aristotle. *Aristotle, on Rhetoric*. Trans. George A. Kennedy. New York: Oxford UP, 1991.

———. *Nichomachean Ethics: The Basic Works of Aristotle*. Ed. Richard McKeon. New York: Random, 1941.

———. *Posterior Analytics*. Trans. Hugh Tredennick. Cambridge: Harvard UP, 1960.

Beale, Walter H. "Rhetorical Performative Discourse: A New Theory of Epideictic." *Philosophy and Rhetoric* 11 (1978): 221–46.

Bellah, Robert, Richard Madsen, William M. Sullivan, Ann Swidler, and Steven M. Tipton. *Habits of the Heart: Individualism and Commitment in American Life*. Berkeley: U of California P, 1985.

Black, Edwin. "Frame of Reference in Rhetoric and Fiction." *Rhetoric and Poetic*. Ed. Donald C. Bryant. Iowa City: U of Iowa P, 1965. 26–35.

———. "The Second Persona." *Quarterly Journal of Speech* 56 (1970): 109–19.

Boas, George. *Vox Populi: Essays in the History of an Idea*. Baltimore: Johns Hopkins UP, 1969.

Calhoun, Craig, ed. *Habermas and the Public Sphere*. Cambridge: MIT P, 1992.

Chase, Richard. "The Classical Conception of Epideictic." *Quarterly Journal of Speech* 47 (1961): 293–300.

Condit, Celeste M. "The Function of Epideictic: The Boston Massacre Orations as Exemplar." *Communication Quarterly* 33 (1985): 284–98.

Connor, W. Robert. *The New Politicians of Fifth-Century Athens*. Princeton: Princeton UP, 1971.

Cope, E. M. *An Introduction to Aristotle's Rhetoric*. London: Macmillan, 1867.

Duffy, Bernard K. "The Platonic Function of Epideictic Rhetoric." *Philosophy and Rhetoric* 16 (1983): 79–93.

Eberly, Rosa. "Andrea Dworkin's *Mercy*: Pain, *Ad Personam*. and Silence in the War Zone." *Pre/Text* 14 (1993): 273–304.

———. "From Readers to Publics." CCCC Convention, Washington, DC, March 1995.

Farrell, Thomas B. *Norms of Rhetorical Culture*. New Haven: Yale UP, 1993.

Forester, John. *Critical Theory and Public Life*. Cambridge: MIT P, 1985.

Fraser, Nancy. "Rethinking the Public Sphere: A Contribution to the Critique of Actually Existing Democracy." *Social Text* 25/26 (1990): 56–80.

———. *Unruly Practices: Power, Discourse, and Gender in Contemporary Social Theory*. Minneapolis: U of Minnesota P, 1989.

Goodnight, G. Thomas. "Opening 'the Spaces of Public Discussion.'" *Communication Monographs* 64 (1997): 270–75.

———. "The Personal, Technical, and Public Spheres of Argument: A Speculative Inquiry into the Art of Public Deliberation." *Journal of the American Forensic Association* 18 (1982): 214–27.

———. "Public Discourse." *Critical Studies in Mass Communication* 4 (1987): 428–32.

Graham, George J., Jr. and William C. Havard, Jr. "The Language of the Statesman: Philosophy and Rhetoric in Contemporary Politics." *Sophia and Praxis: The Boundaries of Politics*. Ed. J. M. Porter. Chatham: Chatham House, 1984. 73–92.

Grimaldi, William M. A., S.J. *Aristotle, Rhetoric I: A Commentary*. New York: Fordham UP, 1980.

Habermas, Jürgen. *Legitimation Crisis*. Trans. Thomas McCarthy. Boston: Beacon, 1975.

———. *The Structural Transformation of the Public Sphere*. Trans. Thomas Burger with the assistance of Frederick Lawrence. Cambridge: MIT P, 1989.

———. *The Theory of Communication Action*. 2 vols. Trans. Thomas McCarthy. Boston: Beacon P, 1984–1987.

Hamlyn, D. W. "Aristotelian Epagoge." *Phronesis* 21 (1976): 166–84.

Hauser, Gerard A. "Aristotle's Example Revisited." *Philosophy and Rhetoric* 18 (1985): 171–80.

———. "Civil Society and the Principle of the Public Sphere." *Philosophy and Rhetoric* 31 (1998a): 19–40.

———. "Features of the Public Sphere." *Critical Studies in Mass Communication* 4 (1987): 437–41.

———. "On Publics and Public Spheres." *Communication Monographs* 64 (1997): 275–79.

———. "Vernacular Dialogue and the Rhetoricality of Public Opinion." *Communication Monographs* 65 (1998b): 83–107.

Herbst, Susan. *Politics at the Margins: Historical Studies of Public Expression Outside the Mainstream*. New York: Cambridge UP, 1994.

Johnstone, Christopher L. "An Aristotelian Trilogy: Ethics, Rhetoric, Politics, and the Search for Moral Truth." *Philosophy and Rhetoric* 13 (1980): 1–24.

Kitto, H. D. F. *The Greeks*. Baltimore: Penguin, 1957.

Loraux, Nicole. *The Invention of Athens: The Funeral Oration in the Classical City*. Trans. Alan Sheridan. Cambridge: Harvard UP, 1986.

Lyotard, Jean-Francois. *The Postmodern Condition: A Report on Knowledge*. Trans. Geoff Bennington and Brian Massumi. Minneapolis: U of Minnesota P, 1984.

MacIntyre, Alasdair. *After Virtue*. 2nd ed. Notre Dame, IN: U of Notre Dame P, 1984.

Moore, Barrington. *Privacy: Studies in Social and Cultural History*. Armonk: M. E. Sharpe, Inc., 1984.

Nussbaum, Martha. *The Fragility of Goodness*. New York: Cambridge UP, 1986.

Oravec, Christine. "Observation in Aristotle's Theory of Epideictic." *Philosophy and Rhetoric* 9 (1976): 162–74.

Perelman, Ch. and L. Olbrechts-Tyteca. *The New Rhetoric* [1957]. Trans. John Wilkinson and Purcell Weaver. Notre Dame: Notre Dame UP, 1969.

Poulakos, John. "Gorgias' and Isocrates' Use of the Encomium." *The Southern Speech Communication Journal* 51 (1986): 300–07.

Poulakos, Takis. "Historiographies of the Tradition of Rhetoric: A Brief History of Classical Funeral Orations." *Western Journal of Speech Communication* 54 (1990): 172–88.

———. "Isocrates's Use of Narrative in the *Evagoras*: Epideictic Rhetoric and Moral Action." *Quarterly Journal of Speech* 73 (1987): 317–28.

Ricoeur, Paul. *Hermeneutics and the Human Sciences*. Ed. and trans. John B. Thompson. Cambridge: Cambridge UP, 1981.

Robbins, Bruce, ed. *The Phantom Public Sphere*. Minneapolis: U of Minnesota P, 1993.

Rosenfield, Lawrence W. "Central Park and the Celebration of Civic Virtue." *American Rhetoric: Context and Criticism*. Ed. Thomas W. Benson. Carbondale: Southern Illinois UP, 1989. 221–66.

———. "The Practical Celebration of Epideictic." *Rhetoric in Transition*. Ed. Eugene E. White. University Park: Pennsylvania State UP, 1980. 131–56.

Ryan, Mary. *Civic Wars*. Berkeley: U of California P, 1997.

———. "Gender and Public Access: Women's Politics in Nineteenth-Century America." *Habermas and the Public Sphere*. Ed. Craig Calhoun Cambridge: MIT P, 1992. 259–88.

Sagan, Eli. *The Honey and the Hemlock*. New York: Basic, 1991.

Self, Lois S. "Rhetoric and Phronesis: The Aristotelian Ideal." *Philosophy and Rhetoric* 12 (1979): 130–45.

Sourvinou-Inwood, Christiane. "Male and Female, Public and Private, Ancient and Modern."
    Pandora's Box: Women in Classical Greece. Ed. Ellen D. Reeder. Princeton: Princeton UP,
    1995. 111–20.
Sullivan, Dale L. "The Ethos of Epideictic Encounter." *Philosophy and Rhetoric* 26 (1993): 113–33.
Taylor, Charles. *Philosophical Arguments*. Cambridge: Harvard UP, 1995.
Walker, Jeffrey. "Aristotle's Lyric: Re-Imagining the Rhetoric of Epideictic Song." *College English* 51
    (1989): 5–28.
Xenophon. *Hellenika I-II.3.0*. Ed. and Trans. Peter Krentz. Warminster: Aris and Phillips, 1989.

III
The Naughts (2000–2009)

Everyone/Everyone is so near/Everyone has got the fear
It's holding on/It's holding on. . . .

—Radiohead, "The National Anthem"

The outgoing president of the Rhetoric Society of America, C. Jan Swearingen, prefaces the first issue of 2000 with a brief assessment of the growing society and the swelling spine of its principle organ. Under the deft navigation of Jeff Walker at Penn State, the journal had emerged as a double-blind, peer-reviewed venue of national stature:

> The past four years have seen a stable, carefully nurtured growth in RSA's membership, and a careful, elegant transformation of *RSQ* as it moved from St. Cloud to Penn State. The journal has come to reflect the growing membership and disciplinary diversity of RSA. More than that, *RSQ* continues to define important new directions for rhetorical studies, and to provide exemplary models for the conduct of scholarship.[1]

Gregory Clark of Brigham Young University in Utah was taking the helm, and would not let go until the decade was almost over and Carolyn Miller stepped in to steer the pages into the twenty-tens of the Gregorian calendar.

During Clark's two-term stewardship—longer than any other but Yoos's—Walker's transformation of the journal into a venue for high-quality, peer-reviewed scholarship was set—and deeply enriched; Clark finished what

Walker started, and their editorships are largely responsible for the journal we enjoy today. With Clark at the helm junior scholars could easily make cases for tenure with their *RSQ* publications. The journal also provided established scholars a respected, national forum uniquely created for *rhetoricians*.

Nearing the end of his first term, Clark was ready to let someone else continue the journal's mission with the reasoning that no member "should have the kind of power and influence the *RSQ* editor has in the field for too long," unquestionably a sentiment that signaled the firmly established, scholarly influence of the journal.[2] Clark's conscience was deftly squelched during a lunch at the 2002 Las Vegas conference with an influential, often behind-the-scenes mover and shaker, Michael C. Leff of Northwestern University, who persuaded him to stay on based on the quality and contribution of his editorship.

In retrospect, the two-term continuity of Clark's editorship helped to ease both the journal and society's radical transition into the digital domain, an evolution hastened by RSA's membership chair for most of the decade, "free-range rhetorician" Rosa Eberly, first while at the University of Texas and then later at Penn State. During this period RSA also hired Kathie Cesa of KOC Member Services to handle the increasingly complex day-to-day operations of the society; Cesa worked with Eberly and others to establish a web presence with a new website and a new blog, ingeniously dubbed by Eberly as "The Blogora."[3] During Clark's tenure negotiations with publisher Taylor & Francis began and were finalized for printing, binding, and mailing the journal, which coincided with the journal "going electronic." All these changes demanded a redesign of the journal and its now unmistakable logo, which was cleverly crafted by Keith Diehl.[4]

Although the essays collected in this part of *Fifty Years* bear no visible signs of the radical transformation of the journal and society during this decade, they do index an almost equally radical shift toward an investment in rhetorical theory and characteristically philosophical topics. The essays collected in this part are also those mentioned most frequently by the membership in our survey and interviews. Bizzell's essay on feminist methods continues both the field's and journal's commitment to feminism, which has never wavered since Jarrett's 1992 guest-edited, special issue on feminist historiography; Rice's essay on "rhetorical ecologies"—cited as the single most influential *RSQ* essay in our survey—inaugurates a continued and abiding interest among rhetoricians in affect and "public feelings"; Haskins's rumination on "public memory" represents a now widespread investment in the topic; and Davis's essay on the differences between Burke and Freud on "identification" completely upends longstanding assumptions about what we think persuasion actually is. With feminism now fully rooted in rhetorical studies, these three essays measure something of a sea change in rhetorical sentiment and new scholarly agendas.

The remaining four essays focus on what seemed to be an obsession for rhetoricians during this period: agency. One would think the most profound, life-changing event of the decade—the attacks of 9/11—would have had a noticeable effect on scholarship in the journal during this time. Perhaps the interest in agency is something of an indirect response to the cultural wounding of the attacks on September 11, 2001, but unquestionably the most direct stimulus was the Alliance for Rhetorical Societies (ARS) conference held in Evanston, Illinois in the fall of 2003. Inspired largely by the efforts of Michael C. Leff and enabled by many members of the society's leadership, the ARS "working conference" had a discernable, weighty influence on the scholarship published in *RSQ* in the 2000s. That the ARS conference happened around the same time as radical changes to the journal's format and delivery is not coincidental: the mid-2000s was a time of big changes in rhetorical studies, marked by a renewed self-consciousness as a field that is bigger than we thought, as well as major (largely corporatizing) transformations in higher education that posed new challenges for the teaching of rhetoric.

The origin of ARS was a business meeting at the 2000 RSA in Washington, DC, during which the membership received a committee report, commissioned by then president Fred Antczak and chaired by Robert Gaines, on the future of rhetorical studies. The concern at that time was the perceived, diminished role for rhetorical studies in our larger, professional organizations (such as the 4Cs and NCA) as well as the general sense that we simply didn't know how many self-identified rhetoricians there were in the world. After this meeting, then board member (and eventual president) Gerard A. Hauser was tasked with helping to grow RSA's membership and convening a meeting between various societies that claimed rhetoric as a subject area. Leff was particularly vocal about the necessity of such a meeting, expressing a concern that rhetorical studies was fragmented across a number of different scholarly societies, thus working against attempts to secure rhetorical studies a continued seat at the table of higher education.[5]

Hauser and Leff helped to broker this meeting in Evanston in the summer of 2001 with nine different societies represented. "The point of the meeting was to determine whether we had enough in common to continue a conversation," remembers Hauser. "The meeting was a success and from it the idea of ARS was born."[6] Concerns arouse among sibling societies that ARS may be trying to poach their members, so a constitution and by-laws were drawn up, stressing that ARS was an association of associations with no core membership of its own.[7] Soon after the first (and only) conference of the Alliance of Rhetorical Societies was hosted by Northwestern University in September, 2003, under the co-direction of Andrea Lunsford and Michael Leff. Jointly sponsored or at least approved by the American Forensic Association, the American Society for the History of Rhetoric, the Coalition of Women Scholars in the History of Rhetoric, the Canadian Society for the History of Rhetoric, the 4Cs, the International Society for the History of Rhetoric, the International Society for the Study of Argumentation, the Kenneth Burke Society, NCA, *and* RSA—whew!—hundreds of teachers and scholars of rhetoric were in attendance.

The ARS conference theme was on "The Status and Future of Rhetorical Studies," and the program was organized around four plenary addresses, spread across the three of the four days of the conference, keyed to four issues:

(1) How we ought to understand the concept of rhetorical agency.
(2) Whether we have a "rhetorical tradition" and how we should use the concept of "tradition" itself.
(3) What the institutional and social goals of academic rhetoric should be.
(4) What it means to teach rhetoric.[8]

Karlyn Kohrs Campbell gave the address for the first question[9]; Jerzy Axer for the second; Steven Mailloux for the third, and Jacqueline Jones Royster for the fourth. Based on previously submitted position statements, attendees were shuffled into smaller but deliberately diverse working groups comprised of graduate students and junior and senior rhetoricians that were to engage one of the four questions (the editors, for example, met for the first time in a working group on "rhetorical agency" led by Karlyn Kohrs Campbell). Each of the working groups was tasked to develop a statement and agenda for teaching and research on their topic by the last day of the conference.

By most accounts the conference was an invigorating success. Clark dedicated an entire issue of *RSQ* to reports and reflections on the work completed and agendas produced at the conference, which remains a frequently consulted touchstone for rhetorical studies today.[10] The two-issue discussion with Lundberg and Gunn, inspired by Cheryl Geisler's report on the "agency" working groups, is reprinted here in its entirety, providing an insightful window into the anxiety provoked by poststructural theory vis-à-vis pedagogy. Carolyn Miller's much cited essay, "What Can Automation Tell Us About Agency?" continues the conversation, locating agency in "rhetorical events," not agents, decentering the longstanding assumptions central to humanism—and the study of rhetoric.

Despite the significant influence the ARS conference seemed to have for rhetorical scholarship, ironically this association of associations petered out only a few years after it began. In part this was because of the continued growth and successes of the Rhetoric Society of America, whose position and influence grew such that many of the functions of the ARS were gradually absorbed by the society (including the leadership of Leff, who eventually assumed the presidency of RSA by decade's end). The agenda-setting function envisioned for ARS was achieved in part through the bi-annual, RSA Summer Institutes that began in 2005; numerous essays hatched or catalyzed at the institutes have subsequently become familiar features in the published pages of *RSQ*.

Chapters in Part III

Patricia Bizzell, "Feminist Methods of Research in the History of Rhetoric: What Difference Do They Make?"

Forum Discussion on Agency:

Cheryl Geisler, "How Ought We to Understand the Concept of Rhetorical Agency? Report From the ARS."

Christian Lundberg and Joshua Gunn, "'Ouija Board, Are There Any Communications?' Agency, Ontotheology, and the Death of the Humanist Subject, or, Continuing the ARS Conversation."

Cheryl Geisler, "Teaching the Postmodern Rhetor: Continuing the Conversation on Rhetorical Agency."

Jenny Edbauer (Rice), "Unframing Models of Public Distribution: From Rhetorical Situation to Rhetorical Ecologies."

Carolyn R. Miller, "What Can Automation Tell Us About Agency?"

Ekaterina Haskins, "Between Archive and Participation: Public Memory in a Digital Age."

Diane Davis, "Identification: Burke and Freud on Who You Are."

Notes

1 C. Jan Swearingen, "Changes," *Rhetoric Society Quarterly* 30 (2000): 5.

2 Gregory Clark, email message to authors, 17 September 2017.

3 The Blogora debuted in the fall of 2004, at a time when "weblogs," or "blogs," were very popular on the Internet, and it quickly became a central hub for the society for over a decade. The Blogora was initially steered by James Arnt Aune of Texas A&M, and Rosa Eberly and Diane Davis of the University of Texas at Austin (the blog was also housed on a UT webserver). During its heyday the Blogora began to cycle in guest bloggers and added a table of "commentators." David E. Beard of the University of Minnesota, Duluth took the helm in 2010 until the society retired the venue—as blogs were replaced by social networking hubs like Facebook and microblogging services like Twitter—in April 2016. The spirit of The Blogora continues as a "public group" today on Facebook.

4 Gregory Clark, "Changes," *Rhetoric Society Quarterly* 34, no. 2 (2004): 5; Rosa Eberly, email message to the authors, 30 September 2017.

5 David Zarefsky, email to authors, 18 September 2017.

6 Gerard A. Hauser, email to authors, 18 September 2017.

7 David Zarefsky, email to authors, 18 September 2017.

8 Clark, "Introduction," 5.

9 For a revised version of Campbell's plenary address, see Karlyn Kohrs Campbell, "Agency: Promiscuous and Protean," *Communication and Critical/Cultural Studies* 2, no. 1 (2005): 1–19.

10 See *Rhetoric Society Quarterly* 34, no. 3 (2004).

9

Feminist Methods of Research in the History of Rhetoric
What Difference Do They Make?

PATRICIA BIZZELL

Ten years of scholarship in the history of rhetoric had to be accounted for when Bruce Herzberg and I undertook to prepare the second edition of our anthology of readings in rhetorical theory, *The Rhetorical Tradition*. It was first published in 1990 and the second edition is now in press. The past decade has seen a tremendous outpouring of work in the history of rhetoric, as researchers in classics, history, philosophy, and speech communication have been joined in unprecedented numbers by scholars from English studies and composition. Herzberg and I have, of course, attempted to reflect this new work in the changes we have made in our anthology. But in my opinion as co-editor, the most significant change in the second edition comprises the presence of women's rhetorics and rhetorics of color. I don't wish to suggest that I think the new book adequately represents these strands in Western rhetoric. But I wish to argue that their increased presence is significant for two reasons. I will explore these reasons primarily in terms of women's rhetorics here, although I believe that similar arguments could be made with respect to rhetorics of color, and as suggested below, there is considerable overlap. On the one hand, as Richard Enos contends in "Recovering the Lost Art of Researching the History of Rhetoric," feminist research in the history of rhetoric is perhaps the best current example of what humanistic scholarship in rhetoric can accomplish. On the other hand, feminist research in the history of rhetoric presents the most trenchant challenges to traditional scholarly practices, opening up exciting new paths not only in the material scholars can study, but also, and perhaps ultimately more significantly, in the methods whereby we can study it.

I

First, what has feminist research in the history of rhetoric produced? Preparing the second edition of the *Rhetorical Tradition* anthology puts me in a relatively good position to answer that question, because of my avowed agenda of representing women's rhetorics in that volume coupled with the anthologist's necessity of relying on already published scholarship. I felt that the state of scholarship in 1989, when the first edition of the book was sent to the printers, permitted me to include only the following: Christine de Pizan and Laura Cereta combined in a single unit, with two brief excerpts, within the Renaissance section; Margaret Fell and Sarah Grimké similarly combined, though with slightly longer excerpts, in what was then the Enlightenment section, covering the eighteenth and nineteenth centuries; and Julia Kristeva and Hélène Cixous also combined, with longer excerpts, in the twentieth-century section. This is not very many women. Furthermore, as many readers have pointed out, combining the women tends to imply a devaluation of their work, as if it were not important or substantial enough to stand on its own. And indeed, the only men presented in combination in the first edition are four nineteenth-century composition textbook authors, representing what is openly treated as a minor genre. The women are presented in combination because I felt the need to preface their work in every case with a rather lengthy headnote justifying their inclusion and providing hints for how to read these texts as rhetorical theory, since they usually do not resemble the kinds of theoretical texts written by men and familiar in the canonical tradition.

The explosion of feminist scholarship in the history of rhetoric over the last ten years has enabled the table of contents of the second edition of the anthology to look very different: first, no women are presented in combination. Second, every section of the book now contains at least one woman: Aspasia in the classical section; Christine de Pizan, with more excerpts, in the medieval section (where she really seems to belong); Madeleine de Scudéry, Margaret Fell, and Sor Juana Inès de la Cruz in the Renaissance section; Mary Astell in the eighteenth-century section; Maria Stewart, Sarah Grimké, Phoebe Palmer, and Frances Willard in the nineteenth-century section; and Virginia Woolf, Hélène Cixous, and Gloria Anzaldúa in the twentieth-century section. Adrienne Rich would have been included here as well if she had given us permission to reprint her work. From six women, we have gone up to thirteen, and moreover, what was the Enlightenment section in the first edition has been split into separate eighteenth- and nineteenth-century sections in large part because my co-editor and I felt that the advent of people of color and white women on the speaker's platform in the nineteenth century constituted a sufficiently significant change in the possibilities for rhetoric that the century—which in traditional histories is usually thought of as advancing little over the theoretical developments of the previous century—demanded its own section. Furthermore, this list is by no means exhaustive. It represents only those women on whom my co-editor and I felt sufficient research had been done to enable us to include them without tendentiousness.

The importance of this research is addressed by Enos. He is concerned to mount a defense of what he calls "the humanistic study of rhetoric" (8). He wishes to argue ultimately for improved graduate training in primary research methods, to correct a situation which, he says, "encourages students to passively respond to research rather than to actively produce it" (13). Lest anyone think that this line of argument identifies Enos as some sort of conservative old fogey in rhetoric scholarship, I want to point out that his position was anticipated, to some extent, by a more recent in-comer to the field of historical research, Linda Ferreira-Buckley, in her essay entitled "Rescuing the Archives from Foucault," which appeared as part of a discussion in a May 1999 *College English* forum, "Archivists with an Attitude." Moreover, and most radically given the state of scholarship only ten years ago, Enos concludes his essay by holding up as models of the kind of historical research he is calling for, feminist scholars Lisa Ede, Cheryl Glenn, Andrea Lunsford, and other contributors to Lunsford's collection *Reclaiming Rhetorica*. Interestingly, Ferreira-Buckley ends up in almost the same place, featuring among her approved examples the feminist work of Elizabeth McHenry, Jacqueline Jones Royster, and Susan Jarratt.

I mean to imply that feminist research in the history of rhetoric has indeed had a tremendous impact, if we find it cited as exemplary in two essays with ultimately rather different argumentative agendas—Enos calling for a sort of return to traditional research while Ferreira-Buckley openly advocates revisionist history while pointing out that "revisionist historians depend upon traditional archival practices" (581). If we think of the tasks of traditional research as discovering neglected authors, providing basic research on their lives and theories, and bringing out critical editions of their work, my survey of current work undertaken for the new edition of the *Rhetorical Tradition* anthology suggests that few, if any, other areas of research in the history of rhetoric have produced such rich results of this kind as feminist research.

II

Enos, however, misses an important implication of this new work in feminist research. As the "Archivists with an Attitude" forum shows us, historical research now, though relying on some traditional methods, must also raise new methodological questions. The problems that arise when the new wine is poured into old bottles can be seen in another *College English* exchange, that in the January 2000 issue between Xin Liu Gale and Cheryl Glenn and Susan Jarratt.

In "Historical Studies and Postmodernism: Rereading Aspasia of Miletus," Gale evaluates three scholarly works on the ancient Greek rhetorician Aspasia, comparing Glenn's and Jarratt's accounts, the latter co-authored with Rory Ong, with Madeleine Henry's book-length treatment. Gale favors Henry's work because, she says, Henry gives us "meticulous treatment of historical sources," "rather than eschewing the traditional historical method or twisting the male texts to suit her feminist needs" (379). Again and again, Gale uses the term "traditional" to characterize what she likes about Henry's approach. From these terms of praise, we may anticipate the terms of reproach used against Glenn, Jarratt and Ong. They are continually accused of distortions and contradictions.

Gale's critique helpfully reminds us of the importance of traditional historical research methods in feminist scholarship. But Gale does not appreciate the extent to which Glenn, Jarratt and Ong employ the traditional research methods she favors. As a glance at their bibliographies will reveal, their arguments are based in detailed scholarship every bit as "meticulous" and textually oriented as that which Gale praises in Henry, although Henry has the advantage of being more exhaustive because she gives Aspasia book-length treatment, as opposed to the limits of an essay or book chapter. Glenn, Jarratt and Ong have all read the classical sources and secondary scholarship carefully. Indeed, their grasp on traditional methods may be seen in their replies to Gale, in which their defense takes the fundamentally traditional tack of accusing Gale of not reading their work carefully and not quoting from it responsibly. This exchange actually testifies to the importance of the position taken by Enos and Ferreira-Buckley that I described above, namely that people who are going to do research in the history of rhetoric do need training in traditional humanistic scholarly methods, even in this postmodern day and age.

At the same time, I think that none of the participants in this exchange adequately address the role of postmodern theory in feminist research methods. They do not adequately bring out just how revolutionary it has been. Gale acknowledges that all of the scholars she analyzes attest to the influence of postmodern theory on their work, but then she forgets about it in Henry's case in order to re-cast her as a more "traditional" researcher, and she forgets about it in the cases of Glenn and Jarratt and Ong in order to damn them for trying to do something that they explicitly said they were not trying to do, namely, to set up a new master narrative—what Glenn calls in her response a "mater narrative" (388)—to establish traditional sorts of truth claims against the truth claims of traditional rhetorical histories that leave Aspasia out. Hence for Gale, there is a deep "contradiction" in the work she attacks:

> on the one hand, we are asked to accept the post-modern belief that we are never able to obtain objective truth in history; on the other hand, we are asked to consider the reconceived story of Aspasia as a "truer" reality of women in history, a rediscovery of the obliterated "truth" independent of the existing historical discourse of men.
>
> (366)

But I would argue that this is a contradiction only if there is only one kind of truth, what Gale calls here the "objective" kind, which might be taken as the object of historical research. That is not the kind of truth that the scholars she attacks are seeking. Here, for example, is how Glenn characterizes her project in her reply:

> Writing women (or any other traditionally disenfranchised group) into the history of rhetoric . . . interrogates the availability, practice, and preservation (or destruction) of historical evidence, [and] simultaneously exposes relations of exploitation, domination, censorship, and erasure.
>
> (389)

Similarly, Jarratt makes no bones about using what she calls an "intertextual interpretive method" that allows her to "take 'Aspasia' both as a rhetorical construct in Plato's text and as a real person" and to make a "speculative leap," as she says Henry does (I believe correctly), "that [allows] scholars to imagine women in relation to the practices of rhetoric, philosophy, and literary production so long considered almost completely the domain of men" (391).

Yet Gale does seem to be aware of this theoretical orientation in her opponents. In spite of accusing them of a contradiction involving objective truth, Gale does know that Glenn, Jarratt and Ong are not after objective truth. In the same paragraph in which she identifies the contradiction, as quoted above, she notes that Glenn is working from a "postmodern conception of truth as relative and contingent" (366), and she similarly acknowledges Jarratt's and Ong's research premises. I guess that what Gale would say is that the contradiction is not in her argument, but in theirs. In other words, she contends that in spite of claiming that they are not after objective truth, they argue as if they were. But it is not clear exactly what they are doing to draw this attack from Gale. Yes, they argue as if they wished to persuade readers of the merits of their positions. But it seems to me we must allow any scholar to attempt to be persuasive, without thereby accusing him or her of closet foundationalism. Indeed, Glenn, Jarratt and Ong might be expected to make more strenuous efforts to be persuasive than scholars who believe in objective truth would do, because their postmodern view of truths-plural-with-a-small-t suggests that only through persuasion do arguments get accepted as normative. They must be persuasive because they cannot count on their audience being moved simply by clearly perceiving the Truth-unitary-with-a-capital-T in their arguments.

I believe that this tangle arises from Gale's not naming accurately what it is that bothers her in the work of Glenn, Jarratt and Ong. I am moving here into the realm of speculation, and I want to be cautious about seeming to put words in Gale's mouth or to appropriate her arguments. But I am trying to tease out a subtle problem in feminist historiography. I suspect that what really bothers Gale is not that Glenn, Jarratt and Ong neglect traditional methods of historical research, because they in fact share these methods with Henry, whom Gale approves. I don't think it really is that they are making unsupportable claims for new objective truths in their scholarship, because as Gale shows that she knows, they are not in fact making any objective truth claims—that is not the kind of truth they are interested in. What, then, is the problem? I believe that it has to do with the role of emotion in feminist historiography.

Gale begins to get at this problem in her complaints about the ways that Glenn and Jarratt define feminist communities. As I have noted, Gale is aware that the scholars she attacks are working from what she calls a "community-relative view of truth" (370). Jarratt describes this view of truth as follows (mixing, as I have already suggested, what might be called traditional along with postmodern criteria):

> Does this history instruct, delight, and move the reader? Is the historical data probable? Does it fit with other accounts or provide a convincing alternative? Is it taken up by the community and used? Or is it refuted, dismissed, and forgotten?
>
> (391)

But, says Gale in discussing Glenn's work, "all women do not belong to the same community, all women are not feminists, all feminists are not women, and even all feminists do not belong to the same community" (371). Gale makes a similar point when discussing Jarratt's work in her book *Rereading the Sophists*:

> If Jarratt has to attribute all the feminist characteristics to the First Sophists to include them in her feminist system, does she risk making the mistake of essentializing women? . . . [This move] may well raise questions such as how the resemblance between the Sophists and women would empower women and whether her feminist sophistic would create new exclusions, such as the exclusion of men.
>
> (377)

It seems that Gale is concerned about exclusions in the communities that Glenn, Jarratt and Ong define as normative—indeed, a very legitimate concern.

The problem here, though, cannot exactly be that Glenn's, Ong's or Jarratt's view of feminism is not inclusive enough. In her reply, for example, Jarratt states that Gale's "warning that my approach in this section of the book could have the effect of erasing differences among women is well taken" (392). Jarratt questions "the specter of a feminism that is One," and she praises the multiplicity of debate in feminist work and calls it to Gale's attention (392). This would appear to agree with Gale's own call "to invite other perspectives to correct our own partiality" (372). But Gale, it appears, wants closure never to be achieved, persuasion never to be accomplished, because she is afraid that the influence of any community values must be oppressive. She quotes Barry Brummett's caution in this regard, "'*Whose* community?'", as if this were a question that was unanswerable (371; emphasis in original). I would argue, on the contrary, that it is answerable by a process of debate and discussion, provisionally but persuasively—though indeed, the process may require the avowal of values and may not rely on supposedly value-neutral logical demonstration. I do not believe that humanistic knowledge can ever be established above debate. That is perhaps the ultimate epistemological question on which Gale and I disagree.

Therefore, I would redefine Gale's problem with the scholars she attacks as being one that arises when persuasion does not work. Glenn, Jarratt and Ong have not drawn Gale in. I am wondering whether an important reason for her resistance is that she feels excluded not so much from their discourse or their arguments as from their emotions. Gale hears in this work expressions of feelings of solidarity that trouble her, as noted in her commentary on feminist communities above. Perhaps, she feels herself to be excluded from these feelings for reasons she does not discuss. It is notable to me that Gale is very sensitive to the emotions animating work she doesn't like. More than once, she calls Glenn's treatment of Aspasia "passionate" (365), a "personal 'truth'" (366), too "assertive" (366 *et passim*). Jarratt is also too emotional, it seems, "intent on writing women into the history of rhetoric for the purpose of exposing male oppression and exclusion in order to liberate and empower women" (375). In contrast, Henry's emotional valence as described by Gale is cool: she is "meticulous," "painstakingly" "sifting, ordering, and evaluating evidence" (379), and arriving at a conclusion that "may not be as exciting as Glenn's or Jarratt's and Ong's" but that "commands respect" (381).

I think Jarratt is right on the money in her reply when she suggests that Gale harbors "aversions to both rhetoric and feminism" (392). But of course, Gale is under no compulsion to value either. My point would be, however, that Gale should clarify the grounds for her attack. It really isn't that the scholars she censures have vitiated traditional research methods. They have extended them in the service of feminist values and relied in part on rhetorical ethos to promote their positions. What Gale really objects to, I suspect, are these values, and she is not moved by the ethos. Let her be clear about that. And this brings me to the methodological point that I do believe is raised by this debate, namely the function of emotions in scholarly work. We perhaps need more discussion of the part played in the setting of scholarly research agendas and the constructing of scholarly arguments by our emotions about our research topics—or subjects— and our imagined readers. Think, for example, about the unexamined role of emotion in the famous debate between Barbara Biesecker and Karlyn Kohrs Campbell over historical research that focuses on individual figures. I believe we need a more thoroughly rhetorical discussion of these complications of research. Fortunately, that discussion has already begun, and I will conclude by pointing to a few examples.

III

We can now find feminist researchers in rhetoric openly discussing their feelings, both positive and negative, about their subjects of study. For example, in her essay "Women in the History of Rhetoric: The Past and the Future," Christine Mason Sutherland has provided us with a nuanced discussion of the difficulties a twentieth-century believer in feminism and democracy encounters in studying Mary Astell, an important eighteenth-century thinker on political and religious questions and on women's rhetoric who was opposed to democratic forms of government and to many of the liberal tenets of the contemporary women's movement. Sutherland walks us through the ways the researcher must negotiate her feelings about a woman whom she can admire but not entirely agree with. A different example can be found in one of Vicki Tolar Collins's first essays on women in Methodism, in which she tells how she was mysteriously drawn to the work of Hester Rogers, first acquiring her journal from Collins's elderly relative who thought Hester might be part of the family, and then having a dream shortly after she began doctoral studies that compelled her in the middle of the night to dig the book out of boxes as yet unpacked from a move, read until dawn, and discover a research subject. Interestingly, Collins chose to omit this moving story from the longer essay on women and Methodism that she published later in Molly Meijer Wertheimer's collection *Listening to Their Voices*: did she fear that, being too personal, it might taint her scholarship in traditional eyes? And one more short example: in her essay on Ida B. Wells published in *Reclaiming Rhetorica*, Jacqueline Jones Royster repeatedly expresses her admiration for Wells, rather than simply recounting the facts of her life and analyzing her rhetorical practices. Royster observes that Wells practiced the rhetorical arts "with flair and style" (169), that she worked for a world "in which we, African American included, could all flourish" (173), and, in short, that "Ida B. Wells was a wonder, personally and rhetorically" (181).

I believe it is to Royster that we owe our most thorough theorizing of the role of emotions in feminist research to date. In her study of African American women's rhetoric and social action, entitled *Traces of a Stream*, Royster concludes with a chapter that addresses in detail the methodological questions I have raised here. She articulates an approach that frankly begins in her identification—she takes the term from Kenneth Burke—with the subjects of her inquiries (see 252, 272). On the one hand, this is a deeply personal identification, springing from a mutual African American heritage. As Roster says, "theory begins with a story" (255), and she shares her story of community allegiances and multiple experiences with extant archives on African American women, with colleagues on the scholarly journal *SAGE*, and with her students at Spelman College. At the same time, Royster pointedly rejects an essentialized notion of identity. She notes:

> There is a constancy in the need for negotiation, beginning with the uncomfortable question of how much I actually do share identities with the women I study and how much I do not. (271) . . . identity is not natural. It is constructed. I have indeed identified multiple connections between these women and myself, despite our not being perfectly matched. (272) . . . However, as full-fledged members of humanity, this work is not by necessity ours alone. Others can also have interests and investments in it that can

be envisioned from their own standpoints, from their own locations. What becomes critical to good practice, however, is that these researchers—who are indeed outsiders in the communities they study—have special obligations that begin with a need to articulate carefully what their viewpoints actually are, rather than letting the researchers' relationships to the work go unarticulated, as is often the case with practices of disregard.

(277)

What becomes critical, in other words, is the acknowledgment of the multiple functions of emotions and experiences in defining one's relationship to one's research, a departure from traditional methods that Royster calls "practices of disregard," which might be the practices that produce the emotional coolness I saw Gale preferring in Henry.

It follows from this acknowledgment of personal connection in Royster's theory that the scholar will care for the subjects being researched. Here is where emotional attachments come most clearly into the open. Royster notes that for students who learned about the history of African American women's rhetoric and social action, "the most frequent types of responses . . . were affective" (266), relating not only to how they felt about the women they studied but also to how they felt about their own lives as intellectuals. Royster observes that over the years of doing archival research herself, "I was developing a habit of caring as a rhetorician" (258)—note how this formulation links caring with disciplinary activity—"caring *as a rhetorician*" (emphasis added). Particularly for African American women engaged in such research, Royster argues, what she calls an "afrafeminist" methodology should "acknowledge a role for caring, for passionate attachments" (276)—there again is that passion that Gale detected, it seems somewhat disapprovingly, in the work of Glenn, Jarratt and Ong.

Lest this kind of attachment lead to what Gale regards as merely "personal truth," however, Royster repeatedly emphasizes the necessity for feminist researchers to ground their work in the collective wisdom of their scholarly community and, importantly, in the community that they are studying. As Royster puts it:

> I recognize as valuable the perspectives of the scholarly fields in which I operate; simultaneously I respect the wisdom of the community with which I identify. I seek to position myself in academic writing, therefore, in a way that merges membership in two communities: the one I am studying and the ones in which I have gained specialized knowledge. (254) . . . [Afrafeminist scholars] speak and interpret *with* the community [of African American women], not just *for* the community, or *about* the community.
>
> (275; emphasis in original)

Royster makes explicit the discursive consequences of this orientation to multiple communities. Traditional academic discourse will not serve to express her research, but rather she must devise a kind of "academic writing" that mixes the cognitive and linguistic styles of her academic and African American communities—what I have called a "hybrid" form of academic discourse. Royster describes it this way:

> Critical to such methodological practices, therefore, is the idea that, whatever the knowledge accrued, it would be both presented and represented with this community [that is, the community being studied], and at least its potential for participation and response, in mind. This view of subjects as both audiences and agents contrasts with a presentation and representation of knowledge in a more traditional fashion. Typically, subjects [in traditional discourse] are likely to be perceived in a more disembodied way. . . .
> (274)

Clearly, this is an attempt to embody in discourse an answer to the question Gale rightly indicates as crucial for all postmodern historiography, namely, *whose* community is normative? Royster gives us more, and more specific, information on how she answers this question than any other researcher I have encountered. She does not rely on any unitary category of "women" to define her communities. Moreover, Royster is at pains to specify that even the values and perspectives of communities she holds dear cannot be allowed to hold uninterrogated sway over critical discourse. She continually stresses the need for cross-questioning among communities, not only, as noted above, between the academic community and the African American women's community (two which obviously overlap, in the person, for example, of Royster herself), but also between these communities and representatives of other standpoints who may be drawn to research in this area. As Royster says:

> the need for negotiation is, therefore, not arbitrary. It is part and parcel of the consubstantial process. The need for negotiation is yoked to the need for a well-balanced analytical view that takes into account shifting conditions, values, and circumstances between human beings.
> (272)

Royster concludes her discussion by articulating a four-part "afrafeminist ideology" or what I would call "methodology," that organizes these insights. It is notable that the first element Royster mentions is "careful analysis" (279 ff), by which she appears to mean the traditional "basic skills" of research for which Enos and Ferreira-Buckley call and which, I contend, Glenn, Jarratt and Ong, as well as Henry, employ. To them, Royster adds three elements that bespeak the emotions and value commitments I have outlined in her theory above: "acknowledgment of passionate attachment" (280) to the subjects of one's research; "attention to ethical action" (280) in one's scholarship, which requires one to be rigorous in the traditional sense and at the same time "accountable to our various publics" (281); and "commitment to social responsibility" (281), which indicates the need not only to think about the social consequences of the knowledge we generate but also to use it ourselves for the greater common good.

In conclusion, I want to stress why Royster needs the new methodology that she theorizes so thoroughly in this book. She articulates the challenges that face her at the outset:

> The first and most consistent challenges have come hand in hand with the very choosing of the work itself, that is, with identifying myself as a researcher who focuses on a multiply marginalized group; whose interests in this group center on topics not typically associated with the group, such as nonfiction and public discourse rather than imaginative literature and literary criticism; and who is called upon by the material conditions of the group itself to recognize the necessity of employing a broader, sometimes different range of techniques in garnering evidence and in analyzing and interpreting that evidence.
>
> (251)

Later on, she explains how these challenges impacted her research methods:

> The project required that I learn something about history, economics, politics, and the social context of women's lives. For the first time, I had to spend more time considering context than text. I had to take into account insights and inquiry patterns from disciplines other than those in which I was trained. I had to take into account the specific impact of race, class, gender and culture on the ability to be creative and to achieve—not in some generic sense, but in terms of a particular group of human beings who chose deliberately to write and to speak, often in public.
>
> (257)

As Royster notes, her techniques are "quite recognizably interdisciplinary and feminist" (257); she also characterizes them as a sort of ethnographic research in which she was unable to interview her subjects, because most of them were already dead (see 282). These techniques enabled her, as she says, to explore how "knowledge, experience, and language merge" in the lives of her research subjects (259). The point I wish to emphasize is that she thus generates scholarly knowledge that clearly could be developed no other way.

Have Royster, and other feminist scholars for whom she has now more completely articulated methodologies already in practice, departed radically from the rhetorical tradition? Yes, and no. No, because their work relies upon many of the traditional tools of research in the history of rhetoric. No, because the rhetors they have added to our picture of the history of Western rhetoric seem to me to be working within this tradition and enriching it, rather than constituting utterly separate or parallel rhetorical traditions. But yes, because in order to get at the activities of these new rhetors, researchers have had to adopt radically new methods as well, methods which violate some of the most cherished conventions of academic research, most particularly in bringing the person of the researcher, her body, her emotions, and dare one say, her soul, into the work. From my perspective as editor of an anthology called *The Rhetorical Tradition*, contemplating the major changes in scholarship over the last ten years, these new methods have made all the difference.

Works Cited

Biesecker, Barbara. "Coming to Terms with Recent Attempts to Write Women into the History of Rhetoric." *Philosophy and Rhetoric* 25 (1992): 140–61.

Bizzell, Patricia. "Hybrid Academic Discourses: What, Why, How." *Composition Studies* 27 (Fall 1999): 7–21.

Bizzell, Patricia and Bruce Herzberg. *The Rhetorical Tradition: Readings from Classical Times to the Present*. Boston: Bedford Books, 1990.

Campbell, Karlyn Kohrs. "Biesecker Cannot Speak for Her Either." *Philosophy and Rhetoric* 26 (1993): 153–59.

Collins, Vicki Tolar. "Walking in Light, Walking in Darkness: The Story of Women's Changing Rhetorical Space in Early Methodism." *Rhetoric Review* 14 (Spring 1996): 336–54.

———. "Women's Voices and Women's Silence in the Tradition of Early Methodism." *Listening to Their Voices: The Rhetorical Activities of Historical Women*. Ed. Molly Meijer Wertheimer. Columbia: U of South Carolina P, 1997.

Enos, Richard. "Recovering the Lost Art of Researching the History of Rhetoric." *Rhetoric Society Quarterly* 29 (Fall 1999): 7–20.

Ferreira-Buckley, Linda. "Rescuing the Archives from Foucault." *College English* 61 (May 1999): 577–83.

Gale, Xin Liu. "Historical Studies and Postmodernism: Rereading Aspasia of Miletus." *College English* 62 (January 2000): 361–86.

Glenn, Cheryl. "Comment: Truth, Lies, and Method: Revisiting Feminist Historiography." *College English* 62 (January 2000): 387–89.

Jarratt, Susan. "Comment: Rhetoric and Feminism: Together Again." *College English* 62 (January 2000): 390–93.

———. *Rereading the Sophists: Classical Rhetoric Refigured*. Carbondale: Southern Illinois UP, 1991.

Lunsford, Andrea, ed. *Reclaiming Rhetorica: Women in the Rhetorical Tradition*. Pittsburgh: U of Pittsburgh P, 1995.

Royster, Jacqueline Jones. "To Call a Thing by Its True Name: The Rhetoric of Ida B. Wells." *Reclaiming Rhetorica: Women in the Rhetorical Tradition*. Ed. Andrea Lunsford. Pittsburgh: U of Pittsburgh P, 1995.

———. *Traces of a Stream: Literacy and Social Change Among African-American Women*. Pittsburgh: U of Pittsburgh P, 2000.

Sutherland, Christine Mason. "Women in the History of Rhetoric: The Past and the Future." *The Changing Tradition: Women in the History of Rhetoric*. Ed. Christine Mason Sutherland and Rebecca Sutcliffe. Calgary: U of Calgary P, 1999.

10
Forum Discussion on Agency

CHERYL GEISLER, CHRISTIAN LUNDBERG AND JOSHUA GUNN

HOW OUGHT WE TO UNDERSTAND THE CONCEPT OF RHETORICAL AGENCY?

Report From the ARS

CHERYL GEISLER

[Editors' Note: Prior to the ARS conference, participants were asked to submit statements or papers addressing one of the conference themes, which were then circulated among conference goers. These papers are cited in the following, however, they were not public and are no longer available.]

One of the primary purposes of last fall's meeting of the Alliance of Rhetoric Societies was deliberation about the future of rhetorical studies. Appropriately, three working groups of over forty scholars with a common concern in rhetoric spent the better part of four days addressing the question, "How ought we to understand the concept of rhetorical agency?"

The form of this question is telling: By melding a question of definition (what is the concept of rhetorical agency?) with one of deliberation (how ought we to understand the concept. . . ?), the question foreshadowed the complex interplay between rhetoric's interpretive project and rhetoric's educational mission, an interplay that would fully occupy us for the next few days. At the same time, it also harkened back to a tension that had surfaced in the discussion of agency prior to the conference (Gaonkar, "The Idea"). This second interplay—between what rhetorical agency, in *fact*, is and what it, in *value*, ought to be—turns out to be a key issue for the future of rhetorical studies, a point to which I'll return at the end of this report.

Any attempt to synthesize the major thrust of these four days of discussion is inevitably doomed to failure. As a member of only one of the three separate working groups, I could not attend and therefore cannot do justice to the engaging conversations that occupied us. Nevertheless, a thoughtful reading of the posted position papers ([URL provided in original essay is now defunct]) and additional readings in the bibliography, supplemented by my notes and memories, provides some basis on which to synthesize the major issues that arise concerning rhetorical agency and its relationship to the future of rhetorical studies.

Significance of the Question of Agency

Most scholars at the ARS acknowledged, explicitly or implicitly, that recent concern with the question of rhetorical agency arises from the postmodern critique of the autonomous agent. As articulated by Gaonkar more than a decade ago, this critique faults traditional rhetoric for an "ideology of agency," viewing "the speaker as origin rather than articulation, strategy as intentional, discourse as constitutive of character and community, ends that bind in common purpose" (263).

In the context of her ARS paper, Wells acknowledges the problem this critique has had for the concept of rhetorical agency: "Since agency is conventionally seen as the activity of a subject pursuing an intention, very little is left of the concept" after the postmodern assault. And, as Herndl explains, this conceptual problem has had consequences: "theorists typically struggle with the dilemma of how to understand the postmodern subject's ability to take purposeful political action without merely recuperating the humanist individual" (see also Herndl and Nahrwold, "Research").

The critique of the ideology of agency, as Leff admits ("Tradition"), is most justified in the contexts of political oratory, contexts that appeared increasingly limited to many participants at the ARS. Feminists like Nan Johnson argued that rhetoricians need to go beyond studies of those whose agency is taken for granted, and attend as well to the "ever present complications of who has access to rhetorical agency and how rhetorical agency is obtained" (see also *Gender and Rhetorical Space*). In response to such concerns, Campbell acknowledged in his ARS paper that, "only a select few have enjoyed the traditional sense of public rhetorical agency." Nevertheless, he goes on, this restriction "is less a problem with the idea of agency per se and more a problem of understanding the varieties of agency and of the available means for achieving a hearing."

For most participants, however, the question of how to amend the concept of rhetorical agency in order to address the ideology of agency was central. Some of the most interesting advances appear to be coming when rhetoricians go beyond traditional political contexts. Indeed, developments on two fronts suggest that the concept of rhetorical agency may be on the cusp of a major rethinking. The first has concerned itself with describing how rhetorical agency functions in subaltern social groups that, as Johnson suggests, have not had access to mainstream public forums. At the ARS, a generation of young scholars were pushing hard on the concept of rhetorical agency to develop a rhetorical understanding of a wide variety of non-traditional phenomenon: the gay body as a public statement about HIV/AIDS (Brouwer, cf. "Precarious Visibility"), the role of physical place in the rhetoric of community action (Blitefield, cf. "Standing"), femicide in postcolonial India (Dube, cf. "Women Without"), and racial politics in the nineteenth century (Wilson, cf[.] "Racial Politics"). Instead of characterizing rhetors in terms of what they lack, these scholars seem to be moving us toward a richer understanding of rhetorical agency by examining how rhetors without taken-for-granted access do, nevertheless, manage to exercise agency.

The second front of scholars making advances in the concept of rhetorical agency concerns itself with another set of nontraditional contexts—those connected with media. Iconic photographs like the flag-raising on Iwo Jima (Hariman and Lucaites, "Performing"), political icons like Willie Horton (Wells), and filmic representations like that of WWII as the "good war" (Biesecker, "Remembering") call attention to the complex ways that rhetorical agency may be "dispersed, as a series of articulated networks that connect speakers and hearers in multiple, sometimes contradictory ways" (Wells). What is interesting here is the interplay of audience and media in constructing and being constructed by these images, an interplay that raises questions concerning who has agency—and therefore responsibility—for these repeatedly circulating cultural products.

In a related move, some scholars have been looking at the implications of digital technology for a theory of rhetorical agency. My own work on personal digital assistants (Geisler, "When Management") has lead me to explore the kind of agency being exercised when a rhetor uses a text such as a "to-do list" to get herself to do something—like folding laundry—that she cannot manage to do otherwise. Here rhetor and audience appear to occupy a subject position strategically fragmented in order to get work done. This fragmentation of agency, I have suggested, is made possible by a combination of the culture of systematic management, the affordances of literate technologies, and the strategic choice of the rhetor who is conscious of what she is "doing" to herself.

Such small investigations are part of a larger agenda calling for an investigation of the impact of digital technologies on rhetorical practice as part of what Welch has called the "techno-liberal-arts." In terms of rhetorical agency, at a minimum, technological literacies of the type that Welch is referring to entail an expansion of available means, but the impact of such technologies of text (Geisler et al., "IText") probably entails more than a simple expansion of resources. As Gunn has suggested at ARS and elsewhere (Beard and Gunn), digital technologies, by altering the human experience of space, appear to alter the sense of human potential or agency.

The question of rhetorical agency, then, appears to have escaped the bounds of a simple reaction to the critique of the ideology of agency and, through work in a variety of nontraditional contexts, promises to enrich our foundational understanding of rhetoric. In the next section of this report, then, we turn to consider the major themes that arose at the ARS concerning what an enriched concept of agency might involve.

Major Themes

At the core of our common understanding of rhetorical agency at the ARS was the capacity of the rhetor to act. As rhetoricians, we generally take as a starting point that rhetoric involves action. This is perhaps the distinguishing characteristic of a rhetorical approach to discourse.

The Illusion of Agency

The critique of the ideology of agency concerns the link between this rhetorical action and social change—in what sense can the actions of a rhetor be linked to consequences in the world. Most rhetoricians at the ARS took for granted some level of efficacy for rhetorical action. Yet others suggested that this was an illusion. Gunn, for example, suggested that the debate about agency is "a central crisis-fantasy particular to U.S. rhetorical studies," a fantasy that both frames our exercise of agency and protects us from "the abject horror of contingency." A better route, suggests Gunn, would be to take the risk of directly confronting our irrelevance.

Condit, on the other hand, argued that agency, if illusionary, is a "necessary illusion": it grounds rhetoricians' efforts "enhancing agency and the means for doing so." Here Condit's argument concerns the centrality of the concept of agency for rhetoricians' sense of purpose as a field. Without the concept of agency, she suggests, we do not have the necessary rationale for our efforts with our students and readers: by "both exposing them to a broader range of symbolic concatenations and by getting them to exercise their capacities for symbolic manipulation, we enhance the potential range of their choices, and hence give greater potential and vitality to their agency."

This tension over the illusionary nature of agency—whether through cowardice as Gunn argues or necessity as Condit suggests—did not exhaust the positions available to scholars at the ARS. Perhaps more productive was the insight that agency can be understood as a resource constructed in particular contexts and in particular ways. While those making these constructions might agree with Gunn and others that agency is socially constructed, they stop short of arguing for its abandonment.

In fact, scholars like McDaniel often favor what he calls "a more modest approach": "Rather than inquiring into the ontological consistency of the concept, the approach I would forward steps back, as it were, to ask how various political systems figure it." For McDaniel, the insight that "agency seems a fundamental fantasy to the democratic ethos," then becomes a starting point for developing an understanding of how agency can function in society. Under this analysis, the agency of the good man speaking well becomes neither necessary fantasy nor liberal delusion, but one of a number of ideological configurations that emerge in specific historical contexts to form, if you will, the landscape of agency. As Lucaites suggested, "every rhetorical performance enacts and contains a theory of its own agency—of its own possibilities—as it structures and enacts the relationships between speaker and audience, self and other, action and structure. . . ." Here, then, agency becomes not a problem to be solved or trouble to be resolved, but a central object of rhetorical inquiry.

The Skill of the Rhetorical Agent

Even if one concedes that rhetorical action is efficacious, a question can still be asked concerning the rhetor herself—to what extent does her skill matter? Here we begin an inquiry into the role of the rhetor's conscious assessment of situations and choices in response to those assessments. In the tradition view articulated by Campbell, "Central to any competent communication is an assessment of audience and a conscious structuring of one's message to maximize the possibilities of evoking from the hearers the desired response." Borrowing a musical metaphor from Bahktin, Jasinski suggests that, "speakers and writers manifest rhetorical agency when they display an ability to identify and manage or . . . orchestrate resources (e.g. styles, lines of argument, traditions, tropes and figures, etc.)." According to Jasinski, an improvisation metaphor may allow us to sidestep the critique of liberal humanism by acknowledging the contingency of all action while at the same time allowing the rhetor the power to respond to those shifting circumstances.

Alternative views on consciousness at the ARS attempted to acknowledge the way the rhetor's consciousness is shaped by arrangements external to that consciousness. Langsdorf draws our attention to the "practice turn" in contemporary sociology recommending its "orientation toward change, contingency, and consequences," that both allows agency to remain with the agent and yet acknowledge its embedding in the externals of communicative interaction. Using the concept of habitus, Atwill attempts a similar reconciliation, accounting "for the shaping forces of power and material circumstances, while retaining 'something like' a subject." As Atwill argues, "Rhetorical interventions (and inventions) are possible in these spaces of indeterminacy where the symbolic definition of the social world is, within limits, up for grabs."

All of these questions about the rhetor, sometimes called the internal questions, can be linked to rhetoric's educational mission. That is, only if we can assent to the role of the rhetor in producing efficacious action can we as a discipline have a mission to educate such rhetors to have agency.

The Conditions for Agency

Many scholars at the ARS suggested that the question of conditions of agency should also be extended to questions of means or resources—a description of conditions under which the rhetor is able to act. A traditional approach finds the constraints on rhetorical action in the audience and in the rhetorical situation. If the rhetor is seen as efficacious, rhetorical action comes through managing these constraints or resources. Most acknowledge that these constraints and resources are historically situated: that is, that tradition forms and/or limits agency (Leff). As a result some have suggested that rhetoric is inherently conventional (Johnson), limited by discursive form or generic constraint (Wilson).

More complex understandings of the conditions for rhetorical agency involve looking at the possibilities created through the arrangement of social conditions, sometimes identified as context (Carpenter) or social networks (Herndl). According to Logie, agency is "the complex process by which a communicative act materializes out of a combination of individual will and social circumstances."

As we have already seen, some of the more interesting research has been looking at the way that material conditions shape rhetorical action—the rhetor's body (Brouwer), the place of rhetorical performance (Blitefield). Interesting questions arise in this regard in connection with technology. Under the impact of digital technologies, we have the ability to be in virtual places beyond our physical reach—how does this affect agency (Gunn)? And in studying the increasing complex impact of popular media, scholars have been hard pressed to find adequate accounts of agency for mediated experiences like iconic photographs (Lucaites) or the Willie Horton story (Wells).

Directions for the Future of Rhetorical Studies

If discussions of the concept of rhetorical agency at the ARS are a harbinger of the future for rhetorical studies, several developments are worthy of note. To begin with, although concern with agency began as a rear guard defensive action against the postmodern critique, the discussion appears to have shifted significance to more productive investigations into both the consciousness and conditions of agency. That is, the term "agency" has moved from marking off the unnoticed foundation for efficacious rhetorical action to opening up its essential mechanisms. Mirroring developments in the humanities and social sciences in general, we have become less concerned with determining the universals for rhetorical action and more interested in the specific local and or historical conditions that undergird it. With this, we acknowledge that rhetorical agency is not universally available to all members of society, but we also make a commitment to developing rhetoric in a way that will account for rather than ignore this disparity. In this way, then, future developments concerning the concept of rhetorical agency must be understood as both an outgrowth of and an answer to the postmodern critique.

One of the stubborn facts to which rhetoricians at the ARS seem to hold fast is that rhetorical inquiry should make a difference in the world. Another way to put this is that rhetoric as a field must have the power to take efficacious action—must itself have agency. Rhetoric's claim to agency is most obvious with respect to its educational mission. Lyne may have put this most poignantly when he suggested that, "a rhetorical education . . . should . . . be about preparing for the 'big moment' that may come only occasionally in one's life, if at all." Here, Lyne ties the mission of the discipline to its educational function, calling for our interventions in the skills of the rhetorical agents with whom we come in contact. We used to call this teaching.

Developments in the concept of rhetorical agency complicate this traditional understanding of our teaching mission. As Crosswhite points out, "To attempt to realize the potential for rhetorical agency in individuals through education without also addressing and developing the cultural means by which agency is realized is misguided." He goes on to suggest, "however, to ignore the ability of the individual to exercise rhetorical agency in relation to cultural means is also misguided." Balancing concern for educating students in rhetorical agency while at the same time developing a society that grants agency more broadly may be one of the major challenges for the future of rhetorical studies.

The fundamental mission of the ARS is to bring into dialogue the diverse subdisciplinary groups across which a commitment to rhetoric has been dispersed. While the ties that bind us are linked to a commitment to rhetoric as action, I was struck during our three days in Evanston by the disparate approaches to the mission of rhetoric. With respect to the concept of rhetorical agency, the mission of rhetoric as a discipline seems to be the unacknowledged elephant in the room. That is, the tie between the question of "what agency does the rhetor have?" and the question of "what agency do we as rhetoricians have?" has not been fully brought to the table.

I would suggest that one of the comforts of the traditional model of humanist agent was its close link between the mission of rhetoric and the concept of the rhetorical agent. Specifically, a rhetorical agent seen to make choices among the available means of persuasion is an agent rhetoricians can educate to make the best choices. The postmodern agent is not so obviously educable and, if not educable, what agency do we as rhetoricians have?

The obvious anguish that often arose in discussions of the concept of rhetorical agency often arose in unacknowledged crises over this question: how can we create a better society through the pursuit of rhetoric? Although some at ARS argued that coming to grips with the illusion of agency is the only honest thing to do, I saw two major arguments in response.

The first I outlined earlier: studies of rhetorical agency in specific contexts seem to show that members of subaltern groups, though circumscribed in terms of their agency, are not without agency altogether; that a number of unacknowledged resources—body, space, and so on—allow for the exercise of agency in ways that rhetoricians can call attention to. This argument is an argument from fact: the facts on the ground do not appear to support the proposition that rhetorical agency is illusionary.

The second argument is an argument from value. Rhetoric, after all, is concerned with the art of *doing* in language. Rhetoric could abandon social mission, give up the goal of being efficacious in the world, but would we be *doing rhetoric* anymore? In this question, the future of rhetoric as a discipline and the future of the concept of rhetorical agency become intimately connected. We can, then, give more specific articulation to the issue at the ARS: if rhetoric *as an interpretive theory* describes a variety of rhetorical positions, some with more and some with less rhetorical agency, how can rhetoric *as a productive art* incorporate that knowledge into our mission? What shall we, as teachers, say to our students about their potential and obligations with respect to becoming rhetorical agents? What shall we, as critics, say to our fellow citizens about their potential and obligations with respect to being rhetorical agents? If neither our students nor our fellow citizens have such potential or obligations—if agency is illusionary—we may sidestep these questions of potential and obligations as irrelevant . . . but only at the cost of the irrelevancy of rhetoric.

The strength of a forum like the ARS is to allow productive conversations to go on across our many subdisciplines, subdisciplines that too often have isolated critical practice and educational mission. By bringing them into contact at meetings like those held this past fall, we create opportunities to see unacknowledged elephants in the room and to benefit from the valuable synergy, if not synthesis, on such questions such as, "How ought we to understand the concept of rhetorical agency?" We should do this again sometime. . . .

Works Cited

Beard, David and Joshua Gunn. "Paul Virilio and the Mediation of Perception and Technology." *Enculturation* 4.2 (2002). http://enculturation.gmu.edu/4_2/beard-gunn/.

Biesecker, Barbara A. "Remembering World War II: The Rhetoric and Politics of National Commemoration at the Turn of the 21st Century." *Quarterly Journal of Speech* 88 (2002): 393–409.

Blitefield, Jerry. " 'Standing for the Whole': Placed Bodies as Rhetorical Text." Talk given at the National Communication Association, 2003.

Brouwer, David. C. "The Precarious Visibility Politics of Self-Stigmatization: The Case of HIV/AIDS Tattoos." *Text and Performance Quarterly* 18 (1998): 114–36.

Dube, Renu, Reena Dube, and Rashmi Bhatnagar. "Women without Choice: Female Infanticide and the Rhetoric of Overpopulation in Postcolonial India." *Women's Studies Quarterly* 27 (1999): 73–86.

Gaonkar, Dilip. "The Idea of Rhetoric in the Rhetoric of Science." *Southern Communication Journal* 58.4 (1993): 258–95.

Geisler, Cheryl. "When Management Become Personal: An Activity-Theoretic Analysis of Palm Technologies." *Writing Selves and Societies: Research from Activity Perspectives*, Ed. Charles Bazerman and David R. Russell. San Diego: Mind, Culture, and Activity and Fort Collins: Academic Writing, 2003. http://wac.colostate.edu/books/selves_societies.

Geisler, Cheryl, Charles Bazerman, Stephen Doheny-Farina, Laura Gurak, Christina Haas, Johndan Johnson-Eilola, David S. Kaufer et al. "IText: Future Directions for Research on the Relationship between Information Technology and Writing." *Journal of Business and Technical Communication* 15 (2001): 269–308.

Hariman, Robert and John Lucaites. "Performing Civic Identity: The Iconic Photograph of the Flag-Raising on Iwo Jima." *Quarterly Journal of Speech* 88 (2002): 263–92.

Herndl, Carl and Cindy Nahrwold. "Research as Social Practice: A Case Study of Research on Technical and Professional Communication." *Written Communication* 17.2 (2000): 258–96.

Johnson, Nan. *Gender and Rhetorical Space in American Life, 1866–1910.* Carbondale: Southern Illinois UP, 2002.

Leff, Michael. "Tradition and Agency in Humanistic Rhetoric." *Philosophy and Rhetoric* 36.2 (2003): 135–47.

Wilson, Kirt. "The Racial Politics of Imitation in the Nineteenth Century." *Quarterly Journal of Speech* 89 (2003): 89–108.

"OUIJA BOARD, ARE THERE ANY COMMUNICATIONS?"

Agency, Ontotheology, and the Death of the Humanist Subject, or, Continuing the ARS Conversation

CHRISTIAN LUNDBERG AND JOSHUA GUNN

> No, I was NOT pushing that time.
>
> —Morrissey, "Ouija Board, Ouija Board"

The Second Great Awakening of the nineteenth century marks an activist shift in Protestant religious practice in the United States, a turn from Calvinist fatalism toward an active, evangelical conviction in the capacity of humans to act morally and secure their own spiritual salvation. This conviction in moral agency catalyzed a growing belief in spiritualism, the idea that mere mortals could talk to the souls or "spirits" of dead people if they concentrated hard enough or employed the appropriate technological extension of the human sensorium. In the obvious idiom of the telegraph, originally nineteenth-century communiqués from the dead came in the form or "rappings" or "knocks" on tables or walls, which a given "medium" would count to discern if they denoted a "yes," a "no," or a letter of the alphabet (Braude 10–31). Excepting toddlers and accountants, counting is a somewhat tiresome exercise of agency, and so it was only a matter of time before a number of enterprising individuals would develop the "talking board" to ease the labor of mediation. Most familiar to us as Parker Brothers' "Ouija Board," a talking board was originally a device whereby one placed his or her hands on a heart-shaped planchette, which was then presumably directed by a spirit to glide across an alphabet painted on a wooden board, spelling out messages of requited love and approaching danger.

As a technology ultimately inspired by the Second Great Awakening, the Ouija Board illustrates the anxiety surrounding our many fantasies about human agency, particularly in respect to communication as a transcendent, or even transparent event (see Gunn, "Refitting"; Peters 63–108). However ironic, the belief that one or another could literally speak with the souls of the dearly departed reflects an evangelical subject enthusiastically wedded to a humanist gospel that has elevated agency to the status of the godly, lording over the material and spiritual universe. This transcendent sentiment, sometimes discussed as "ontotheology," was heavily critiqued by Heidegger, who lamented that "it seems as though man everywhere and always encounters himself," even beyond death (Heidegger, "Question" 332).[1] Such a narcissistic "ideology of agency," perhaps born of grief, a fear of death, and/or dreams of divine omnipotence, manifests itself in a technology of instrumentality that treats even our spectral doubles as mere objects or extensions of the human subject's will (ghosts as *Bestand*, "standing-reserve"). From a Heideggerian vantage, the folly of spiritualism points to a critique of the humanist agent as autonomous, the so-called "transcendental subject" rooted in the Kantian tradition.

The practice of a séance also directs our attention to a problem implied in (but also somehow beyond) the transparency or transcendence of the moment of communication: the instabilities of the Cartesian self, or the self-transparent and self-possessed subject of thoroughly conscious intention (the *cogito*; see Descartes). Using a Ouija board, for example, demonstrates that while the exercise of agency takes place in the movement of the planchette, the status and possibly even the existence of the agent who originates the action is undecidable. Consider a story from a March 28, 1886 edition of the *New-York Daily Tribune*, which underscores the way in which the uncanny talking board séance might call our accounts of our own and others' agency into question:

> You take the board in your lap, another person sitting down with you. You each grasp the little table with the thumb and forefinger at each corner next to you. Then the question is asked, "Are there any communications?" Pretty soon you think the other person is pushing the table. He thinks you are doing the same. But the table moves around to "yes" or "no." Then you go on asking questions and the answers are spelled out by the legs of the table resting on the letters one after the other. Sometimes the table will cover two letters with its feet, and then you hang on and ask that the table will be moved from the wrong letter, which is done. Some remarkable conversations have been carried on until men have become in a measure superstitious about it.
>
> (quoted in "History of the Talking Board," par. 6)

As anyone who has "played" with a talking board will attest, the fun orbits suspicion: either one deceives, or is deceived by, the co-medium, or one is relatively unable to locate the seat of agency: is my partner moving this thing? Am

I moving it without knowing it? Is it possible that some unseen spirit—a passed relative or worse, an evil genius—is moving the planchette (and therefore, us)? Although the somewhat admittedly perverse practice of talking to the dead is born of Kantian and Cartesian convictions, it nevertheless opens the question of an uncertain and unsettled subject position or disposition.[2]

Indeed, the Ouija's capacity to demonstrate the unsettled subject becomes apparent as soon as one thinks about the variety of possible assumptions underlying the talking board séance. One could play the game presuming that living human subjects move the planchette, and that they do so either by conscious choice, unconscious choice, or in an act of mutual deferment to the conscious or unconscious movements of their partner. The players could also presume that there is an unspecified ratio of cooperation in moving the planchette between human subjects who sit at the table and dead subjects from the Beyond. Players could also invoke the idea of possession by a spirit who temporarily inhabits one or more of the players at the table and directs the movement of the planchette (viz., "channeling"). Players uncomfortable with the possibility that they are being "played" might decide to give up the Ouija board altogether. Yet, each of these options seems mildly *inhospitable* (none more so than packing up your Ouija board and going home). The idea that the game is solely played out among the living is inhospitable toward the spirits who may wish to join the living in communion; the idea that the spirits "possess" the body of one or more people at the table is inhospitable toward the participation of the living subject who is dispossessed. Finally, the ratio seems a hospitable compromise, but also contains the inherent inhospitality of specifying just how much influence living and dead subjects are allowed to have on the play ("sorry dead spirit, my turn to move the planchette"). Perhaps hospitality toward living and the dead implies that we give up our anxieties about the game and just play, never certain who will be manifest in the communion of the game, and never sure just how they will be manifest. Such an agnostic disposition does not imply that the players should ignore the moves of the planchette or the flows of the spirit; it simply means that players should pay attention to the movements of the game without prefiguring the meaning of the movements, reducing them to an absolutist causal account. This disposition of openness to the Other—to an unconditional "what if"—is what Derrida eventually described as the posture of hospitality (see Caputo, *Prayers*; Derrida, *Specters*).

In joining the sometimes overly serious conversation concerning the question, "how ought we to understand the concept of rhetorical agency?" we would prefer that the answer was more hospitable to those of us who find "post-" theory useful, truthful, or productively troubling. We favor an uncertain posture towards the flows of agency and agents implied by an open disposition toward the séance, a posture that embraces a restless and roving insecurity as an antidote or even perhaps a subversive supplement to any civil pedagogy. Although Cheryl Geisler rightfully notes that the discussion question of rhetorical agency often melds the ontological (what?) with the ethical (how?), she and others nevertheless seek to infer the former by presenting the latter evangelically, stressing the fundamental necessity of moral activism for civic salvation and charging those with poststructural and/or posthumanist sympathies as advocating a nihilistic brand of Calvinist passivity, often erroneously dubbed "postmodernism." In what follows, we argue that the humanist/evangelical discussion of agency in Geisler's report, published in last summer's issue of *Rhetoric Society Quarterly*, suffers from three, interrelated shortcomings: (1) the report repeatedly confuses the subject or agent and agency;[3] (2) this confusion lends credence to a conflation of posthumanism and "postmodernism"; and (3) such a conflation contributes to a misleading account of agential fantasy as a mere "illusion." Insofar as few would deny agency exists, we suggest the debate over status of the humanist subject is actually one-sided and phantasmic, serving to disguise the ghost of ontotheology.

Of Agents and Agency: Confronting Ontotheology

To begin we provide a set of brief background sketches of three representative "postmodernists." We pose sketches of these three exemplars to situate our critique of Geisler's report, for if there is one commonality in the haunting specter of "postmodern" thought, it can be found in the treatment of the human subject. The usual suspects whose thinking we refer to in this essay share a concern with accounts of the human subject as "given" and godly instead of as *produced*. To counter this tendency, building on the critique of humanism begun by Heidegger, thinkers such as Jacques Derrida, Jacques Lacan, and Michel Foucault have produced accounts of the human subject that specify its radical contingency, its fragmentary qualities, and/or its dependence on generative systems beyond the seat of an insular individual consciousness.[4]

One of the points underlying Derrida's employment of *différance*, which strategically applies Saussure's structural linguistics, is that

> language [which only consists of differences] is not a function of the speaking subject. This implies that the subject (in its identity with itself, or eventually in its consciousness of its identity with itself, its self consciousness) is inscribed in language, is a function of language, becomes a *speaking* subject—even in so-called 'creation,' or in so-called 'transgression—to the system of the rules of language as a system of differences.
>
> (Derrida, *Margins* 15)

Given this account, the subject is never fully present to itself because it is only a product of the functioning of differential signification. This subject does not possess an ontologically stable form or identity other than the one contingently produced in the play of *différance* (see Biesecker, "Rethinking"). Similarly, Lacan situates the genesis of the subject within structures of language, but roots it specifically in the subject's alienating encounter with signification.

Lacan's varied and often contradictory corpus presents a picture of the subject as a kind of excess that is generated by the trauma of insertion into the Symbolic order. For Lacan, the condition for the articulation of the subject is its emptiness; subjects come to life within a language that they do not choose and that cannot fully represent or express their affective desires. The subject, or rather the idea of an identity that is presumed synonymous with the human subject, is produced as a suture that attempts to mediate the alienating process of signification. In ways that resemble Derrida's understanding of the speaking subject, for Lacan the subject is an effect of discourse and the surplus generated by continuously negotiating a relationship to the Symbolic order (Lacan, *Écrits* 3–9). Finally, Foucault's work interrogates the givenness of the subject by questioning the presupposition made in various discursive domains (the prison, the mental institution, technologies of sexuality, and so on), that one could render an essential description of the subject or "tell the truth" about it. His general method is one of "problematization," a process that usually entails contradicting the claim that a mode of subjectivity is a natural one by revealing that it is a set of historically specific habits, practices, or performances. To deny the truth of the subject, however, is *not* to deny the existence of subjects. Rather, in problematizing subjectivity Foucault hopes to demonstrate that our doctrine of agency is more the result of the application of *techne* than of the result of metaphysical pre-determination.[5]

These sketches of three critiques of the subject are overly simple, and undoubtedly suppress significant differences and disagreements both within and among the works of Derrida, Lacan, and Foucault. Yet, a thoughtful reading of their work supports some provisional claims about the question of agency vis-à-vis the project of the posts (posthumanism, post-Marxism, postmodernism, poststructuralism, and so on). First, none of these critics of a common-sense doctrine of agency deny that the subject or representations of the subject exert significant effects, nor do they deny the subject a kind of social effectivity or agency. To the contrary, to point out that the subject is constructed and not naturally given helps to delineate one of our scholarly tasks as that of tracking the rhetorical effects of doctrines of agency. Instead of asking the question of the subject in terms of truth or the veracity of our representations, they demand that we give an account of how our interpretations of actions (of agency) are often read through, or even prescripted by, a doctrine that centers the agent or the subject as the self-possessed seat of agency. The work of these three "post-" thinkers and their heirs requires that we make a decisive analytical cut between *agency*, understood as the production of effect or action, and the *agent* as the presumed origin of effect or action, which can be a subject, language, ideology, perhaps even a spirit. Because addressing the question of rhetorical agency solely in terms of "agent" and "agency" implies that material change is both naturally and rightfully reducible to the action of the agent, we prefer reframing the question in terms of subjectivity and effect. In other words, we worry that defining the problem of subject and effect as the question of agent and agency prefigures the answer by presuming, by definition, that the agent is directly linked to agency (the potential for action).

Derrida, Lacan, and Foucault's strategies for denaturalizing the subject confound the idea that the simple existence of agency-effects allows us to posit the necessary existence of an agent who initiates these effects. Their critiques of humanist notions of agency combat what Heidegger identified as ontotheology, a kind of thinking that ultimately roots being and truth in divinity. In other words, the habit of reducing agency to the self-transparent human agent is homologous on some level to the cosmological argument for God's existence. Beginning with Aristotle's argument for presuming an unmoved first mover, through Aquinas's reappropriation of his Greek master's account of the first cause, to modern day discourses of creationist evangelicals, the idea that God can be inferred from the presence of movement has been a faithful companion of those theists seeking to reconcile *fides* and *ratio*. The idea that one could infer the existence of something called the "rhetorical agent" from the multiplicity of rhetorical effects has obvious affinities with the argument from first causes. Rendered in the terms of the talking board séance, the ontotheological habit is akin to presuming that the movement of the planchette *proves* the agency of determinate subjects, dead or alive. The interventions of thinkers like Lacan, Foucault, and Derrida caution us from making facile inferences from effect to cause in the form of a characteristically theistic doctrine of rhetorical agency.[6]

Of Ectoplasm, or, the Possession of Agency

Having reframed the "question of rhetorical agency" as a negotiation of subject and effect, we are better prepared to consider the extent to which Geisler's framing of the Evanston discussions is grounded in a natural connection between agency as effect and the inference of a naturally given agent. After a thoughtful reading of Geisler's report, we find that the concept of "possession" surfaces throughout as a trope that yokes agency and agent in the service of an ontotheological humanism.

In her report on the four days of discussion at the ARS revival, Geisler admits that "any attempt to synthesize" or "do justice to the engaging conversations that occupied us" on the topic of agency is "doomed to failure," but that a "thoughtful reading of the posted position papers" and related documents helps to frame the discussion. Geisler continues that the significance of the question of agency is reducible to an engagement with "the post-modern critique of the autonomous agent," which she locates in a 1993 article by Dilip Gaonkar on the "rhetoric of science" (10; see Gaonkar).[7] Ultimately, Geisler frames the discussion on agency at the ARS conference as a reactive *and* productive response to "the post-modern assault" (10). Geisler suggests that the productive responses to the critique of the "ideology of agency," understood here as the humanist subject assumed in Gaonkar's critique, are located in three types of scholarship: scholarship that details and documents the ways in which "subaltern groups" cause social change (10–11; 15); scholarship that explores the conditions and constitution of agency in mass mediated contexts (e.g., as constituted in visual and digital texts; 11–12); and scholarship that explores the teaching of skills and classical norms of citizenship (13–16). In other words, a "consideration of the postmodern critique has stimulated not just 'rear guard' action but a constructive and productive inquiry into the nature of agency and the conditions attached to it" (Leff and Lunsford 63). We do not disagree in total, although we believe that theorizing the relation of rhetoric to subjectivity through the conceptual pair of agent/agency creates interpretive biases that merit closer scrutiny.

As Lynne Clark notes in her position statement, the *OED* defines "agency" as "the faculty of an agent or of acting." Despite a number of alternate accounts of agency at the ARS conference, most of the position papers that Geisler chooses to highlight adopt this "possession" metaphor of agency, explicitly in some cases, and implicitly in others. Throughout her remarks Geisler presents agency as a kind of substance, a quantifiable ectoplasm that can be taken from the agent by the presence of social constraints, as well as something that can be given to the agent by the application of appropriate methods. For instance, in her report Geisler relies on the notion of possession to aggressively advance the connection between pedagogy and substantive agency: "only if we can assent to the role of the rhetor in producing efficacious action can we as a discipline have a mission to educate such rhetors to *have* agency" (8; italics ours). Further, agency is not only a possession in that it is something the agent can have, it is also a possession that can be granted, since "developing a society that *grants* agency more broadly may be one of the major challenges for the future of rhetorical studies" (Geisler 10; italics ours). This understanding of agency as a possession is central to reproducing the humanist model of the intentional agent who owns the capacity to make agential choices.[8] The possessive understanding of agency also appears implicitly in Geisler's recognition that agency can be understood as a "*resource* constructed in particular contexts and in particular ways" (Geisler 7; italics ours). Although this particular employment of the metaphor recognizes that agency is socially constructed, it only does so at the cost of employing a trope that implies that the agent who receives access to this resource is not socially constructed in the same way that the resource may in fact be; the social mediation of agency begs the question of the social construction of the *agent*. Given the tropological structure of the possession metaphor employed here, there must be a pre-given agent who receives access to and employs the resource (here we find echoes of the idea of agency as the *Bestand*, or the standing-reserve of the agent alluded to earlier).[9]

Geisler's text comes closest to specifically addressing the social construction of the agent in her discussion of Atwill's and Langsdorf's papers, which situate the agent in communicative interaction. In response to the situation of the agent in structures of language or, more appropriately for us, the marking of the agent as a rhetorical effect, Geisler hopes for a moderate approach to the implication of the agent's contingency. In a final employment of the possession metaphor, Atwill's and Langsdorf's approaches are praised because they allow the agent to maintain its agency. Geisler claims that their approach would allow the agent to keep its agency, that it allows "agency to remain with the agent and yet acknowledge *its* embedding in the externals of communicative interaction" (Geisler 8; italics ours). Demonstrating remarkable figural acumen, Geisler's amphibolous "its" is a delicious example of the conflation that enables the slippage between agent and agency. Does the "its" refer to agent or agency? Which of the two is embedded in the externals of communicative action? Perhaps, if we are to maintain the doctrine of agency as a possession of the agent, it is more productive to let the amphiboly lie as it is. Such a reading practice, however, would make the decisive analytical cut that we call for difficult.

(D)illusions of Rejection

Opposing the equivocation of agent as an unverified conceptual possibility and agency as the real presence of action, we part ways with Geisler's characterization of postmodern theory. In her report Geisler strongly argues against what she sees as an unproductive response to the critique of the self-transparent, autonomous agent: the "abandonment" of the concept or idea of agency. Exclusively basing her observations on one, short position paper, Geisler notes that although "most rhetoricians at the ARS took for granted some level of efficacy for rhetorical action . . . others suggested that this was an illusion" (12).[10] Gunn is singled out for suggesting that agency is a sham and for suggesting that the failure of rhetoricians to jettison the concept is "cowardice."[11] "Although some at ARS argued that coming to grips with the illusion of agency is the only honest thing to do," Geisler reports she observed two important rejoinders, one ontological ("is"), the other, ethical ("ought"): first, those studying the subaltern have demonstrated that agency exists; and second, abandoning agency entails the "cost of the irrelevancy of rhetoric" (15–16).

Although Geisler's report may reflect a "thoughtful reading," it certainly is far from a charitable one, particularly in respect to those rhetoricians who have embraced so-called postmodern theory.[12] The equivocation of agent and agency enables a strategic conflation of the critique of humanism with postmodernism, the latter serving alternately as a scapegoat ("postmodernism will destroy rhetorical studies!") and epithet ("damn you postmodernists!"). Although it is certainly the case that we can identify a number of thinkers associated with the category of the postmodern (e.g., Deleuze, Derrida, Foucault, Jameson, Lyotard, and so on), and although we suspect a number of rhetoricians would identify their work as participating in a postmodern idiom, there is little consensus in the academy about what postmodernism means (see Best and Kellner, *Postmodern Theory*; Best and Kellner, *Postmodern Turn*; and Jameson). The only common thread that seems to hold the idiom of postmodernity together is the critique of the humanist subject as the center of the universe and, as Protagoras has said, the measure of all things, "of things that are that they are, and of things that are not that they are not" (Sextus 18). In other words, Geisler is overly ambitious in her application of the term "postmodern" or "post-modern" to the critique of humanism, or posthumanism. As we noted earlier, this critique is often traced to the work of Heidegger on ontotheology, and later, to that of Derrida, Foucault, and Lacan. Heidegger critiques Sartre's existentialism as an arrogant, romantic humanism that leads to a ruthless, righteous instrumentality; Derrida's theory of deconstruction demonstrates the violence of notions of unity, presence, self-mastery, and transcendence; Foucault's work collectively points to the subject as a function or fold of discourse; and Lacan's theory suggests that the Symbolic itself is an agent. None of these thinkers, however, would argue that rhetors do not produce effects. Instead, they focus on the implications of making reference to an "acting subject" as the exclusive means for theorizing the capacity to act. For example, to return to our séance allegory, Lacan might insist that the Symbolic is more in control of the people in a séance than they know, that the planchette as the *objet a* has more agency than the medium, or that the enjoyment in playing the game produces the fantasy of acting agents. Yet, insofar as Lacan wrote and lectured about his ideas, it is simply silly to insist that he or his compatriot critics of humanist agency were flippant about the capacity for rhetorical action.[13]

Despite the absurdity of the move, Geisler repeatedly and mistakenly reduces the critique of the humanist subject to a kind of pomo flippancy, to the inability of an individual to engender social change, and ultimately to a denial of the capacity to act altogether.[14] In the same issue Leff makes a similar inference, amplifying the cries of moral censure in Geisler's account:

> It is possible, of course, to declare that rhetoric should break entirely with tradition, toss concerns about agency into the trash heap of obsolete ideologies, and go about the business of interpretation without any qualms of conscience. This option, however, proves to have limited appeal. In the first place, it is dangerous. Teachers of writing and speaking can pursue an unrestrained deconstruction of agency of speakers and writers only at the risk of theorizing themselves out of jobs. Secondly, qualms of conscience— perhaps even of collective consciousness—assert themselves.
> (Leff and Lunsford 62)

To return to our séance allegory, for Geisler and Leff, those who embrace the "postmodern" critique are somehow mindlessly moved around by the agency of the planchette (the Symbolic, ideology, discourse, History, and so on), while those who find "comfort" in the "traditional model of [the] humanist agent" can plainly see that *someone* is moving it around (Geisler 14). Yet we would respond that even though someone or something is acting on the planchette in a séance, it does not follow that agency must necessarily be rooted in an autonomous, intending human agent—however conscious or stricken with conscience she may be. Nor does the mere fact of movement allow for a discernment of the movement's cause without pre-reading the situation through the lens of a humanist account of an agent producing agency; the undeniable existence of agency, in other words, does not prove that the autonomous subject is therefore its source.

Our concern is that rhetorical theorists should be more honest about the secret interpretive work done by their ontotheological framework for interpreting agency as an extension of the agent. Even Leff has argued that the classical rhetorical agent comprises a fundamental ambivalence between rhetoric and audience, contradicting claims that "humanistic rhetoric valorizes and centers itself on the individual agent" ("Tradition" 138; also see Gunn, *Modern* 136–137). In other words, rhetoricians have long accepted some form of the argument that subjectivity is *not* autonomous and have rejected the self-sufficiency of the subject. Indeed, that there is a discussion about "agency" at all means, at least tacitly, that we have rejected "an ontology of agency that freezes the concept in static theoretical space" (Leff and Lunsford 63). What remains to be seen is a rigorous rejection of the ontotheological, despite the well-known (and tacitly accepted) problematization of the ontology of agency. What is really at issue is not so much the "is" of agency but the "how," as well as the way in which the two are linked.

The Second Great Equivocation, or, Rhetoric's Ethical Righteousness

We are suggesting that the threat of posthumanism (or as it is known in rhetorical studies, "postmodernism") is a phantom paper tiger, a specter that haunts and causes great trembling, but only because it is mistakenly said to bring the plague of agential paralysis. Geisler's claim that "the facts on the ground do not appear to support the proposition that rhetorical agency is illusionary" presumes such a proposition was made; to our knowledge, the only thinker who has come close to this suggestion is Jean Baudrillard, and we're fairly confident his claims are strategically mischievous and provocative. Just because we might argue that the posthumanist subject is performed, split, interpellated, or a function of discourse, tropology, rhetoric, and so on does not mean rhetors do not exert agential effects in pursuit of their interests; indeed, we certainly have a well-documented history of our acting against them.

Insofar as the first "argument from fact" offered in response to the pseudo-problem of the existence of agency is much ado about something, that something must be the second "argument of value" (Geisler 15–16). In this respect, the argument of straw regarding the "illusion of agency" participates in a consequentialist logic designed to lead us to ethical imperatives. In the ARS discussions in print and during the conference, rhetorical humanists tended to hitch ethical questions to issues of pedagogy. Leff's commentary on Geisler's report strongly emphasizes the ethical import of teaching rhetoric:

> Rhetoricians believe that their work ought to make students more effective agents in the public world, and rhetoric is, Geisler recalls, "the art of doing in language." The exercise of agency in and through language is close to the core of this art, and should it abandon the goal of being efficacious in the world, Geisler wonders whether its teachers would still be rhetoricians. In the face of this pedagogical undercurrent, it is no surprise that rhetoricians have reacted against doctrines that thoroughly suppress the exercise of individual agency through language.
>
> (Leff and Lunsford 62)

In other words, the "ought" is driving the humanist critique of the posthumanist critique of the "is." And this ought *is* heavily indebted to a romantic understanding of the subject, rooted less in the figure of the classical rhetor in Aristotle and Cicero than in the anxious character of Antoine Roquentin in Sartre's *Nausea*: if humans are the measure of all things, if it seems as though we everywhere and always encounter ourselves in this world by means of *rhetoric*, then invention entails a tremendous responsibility (also see Scott 14–17).

The enthymematic element here is that responsibility confers agency, and to recoil from the freedom that demands choice is, in some sense, to suffer social death or rhetorical impotence. Hence our characterization of the pomo specter as a Calvinist harbinger of radical passivity and the trauma of a totalizing determinism: from the humanist vantage, symbolic action or rhetoric as "doing in language" assumes contingency and freedom; freedom demands making choices and locating responsibility in the individual who chooses; failing to make choices presumably because they are always already scripted in the illusion of agency is therefore failure to understand rhetoric and assume responsibility for one's symbolic choices. For Geisler, separating the fact of agency from the value of responsibility and choice is fundamentally *immoral*. Hence she asks,

> What shall we, as critics, say to our fellow citizens about their potential and obligations with respect to becoming rhetorical agents? What shall we, as critics, say to our fellow citizens about their potential and obligations? If neither our students nor our fellow citizens have such potential or obligations—if agency is illusory—we may sidestep these questions . . . as irrelevant.
>
> (16)

What emerges from Geisler's report is ultimately a variation of "is/ought" problem first identified by Hume and later dubbed the "naturalistic fallacy" by G. E. Moore. Here we find the specific moral incarnation of inferring cause from effect, the equivocation of agency as the capacity to act and participatory citizenship as a moral duty.

In light of the tacit acceptance of the critique of the autonomous subject, the question is not really "how ought we to understand the concept of rhetorical agency?" but "where do we locate responsibility when agency is exercised?" If as subjects we are interpellated by ideology to invest in our own unhappiness, who is responsible? Further, if we are unable to determine the seat of agency, then are we robbed of our ability to locate lying and to censure deception? And perhaps most importantly, who or what gives us the right as teachers and critics to determine good and bad norms of civic engagement? For Geisler, to answer these kinds of questions simply by arguing that agency exists *is not enough*, because rhetorical ontotheology demands some locus of agency to secure the gospel of rhetoric *as* civic responsibility. This understanding of rhetoric partic-ipates in what we term rhetorical evangelicalism, an approach to the study and teaching of rhetoric that is ethically righteous in respect to the classical norms of civic culture, and particularly the moral responsibility of "civic engagement." Because of "the attachment of rhetorical agency to a vision of political change," Ronald Walter Greene argues that rhetorical critics and theorists have been increasingly pushed into "becoming moral entrepreneurs scolding, correcting, and encouraging the body politic to improve the quality and quantity of politi-cal participation" (189). From Greene's perspective, the problem with insisting that rhetorical agency always concerns political (or civic) effectivity is that it puts us into an intellectual straitjacket:

> whether the model [of political communication] imagines rhetorical agency in terms of reinventing cultural traditions (hermeneutics) or in terms of collective action (social movements), the emphasis on rhetorical agency as a model of political communication, prefigures the significance of rhetorical agency as always already in support of, or opposition to, the institutional structures of power. Thus a permanent anxiety about the char-acter of rhetorical agency is made inevitable, because [it] suspends dialec-tically between structures of power . . . and the possibility of social change. To break out of this dialectical anxiety requires more than an alternative model of communication; it requires the abandonment of the dialectical interface between structure and change.
>
> (198)

Although we think that the idea of "breaking out" from the project (if not con-dition) of mediation, of finding an "escape route" from a reckoning with the dia-lectic of structure and struggle, is a too romantic for our tastes, Greene's claim that a dogged commitment to conflating agency and responsibility leads to a permanent anxiety is well taken.[15] If we locate the First Great Awakening to the post-idioms in rhetorical studies as a shift toward hermeneutics (see Leff; Leff and Kauffeld; Leff and Lunsford, 62), then the Second Great Awakening is the characteristically evangelical response to the neurosis that Greene identifies, an increasingly apocalyptic humanism and an enterprise of moral entrepreneurship that would extend our role as teachers and critics to that of lording over civic space.[16] We do not necessarily disagree with an understanding of rhetorical studies as having an ethical mission (defined by the imperative to generate normatively good civic action), but we do urge a consideration of *our* qualms of conscience concerning a characteristically conservative claim to moral righteousness in response to post-theory. Although some rhetoricians may find moral entrepreneurship a "productive" direction, we are not so converted.

Concluding Remarks: Giving up the Geis(t)ler?

In our response to Geisler's report on the ARS conference discussions concerning rhetorical agency, we have attempted to provide a more faithful account of the posthumanist critique of the subject or agent, which we think functions as a straw person in her argument. We suggested that an equivocation of agent and agency is at the center of Geisler's report, and that the agency-as-possession metaphor indicates that this equivocation is ontotheological in aim and scope. Ultimately, we concluded that ethical righteousness, couched in the language of pedagogy, is behind the claim that agency proves the existence of the humanist agent, that the "how" determines the "is." Although we do not necessarily disagree with claiming an ethical mission for rhetorical studies, we suggest that the allegory of ARS tent revival ought to be replaced with the allegory of the séance, with the possibility that the specter of language and other ghosts move us more than we know.

We would be remiss, however, if we did not point out that problematizing the idea of the agent does not necessarily create an a priori rejection of the doctrine of responsibility. In fact, we suggest that responsibility demands such a problematization *and* that such a problematization can generate an alternate model of responsibility. For example, Derrida borrows from the Heideggerian maxim that "speaking is responding" to argue that responsibility ought not be framed as a normative imperative on the agent to own up to the consequences of its intentions and actions. Instead, "response"-ability marks the idea that every action, discursive or otherwise, is only born of an engagement with the set of conditions that produced it. This is the logical implication of the idea that every act of speaking is an act of response. Thus, argues Caputo,

> if Derrida is a renegade . . . he is a highly responsible one. The work of deconstruction is set in motion, engaged (engage) only by a pledge of responsibility, indeed of unlimited responsibility, because a "limited responsibility" (drawing oneself into a corporate circle) is just an excuse to credit oneself with a good conscience . . . deconstruction is set in motion by something that calls upon us and addresses us, overtakes and even overwhelms us, to which we must respond, and so be responsive and responsible . . . such questioning, be assured, arises from the height—or depths—of responsibility.
>
> (Caputo, *Deconstruction* 51)

The implication of this claim is that any call for normative doctrines of responsibility determined by the agential choices of the subject paradoxically entails a *deferral* of responsibility. The deferral concerns the tendency of accounts of the responsible subject to predetermine the choices of the subject by the force of metaphysical law. An unconditional responsibility, here entailed in the call to deconstruction, rejects the casuistry that tethers the future actions of an agent to a doctrine about that agent's naturalness or givenness, and therefore to a set of protocols to which the agent must adhere to exercise responsibility. We suggest that instead of avoiding responsibility, a relentless questioning of the conditions of the production of the agent, and a close textual engagement with the agential narrative and the agent's texts, affirms an unconditional commitment to responding, and ultimately to responsibility, despite the threat of undermining our corporate attempts to credit the rhetoric community with good conscience.

In bringing our response to a close, we suggest that a more hospitable conversation about the rhetorical agent might entail three moves. First, we propose an alternate discourse of possession that can be read against the trope of agents possessing agency. Rosemary Ellen Guiley's entry in the *Harper's Encyclopedia of Mystical and Paranormal Experience* notes that "some demonologists say the Ouija opens the door to possession by evil spirits" (Guiley 419). Although we will stop short of advocating a rhetorical demonology (necromancy is perhaps more apt), we hope that our séance allegory—the spiritualist idiom of possession from without—helps to encourage a discourse counter to the hegemony of possessing agency. What happens to the conventional rhetorical account of agency if it starts out by presuming that the agency possesses the agent, as opposed to the agent possessing agency as an instrument or substance? Such a narrative refocuses our attention on the ways that the subject is an effect of structures, forces, and modes of enjoyment that *might* precede or produce it. This reversal of agent's relation to agency directs attention to quintessentially rhetorical concerns: to the constitutive function of trope, to modes of address, to the dialectics of identification and difference, and even to the power of concealing exercises of *techne* under the veil of the natural.

Second, to the extent that we rhetoricians ought to worry about such things, the reversal of "possessing" to "possessed" is obviously more hospitable to the concerns of posthumanist thinking, and none more so than Lacan's. The French psychoanalyst's earliest work dealt with the phenomena of "automatism," the perception by paranoid patients that something outside of them controlled their thought processes (Lacan, *Seminar III* 29–43). In response to the problem of accounting for automatism while denying the external reality of the paranoid delusion, Lacan began to theorize the agency of the structures that produced both the perceptions of the subject and the perceiving subject. Lacan thus ultimately attributes agency to tropes, to the Symbolic, and to enjoyment (Lacan, *Écrits* 138–168; also see Lacan, *Seminar XX* 3, 56). This agency possesses the subject, thereby bringing the fantasy of the agent to life. For Lacan, the "response"-ible reading of the dynamics of subjectivity requires reference to rhetoric (Lundberg 500–01). In short, Lacanian psychoanalytic theory can help rhetoricians navigate the posthumanist theoretical landscape in a characteristically rhetorical way.

Third, if we are in fact dealing with a covertly theistic discourse of the subject (paired with all the evangelistic fervor that one might expect), perhaps reference to the ontotheological is more helpful than some may realize. Atheism, of course, is one possible response to posthumanism, as if to withdraw from a séance, or worse, as if to join our doggedly positivistic colleagues in the hard sciences.[17] We think that there is another, characteristically agonistic possibility: a negative theology of the subject (see Bernauer). *Prima facie*, negative theology seems like a kind of atheism: it begins by pointing out that the particularity of language necessitates that all descriptions on an infinite God (even positive ones) do violence to God, and thus calls for a stripping away of the names and presumed qualities of the divine.[18] All representations of God in this system, though necessary for devotional practice, participate in a subtle idolatry. Yet, it should go without saying that to deny the existence of God also participates in violence toward God, and an idolatry of its own. In marking the impossibility of truth in describing God, the *via negativa* opens a hospitable and responsible horizon for receiving the divine. By analogy, Foucault argues that a negative theology of the subject does not deny the possibility of subjectivity, but instead demands that we strip away all the various discursive attributions of qualities and possessions to the subject with the hope of liberating subjectivity from the ossified bounds of the agent as a technology for organizing the experience of subjectivity. Perhaps a similar negative theology of the rhetorical agent would allow rhetoric to be practiced without the agent as the decisive horizon for rhetorical agency? This project would call for a thick theorization of the rhetorical effects of doctrines of agency, and for inquiry into the function of persuasion as a systemic effect/affect beyond the individual agent—in collectivities, discursive formations, new technologies, and so on. Far from denying rhetorical study the fruits of its labor, such an agnostic disposition of hospitality asks for nothing more than a restless and relentless thinking. Casting the problem of rhetorical agency as a rhetorical affect, instead of as a point of origin for rhetorical effect, requires us to think about the agent and its relation to agency as one trope among others that productively and destructively constrains the exercise of our critical imagination. This move requires faithfulness to the analytical cut separating the doctrine of the subject or agent as an ontological claim from the social and rhetorical effects that are wrought by presuming a specific configuration of the subject. Adopting such a disposition, we sit patiently and with wonder, ready for surprise, open to possible joy, to the Messianic return (even if joy or the Messiah never come). We wait openly, as if having just asked, "Ouija Board, are there any communications?"

Notes

1 Foucault, following Heidegger, also diagnoses a latent theistic tendency in humanism. Framing the gospel of humanism as an "absolutization" of the human subject, he observes that in the wake of the oft proclaimed death of God, the image of "man (sic)" had become that of a "God incarnated in humanity" (Bernauer 68; Foucault, "Foucault Response" 38).

2 As Karlyn Kohrs Campbell notes, rhetorical agency "is perverse, that is, inherently protean, ambiguous, open to reversal" (2).

3 Technically speaking, we should make a strict separation between the "subject" and "the agent," insofar as we will eventually claim, following Lacan, that language is an agent itself. We recognize, however, that most people mean "subject" when using the term "agent" and so we will continue the habit.

4 For the beginning of this posthumanist line of thought, see Heidegger's "Letter on Humanism."

5 Thus, Foucault suggests an alternate term "subjectivization" which is "the procedure by which one obtains the constitution of a subject, or more precisely, of a subjectivity which is, of course *only one of the given possibilities* of organization of a self consciousness" (Foucault, "Return of Morality" 253; italics ours).

6 We do not need to turn to the reflections of continental thinkers to make these points. In fact, upon reading the ARS position statements we found many voices that resonate with this general line of argument. Lundberg's position statement points out that

> subjectivity (the question of the agent) implies a question of the ontological foundations (or lack thereof) of human being, and subsequently (but not exclusively) action. Agency implies a functional account of action or the potential for action, and as a functional account one does not necessarily have to rely on a firm answer to the question of subjectivity to address agency. Thus the question of agency brackets the question of subjectivity in a significant way, though a view of subjectivity is necessarily implied in thinking about agency.

We find similar concerns with the production of subjectivity or the agent as analytically separate from the question of agency in the statements of Barbara Biesecker, Diane Davis, Renu Dube, Randall Iden, John Kirby, James McDaniel, John Lucaites, and Brett Ommen. This is not an exhaustive list, but this sampling does provide evidence that this line of criticism exerted a significant voice in the Evanston discussions on agency.

7 The more significant critique of "the ideology of agency," however, is Barbara Biesecker's "Coming to Terms with Recent Attempts to Write Women into the History of Rhetoric."

8 Geisler's argument for the desirability of this model is consistently made in the name of teaching: "a rhetorical agent seen to make choices among the available means of persuasion is an agent rhetoricians can educate to make the best choices" (11). Despite claims to a polysemous presentation of agency and caveats about the productive influence of "postmodernism," the "comfort of the traditional model of the humanist agent" stealthily slides from a consoling presupposition of the tradition to a formal imperative for the future (11). When combined with the claim that if rhetoric is avert the risk of irrelevance it must be able to generate change, comfort in the traditional, possessive view of the subject sounds like a precondition for the relevance of the discipline or, more menacingly, an argument *ad consequentiam*.

9 Geisler's summation of McDaniel's call for one version of the analytical cut we develop in this essay follows a similar figural pattern: "the agency of the good man speaking well becomes neither necessary fantasy nor liberal delusion, but one of a number of ideological configurations that emerge in specific historical contexts to form, if you will, the landscape of agency" (Geisler, 7). Here again, there is a fundamental recognition that *agency* is the product of social construction, but it is still presented as a possession of "the good man speaking well," though the context for the exercise of agency changes in this configuration, the basic assertion that agency is a possession of the human subject does not change: agency is the possession of the

agent. This same configuration is present in her representation of John Angus Campbell's and James Jasinski's position statements: "According to Jasinski, an improvisation metaphor may allow us to sidestep the critique of liberal humanism by acknowledging the contingency of all action while at the same time allowing the rhetor the power to respond to those shifting circumstances" (Geisler, 7). Yet again, agency is figured as context dependent, but this is only a mild impediment to be overcome by the power of invention, here unquestionably possessed by the rhetor.

10 That paper is Gunn's, which we produce here in full because it is brief:

> In their epilogue to the popular textbook, *Contemporary Rhetorical Theory: A Reader*, John Louis Lucaites and Celeste Michelle Condit sketch an imaginary debate among two camps of rhetorical scholars: On the left, we have a number of "postmodern" rhetoricians who argue that the agency of rhetors is "prestructured" by ideology; on the other left, we have "modernists" who claim empirical evidence for human agency in the social and material world. Because of the assumed incommensurability of each position, Lucaites and Condit characterize the debate as a contemporary theoretical impasse that can be resolved only by "reconstituting our understanding of agency as a function of complex speaker-audience interactions." This magical third way is said to situate agency among lived relations in a "social interaction," thereby mediating the tensions between determinism and free will. Whether such a solution makes sense (in the words of Edward Schiappa, this seems to me like another proposal for "sophisticated modernism"), this imaginary debate continues to fuel the current hand-wringing over agency that the ARS Conference is designed to address. My position is that this debate is, in fact, a discipline-specific misrecognition or fantasy. Fantasies provide, simultaneously, a frame within which to exercise agency as well as a shield from the abject horror of contingency. In this light, my position on the concept of rhetorical agency is that it only became a critical concept at the threshold of its own fictional dissolution. As the caption point of a central crisis-fantasy particular to US rhetorical studies, the questioning of the rhetorical agent is, in fact, a generative or productive scholarly neurosis; in other words, the "question" of rhetorical agency is a fundamental topos for scholarly invention that forestalls any satisfactory answer. The debate-fantasy over the possibility of agency has also been a shield from the investigation of unconscious suasive processes as well (processes that challenge the assumptions of the debate, of course). Functioning much as the concept of "text" did the late 1970s and 1980s (documented in the widely read edited collection, *Texts in Context*), the question of rhetorical agency provides a frame for scholarly endeavor that, if dissolved, risks a direct confrontation with the madness of irrelevance.

11 Douglas Walton notes that "the straw man fallacy occurs when an arguer's position is misrepresented by being misquoted, exaggerated, or otherwise distorted" (22). Claiming that agency is a fantasy is not the same as claiming it is not real, nor does a failure to recognize the phantasmic nature of subjectivity reduce to the charge of cowardice.

12 In fact, her reading is far from correct as well. Gunn never says agency is an illusion, nor does he advocate its abandonment, yet his position is characterized as an amoral, nihilistic embrace of a ridiculous "postmodern" position. Part of the problem is semantic: "illusion" is a misreading of "fantasy," which in psychoanalytic theory is not "fancy" but that which yields the self or "I" a positive consistency. Fantasy can be understood as a rhetorical structure that retroactively assigns meaning to human, sensory encounter and explains to us what we desire (see Gunn, "Refitting Fantasy"; Gunn, "On Dead Subjects"; Lundberg; Žižek, *Plague* 3–44).

13 Nor do any of these thinkers have an easy relationship with the term "postmodern," or with many of the presuppositions attached to postmodern theories by anxious rhetoricians. Foucault, for example, was suspicious of the imprecision and arbitrariness associated with the term. In response to a question regarding the specter of postmodernity he quips:

> What are we calling postmodernity? I am not up to date. . . . I've never understood what
> was meant . . . by the word modernity . . . neither do I grasp the kind of problems intended
> by this term—or how they would be common to people thought of as being "postmodern."

(Foucault, "Critical Theory," 33–34) Lacan (a thinker whose work informed much of Gunn's original statement on agency) can also only be framed as a "postmodernist" by ignoring significant portions of his work on the significance of the symbolic, the name of the father, and his account of subject formation (see Gunn, "On Dead Subjects"; Lundberg). Secondary interpreters of Lacan's such as Žižek, Badiou, and Laclau argue that his work provides an *antidote* to the problems of postmodernism by allowing a new theorization of the universal or by preventing a descent into sheer romanticism (see Badiou; Žižek, *Ticklish*).

14 We find the absence of any mention of Karlyn Kohrs Campbell's plenary session paper conspicuous. In "Agency: Promiscuous and Protean," Campbell likens herself to Odysseus steering among the rhetorical tradition, the Charybdis of poststructural feminist theory, and the Scylla of "Barthes, Derrida, and Foucault" (1). The result is a provocative and insightful rumination on rhetoric's relation to social change. Although we disagree with some of her claims, Campbell's paper most clearly and directly articulates the challenge that we face as rhetorical critics in an increasingly "postmodern" world, and is the most faithful report of the agency issues discussed at the ARS conference.

15 Many so-called "postmodern" positions seem to call for, paradoxically, the transcendence of transcendence, for escaping or breaking free from any dialectical ontology. Nevertheless, in fairness to Greene we should underscore that his materialist project includes both a critique of the romantic doctrine behind the turn to hermeneutics (ethics) as well as a "de-Hegelizing" of Marxism (politics). In personal communication, Greene noted that his political commitments and "theory work together to challenge the ontology of mediation that is the real locus of the disciplinary debate on such things as humanist/posthumanist," and warned us not to disarticulate the political and ethical. We agree that mediation is central to the disciplinary debate on agency; however, we are not ready to abandon it as a method, an aim, or as a general rhetorical project.

16 This is obviously related to Gaonkar's global warning about "big" rhetoric (see Gaonkar; and Schiappa).

17 Regrettably, atheism has been the unfortunate tendency in rhetorical studies. As a result, our understanding of religion and theology is overly-simplistic and narrow. We are encouraged, however, by the Spring 2005 issue of *Rhetoric and Public Affairs*, which explores the relationship between religious faith and scholarly invention.

18 The most significant founding work in this regard is Pseudo-Dionysius the Areopagite's "Divine Names."

Works Cited

Badiou, Alain. "Manifesto of Affirmationism." Trans. Barbara Fulks. *Lacanian Ink* 24 (12 March 2005). www.lacan.com/frameXXIV5.htm.

Bernauer, James. "Michel Foucault's Ecstatic Thinking." *The Final Foucault*. Ed. James Bernauer and David Rasmussen. Cambridge: MIT P, 1988. 45–82.

Best, Steven and Douglas Kellner. *Postmodern Theory: Critical Interrogations*. New York: Guilford, 1991.

———. *The Postmodern Turn*. New York: Guilford, 1997.

Biesecker, Barbara. "Coming to Terms with Recent Attempts to Write Women into the History of Rhetoric." *Philosophy and Rhetoric* 25.2 (1992): 140–61.

———. "Rethinking the Rhetorical Situation from within the Thematic of Difference." *Philosophy and Rhetoric* 22.2 (1989): 110–30.

Braude, Ann. *Radical Spirits: Spiritualism and Women's Rights in Nineteenth-Century America.* Boston: Beacon P, 1989.

Campbell, Karlyn Kohrs. "Agency: Promiscuous and Protean." *Communication and Critical/Cultural Studies* 2.1 (2005): 1–19.

Caputo, John. *Deconstruction in a Nutshell.* New York: Fordham UP, 1997.

———. *The Prayers and Tears of Jacques Derrida: Religion without Religion.* Bloomington: Indiana UP, 1997.

Derrida, Jacques. *Margins of Philosophy.* Trans. Alan Bass. Chicago: U of Chicago P, 1982.

———. *Specters of Marx: The State of Debt, the Work of Mourning, and the New International.* Trans. Peggy Kamuf. New York: Routledge, 1994.

Foucault, Michel. "Critical Theory/Intellectual History." Trans. Jeremy Harding. *Michel Foucault: Politics, Philosophy, Culture.* Ed. Lawrence Kritzman. New York: Routledge, 1988. 17–46.

———. "Foucault Response to Sartre." *Foucault Live.* Trans. and Ed. Sylvere Lotringer. New York: Semiotext(e), 1989. 35–44.

———. "The Return of Morality." Trans. David Levin and Isabelle Lorenz. *Michel Foucault: Politics, Philosophy, Culture.* Ed. Lawrence Kritzman. New York: Routledge, 1988. 242–54.

Gaonkar, Dilip Parameshwar. "The Idea of Rhetoric in the Rhetoric of Science." *Southern Communication Journal* 58.4 (1993): 258–95.

Geisler, Cheryl. "How Ought We to Understand the Concept of Rhetorical Agency? Report from the ARS." *Rhetoric Society Quarterly* 34.3 (2004): 9–17.

Greene, Ronald Walter. "Rhetoric and Capitalism: Rhetorical Agency as Communicative Labor." *Philosophy and Rhetoric* 37.3 (2004): 188–206.

Guiley, Rosemary Ellen. *Harper's Encyclopedia of Mystical and Paranormal Experience.* New York: HarperSanFrancisco, 1991.

Gunn, Joshua. "On Dead Subjects: A Rejoinder to Lundberg on (a) Psychoanalytic Rhetoric." *Quarterly Journal of Speech* 90.4 (2004): 501–14.

———. *Modern Occult Rhetoric: Mass Media and the Drama of Secrecy in the Twentieth Century.* Tuscaloosa: U of Alabama P, 2005.

———. "Refitting Fantasy: Psychoanalysis, Subjectivity, and Talking to the Dead." *Quarterly Journal of Speech* 90.1 (2004): 1–23.

Heidegger, Martin. "Letter on Humanism." *Basic Writings.* Rev. ed. Trans. Rank A. Capuzzi and J. Glenn Gray and Ed. David Farrell Kress. San Francisco: HarperSanFrancisco, 1993. 217–65.

———. "The Question Concerning Technology." *Basic Writings.* Rev. ed. Trans. William Lovitt and Ed. David Farrell Krell. San Francisco: HarperSanFrancisco, 1993. 311–41.

"History of the Talking Board." *Museum of Talking Boards.com* (3 March 2005). http://museu moftalkingboards.com/history.html.

Jameson, Fredric. *Postmodernism, or, the Cultural Logic of Late Capitalism.* Durham: Duke UP, 1992.

Lacan, Jacques. *Écrits: A Selection.* Trans. and Ed. Bruce Fink. New York: W. W. Norton and Company, 2004.

———. *Encore: The Seminar of Jacques Lacan, Book XX: On Feminine Sexuality, the Limits of Love and Knowledge, 1972–1973.* Trans. Bruce Fink and Ed. Jacques-Alain Miller. New York: W. W. Norton, 1998.

———. *The Seminar of Jacques Lacan, Book III: The Psychoses, 1955–1956.* Trans. Russell Grigg and Ed. Jacques-Alain Miller. New York: W. W. Norton and Company, 1993.

Leff, Michael C. "The Idea of Rhetoric as Interpretive Practice: A Humanist's Response to Gaonkar." *Southern Communication Journal* 58.4 (1993): 296–300.

———. "Tradition and Agency in Humanistic Rhetoric." *Philosophy and Rhetoric* 36.2 (2003): 135–47.

Leff, Michael C. and Fred J. Kauffeld, eds. *Texts in Context: Critical Dialogues on Significant Episodes in American Political Rhetoric.* Davis: Hermagoras P, 1989.

Leff, Michael C. and Andrea A. Lunsford. "Afterwords: A Dialogue." *Rhetoric Society Quarterly* 34.3 (2004): 55–67.

Lucaites, John Louis, Celeste Michelle Condit, and Sally Caudill, eds. *Contemporary Rhetorical Theory: A Reader.* New York: Guilford, 1999.

Lundberg, Christian. "The Royal Road Not Taken: Joshua Gunn's 'Refitting Fantasy: Psychoanalysis, Subjectivity, and Talking to the Dead' and Lacan's Symbolic Order." *Quarterly Journal of Speech* 90.4 (2004): 495–501.

Morrissey, Stephen and Stephen Street. "Ouija Board, Ouija Board." Perf. Morrissey. *Bona Drag.* New York: Sire, 1989.

Peters, John Durham. *Speaking into the Air: A History of the Idea of Communication.* Chicago: U of Chicago P, 1999.

Pseudo-Dionysius the Areopagite. "Divine Names." *Pseudo Dionysius: The Complete Works.* Trans. and Ed. Jean Leclercq. Mahwah: Paulist P, 1987. 47–132.

Sartre, Jean-Paul. *Nausea.* Trans. Lloyd Alexander. New York: New Directions, 1964.

Schiappa, Edward. "Second Thoughts on the Critiques of Big Rhetoric." *Philosophy and Rhetoric* 34.3 (2001): 206–74.

Scott, Robert L. "On Viewing Rhetoric as Epistemic." *Central States Speech Journal* 18.1 (1967): 9–17.

Sextus. "Against the Schoolmasters" [excerpt]. *The Older Sophists.* Trans. Michael J. O'Brien and Ed. Rosamond Kent Sprague. Columbia: U of South Carolina P, 1972. 18.

Walton, Douglas. *Informal Logic: A Handbook for Critical Argumentation.* New York: Cambridge UP, 1989.

Žižek, Slavoj. *The Plague of Fantasies.* New York: Verso, 1997.

———. *The Ticklish Subject: The Absent Centre of Political Ontology.* New York: Verso, 2000.

TEACHING THE POSTMODERN RHETOR

Continuing the Conversation on Rhetorical Agency

CHERYL GEISLER

A compliment must be paid to Gunn and Lundberg for inviting readers to consider what Ouija Board experiences can tell us about rhetorical agency. Though they have found little to compliment in my synthesis of the discussion of rhetorical agency at the ARS in 2003, I believe readers can find something interesting in pursuing their analogy between the Ouija Board and rhetoric.

My own time with the Ouija Board was short. Eight years old, visiting a more sophisticated cousin, I gingerly touched the planchette with all the emotions Gunn and Lundberg's piece reawakened. As the planchette haltingly spelled out responses to my cousin's questions, my conviction grew that we were in contact with demonic forces. Finally, and over my cousin's protests, I pulled away . . . and I haven't been back since.

Gunn and Lundberg suggest that a fear of duplicity drives a great deal of the ambivalence we feel about the Ouija Board—we worry about being tricked into believing we have made contact with the world beyond. Mired in the humanistic belief that some*one* must be pushing the planchette, our unease grows as we cannot pin down the culprit. Like Ouija players, Gunn and Lundberg suggest, many rhetoricians do not feel at ease until they can associate the cause of rhetorical movement with a specific rhetor. This interesting analysis provides much food for thought as we continue the conversation on rhetorical agency.

Rhetor as Postmodern Agent

Before we delve a bit more into the Ouija metaphor, I want to address some concerns that Gunn and Lundberg have raised in their response to my ARS report. From my perspective, they have engaged in an interesting misreading of my synthesis when they accuse me of an uncharitable treatment of rhetoricians who have embraced postmodern theory. Readers of the ARS papers on agency (www.comm.umn.edu/ARS/) will find that it does not take long to feel how long a shadow has been cast on the discussion of agency by the debate over postmodernism. For this reason, in my synthesis, I portrayed postmodernism as the historical starting point for the issue of agency, beginning with Dilip Gaonkar's 1993 piece arguing against a humanistic "ideology of agency" and for a concept of agency more in keeping with the "postmodern condition" (263).

Rather than rejecting that critique, however, I suggested that most of the interesting work at the ARS had taken it as a departure point, including my own work describing rhetors as occupying "a subject position strategically fragmented in order to get work done." Gunn and Lundberg seem both to acknowledge and agree with this analysis. Despite these agreements, however, much of their response is aimed at chastising me for singling Gunn out as a representative of the postmodernist position and ridiculing him and other postmodernists for entertaining the claim that agency is illusionary.

I take as useful both Gunn and Lundberg's suggestion that postmodernism is too variable to pigeon-hole and that the term itself may be inappropriate. But I would demur to their characterization that I "strongly argue[d] against what [I]/she sees as an unproductive response to the critique of the self-transparent, autonomous agent: the 'abandonment' of the concept or idea of agency." A more careful reading of my piece would suggest that while I do report on the discussion concerning the claim that agency is illusionary, I do not attribute this claim to Gunn alone, I do not identify this claim as a particularly postmodern claim, and I do not treat this claim flippantly. Indeed, I saw numerous participants at the ARS struggling with this possibility—in particular, I named Condit as well as Gunn.

Gunn and Lundberg suggest that no postmodernist ever seriously entertained the idea that "rhetors do not produce effects." Whether they consider themselves postmodernists, I cannot say, but the lack of rhetorical efficacy seems to me to be just the possibility that their Ouija Board metaphor invites us to consider:

> As anyone who has "played" with a talking board will attest, the fun orbits suspicion: either one deceives, or is deceived by, the comedium, or one is

relatively unable to locate the seat of agency: is my partner moving this thing? Am I moving it without knowing it? Is it possible that some unseen spirit—a passed relative or worse, an evil genius—is moving the planchette (and therefore, us)?

As Gunn and Lundberg here suggest, unease over who moves the planchette is at the heart of the Ouija Board experience. One of the possibilities that we entertain, they suggest, is that we, the rhetor, do not move it: that it may be our "co-medium" or "some unseen spirit" who is "moving the planchete (and therefore, us)." Ultimately Gunn and Lundberg argue that we must remain "undecided" or "agnostic" about who is moving the planchette, a point to which I will return.

As Gunn and Lundberg clearly understand, I and many others at the ARS find the teaching mission of rhetoric as a profession to be problematized by the postmodern agent. Leff and Lunsford may find these problematics to be grounds for rejecting the postmodern critique, as Gunn and Lundberg suggest—I will let them speak for themselves. I do not. Indeed, I raised the following questions about what our profession should do—questions which Gunn and Lundberg seem to take as merely rhetorical—in all seriousness:

> If rhetoric *as an interpretive theory* describes a variety of rhetorical positions, some with more and some with less rhetorical agency, how can rhetoric *as a productive art* incorporate that knowledge into our mission? What shall we, as teachers, say to our students about their potential and obligations with respect to becoming rhetorical agents? What shall we, as critics, say to our fellow citizens about their potential and obligations with respect to being rhetorical agents?

That is, I am *not* here asserting that we should abandon the lessons of the postmodern agent because we might, as Leff and Lunsford have it, run "the risk of theorizing [our]selves out of jobs." Gunn and Lundberg, correctly I think, reject that argument that we should tailor our scholarship in order to remain comfortable as a profession. I *am* asserting, however, that the postmodern agent creates problems for rhetoric as a teaching profession, problems that I firmly believe we need to take seriously. Sadly, however, Gunn and Lundberg do not take up this challenge of retheorizing teaching. Thus, their response, while useful in clarifying the nature of rhetorical agency, is not yet up the challenge of following out its implications.

Whether one finds the implications for teaching compelling or not may depend upon the disciplinary differences that I noted to be right below the surface at the ARS meeting. Even in Gaonkar's original terms, the pursuit of a critique of humanism seemed to require that we set aside questions of rhetoric as a practical or design art.[1] Gunn and Lundberg seem to make much the same point when they in effect say, "if the postmodern agent causes problems for the teaching of rhetoric, so be it!" Saying anything else, they claim, would be "less than honest."

I want to suggest, however, that accepting the mantle of "rhetorician" will ultimately require more from us than just "sit[ting] patiently and with wonder" to see what happens next. We have some real work to do as a profession to retheorize teaching in a way that we can both explain to those outside the profession and justify to each other. My own work on the history and practices of the professions (Geisler, *Academic*) has taught me that the long-term health of any academic profession depends on a close yoking of the generation of new knowledge through scholarship and the teaching of knowledge and practice in the classroom. I recognize that many of my colleagues are uncomfortable with this forthright embrace of a teaching mission. I remember years ago hearing the advice of one colleague to another at an NCA convention: "Never admit you teach speech!" Gunn and Lundberg have asked that we take the postmodern critique seriously. I agree. But I would also ask that they and others take the question of teaching just as seriously in return. And, indeed, Gunn and Lundberg's Ouija Board metaphor helps us make some real headway in this direction.

Teaching the Postmodern Rhetor

Some might argue that the acceptance of the postmodern critique has no serious consequences for the classroom. Accepting that we are always already fragmented, we could argue that it is not necessary to follow out the logic of our scholarly beliefs when we turn to the pursuit of daily bread through teaching. Yet if we demand consistency in the scholarly sphere—in the form of the kind of good sound argument that Gunn and Lundberg are calling for—I can see no good grounds for abandoning it when we move to the teaching sphere. So, if you will allow me, for the moment, to pursue consistency, it has seemed to me for a long time entirely uncomfortable to recognize the emerging scholarship on agency and pursue teaching in the traditional way.

Gunn and Lundberg's Ouija Board metaphor has been particularly useful in pushing further at the issues involved with teaching rhetoric. That is, what might it mean to teach the Ouija player? How is teaching students to engage in rhetorical performance like teaching the Ouija Board performance? There are two implications I would like to explore here.

To begin with, the comparison between rhetoric and the Ouija Board brings to the fore the conditions for performance. If touching the planchette is equivalent to engaging with a situation in which rhetorical agency is at work—the planchette is moving—what about all those situations in which one of us, like my 8-year-old self, just walks away?

As rhetoricians, we have tended to assume that students come to us already positioned for rhetorical work—or, sometimes, already positioned outside of it. But does not such an assumption incorrectly accept as "natural" students' own sense of positioning? Pursuing the Ouija Board metaphor productively, once we recognize that all kinds of things have to be in place before the student can place her hands on the planchette, what might that mean for the way we teach her?

I have been teaching proposal writing for nearly a decade now. Interestingly the same issue of engagement comes to the fore in proposal writing as it does with the Ouija. A few of my students come to the course ready to touch the planchette—that is, eager to make a proposal. The majority, however, are more ambivalent. Most think they have nothing to offer, no ideas worth proposing, no one interested in hearing their proposals, no credibility in putting a proposal forward. As if that planchette were better reserved for other more exalted beings. So teaching proposal writing is, to begin with, a recruitment task, "Come on, you can do it. Just give it a try." Just like my cousin recruited me to the Ouija Board all those years ago. . . .

Obviously, if my recruitment fails, the planchette will not be moved. I do find students in my proposal writing class who cannot be convinced to "give it a try." In essence, they take a pass on rhetoric; occasions for rhetorical performance never develop; the karotic moment never materializes. I am not sure how Gunn and Lundberg feel about such developments, but I worry about them in my classroom, especially if they happen too often.

So I do think we want to make a case, most of the time, for taking hold of the planchette. On what grounds can that recruitment be undertaken? How, in other words, might we answer my earlier question,

> What shall we, as teachers, say to our students about their potential and obligations with respect to becoming rhetorical agents?

Looking at the Ouija Board player, minimally I think we could say that we don't know whether, if you put your hands on the Ouija Board, you will move it. But we do know that if you don't put your hands on the Ouija Board, it won't move. By extension, we can say to the potential rhetor: I don't know whether, if you engage with this rhetorical situation, you will succeed in the way you intend. But we do know that if you don't engage, nothing will happen.

Although such an assurance may seem too mild to engender the kind of enthusiastic engagement with rhetoric that some would desire, it does have the kind of honesty that Gunn and Lundberg call for. Furthermore, repeated over and over again to a whole generation of students, it might just serve as at least part of an account for rhetoric as a profession.

The Ouija Board metaphor suggests we can go even a bit further than this minimalist argument. For teaching has to involve more than just recruitment, more than just getting the player to latch on and then standing back to see how things turn out. Once the student is in the game, so to speak, there is still work to be done.

In a traditional classroom where we assumed that our students were driving the planchette, our tasks as teachers were fairly obvious. We would try to teach them how to steer the planchette to their purposes. We would try to inform them of the ethical responsibilities of driving. We would try to show them the pragmatic consequences of different moves. All of this changes once we accept that our students are not in control. Unlike what some of the hand-wringing at the ARS might suggest, however, there are things we can endeavor to do.

What I so like about the Ouija Board metaphor, in fact, is that it suggests exactly the situation in which I try to place my students when they write proposals. Agency does not lie in the hands of any one person at the proposal writing table, but rather lies in the interaction among them. It is a complex interplay as one player at the planchette makes subtle movements, the other player picks up and responds, reinforcing or resisting, back and forth through minute by minute adjustments that eventually lead to an outcome that neither player could have, in advance predicted. But the unpredictability of the outcome does not preclude teaching—in fact, it demands it.

While the act of writing a proposal may culminate in a rhetorical performance, in many if not most cases, the argument is won or lost in the interactions leading up to that performance rather than in the performance itself. Prosaically, I tell my students they must do the "legwork" to see a proposal succeed—they must get out there and talk to the players, find out what they are thinking, considering, and how they may feel about the proposal they have in mind. But such legwork does far more than inform them of what their co-medium is thinking. It actually sets in motion a process of interactive engagement in which neither the rhetor nor her audience remains unchanged. The student usually learns of issues, circumstances and concerns that lead to modifications of the proposal itself. The so-called audience learns about the proposer herself, measures her credibility, considers her ideas, and deepens her understanding of the current exigency as the rhetor sees it. If all is working well, by the time of the actual proposal, the text has become confirmatory of an understanding of common purpose that has already been worked out between rhetor and audience.[2] In Ouija Board terms, both players have cooperated to bring about the performance in ways that make accounting for the source of agency a moot point.

The strategies for recruitment and legwork I've described here may not be part of the traditional cannons of rhetoric, but they do seem to be useful additions for teaching the postmodern rhetor. Once the autonomous agent has been denaturalized, once we recognize the complex and fragmented forces that necessarily come into play in any rhetorical performance, we as members of the profession of rhetoric are far from in danger of losing our jobs. Indeed, tasks such as helping students first to engage with and then to participate in a more appropriately theorized rhetoric leave us plenty to do. And, like the Ouija Board player, we may not be able to know how the movements of our classroom planchette will be related to our teaching intentions. But—like every other rhetor—we do know the costs of walking away from the game.

Acknowledgments

I would like to thank Diane Davis, Jeff Rice, and Collin Brooke for their feedback on earlier drafts of this article.

Notes

1 Much attention has actually been paid lately in the pages of *RSQ* to the roots of the disciplinary ambivalence over teaching. See for example, Crowley and, of course, Leff and Lunsford.

2 The importance and function of interaction in advance of rhetorical performance may have been best understood in the field of technical and professional communication. See work by Spilka and Harper for examples.

Works Cited

Crowley, Sharon. "Communications Skills and a Brief Rapprochement of Rhetoricians." *Rhetoric Society Quarterly* 34.1 (2004): 89–104.

Gaonkar, Dilip. "The Idea of Rhetoric in the Rhetoric of Science." *Southern Communication Journal* 58.4 (1993): 258–95.

Geisler, Cheryl. *Academic Literacy and the Nature of Expertise: Reading, Writing, and Knowing in Academic Philosophy*. Hillsdale: Lawrence Erlbaum Associates, 1994.

———. "How Ought We to Understand the Concept of Rhetorical Agency? Report from the ARS." *Rhetoric Society Quarterly* 34.3 (2004): 9–18.

Harper, Richard H. R. *Inside the IMF*. San Diego: Academic P, 1998.

Leff, Michael and Andrea A. Lunsford. "Afterwords: A Dialogue." *Rhetoric Society Quarterly* 34.3 (2004): 55–68.

Spilka, R. (1990). "Orality and Literacy in the Workplace: Process- and Text-Based Strategies for Multiple Audience Adaptation." *Journal of Business and Technical Communication* 4.1 (1990): 44–67.

11

Unframing Models of Public Distribution[1]

From Rhetorical Situation to Rhetorical Ecologies

JENNY EDBAUER (RICE)

[P]laces . . . are best thought of not so much as enduring sites but as *moments of encounter*, not so much as "presents", fixed in space and time, but as variable events; twists and fluxes of interrelation. Even when the intent is to hold places still and motionless, caught in a cat's cradle of networks that are out to quell unpredictability, success is rare, and then only for a while. Grand porticos and columns framing imperial triumphs become theme parks. Areas of wealth and influence become slums.

—Ash Amin and Nigel Thrift (30)

Elemental Frameworks

In his multifaceted description of what constitutes a public, Michael Warner explains why certain notions of "public communication" have done us such a disservice. He writes:

No single text can create a public. Nor can a single voice, a single genre, or even a single medium. All are insufficient . . . since a public is understood to be an ongoing space of encounter for discourse. It is not texts themselves that create publics, but the concatenation of texts through time. . . . Between the discourse that comes before and the discourse that comes after, one must postulate some kind of link. And the link has a social character; it is not mere consecutiveness in time, but a context of interaction.

(62)

Warner tells us that this is why the overly simplified models of communication— often represented through the triangulated terms *sender, receiver, text*—are nothing short of a conceptual paradox. He continues, "A public seems to be self-organized by discourse, but in fact requires preexisting forms and channels of circulation" (75). Herein lies the paradox: sender-receiver models of public communication tend to identify a kind of homeostatic relationship, which simultaneously abstracts the operation of social links and circulation. The triangle of sender, receiver, text misses the concatenations that come to constitute Warner's version of a public.

Of course, oversimplified sender-receiver models of public communication have been productively complicated by theories like Lloyd Bitzer's notion of the rhetorical situation, which theorized the contextual dimensions of rhetoric. As Bitzer explains, "When I ask, What is a rhetorical situation?, I want to know the nature of those contexts in which speakers or writers create rhetorical discourse" ("Rhetorical" 382). This starting point places the question of rhetoric—and the defining characteristic of *rhetoricalness*—squarely within the scene of a situational context. In his explicit definition, Bitzer writes that a rhetorical situation is "a natural context of persons, events, objects, relations, and an exigence which strongly invites utterances" (385). As many commentators of Bitzer have pointed out, his definition locates exigencies in the external conditions of material and social circumstances. Bitzer himself tells us that exigencies are "located in reality, are objective and publicly observable historic facts in the world we experience, are therefore available for scrutiny by an observer or critic who *attends to them*" ("Rhetorical" 390; emphasis mine). In Bitzer's schema, rhetoricians answer an invitation to solve a problem through discourse, which is then rendered as rhetorical discourse. Richard Vatz's infamous critique against Bitzer's "realism" challenges the notion that exigencies exist in any autonomous sense. Whereas Bitzer suggests that the rhetor *discovers* exigencies that already exist, Vatz argues that exigencies are *created* for audiences through the rhetor's work.

In yet another critique of Bitzer, Craig Smith and Scott Lybarger argue that rhetorical situation involves a plurality of exigencies and complex relations between the audience and a rhetorician's interest. In this way, Smith and Lybarger revise Bitzer's relatively autonomous notion of exigence by making it more interactive with other elements of the situation. They offer an example of this reconceptualized situation in their analysis of two 1989 speeches from President George Bush concerning the "war on drugs." Using a modified version of Bitzer's model, Smith and Lybarger identify three main elements of Bush's speeches: exigences, audiences, and constraints. At the time of these speeches, they write, polls reported that the public felt drug abuse was a serious problem. Media reports "helped increase the interest in the problem by providing direct knowledge of it. Bush took advantage of an attitude that the press reinforced" (203). Accordingly, this public concern constrained Bush's choices of which public exigences to address in his official attention. At the same time, of course, Bush's articulation of "the drug crisis" helped to reinforce this exigence *as* a rhetorical problem that must be addressed. Smith and Lybarger emphasize the mutuality of exigence from the positions of rhetorician and audience, reflecting how both elements help to create the sense of problem. This is a careful modification of Bitzer's model in that the authors link the articulation of exigence(s) to multiple agents and constraints.

In short, Bitzer's theories, as well as the critiques and modifications like those above, have generated a body of scholarship that stretches our own notions of "rhetorical publicness" into a *contextual* framework that permanently troubles sender-receiver models. Returning to Warner for just a moment, however, we might still ask whether notions of rhetorical situation adequately account for the "constitutive circulation" of rhetoric in the social field. Do theories of rhetorical situation allow us to theorize how "concatenation of texts through time" help to create publics? Barbara Biesecker's critique of these models suggests that perhaps the answer is *no*. According to Biesecker, the problem with many takes on rhetorical situation is their tendency to conceptualize rhetoric within a scene of already-formed, already-discrete individuals. For Biesecker, this problem can be seen in the way these models often treat "audience" as a rather unproblematic and obvious site. The trouble, she writes, is that:

> if we posit the audience of any rhetorical event as no more than a conglomeration of subjects whose identity is fixed prior to the rhetorical event itself, then . . . the power of rhetoric is circumscribed: it has the potency to influence an audience, to realign their allegiances, but not to form new identities.
>
> (111)

Here we arrive at an un(der)explored line of inquiry into one of rhetoric's most familiar and most revered theoretical-pedagogical paradigms. Biesecker's critique points to the way in which various models of rhetorical situation tend to describe rhetoric as a totality of discrete elements: audience, rhetor, exigence, constraints, and text. In other words, despite their differences, these various takes on rhetorical situation tend to be rooted in the views of rhetorics as *elemental conglomerations*.

Louise Weatherbee Phelps proposes a similar critique in her argument that many theories of discourse (and, by extension, we could also say of rhetoric) represent discourse as "a set of discrete components (units and correlated functions) based on variations and elaborations of the traditional communication triangle" (60). Rhetoric and discourse thus become conceptualized as a collection of elements—often called by such names as speaker-audience-message, ethos-pathos-logos, or rhetor-audience-constraints-exigence. Although such element-based theories of discourse have important explanatory power, continues Phelps, there is also great power in describing

> how an element (e.g., the writer as "ethos") *is discriminated from a flux* and perceived as invariant, stable, and autonomous. . . . Natural and traditional categories acquire greater depth and scope when we . . . temporalize them, interpret them as metaphors, expand their range of variation, multiply their interpretants, pursue their logic to the limit, or treat them in historical-institutional terms.
>
> (60; emphasis mine)

Rather than seeing rhetoric as the totality of its discrete elements, Phelps's critique seeks to recontextualize those elements in a wider sphere of active, historical, and lived processes. That is, the elements of a rhetorical situation can be reread against the historical fluxes in which they move. While the incarnations of rhetorical situation create complex frameworks for understanding a rhetoric's operation in a particular social scene, therefore, both Biesecker and Phelps interrogate the effects of building a model around a "conglomeration" of distinct elements in relation to one another.

The weakness of "conglomeration" models is tacitly exposed in Smith and Lybarger's analysis of Bush's "war on drugs" speeches, for instance. When Smith and Lybarger discuss the exigences involved in the "war on drugs," they point to audience perceptions, Bush's speeches, media images, and the various constraints of all participants. They emphasize the important role that perception plays, since "each auditor will have a perception of the rhetor *and* the message in addition to a perception of the issues, [which means that] rhetorical communication is always in a state of flux that requires the critic to move beyond the strict realism of Bitzer" (200). The exigence is more like a complex of various audience/speaker perceptions and institutional or material constraints. Indeed, because "exigencies are everywhere shot through with perceptions" (197), there can be no pure exigence that does not involve various mixes of felt interests. Their analysis thus suggests a problem of location; the exigence does not exist per se, but is instead an amalgamation of processes and encounters: concerns about safe neighborhoods, media images, encounters of everyday life in certain places, concerns about re-election, articulations of problems and the circulation of those articulations, and so forth. The exigence is not properly located in any element of the model. Instead, what we dub *exigence* is more like a shorthand way of describing a series of events. The rhetorical situation is part of what we might call, borrowing from Phelps, an ongoing social flux. Situation bleeds into the concatenation of public interaction. Public interactions bleed into wider social processes. *The elements of rhetorical situation simply bleed.*

In order to rethink rhetorical publicness as a context of interaction, therefore, this article proposes an augmentation to our popular conceptual frameworks of rhetorical situation. Rather than primarily speaking of rhetoric through the terministic lens of conglomerated elements, I look towards a framework of *affective ecologies* that recontextualizes rhetorics in their temporal, historical, and lived fluxes. In what follows, I want to propose a revised strategy for theorizing public rhetorics (and rhetoric's publicness) as a circulating ecology of effects, enactments, and events by shifting the lines of focus from *rhetorical situation* to *rhetorical ecologies*. Like Biesecker, Phelps, and Warner, I want to add the dimensions of history and movement (back) into our visions/versions of rhetoric's public situations, reclaiming rhetoric from artificially *elementary* frameworks. While one framework does not undermine the other, I argue that this ecological model allows us to more fully theorize rhetoric as a public(s) creation.

Situs, Situation, and the Idea of Place

We might begin this conceptual augmentation by exploring some etymological tropes that remain buried within our popular theories. Consider the following: tracking the Latin roots of "situation" brings us to the key words *situare* and *situs*, both of which resonate with our definitions for location, site, and place. The Latin word *situs* is closely tied to the originary position of objects. (Significantly, this term still has currency in legal vocabulary as reference to the places in which a crime or accident occurs, or the location of property.) By definition, then, *situs* implies a bordered, fixed space-location. Consequently, the concept of "rhetorical situation" is appropriately named insofar as the models of rhetorical situation describe the scene of rhetorical action as "located" around the exigence that generates a response. We thus find a connection between certain models of rhetorical situation and a sense of *place*. But the public existence of *situs* is complicated. As Steven Shaviro points out in *Connected*, the social does not reside in fixed sites, but rather in a networked space of flows and connections. "The predominant form of human interaction . . . is *networking*," he writes (131). Moreover, this "networked life" is a matter of actual, historically shaped forces of flows themselves. Shaviro explains:

> [T]he network is not a disembodied information pattern nor a system of frictionless pathways over which any message whatsoever can be neutrally conveyed. Rather, the force of all messages, *as they accrete over time*, determines the very shape of the network. The meaning of a message cannot be isolated from its mode of propagation, from the way it harasses me, attacks me, or parasitically invades me.
>
> (24; emphasis mine)

Temporarily bracketing the rather ominous perspective that Shaviro brings to this sense of connection, we find that networks involve a different kind of habitation in the social field. To say that we are connected is another way of saying that we are never outside the networked interconnection of forces, energies, rhetorics, moods, and experiences. In other words, our practical consciousness is never outside the prior and ongoing structures of feeling that shape the social field.

At the same time, life-as-network also means that the social field is not comprised of discrete *sites* but from events that are shifting and moving, grafted onto and connected with other events. According to Shaviro, "The space [of networks] can be exhilarating, disorienting, or oppressive, but in any case it is quite different from the space of places" (131). Our sense of place tends to remain rooted in an imaginary that describes communities as a collection of discrete elements, like houses, families, yards, streets, and neighborhoods. Nevertheless, Shaviro explains that place should be characterized less in terms of this sense of community (discrete elements taken together), and more in the interactions *between* those elements—their encounters in the crease and folds:

> What's crucial about the space of places is rather something other than "community": the fact that, in large urban agglomerations, networking is less important than . . . *contact*: the serendipitous encounters between strangers. . . . These sorts of encounters happen in the pedestrian-friendly spaces of older large cities. . . . The space of places is less that of nostalgically idealized traditional communities than that of turbulent urban modernity.
>
> (132–33)

In this way, place becomes decoupled from the notion of *situs*, or fixed (series of) locations, and linked instead to the in-between en/action of events and encounters. Place becomes a space of contacts, which are always changing and never discrete. The contact between two people on a busy city street is never simply a matter of those two bodies; rather, the two bodies carry with them the traces of effects from whole fields of culture and social histories. This is what it means to say that the social field is networked, connected, rather than a matter of place, sites, and home.

The notion of place has also recently become much more complicated in the theoretical frameworks of both cultural geographers and rhetoricians. In *Geographies of Writing*, for example, Nedra Reynolds argues that it is important "to understand geographies as embodied, and how the process of social construction of space occurs at the level of the body, not just at the level of the city or street or nation" (143). What we normally take as "sites" are not only comprised in a *situs* or fixed location. Reynolds explains that these "sites" are made up of affective encounters, experiences, and moods that cohere around material spaces. This is why sites are not just seen, but (perhaps even more so) they are felt (147). She gives the example of certain students with whom she worked during her study in Great Britain. When questioned about their city, the students had no trouble at all identifying the "bad" and "good" parts of town. Although these "good/bad" sites may even have fairly solid boundary markers (*east of the freeway, downtown, southside of town*), we might argue that these sites are not only comprised *as such* through their location or collection of elements. Instead, they obtain their descriptions as good/bad sites from the affective and embodied experiences that circulate: feelings of fear or comfort, for instance.

Even in those spaces that are more obvious examples of bordered sites, we find it increasingly difficult to speak in terms of fixed place. Take the example of cities, which cultural geographers Ash Amin and Nigel Thrift thoroughly rework in *Cities: Reimagining the Urban*. According to Amin and Thrift:

> [C]ontemporary cities are certainly not systems with their own internal coherence. The city's boundaries have become far too permeable and stretched, both geographically and socially, for it to be theorized as a whole.

The city has no completeness, no centre, no fixed parts. Instead, *it is an amalgam of often disjointed processes and social heterogeneity, a place of near and far connections, a concatenation of rhythms.*

(8; emphasis mine)

The city itself is less a *situs*, say Amin and Thrift, than a certain way of processing. In fact, it may be more appropriate to rethink "city" less as a noun (implying a *situs*) and more of a verb, as in *to city*. We *do city*, rather than exist *in the city*. Amin and Thrift argue that cities are more about movements and processes than the elements that materially construct their borders. They explain, "We certainly take circulation to be a central characteristic of the city. . . . [C]ities exist as a means of movement, as means to engineer *encounters* through collection, transport, and collation. They produce, thereby, a complex pattern of traces, a threadwork of intensities" (81). Amin and Thrift thus move away from the site-model framework of urban spaces, which renders the city as a kind of "container" for the unique elements that the city envelops.

The site-model would imagine, for example, that Austin is a container for the local elements within a given space, much as New York is a container for another set of local elements. Talking about those two different cities merely involves talking about the different elements held by the same (kind of) container called "city." New York might thus be described as containing more diverse population elements than Austin; or perhaps Austin could be described as a container for more conservative political elements. Yet Amin and Thrift suggest that the city-as-container does not adequately describe the city as an *amalgam of processes*, or as a circulation of encounters and actions. Rather than relying upon the container metaphor, therefore, they offer up an ecological metaphor in order to read the city:

[I]t is only by moving beyond the slower times of the city's built fabric—which seem to form a container—to the constant to and fro of the movements which sustain that fabric that we can begin to understand what a city is. . . . The city becomes a kind of weather system, a rapidly varying distribution of intensities.

(83)

Though cities are indeed *sites* (or can even be described in terms of borders, boundaries, and containers), Amin and Thrift suggest that these *sites* (the *situs*) are sustained by the amalgam of processes, which can be described in ecological terms of varying intensities of encounters and interactions—much like a weather system.

From Situs to Distribution

What does this discussion of cities and sites have to do with the rhetorical situation? For one thing, we find in the early models of rhetorical situation a notion of rhetoric as *taking place*, as if the rhetorical situation is one in which we can visit through a mapping of various elements: the relevant persons, events, objects, exigence, and utterances. But this place-based perspective becomes troubled when attending to the ecological models that cultural theorists (such as Shaviro, Reynolds, and Amin and Thrift) have developed alongside site-specific models of social processes. In *The Wealth of Reality: An Ecology of Composition*, Margaret Syverson performs one such alternative framework by arguing that writing is a radically *distributed* act, rather than an isolated act of creation among individual elements. According to Syverson:

> [T]he knowledge involved in "writing" . . . depends on activities and communications shared in interactions not only among people but also interactions between people and various structures in the environment, from physical landmarks to technological instruments to graphical representations. . . . Our theories of composition have been somewhat atomistic, focusing on individual writers, individual texts, isolated acts, processes, or artifacts.
>
> (8)

Syverson argues that rhetoric and composition "has posited a triangle of writer, text, and audience," which "has tended to single out the writer, the text, or the audience as the focus of analysis" (23). This isolated view fails to highlight what Syverson calls the emergent ecological process of writing. Rather than focusing on the familiar "triangle" that places various elements into a static relation with the other elements, Syverson maintains that "we can speak of the distribution of . . . [text composing] across physical, social, psychological, spatial, and temporal dimensions. . . . [T]he social dimensions of composition are distributed, embodied, emergent, and enactive" (23). Syverson's ecological approach places the "scene" of writing into a field that is distributed and socially situated. Writing is thus more than a matter of discrete elements (audience, a writer, text, tools, ideas) in static relation to one another (a writer types her ideas into a computer for an audience who reads the text). Rather, writing is distributed across a range of processes and encounters: the event of using a keyboard, the encounter of a writing body within a space of dis/comfort, the events of writing in an apathetic/energetic/distant/close group. A vocabulary of "distribution" points to how those elements are enacted and lived, how they are put into use, and what change comes from the in-processes-ness itself.[2]

Much like Syverson has done in her own work, we can tune to a model of public rhetoric that sets its sights across a wider social field of distribution. Such attunement is important if we want to account for rhetoric's (public) operation in the social field. That is, if we are to explore how rhetoric circulates in a "practical consciousness of a present kind, in a living and interrelating continuity," as Raymond Williams puts it (132), we need a model that allows us to discuss such movement. Rather than imagining the rhetorical situation in a relatively closed system, this distributed or ecological focus might begin to imagine the situation within an open network. Returning to Amin and Thrift's notion of a city as a weather system, or an agglomeration of processes, we recall how we saw that "city" might better be conceptualized in terms of a verb—as in *to city*—as opposed to a noun. This grammatical oddity parallels the ways we speak in terms of *rhetoric* as a verb: we *do rhetoric*, rather than (just) finding ourselves *in a rhetoric*. By extension, we might also say that rhetorical situation is better conceptualized as a mixture of processes and encounters; it should become a verb, rather than a fixed noun or *situs*. This kind of foregrounding within an affective field offers the possibility of a vocabulary that reveals a wider context for public rhetorics.

To borrow another conceptual metaphor, we are speaking about the ways in which rhetorical processes operate within a viral economy. The intensity, force, and circulatory range of a rhetoric are always expanding through the mutations and new exposures attached to that given rhetoric, much like a virus. An ecological, or *affective*, rhetorical model is one that reads rhetoric both as a process of distributed emergence and as an ongoing circulation process. Deleuze and Guattari give us one example of such an affective rhetoric in their introduction to *A Thousand Plateaus*, where they write about the *becoming* of evolutionary processes that happen between two or more species. Rather than a hierarchical transmission of genetic information, evolution involves a kind of sharing and an emergence that happens in the in-between of species. This is what Remy Chauvin describes as an "*aparallel evolution* of two beings that have absolutely nothing to do with each other" (quoted in Deleuze and Guattari, 10). For example, write Deleuze and Guattari:

> [Consider] Benveniste and Todaro's current research on a type C virus, with its double connection to baboon DNA and the DNA of certain kinds of domestic cats. . . . [T]here is an *aparallel evolution* . . . [between] the baboon and the cat; it is obvious that they are not models or copies of each other (a becoming-baboon of the cat does not mean that the cat "plays" baboon). . . . [T]ransfers of genetic material by viruses of through other procedures, fusions of cells originating in different species, have results analogous to those of "the abominable couplings dear to antiquity and the Middle Ages." Transversal communication between different lines scramble the genealogical trees.
>
> (10–11)

The image of a viral/genetic connection between baboon and cat (two beings that, in Chauvin's words, have absolutely nothing to do with each other) suggests a new kind of model for thinking of rhetoric's "transversal communication" and travel in the world. A given rhetoric is not *contained* by the elements that comprise its rhetorical situation (exigence, rhetor, audience, constraints). Rather, a rhetoric emerges already infected by the viral intensities that are circulating in the social field. Moreover, this same rhetoric will go on to evolve in *aparallel* ways: between two "species" that have absolutely nothing to do with each other. What is shared between them is *not* the situation, but certain contagions and energy. This does not mean the shared rhetoric reproduces copies or models of "original" situations (any more than the shared C virus turns a cat into a baboon). Instead, the same rhetoric might manage to infect and connect various processes, events, and bodies.

Situations Unbound: City Problems

In order to explore what this shifted emphasis on rhetorical ecologies might look like in our scholarship, I would like to take an example of a public rhetoric from my adopted Texas hometown, Austin. When I first moved to Austin in 1992, the economy was less than ideal. While Austin is a place of state government affairs and bureaucracy, the city economy was far from being competitive with larger Texas cities like Dallas or Houston. Few graduates from the University of Texas remained in Austin for the jobs; you stayed because you loved Austin.[3] But this all changed in the mid to late 1990s, when the technology boom brought new infrastructure into the city. Thanks to an onslaught of dot com startup companies in the area, as well as bigger companies like Dell Computers, Austin quickly became a major player in the technology sector. The city earned the nickname "Silicon Hills," which echoed its close connection with the technologically saturated areas known as "Silicon Valley" and "Silicon Alley." Almost overnight, Austin became a major player in the financial and technological sector.

As a result of this growth, Austin experienced significant changes to its entire economy. Not only did the city's population explode, but real estate prices and median income also began to climb. According to a 2002 city council white paper on Austin economic development:

> Local economic growth in Austin has been extraordinary in recent years. A combination of corporate relocations and expansions, rapid population growth, extensive investment in technology and Internet-related start-ups, and the meteoric rise of Dell helped make Austin among the five fastest growing metropolitan areas in the United States over the last decade. Since 1990, per capita personal income has risen from $18,092 to $32,039 (during 2000), more than 280,000 jobs have been created, and the average price of a home sold has grown from $87,600 to a current estimate of $199,500, a gain of almost 130 percent.
>
> ("Austin's Economic Future" 5)

Because of the growth in income levels and a more professional population, many large chain stores began to view Austin as a viable market for retail outlets like Home Depot, Barnes and Nobel, Starbucks, Target, Borders, and other "big box" franchises. Locally owned businesses in Austin quickly began to feel the sting of increased rents in those areas that had previously been affordable. Higher costs of operation forced many smaller local businesses to either move outside of their long-established sites in central Austin or close down business completely. Sound Exchange, a popular local record store in the heart of central Austin (commonly referred to as "the Drag"), is one example of a business that was forced to shut down its operation due to higher rent. Whereas Sound Exchange's rent had previously been $2800 throughout the 1990s, the new lease in 2003 climbed to $4369 per month (Gross). After serving as one of the most unique independent record stores in Austin since 1977, Sound Exchange finally closed its doors in January 2003. The business was quickly replaced by Baja Fresh Mexican Grill, a national fast food chain.

In Austin, the experience of Sound Exchange is hardly unusual. As journalist Lacey Tauber writes in a story for the Austin Independent Media Center about local businesses along the Drag:

> On the south end, Captain Quackenbush's (aka Quack's) coffee house moved out more than two years ago to Hyde Park. The smell of incense no longer wafts down the street from the A-frame of Good Gawd, what used to be a filled-to-overflowing vintage and costume shop, now relocated to South Lamar. Banzai Japanese and sushi restaurant and its smiling Buddha mural are nowhere to be found. In their place sits the new home of Diesel clothing company, a branch of a major corporation that can set shoppers back more than $130 for a pair of jeans. . . . Continuing up the Drag, more corporate faces appear. A long-vacant area is now home to Chipotle Mexican Grill, a business that is partially owned by the McDonalds corporation. Where the old Texas Textbooks once stood, Tyler's shoe and beach shop . . . displays a giant Nike logo.
>
> ("Is Austin Slowly Losing its Character?")

By the time I began teaching first-year writing at The University of Texas in 2001, the Drag's main businesses consisted of The Gap, Chipotle Mexican Grill, Diesel, Urban Outfitters, Barnes & Noble, and Tower Records. In less than a decade, the Drag lost several independent bookstores, music stores, coffee shops, and other small businesses. It was difficult not to sense the palpable transformation that was moving throughout the city.

In 2002, two local businesses, BookPeople Bookstore and Waterloo Records, decided to take a stand against the city's plan to give tax breaks for a large Border's Bookstore to open up directly across from the two shops. According to Steve Bercu, the owner of BookPeople:

> I was talking with the owner of Waterloo Records about our struggle to stop the City of Austin from providing incentives for a developer who planned to put a chain bookstore across the street from our stores. I suggested that

we get some bumper stickers that said "Keep Austin Weird," put both our logos on them, and then give them away at our stores. We decided that we should buy 5,000 stickers and see what our customers thought.

(Bercu)

These 5,000 stickers were so popular that the stores immediately ordered another 10,000 and then 25,000 stickers. Almost a year later, nearly 60,000 stickers had been distributed. Soon enough, other Austin businesses joined the call to weirdness. Local businesses began to sell t-shirts that featured their individual logos on front and the same "Keep Austin Weird" logo on the back.

The phrase "Keep Austin Weird" quickly passed into the city's cultural circulation, taking on the importance of a quasi-civic duty. One pledge pitch for a local public radio station told listeners, "You too can work towards keeping Austin weird by pledging to keep KOOP Radio 91.7FM on-the-air." In certain parts of Austin, it is nearly impossible to go for very long without finding some display of the slogan on a t-shirt, bumper sticker, tote bag, mug, or a local business's billboard vowing to "keep it weird." Ironically enough, the injunction to "Keep Austin Weird" has even erupted at the level of city politics. In a 2002 white paper on Austin's economic development, the city council formally acknowledged the reality of "weird Austin" and its effect on the life of the city itself:

[Q]uality of life, an umbrella term that loosely covers variables such as recreational and cultural amenities, overall cost of living, diversity of local residents, and a sense of place . . . is an increasingly important asset. This is especially the case in Austin, where there is a strong sense that the above factors combine in a unique and special way.

("Austin's Economic Future" 7)

The white paper footnotes that this "strong sense" of uniqueness is "[e]ncapsulated in the popular bumper sticker 'Keep Austin Weird'" ("Austin's Economic Future"). With this public incorporation of the slogan, the city council legitimated the rather intangible weirdness as a very real element of Austin's everyday existence.

At this point, one familiar question seems appropriate: *what is the rhetorical situation here?* Using Bitzer's model of rhetorical situation to read Austin's "weird rhetoric," we might describe the "big box" influx as (in the eyes of many Austinites) an exigence, or an imperfection marked by urgency. Certain rhetorical bodies involved in this scene, like BookPeople and Waterloo, chose to make the exigence salient by evoking it specifically as a problem to a number of audiences—Austin residents, city government, etc. There were also a number of constraints upon anti-big boxers, including a reluctance to be seen as undermining free and fair competition. While this is only one possible (and quite truncated) reading of this scene's rhetorical situation, we can already begin to see how this model can be useful for reading the complex relation of elements within public scenes.

But, at the same time, we can also bracket these analytical terms in order to bring something else into focus: the lived, in-process operations of this rhetoric. Here we're simply shifting field and ground of the same scene. Because the rhetoric of "weirdness" is distributed through ecologies that expand beyond audience/rhetor/exigence, we begin to see more about its public operation by bracketing these terms for a moment. Consider the ways in which this rhetoric has circulated in the social field. The original rhetoric has been expanded in the course of new calls, which adopt the phrase and transform it to fit other purposes. The University of Texas Liberal Arts' [sic] college gives away shirts that are very similar to the "weird" shirts, though they feature the slogan "Keep Austin Liberal Arts" in place of the earlier motto.

Likewise, the Austin Public Library circulated many popular bumper stickers that also kept the same "weird" font, but instead featuring the words, "Keep Austin Reading." Similarly, new businesses that emerged as replacements of older local businesses have begun to adopt the "Keep Austin Weird" slogan as advertisement. Older businesses, too, have started using the phrase as a way of promoting themselves in local publications. Even the corporate giant Cingular Wireless has created an advertisement in local publications that prominently features the phrase "Keepin' Austin Weird" beside their corporate logo. The obvious irony in Cingular's use of this phrase relates to the "weird" slogan's origination in a movement against big business and non-local corporate interests in Austin. These various rhetorics overlap through a kind of *shared contagion*, though the calls for local business support, the promotion of Liberal Arts, and the encouragement of literacy are hardly overlapping in terms of their *exigencies* or even their *audiences*. At the same time, of course, the "weird rhetoric" receives an increased circulation through these kinds of affective transmission.

In fact, even the increasingly popular counter-slogans manage to illustrate a kind of distributed ecological spread of this rhetoric. Appearing on t-shirts and bumper stickers throughout Austin, there is the "Make Austin Normal" campaign, which was the brainchild of a University of Texas business student who wanted to make a point of (and a profit from) what he sees as the ironic popularity of the "Keep Austin Weird" slogan. Of course, the "Make Austin Normal" campaign is hardly unique. While walking along the one of the main city streets of central Austin one spring day, I stumbled across a piece of white paper pasted on the side of a newspaper stand. In all block letters, the words read: "Keep Austin fucking normal. Conform. It's just easier." Upon seeing a picture of this homemade sign, my friend laughingly commented, "Doesn't this person realize just how *weird* this sign is?" While my friend meant this comment in jest, it addresses another aspect of what I call "rhetorical ecologies." Not only do these counter-rhetorics directly respond to and resist the original exigence, they also expand the lived experience of the original rhetorics by *adding* to them—even while changing and expanding their shape. The anti-weird rhetorics of Austin add to the "weird rhetoric" ecology through a practice of mixture and encounters of extended proximity.

Distribution, concatenation, encounter. This public scene forces us into a rather fluid framework of exchanges—a fluidity that bleeds the elements of rhetorical situation. Indeed, the (neo)Bitzerian models cannot account for the amalgamations and transformations—the *viral spread*—of this rhetoric within its wider ecology. When we temporarily bracket the discrete elements of rhetor, audience, and exigence in the "Keep Austin Weird" movement, we attune to the *processes* that both comprise and extend the rhetorics. Indeed, the rhetorical process itself plays out between the sites of these elements: the call is currently circulating on shirts and cars, it is mocked and pushed against, and it is distributed across purposes and institutional spaces. It circulates in a wide ecology of rhetorics. To play off Shaviro's words, the force of "messages," as they accrete over time, determine the shape of public rhetorics.

A New Model: Distributed Rhetorical Ecologies

Although the standard models of rhetorical situation can tell us much about the elements that are involved in a particular situation, these same models can also mask the fluidity of rhetoric. Rhetorical situations involve the amalgamation and mixture of many different events and happenings that are not properly segmented into audience, text, or rhetorician. We must therefore consider whether our popular models reflect the fullness of rhetoric's operation in public. Rhetorical ecologies are co-ordinating processes, moving across the same social field and within shared structures of feeling. The original call of Austin's "weird" rhetoric, for example, has been affected by the actions, events, and encounters that form "small events loosely joined"[4] as a kind of rhetorical-event neighborhood. Even when a multi-national corporation like Cingular coopts the phrase, placing it within a completely antithetical context from its origin, we find that Cingular's rhetoric *adds* to the (original) rhetoric of "weirdness" in Austin. They mark two different situations, of course—complete with different exigence, audience, rhetors, and constraints. But Cingular's rhetoric co-ordinates within the same neighborhood as the anti-corporate rhetoric. Thus, in the course of this evolution, the "weird rhetoric" receives what we might call an extended half-life in its range of circulation and visibility, as well as a changed shape, force, and intensity. Like a neighborhood, the amalgamation of events can both extend the street's visibility (or impact) and its very contours.

Consequently, though rhetorical situation models are undeniably helpful for thinking of rhetoric's contextual character, they fall somewhat short when accounting for the amalgamations and transformations—the spread—of a given rhetoric within its wider ecology. Rather than replacing the rhetorical situation models that we have found so useful, however, an ecological augmentation adopts a view toward the processes and events that extend beyond the limited boundaries of elements. One potential value of such a shifted focus is the way we view counter-rhetorics, issues of cooptation, and strategies of rhetorical production and circulation. Moreover, we can begin to recognize the way rhetorics are held together trans-situationally, as well as the effects of trans-situationality on rhetorical circulation. As urban scholar Helen Liggett writes, "presentations of situation [can be] understood as somewhat open-ended processes involving relays and connections that are both theoretical and practical" (2). In other words, we begin to see that public rhetorics do not only exist in the elements of their situations, but also in the radius of their neighboring events.

By shifting the ground and field in this manner, we add the dimension of movement back into our discussions of rhetoric. Brian Massumi illuminates the dilemma of movement's absence in our theories: "When positioning of any kind comes a determining first [in our theories], movement comes a problematic second. . . . Movement is entirely subordinated to the positions it connects. . . . The very notion of movement as qualitative transformation is [therefore] lacking" (3). We hear echoes of Biesecker's critique here that rhetorical situation too often imagines an audience as a "conglomeration of subjects whose identity is fixed prior to the rhetorical event itself," which circumscribes the power of rhetoric as movement. Massumi's hope is that

> movement, sensation, and qualities of experience couched in matter in its most literal sense (and sensing) might be culturally-theoretically thinkable, without falling into either . . . naïve realism or . . . subjectivism and without contradicting the very real insights of poststructuralist cultural theory concerning the coextensiveness of culture with the field of experience and of power with culture.
>
> (4)

Our rhetorical theories can thus acknowledge the affective channels of rhetorical communication and operation by "testifying" to them. Such testimonies would invent new concepts and deploy them in order to theorize how publics are also created through affective channels.

Producing Rhetorical Pedagogies

One implication of conceiving rhetorics in ecological or event-full terms relates to rhetoric and composition pedagogies. More specifically, I argue that this augmented framework can emerge at the level of *production*. In her discussion of classrooms as (potentially) protopublic bodies, Rosa Eberly argues that rhetoric is a process, not a substance that inheres in the collection of traits within a given text. Instead, she continues, "Rhetoric is thus *not only understood but practiced* as the powerful architectonic productive art that it is" (293; emphasis added). Emphasizing production should not mean falling into the trap of "real vs. artificial" writing situations, but instead should stress the ways in which rhetorical productions are inseparable from lived encounters of public life. Richard Marback calls this inseparability a "material theory of rhetoric," which "would articulate the impact of material and representational practices on each other" (87). The kinds of pedagogies I would like to pursue attune to this *mutuality* of material practice, embodied experience, and discursive representation that operate in public spaces every day. By way of concluding my discussion, I want to briefly highlight one way that this ecological publicness can inform our pedagogical *practices* in order to place greater emphasis on production in the classroom.

Whereas research is often considered by students (and even some teachers) as a process *leading to* public production and circulation (a means to an end, so to speak), we can look to the logics of a generative research method that takes the circulation of effects *as* an aim. Some of the most compelling "live" examples of generative research are city blogs, or weblogs (often written by individuals) that track the life of a place through images, text, comments, and links to relevant stories and sites. Take the example of G. Schindler's photoblog, which documents the life of Austin and its urban spaces through images. The blog writer, or "blogger," tracks the city in what we might recognize as a kind of local-research-in-the-wild. Schindler is a stalker of sorts, documenting local places without any other *telos* beyond the documentation itself. His images are unframed by extra commentary or descriptions, allowing the reader to simply drift through the city in a kind of *derive*. Through his images of signs, storefronts, abandoned couches, and handmade lost pet flyers, Schindler captures the (extra)ordinary details of life in the city. Instead of attempting to give readers the "true" version of Austin, he documents his own encounters with/in the city.

Call it generative research. These encounters can be tracked among (student) users as an example of how representations of place—like Austin—are constructed discursively, visually, affectively, and link-fully. Moreover, because this kind of documentation is public, often open to comments and citation in other blogs and websites, the "research" grows in social waves. The networked nature of blogs puts research into a circulation that becomes linked, put to other uses, transformed. In fact, without such citation and use by others, a blog is as good as dead. After a bit of caveat-ing, we might even dub it an act of "open source" research, exposing the myth of research as a personal process that only *later* leads to a public text. The photoblog's logic turns documentation into a kind of social production in itself.

Rather than thinking *only* in terms of audience, purpose, clarity, and information, therefore, the logic of the photoblog focuses on the *effects* and *concatenations* of our local ecologies. Bringing this logic into the realm of our own rhetorical pedagogy, we are reminded that rhetorically grounded education can mean something more than learning how to decode elements, analyze texts, and thinking *about* public circulations of rhetoric. It can also engage processes and encounters. Not "*learning* by doing," but "*thinking* by doing." Or, better yet, *thinking/doing*—with a razor thin slash mark barely keeping the two terms from bleeding into each other. This is a rethinking of the "in order to later" model, where students learn methods, skills, and research *in order to later* produce at other sites (other sites in the university or workplace, for example). This one-way flow can be radically revised in everyday settings, where rhetorical ecologies are already spatially, affectively, and conceptually in practice. As Eberly puts it, "[r]hetoric matters because rhetoric—*which demands engagement with the living*—is the process through which texts are not only produced but also understood to matter" (296; emphasis mine). This "mattering" is not fully explained only by a text's elemental properties, but also in the sense of *material effects and processes*. When we approach a rhetoric that does indeed engage with the living, hooking into the processes that are already in play, then we find ourselves theorizing rhetorical publicness. We find ourselves engaging a public rhetoric whose power is not circumscribed or delimited. *We encounter rhetoric.*

Notes

1 Editor's Note: The original essay contains a number of illustrations that could not be reproduced in this volume. Readers are encouraged to consult the original essay in print or online.
2 Perhaps we can rephrase this notion of distribution in terms of music: the lived experience of listening to a song cannot be framed only in terms of its constituent parts; the experience also includes the distributed processes of *hearing*—and, in my apartment with the bass turned up, even *feeling* the song.
3 Jokes used to circulate about Austin being the only city in the United States where the 7-11 employees also happened to have PhDs.
4 Here I purposefully play off David Weinberger's *Small Pieces Loosely Joined*, which makes a similar kind of argument about networking and social ecologies.

Works Cited

Amin, Ash and Nigel Thrift. *Cities: Reimagining the Urban.* Polity: Cambridge, 2002.
Bercu, Steve. "Letter to the Editor: Keep Everywhere Weird." *Publishers Weekly* (5 December 2003). http://print.google.com/print/doc?articleid=f3ypx1QKhYE
Biesecker, Barbara A. "Rethinking the Rhetorical Situation from within the Thematic of Différance." *Philosophy and Rhetoric* 22.2 (1989): 110–30.
Bitzer, Lloyd F. "The Rhetorical Situation." *Philosophy and Rhetoric* 1.1 (1968): 1–14.
City of Austin. "Austin's Economic Future." (20 November 2002). www.ci.austin.tx.us/redevelop ment/whitepaper1.htm
Deleuze, Gilles and F. Guattari. *A Thousand Plateaus: Capitalism and Schizophrenia.* Minneapolis: U of Minnesota P, 1987.
Eberly, Rosa A. "Rhetoric and the Anti-Logos Doughball: Teaching Deliberating Bodies the Practices of Participatory Democracy." *Rhetoric & Public Affairs* 5.2 (2002): 287–300.
Gross, Joe. "Say Goodbye to Sound Exchange." *Austin-American Statesman* (9 January 2003): 11–12.
Liggett, Helen. *Urban Encounters.* Minneapolis: U of Minnesota P, 2003.
Marback, Richard. "Detroit and the Closed Fist: Toward a Theory of Material Rhetoric." *Rhetoric Review* 17.1 (1998): 74–91.

Massumi, Brian. *Parables for the Virtual: Movement, Affect, Sensation.* Durham: Duke University Press, 2002.

Phelps, Louise W. *Composition as a Human Science.* New York: Oxford UP, 1988.

Reynolds, Nedra. *Geographies of Writing: Inhabiting Places and Encountering Difference.* Carbondale: Southern Illinois UP, 2004.

Schindler, G. www.gschindler.com/blog.htm.

Shaviro, Steven. *Connected, or, What It Means to Live in the Network Society.* Minneapolis: U of Minnesota P, 2003.

Smith, Craig R. and Scott Lybarger. "Bitzer's Model Reconstructed." *Communication Quarterly* 44.2 (1996): 197–213.

Syverson, Margaret A. *The Wealth of Reality: An Ecology of Composition.* Carbondale: Southern Illinois UP, 1999.

Tauber, Lacey. "Is Austin Slowly Losing Its Character?" *Austin Independent Media Center* (4 December 2002). http://austin.indymedia.org/newswire/display/9888/index.php

Vatz, Richard. "The Myth of the Rhetorical Situation." *Philosophy and Rhetoric* 6 (1973): 154–61.

Warner, Michael. "Publics and Counterpublics." *Public Culture* 14.1 (2002): 49–71.

Weinberger, David. *Small Pieces Loosely Joined: A Unified Theory of the Web.* New York: Basic Books, 2003.

Williams, Raymond. *Marxism and Literature.* Oxford: Oxford UP, 1977.

12
What Can Automation Tell Us About Agency?

CAROLYN R. MILLER

According to the editors of a recent book about the computerized assessment of writing, "Machine scoring no longer has a foot in the door of higher education. It's sitting comfortably in the parlor. In K–12 schools, machine scoring has become even more of a permanent resident" (Ericsson and Haswell 4). Automated scoring systems are being used for placement, for program assessment, and for classroom instruction, and there are four or five well-established and aggressively promoted systems on the market. Their appeal is that they save time and money and are reliable and consistent. For administrators, automation is easier to justify to budget officers and more reliable than cumbersome systems of faculty-based assessment. For faculty, automation saves time and energy that can be put to uses other than the drudgery of reading hundreds of student papers. For students, automation provides immediate feedback on their rhetorical efforts in an appealing form; according to one pitch, "Most of today's students have had experience with instant feedback in computer programs and are becoming more comfortable with the idea of computerized scoring."[1]

Automated writing assessment is an applied branch of natural language processing, which in turn is a branch of artificial intelligence. The commercial systems all have proprietary software such as a parser or an inference engine in addition to a lexicon or dictionary that allow for interpretation of word strings and comparison with models or criteria. According to Ericsson and Haswell, by October 2004, over 900 colleges and universities were using the College Board's ACCUPLACER service with WritePlacer® Plus, which measures student writing skills,[2] and over five million tests had been administered in the previous year (3). The advent of the new SAT in 2006, with an expanded section on writing, has prompted speculation that automated assessment will inevitably be used to score the required writing samples from the hundreds of thousands of students who take it each year (Baron).

Here's a brief survey of some of the other available products and their sales pitches:

- The Educational Testing Service is marketing a new Web-based product, CriterionSM Online Writing Evaluation, available in two versions, for K–12 and higher education. The higher education version provides "writing instructors and administrators at community colleges and four-year institutions with reliable evaluations of their students' writing abilities. Students draft and submit essays and receive immediate feedback in the form of a holistic score and diagnostic annotations within each essay that guide instruction."[3] According to the testimonials on the ETS website, CriterionSM is being used for placement, remediation, and exit assessment.

- MY Access!® by Vantage Learning is marketed for grades 4–12 and higher education. According to the website, "With MY Access!®, students are motivated to write more and attain higher scores on statewide writing assessments. . . . The program's powerful scoring engine grades students' essays instantly and provides targeted feedback, freeing teachers from grading thousands of papers by hand." The IntelliMetric™ artificial intelligence scoring engine "emulates the process carried out by human scorers."[4]

- Pearson Knowledge Technologies is promoting its product the Intelligent Essay Assessor. According to its website, the IEA "automatically assesses and critiques electronically submitted essays, providing assessment and instructional feedback. . . . IEA is a back-end service using the KAT™ engine and a customer's Web interface to evaluate essays as reliably as skilled human readers."[5]

The market for automated writing assessment is active and growing. But now there's a new product of interest to rhetoricians, so new that it has not yet received much attention: a computer system for the automated assessment of oral performance in public speaking. Instructors in public speaking will be able to handle many more students with less classroom time devoted to individual presentations and critiques. Program directors will be able to use the system for placement and credit by exam. Assessment of speaking required the solution of multiple technical and mechanical problems because the computer system must account for not only the stream of oral language but also visual data about body language and auditory data about expressiveness, and the like. This new system will soon be marketed as AutoSpeech-Easy™.[6]

To use AutoSpeech-Easy™, students deliver their speeches to a videocam connected to a computer, and the system then delivers an assessment (or score) to the student and to the instructor or placement administrator, who records it without ever having to hear or see the student's work. Just like many of the writing assessment programs, AutoSpeech-Easy™ can be used for placement, for coaching, or for course assignments. It can provide comments on specific features, suggestions for improvement, and justifications for its ratings.

It is customizable, so that instructors can select the features that are subject to assessment and the criteria for the ratings.

Needless to say, AutoSpeech-Easy™ is a revolutionary technology, which has benefited from major advancements in computer science and cognitive engineering: rasterization of video input for realtime face and expression detection; an extensive database of haptics, oculesics, and proxemics; speech-recognition algorithms with matrix analysis of vocalics; and a patented inference engine for emotion recognition. These new programming achievements have been combined with established parsers for syntax, semantic cohesion, and logic. AutoSpeech-Easy™ thus offers a direct analogue to what has already been available for automated assessment of student writing.

The changing economics and politics of higher education are driving the development and adoption of automated writing assessment, but it remains to be seen whether automated assessment of speaking will follow this same pattern. Most rhetoricians have severe reservations about the use of automated writing assessment, and the Ericsson and Haswell collection includes excellent arguments against the practice. I want to generalize the analysis here to include speaking as well as writing. By positing a machine as audience, automated assessment systems for both writing and speaking denaturalize rhetorical action, challenging and uncovering our intuitions about its necessary conditions. In effect, automated assessment systems create a situation in which Burkean symbolic action directly confronts nonsymbolic motion in the form of the machine. This confrontation suggests that rhetorical agency is exactly what is at stake in automated assessment. It raises questions about the action and agentive capacity of the writer or speaker in the context of the presumably agentless motion of the mechanized audience. What I want to explore here is how our resistance to automated assessment can inform the current debate about the nature of rhetorical agency. Thus, I'm interested in our rhetorical intuitions about these systems.

A Thought Experiment

To gather some of those intuitions, I asked instructors of composition and public speaking at my university what they thought about AutoSpeech-Easy™ as well as about the products for automated writing assessment. One of the strongest themes in the twenty-five responses I received to this informal survey was sheer incredulity about the technical capacities of writing assessment systems and AutoSpeech-Easy™. I should note that, in the latter case, the incredulity is fully justified, because AutoSpeech-Easy™ is a complete fiction.[7] But I was interested in what forms the incredulity would take in general and in particular whether it would take different forms for the automated assessment of speaking and of writing.

Even though automated writing assessment is now a bureaucratic fact, and even though AutoSpeech-Easy™ was presented in my survey not as a fact but as a "thought experiment," the level of incredulity about the capacities of both kinds of system was quite high, with writing teachers generally being more sensitive to the difficulties involved in writing assessment, and speech teachers more sensitive to those involved in assessment of speaking. The reasons for skepticism included the belief that computers could never take into account communicative complexities such as creativity, appropriateness to context, the expression of emotion, and individual and cultural differences. Some respondents expressed qualms about abandoning their own pedagogical responsibilities to a machine (although a few said they would welcome the opportunity), with comments like, "If there were no high-stakes decisions tied to the assessment, it would be okay for formative assessment and practice" (respondent #W21).[8]

The second major theme in the responses concerned the damage that automated assessment does to rhetoric's audience, a reaction that focuses directly on the confrontation between action and motion. This theme was tied to some respondents' incredulity, because they just could not believe that a computer system could simulate a real audience. They said, for example, "Can the Program differentiate between audiences defined by each Instructor for each assignment?" (#S13) and, "Similar to written communication, speeches are used to express one person's ideas to other people. Computer assessment cannot be made sensitive enough to truly distinguish how a message is received by human beings" (#S11). But the concerns about audience go further than skepticism about technological capability. For one thing, there was a practical concern that was particularly obvious in the case of public speaking: "To grade via computer takes away one of the hardest parts of public speaking: the public part" (#W25). Speaking to a computer would "sanitize the speaking environment" and "negate all that is 'public speaking'" (#S15). Several respondents mentioned the dynamic interaction with audience that is the essence of a speaking situation: "A speaker's response to audience feedback needs the living dynamics of actual listeners" (#S12). And further, respondents spoke of the need for "engagement" with audience in both writing and speaking: "student writers," one said, should "engage in conversation with other academics" (#W18). And the concerns were also conceptual and even moral. One respondent said, "I think students need a sense of audience. . . . Even if the computer was able to . . . somehow grade based on audience awareness, I think the very notion of computer assessment would negate that idea" (#W24). Another said, "Each student comes to the lectern with different skills, backgrounds, and experiences. I believe assessing human beings require[s] human judgment" (#S9).[9]

These survey results have no statistical significance whatsoever, of course, so I treat them as informative supplements to my own speculations. These collective intuitions suggest that our resistance to automation is rooted in a commitment to agency, or more specifically that we find it difficult (and perhaps perverse) to conceive of rhetorical action under conditions that seem to remove agency not from the rhetor so much as from the audience. The concern for agency might seem misplaced, or futile, since rhetoric under the conditions of placement testing or classroom performance strikes many of us as having minimal agentive potential. Accordingly, these intuitions should perhaps be treated as unreliable mystifications, delusional vestiges of a humanist ideology. But on the possibility that they might instead provide a way to reconcile the everyday lifeworld with the collision between modernist-humanism and post-modernity that has troubled rhetoric's understanding of agency, I will pursue their implications here and hope that the discussion to follow can put these intuitions in their place.

Because the conditions for rhetorical performance in writing and speaking are different, it is through a contrastive analysis that we may come to appreciate both the wisdom and the weaknesses of our intuitions about the nature of rhetorical agency. My initial hunch was that automated assessment is much more problematic for speaking than for writing, and there is some agreement with this in the survey. Asked whether automated assessment could be acceptable under some circumstances, assuming technical advances could make it as reliable as human assessment, more respondents said no for speaking than said no for writing. Asked directly whether they think there are any specifically rhetorical issues that will make computer assessment of speaking less satisfactory than computer assessment of writing, more said yes than no. Their comments suggest that the heightened resistance to automated assessment of speaking derives partly from first-hand experience that the performative aspects of speaking are more complex than those of writing, and thus that the technology that tracks or models them is less likely to be valid or reliable (the incredulity factor, again); but resistance also derives from the greater visibility and materiality of the audience for speaking and the perception that speaking therefore requires interaction between rhetor and audience. The survey responses thus point to three dimensions of rhetoric that may help us understand what we want from a concept of agency, that is, what is missing from the confrontation of action with motion: these are performance, audience, and interaction. These are certainly not new ideas, but what I hope to do here is to suggest what we can learn from their conjunction.

First, however, I should review the conceptual problem that the AutoSpeech-Easy™ thought experiment was designed to illuminate (though certainly not to solve). Agency has been prominent on the agenda of rhetorical studies recently, the cause of what Ronald Greene has characterized as an "anxiety . . . lodged in the critical imagination" of the field (188). Traditional rhetoric presupposes—even celebrates—agency, as the power of the rhetor, of invention, of eloquence itself; poststructuralist rhetoric debunks agency as "ideology" (Gaonkar)[10] or "ontotheology" (Lundberg and Gunn). How we ought to understand agency was one of four "pressing questions" featured at the 2003 Alliance of Rhetorical Societies (ARS) conference (Clark 5), and the report about the discussions on this question became the subject of an award-winning debate in these pages (Geisler "How Ought"; Lundberg and Gunn; Geisler "Teaching").[11] *Philosophy and Rhetoric* published a special issue on agency in 2004. Conference panels and other forms of rumination on the topic abound.[12] And rhetoric is not alone in its preoccupation with agency: cultural studies, gender studies, literary studies, and political and social theory have been worrying for some time about the relative effectivity of the "subject" and the social order (or "structure" or "ideological state apparatuses") and about the nature of their relationship. One protracted discussion, in the area of science and technology studies, challenges the Burkean distinction between action and motion by positing two forms of agency, human and nonhuman (or material), the latter including both machines and natural forces. These are understood to be complexly interrelated in what Pickering calls the "mangle of practice" and what Latour calls "hybrids" or "networks" (*We Have Never*). Whether these two forms should be treated symmetrically in inquiry and theorizing remains a point of contention.

Within rhetorical studies, three related sets of concerns—theoretical, ideological, and practical—prompt this anxious attention to agency. The theoretical concerns arise from the struggle of rhetoric to come to terms with the postmodern condition, or at least with poststructuralist theorizing. Since agency has traditionally been understood as a property of an agent, the decentering of the subject—the death of the author/agent—signals a crisis for agency, or perhaps more accurately, for rhetoric, since traditional rhetoric requires the possibility for influence that agency entails. Poststructuralist or posthumanist theories detach agency from the agent, challenging our syntactic habits of treating agency as a possession (Lundberg and Gunn 89) and of using agency after transitive verbs (Herndl and Licona)—tropes that reify the agent. Agents do not "have" or "acquire" agency. Instead, agency is said to "possess" the agent (Lundberg and Gunn 97), or to "precede" the agent (Herndl and Licona 13); agency is dispersed to the "intersection of the semiotic and the material" (Herndl and Licona 13), to "discursive and aesthetic conditions" (Vivian 241), to Lacanian tropes or the Symbolic (Lundberg and Gunn 97), to "the spaces in and from which rhetorical situations take shape and meaning" (Barnett 3), to "the structures and dispositions that constitute the habitus" (Atwill). Many have questioned whether rhetoric can survive this dispersion of agency.

The ideological concerns arise from the conflict between realities of political and economic power and ideals of civic participation and social justice. According to Greene, the "root cause of the anxiety over agency" is its "attachment . . . to a vision of political change" (189). Rhetorical agency is important because it would give voice to the voiceless, empowering subaltern groups, and thus, presumably, weakening structures of institutional, corporate, and ideological domination. This set of concerns tends to produce resistance models of agency, models that usually rely on a metonymy between agent and agency. Thus, Paul Smith has understood the term *agent* as "a form of subjectivity where . . . the possibility (indeed, the actuality) of resistance to ideological pressure is allowed for" (xxxv). Feminism in particular, according to Smith, has seen in the fragmentation of the subject into multiple subject positions the opportunity, even the necessity, for "contradiction and negativity" that produce resistance (152). Thus, agency-resistance is both the product of domination and the negation of the same: it is agency-against-patriarchy, or agency-against-capitalism. In the work of Judith Butler, for example, agency takes the form of "a strategy of displacement of constraining symbolic norms" and is thus, according to Lois McNay, negative and uncreative (189). For rhetoric, the ideological approach to agency results in what Lundberg and Gunn call "rhetorical evangelicalism" (94), a self-righteousness about civic engagement, or what Greene calls "moral entrepreneurship," a presumption that agency is "always already in support of, or opposition to, the institutional structures of power" (189, 198).

The pedagogical concerns about agency arise from the efforts of teachers to make rhetoric matter. These efforts are frequently tied to the ideological concerns described above; for example, Gerard Hauser's reflections on the ARS discussions on the theme of teaching ends with the claim that faculty in rhetorical studies "have a birthright: rhetoric's role in civic education. That role is not just in the public performance of political discourse but in the education of young minds that prepares them to perform their citizenship" (52). The pedagogical concerns are also tied to the theoretical concerns; Leff and Lunsford's reflection on the ARS conference notes that "Teachers of writing and speaking can pursue an unrestrained deconstruction of the agency of speakers and writers only at the risk of theorizing themselves out of their jobs" (62). It is the agency of students (another subaltern group) that is the focus of these concerns, and the pedagogical situation highlights the conjunction of two dimensions of agency: the student's developing competence (agency as capacity) and the goals of social change (agency as effect). Karlyn Campbell's ARS plenary address illustrates this doubleness: "Rhetorical agency refers to the capacity to act, that is, to have the competence to speak or write in a way that will be recognized or heeded by others" (4). Similarly, Geisler's report on the ARS conference uses a doubled definition, beginning with an understanding of agency as the "capacity to act" and going on to note that agency is necessary because of rhetoric's "social mission, . . . the goal of being efficacious in the world" ("How Ought" 12, 16). Because in this view agency must be not only a capacity of the rhetor but also in some way a capacity of the audience, the issues become considerably more complicated.

The AutoSpeech-Easy™ thought experiment challenges this double understanding of agency by radically truncating the pedagogical situation, leaving the student in a rhetorical desert, demonstrating her capacities to an "audience" capable only of motion, turning effects into algorithms. Can agency as rhetorical capacity survive when the possibility of agency as effectivity has completely dried up? (We might, of course, ask the same question about many other situations we put students into.) Automated assessment systems also cut to the heart of the theoretical and ideological concerns about agency. Can posthumanist theory disperse agency to a machine? What are our moral obligations to such hybrids? Is our resistance to the mechanized audience simply another example of rhetorical evangelicalism? A consideration of what the survey responses suggest about performance, audience, and interaction provides some perspective on such questions.

Performance/Performativity

Although it wasn't identified as one of the "pressing issues" for the ARS conference, Andrea Lunsford found that "performance" served as a key term in the discussions there (Leff and Lunsford 55). Similarly, Michael Leff has noted that terms like "performance" and "action" have gained priority over earlier preoccupations with "substance" and "theory" ("Up from Theory"), and Susan Jarratt recently identified a "turn to the performative" in rhetorical scholarship. The survey responses quoted above about the specifically *public* nature of public speaking also draw our attention here to the performative dimension of rhetoric. Speaking strongly resists automation because we understand it intuitively it as a performance, meaning that it is dynamic and temporal, that it requires living presence; as one respondent put it, "We are training students to present live speeches to living audiences" (#S12). Speaking is understood as *im*-mediate, both in the sense that it happens in the instant and in the sense that it is not mediated but direct. Speaking-performance highlights consciousness of the co-present subject and other, even as the possibility of self-consciousness and the knowability of the other come under question.

The bias of the speaking situation is to foreground the agent, the performing subject as the seat of rhetorical origin, seizing the *kairos* (capacity) to instigate change (effect). This bias arouses suspicions of performative conceptions of agency and of what Leff has called the "homage to the rhetor" paid by much of the classical tradition of rhetoric ("Tradition and Agency" 137). As agency has been disconnected from the agent, these suspicions have disconnected performance from the performer-agent and dispersed it to structures of power and ideology; unlike agents, the "points of articulation" for these structures do not perform; rather, they exhibit performativity. Leff goes on, however, to urge us not to jettison the classical treatment of agency in our postmodern enthusiasm, by showing us how the classical tradition tempers the power of the rhetorical agent. Both Isocrates and Cicero, who celebrate the agential power of the speaker, also point to powerful constraints on the speaker, those of the audience and of communal tradition ("Tradition and Agency" 138–39). The rhetor cannot be an autonomous originator and expect to succeed in persuasion—and never could.

And indeed, performative conceptions of agency are tempered by other considerations like the ones I take up below, audience and interactivity. Like agency, performance points both to the rhetor and to the audience, and this doubleness is embedded in the tradition of performance studies. Foundational work by Erving Goffman characterized performance as behavior aimed at producing an impression on an observer but at the same time called attention to the performer's efforts to control that behavior. A recent review of performance theory notes its roots in both psychoanalytic theory and social theory and its association with "consciousness and reflection" as well as with a theatrical focus on audience reception (Carlson 80).

In contrast to the speaking situation, the bias of writing is to obscure performance, kairos, and audience.[13] Writing, as Burke might put it, essentializes temporality, just as speech temporalizes essence. Jenn Fishman, Andrea Lunsford, Beth McGregor, and Mark Otuteye have recently urged us to attend to writing as performance and to learn from the anthropologists, linguists, and theater scholars who have made performance studies a lively field in the past fifty years. Fishman and Lunsford focus on enactments of writing, "scripted forms of oral communication" that put the rhetor and the audience together into a lived event (226–27). But a useful concept of agency could help us go beyond this to view all text as having a performative dimension, just as J. L. Austin finally concluded that all locutions are speech acts, that even constatives are performatives (150).

If the writing situation mystifies us with the absence of the performed event, however, the speaking situation mystifies us with its material presence. Speech tempts us to focus exclusively on bodily motion, personal presence, eye contact—and to neglect symbolic action, mental presence, emotional contact, all of which are manifested in both writing and speaking and all of which are means through which we can infer rhetorical action and agency. I suggest, then, that we think of agency as the *kinetic energy* of rhetorical performance. The Greek root of energy is *ergon*, deed or work, and *energeia* is the deed in the doing, action itself. In invoking the distinction that physics makes between potential and kinetic energy, I'm comparing agency not to the energy of a stone sitting at the top of the cliff but rather to the energy it has as it falls, the energy of motion.[14] But in this case, we're interested not in the motion of stones but in the symbolic actions of rhetorical performers. If agency is a potential energy, it will be thought of as a possession or property of an agent (like a stationary stone), but if agency is a kinetic energy, it must be a property of the rhetorical event or performance itself. Agency thus could not exist prior to or as a result of the evanescent act. Our talk about agency has tended to essentialize the temporal, condensing into a property or possession of the hypostatized agent what more productively should remain temporalized in the act or performance. As the kinetic energy of performance, agency resolves its doubleness, positioned exactly between the agent's capacity and the effect on an audience. Our task is to understand how the kinetic energy of performance works in writing as well as in speaking.

Audience/Addressivity

Audience is inherent in our understanding of performance, and one of the purposes of my thought experiment with AutoSpeech-Easy™ was to test that understanding with a limit case by turning the speaker's audience into a literal black box. But the responses to the survey unpacked the black box by indicating different forms of resistance to its two components, the camera and the computer. Both are instructive.

The videocam mediates the speaking event, removing the audience from the rhetor, an absence to which several respondents specifically objected: "I can't imagine actually having a student deliver a speech to a camera . . . since that would defeat the purpose of communicating with an audience!" (#W1); "Audience is lost when one stands in front of a camera. Even though I assume the presenter has been prepped to visualize his intended audience . . . that seems a bit far-fetched considering he will be staring into a video camera" (#W8); "When you are speaking into a camera, my personal experience is that you lose the connection to the audience because there is no one to talk to, thus you will often lose your tone and impact, often speaking faster than normal and without much affect" (#S15); "The camera doesn't nod, smile or frown. Speeches need a certain amount of instant feedback" (#S16).

However, none of the respondents noted the widespread use of camera-mediated oral communication, in both broadcast and online environments. Even when there is an audience present with the camera, it may be much less important (as well as less numerous) than the audience mediated by the camera. Moreover, the mediating role of the camera makes the speaking situation similar to writing, where audience is more remote, less insistently present and visible, than in unmediated speaking. Mediation of either sort draws attention to the rhetorical effort required to anticipate an audience, effort we easily forget is also required for unmediated audiences. Just because we can see and enumerate our audience doesn't ensure that we can understand their presumptions and convictions. On these grounds it is difficult to condemn the camera itself as rhetorically destructive to audience.

Speaking *through* a camera *to* a computer also provoked objections, although respondents said little to explain these responses. For example, there were no comments to the effect that the computer might be more inscrutable or more intimidating to students than a human audience.[15] It was the simple absence of audience that was objectionable: "Students need an audience in order to give a speech. If the student gives a speech to a computer, then s/he is not getting the full speech experience" (#W10). However, asking students to perform in the absence of audience is not much different from the typical mass testing situation or even many classrooms. As one respondent noted: "It honestly doesn't seem like computers would be that different from the human readers of standardized tests" (#W25). In most educational situations, the possibilities for agency as rhetorical effect are artificially truncated: there is no exigence beyond educational accounting, and the teacher's role is that of grader, not that of a rhetorical audience capable of enacting change. In such conditions, rhetoric can be little more than declamation. But neither declamation nor our dissatisfaction is new, and it seems that, rather than being a new obstacle to agency, the computer serves as a surrogate for our dissatisfaction with declamation.

If it's not the literal machine—either camera or computer—that makes the mechanized audience so rhetorically objectionable, what does? A clue is provided by several respondents who objected to computer assessment of public speaking because it would alleviate "communication apprehension": "students would most likely be less nervous speaking to a machine" (#W10); "a public speaking course should be teaching them skills to manage and/or overcome speaking anxiety. The effect of a computer 'audience' would be different for writing because the element of anxiety about receiving public attention does not exist as keenly for writers as for speechmakers" (#S11); "by having the student speak into a computerized recorder you are changing the entire process, which might for some lessen the anxiety, while for most I think it will greatly reduce performance and grades" (#S15).

I suggest that what makes us apprehensive about public speaking is precisely the energy that signals the presence of agency. What is unmistakably present in the live speaking situation is an Other, someone who may resist, disagree, disapprove, humiliate—or approve, appreciate, empathize, and applaud. The problem with the mechanized audience is not that it is inscrutable—audience is always inscrutable to at least some degree—but that we are unwilling to grant it such presence and therefore cannot, in an important sense, perform. To produce kinetic energy, performance requires a relationship between two entities who will *attribute* agency to each other. Indeed, much of what inexperienced writers and readers have to learn is how to attribute agency to the invisible, mediated other within a written text, how to produce kinetic energy in a textual performance.

By the same token, what both speakers and writers in most pedagogical situations must learn is how (and how to be willing) to attribute agency to a mediating audience, one that is standing in for an audience that might change or enact change. In other words, they must learn how to engage in productive *imitatio*, how to benefit from the imaginative (re)construction of rhetorical situations in which agency is willingly attributed. This is the pedagogical value of declamation, which operates not in the dimension of effectivity but in the other dimension of agency, the student's developing capacity. As Jeff Walker explains it in his response to the ARS plenary on rhetorical traditions, "the purpose of declamation is . . . to develop a capacity, a *dunamis* of thought and speech, a deeply habituated skill, that can be carried into practical, grown-up, public life—as the student gathers experience and matures" (8). If pedagogically successful, declamation teaches agency-attribution through imitation.

Interaction/Interactivity

As audience is inherent in our understanding of performance, so interaction is fundamental to our understanding of audience. The energy of agency (whether direct or mediated) is rhetorically functional only through interaction. Leff's discussion of how agency is represented within the classical tradition notes the essential role of interaction. Because the rhetor must adapt to the social context and to the audience's knowledge, values, conventions, and expectations, the speaker's power in effect derives from the power of the audience; Leff cites the example of Crassus in the first book of the *de Oratore*, confessing to his fear of the audience and concludes, "Paradoxically, then, this man who strikes awe into the heart of his listeners is himself awed by his audience" ("Tradition and Agency" 139). Perhaps the example is not so much paradoxical as paradigmatic.

Many of the responses to my survey insisted that a speaker's audience must be rhetorically available to the speaker through interaction—this was by far the most important aspect of audience for this group of instructors. They talked about "feedback" (#S12, #S16, #W12), "reactions" and "responses" (#S12, #W8, #W19, #W24), the "ongoing relationship" between the speaker and audience (in contrast to that between writer and reader) (#S15), the "chemistry between a speaker and the audience" (#S9). They spoke of audiences as "live" and "living" (#W8, #W12). These respondents were unwilling to attribute agency to the AutoSpeech-Easy™ system—and assumed that their students would be similarly unwilling, or unable—in large part because it evidently would not offer any ongoing interaction with the speaker. It's an interesting corroboration of my claim here that computer scientists began to call their systems "intelligent agents" only when they achieved the capacity for the machines to "interact" with users.[16]

Interaction is necessary for agency because it is what creates the kinetic energy of performance and puts it to rhetorical use. Agency, then, is not only the property of an event, it is the property of a relationship between rhetor and audience. There are at least two subjects within a rhetorical situation, and it is their interaction, through attributions they make about each other and understand each other to be making, that we constitute as agency. Crassus is awed by his audience not so much because of anything they are doing but because he attributes to them the capacity to do something, including attributing agency to him. The interactive process of mutual attribution generates the kinetic energy of performance. In this sense, agency is, as Campbell says, "communal, social, cooperative, and participatory" (5). It is, as Lucaites and Condit put it, "bound in relationship, rather than [being] the solitary product of some sort of determinism" (612).

The shorthand version of all this is that we understand agency as an attribution made *by another agent*, that is, by an entity to whom we are willing to attribute agency. It is through this process of mutual attribution that agency does, indeed, produce the agent, much as Herndl and Licona put within their somewhat different explanatory framework: "it is the social phenomenon of agency that brings the agent into being" (13). Herndl and Licona go on to posit what they call the "agent function," which we can understand as a specialized or constrained version of the process of attribution that I have been describing. Developed by analogy with Foucault's "author function," the agent function "arises from the intersection of material, (con)textual, and ideological conditions and practices" (14). The agent function operates as a principle of discursive economy and control, constituting a position *into* which subjects are articulated. In the terms that I have been using, attributions of agency may rely on prefabricated conventions, ideologically imposed or culturally given. In other words, rather than having to posit an agent function existing in a totally abstract space, we can position it within the habitual or imposed patterns of attributions that rhetor or audience is prepared to make. The agent function, then, would be simply an indication of the ability or willingness of participants to attribute a particular form of agency.

Another analogy to the process of attribution that I am describing here can be found in the classical tradition, in what the ancients called *ethopoeia*, the construction of character in discourse (sometimes called "impersonation"). The early Sophists recognized that character (*ethos*) was an important dimension of speeches they wrote for others to deliver: they knew that character was not so much represented as constructed, and the best speechwriters were adept at persuasive impersonation. Aristotle described ethos as not only a matter of prior reputation (an inartistic proof) but also a dimension of a performative event, an effect of delivery and reception, in other words, an attribution (I.viii.6, II.i.2). In these conceptions, ethos appears very much as I described agency earlier—as an energy within performance produced by ethopoetic attributions, which in turn are necessary for rhetorical effects to occur.

Research in interpersonal communication, human–computer interaction, and computer-mediated communication has suggested that we have a very low threshold for ethopoeia: in other words, it doesn't take much for us to be willing to attribute character to an interlocutor, no matter how primitive the cues are.[17] We go out of our way to construct a human relationship: the "Eliza effect," or the attribution of intelligence and sympathy to an early computer program that simulated a psychotherapist is perhaps the most notorious example (Weizenbaum). Our predilection for ethopoeia results in frequent attributions of agency to machines: people name their cars, others talk to their computers, gamblers attribute beneficence or malevolence to slot machines,[18] and so on. And, like agency, ethopoeia can involve both rhetorical capacity and rhetorical effect. Discussions of "material agency" focus our attention on the single dimension of effect (this is Pickering's position), though the full ethopoetic impulse of the everyday practices exemplified just above adds the second dimension by endowing nature and machines with a human-like capacity for intentional action. A natural predilection for ethopoeia is necessary to the development of trust in infants (Baier), and a trained or cultural predilection of the same sort is necessary for mediated texts to operate as rhetorical performances.

We might expect, then, that automated assessment technologies could take advantage of our eagerness to attribute agency, and perhaps they can—and will. For now, though, many of us are culturally and economically positioned to deny agency to machines in this particular situation, especially if the machines threaten to substitute for our own agency. Others, like educational administrators, are culturally and economically positioned to welcome mechanized agency, to posit an agent function that will position the machine as an adequate reader of placement essays, for example. Better system design with more interactivity could help bring the rest of us around to this view, as could simple habituation on our part: given sufficient experience and exposure, we may accept these machines as Latourian hybrids to which we unproblematically delegate rhetorical agency, just as we delegate the functions of a doorman to an automatic door closer (Latour "Mixing Humans"). On the other hand, perhaps a better understanding of agency will help us determine how and where to draw the line—between the human and the nonhuman, between the symbolic and the material—and how to make our case to others.

Conclusion

The attributing of motives, said Burke, produces "basic forms of thought" that underlie all kinds of symbolic action, and the basic forms of thought he worked with were the pentadic terms of dramatism, which together "treat language and thought primarily as modes of action" (xv, xxii).[19] In other words, the attribution of motives is a generative process, generative of rhetorical action. The process that I have been sketching, the attribution of agency, resembles what Burke is talking about. Our attributions of agency produce the kinetic energy of performance and thereby engage the performance *as* action.

Celeste Condit has called agency a "necessary illusion":[20] I have tried to suggest something about why it is necessary—it makes symbolic action possible— and also to pin down what sort of illusion it is. It's an illusion not in the sense that it's a theoretical fiction but rather in the sense that it's an attribution, an attribution that's not determined but constructed (or pre-constructed) and offered in answer to Burke's question in the opening of the *Grammar of Motives*, "What is involved when we say what people are doing and why they are doing it?" (xv). Agency is also an illusion in the sense that it's an ideological construct: it arises from the "nature of the world as all [humans] necessarily experience it" (xv). In other words, agency is a product of the inescapable ideology of the Human Barnyard. Prefabricated agent functions are the products of more provincial ideologies. But if agency is an attribution, our ideological concerns have been misplaced. We should be concerned less about empowering subaltern subjects and more about enabling and encouraging attributions of agency *to* them by those with whom they interact—and accepting such attributions *from* them. We should examine the attributions we ourselves are willing to make and work to improve the attributions that (other) empowered groups are willing to make.

This same point applies to our pedagogical concerns. Part of our responsibility is to be willing to attribute agency to students and part is to educate their capacities of attribution. This requires both technical and moral education, for our attributions of agency are ultimately moral judgments, matters of human decency and respect, matters of "acknowledgment," to use Michael Hyde's more theological term. Acknowledgment, he says, is a "life-giving gift" (23), and attribution gives the gift of rhetorical agency. Do we owe such acknowledgment, such agency-granting attribution, to automated assessment systems? Right now, I suspect that most of us agree that we do not, and moreover that out of respect for our students we should not ask them to make such attributions either.

Acknowledgments

I am grateful to the twenty-five instructors who responded to my survey; their thoughtful comments proved to be highly productive stimulants to my own thinking. Christian Casper assisted with the setup of the survey questions on the SurveyMonkey site and retrieved and organized the responses. I benefited from discussions of agency with Scot Barnett during an independent study we undertook in 2005 and from his comments and those of Carl Herndl, Jerry Blitefield, and Lisa Keranen on an earlier draft of this article.

Notes

1 www.ets.org/portal/site/ets/menuitem.1488512ecfd5b8849a77b13bc3921509/?vgnextoid=f 5d9af5e44df4010VgnVCM10000022f95190RCRD&vgnextchannel=6aae253b164f4010Vgn VCM10000022f95190RCRD#q20; accessed 8 June 2006.

2 www.collegeboard.com/highered/apr/accu/accu.html; accessed 8 June 2006.

3 www.ets.org/portal/site/ets/menuitem.1488512ecfd5b8849a77b13bc3921509/?vgnextoid=ef 972d3631df4010VgnVCM10000022f95190RCRD&vgnextchannel=d07e253b164f4010Vgn-VCM10000022f95190RCRD; accessed 8 June 2006.

4 www.vantagelearning.com/myaccess/index.php; accessed 8 June 2006; www.vantagelearning. com/myaccess/faqs.php; accessed 8 June 2006.

5 www.k-a-t.com/prodIEA.shtml; accessed 8 June 2006.

6 This product is many steps beyond the only other effort I am aware of so far, Speech-Grader™, which is a spreadsheet designed for teacher grading; see www.speechgrader.com; accessed 8 June 2006.

7 At least for now. Some of the features described earlier are not quite as ridiculous as I had intended when I started making them up. See "HCI and the Face," www.bartneck.de/workshop/ chi2006/index.html; the "Affective Computing Portal," www.bartneck.de/link/affective_portal. html; the "Face Detection Homepage," www.facedetection.com/; all sites accessed 8 June 2006.

8 The survey was conducted at www.surveymonkey.com. An explanation and link were sent to the listserv for first-year writing instructors and to the director of the basic course in public speaking, who forwarded it to instructors. At the end of the anonymous survey, respondents were asked to indicate whether they were teachers primarily of writing or of public speaking. Quotations are identified by the respondent number assigned by SurveyMonkey and by W for those who identified themselves as writing instructors or S for speaking instructors.

9 Another respondent identified the issue in moral terms but said, "I have no moral dilemma with letting a machine save me what amounts to about a month of hours [sic] worth of grading per academic year" (#W22).

10 Sometimes this ideology seems to be "humanist," however, and sometimes it seems to be "modernist."

11 This exchange won the 2005 Charles Kneupper award for the "most significant contribution to scholarship in rhetoric" in the pages of the *Rhetoric Society Quarterly* (see Awards and Honors at http://rhetoricsociety.org/). Information about the Alliance is available at www.rhetoricalliance.org/.

12 Interestingly, however, "agency" appears as a main entry in none of the three recent reference works on rhetoric and as an index entry only in Enos (under "Marxist rhetoric" and "Voice") (Enos; Jasinski; Sloane).

13 The effects on rhetoric of the bias of writing have been characterized in many ways; useful discussions are by George Kennedy (*Classical Rhetoric*), Walter Ong, and Jan Swearingen.

14 My suggestion here is reminiscent of George Kennedy's definition of rhetoric itself as "the energy inherent in an utterance" (*Comparative Rhetoric*, 5).

15 In fact, some thought the computer would be *less* inscrutable (several speculated that students would learn to "game" the system) and less intimidating.

16 See my earlier discussions of intelligent agents such as the software robot "Julia" and pedagogical agents ("Writing in a Culture of Simulation"; "Expertise and Agency").

17 See my discussion of ethopoeia in the context of artificial intelligence ("Writing in a Culture of Simulation"), where I cite some of the research referred to. See also Stewart Guthrie's discussion of anthropomorphism as a cognitive bias with survival value and Justin Barrett's hypothesis that humans possess a "hyperactive agent-detection device," or HADD (31).

18 Thanks to Scot Barnett for this example.

19 It should be remembered that Burke's "agency" differs from the agency under discussion here. Burke defines agency as the instrumental means in an action and usually exemplifies it as a tool or machine (although of course it has considerable flexibility) (xx), whereas its central use in the ongoing conversation I have referred to is much closer to Burke's own "motive."

20 See also Sharon Crowley's contention that "sound and useful theories of rhetorical agency are important to the survival of rhetorical studies" (Crowley, 7).

References

Aristotle. *On Rhetoric: A Theory of Civic Discourse.* Trans. and Ed. George A. Kennedy. New York: Oxford UP, 1991.

Atwill, Janet M. "Rhetorical and Political Agency in the Habitus." *Alliance of Rhetoric Societies.* Evanston, 2003. www.comm.umn.edu/ARS/Agency/Atwill,agency.htm.

Austin, J. L. *How to Do Things with Words.* 1962. 2nd ed. Cambridge: Harvard UP, 1975.

Baier, Annette C. *Moral Prejudices: Essays on Ethics.* Cambridge: Harvard UP, 1994.

Barnett, Scot. "Spatializing Rhetorical Agency: Capacities for Action in Non-Place." *Rhetoric Society of America.* Memphis, 2006.

Baron, Dennis. "The College Board's New Essay Reverses Decades of Progress Toward Literacy." Opinion. *Chronicle of Higher Education* (6 May 2005). http://chronicle.com/weekly/v51/i35/35b01401.htm

Barrett, Justin L. "Exploring the Natural Foundations of Religion." *Trends in Cognitive Sciences* 4.1 (2000): 29–34.

Burke, Kenneth. *A Grammar of Motives.* 1945. Reprint ed. Berkeley: U of California P, 1969.

Campbell, Karlyn Kohrs. "Agency: Promiscuous and Protean." *Alliance of Rhetoric Societies.* Evanston, 2003. www.comm.umn.edu/ARS/

Carlson, Marvin. *Performance: A Critical Introduction.* 1996. 2nd ed. New York: Routledge, 2004.

Clark, Gregory. "Introduction [to the Special Issue on the Alliance of Rhetoric Societies Conference]." *Rhetoric Society Quarterly* 34.3 (2004): 5–7.

Condit, Celeste. "Why Rhetorical Training Can Expand Agency." *Alliance of Rhetoric Societies.* Evanston, 2003. www.comm.umn.edu/ARS/Agency/Condit,%20agency.htm

Crowley, Sharon. "Response to Karlyn Kohrs Campbell, 'Agency.'" *Alliance of Rhetoric Societies.* Evanston, 2003. www.rhetoricalliance.org

Enos, Theresa, ed. *Encyclopedia of Rhetoric and Composition: Communication from Ancient Times to the Information Age*. New York: Garland Publishing, 1996.

Ericsson, Patricia Freitag and Richard Haswell, eds. *Machine Scoring of Student Essays: Truth and Consequences*. Logan: Utah State UP, 2006.

Fishman, Jenn, Andrea Lunsford, Beth McGregor, and Mark Otuteye. "Performing Writing, Performing Literacy." *College Composition and Communication* 57.2 (2005): 224–52.

Gaonkar, Dilip Parameshwar. "The Idea of Rhetoric in the Rhetoric of Science." *Rhetorical Hermeneutics: Invention and Interpretation in the Age of Science*. Ed. Alan G. Gross and William M. Keith. Albany: SUNY P, 1997. 25–85.

Geisler, Cheryl. "How Ought We to Understand the Concept of Rhetorical Agency? Report from the ARS." *Rhetoric Society Quarterly* 34.3 (2004): 9–17.

———. "Teaching the Post-Modern Rhetor: Continuing the Conversation on Rhetorical Agency." *Rhetoric Society Quarterly* 35.4 (2005): 107–13.

Goffman, Erving. *The Presentation of Self in Everyday Life*. Garden City: Doubleday, 1959.

Greene, Ronald Walter. "Rhetoric and Capitalism: Rhetorical Agency as Communicative Labor." *Philosophy and Rhetoric* 37.3 (2004): 188–206.

Guthrie, Stewart. *Faces in the Clouds: A New Theory of Religion*. New York: Oxford UP, 1993.

Hauser, Gerard A. "Teaching Rhetoric: Or Why Rhetoric Isn't Just Another Kind of Philosophy or Literary Criticism." *Rhetoric Society Quarterly* 34.3 (2004): 39–53.

Herndl, Carl G. and Adela C. Licona. "Shifting Agency: Agency, Kairos, and the Possibilities of Social Action." *Communicative Practices in Workplaces and the Professions: Cultural Perspectives on the Regulation of Discourse and Organizations*. Ed. Mark Zachry and Charlotte Thralls. Amityville: Baywood Publishing Company, In Press.

Hyde, Michael J. "Acknowledgment, Conscience, Rhetoric, and Teaching: The Case of *Tuesdays with Morrie*." *Rhetoric Society Quarterly* 35.2 (2005): 23–46.

Jarratt, Susan C. "A Matter of Emphasis." *Rhetoric Society Quarterly* 36.2 (2006): 213–19.

Jasinski, James. *Sourcebook on Rhetoric: Key Concepts in Contemporary Rhetorical Studies*. Rhetoric and Society. Ed. Herbert W. Simons. Thousand Oaks: SAGE Publications, 2001.

Kennedy, George A. *Classical Rhetoric and Its Christian and Secular Tradition from Ancient to Modern Times*. 1980. 2nd ed. Chapel Hill: U of North Carolina P, 1999.

———. *Comparative Rhetoric: An Historical and Cross-Cultural Introduction*. New York: Oxford UP, 1998.

Latour, Bruno. "Mixing Humans and Nonhumans Together: The Sociology of a Door-Closer." *Social Problems* 35.3 (1988): 298–310.

———. *We Have Never Been Modern*. Trans. Catherine Porter. Cambridge, MA: Harvard UP, 1993.

Leff, Michael. "Tradition and Agency in Humanistic Rhetoric." *Philosophy and Rhetoric* 36.2 (2003): 135–47.

———. "Up from Theory: Or I Fought the Topoi and the Topoi Won." *Rhetoric Society Quarterly* 36.2 (2006): 203–11.

Leff, Michael and Andrea A. Lunsford. "Afterwords: A Dialogue." *Rhetoric Society Quarterly* 34.3 (2004): 55–67.

Lucaites, John Louis and Celeste Michelle Condit. "Epilogue: Contributions from Rhetorical Theory." *Contemporary Rhetorical Theory: A Reader*. Ed. John Louis Lucaites, Celeste Michelle Condit, and Sally Caudill. New York: Guilford P, 1999. 609–13.

Lundberg, Christian and Joshua Gunn. "'Ouija Board, Are There Any Communications?' Agency, Ontotheology, and the Death of the Humanist Subject, or, Continuing the ARS Conversation." *Rhetoric Society Quarterly* 35.4 (2005): 83–105.

McNay, Lois. "Subject, Psyche and Agency: The Work of Judith Butler." *Theory, Culture, & Society* 16.2 (1999): 175–93.

Miller, Carolyn R. "Expertise and Agency: Transformations of Ethos in Human–Computer Interaction." *The Ethos of Rhetoric*. Ed. Michael Hyde. Columbia: U of South Carolina P, 2004. 197–218.

————. "Writing in a Culture of Simulation: Ethos Online." *Towards a Rhetoric of Everyday Life: New Directions in Research on Writing, Text, and Discourse.* Ed. Martin Nystrand and John Duffy. Madison: U of Wisconsin P, 2003. 58–83.

Ong, Walter J. *Orality and Literacy: The Technologizing of the Word.* London: Methuen, 1982.

Pickering, Andrew. *The Mangle of Practice: Time, Agency, and Science.* Chicago: U of Chicago P, 1995.

Sloane, Thomas O., ed. *Encyclopedia of Rhetoric.* Oxford: Oxford UP, 2001.

Smith, Paul. *Discerning the Subject.* Minneapolis: U of Minnesota P, 1988.

Swearingen, C. Jan. *Rhetoric and Irony: Western Literacy and Western Lies.* New York: Oxford UP, 1991.

Vivian, Bradford. "Style, Rhetoric, and Postmodern Culture." *Philosophy and Rhetoric* 35.3 (2002): 223–43.

Walker, Jeffrey. "On Rhetorical Traditions: A Reply to Jerzy Axer." *Alliance of Rhetoric Societies.* Evanston, 2003. www.rhetoricalliance.org

Weizenbaum, Joseph. *Computer Power and Human Reason: From Judgment to Calculation.* San Francisco: W. H. Freeman, 1976.

13

Between Archive and Participation
Public Memory in a Digital Age

EKATERINA HASKINS

In sizing up the notion of public memory, rhetoricians would be remiss not to consider the increasing importance of new media in shaping our contemporary remembrance culture. Whereas mediation in one form or another has always imprinted itself on memory work, the rising popularity of the internet as a vehicle of memory and as a supplement to older forms of commemoration deserves a closer look. This article proposes to examine memorial functions of the internet in light of recent scholarly debates about virtues and drawbacks of modern "archival memory" as well as the paradoxical link between the contemporary public obsession with memory and the acceleration of amnesia. I suggest that "digital memory," more than any other form of mediation, collapses the assumed distinction between modern "archival" memory and traditional "lived" memory by combining the function of storage and ordering on the one hand, and of presence and interactivity on the other. Although on its face such synthesis seems to posit the internet as a panacea for both ideological reification associated with official memory practices and the fragility of popular memory, the medium's potential cannot be discussed in the abstract, separate from its cultural and political milieu and institutions that have deployed it in the service of memory work. Accordingly, to illustrate the merits and limitations of electronic media as vehicles of collecting, preserving, and displaying traces of the past, I will examine *The September 11 Digital Archive*, a comprehensive online effort to document public involvement in commemorating the tragedy of 11 September 2001.

Archival Memory and Its Discontents

In his influential work *The Past Is a Foreign Country*, David Lowenthal remarks, "The past is integral to our sense of identity. . . . Ability to recall and identify with our own past gives existence meaning, purpose, and value" (41). Although most public memory scholars begin with this premise as a point of departure, their analyses of commemorative activity often raise questions of representation and agency. Which past is identified as worthy of remembrance? Who carries out the work of recalling it? What forms does commemoration take?

As French historian Pierre Nora famously observed, "Modern memory is, above all, archival. It relies entirely on the materiality of the trace, the immediacy of the recording, the visibility of the image" (13). In choosing what to preserve as traces of the past, museums and archives have traditionally valued objects and texts, selected for their enduring cultural value, over ephemeral manifestations of cultural heritage. Not incidentally, artifacts and texts selected for preservation and veneration were typically products of intellectual and artistic elites rather than illiterate artisans and performers. This preference, furthermore, contributed to the loss of contexts in which artifacts and texts were produced in order to subordinate them to legitimizing narratives of historical progress and national identity.[1]

Furthermore, relegating the task of remembering to official institutions and artifacts arguably weakens the need for a political community actively to remember its past. Instead of continuous transmission of shared past through participatory performance and ritual, memory work is carried out by "compensatory organs of remembrance" (Huyssen 252) such as museums, archives, and memorials.[2] Associated with the rise of capitalism and the modern nation-state, these institutions of memory have tended to promulgate official ideologies of the ruling elites while claiming to speak on behalf of the people. As John Gillis points out, until the late 1960s, memory work was "the preserve of elite males, the designated carriers of progress. . . . Workers, racial minorities, young people, and women gained admission to national memories at an even slower pace than they were admitted to national representative and educational institutions" (10). In other words, until recently, public memory was constructed and disseminated for the people but not by the people.

Stylistically, official memorial culture has relied on " 'dogmatic formalism' and the restatement of reality in ideal rather than complex or ambiguous forms" (Bodnar 13). Monuments and memorials erected throughout the nineteenth and first half of the twentieth centuries employed representational symbolism to convey narratives of victory and valor.[3] Museums of history and public art, similarly, were fashioned after Greek and Roman architectural forms to emphasize the affinities between modern nation-state and classical forms of government (Duncan). The scale of memorials and museums, too, played its role in instilling a sense of awe and distance in their audience: dwarfed by their size, the visitor was cast in the role of observer and spectator rather than participant.

In contrast with the hegemonic official memory, vernacular practices of public remembrance typically assume decidedly ephemeral forms such as parades, performances, and temporary interventions. Instead of somber monumentality, they employ non-hierarchical, sometimes subversive symbolism and stress egalitarian interaction and participation. According to Bodnar, such practices convey "what social reality feels like rather than what it should be like" (14). Although vernacular forms of cultural expression have existed alongside the official culture for a long time (think of Medieval carnival), it is only recently that they acquired cultural respectability in Western democracies. The traveling NAMES project AIDS Memorial quilt is often cited as an example of a vernacular commemoration that acts both as an intimate tableau of private grief and a compelling form of public address. The multiplicity of individually crafted panels comprising the quilt as well as the variety of messages and images inscribed on them underscored the plurality of voices united in the act of grieving and the enormity of the problem that the audience was encouraged to grasp. The quilt's material and its formal configuration also made a vivid statement: fabric by nature frays and decays with time, so fresh panels must replace the worn ones and new panels must be added as more lives are claimed by the AIDS epidemic (Hawkins 141). By its very impermanence and contingency, then, this memorial gesture reminded its audience about the frailty of memory and its dependence on the continuing communal participation.

The line between official and vernacular memory practices, however, is becoming blurry, as designers, museum professionals, and art critics begin to ponder how "permanent" memorials might engage their popular audiences instead of imposing on them the ossified values of political and cultural elites. Many scholars agree that official "archival" memory no longer exclusively relies on idealized representational forms and dogmatic iconography. Projection artist Krzystof Wodiczko, a champion of ephemeral public gestures, describes this shift from official to vernacular tendencies in public memorials:

> The previously respectful distance ("historical perspective") of the memorial from everyday life is now being broken. Cold, tombstone benches, regimenting, mountainous stairways, brainwashing fountains, architortured bushes, and windswept floors were intended to banish unofficial life from the memorial's territory. Today, the authorities want to add life and "social function" to the memorial site, to turn it into a "humanized" space for cultural relaxation, a zone of free festivity, tourism, permanent recreation, and so-called art in public spaces.
>
> (49)

The precedent, at least in the United States, appears to have been set by Maya Lin's design for the Vietnam Veterans Memorial in Washington, DC. Instead of glorifying the Vietnam conflict, the black granite chevron laconically conveys the cost of war by listing all American casualties in chronological order. Explaining its impact on subsequent commemorations, Gillis states, "the Vietnam Memorial, with its wall of names is generally agreed to represent a turning point in the history of public memory, a decisive departure from the anonymity of the Tomb of the Unknown Soldier and a growing acknowledgement that everyone now deserves equal recognition at all times in wholly accessible places" (13).

In addition to its strategy of naming names, the memorial's physical form invites participation: its polished black surface reflects the visitor's image and its modest scale allows one to reach out and touch the names inscribed on the wall. Although its non-heroic stance initially angered some officials and veterans who wished to see an unambiguous affirmation of military valor, the memorial has become an iconic site of popular remembrance. To mark their pilgrimage to the wall, many visitors leave behind mementos that temporarily become part of the memorial composition. At first, the National Park Service classified these ephemera as "lost and found" but later on began collecting and archiving them for posterity, thus moving them "from the cultural status of being 'lost' (without category) to historical artifacts" (Sturken 173). In the case of the Vietnam Veterans Memorial, then, "written in stone" official memory and ephemeral public participation are continuous with each other.[4] This happy coexistence seems to guard against the twin dangers of ideological reification and amnesia. In the age of electronic media, however, these dangers haunt all efforts to include the public into the memorial process and to preserve the ephemera of popular expression.

Promises and Problems of Digital Memory

Although even "permanent" memorials and museums are now being built with an eye to stimulating public engagement, their capacity to share memory work with ordinary people pales in comparison with "digital" memorials and archives. Still, the internet's promise of representational diversity, collective authorship, and interactivity is in need of exploration and critique.

At least in theory, online memorializing can accommodate an infinite variety of artifacts and performances. Because all new media objects are composed of digital code (Manovich 27), it becomes possible to collect, preserve, sort, and display a vast amount of texts, drawings, photography, video, and audio recordings. In addition to this capacity to "translate" other media into digital code, the function of hyperlinking facilitates interconnectedness among different sources, producing a cacophonous heteroglossia of public expression (Warnick, *Critical Literacy* 107). Instead of only official accounts disseminated by mainstream media and the government, all kinds of stories can now become part of an evolving patchwork of public memory. Formerly limited in time and space, ephemeral gestures can be preserved in still and moving images, ready to be viewed and replayed on demand. Previously banished to dark storage rooms, mementos left at memorial sites can be displayed for all to see. The boundaries between the official and the vernacular, the public and the private, the permanent and the evanescent will cease to matter, for all stories and images will be equally fit to represent and comment on the past.

Perhaps like no other medium before, the internet has made collective authorship a practical reality, fulfilling many literary critics' desire to free texts from authorial constraints. Most new media texts are products of collaboration among multiple designers and users. According to Warnick,

"A hyperlinked, multi-media site including user contributions as part of its text is best described in Barthes' words as a de-centered 'tissue of quotations drawn from innumerable centers of culture'" ("Looking to the Future" 146). It functions as "text" and not as "work," in that it appropriates and reproduces content from the networked system of which it is a part and may not lend itself well to critical approaches that assume authorial intent and linear structure" ("Looking to the Future" 330–331). Landow elaborates this point when he compares the process of generating digital hypertext with the tradition of appropriating or paraphrasing other discourses in print: "The text of the Other may butt up against that by someone else; it may even crash against it. But it does seem to retain more of its own voice. In print, on the other hand, one feels constrained to summarize large portions of another's text, if only to demonstrate one's command (understanding) of it and to avoid giving the appearance that one has infringed copyright" (158). The internet levels the traditional hierarchy of author-text-audience, thereby distributing authorial agency among various institutions and individuals involved in the production of content and preventing any one agent from imposing narrative and ideological closure upon the data. As Web memorials depend on "the joint production of Web-accessible materials by disparate actors" (Foot, Warnick, and Schneider), they represent an evolving, multidimensional narrative of historical events and responses to them.

Similar to multiple authorship, "interactivity" has been hailed as a democratizing attribute of new media. Simply put, interactivity embodies "one of the biggest potentials of cyberspace"—to act as "a two-way street in a world where the dominant medium (television) has been unidirectional" (Gurak 44). Although some consider the term itself too broad and even misleading,[5] the users' ability to supply content, provide feedback, and choose their own paths through the system of hyperlinks marks the experience of navigating the internet as more participatory and active than that of flipping through television channels, scanning a newspaper, or following an audio tour through a museum. The audience no longer acts as a consumer of a linear story—it takes part in the experience by making choices to connect particular messages and images as well as to register responses to them.

Although diversity of content, collective authorship, and interactivity hold a potential of stimulating broad public engagement in memory work, these features work in tandem with a larger cultural context and are subject to medium-specific constraints. One cannot ignore that today's memorializing occurs in a climate of rapid obsolescence and the disappearance of historical consciousness, that much of computer-mediated communication serves commercial and entertainment purposes, and that interactivity can nurture narcissistic amnesia no less than communal exchange.

Contemporary "democratization of the past" (Gillis) is paradoxically entwined with the disappearance of historical consciousness. According to Andreas Huyssen,

> Both personal and social memory today are affected by an emerging new structure of temporality generated by the quickening pace of material life on the one hand and by the acceleration of media images and information on the other. Speed destroys space, and it erases temporal distance. In both cases, the mechanism of physiological perception is altered. The more memory we store on data banks, the more past is sucked into the orbit of the present, ready to be called up on the screen.
>
> (253)

The glut of archival memory is a by-product of rapid obsolescence. In the words of Gillis, "The past has become so distant and the future so uncertain that we can no longer be sure what to save, so we save everything. . . . The scale of collecting increases in inverse proportion to our depth perception. Now that old is equated with yesterday we allow nothing to disappear" (15). The common worry about this expanding dossier is that active memory work—not just compulsive collection of traces—would be thwarted by the sheer volume of stuff that is being preserved as well as the ease of retrieving the past at will. When technology offers the ability of instant recall, individual impulse to remember withers away. If archival preservation and retrieval are not balanced by mechanisms that stimulate participatory engagement, electronic memory may lead to self-congratulatory amnesia.[6]

Another concern is that the typical user's participation in online interaction has been to a large extent shaped by commercial patterns of experience. As Manovich reminds us, "the logic of new media fits the logic of the postindustrial society, which values individuality over conformity" (41). The rhetoric of individual choice permeates contemporary commercial culture, reassuring consumers of their uniqueness and stimulating compulsive shopping as a form of identity-shaping performance. Perhaps it is not coincidental that a good portion of user-supplied Web content consists of self-expression, most vividly represented by the genre of Weblog (Miller and Shepherd). Although some bloggers engage in a sort of editorial activity by providing links and annotating other sources, the majority of blog authors relate their own experiences (whether real or imaginary) to a potentially limitless number of people (Blood).

Blogging can be seen as a form of self-memorialization, and an impulse to save the most trivial details of one's past, however recent it might be, is one manifestation of contemporary remembrance culture in the West: "Both Americans and Europeans have become compulsive consumers of the past, shopping for that which best suits their particular sense of self at the moment, constructing out of a bewildering variety of materials, times, and places the multiple identities that are demanded of them in the post-national era" (Gillis 17–18).

However, this "customized" approach to one's past and sense of belonging, enabled by electronic media, may breed cultural and political insularity and lead to a fragmented body politic. Scholars of political communication caution that some of the internet's assets as a political medium could also be its greatest weaknesses. The ability to narrow down one's Web search thematically, for example, while allowing to magnify one's exposure to information on a particular topic, simultaneously promotes a narrow focus on certain issues at the expense of a broad awareness of political matters (see Selnow, Gronbeck).[7]

The intersection of contemporary remembrance culture and new media technologies presents a mixed bag of promises and problems. Storage and sorting capacities of the internet are certainly helpful in preserving, organizing, and linking vast amounts of data. Everyone can now engage in a free search for one's past and identity, becoming her own historian. Thanks to interactivity, virtually everyone can also leave an imprint on the fabric of public memory by sharing images and stories with millions of other users. As a result of these technologically abetted cultural changes, professional historians, archivists, and museum curators find themselves compelled both to acknowledge the role of ordinary people in history making and to include diverse forms of popular expression into the "official" record of history. In so doing, however, they are facing a challenge to their traditional role as stewards of public memory. To remain relevant, they must strike a delicate balance, as it were, between a desire to accommodate as many different voices as possible, on the one hand, and a responsibility to provide a common ground for this diversity, on the other. It is one thing to collect and digitize large quantities of memorial artifacts; it is quite another to display them in ways that stimulate not only spectatorship but also meaningful participation. Although online interactivity has been extolled for its potential to foster communitarian intimacy, it is necessary to ask what kind of exchange actually occurs—whether it indeed creates bridges between demographically and politically diverse audiences or promotes balkanization.

Between Archive and Public Participation:
The September 11 Digital Archive

11 September 2001 became deeply etched in collective imagination not only because of the brutality of the terrorist attacks and the magnitude of human loss, but also because it was one of the most mediated disasters in history. Broadcast live on television, the sudden collapse of the World Trade Center towers was witnessed by a global audience. Yet mainstream media were not the only narrators of the unfolding drama of those tragic events and their aftermath. Thousands of people, armed with digital cameras and personal computers, were recording history and reporting it on the internet. In Dan Gillmor's description, "Another kind of reporting emerged during those appalling hours and days. Via e-mails, mailing lists, chat groups, personal web journals—all nonstandard news sources—we received valuable context that the major American media couldn't, or wouldn't, provide" (x).

Like grassroots journalism, the proliferation of memorial and discussion websites created in response to the trauma of 11 September 2001 and its aftermath pointed to the diversity and robustness of vernacular expression.

Memorializing online was often an extension of the spontaneous process begun in the streets, squares, and train stations of New York City and Washington, DC. Thousands of ephemeral artifacts from posters and graffiti to makeshift memorials filled public spaces, interrupting quotidian time and space of city life and creating a vivid counterpoint to mainstream media coverage. These unregulated displays of mourning, sympathy, pride, and protest not only represented a range of responses to the events—"intervening into the rhythm of the metropolis, the vernacular utterance of street memorials jolted lunch-hour pedestrians and commuters into realizing the significance of public spaces" (Haskins and DeRose 383). City residents, commuters, and tourists alike were made into witnesses of history as it was unfolding not on television or front pages of newspapers but directly in front of them. This liminal experience momentarily transformed a collection of passersby into a community of people who were, to paraphrase S. Michael Halloran (5), self-consciously present to each other as well as to the spontaneous spectacle that brought them together. Before commemorative process migrated to cyberspace, it was actively experienced by thousands of people as they witnessed and contributed to the ephemeral tableau of vernacular gestures.

When temporary memorials and posters of missing began to be removed, many museums and organizations stepped in to preserve these and other ephemera of 9/11 for posterity in order to add them as historical evidence to an already ample set of individual and corporate efforts to memorialize the victims of the attacks. The *September 11 Digital Archive*, organized by the American Social History Project at the City University of New York and the Center for History and New Media at George Mason University and now supported by the Library of Congress, represents a comprehensive attempt to "collect, preserve and present the history of September 11 attacks" (*The September 11 Digital Archive*). The Archive's stated purpose summarizes its desire to act as a mediator of a historical event as it was witnessed by regular people, to provide a well-sorted repository of materials for future historians, and to furnish a space where the disparate experiences and reactions could be relived and reflected on. Accordingly, the following discussion of the Archive will focus on these three aspects of its mission—to collect, to organize, and to display—in light of this article's concern with the promises of "digital memory."

"The utterly objective exhibition, like the completely unmediated photograph, is a phantasm" (Livingston and Beardsley 105). Archivists and museum curators always mediate between the artifacts they choose for display and their audiences but rarely do they explicitly acknowledge their own motives or recognize the role that visitors play in parsing an exhibit's narrative. As Bruce Ferguson argues, "Exhibitions are publicly sanctioned representations of identity, principally, but not exclusively, of the institutions which present them. They are narratives which use art objects as elements in institutionalized stories that are promoted to an audience" (9). For example, the Museum of the City of New York, one of the institutions that participated in salvaging ephemeral artifacts of 9/11 for posterity, organized an exhibit of these objects on the first anniversary of the attacks to "underscore the role of museums as stewards of the nation's stories and as special places where communities can examine and reaffirm our basic freedoms" (quoted in Haskins and DeRose 384).

It is therefore noteworthy that the organizers of the *September 11 Digital Archive* not only "exhibit [their] intention" but also show their awareness of being "only one of three agents" in the field of exhibition (the other two being the maker of objects on display and the viewer) (Baxandall 39). In so doing, they do not promote a univocal, self-aggrandizing narrative. Their goal, instead, is to "foster some positive legacies of those terrible events by allowing people to tell their stories, making those stories available to a wide audience, providing historical context for understanding those events and their consequences, and helping historians and archivists improve their practices based on the lessons we learn from this project" ("About This Site").

Unlike traditional exhibitions, where the curator often exercises full control over the selection of materials, the *September 11 Digital Archive* epitomizes inclusiveness, which is made possible in no small degree by the interactive capacities of electronic media. The Archive's "Contributor Information" link welcomes submissions in multiple forms and media (stories, e-mails, and images) and allows for participation by anyone who had been touched by the events of 11 September. In particular, the wording of answers to frequently asked questions invites collaboration, positioning audience members as active participants in the unfolding of history regardless of their age, nationality, or location on the day of the attacks. For example, those who may have doubted their story's importance because they were not at Ground Zero, the Pentagon, or in Pennsylvania, were reassured as follows: "Please! We want to hear from you. Your experiences need not have been at or near the directly affected locations, not [*sic*] do they need to be particularly heroic or harrowing tales. They can be short or much longer personal reminiscences about how you or the people you knew were affected by 9/11" ("Contributor Information"). Foreigners, too, were encouraged to contribute to the archive: "September 11 was an event that evoked many kinds of responses in many parts of the world. The internet is similarly a global phenomenon. As such, we are eager to receive contributions of all kinds from all parts of the world" ("Contributor Information").

The Archive's strategy of democratic openness yielded a plethora of submissions, especially in the form of personal stories and images (both still and moving), which reached nineteen thousand and three thousand, respectively. In addition to these, the archive organized quantities of already existing individual, corporate, and government websites, documents, and online collections related to 11 September and its aftermath. Finally, in a section "Frequently Asked Questions about the September 11 attacks" it provided links to a step-by-step account of the event by the *New York Times*.

In its sprawling totality, this collection of stories, images, and points of view reflects the unsettled and still evolving quality of public memory of the 9/11 trauma. Although mainstream media accounts assembled by the Archive provide a factual overview of the events themselves, personal stories, photo essays, and artwork present a motley tapestry of sentiments and attitudes in response to the events. They echo the spontaneous vernacular commemoration begun in public spaces in the days after the attacks as well as testify to the connection between privately shaped memories and those furnished for public consumption by mainstream media.

Individual stories, arranged in reverse chronological order by the date of submission (similar to the way entries are displayed on electronic discussion lists), reveal a mix of the extraordinary and the banal. On the one hand, family members tell of their loved ones who perished, survivors recount the circumstances of their escape from the Twin Towers or the Pentagon, and volunteers relate their experiences of helping rescue and cleaning crews at Ground Zero or working at hospitals and blood banks. On the other hand, entry after entry describes its author's memory of television coverage of the terrorist attacks. Many of these register their shock at realizing that what they were watching was not an action movie but a live broadcast.

Although scores of stories simply recall their authors' first emotional reactions—disbelief, terror, and sympathy for victims and their families are the most common sentiments—some also go on to reflect on the meaning of the tragedy and its aftermath. A sense of vulnerability and loss pervades many entries, especially those by schoolchildren, for whom 11 September was the first exposure to organized violence on a large scale. As one high school student puts it, "Sometimes we take things for granted and my generation really didn't know what it felt like to be under attack but now we do" (Pichoff). A ski patroller from Colorado recalls the confusion and misplaced jingoism that characterized the months after the attacks:

> The desire to take revenge was very strong, although there seemed to be nobody to take revenge against. In this atmosphere calling French fries "freedom fries", or singing "God Bless America", were seen as dynamic actions rather than being auxiliary to the matter at hand, simply because it was unclear as to what, exactly, the matter at hand was.
>
> (Oien)

There are, of course, more emphatic statements that express politically polarized attitudes in support of or in opposition to the US government's domestic and foreign policy in the wake of 9/11. For example, a Chicago businessman who stockpiled firearms in case US residents of Middle-Eastern descent become "sleeper warriors" and take to the streets, intones:

> In short order—our Commander in Chief, George W. Bush, did what needed to be done in a very pragmatic and reasonable way. He went about the job he had to do and now the evil people that brought terror to us—are

either dead, terrified or on the run and in hiding. They may well attack again. But for every one of us they kill, we will bring the wrath of God down on them thousandfold.

(Hiley)

On the other end of the spectrum, a college student who became an anti-war activist after 11 September, voices her anger at the Bush administration:

September 11th made clear to me the importance of challenging and criticizing our governments [sic] blind move to bomb and murder thousands of innocent Afghanistani, and soon, Iraqi citizens. When the towers first fell I was in a state of shock, but as I listened to President Bush's rhetoric (laced heavily with calls for American Manifest Destiny), I found myself enraged and energized for action.

(Jaeger)

Similar to verbal accounts, images submitted to the Archive represent a collage of perspectives. Among still photographs, which dominate the category, many document the devastation of Ground Zero and the neighborhoods around it, the recovery and clean-up work of the police and firefighters, and the proliferation of missing posters and impromptu remembrance shrines around New York City and the country. Some pictures capture the sights familiar to many through mainstream media coverage, such as the smoldering pile of wreckage that used to be the World Trade Center, whereas others focus on smaller details of the changed landscape, such as a poison dust warning posted in a Tribeca park near North Tower days after 9/11 (Vogler) or a Burger King that became a makeshift triage center (Occi).

Photographic entries often "voice" their authors' rhetorical intent, clarified by captions or short narratives. These commentaries tend to situate their subjects within some narrative frame, casting the events in a different light depending on the author's attitude. For instance, an image depicting a unit of National Guardsmen arriving at the World Trade Center site on 12 September is titled "Redeemers" (G. N. Miller) and as such contributes to a narrative of heroic sacrifice, which came to dominate the memory of 9/11 as it has been constructed in mainstream US culture in the following years. A narrative of a community coming together to grieve and remember is reflected in captions accompanying photographs of makeshift memorials, as in the one describing the temporary shrine in Union Square Park just twenty blocks from Ground Zero: "Every day, all day hundreds of people would gather" (Selders). Some authors attempt to account for the presence of revenge symbolism that dotted the landscape in the weeks following the tragedy. Commenting on the picture of a life-size doll of Osama bin Laden that was hanging by its neck out of a window of a house in Massachusetts, the photographer explains:

For the last eight years I have driven by Wallaston Beach in Quincy, Massachusetts on my way to work. A couple of days after 9/11 this appeared on one of houses along the beach. It was an erie [*sic*] image considering that you can watch planes take off and land from Logan airport at the beach. They fly right over-head.

(Anonymous)

A dissenting anti-war narrative is represented by a submission called "Liberty Street Protest," whose author interprets the significance of a Liberty Street building whose windows displayed "No War" signs and peace symbols:

Overlooking the memorial plaques and area where most tourists and onlookers from around the world visit when they want to see the emptiness that is now Ground Zero and the WTC site as well as pay their respects. Conceived by local artist Glen E. Friedman, . . . to let people of the world know that New Yorkers, who live so close to the actual destruction of 9/11/01, do not agree with the "War on Terror" being waged in their name.

(Dominguez)

The most prevalent narrative by far, however, is that of nostalgia for the World Trade Center and the postindustrial utopia it symbolized. Dozens of people sent in pictures of themselves and their family members photographed against the panoramic backdrop of the Manhattan skyline anchored by the Twin Towers. Criticized as the epitome of bad urban planning and architectural hubris during their lifetime, in their haunting absence the towers became beloved martyrs whose resurrection was viewed by many as essential to the restoration of New York City and the old world order.

In gathering together these disparate fragments of post-9/11 discourse, the Archive offers a panoramic view of the fractious cacophony of public expression that cannot be accommodated by a permanent, professionally designed memorial. Cultural geographer Kenneth Foote stresses the difficulty of constructing such a memorial to 9/11 because of "the magnitude of the losses, the diversity of the victims, and the fact that the entire nation feels it has a stake in the commemorative process" (344). Although a physically tangible memorial is necessary, a virtual space such as the one provided by the Archive can play a crucial role in "forcing emotion and competing interpretations into the open" (Foote 343). By granting the authority to determine what's important (or appropriate) to individual contributors, *September 11 Digital Archive* refrains from taking sides and imposing closure upon the audience's interpretation of the different narratives. And, by allowing readers to continue submitting their stories and images, the Archive acknowledges that public memory is, in fact, an evolving process.

Beyond providing a forum for public expression, the Archive aims to offer a usable set of materials for professional historians who will revisit 11

September in the future. Toward this end, the collection is sorted and organized by medium and subject matter, allowing one to search through the cornucopia of submissions and links. Brief annotations describe many an item's content and occasionally indicate whether certain entries might offend some visitors, as in the case of several digital animation submissions that revel in the fantasy of violent retaliation against Osama bin Laden and al Qaeda. In other instances, the Archive's wording more explicitly distances its professional agenda from those of its many sources: "The September 11 Digital Archive collects reports, studies, and white-papers written by a variety of organizations and institutions in response to the September 11, 2001 attacks and the public reaction to them. The Archive gathers and presents these items to preserve the historical record. These materials do not necessarily reflect the opinions and views of the Archive or its staff."

Perhaps the clearest sign of the Archive's desire to assert its status as a steward of history while allowing unrestricted public participation can be seen in the effort to distinguish between fact and fabrication. At the bottom of each individual submission, whether it's email, story, or image, one finds a highlighted question, "How do I know that this item is factual"? Clicking on the question leads one to a manifesto of sorts that signals a tension between the Archive's populist commitment to grassroots history making and its professional obligation to maintain impartial factuality:

> Every submission to the September 11 Digital Archive—even those that are erroneous, misleading, or dubious—contributes in some way to the historical record. A misleading individual account, for example, could reveal certain personal and emotional aspects of the event that would otherwise be lost in a strict authentication and appraisal process. That said, most people who take the time to submit something to the September 11 Digital Archive share the goal of its organizers—that is, to create a reliable and permanent record of responses to the 9/11 attacks—and therefore most contributions are authentic. Nevertheless, as with any historical sources (including, for example, newspaper accounts), there are always questions about reliability, and all researchers need to evaluate their sources critically. It is for this reason that the Archive harvests metadata from every contributor—including name, email address, location, zip code, gender, age, occupation, date received—and suggests that these metadata be examined in relation to one another, in relation to the content of the submission, and in relation to other authenticated records. Sound research technique is the basis of sound scholarship.
>
> ("Frequently Asked Questions")

The Archive thus fashions itself as a space of interplay between vernacular and official interests, between the lay public and trained historians. It is a balancing act, however, and reservations in the quoted passage ("That said," "nevertheless") indicate how delicately one must tread to employ popular memory as a source of professional history writing.

If in its role as a database of historical materials the Archive seeks to respect the authorial agency of contributors, in the role of a tour guide it strives to educate its audience while respecting its autonomy. As distinct from brick-and-mortar exhibitions, digital displays do not offer a spatially continuous sequence of artifacts but instead work by inviting one to choose an item for display from a menu. It is the viewer's own preferences and interests, then, that ultimately shape her experience, even though the Web designer is responsible for the range of her choices.

To guide visitors' exposure to the variety of sources in its vast repository, *September 11 Digital Archive* makes use of several display mechanisms. First, an interactive menu breaks down the collection into main categories—stories, email, still images, moving images, audio, documents, and guide to websites. Clicking on any of these links conjures another subdivision; "moving images," for example, comprises video, digital animations, and image collections from groups and individuals. Annotations further aid the visitor in choosing which item to view. If one is inclined to browse through "digital animations," labels do not so much dictate how one should interpret their content but direct the visitor's attention by noting the satirical quality of certain entries or warning that "viewers may find the content of this digital creation offensive."

Leaving it up to the audience to decide how to proceed in their interaction with the objects on display, the Archive assigns the responsibility for the content of individual entries to their authors. In some cases, the audience reaction to certain submissions was so voluminous and polarized that their authors were compelled to add a formal reply. Thus, the author of "America Attacked 9/11," a digital creation that combined a tribute to victims and heroes of 11 September with a call for military retaliation, posted a form letter to answer his critics' objections:

> Please don't e-mail me about trying to understand the folks that did this. I have no interest in understanding them. I want them dead. Don't e-mail me about innocent people being accidently [sic] killed in a war zone. I am uninterested in their plight and if that sounds cold, go review my website again. None of THOSE people were at war on 11 September and they are not casualties of war. They were murdered. I don't want their murderers treated as war criminals; I want them treated as they are—subhuman criminals who committed crimes against humanity. I don't want to hug them, analyze them or anything other than annihilate them. Wipe them off the face of the earth.
>
> (Golding)

The letter not only reveals the author's frame of mind but also points to a deep political division that marked public response to the US government's policies in the aftermath of the attacks. After all, "depending on your political inclinations, the events of September 11, 2001 were either unique or inevitable, richly deserved or entirely unprovoked, a predictable product of generations of conflict or the dawn of an entirely new age" (Mandel). The Archive's judiciously neutral stance with regard to submissions' content, in this case, allows for a clash of these political perspectives, ignited by one contributor's inflammatory rhetoric.

Still, the Archive conspicuously exercises its control over the arrangement of items on display to draw attention to entries that may otherwise go unnoticed. Similar to temporary special exhibits mounted by regular museums, *September 11 Digital Archive* presents "featured items" that underscore its public mission to give voice to underrepresented views. The main page, for example, highlights experiences of Chinatown residents, "largely neglected by national media following 9/11," by providing a link to a collection "Ground One: Voices from Post-911 Chinatown." Under the "Documents" rubric, the featured item is "American Backlash," a "report documenting press coverage of bias incidents and violent hate crimes that occurred in the first week after the September 11 attacks." Until the fifth anniversary of the attacks, the video collection gave center stage to a film featuring interviews with Arab American residents of Bay Ridge, Brooklyn ("Arab American Responses"), after which a commemorative montage "September 11 Hero Tribute" took the spotlight. The "featured item" strategy, then, can be a mechanism for leveling the playing field by allowing politically marginalized groups to have their say. Ironically, in so doing the Archive is trying to balance its open submission policy that generated plenty of politically incorrect and even offensive material in the name of popular participation.

Perhaps because of the tension between its commitment to unbridled populism, on the one hand, and political fairness on the other, the Archive seems reluctant to lend its curatorial credibility to a particular way of commemorating 11 September. An example of this seeming objectivity is an "interactive map" of Manhattan unveiled on the fourth anniversary of 9/11 attacks. The Archive selected from its collection photographs and stories that captured the attacks against the World Trade Center and overlaid them on the map of Manhattan. Each photograph is represented by a blue marker and each story by a red marker. Visitors can click on them to relive, in painful detail, the events of that fateful day from the perspective of people who witnessed them first hand. The virtue of this display is that it presents, in a visually compelling and dynamic way, images and accounts that until then had been separate fragments of a larger story. Seeing the burning towers of the World Trade Center photographed from various vantage points and reading accounts of commuters, train operators, and policemen gives one a sense of the event as it unfolded. However, the display offers little beyond the now familiar spectacle of impending devastation, freezing in memory the moment before the towers' collapse. Reproduced repeatedly in various news media, the image of the World Trade

Center still standing became iconic in the weeks and months following the attacks. As Barbie Zelizer explains its rhetorical power,

> Not only did the images [of the towers] offer the appropriate degree of contingency for a message too harsh to be seen with the brute force of reality's depiction. . . . But the image also cut—and depicted—the story at precisely its most powerful moment, pushing spectators to recognize what came later while allowing them to prolong the experience of what had been before. The images hence created a space of (im)possibility, whereby spectators were able to linger in a moment when the full scope of the tragedy was not yet upon them.
>
> (178–79)

Focusing on this moment in an anniversary display, then, the Archive assimilated its audience's contributions into the mainstream media's strategy that can be described as a symbolic refusal to come to terms with the events of 11 September.

Conclusion

This article began with a premise that any discussion of public memory ought to take into account the issue of mediation. The rising popularity of the internet as a medium of both private remembrance and public commemoration calls for a reconsideration of traditional distinctions between official memory, embodied by "compensatory organs of remembrance" such as memorials, monuments, and museums, and vernacular forms of memory that depend on active communal participation. Online memorializing, thanks to the technology's capacity for virtually unlimited storage and potential to engage many diverse audiences in content production, appears to mitigate against the ideological ossification associated with official memory practices and the fragility of vernacular memorial gestures.

At the same time, in exploring the internet's promise as a medium of public memory, it is important to realize that the contemporary Western obsession with recording traces of the past is an ambivalent cultural trend—it signals not only the "democratization" of memory work but also the acceleration of amnesia. Moreover, the very features of electronic communication that make the technology friendly to popular participation in cultural politics can also abet political fragmentation.

As the most comprehensive effort to collect, organize, and display discursive traces of the momentous historical event commonly referred to as 9/11, the *September 11 Digital Archive* illustrates both the virtues and limitations of digital memory. Launched by professional historians, it is presented as an inclusive collection of contributions from both individuals and institutions. According to the Archive's director, Tom Scheinfeldt, there is a direct link between the size of digital storage and its democratic potential: "Unlike traditional 'brick and mortar' archives, there are no physical limits to the size of the September 11 Digital Archive's collection. If it needs to expand, it just adds more disk space. This means that no digital object is too trivial for the Archive to accept" ("Memories"). Indeed, the strategy of defining any submission related to 9/11 as "historical record" allowed the Archive to solicit and preserve a vast and diverse set of stories, images, and points of view that otherwise would have been lost or dispersed in cyberspace and private archives.

At first glance, there is no downside to inclusiveness: the Archive encourages ordinary people to participate in the production of public memory, furnishes future historians with a wealth of data, and generates a robust multiplicity of perspectives on the same event. Preservation of large quantities of digitized materials does not translate into a usable past, however. The task of interpreting this "burgeoning dossier," to use Nora's phrase, is decentralized and entrusted to the Archive's users, be they future professional historians or lay visitors. The Archive gives minimal guidance to either group: historians are admonished to distinguish between fact and fabrication when sifting through the submissions; visitors are reminded to pay attention to underrepresented voices and to be wary of voices that may offend them. There is no other mechanism, however, for encouraging the audience to explore views different from their own, in the manner that pedestrians in the streets of New York City were in the weeks following 11 September.

Such decentralized approach to historical research and remembrance may indeed be a self-conscious reaction against the traditional dictatorial role of official institutions of memory. By allowing users to participate in the shaping of the historical record and by enabling them to take charge of their journey through its collection, the Archive undoubtedly preempts possible accusations of professional elitism and political bias. Although making multiple fragments of the 9/11 discourse publicly visible and accessible, however, this approach also shifts the burden of active remembrance to individuals and groups, effectively disavowing the *public* nature of the enterprise.

Notes

1 The narrative orientation of archives and museums is evident both in their acquisition policies and display strategies. On the archive's role in constructing a connection between past and present, see Brothman. Mieke Ball similarly argues that what is being collected is guided by what story the objects on display can tell.

2 Nora distinguishes between *lieux de memoire*, sites of memory, and *milieux de memoire*, environments of memory, noting that the former have largely displaced the latter "by virtue of the de-ritualization of our world" (12).

3 See Savage on official commemorative practices after the Civil War and Bodnar on the tension between official and vernacular commemorations in the twentieth century. Foote's study of how Americans have marked sites of tragic and violent events in the last three centuries also suggests that the monumental veneration of heroes and martyrs has been the preferred method of dealing with traumatic memories.

4 Blair, Jeppeson, and Pucci interpret the Vietnam Veterans Memorial as a prototype of post-modern memorializing, given its openness to multiple interpretive gestures, its sensitivity to its environment, and its interrogative, critical stance.

5 Manovich maintains that "to call computer media 'interactive' is meaningless—it simply means stating the most basic fact about computers" (55). He further cautions,

> when we use the concept "interactive media" exclusively in relation to computer-based media, there is the danger that we will interpret "interaction" literally, equating it with physical interaction between a user and a media object (pressing a button, choosing a link, moving the body), at the expense of psychological interaction. The psychological processes of filling-in, hypothesis formation, recall, and identification, which are required for us to comprehend any text or image at all, are mistakenly identified with an objectively existing structure of interactive links.
>
> (57)

Upon reviewing recent literature on "interactivity" and synthesizing the various definitions of it, Kiousis suggests that interactivity is both a media and psychological factor that varies across communication technologies, communication contexts, and people's perceptions.

6 At the same time, historians and archivists are concerned that digital data in particular lacks durability. As Web enthusiasts Daniel Cohen and Roy Rosenzweig point out, "we are rapidly losing the digital present that is being created because no one has worked out a means of preserving it" (9–10).

7 Noting "passivity" (the downside of "interactivity") as one of the major challenges to doing history online, Cohen and Rosenzweig paraphrase literary critic Harold Bloom who argues that "whereas linear fiction allows us to experience more by granting us access to the lives and thoughts of those different from ourselves, interactivity only permits us to experience more of ourselves" (12).

References

Anonymous. Image #2603. *The September 11 Digital Archive* (7 September 2004). http://911digita larchive.org/images/details2603

Ball, Mieke. "Telling Objects: A Narrative Perspective on Collecting." *The Cultures of Collecting*. Ed. John Elsner and Roger Cardinal. Cambridge: Harvard UP, 1994. 97–115.

Baxandall, Michael. "Exhibiting Intention." *Exhibiting Cultures: The Poetics and Politics of Museum Display*. Ed. Ivan Karp and Steven D. Lavine. Washington, DC: Smithsonian Institution P, 1991. 33–41.

Blair, Carole, Martha S. Jeppeson, and Enrico Pucci. "Public Memorializing in Postmodernity: The Vietnam Veterans Memorial as Prototype." *Quarterly Journal of Speech* 77 (1991): 263–88.

Blood, Rebecca. "Weblogs: A History and Perspective." *Rebecca's Pocket* (7 September 2000). www.rebeccablood.net/essays/weblog_history.html; accessed 10 July 2006.

Bodnar, John. *Remaking America: Public Memory, Commemoration, and Patriotism in the Twentieth Century*. Princeton: Princeton UP, 1992.

Brothman, Brien. "The Pasts That Archives Keep." *Archivaria* 51 (2001): 48–80.

Cohen, Daniel J. and Roy Rosenzweig. *Digital History: A Guide to Gathering, Preserving, and Presenting the Past on the Web*. Philadelphia: U Pennsylvania P, 2005.

Dominguez, Vida. Image #2673. *The September 11 Digital Archive* (12 October 2004). http://911digitalarchive.org/images/details/2673

Duncan, Carol. "Art Museums and the Ritual of Citizenship." *Exhibiting Cultures: The Poetics and Politics of Museum Display*. Ed. Ivan Karp and Steven D. Lavine. Washington, DC: Smithsonian Institution P, 1991. 88–103.

Ferguson, Bruce W. "Exhibition Rhetorics: Material Speech and Utter Sense." *Thinking About Exhibitions.* Ed. Reesa Greenberg, Bruce W. Ferguson, and Sandy Nairne. London: Routledge, 1996. 175–90.

Foot, Kristen, Barbara Warnick, and Steven M. Schneider. "Web-Based Memorializing after September 11: Toward a Conceptual Framework." *Journal of Computer-Mediated Communication* 11 (2005): article 4. http://jcmc.indiana.edu/vol11/issue1/foot.html, June 4, 2006.

Foote, Kenneth E. *Shadowed Ground: America's Landscapes of Violence and Tragedy.* Rev. ed. Austin: U of Texas P, 2003.

Gillis, John R. "Memory and Identity: A History of a Relationship." *Commemorations: The Politics of National Identity.* Ed. John R. Gillis. Princeton: Princeton UP, 1994. 1–24.

Gillmor, Dan. *We the Media: Grassroots Journalism by the People, for the People.* Sebastopol: O'Reilly Media, 2004.

Golding, Steve. "Creator's Statement." *The September 11 Digital Archive* (20 February 2002). http://911digitalarchive.org/moving/moving_collections.html

Gronbeck, Bruce E. "Citizen Voices in Cyberpolitical Culture." *Rhetorical Democracy: Discursive Practices of Civic Engagement.* Ed. Gerard A. Hauser and Amy Grim. Mahwah: Lawrence Erlbaum, 2004.

Gurak, Laura J. *Cyberliteracy: Navigating the Internet with Awareness.* New Haven: Yale UP, 2001.

Halloran, S. Michael. "Text and Performance in a Historical Pageant: Toward a Rhetoric of Spectacle." *Rhetoric Society Quarterly* 31 (2001): 5–17.

Haskins, Ekaterina V. and Justin P. DeRose. "Memory, Visibility, and Public Space: Reflections on Commemoration(s) of 9/11." *Space and Culture* 6 (2003): 377–93.

Hawkins, Peter S. "Naming Names: The Art of Memory and the NAMES Project AIDS Quilt." *Thinking About Exhibitions.* Ed. Reesa Greenberg, Bruce W. Ferguson, and Sandy Nairne. London: Routledge, 1996. 133–55.

Hiley, Richard. Story #10532. *The September 11 Digital Archive* (11 April 2004). http://911digitalarchive.org/stories/details/10532

Huyssen, Andreas. *Twilight Memories: Marking Time in a Culture of Amnesia.* New York: Routledge, 1995.

Jaeger, Elizabeth. Story #8483. *The September 11 Digital Archive* (17 October 2002). http://911digitalarchive.org/stories/details/8483

Kiousis, Spiro. "Interactivity: A Concept Explication." *New Media and Society* 3 (2002): 355–83.

Landow, George. "Hypertext as Collage-Writing." *The Digital Dialect.* Ed. Peter Lunenfeld. Cambridge: The MIT P, 2000. 150–70.

Livingstone, Jane and John Beardsley. "The Poetics and Politics of Hispanic Art: A New Perspective." *Exhibiting Cultures: The Poetics and Politics of Museum Display.* Eds. Ivan Karp and Steven D. Lavine. Washington, DC: Smithsonian Institution Press, 1991. 104–20.

Lowenthal, David. *The Past Is a Foreign Country.* Cambridge: Cambridge University Press, 1999.

Mandel, Naomi. "To Claim the Mandane." *The Journal of Mundane Behavior* 3.3 (2002). http://mundanebehavior.org/issues/v3n3/mandel33.htm; accessed 10 July 2006.

Manovich, Lev. *The Language of New Media.* Cambridge: MIT P, 2001.

Miller, Carolyn R. and Dawn Shepherd. "Blogging as Social Action: A Genre Analysis of the Weblog." *Into the Blogosphere: Rhetoric, Community, and Culture of Weblogs.* Ed. Laura Gurak, Smiljana Antonijevic, Laurie Johnson, Clancy Ratliff, and Jessica Reyman. http://blog.lib.umn.edu/blogosphere/blogging_as_social_action_a_genre_analysis_of_the_weblog.html; accessed 10 July 2006.

Miller, G. N. Image #2757. *The September 11 Digital Archive* (1 June 2005). http://911digitalarchive.org/images/details/2757

Nora, Pierre. "Between Memory and History: Les Lieux de Memoire." *Representations* 26 (1989): 7–25.

Occi, Jim. Image #1760. *The September 11 Digital Archive* (14 November 2002). http://911digitalarchive.org/images/details/1760

Oien, Niles. Story #11163. *The September 11 Digital Archive* (17 November 2004). http://911digi talarchive.org/stories/details/11163

Pichoff, Lisa. Story #11549. *The September 11 Digital Archive* (24 June 2005). http://911digitalar chive.org/stories/details/11549

Savage, Kirk. *Standing Soldiers, Kneeling Slaves: Race, War and Monument in Nineteenth-Century America*. Princeton: Princeton UP, 1999.

Scheinfeldt, Tom. "Memories: September 11 Digital Archive." (9 September 2002). http://hnn.us/ articles/959html (10 July 2006)

Selders, Paul. Image #1742. *The September 11 Digital Archive* (3 November 2002). http://911digi talarchive.org/images/details/1742

Selnow, Gary W. *Electronic Whistle-Stops: The Impact of the Internet on American Politics*. Westport: Praeger, 1998.

Sturken, Marita. "The Wall, the Screen, and the Image: The Vietnam Veterans Memorial." *The Visual Culture Reader*. Ed. N. Mirzeoff. London: Routledge, 1998. 163–78.

Vogler, David. Image #2691. *The September 11 Digital Archive* (1 November 2004). http://911digi talarchive.org/images/details/2691

Warnick, Barbara. *Critical Literacy in a Digital Era: Technology, Rhetoric, and the Public Interest*. Mahwah: Erlbaum, 2002.

———. "Looking to the Future: Electronic Texts and the Deepening Interface." *Technical Communication Quarterly* 14 (2005): 327–33.

Wodiczko, Krzysztof. *Critical Vehicles: Writings, Projects, Interviews*. Cambridge: MIT P, 1999.

Zelizer, Barbie. "The Voice of the Visual in Memory." *Framing Public Memory*. Ed. Kendall R. Phillips. Tuscaloosa: U of Alabama P, 2004. 157–86.

14

Identification
Burke and Freud on Who You Are

DIANE DAVIS

Identification is affirmed with earnestness precisely because there is division. Identification is compensatory to division. If men were not apart from one another, there would be no need for the rhetorician to proclaim their unity.

—Kenneth Burke, *A Rhetoric of Motives*

Identification, in fact, is ambivalent from the very first; it can turn into an expression of tenderness as easily as into a wish for someone's removal. It behaves like a derivative of the first, *oral* phase of the organization of the libido, in which the object that we long for and prize is assimilated by eating and is in that way annihilated as such. The cannibal, as we know, has remained at this standpoint; he has a devouring affection for his enemies and only devours people of whom he is fond.

—Sigmund Freud, *Group Psychology and the Analysis of the Ego*

According to Jack Selzer's delightful early history, *Kenneth Burke in Greenwich Village*, Burke's friends at *The Dial* probably introduced him to Sigmund Freud's work sometime in the early 1920s. The impact was profound and sustained: Burke loved Freud. In a 1939 essay called "Freud—and the Analysis of Poetry," for instance, Burke writes: "the reading of Freud I find suggestive almost to the point of bewilderment. Accordingly, what I would most like to do would be simply to take representative excerpts from his work, copy them out, and write glosses upon them" (*Philosophy* 258). I'm not the first to observe that Burke spent much of his career, in fact, tweaking, applying, and extending Freud's ideas. Ellen Quandahl, David Blakesley, and others have demonstrated that Burke, in Freud's footsteps, set out to expose human motivations by analyzing language, and that he lifted several of his own key terms, such as "identification" and "motive," from *The Interpretation of Dreams*. As Roderick Hart and Suzanne Daughton bluntly put it, Burke "was Freudian to his core" (262).

And yet, anyone who has studied Freud's work on identification (or anyone who has seen the film *All About Eve*, for that matter) will already have detected the tell-tale signs of a simmering rivalry. Although Burke never denounced Freud and loved him to the end, his anxiety of influence did take a parricidal turn, which expressed itself—in part and interestingly enough—in Burke's own theory of identification, which he himself described as "*post*-Freudian" ("Methodological Repression" 407–408).[1]

Burke based his theory on Freud's, and the overlap is readily discernable.[2] According to the more or less "official" interpretation, Freud maintains a clean distinction between desire and the purely secondary motivation of identification: Boy *wants* Momma, Daddy *has* Momma, so Boy wants to *be* Daddy, identifies with him, takes him as the ideal model (*Group Psychology* 47). Burke agreed with Freud that humans are motivated by desire at least as much as by reason, but he ditched the Oedipal narrative, arguing that the most fundamental human desire is social rather than sexual, and that identification is a response to that desire. By all appearances, then, the disagreement is in the details, because both Freud and Burke describe identification as a social act that partially unifies discrete individuals, a mode of "symbolic action" (as Burke would say) that resides squarely within the representational arena (or the dramatistic frame).

What gets deep-sixed in Burke's articulated revision, however, are Freud's less "official" reflections on an immediate, *affective* identification with the other (the "m/other"), who is not (yet) a discrete object or image or form. This "primary identification," as Freud sometimes calls it, precedes the very distinction between ego and model, and inasmuch as it is precisely *not* compensatory to division, it remains stubbornly on the motion side of Burke's action/motion loci. Burke had studied at least two of the works in which Freud explicitly addressed the problem of a nonrepresentational identification (*Group Psychology* and *The Ego and the Id*), so it may be telling that he never directly challenges it—or even mentions it. In any case, we will be interested here in digging up something of what Burke buried, because he covers over a more radically generalized rhetoricity, an a priori affect*ability* or persuad*ability* that precedes and exceeds symbolic intervention.

Dramatizing Identification

In *A Rhetoric of Motives*, published in 1950, Burke follows Aristotle's lead in suggesting that rhetoric's "basic function" is persuasive, but he also argues that persuasion's very condition of possibility is identification; indeed, that any persuasive act is first of all an identifying act: "You persuade a man only insofar as you can talk his language by speech, gesture, tonality, order, image, attitude, idea, identifying your ways with his" (55). According to Burke, the father of modern rhetorical studies, the primary aim of rhetoric is not to win an argument but to make a connection, shifting the imagery of the persuasive encounter from a duel to a "courtship":

> A is not identical with his colleague, B. But insofar as their interests are joined, A is *identified* with B. Or he may *identify himself* with B even when their interests are not joined, if he assumes they are, or is persuaded to believe so.
>
> Here are the ambiguities of substance. In being identified with B, A is 'substantially one' with a person other than himself. Yet at the same time he remains unique, an individual locus of motives. Thus he is both joined and separate, at once a distinct substance and consubstantial with another.
>
> (*Rhetoric* 20–21)

According to Burke, it is because neither A nor B is an absolute identity, because they share *no* essence-in-common, and because they are *not* identical or conjoined in any actual sense, that there can and must be rhetorical identification, a "mediatory ground" that establishes their consubstantiality without accomplishing their complete unity.[3] Identification, or what Burke also calls "consubstantiation," is both the mode by which individual existents establish a sense of identity and the mode by which they establish a relation to one another. As he puts it in *Attitudes Toward History*, identification "is hardly other than a name for the function of sociality" (267).

It can also go wrong, of course. Too much identification, too much unification, too much cooperation within any group, Burke warns, can be deadly for everyone else: he calls the "ultimate *disease* of cooperation: *war*" and notes that "you will understand war much better if you think of it, not simply as strife come to a head, but rather as a disease, or perversion of communion" (*Rhetoric* 22). Burke, writing the *Rhetoric* in the aftermath of a devastating war, pins his hopes for a survivable coexistence not so much on the act of identification, which is ontologically guaranteed, but on the human capacity to *resist* a little, to maintain a crucial distance through reasoned critique.[4] As Timothy Crusius puts it, for Burke "the problem, then, is not with identification *per se* (trust, faith) but with faulty or malign identifications, which must be exposed, critiqued, discarded, and replaced with sounder loyalties" (86). Burke's quiet rivalry with Freud drops anchor here, in Burke's insistence that identification is a symbolic act—whether conscious or unconscious—which therefore remains available for sober critique and reasoned adjustment.

According to Burke, there is no essential identity; what goes for your individual "substance" is not an essence but the incalculable totality of your complex and contradictory identifications, through which you variously (and vicariously) become able to say "I." Like the "official" Freudian version on which it's based, "rhetorical identification" depends on symbolic representation, on the production and intervention of meaningful figures, which Burke says are already persuasive: "wherever there is 'meaning,' there is 'persuasion,'" he writes

(*Rhetoric* 172). Or, as Crusius observes, in Burke, "shared meaning is the very basis for identification" (86). There can be no identity without identification, and there can be no identification without figuration, without the suasive force of meaningful figures.

Now, we will need to catch two non-harmonious Burkean drifts here: first of all, this indicates that what I habitually call "my" identity is the product of an identification with figures or symbols that reside outside my self, that the relation to symbolic structure precedes the relation to the self. Inasmuch as "my" identity is an effect of "my" inscription by this structure, "I" am always already other than myself, non-present to myself, inessential. Or, from another angle, "I" am *essentially* an actor, says a very Nietzschean Burke, "enact[ing] rôles" that are available to me as a "member of a group," which "is the only active mode of identification possible," he writes, since "all *individualistic* concepts of identity dissolve into the nothingness of mysticism and the absolute" (*Philosophy* 310–11). "Identity is not individual," Burke insists; it is constituted via the enactment of a series of dissociated and frequently contradictory roles defined by the groups with which one identifies (*Attitudes* 263). And my identification with other existents necessarily triangulates through the symbolic structures that grant my identity.

Paradoxically, however, and here's the second drift, to say that identification depends on shared *meaning*, on the intervention of already meaningful figures, is also to presume—as the condition for identification—a subject or ego who knows itself as and through its representations. It is to presume the prior activation of a human *tupos* itself, which covertly operates as the figure *of* meaning as well as the ground for any possible relation.[5] Indeed, for Burke, everything begins with an "individual" who is individuated by nature itself: the figures of self and other are not first of all a function of symbolic structure but of biology, says Burke. Each human organism is given as such in the material separation of one central nervous system from another, which results in the "*divisiveness* of the individual human organism from birth to death" (*Rhetoric* 130)[6] Prior to language acquisition, psychosexual development, and class consciousness, Burke proposes, there is biological estrangement, ontology's insurance premium for securing his entire rhetoric of relationality.[7] And any reference to some "Edenic" existence before this "fall" into divisiveness, Burke writes, belongs to mythology, to the "myth of a power prior to all parturition," in which "divided things were not yet proud in the private property of their divisiveness" (*Rhetoric* 140). For him, the division between self and other is the "state of nature" that is identification's motivating force: identification's job is to transcend this natural state of division, and rhetoric's job is identification.

In an exemplary instance of the way in which texts, as he says, can embody contradictory "*wishes*, each proclaimed in its own right, without regard to the others" (*Language* 68), Burke describes identity as an effect of the processes of identification *and* identification as the achievement of an already discernable (biological) "identity." The itinerary is complicated, and these descriptions contest and check each other throughout the *Rhetoric*, but whenever Burke feels forced to make a decision, to lay out the "ultimate" order of things, he comes down on the side of originary divisiveness, and there is no other choice.[8] From the moment he determines that identification is a function of (rather than the condition for) shared meaning—as soon as he situates identification *within* the arena of representation, in other words—he has already presumed a prior divisiveness and engaged the necessary contradiction.

According to Burke, "in parturition begins the centrality of the nervous system" (*Rhetoric* 146), and our very concepts of ownership and private property—indeed, of all our egoistic impulses—originate in this irreparable biological predicament: "What the body eats and drinks becomes its special private property; the body's pleasures and pains are exclusively its own pleasures and pains." But if you then "bring together a number of individual nervous systems, each with its own centrality," he says, relational impulses intervene; there will be "vicarious sharing by empathy, by sympathy, the 'imaginative' identification with one another's states of mind." This scramble of egoistic and relational motives is the rhetorical situation into which "man" is born, says Burke, an endless dialectical struggle between "the original biological goading that is located in the divisive centrality of the nervous system" and the inborn desire to transcend this state of nature through the mediatory ground of identification (*Rhetoric* 130).

Barbara Biesecker surmises, correctly I think, that "Burke's thinking of the social finds its resources in the newly determined space of the individual: in the predication of the human being *per se* is the possibility for the social" (47). And there is the problem. Who is this "individual," this human being *per se* who precedes predication and/so predates the processes of identification? Who is *there*, there *already*, to experience alienation, to desire sociality? Burke's response: "*homo dialecticus*," whose inborn rationality includes the superpersonal "resources of classification, of abstraction, of comparison and contrast, of merger and division, of derivation, and the like [which] characterize the thinking of man *generically*" (*Rhetoric* 276, 285). Essentially enclosed and alienated, *homo dialecticus* already desires to transcend this state of nature—"[b]iologically, it is of the essence of man to desire," Burke writes (*Rhetoric* 275)—and is ontologically equipped to do so via the inborn powers of his or her own imagination. So although Burke challenges psychoanalytic criticism for reducing the desire for social intercourse to a sexual desire, he is very much with the "official" Freud in his refusal to question the ontological priority of desire itself, which, despite it all, presumes a subject who *has* desires, be they conscious or unconscious.

In his response to Fredric Jameson, who suggests that the "centrality of the self" is an "optical illusion" (520), Burke rather impatiently explains again that he makes a clean distinction between the individual as a biological organism and the individual as a social/ideological construct, presumably contending that the former is *not* already a construct: "I locate the *individual* (as distinct from the kind of "ideological" identity that is intended in a social term, such as "individualism") in the human body, the "original economic plant" distinct from all others owing to the divisive centrality of each body's particular nervous system" ("Methodological Repression" 404). Inasmuch as the "individual" is biologically individuated, Burke continues, it exists "as a separate organism possessing immediate sensations, not thus shared in their immediacy by other organisms." He grants that "the individual, as a 'person,' dissolves into quite a complexity of *identifications* in the sociopolitical realm," but he insists that this individual is first of all an irreparably *separate* organism (413).[9]

That somewhat puzzling proposition deserves our attention precisely because it seems so improbable coming from Burke—the thinker, *par excellence*, of the paradox of substance—and because he repeats it over and over like a refrain, as if it were deflecting a traumatic insight. Now, it would not be my first choice to venture into the arena of neuroscience here, but I feel compelled to try to speak Burke's language, to identify my ways with his. So: who can deny that sense organs and sensory neurons, which operate together not so much *at* but *as* threshold, already indicate an excentric structure, an inside-outside similar to a Klein jar or möbius strip?[10] Mirror neurons, which were discovered in the last decade of Burke's life, offer further confirmation: mirror neurons reside in the premotor area of the brain, which is the area that primes the next movements in a motor sequence. What's so interesting about them is that they act as both sensory and motor neurons, firing in association not only with the execution but also with the observation of an action. This means that the same mirror neurons fire in my brain whether I actually grab a pencil myself or I see you grab one, indicating no capacity to distinguish between my grasping hand and what is typically (and hastily) described as a visual representation of it: *your* grasping hand.

The same basic thing purportedly happens with non-goal directed "biological movements": neurons in my motor areas start to "resonate" when *you* move.[11] And this is not learned activity, at least not in the beginning. Almost immediately after birth (42 minutes after, according to recent studies) infants will imitate a number of facial gestures: when an infant witnesses an adult open her mouth or stick out her tongue, for example, the mere observation often triggers the related neurons in the motor cortex that physically mime that action: the infant's mouth opens and the tongue comes out.[12] Here, identification surely does not depend on shared meaning: a mimetic rapport precedes understanding, affection precedes projection.

Despite the authors' distinctly humanist frame-ups, published reports on the activity of mirror neurons and resonance mechanisms can be read as eloquent deconstructions of Burke's ultimate order of things, shattering the presumption of an originary biological disconnect between self and other. The "centrality" of each individual nervous system can hardly be characterized as "divisive" when it doesn't manage consistently to distinguish between self and other; indeed, at the level of the organism, a rather astonishing condition of indistinction announces itself. It's not only that "I" appear to be hardwired to mime "your" actions but, more disturbingly perhaps, that "I" may *be* "your" actions, that there may be no "me" until "I" perform "you." What is at issue here, maybe, is what Philippe Lacoue-Labarthe has termed a "constitutive mimesis," an originary mimetic rapport that exposes "the primitive, native lapse or default of identity," even at the level of the organism (116).

What's so confusing about all of this is that Burke himself suggests much the same thing in other terms. To say that the subject is *essentially* an actor, as Burke does, is already to imply its general absence of identity, as well as its "pure and disquieting plasticity," as Lacoue-Labarthe puts it, "which potentially authorizes the varying appropriation of all characters and all functions (all the roles), that kind of 'typical virtuosity' which doubtless requires a 'subjective' base—a 'wax'—but without any other property than an infinite malleability: instability 'itself'" (115). Nonetheless, Burke insists that the organism, the "wax," both is estranged and knows it's estranged, which allows him to interpret identification as an active response to a passive estrangement. This is why Burke can write in the *Rhetoric* that empathy and sympathy are "'imaginative' identifications" with another's state of mind (130), that they are affects that one "individual" *has* in regard to another, imaginative projections based on comparison or analogy—rather than that these affects are affections, that the "other" with whom "I" identify affects me with "my" affect precisely because "I" have no affect of my own—indeed, that there is no "my own" prior to identification.

By positing an estranged and desiring "individual" holding steady beneath the swirl of identifications, Burke is able to preempt any consideration of this "individual's" *genesis* in identification.[13] What this uncharacteristic lapse into metaphysical prejudices buys him, then, is a strategic pick against the rush of impossible questions: what if identification precedes not only any sense of identity but also, and *therefore*, any sense of divisiveness, as well? What if the identity of the organism *itself* is in the other? What if repetition is originary? In short, what if the real question, as Avital Ronell puts it in *The Telephone Book*, is not how to make a connection (that was the beginning) but "*how to make a disconnection*" (194)?[14]

These questions, blocked by the barricade of biological estrangement, imply that the entire logic of identification has to be rethought: it can no longer be understood as an identification *of* one *with* another, at least not at first, because it would necessarily precede the very distinction between self and other. Identification could not operate among self-enclosed organisms; it would have to belong to the realm of affectable-beings, infinitely open to the other's affection, inspiration, alteration; it would have to belong to the realm of a radically generalized rhetoricity, then, an a priori affect*ability* or persuad*ability* that is at work prior to and in excess of any shared meaning. As Lacoue-Labarthe and Jean-Luc Nancy observe in a very early piece on identification in Freud, "to be affectable is to be always already-affected," to be nothing other than affected, nothing other than this endless repetition of each time originary alterations ("The Unconscious" 199).

To get a sense of what Burke is avoiding here, we will need to go back to his most important source—to Freud—who never stopped wrestling with precisely what Burke's "post-Freudian" notion of identification silently sheers off. It's true that even when Freud describes an Oedipal *prehistory*, he tends to maintain the distinction between identificatory and libidinal bonds and to depend on his cast of usual suspects—the Mother, the Father, and an ego who takes the Father as a model and the Mother as an object. However, Freud also had the guts—here and there, against the grain—to explore a prehistory *to* that prehistory in which identification is "anterior and even interior to any libidinal bond" (Borch-Jacobsen, *Emotional* 8).

Primary Identification

> To say *what* I am is relatively easy—that is even how I assure myself of myself beyond all possible doubt: to paraphrase Descartes, I am what I think, wish, fantasize, feel, and so on. But to say *who* I am—who thinks, who wishes, who fantasizes in me—is no longer in *my* power. That question draws me immediately beyond myself, beyond my representations, toward a point—we shall name it . . . the "point of otherness"—where I am another, the other who gives me my identity. That is, the other who gives birth to me.
>
> —Mikkel Borch-Jacobsen, *The Freudian Subject*

Freud begins the seventh chapter of *Group Psychology* with a revelation that, save the reference to psychoanalysis, Burke could easily have written: "Identification is known to psycho-analysis as the earliest expression of an emotional tie with another person" (105). However, as we saw in the second epigraph, Freud goes on to indicate that this very first "emotional tie" is formative of the ego—so we are really talking about the "passionate attachment," as Judith Butler puts it, of something or someone who doesn't yet exist, a relation (without relation) to the other that is older than and productive of the relation to the self. This identification, Freud continues, "behaves like a derivative of the first, *oral* phase of the organization of the libido, in which the object that we long for and prize is assimilated by eating and is in that way annihilated as such" (105). According to him, you are *who* you eat: the genesis of the ego involves a devouring affection, a fusional sort of cannibalism that you are not yet around to remember (or even to repress).

"The effects of the first identifications made in earliest childhood will be general and lasting," Freud writes a few years later in *The Ego and the Id*.

> This leads us back to the origin of the ego-ideal, for behind it there lies hidden an individual's first and most important identification, his identification with the father in his own personal prehistory. This is apparently not in the first instance the consequence or outcome of an object-cathexis; it is a direct and immediate identification and takes place earlier than any object-cathexis.

(31)

Although Freud stubbornly describes this "first and most important identification" as an "identification with the father"—or even, according to his footnoted second choice, with "the parents"—the qualifiers "directly and immediately" imply that Freud is trying to suggest something else: that this formative identification would precede any representational scission between identity and alterity and so would be prior to the intervention of a specular object or ideal model. In a sociality or collectivity prior to all individual history, ego is formed "directly and immediately" through a *blind* identification in which a not-yet-I swallows the not-yet-other alive.[15]

Seventeen years later, in "An Outline of Psycho-Analysis," Freud drops all reference to ego-model pairs and explicitly details a pre-egoic identification: "To begin with," he writes, "the child does not distinguish between the breast and its own body," but "when the breast has to be separated from the body and shifted to the *outside* because the child so often finds it absent, it carries with it as an *object* a part of the original narcissistic libidinal cathexis" (188).[16] There is first an objectless identification with the nurturing breast, Freud is suggesting—the breast is part of "me"—and it's only afterwards, after it has gone MIA too many times, that this breast is "shifted to the outside," becoming an object of desire. Both self and other would be established in this crucial "shift," which could be described as a separation of "me" from "myself," except that there would be no "me" at all prior to this separation. The almost unthinkable claim being posited here is that both individuation and the relation to alterity are born in this experience of dis-identification: a dis-sociation that takes place at the very moment of association, an untying tie in which identity appears in (or as) the movement of its disappearance.

And/but apparently this "birth" is itself a repetition. Already in *Inhibitions, Symptoms and Anxiety*, Freud had proposed that the birth event is the first (and paradigmatic) instance of anxiety, which stems not from the fetus's conscious perception of danger (because how could it know?), but from an awareness "of some vast disturbance in the economy of its narcissistic libido" (135). This "disturbance" is birth itself, the separation of "me" from "myself" in the very advent of becoming a self. In contradistinction to Burke's clean snip of the umbilicus, Lacoue-Labarthe and Nancy observe that

> what is at stake here is the incision of an outside in an inside, a withdrawal of identity in the advent of identity. Or again, it is a dependence in the advent of autonomy: the dependence of birth, that of pre-maturation, and finally that which lasts an entire life.
>
> (200)

Perhaps Burke's "individual" finally comes into play here, as a product of the experience of dis-identification and individuation, and perhaps that sets the stage for the secondary or "post-Oedipal" identification that both Freud and Burke define as "social"—the identification *of* one *with* another. There is, of course, no denying that specular and symbolic identifications take place, every-where and all the time, but as Mikkel Borch-Jacobsen observes, they "cannot really be produced elsewhere than on the (abyssal, non-'subjectal') ground of a preliminary *affection*, by the 'other' that 'I' *am* 'myself,'" prior to any perception or representation (*Lacan* 66). And nothing indicates that the originary narcissistic tendency upon which "social" identifications are produced can be permanently displaced or overcome. If identification precedes and is the condition for identity, then how could there be any biological, ontological, or symbolic prophylactic against devouring affection, any way retroactively to switch off the swallowing machine? Although he ultimately protects his Oedipal narrative, Freud does attempt several times to tackle this problem, both in his descriptions of melancholia (which we cannot explore here)[17] and in his career-long struggles with what he calls "the riddle of suggestive influence" (*Group Psychology* 117). And what gets exposed, each time, is the repetitive nature of "primary identification," which confounds all attempts at chronological description.

The Hypnosuggestive Technique

Between 1886 and 1896, Freud employed the therapeutic technique of hypnosis, which typically counts on a series of verbal suggestions through which the hypnotist talks the patient into a state of "mental compliance," literally persuading the patient to become persuadable, affectable, suggestible vis-à-vis the hypnotist ("Psychical Treatment" 293–95). When the patient falls into a hypnotic state, Freud explains, he demonstrates an extreme "docility" in his relation to the hypnotist, becoming "obedient and credulous—in the case of deep hypnosis, to an almost unlimited extent" (294–95). "Suggestion" is the technical name for "the words spoken by the hypnotist which have the[se] magical results," Freud writes, and he confirms all of Plato's suspicions about rhetoric when he says that in the suasive force of suggestion, "words have once more regained their magic" (296). Why magic? Because suggestion names the power of an "influence without logical foundation" (*Group Psychology* 88–90). In his preface to the German edition of Bernheim's *Suggestive Therapeutics*, Freud writes:

> What distinguishes suggestion from other kinds of psychical influence, such as a command or the giving of a piece of information or instruction, is that in the case of suggestion, an idea is aroused in another person's brain which is not examined in regard to its origin but is accepted just as though it had arisen spontaneously in that brain.
>
> (82)

Suggestion, as Borch-Jacobsen observes, "possesses the remarkable property of annulling (at least for the hypnotized person) the distance between locutor and listener, emitter and receiver."[18] Whereas the other sorts of "psychical influence" that Freud mentions consist in communication with the other, suggestion consists in the constitution of that other—*again*. It involves "the birth of the subject," Borch-Jacobsen writes, "perhaps not a repetition of the birth event— but birth as repetition, or as primal identification: in it the subject comes into being (always anew: this birth is constantly repeated) as an echo or duplicate of the other, in a sort of lag with respect to its own origin and its own identity" (*Freudian* 231).[19]

In a piece called "Psychical Treatment" published in 1905, Freud noted that suggestion's capacity to "cure" hysteria and certain other ailments points to the astonishing "physical influence of an idea," to the "magical" power of language to "remove the symptoms of illness" (296, 292). By then Freud had already ditched hypnosuggestion as a therapeutic technique, but not because it didn't work; sixteen years later in *Group Psych* he was still convinced that suggestibility is "an irreducible, primitive phenomenon, a fundamental fact of the mental life of man" (89). On the contrary, Freud felt compelled to give up the use of suggestion in his practice because it worked too well, so well that it offended his humanist sensibilities, or, as Burke puts it, his "individualistic libertarianism" (*Language* 79): a patient, Freud tells us, should not be subjected to the suggestions of analysts, at least not without recourse to counter-suggestion. But Freud also felt compelled to give up the practice of suggestion because its undeniable success couldn't be adequately explained; what Freud couldn't tolerate, he tells us in *Group Psych*, was that "suggestion, which explained everything, was itself to be exempt from explanation" (87). "The hypnosuggestive technique was expressly rejected by Freud," Borch-Jacobsen observes, "for a very simple reason, which is, at bottom, reason itself. . . . [F]or how is one to say the truth about this false power, this *pseudologos* that makes one believe in no-matter-what?" (*Emotional* 68). Analysts who use hypnosuggestion are like the rhetoricians in Plato's *Phaedrus*: they do not *know* what they are doing, "they can't produce the truth of their own psychagogic discourse" (*Emotional* 68). Freud founds the "science" of psychoanalysis by trading in the analyst's suggestions for the patient's "free-associations"—that is, by trading in persuasion for interpretation, performative for constative language, or again, by trading in rhetoric as persuasion for rhetoric as trope—and from then on the analyst was for the most part to keep his or her mouth shut.

Nonetheless, and to Freud's great consternation, the problem of suggestibility shows up again spontaneously in analysis in the form of the transference. No matter how tightly the analyst zips it, Freud discovers, the patient still submits to his or her influence, demonstrating "the same dynamic factor which the hypnotists have named 'suggestibility,' which is the agent of hypnotic rapport" (*An Autobiographical Study* 42). Indeed, Freud finally has to admit, with Gustav Le Bon, that the paradigmatic relation to others is hypnosis, that the social tie is comprised not of thinking subjects but of *hypnotized things*: "Hypnosis is not a good object for comparison with a group formation because it is truer to say that it is identical with it" (*Group Psychology* 114–15). Group formation involves a collective hypnosis, and the hypnotist, says Freud, could be a Chief,

Father, or *Führer*, could be a party or an ideology or some other "leading idea," such as that of "country" or "national glory." However, according to him—and here is the recuperative gesture—the identifications among group members result from a prior love for the hypnotist, the unifying figure. There is no herd instinct, he still argues, no natural sociability; there is instead a *horde* instinct. Love for the same Leader holds the group together, and when that Leader goes down, Freud insists, panic sets in, prompting the group to dissolve into its constitutive parts: individual Narcissi estranged and opposed to one another.

Paradoxically, however, the defining feature of the phenomenon of "panic fear" is contagion, which indicates not estrangement but exposedness. As Borch-Jacobsen observes, "panic fear" announces "an uncontrollable breaching of the ego by (the affects of) others; or, if you will, a mimetic, contagious, suggested narcissism" (*Emotional* 9; also *Freudian Subject* 166–67). The infectious nature of panic indicates "a gaping, more or less bewildered opening toward others," as he puts it, in which "each imitates the 'every man for himself' of the others" (*Emotional* 9). What Freud shows but cannot quite embrace is that "the sympathetic (suggestive, imitative) bond" of identification is precisely what remains when the Leader/hypnotist is subtracted from the equation (*Freudian Subject* 167). "What is the transference," Borch-Jacobsen asks, "if not hypnosis without a hypnotist, persuasion without a rhetorician, since it is produced in the absence of any direct suggestion?" The phenomenon of positive "transference reveals that the influence of the hypnotist" is grounded not in some specific hypnotic technique but in "an a priori affectability (a 'spontaneous receptivity') in the patient—that is to say, [in] the 'rhetoricity' of the affect as such, a rhetoricity anterior to any verbal persuasion and also to any metaphoric expression of passions" (*Emotional* 71).[20] And we will not even mention the equally impressive phenomenon of countertransference.

The "Suggest" of Desire

> What would be inexplicable, unacceptable . . . would be the absence of anyone to want or desire anything at all—except the strange and disquieting *suggest* of hypnosis, always already in submission, subjected to the will of another.
>
> —Mikkel Borch-Jacobsen, *The Freudian Subject*

Another way to say all of this is that the subject is always already a "suggest," as Borch-Jacobsen puts it, and Burke just cannot go there, not without throwing into question his entire ontology of the social. He stumbles onto but then artfully dodges the problem when he mentions, seemingly in passing, the "rhetoric of hysteria." Because even an hysterical fit is addressed to an audience, Burke observes, it must be situated squarely within the dramatistic frame: "even a catatonic lapse into sheer automatism, beyond the reach of all normally linguistic communication, is in its origins communicative, addressed, though it be a paralogical appeal that ends all appeals" (*Rhetoric* 39). This observation is followed by a new heading on a new page: "Rhetoric and Primitive Magic." So by all appearances, Burke has finished with the topic of hysterical rhetoric, finished without so much as touching on the question of "suggestibility," which is both the chief feature of hysteria and what could quite possibly be the "ultimate" rhetorical question. What suggestibility suggests is a human capacity to be "directly and immediately" induced to action or attitude by another, *sans* all logical foundation and cognitive discretion; it involves a nonrepresentable and each time originary identification that takes place behind the back and beyond the reach of critical faculties.

So we witness Burke bring up but then very quickly drop the "rhetoric of hysteria." And when he argues, two pages later under the new heading "Rhetoric and Primitive Magic," that the "art" of rhetoric is "not 'magical'" (41), he appears to be making an unrelated and fairly commonsensical observation:

> The approach to rhetoric in terms of "word magic" gets the whole subject turned backwards. Originally, the magical use of symbolism to affect natural processes by rituals and incantations was a mistaken transference of a proper linguistic function to an area for which it was not fit. The realistic use of addressed language to *induce action in people* became the magical use of addressed language to *induce motion in things* (things by nature alien to purely linguistic orders of motivation).
>
> (*Rhetoric* 42)

This important reclaiming of the properly rhetorical use of language also instantly forecloses any thinking of the problem of suggestion, which is something like the ability of addressed language to induce *motion* in *people*, even when the addressor says nothing, that is, even when the magic words, as Cheryl Glenn might say, go "unspoken." But this impossible possibility, which becomes necessary as soon as identification is understood as the condition for identity, is precisely what the principle of ontobiological divisiveness stiffens against. Unlike political persuasion, suggestion is an improper rhetoric, a bastard form that induces action (or attitude) without properly persuading, a directly suasive "discourse" that dissolves the presumed distance between self and other, evading cognitive discretion and so all possibility for deliberation.

A few years later in *Language as Symbolic Action* (1966), Burke explicitly articulates the problem of suggestibility in terms of ideology. Citing psychogenic illnesses as an example of symbol-misuse, he argues that when symbolic action is "improperly criticized," "the realm of symbolicity may affect the sheerly biologic motions of animality" (6). You may actually gag or spew, for instance, if you try to eat foods that are "perfectly wholesome" and "prized" in other cultures but considered disgusting in your own. And then this: "Instances of 'hexing' are of the same sort (as when a tribesman, on entering his tent, finds there the sign that for some reason those in authority have decreed his death by magic, and he promptly begins to waste away and die under the burden of this sheer thought)" (7). Here, Burke affirms the astonishing "physical influence of an idea," that is, language's capacity (as ideology) to induce *motion* in *people*, but he nonetheless retains an almost absolute faith in the power of reason. Persuadability remains a function of shared meaning; symbolic structure still mediates between listener and locutor, which leaves a space for cognition and so for a more *proper* critique.

Freud's work demonstrated, however, that suggestive influence is less rational, less manageable, less consciously *correctable* than Burke allows. What Freud rediscovers, mostly despite himself, is basically a new version of "the 'pathic' part of ancient rhetoric"—except that this version involves not an emotional appeal but an immediate affection, a kind of "mimetico-affective contagion," as Borch-Jacobsen puts it, that indicates, once again, the absence of any proper divisiveness, of any *subjectum*, and finally of any subject—including any subject *of* representation (*Emotional* 67). What suggestibility suggests, in other words, is that identification is not simply rhetoric's most fundamental aim; it's also and therefore rhetorical theory's most fundamental *problem*. This problem, which is not simply solvable, effectively undercuts any theory of relationality grounded in representation, and therefore any hope of securing a crucial distance between self and other through reasoned critique or other forms of symbolic action.

The Voice of Conscience

Perhaps Burke's theory of ontobiological divisiveness, along with its attendant faith in critique, was installed as a defense against the threat that Freud's scattered insights posed, the threat of an originary repetition, of an abyssal mimesis propelled along by an irrepressible narcissistic tendency from which symbolic structure could provide no real transcendence. However, the laceration one suffers when the breast goes MIA or when one encounters the dead other (Freud's *der Tote*) or when one engages in conversation (Levinas's *entre-tien*) with an/other, for example, is not the effect of a critical intervention; it emerges instead from a *failure* of identification, an interruption in narcissistic appropriation. According to a certain Freud, devouring affection is interrupted (temporarily) not by the Law or by the will or by the unstoppable powers of the critical faculty but by a surplus of alterity that remains indigestible, inassimilable, unabsorbable. Burke insisted in *Language as Symbolic Action* that "there are no negatives in nature and that this ingenious addition to the universe is solely the product of human symbol systems" (9). However, what Freud gives us to think is a pre- or extra-symbolic "experience" of the negative, a "thou shalt not" that issues not from human symbol systems or the Law (of the father) but from an originary dissociation that operates as the condition for both.[21] The other *as* other shows up in this interruption in identification, which installs a bewildering and (temporarily) ineffaceable distance. What Freud calls the "voice of conscience" owes itself to this failure of identification, to this self-shattering dissociation, in which "I" experience my vulnerability, my destitution, my debilitating dependence: my finitude. And yours.

In "Thoughts for the Times on War and Death," Freud writes:

> What came into existence beside the dead body of the loved one was not only the doctrine of the soul, the belief in immortality and a powerful source of man's sense of guilt, but also the earliest ethical commandments. The first and most important prohibition made by the awakening conscience was "Thou shalt not kill." It was acquired in relation to dead people who were loved, as a reaction against the satisfaction of the hatred hidden behind the grief for them.
>
> (295)

The voice of conscience and the experience of guilt emerge in the anxious apprehension of death "beside the dead body of the loved one." Contrary to the myth elaborated in *Totem and Taboo*, Freud here indicates that this dead one need not be a murdered "father" but anyone with whom one is identified.[22] When "primeval man" is confronted with a dead loved one, any dead loved one, Freud continues, "in his pain, he [is] forced to learn that one can die, too, oneself, and his whole being revolt[s] against the admission; for each of these loved ones was, after all, a part of his own beloved self" ("Thoughts" 293). You necessarily gain a particular sense of certitude in an encounter with *der Tote*, but it can only be an unsettling one: "the certainty of a *cogito* whose formula is not 'I am' but 'he is/you are dead,'" as Nancy and Lacoue-Labarthe put it ("La panique," 27)—"he is," and so, given your devouring affection, "*you* are," you are *too*. How to throw up the dead one? Facing "the dead body of the loved one" means facing what is absolutely inappropriable: your own death, your own dying (*le mourir*), your finitude—which is to say your non-self-sufficiency, your exposedness, your "infinite lack of an infinite identity," as Nancy has put it (*Inoperative* xxxviii).

According to Freud, the *relation* to alterity (already ethical) is born here, in the interruption of narcissistic appropriation, in a disidentification that serves as the condition for symbolic intervention.[23] What's at stake in Burke's truncated rearticulation of Freud's theory of identification, then, is "social feeling" itself. It is not in identification but in its failure, in the withdrawal of identity, that I am exposed to my predicament of exposedness and become capable of demonstrating concern for another finite existent. In Freud the social tie, Lacoue-Labarthe and Nancy write, amounts to this dissociating association, an untying tie that "would therefore be formed of this identification with the withdrawal" ("The Unconscious" 203). As non-intuitive as this may sound, what Freud gives us to think is that *dissociation* is productive of the exteriority that sociality implies, that it is through disidentification, dislocation, depropriation that social feeling emerges and (so) something like society becomes possible. It's only in the failure of identification, each time, that "I" am opened to the other *as* other and get the chance to experience something like responsibility for the other that exceeds (and conflicts with) my narcissistic passions.

But this failure cannot be *produced* through reason or critique. Indeed, what Burke censored in Freud—consciously or unconsciously—is the possibility that no flex of reason, no amount of proper critique, can secure the interpersonal distance on which Burke had pinned his hopes. According to Freud, an a priori affectability or persuadability operates irrepressibly and below the radar of the critical faculties. None of this suggests, of course, that critiquable (symbolic) identifications do not take place (everywhere and all the time), nor does it suggest that symbolic identifications are insignificant or that critiquing them is unnecessary. It is surely one task of rhetorical studies to soberly analyze and to provoke resistance to certain dangerous (or simply distasteful) alliances when they disclose themselves to consciousness. However, there may be nothing more dangerous than too much faith in reasoned critique. It seems to me that Freud presents rhetorical studies with another, equally important task: to think the limits of reason by tracking the implications—for society, for politics, for ethics—of a radically generalized rhetoricity that precedes and exceeds symbolic intervention. It seems necessary today, at the very least, to begin exploring the sorts of rhetorical analyses that become possible only when identification is no longer presumed to be compensatory to division.[24]

Notes

1 There was no clean break, no moment at which Burke suddenly turned against Freud. What I hope to demonstrate here, rather, is that according to the subtle registers of the Freudian ambivalence machine, Burke's love harbored within it a desire to take out his teacher, to take his place, to *re*place him and his theory of identity. "Ambivalent from the very first," identification in Freud is simultaneously loving and rivalrous, a *devouring* affection. It's not only that identification involves inclusion by virtue of exclusion, congregation by virtue of segregation; it is also that identification by definition involves seizing the other's place, ousting the other from the position that "I," having devoured the other, now presume to occupy. According to Freud, wherever there is identification, there is already and intrinsically *war*.

2 For another approach to this issue, see Mark H. Wright's very fine and very early essay, "Burkean and Freudian Theories of Identification." Burke was obviously under the influence of other thinkers, as well; Marx, for example. And in her fascinating essay "Language as Sensuous Action," Debra Hawhee makes a strong case for Sir Richard Paget's influence on Burke's theory of identification.

3 Burke zooms in on the productive tension between fusion and division in his analysis of "the principle of courtship in rhetoric," which he defines as the "use of suasive devices for the transcending of social estrangement" (*A Rhetoric* 208). The principle of courtship maintains and perpetuates itself, he says, thanks to the unending "mystery" sparked by identification's inability finally to accomplish itself, to achieve complete unity. The "precondition of all appeal," Burke writes, is the "purely technical pattern" in which the speaker shapes "his speech as to 'commune with' the spoken-to." And the irreducible distance between existents, the "standoffishness," as he puts it, "is necessary to the form, because without it the appeal could not be maintained. For if union is complete," he writes, "what incentive can there be for appeal? Rhetorically, there can be courtship only insofar as there is division" (271). This drive to keep the appeal or the "courtship" alive, Burke says, is a "motivational ingredient in any rhetoric," and the "standoffishness"

through which it operates is a purely formal or technical "self-interference" that is inherent in language itself (*A Rhetoric*, 269):

> There is *implicit in language itself*, the act of persuasion; and *implicit in the perpetuation of persuasion* (in persuasion made universal, pure, hence paradigmatic or found) *there is the need for interference*. For a persuasion that succeeds, dies.
>
> (274; his emphasis)

The "ultimate rhetorical grounds for the tabus of courtship," Burke writes, resides in the conditions of "standoffishness" (274), in the principle of interference that deflects the goal, preventing the persuasion, the identification, from finally accomplishing itself. "When the plea is answered," Burke writes, "you have gone from persuasion into something else" (274).

4   We can all name affiliations that seem to define who we are, as well as certain loose affiliations that we could take or leave. Most of us are also aware that we are identified by affiliations that are less palatable, less direct, and/or less conscious to us than the ones we specifically choose, and Burke zeroes in on those as well:

> The fact that an activity is capable of reduction to intrinsic, autonomous principles does not argue that it is free from identification with other orders of motivation extrinsic to it. . . . Any specialized activity participates in a larger unit of action. "Identification" is a word for the autonomous activity's place in this wider context, a place with which the agent may be unconcerned. The shepherd, *qua* shepherd, acts for the good of the sheep, to protect them from discomfiture and harm. But he may be "identified" with a project that is raising the sheep for market.
>
> (*A Rhetoric* 27)

Burke's point is that even these indirect identifications are available for critique; they are critiquable—and so perhaps resistible—precisely because they are products of representation.

5   Heidegger illuminates the subject of representation in his discussion of Descartes and representation in *Nietzsche*, IV, ch. 16.

6   Burke scholars rarely challenge his claim that the "centrality" of the nervous system is intrinsically divisive. "Estrangement," Biesecker writes, "is a biological, indeed ontological, fact; it is inscribed in the nature of the human being proper" (46). Robert Wess concurs: "Prior to the identifications and divisions of rhetoric, there is the biological division of one central nervous system from another" (204–05). And so on.

7   Biesecker argues quite compellingly that part three of Burke's *A Rhetoric of Motives* offers an "ontology of the social," an attempt to ground the ultimate condition for sociality in the predicament of the human organism.

8   Burke most fully explicates what he calls the "ultimate" ground of the individual in the *Rhetoric*:

> "Man" arises out of an extrahuman ground. His source is, as you prefer, "natural," or "divine," or (with Spinoza) both. In any case, the scene out of which he emerges is *ultimate*. And in this respect it must be "super-personal," quite as it must be "super-verbal." For it contains the principle of personality, quite as it contains the principle of verbalizing. The distinction between personal and impersonal, like that between verbal and nonverbal, is scientific, pragmatic, and thus is justified when our concerns are pragmatic. But from the standpoint of ultimate speculation, there must be an *order* here: First, there is "nature" in the less-than-personal sense; next, there is the "personal" distinguished from such impersonal nature as an idea of something is distinguished from the thing. But ultimately there must be nature in the "over-all" sense; and nature in this sense must be "superpersonal," since it embraces both "personality" and "impersonality."
>
> (289)

This "ultimate" ground, in other words, is an extra-personal and extra-linguistic *nature*, which already contains the potential for both language and personality—and so for identification (290). It is out of this not-yet-human ground of biological estrangement (motion pole), that "man" arises as the linguistically enabled agent/actor whose essence it is to "transcend" this estrangement.

9   In the *Rhetoric* Burke also notes that there may be no such thing as

> "personality" in the human realm. And when you get through dissolving personality into the stream of consciousness, or into dissociated subpersonalities, or into "conditioned reflexes," or into appearances of substance that derive purely from such extrensic factors as status and role, there may not seem to be any intrinsic core left.
>
> (290)

Still, Burke never stops positing the biological *as* this core, not of individual personality but of *separate* personalities, which themselves may be completely constructed, products of identification, ideology, and so on. Division is the ontological condition for identification, according to him, and so for rhetorical exchange, for sociality itself.

10   A quick biology refresher: sensory or afferent neurons send impulses from the sense organs (the exposed receptors) to the brain and spinal cord; motor or efferent neurons carry impulses from the brain and spinal cord to muscles and glands (the effectors); and interneurons, located only within the central nervous system, *connect* sensory and motor neurons, carrying impulses between them.

11   For a fascinating review of recent research on mirror neurons and resonance mechanisms, see Rizzolatti, Fadiga, Fogassi, and Gallese, especially pp. 252–53.

12   See, for example, the 1977, 1983, 1989, 1994, and 1997 studies by Meltzoff and Moore.

13   By positing an essence of the organism, in other words, Burke deflects the more radical implications of originary exposedness. If an organism is always already exposed, affected—open to the other's affection—then there is no essence of that organism, no way even to pose the ontological question: what is it? And yet, Burke's own unfolding of the paradox of substance had already suggested this, which makes his position on the body, "the original economic plant," all the more puzzling.

14   This was Heidegger's question, obviously, but it was Freud's too: a question of finitude. The first other, they both say, is a dead other, because death sets the absolute limit on identification. Levinas did not pose this question as such, but he did propose that the language relation, as "discourse" or "conversation" (*entre-tien*), was ethical inasmuch as it instituted a *distance* between the interlocutors, thereby opening the possibility for proximity. The distance, the interruption in identification, they all separately suggest, must be *achieved* somehow—which is not to say that it would amount to an achievement of the will.

15   In *Les complexes familiaux* (originally written in 1938 for *L'Encyclopédie française* VII), Lacan addressed this direct and immediate identification, acknowledging that it must precede even the specular representation of the "mirror stage." Mikkel Borch-Jacobsen notes that this insight "should have ruined the whole *theory* of the imaginary in advance" (Lacan 69).

16   This process involves what Freud called "reality testing." For a brilliant discussion of this phenomenon and its implications, see "Prototype 3" in Avital Ronell's *The Test Drive*, 64–71.

17   I'll venture only a few preliminary remarks. In "Mourning and Melancholia," Freud described melancholia as the pathological result of an inability to mourn: whereas successful mourning names a normal process whereby libidinal cathexes are eventually withdrawn from a lost love object and re-invested in another, melancholia involves an incorporation of the object, so that libido, rather than finding a substitute, "withdraws into the ego" and the object-cathexis is replaced by an identification—a process Freud describes as "a *regression* to narcissism." The "shadow of the object" falls upon the ego, as Freud puts it, which swallows but cannot or will not digest the foreign body; ego becomes a little tomb for the dearly departed, who refuses finally to depart (249). Later, however, in *The Ego and the Id*, Freud confesses that he had failed to "appreciate the full significance of this process," which he now recognizes as "common" and "typical" rather than pathological (28). Here, he describes the melancholic structure as both internal to the process of mourning and crucial to the formation of ego's character.

It may be that by this introjection, which is a kind of regression to the mechanism of the oral phase, the ego makes it easier for the object to be given up or renders that process possible. It may be that this identification is the sole condition under which the id can give up its objects. At any rate the process, especially in the early phases of development, is a very frequent one, and it makes it possible to suppose that the character of the ego is a precipitate of abandoned object-cathexes and that it contains the history of those object-choices.

(29)

So ego turns out to be a kind of crypt for lost or abandoned objects, where they are preserved through incorporation and so never quite lost or abandoned enough. Laurence Rickels and Avital Ronell—two *other* American readers of Freud—follow Abraham and Torok, as well as Derrida, in exploring this inability to let go under the name "cryptonymy." "The *primal* pre-condition of every so-called self-relation," Rickels observes in *The Case of California*, is that "it must always take a detour via the dead other" (5). "Even the most ancient theories of ghosts see the specter," he continues in *Aberrations of Mourning*, "as a dead person who has been improperly buried" (4). And in this case, the "dead people" (the unmournable) are improperly buried in the ego, the "character" of which turns out to be the prototypical horror flick and thriller—not just *The Night of the Living Dead* but also *When a Stranger Calls*: the tale of an outside that affects from within, and of an inside that affects itself on the outside. I think, for instance, of Ronell's famous reading of Emma Bovary, whose self-relation detours through the double-incorporation of a dead [m]other "on which Emma continues symbolically to feed," and a dead [br]other who "remote controls her" (*Crack Wars* 118). According to Freud, the contamination is primary: ego is *constituted* through and by its identifications. Indeed, in "Mourning and Melancholia" when Freud describes the shift from object-relation to identification as a "regression," he suggests that the object-relation was *already* identificatory, already a narcissistic object choice. If the loss of the object provokes an identification, in other words, it's due, apparently, to the profoundly identificatory nature of the relation to the object (cf. Borch-Jacobsen, *Freudian Subject* 185).

18 In *Group Psychology*, suggestion becomes a synonym for identification: "The other members of the group, whose ego ideal would not, apart from this, have become embodied in his person without correction, are then carried away with the rest by 'suggestion,' that is to say, by means of identification" (79).

19 In the 1990s, the ethical and political implications of the predicament of suggestibility were exposed more generally when the tragic "science" of Recovered Memory Therapy (RMT)—a.k.a., False Memory Syndrome—which ignored all Freud's warnings, made international headlines. In *A Dictionary of Psychology* (Oxford, 2001), Andrew Colman defines RMT as "An apparent recollection of something that one did not actually experience, especially sexual abuse during infancy or childhood, often arising from suggestion implanted during counseling or psychotherapy." In an RMT session, the therapist uses various suggestive techniques (hypnosis, guided imagery, etc.) to "assist" the patient in imaging/figuring/piecing together what are presumed to be the repressed traumatic memories triggering current psychogenic illnesses (bulimia, anorexia, and so on). Between the late 1980s and early 1990s, and to the utter bewilderment of their families of origin, hundreds of thousands of RMT patients in the United States and Canada suddenly "remembered" horrific incidents of childhood abuse, which was typically sexual and often also involved ritualistic and/or satanic elements. These recovered "memories," of course, almost always turned out to have originated in fantasy (in nightmares, horror flicks, novels, etc.), something Freud had already taught us. (Burke was also alert to the possibility that fantasy can be experienced as reality: "the symbolic consummations in forgotten or vaguely remembered dreams might serve as motivational incentives [as sources of guilt, and the like]. The dreams might secretly have the effect of profoundly experienced actualities" [*Language* 69].) Yet, for almost a decade grown children hauled their aged parents into court en masse to answer for these suddenly "remembered" crimes, and they often won.

20 For an exhilarating examination of the way that Freud's argument self-destructs, see both versions of Borch-Jacobsen's "The Primal Band," in *The Freudian Subject* (127–239) and *The Emotional Tie* (1–14).

21 After Freud, but with no reference to his work, Levinas more fully and compellingly elaborates this extra-symbolic limit, proposing that an originary "You shall not kill" operates not only as a "simple rule of conduct" but as "the principle of discourse itself," the very condition for symbolic systems. According to him, the only content that can be attributed to the saying of the face is a "No" that comes through, along with an invitation to speak, as an interdiction against murder: "To see a face is already to hear: 'You shall not kill'" (*Difficult Freedom* 8–9). And/but in this prohibition—"You shall not kill," or simply "No"—there sounds also a kind of declaration of victory: you *cannot* kill me; you *cannot* absorb me completely. The surplus of alterity expressed in the saying of the face paralyzes my power, not by opposing it with greater force but by transcending all force.

22 But see Borch-Jacobsen's stunning rereading of the *Totem and Taboo* myth as an ethics of finitude in the second chapter of *The Emotional Tie*, "The Freudian Subject: From Politics to Ethics," 15–35.

23 As I suggested earlier, Freud proposes that this originary disidentification takes place not only beside the dead body of a loved one but also, for example, in the separation of birth or when the breast will not stay put. That is, it takes place wherever narcissistic appropriation is interrupted, wherever an inassimilable surplus announces itself. Levinas proposes something slightly different: that this interruption takes place in the language relation, whenever a "you" and an "I" engage in "conversation" (*entre-tien*). I have discussed the implications of the (ethical) relation for rhetorical studies in several previous essays, most recently in "Addressing Alterity" and "The Fifth Risk." In my book-in-progress, *Inessential Solidarity*, I focus specifically on the necessary tension between identification and ethics.

24 Let me note that Jenny Edbauer's recent examination of the affective force in the second President Bush's incomprehensible orations would be one example of a rhetorical analysis that does not presume that identification is compensatory to division.

References

Biesecker, Barbara. *Addressing Postmodernity: Kenneth Burke, Rhetoric, and a Theory of Social Change*. Tuscaloosa: U of Alabama P, 1997.

Blakesley, David. *The Elements of Dramatism*. New York: Longman, 2002.

Borch-Jacobsen, Mikkel. *The Emotional Tie: Psychoanalysis, Mimesis, and Affect*. Trans. Douglas Brick. Stanford: Stanford UP, 1992.

———. *The Freudian Subject*. Trans. Catherine Porter. Stanford: Stanford UP, 1988.

———. *Lacan: The Absolute Master*. Trans. Douglas Brick. Stanford: Stanford UP, 1991.

Burke, Kenneth. *Attitudes Toward History*. 3rd ed. Berkeley: U of California P, 1984.

———. *Language as Symbolic Action: Essays on Life, Literature, and Method*. Berkeley: U of California P, 1968.

———. "Methodological Repression and/or Strategies of Containment." *Critical Inquiry* 5.2 (Winter 1978): 401–16.

———. *The Philosophy of Literary Form*. 3rd ed. Berkeley: U of California P, 1974.

———. *A Rhetoric of Motives*. Berkeley: U of California P, 1969.

Butler, Judith. *The Psychic Life of Power: Theories in Subjection*. Stanford: Stanford UP, 1997.

Colman, Andrew. *A Dictionary of Psychology*. 2nd Edition. Oxford: Oxford University Press, 2006. 273.

Crusius, Timothy. "Neither Trust Nor Suspicion: Kenneth Burke's Rhetoric and Hermeneutics." *Studies in the Literary Imagination* 28.2 (Fall 1995): 79–90.

Davis, Diane. "Addressing Alterity: Rhetoric, Hermeneutics, and the Non-Appropriative Relation." *Philosophy and Rhetoric* 38.3 (2005): 191–212.

———. "The Fifth Risk: A Response to John Muckelbauer's Response." *Philosophy and Rhetoric* 40.2 (2007): 248–56.

Edbauer, Jenny. "Executive Overspill: Affective Bodies, Intensity, and Bush-in-Relation." *Postmodern Culture* 15.1 (September 2004). http://muse.jhu.edu/journals/postmodern_culture/toc/pmc15.1.html

Freud, Sigmund. *An Autobiographical Study. The Standard Edition of the Complete Psychological Works of Sigmund Freud* (hereafter: *SE*). Ed. James Strachey. London: Hogarth P and the Institute of Psychoanalysis, 1953–1974 20: 3–76.

———. *The Ego and the Id. SE* 19: 3–68.

———. *Group Psychology and the Analysis of the Ego. SE* 18: 67–145.

———. *Inhibitions, Symptoms, and Anxiety. SE* 20: 77–178.

———. "Mourning and Melancholia." *SE* 14: 237–60.

———. "An Outline of Psycho-Analysis." *SE* 23: 141–208.

———. "Preface to the Translation of Bernheim's Suggestion." *SE* 1: 73–88.

———. "Psychical (or Mental) Treatment." *SE* 7: 283–304.

———. "Thoughts for the Times on War and Death." *SE* 14: 275–301.

Hart, Roderick P. and Suzanne M. Daughton. *Modern Rhetorical Criticism*, 3rd ed. Boston: Allyn & Bacon, 2005.

Hawhee, Debra. "Language as Sensuous Action: Sir Richard Paget, Kenneth Burke, and Gesture-Speech Theory." *Quarterly Journal of Speech* 92.4 (November 2006): 331–54.

Heidegger, Martin. *Nietzsche.* Volume IV: *Nihilism.* Trans. Frank A. Capuzzi. San Francisco: Harper & Row, 1982.

Jameson, Fredric. "The Symbolic Interference; or, Kenneth Burke and Ideological Analysis." *Critical Inquiry* 4 (Spring 1978): 507–23.

Lacan, Jacques. *Les complexes familiaux. L'Encyclopédie française* VII (March 1938). This work was published again in 1984 by Navarin éditeur, and again in *Autres écrits.* Paris: Le Seuil, 2001. 23–84.

Lacoue-Labarthe, Philippe. *Typography.* Ed. Christopher Fynsk. Stanford: Stanford UP, 1989.

Lacoue-Labarthe, Philippe and Jean-Luc Nancy. "The Unconscious Is Destructured Like an Affect." *Stanford Literature Review* 6 (Fall 1989): 191–209.

Levinas, Emmanuel. *Difficult Freedom: Essays on Judaism.* Trans. Seán Hand. Baltimore: Johns Hopkins UP, 1990.

Meltzoff, A. N. and M. K. Moore. "Explaining Facial Imitation: A Theoretical Model." *Early Development and Parenting* 6 (1997): 179–92.

———. "Imitation in Newborn Infants: Exploring the Range of Gestures Imitated and the Underlying Mechanisms." *Developmental Psychology* 25.6 (1989): 954–62.

———. "Imitation, Memory, and the Representation of Persons." *Infant Behavior and Development* 17 (1994): 83–99.

———. "Imitation of Facial and Manual Gestures by Human Neonates." *Science* 198 (1977): 74–78.

———. "Newborn Infants Imitate Adult Facial Gestures." *Child Development* 54 (1983): 702–09.

Nancy, Jean-Luc. *The Inoperative Community.* Ed. Peter Connor, Trans. Peter Connor, Lisa Garbus, Michael Holland, and Simona Sawhney. Minneapolis: U of Minnesota P, 1991.

Nancy, Jean-Luc and Philippe Lacoue-Labarthe. "La panique politique." *Retreating the Political.* Ed. Simon Sparks. New York: Routledge, 1997. 1–31.

Quandahl, Ellen. "More Lessons in How to Read: Burke, Freud, and the Resources of Symbolic Transformation." *College English* 63.5 (May 2001): 633–54.

Rickels, Laurence. *Aberrations of Mourning: Writing on German Crypts.* Detroit: Wayne State UP, 1988.

———. *The Case of California.* Minneapolis: U of Minnesota P, 2001.

Rizzolatti, G., L. Fadiga, L. Fogassi, and V. Gallese. "From Mirror Neurons to Imitation: Facts and Speculations." *The Imitative Mind: Development, Evolution, and Brain Bases.* Ed. A. N. Meltzoff and W. Prinz. Cambridge: Cambridge UP, 2002. 247–66.

Ronell, Avital. *Crack Wars: Literature Addiction Mania*. Lincoln: U of Nebraska P, 1992.

———. *The Telephone Book: Technology, Schizophrenia, Electric Speech*. Lincoln: U of Nebraska P, 1989.

———. *The Test Drive*. Urbana: U of Illinois P, 2005.

Selzer, Jack. *Kenneth Burke in Greenwich Village: Conversing with the Moderns, 1915–1931*. Madison: U of Wisconsin P, 1996.

Wess, Robert. *Kenneth Burke: Rhetoric, Subjectivity, Postmodernism*. Cambridge: Cambridge UP, 1996.

Wright, Mark H. "Burkean and Freudian Theories of Identification." *Communication Quarterly* 42.3 (Summer 1994): 301–10.

IV

RSQ Lately (2010–Present)

You know you that bitch when you cause all this conversation
Always stay gracious, best revenge is your paper.

—Beyoncé, "Formation"

Although *2010: The Year We Make Contact* (1984) seemed to bring a sense of pragmatic closure to a creative, cinematic era, as the sequel to Arthur C. Clarke and Stanley Kubrick's original, 1968 kaleidoscopic, science fiction foray, it murdered the mystery and wizened the wonder. Measured in decades, *RSQ*'s sequels are quite the opposite, successively bigger and better, ever-more curious, and widening the field of rhetorical objects beyond word and speech to screens, sounds, and . . . brain scans.

In 2009, then editor Carolyn Miller and the RSA Board of Directors established the position of Associate Editor of Special Issues for *RSQ*, and they quickly filled the post with Debra Hawhee, who brought out the first special issue in 2010. In her "Editor's Note" to that issue, Hawhee glosses the exigency:

The idea for an annual special fifth issue responds to a number of circumstances: the growth of rhetorical studies and RSA in particular; the organization's unique intertwining of rhetoric's "home" and allied disciplines (English, Communication, Composition, even Anthropology and Law); the need to approach pressing topics from prismatic perspectives, and to do so in a sustained manner; and the need for more publishing outlets in rhetorical studies.[1]

The theme of this inaugural fifth issue is Neurorhetorics, guest edited by Jordyn Jack, whose own contribution with Gregory Appelbaum is reprinted in this section.

The decision to devote *RSQ*'s first special issue to the intersections of rhetoric and brain science was in part due to a trend in rhetorical studies that gained prominence during this most recent decade: a "new" materialist turn. According to a 2011 study conducted by S. Scott Graham, an associate professor in scientific and technical communications at the University of Wisconsin–Milwaukee, between 2008 and 2010 the number of articles in *RSQ* that focused on "rhetorics of (social) science, technology, engineering, the environment, mathematics, and medicine" increased by 40%.[2] There is little doubt that this increase is in part due to Carolyn Miller, Distinguished Professor of Rhetoric and Technical Communication, stepping into the role of *RSQ* editor in 2008. It's also, however, the function of a more general shift in the field itself: whereas the 1990s saw the emergence of a critical interest in the *rhetorics* of science and technology,[3] this current decade demonstrates a new fascination with science, with big data, with biotechnologies, with objects and things, animals and plants, bodies and ecosystems.

As Michele Kennerly puts it in her 2013 essay "The Mock Rock *Topos*," also reprinted in this section, "Bodies, brains, borders, and beasts, and also quilts, museums, statues, and cafés have become objects of rhetorical analysis" (48).[4] Indeed, three of the four *RSQ* essays our survey participants selected as "most significant" from 2010 to the present directly engage this "new" materialist turn, attending, respectively, to neuroscience,[5] the environment,[6] and stones[7]— though, this is of course putting it too quickly. Nonetheless, the fourth essay collected here deals with Michel Foucault's take on *parrēsia*, and so with a more traditional rhetorical materialism.[8] This latter piece was the subject of a special Forum in *RSQ* 43 no. 4, in which Pat J. Gehrke, Susan C. Jarratt, Bradford Vivian, and Walzer himself participated.

As these selections make clear, rhetoric's transdisciplinary character is at this point undeniable: the radical diversity of scholarship that describes itself as rhetorical is mind-boggling. RSA responded, in part, by partnering with Penn State University Press in 2015 to develop a highly selective new book series: *RSA Series in Transdisciplinary Rhetoric*. *RSQ* responded, too, at first with a certain amount of hand-wringing. In his "Editor's Note" to the first volume of 2012, then incoming *RSQ* editor James Jasinski wrote that that he hoped the journal would "continue to change and evolve" under his editorship, but also that he hoped the proliferation of various theoretical and substantive interests would not result in too much fragmentation.[9] In her first "Editor's Message" in 2016, Susan Jarratt expressed a similar sentiment: "I have been dazzled, and I must admit, at times, dazed by the range of work coming across the journal's electronic transom. The curatorial challenge of this job is invigorating and daunting. What belongs? And in relation to what?"[10] Jarratt's response to this dizzying diversity was to institute "an experiment in curation" in which each of the 2016 issues of *RSQ* would be "organized as a group of essays clustered loosely on the basis of a family resemblance" and would be accompanied by a new feature she called "Counterpoint," in which a respected rhetorical scholar would respond to the essays in relation to one another.[11] This proved an interesting but—from a publishing perspective—unstainable response to what may or may not be an actual and continual issue for the journal and the field.

In January 2017, embracing the opportunities of digital publication, *RSQ* introduced a "Latest Articles" section on the Taylor & Francis website, which began "publishing accepted work on a rapid online basis, before print editions come out," Jarratt notes in her "Editor's Message" for that issue.[12] And to close with a delicious, forward-looking instance of repetition with difference, the RSA board is currently planning a new publication venue, *Rhetoric Society Monthly* [*RSM*], which will be an online-only newsletter designed, this time around, to be outward facing. According to Casey Boyle, RSA's Electronic Communications Officer, *RSM* will "circulate its members' expertise and scholarly production towards a more general audience."[13]

Chapters in Part IV

Jordynn Jack and L. Gregory Appelbaum, "'This is Your Brain on Rhetoric': Research Directions for Neurorhetorics."

Michele Kennerly, "The Mock Rock *Topos.*"

Arthur E. Walzer, "*Parrēsia*, Foucault, and the Classical Rhetorical Tradition."

Nathaniel A. Rivers, "Deep Ambivalence and Wild Objects: Toward a Strange Environmental Rhetoric."

Notes

1 Debra Hawhee, "Editor's Note." *Rhetoric Society Quarterly* 40, no. 5 (2010): ii.

2 S. Scott Graham, "How Big Is Rhetoric of Science and Medicine?" *S. ScottGraham.com* (31 March 2011). http://sscottgraham.com/archives/236. Graham also presented this work at the Association for the Rhetoric of Science and Technology in New Orleans in 2011 under the title "Rhetoric of Science and Interdisciplinarity: A Citational Analysis."

3 *RSQ* 26 no. 4 is a special issue devoted to "The Rhetoric of Scientific and Technological Practice," which guest editors Leah Ceccarelli, Richard Doyle, and Jack Selzer describe as "a growing subfield of rhetorical inquiry" (7).

4 *Rhetoric Society Quarterly* 43, no. 1 (2013): 46–70.

5 Jordyn Jack and L. Gregory Appelbaum, "This Is Your Brain on Rhetoric: Research Directions for Neurorhetorics," *Rhetoric Society Quarterly* 40, no. 5 (2010): 411–37.

6 Nathaniel Richards, "Deep Ambivalence and Wild Objects: Toward a Strange Environmental Rhetoric," *Rhetoric Society Quarterly* 45, no. 5 (2015): 420–40.

7 Michele Kennerly, "Mock Rock *Topos,*" *Rhetoric Society Quarterly* 43, no. 1 (2013): 46–70.

8 Arthur Walzer, "*Parrēsia*, Foucault, and the Classical Rhetorical Tradition," *Rhetoric Society Quarterly* 43, no. 1 (2013): 1–21.

9 James Jasinski, "Editor's Note," *Rhetoric Society Quarterly* 42, no. 1 (2012): ii.

10 Susan C. Jarratt, "Editor's Message," *Rhetoric Society Quarterly* 46 (2016): 1.

11 Ibid., 2–3.

12 Susan C. Jarratt, "Editor's Message," *Rhetoric Society Quarterly* 47, no. 1 (2017): 2.

13 Casey Boyle, email message to authors, 26 September 2017.

15

"This Is Your Brain on Rhetoric"
Research Directions for Neurorhetorics

JORDYNN JACK AND L. GREGORY APPELBAUM

At a time when cultural critics lament declining popular interest in science, neuroscience research findings are only gaining in popularity. Highly persuasive neuroscience-related findings are touted for their potential to transform advertising, political campaigns, and law (for example, through new brain-based "lie detectors").[1] Those hoping to improve their own brains can read self-help books, play "brain training" computer and video games, listen to specially designed meditations, and train their children's brains with Baby Einstein, Beethoven for Babies, and similar devices.[2] Neuroscientific research findings are reported in mainstream news outlets with striking regularity. Through scientific and technical developments, researchers can now track active neural systems and document the relationship between brain chemistry, human behavior, and mental activities. These undertakings seem to offer concrete, material proof of concepts previously considered ephemeral, especially when claims are supported with showy, multicolored brain scan images.[3]

In rhetorical studies, there seem to be two main approaches to studying this bourgeoning attention to all things *neuro-*. One area of study under the rubric of neurorhetorics might be *the rhetoric of neuroscience*—inquiry into the modes, effects, and implications of scientific discourses about the brain. To take up a recent example, on 3 February 2010, a Reuters news report featured the following headline: "Vegetative patient 'talks' using brain waves" (Kelland). According to reports carried in nearly every major news outlet, British and Belgian researchers used functional magnetic resonance imaging (fMRI) to demonstrate that a comatose man was able to think "yes" or "no," intentionally altering his brain activity to communicate with the researchers. Newspapers and magazines reprinted the dramatic images of brain activation that appeared in the original scientific report in the *New England Journal of Medicine*, with "yes" answers featuring orange and "no" answers showing blue spots. The findings immediately prompted debates in popular venues. As is often the case with widely reported neuroscience findings, this announcement reinvigorated public arguments about medical care, governmentality, and the politics of life itself. Rhetoric scholars should certainly pay attention to how scientific appeals function in these debates.

A second approach might be *the neuroscience of rhetoric*, drawing new insights into language, persuasion, and communication from neuroscience research. Findings such as this study of noncommunicative patients can prompt us to broaden our very definitions of rhetoric to include those with impaired communication (such as autism, aphasia, or "locked-in syndrome"), asking how communication occurs through different means, or how brain differences might influence communication. Cynthia Lewiecki-Wilson argues that "we need an expanded understanding of rhetoricity as a potential, and a broadened concept of rhetoric to include collaborative and mediated rhetorics that work with the performative rhetoric of bodies that 'speak' with/out language" (157). Surely, cognitive neuroscience findings can play an important role in such an endeavor. Neuroscience findings might also add new insights to longstanding rhetorical issues, such as the relationship between *pathos* and *logos*, or emotion and logic, or other cognitive dimensions of rhetoric (Flower; Arthos; Oakley). Indeed, Mark Turner goes so far as to suggest that "If Aristotle were alive today he would be studying this [neuroscience] research and revising his work accordingly" (10).

In this article, we, a neuroscientist and a rhetoric-of-science scholar, argue that the rhetoric of neuroscience and the neuroscience of rhetoric should be intertwined. In other words, to work with neuroscience research findings one should carefully analyze that work with a rhetorical as well as a scientific lens, paying attention to the rhetorical workings of accounts of cognitive neuroscience research. Rhetoricians who would like to do work in neurorhetorics should understand how knowledge is established rhetorically and empirically in the field of cognitive neuroscience, how to interpret scientific findings critically, and how to avoid pitfalls of interpretation that could lead to misleading arguments about rhetoric. Here we demonstrate the kinds of considerations rhetoric scholars should use to examine neuroscience research. First, in order to highlight the complex methodological choices that go into neuroscience research studies, we introduce a contentious debate concerning common analytical practices for functional magnetic resonance imaging. To give rhetoric scholars a set of tools for understanding these complex arguments, we highlight key topoi scientists use to negotiate methodological argument, such as accuracy, efficiency, and bias. Second, we examine how neuroscience researchers define key concepts that may also be of interest to rhetorical scholars, such as emotion, reason, and empathy, considering whether those definitions square with traditional rhetorical concepts of pathos, logos, and identification. In the third section, we consider how a single research article in neuroscience is framed rhetorically, including how decisions about terminology, research questions, and research subjects are rhetorical as well as empirical decisions. In the final section we identify common tropes used in popular accounts of neuroscience research findings. We offer guidelines in each section for rhetorical scholars who would like to work with neuroscience findings, and conclude by offering a set of suggested topics for future research that can constitute what we call neurorhetorics.

Accuracy, Bias, and Efficiency: Methodological Topoi in Human Brain Imaging

As scholars in the rhetoric of science have demonstrated, research findings are shaped rhetorically to fit with scientists' shared expectations. As Lawrence Prelli has argued, scientists use "an identifiable, finite set of value-laden topics as they produce and evaluate claims and counterclaims involving community problems and concerns" (5). Some of these topics (or *topoi*) include accuracy (200), quantitative precision (195), and bias. The accuracy *topos* focuses on the degree to which methods, procedures, and statistical calculations match what is being measured, while the precision *topos* focuses attention on the degree of reliability of the experimental method. Bias refers to the potential for the results to be influenced by factors unrelated to the variable being tested.

In the case of neuroscience, researchers use these three topoi to argue for methods that can usefully extend existing knowledge of the brain's structures and functions. One approach involves using case studies of individuals with brain deficits to draw inferences about normal brain functions. A second approach requires careful, statistical analysis of digitized data generated through imaging technologies such as fMRI or positron emission tomography (PET) (Beaulieu "From Brainbank"). As Michael E. Lynch explains, this data becomes visible through various technologies that transform specimens (animal or human brains) such that "[t]he squishy stuff of the brain becomes a subject of graphic comparison, sequential analysis, numerical measure, and statistical summary" (273). The methods used to accurately extract data from squishy brains are rhetorically negotiated through ongoing debates.

In order to understand these debates, a brief overview of neuroimaging research techniques is important. Through recent advancements in fMRI capabilities, researchers have been able to gain advanced understanding of the activity, structure, and function of the human brain on a fine spatial scale (Bandettini; Poldrack et al.). In most instances, the primary objective in acquiring fMRI data is to infer information about the brain activity that supports cognitive functions (such as perception, memory, emotion) from local changes in blood oxygen content. Increases in neural activity cause variations in blood oxygenation, which in turn cause changes in magnetization that can be detected in an MRI scanner. While these changes (called Blood Oxygenation Level Dependent or BOLD activity) offer a somewhat indirect measure of neural activity, they are widely accepted as a close proxy for the synaptic activity assumed to underlie neuronal communication, brain function, and ultimately cognition (Logothetis and Wandell; Logothetis et al.; Bandettini).[4]

In the hands of cognitive neuroscientists, an fMRI experiment is typically carried out by presenting a subject with a stimulus (such as an image, word problem, or even scent) and a task that requires some kind of response (answering a simple multiple choice question, choosing yes or no, etc.). Neuroscientists analyze the resulting data with regard to specific experimental contrasts designed to isolate, in a meaningful way, specified cognitive functions (e.g., subtraction between remembered and forgotten items from a list). As a result of a single experimental session, researchers can identify minute, specific regions of BOLD activation that correlate with the task at hand in one individual's brain.[5] However, given the inherent variability between individuals in brain anatomy, these activations can not easily be generalized across individuals. The activation patterns may not land consistently in the same place in different brains, nor can they be defined by any set of standard anatomical co-ordinates (see Saxe et al.). In order to draw conclusions about brains in general, and not about single individuals, neuroscientists need to establish some basis of comparison across brains, even though they differ in anatomy, size, and arrangement. This is where methodological arguments come in, since neuroscientists must argue for the accuracy and efficiency of their preferred techniques for addressing this challenge.

One approach involves acquiring information from separate "localizer" scans in each subject. Neuroscience researchers Rebecca Saxe, Matthew Brett, and Nancy Kanwisher argue such an approach can "constrain the identification of what is the same brain region across individuals," allowing researchers to more easily "combine data across subjects, studies, and labs" (1089). In rhetorical terms, these researchers argue from the accuracy topos. By identifying regions that function similarly across subjects, they claim that localizer scans allow for more accurate representations of how the brain works. In addition, Saxe, Brett, and Kanwisher argue from efficiency and bias, claiming that the functional regions-of-interest (fROI) approach allows researchers to "specify in advance the region(s) in which a hypothesis will be tested," which "increases statistical power by reducing the search space from tens of thousands of voxels to just a handful of ROIs" (1090). In contrast, the authors claim that whole-head comparisons will "produce an explosion of multiple comparisons, requiring powerful corrections to control false positives" (1090). In this way, they position the fROI approach as more accurate, more efficient, and less likely to lead to biased results (such as false positives). By bias, they mean statistical bias (not personal bias), which can result simply from taking multiple measurements of the whole head. Given the complexity of the brain and the sheer number of neurons it contains, some voxels might indicate brain activity that appears to correlate with the task in question, but that is actually due to sheer chance. In debates about fMRI methodology, the accusation that one technique or another might lead to more false positives serves as a way to position that technique as less sound than the preferred technique.

Using functional localizers, or fROIs, represents a dramatic shift away from more traditional analytical approaches that take into account all measurements from the whole recorded volume, so-called whole-head measurements. Notably, those who support a whole-head approach argue from the very same topoi as those who argue for the fROI approach. For instance, Karl Friston is a vocal proponent of the whole-head approach, which he claims allows for greater accuracy precisely because it does not pinpoint a region of interest a priori (Friston et al.; Friston and Henson). Friston points out that the only way to guarantee one has not overlooked potentially interesting activations is to test every voxel (the 3-D unit of measurement in fMRI), a tactic that cannot be done by limiting analysis to only those areas pre-defined in a localizer scan. Drawing on the efficiency topos, Friston et al. argue that whole-brain approaches provide "increased statistical efficiency," making it possible to report results for all locations in the brain while statistically accounting for the multiple tests performed across the whole volume (Friston et al. 1086). In their defense of the whole-head approach, Friston et al. also argue from the topos of bias, claiming that in the whole-head approach, "the test for one main effect cannot bias the test for other main effects or interactions" (Friston and Henson 1098).

As is the case with any scientific method, claims based on fMRI data rely on chain of inferences that link the data to the psychological function or construct of interest. Each step of this chain raises potential questions about the inferences that can be garnered from the data. The nature and meaning of data are in turn shaped by a series of methodological and conceptual choices made by scientists. This ongoing debate regarding the appropriate tactics to use in fMRI data analysis highlights the fact that neuroscientists have not yet established consensus on these underlying assumptions. It is therefore up to the author to adequately communicate their methodology (Poldrack et al.) and to the reader to be versed in the meaning, trends, and nuances of the methodologies employed.

For researchers hoping to discover new insights into rhetoric and communication from brain studies, it might be tempting to lump together a number of research findings on a topic (such as desire or reason). Yet, each of those studies, individually, might use a different technology (such as PET vs. fMRI), employ a different methodology (such as fROI or whole-brain analysis), and use different kinds of stimuli to evoke a given mental state (images, sounds, smells, etc.). To draw conclusions from such a disparate group of studies requires significant technical knowledge. While rhetoric scholars might find neuroscience methods difficult to understand, they can start by paying attention to these topoi. By looking for terms such as "false positive," "bias," or "assumptions," rhetoric scholars can ferret out places where neuroscientists argue for their methods (or argue against others).

Same Words, Different Meanings: Neurorhetorics of Reason and Desire

Rhetorical scholars have long held a principal interest in reason, emotion, and how they work together to achieve persuasion. These fundamental aspects of human behavior have recently emerged into a rapidly growing branch of empirical neuroscience, called neuroeconomics. As the name implies, neuroeconomics employs both neuroscience techniques and economic theory to test how desire, reason, and choice are represented in the human mind, and, ultimately, why humans make the choices that they do. Neuroeconomics may therefore hold a particularly promising avenue for rhetorical scholars to explore questions that have traditionally been tied to verbal appeals: how people are ultimately persuaded toward a particular course of action.

Rhetoric scholars might be particularly interested in how terms like emotion and reason (which evoke the ancient rhetorical proofs, *pathos* and *logos*) can be studied experimentally in neuroeconomics. In this way, we might gain a deeper understanding of what parts of the brain are activated by emotional stimuli (such as memories of events that signal threat) or by reasoning tasks (such as decision/reward tasks involving the anticipation of gains and losses) (Labar; Carter et al.). Nevertheless, neuroeconomics must be approached with care, since reason and emotion can be difficult concepts to pin down. In this section, we examine how researchers in neuroeconomics understand reason and emotion, how they operationalize those qualities in experiments, and how those understandings do or do not line up with how rhetoricians understand reason and emotion.

Of course, the word "neuroeconomics" itself suggests that the field draws on a specific understanding of human action, one that frames such issues primarily in economic terms. The assumption underlying much of this research is that humans make decisions according to calculations of rewards, risk, and value, and that these are represented in concrete and testable psychological and neural terms. If the brain is responsible for carrying out all of the decisions that humans make, understanding the physiological functions of the brain will help explain why people make specific choices and why they often fail to make optimal decisions.

The interplay between such theory and neurobiology has led to productive insights. Over the past several years, neuroscientists have begun to identify basic computational and physiological functions that explain how reasoning works. One common model is a compensatory one, where individuals make decisions based on calculations of positive versus negative outcomes (Rangel). In this model, decision makers must first form mental representations of the available options, and then assign each option some value according to a common currency (such as monetary gain). Next, the organism compares the values of different options and chooses a specific course of action. After the action is completed, the organism measures the benefit gained, and this information is fed back into the decision mechanism to improve future choices.

A growing body of neuroscientific evidence supports this framework. For example, researchers have found that some neurons in the brain adjust their firing rate with the magnitude and probability of reward (Platt and Glimcher). Similarly, researchers have shown that neurons in the monkey orbitofrontal cortex encode the value of goods (Padoa-Schioppa and Assad), while others have suggested that the frontal cortex neurons represent decision variables such as probability, magnitude, and cost (Kennerley et al.). Collectively, this evidence suggests that subjective value is represented in the nervous system, and that individuals make choices by weighing these values. In this model, decisions are made primarily through rational calculations of value, with the goal being for organisms to maximize their reward (whether it be money, food, or something else).

But does this understanding of reason and emotion line up with the assumptions rhetorical scholars might make about those concepts, which since Aristotle's *Rhetoric*, have been associated with logos and pathos? We might be tempted to take these studies as outside proof that such concepts exist, or to suggest the possibility of someday teasing out rhetorical appeals scientifically (an idea being implemented in the field of neuromarketing). Yet, rhetorical scholars should be careful to distinguish our own understandings of emotion and logic from those supposed by neuroscientists. Daniel Gross argues that Aristotle understands the passions as a sort a "political economy," but the emotions in this theory are decidedly public and rhetorical (6). Anger, for Aristotle, "is a deeply social passion provoked by perceived, unjustified slights," presupposing "a public stage where social status is always insecure" (2). According to Gross, emotions that were at one time treated as "externalized forms of currency" have been folded into the brain, where they are now understood as hardwired and biological, not political and rhetorical (8). While the notion of an emotional economy might appear in both fields, then, the nature of that economy varies significantly.

To determine how, exactly, neuroscientific understandings of reason and logic might match up with rhetorical ones, we searched PubMed for articles that contained the terms *reason, emotion,* and *fMRI*. Out of 83 articles, we chose 20 that attempted to track individuals' response to emotional stimuli and/or reasoned judgments. For each article (see Appendix 15.1), we tracked whether or not definitions were provided for the terms *reason* and *emotion,* noted what definitions were given, and determined how those fuzzy concepts were *operationalized,* or rendered scientifically measurable. The studies we selected focused on such topics as gender differences in cognitive control of emotion, the "neural correlates" of empathy, and the recruitment of specific brain regions in inductive reasoning. Obviously, direct comparison of these articles is impossible, and that is not our intent. Our aim was not to conduct an exhaustive study of how scientists operationalize these concepts, but simply to get a preliminary sense of how scientific understandings of reason and emotion might square with rhetorical conceptions.

In many cases, researchers did not define what was meant by key terms such as *emotion* or *reason*—only six of the articles in our sample did so. Perhaps the writers assumed that their readers already shared a common, disciplinary definition. For non-neuroscientists, then, this poses a challenge: what do the authors mean by a term like *emotion* if it is not defined? Is there a standard definition or understanding about this term as it is used in the field? And might these definitions differ between sub-fields?

When definitions were given, they varied in format and content. For instance, studies of reason usually offered provisional definitions, as in these four:

- reasoning "combines prior information with new beliefs or conclusions and usually comes in the form of cognitive manipulations . . . that require working memory" (Schaich Borg et al. 803)
- "a combination of cognitive processes that allows us to draw inferences from a given set of information and reach conclusions that are not explicitly available, providing new knowledge" (Canessa et al. 930)
- "By 'reasoning,' we refer to relatively slow and deliberative processes involving abstraction and at least some introspectively accessible components" (Greene et al. 389)
- "Inductive reasoning is defined as the process of inferring a general rule (conclusion) by observation and analysis of specific instances (premises). Inductive reasoning is used when generating hypotheses, formulating theories and discovering relationships, and is essential for scientific discovery" (Lu et al. 74).

Anyone hoping to draw conclusions about reason as an element of rhetoric would need to take into account these differing definitions, weighing whether or not they are similar enough to warrant generalizations to rhetorical study. While rhetoricians may wish to associate reason with *logos*, none of these articles considers how individuals are persuaded by logical arguments. In these studies, participants are usually presented with logical puzzles or problems they must solve individually. It would be difficult for a rhetorical scholar to draw clear inferences about logical persuasion from these studies, since they do not focus specifically on how the brain responds to logical appeals.

In the studies mentioning empathy, one cited *Encyclopedia Britannica*'s definition of empathy—"the ability to imagine oneself in another's place and understand the other's feelings, desires, ideas, and actions"—along with criteria from a previous study (Krämer et al. 110). A second defined empathy as "the capacity to share and appreciate others' emotional and affective states in relation to oneself," drawing on previous work by other researchers (Akitsuki and Decety 722). While these definitions are similar, in the first one, empathy involves propelling oneself outward into another's "place," while the second involves the opposite movement of considering another's emotions "in relation to oneself"—the first is outer-directed, the second inner-directed.

For rhetoric scholars, the next step might be to consider how these definitions compare to rhetorical ones. Both of the definitions cited here envisioned empathy as an ability or capacity, something one presumably either has or does not have. On the face of it, these definitions might square with Quintilian's notion that the most effective rhetors possess a capacity to feel the emotions they seek to evoke (Quintilian 6.2.26). For Quintilian, though, empathy is a distinctly performative skill, since orators who can "best conceive such images will have the greatest power in moving the feelings" (6.2.29). In his formulation, empathy represents a capacity to conjure for oneself the emotional states that move the feelings, and to project those emotional states to an audience. Alternately, we might be tempted to line up these fMRI studies with Kenneth Burke's concept of identification, which suggests that "You persuade a man only insofar as you can talk his language by speech, gesture, tonality, order, image, attitude, idea, *identifying* your ways with his" (Burke 55; his emphasis). In any case, both Quintilian and Burke add a dimension to empathy that is lacking in the scientific accounts—the capacity not only to put oneself in another's shoes, but then to *take on* or perform that person's emotions, to "talk his language," as Burke suggests, or to paint an image that evokes those emotions, in Quintilian's conception.

In order for an fMRI study of empathy to map neatly onto these definitions, the study would have to operationalize this specific, rhetorical definition of empathy—not just any study of empathy will necessarily apply. The choice of stimulus would also be significant. In our sample, emotion was evoked using images of neutral or emotional faces (Kompus et al.), faceless cartoons in emotional or neutral situations (Krämer et al.), negative olfactory stimulation (by means of rotten yeast) (Koch et al.), and angry or neutral voices reading nonsense utterances (Sander et al.). Only in a few cases did studies focusing on emotion involve subjects reading or listening to meaningful text—usually a few lines only (Harris, Sheth, and Cohen; Ferstl and von Cramon; Schaich Borg et al.). To date, no fMRI studies that we could find studied individuals' neuronal responses to explicitly rhetorical stimuli— there have been no "this is your brain on Martin Luther King's 'I Have a Dream' speech" studies (although perhaps it is only a matter of time before such a study appears).

In the remaining articles, the terms *emotion* or *reason* were either taken as given, or were implicitly defined. For instance, in Harris et al., a study of belief and disbelief, participants were asked to rate phrases as "true" or "false" while their brain activation was measured with fMRI. Because this is how the authors chose to operationalize belief and disbelief, we can surmise that they defined those values, implicitly, as being akin to truth and falsity (as opposed to some other definition of belief emphasizing faith, trust, or confidence). While our survey was not exhaustive, it does suggest that rhetoricians seeking to incorporate neuroscience findings must do considerable work to unpack the assumptions underlying any single study, to put those in the context of other studies, and then to compare neuroscience understandings with those common to our own field. This preliminary survey suggests that we need to be careful not to assume that terms like "reason" or "emotion" have stable definitions, that they are defined in the same way across studies, or that they necessarily align with the preferred rhetorical definitions.

Empathy and Neurological Difference

As we have shown, neuroscience research is replete with methodological and terminological variability, so that writers of research articles must make careful choices about the terms and methods they describe. By drawing on rhetoric of science studies, readers of these articles can examine research articles carefully, considering alternative interpretations and the broader cultural debates in which such articles participate (Bazerman; Berkenkotter and Huckin; Myers; Schryer; Swales). The example we consider here is an article titled "Neural Mechanisms of Empathy in Adolescents with Autism Spectrum Disorder and Their Fathers," published by Ellen Greimel et al. in a 2010 issue of *NeuroImage*. We chose this article because it deals with a topic of great cultural interest at the moment, one suited to the emphasis of this special issue on neurological difference: autism. Not only is autism a highly debated topic in popular spheres, but, as a communicative disorder, it is sometimes posited as a kind of touchstone against which rhetorical ability can be measured (see, for instance, Oakley 102).

Formerly seen as a rare disorder, autism diagnosis rates have risen dramatically over the last 20 years, with current prevalence estimates at 1 in 110, according to the Center for Disease Control. In the *Diagnostic and Statistical Manual* (DSM-IV) of the American Psychological Association, autistic disorder (sometimes called Autistic Spectrum Disorder, or ASD), is defined in part by a list of impairments in communication and social interaction, combined with repetitive and stereotyped behavior.[6] This increase in diagnosis has led to many cultural developments: the rising influence of parent organizations arguing for biomedical treatment options; the increasing presence of autistic characters in television and film;[7] and the growing self-advocacy movement among autistic individuals who seek a greater voice in shaping directions for research and advocacy (O'Neil; Solomon; Sinclair). Scientific articles about autism necessarily participate in this broader cultural milieu. New findings about autism tend to be widely reported in the media, especially when they suggest either anatomical or genetic differences that may explain the behavioral criteria that distinguish autism.

One of these broader cultural trends is the position of ASD as a male disorder. The first thing to notice from the title of Greimel's study is that the study focused on adolescents and their *fathers*. From the abstract, we learn that the study examined high-functioning boys with a diagnosis of ASD. While the writers do not remark on their choice of male subjects, from a rhetorical standpoint these facts situate the article within a broader cultural depiction of autism as a disorder affecting males. Studies suggest that boys are four times more likely than girls to receive a diagnosis of ASD, a fact that has led some researchers to posit that autism is a disorder of the "extreme male brain" (Baron-Cohen, *The Essential Difference*; Baron-Cohen, "The Extreme-Male-Brain"). In this theory, ASD simply represents an exaggeration of qualities taken to be typically male. In Baron-Cohen's theory, brains tend to be either "systematizing" or "empathizing." Women tend to score higher on tests of empathizing, while men tend to score higher on tests of systematizing. Nonetheless, Baron-Cohen insists that it is *brains* that are male (systemizing) or female (empathizing), not necessarily the bodies in which those brains exist.[8] At any rate, individuals with ASD, according to Baron-Cohen, get exceedingly high scores on systemizing tests. In fact, Greimel et al. used Baron-Cohen's survey of systematizing and empathizing tendencies, called the "Autistic Quotient," or AQ, to determine whether the fathers in the study possessed autistic qualities.

Rhetoric researchers might be interested in examining this broader debate about gender and autism and how it is inflected in a particular article. By focusing on male subjects, Greimel et al. subtly appeal to the dominant depiction of the disorder as fundamentally male—a depiction that also plays on the ever-popular suggestion that male and female brains are fundamentally different (Condit). This is not necessarily a shortcoming of Greimel et al.'s paper. After all, it is quite commonplace to constrain one's sample size by looking only at one sex. Recently, though, some researchers have suggested that girls and women with ASD are underdiagnosed, that the definition of the disorder itself overlooks how ASD may present in females differently (Koenig and Tsatsanis). Scientific articles like the one by Greimel et al. participate in this gendering of autism as a male disorder, a process that draws on cultural discourses about masculinity, technology, and geekiness.

By focusing on empathy, the authors of this study make a rhetorical, as well as a scientific, choice, framing their article as an intervention into that particular theory of autism's etiology. Autism presents interesting questions for neuroscientists who seek to identify differences in brain structure and function between people with and without autism. One of these proposed differences is a lack of empathy, often called mindblindness, in individuals with autism (Baron-Cohen, *Mindblindness*; Happé). Accordingly, studies of empathy constitute a large proportion of autism research studies in psychology or neuroscience. Drawing on Baron-Cohen's work, Greimel et al. open by identifying "difficulties inferring their own and other persons' mental states" as among the core deficits of autism (1055). While the writers present this as a statement of fact, there are competing theories, such as the intense world hypothesis (Tager-Flusberg) or weak central coherence theory (Frith and Happé) which are not mentioned in this article. Further, the term empathy does not appear in the APA's diagnostic criteria for autism; the closest terminology in that text refers to difficulty with social reciprocity. Empathy may be an attractive concept to neuroscience researchers interested in autism because it can be operationalized in an fMRI study via quizzes or images, and because it has been studied in non-autistic individuals. In contrast, social reciprocity may seem fuzzier or more difficult to operationalize, and therefore more difficult to justify in a research article.[9] Rhetorical scholars should pay careful attention to how and why scientists choose specific concepts to test, how they are defined, and whether they may (or may not) apply to rhetorical concepts.

Rhetoric scholars should also pay close attention to the terminology used to describe research findings. In their study, Greimel et al. draw on genetic explanations for autism, suggesting that "[s]imilarities in neurocognitive and behavioural profiles [between individuals with ASD and their family members] strongly suggest a common biological substrate underlying these disturbances. Thus, exploring the neural underpinnings of altered social cognition in persons with ASD and their first-degree relatives might be a valuable approach to identifying familial influences on autistic pathology" (1055–56). Here, the writers first suggest a "common biological substrate" and then replace that term, in the second sentence, with "neural underpinnings," a move that concretizes their suggestion that there may be identifiable neurological similarities between the boys with ASD and their fathers. The writers suggest that their results indicate "that FG [fusiform gyrus] dysfunction in the context of empathy constitutes a fundamental neurobiological deviation in ASD" (1062). The transformation is subtle, but what are understood to be neural *correlates* of empathy become located in the fusiform gyrus (FG), a particular site in the brain, which then becomes (potentially) a concrete, physical predictor of ASD. The term *neural correlates* is particularly slippery in this way—while it suggests correlation, not causation, the noun phrase *neural correlates* makes the phenomenon seem more concrete. To a non-scientist, especially, neural correlates may easily be confused with "neural substrates" or something similarly tangible. It is easy to overlook the fact that the researchers are mapping BOLD activity, a proxy for neurological function, to behavior under particular experimental circumstances. Rhetoric scholars, then, should pay close attention to terms such as neural correlates, neural substrates, and the like, being sure to tease out what these terms mean and the potential suasory impact of such terms.

With regards to the methodology used, Asperger's syndrome serves an interesting rhetorical and methodological function. It is also notable that the authors studied adolescent boys diagnosed with Asperger's syndrome, usually considered a high-functioning variant of autism, but one that is currently listed as a separate disorder in the DSM-IV. The writers posit that Asperger's may serve as an appropriate analogy to other forms of autism: "One way to overcome the barriers associated with such complexity [in autistic disorders] is to examine qualitatively similar but milder phenotypes in relatives of affected individuals" (1056). The rhetorical figure at hand is the *incrementum*, which Jeanne Fahnestock suggests orders subjects who presumably share some kind of attribute to differing degrees (*Rhetorical Figures in Science* 95). The notion that individuals with classic autism and with Asperger's syndrome exist on a spectrum, or *incrementum*, implies that they differ in degree of impairment, but have the same underlying biological condition. It is this figure that grounds studies such as this one, which allow boys with Asperger's to stand in for all individuals with autism.

The notion of incrementum can help to explain the language that writers use to describe autism and Asperger's. While they portray Asperger's as a "milder phenotype" of autism, they nevertheless described the test group as "affected individuals" (1062), while the control group was called "healthy adolescents" (1063) or "healthy controls" (1063). Individuals with ASD were characterized as having "*aberrant* neural face and mirroring mechanisms" (1055; emphasis ours) and "socioemotional *impairments*" (1063; emphasis ours). This terminology, common to scientific articles about autism, also constitutes a rhetorical choice among available terms. By choosing this language, the writers position their work clearly within a scientific conversation surrounding the deficits apparent in autism. A different choice of language might signal a different approach. For instance, individuals who argue for neurodiversity, or the notion that neurological differences are at least partially culturally produced, might use terms such as *difference, condition* (as opposed to disorder), and *acceptance* rather than *therapy* or *cure*. Meanwhile, parents who advocate biomedical treatments for autism tend to use terms connoting *disease* and *devastation*, on the one hand, and *cure* or *recovery*, on the other, to argue for their case. For rhetoric scholars, the point may not be to weigh in on this debate, but to pay attention to the kinds of language used to describe a neurological difference such as autism, and to the different meanings they carry in different contexts.

The implications of any scientific article, which usually appear in the discussion section, are key considerations. In scientific articles on autism, diagnosis and genetics tend to appear in discussion sections, serving as commonplaces to help writers address the so-what question. The upshot of Greimel et al.'s implications is that autism might be corrected through medical intervention, particularly early diagnosis and genetic identification. Greimel et al. suggest that "Illuminating aberrancies such as reduced activation of the amygdala and the FG in persons presenting with mild autistic traits might prove beneficial for the identification of neurobiological endophenotypes of ASD and may provide future directions for molecular genetic studies" (1063). These commonplaces are disputed in other circles, such as in the neurodiversity movement, where they are interpreted as portending the possibility of fetal screening and selective abortion of fetuses identified as "autistic." Meanwhile, parents who write about autism often embrace early diagnosis and screening techniques, since they may help them to argue for appropriate therapies and resources. For rhetoric scholars, then, it is key to consider how these topoi function as rhetorical choices, and how those topoi might be interpreted in other contexts.

One might be inclined to conclude from Greimel et al.'s study that the fusiform gyrus (FG) can verify the fundamentally human capacity for empathy, or the lack thereof in autistic individuals, and hence rhetoric. As we mentioned earlier, empathy underlies a number of rhetorical theories, including those of Quintilian and Burke. Indeed, Dennis Lynch argues that "The concept and practice of empathy insinuates itself into most modem rhetorical theories, under one guise or another" (6). It might be tempting, then, to use the case of autism as a kind of test case or touchstone against which "normal" human rhetorical capacities might be measured. Using empathy as a marker of rhetorical potential might seem to exclude individuals with autism from human rhetorical capacity on almost every level, a fact that can be ethically objectionable. A more responsible move, then, might be to question whether it is ethical for rhetoricians to assume a lack of empathy in other humans, or to consider whether rhetorical theories should be revised in order to better account for the full range of human rhetorical capacities, including those with neurological differences.

Any research article is situated both with relation to a scientific conversation and a broader cultural one. In the case of neurological differences, these contexts are increasingly convergent, in that non-scientists are gaining a voice in research decisions about autism, bipolar disorder, depression, and the like. However, readers must be quite familiar with such debates, both within scientific communities and outside of them, in order to understand the rhetorical choices, as well as elisions, within a given article.

Rhetorical Considerations: Neuroscience Findings in the Popular Media

Given the complexities of scientific texts, rhetoric scholars might be drawn to popular texts about neuroscience, since they provide accessible overviews of current findings. In general, though, popular science reports often repackage scientific findings by drawing on topoi such as application or wonder (Fahnestock "Accommodating"). In their study of popular news reports about neuroscience, in particular, Eric Racine, Ofek Bar-Ilan, and Judy Illes, categorize claims as falling into three types, which they call neurorealism, neuroessentialism, and neuropolicy. Readers should be aware of these three commonplaces, how they work on audiences, and how they might relate to the scientific reports themselves, rather than taking them at face value. Moreover, readers might also look for these tendencies in scientific articles, where they may appear in the discussion section as a way to signal the importance of a given research study.

As described by Racine, Bar-Ilan, and Illes, neurorealism occurs when "coverage of fMRI investigations can make a phenomenon uncritically real, objective or effective in the eyes of the public" (160), or when reports invalidate or validate our ordinary understanding of the world. We would suggest that neurorealism can occur in popularization of all kinds of neuroscience research, not just those that report on fMRI research. Rhetorically, neurorealism operates through metaphors that work to spatially locate specific functions in the brain. One example of neurorealism is this headline from *New Scientist*: "Emotional speech leaves 'signature' on the brain" (Thomson). In this study, scientists examined patterns of brain activation in 22 individuals who listened to a single sentence, read with different emotional inflections. In the article, Thomson suggests that the scientists observed "signatures," a term that implies that the results in question somehow left a mark on the brain, rather than interpreting them as momentary patterns of activation. The usage reflects the underlying metaphor of the brain as text, inscribed by sensory experiences. A correlate of this metaphor tends to be the suggestion that scientists can therefore "read minds" in a popular sense, as though scientists could literally read a transcript of someone's thoughts rather than *interpret* visual images or data. Such usage, along with references to regions of the brain such as a "emotion center," "neural architecture," or "god spot," also involve spatial metaphors, which, like textual metaphors, seek to fix brain functions in particular spaces.

The second tendency, neuroessentialism, refers to "how fMRI research can be depicted as equating subjectivity and personal identity to the brain" (160). The key rhetorical figure for neuroessentialism might be a double synecdoche, wherein both the brain and the quality to be measured stand in for a complex of biological and cultural factors. An example of might be this claim from a MSNBC report: "Two new brain-imaging studies describing the origins of empathy and how placebos work provide insights into the nature of pain, the mind-body connection and what it means to be human" (Kane). The "brain" stands in for the complex network of neurons, blood flow, bodily actions, and cognitive processes that might actually make up something like pain or the "mind-body connection." Once the brain takes over for this complex, it can be given tasks like "handling love and pain" or telling us "what it means to be human." In this way, the brain represents the *essence* of human experiences (love, pain), or even of humanness itself. Such reports often anthropomorphize the brain, making it an active agent, as in the headline for the Kane article, "How your brain handles love and pain."

Finally, neuropolicy refers to "attempts to use fMRI results to promote political and personal agendas" (Racine, Bar-Ilan, and Illes 161). Often, neuropolicy arguments rely on weak analogies that extend the initial research findings far beyond their original contexts. For example, a recent report in *Popular Science* suggested that a new study showing neural correlates of pain in 16 men undergoing oral surgery held implications for animal rights: "applications of this technology for fields beyond medicine, such as animal rights, may prove more transformative than any medical use. Using the fMRI on animals could quantify the pain levels of veterinary and slaughter procedures, potentially changing the way we both heal and kill animals (Fox). Here, the writer extends the research findings beyond their immediate context (research on humans undergoing oral surgery) to a very different context—animals being treated by a veterinarian or slaughtered for food. This is not to say that such an application might not be possible, or warranted, but these kinds of statements tend to minimize the time, effort, and technological innovation required for these applications. A weak analogy can also occur when writers extend animal studies to humans, since the biological and social factors influencing human cognition vary from, say, rats. Whether or not the comparison is apt depends on the situation.

Given these tendencies in popular and scientific articles, researchers in rhetoric should carefully question the interpretations writers give for neuroscience findings. More generally, both popular and scientific texts take advantage of the persuasiveness of visual images of the brain (McCabe and Castel; Johnson;

Beaulieu "Images"; Weisberg et al.), sometimes leading audiences to grant greater credibility to scientific claims than they might otherwise. These images, nearly ubiquitous in popular reports, act as the warrant for the scientific claims, offering what Anne Beaulieu calls "a concrete unit of scientific knowledge" in an attractive, visual form ("Images" 54). Rhetoricians seeking to rely on popularized accounts of neuroscience need to carefully read such texts with a rhetorical lens, considering how authors frame their research, what arguments they make, and what other viewpoints might exist in the field.

Guidelines and Future Directions

Neuroscience research holds tantalizing possibilities for rhetorical scholarship; however, there exists a deep divide in how rhetoricians and neuroscientists communicate. Paying attention to the fundamental differences in discourse between these communities will help rhetoric scholars to work with neuroscience findings in a responsible manner. To conclude, we offer here some guidelines for scholars in rhetoric who plan to use neuroscience research in their work.

First, as we showed in the initial section, it is important to understand the methodological assumptions and debates driving neuroscience research. While neuroimaging technologies provide powerful tools, their interpretation is also guided by complex, ongoing arguments about specific methodological practices. In fact, untangling how methodological assumptions influence neuroscientific analyses sometimes reveals that these assumptions may predetermine results to some extent. By focusing on the topoi of *accuracy*, *precision*, and *bias*, we showed how neuroscientists negotiate the empirical parameters out of which claims about the brain can be made. Since these parameters are not yet settled, it is important for outside readers to be careful about applying scientific results to new contexts, such as rhetorical ones.

Second, rhetoric scholars should carefully compare their own terms and definitions with those used in neuroscience fields. As we showed in our second section, the neuroscience concepts of emotion, reason, and empathy might seem to match rhetorical concepts of pathos, logos, and identification; yet this assumption would be false in many cases. In order to draw conclusions from neuroscientific studies, rhetoric scholars will either have to make judgments about what qualifies as a close enough operationalization of a given concept or work directly with neuroscientists to operationalize our own concepts. Rhetoric scholars might work with neuroscientists to empirically test rhetorical effectiveness of, say, campaign speeches. However, both of us are skeptical of this approach, which could easily fall into the traps of neurorealism or neuroessentialism.

Third, scholars should draw on the insights of rhetoric of science scholarship when examining any particular scientific article. Rather than simply extracting the findings from an abstract, we should be careful to consider the framework the writers create for their data, asking what other scientific frameworks or explanations might be possible, and how those frameworks relate to broader debates. Such an approach requires at least some familiarity with the conceptual or methodological debates going on within a given field of study. For neuroscientists, evaluating a single article depends on the ability to fit that article within a body of converging evidence. For scholars doing interdisciplinary work, this poses a significant challenge. Ideally, collaborative work with neuroscience researchers could provide an avenue for rhetoric scholars to use neuroscience insights responsibly in their own work. In lieu of a direct collaboration, rhetoric scholars will need to do significant outside reading in order to situate a given research finding within its discourse community.

Finally, rhetoric scholars should be wary of repeating (or making their own) claims that fall into the trap of neurorealism, neuroessentialism, or neuropolicy. While we locate these pitfalls in popular accounts, they may also be tendencies in the cross-disciplinary endeavor we are calling neurorhetorics. For instance, we might be apt to argue that a given rhetorical concept (pathos, ethos, identification, or what have you) can be proven to exist due to neuroimaging studies— an instance of neurorealism. Or, we might lean toward neuroessentialism by claiming that brain scan studies attest to different types of brains—the "pathos-driven brain" or the "logos-driven brain"—based on how individuals respond to emotional versus logical kinds of arguments. The third pitfall, neuropolicy, may be especially likely to ensnare scholars interested in rhetorical production. Suggesting that brain studies offer proof of the effectiveness of a specific method of instruction will often fall into the trap of neuropolicy. Clearly, the classroom is a much more complex place than can be simulated inside an fMRI machine, so we should be wary of weak analogies that seek to offer scientific proof of the effectiveness of any given pedagogical method.

Given these caveats, we return to our initial claim that neurorhetorics research should involve both careful rhetorical analysis of neuroscience arguments as well as consideration of how neuroscience can inform rhetorical theory and practice. Accordingly, we suggest the following directions for future research.

We may consider how scientific research about the brain is used to support arguments in all kinds of venues (political, legal, literary, medical, and so on). In this issue, for instance, Katie Guest Pryal, John P. Jackson, and Jenell Johnson each examine the rhetorical controversies that often surround attempts to define (or exclude) individuals on the basis of cognitive functioning or difference. Rhetoricians might also consider why neuroscientific explanations and images hold particular sway over audiences, an issue neuroscientists have themselves been debating. In one recent study, researchers David McCabe and Alan Castel found that people ranked descriptions of brain research as more credible if it included images of brain scans. In another study, researchers found that even including the words "brain scans indicate" increased readers' confidence in explanations of brain phenomena, leading researchers to question the "seductive allure" that neuroscience seems to hold (Weisberg et al.). Rhetoricians might help us to understand why neuroscience findings seem to hold this allure, and to what effect.

While scholars have shown that popular news accounts tend to overemphasize or decontextualize neuroscience research findings (McCabe and Castel; Weisberg et al.), we know of no studies that question whether neuroscience research articles themselves reflect popular science preoccupations. In other words, do publication and funding pressures encourage authors to frame their research in ways that will lead to attractive headlines? A related project might consider how rhetorical theory can account for the persuasiveness of neuroimaging and neuroscience findings noted by McCabe and Castel and Weisberg et al.

Applications of neuroscience research to legal contexts should also interest rhetorical scholars, since forensics have always been part of rhetoric's domain. Brain data are already being offered as evidence in trials, but we contend that such data must be interpreted by expert witnesses.[10] For rhetoric scholars this means that expert ethos becomes a key issue—who is trusted to make these judgments in court (and in other venues)? How do legal and scientific arguments coincide in these cases? The legal venue is just one of many in which neurological difference is produced, identified, and realized in specific brains. As the articles in this issue demonstrate, the production of neurological difference never happens exclusively within scientific realms, but it nonetheless draws on neuroscience evidence for its power.

Finally, we hope more researchers in both rhetoric and neuroscience will undertake collaborative, interdisciplinary research. As we have shown, these two fields do have much to say to one another. While great differences in research methodologies, foundational concepts, discourse practices, and publication venues exist between these fields, we hope that the two-sided approach proposed in this article can help rhetoric scholars to use neuroscience insights in a responsible manner to yield productive insights into rhetoric while minimizing potential pitfalls of interdisciplinary work. We have highlighted a number of strategies here, such as carefully considering neuroscience research methods, comparing neuroscientific with rhetorical understandings of similar terms, or grounding any borrowings in a broader understanding of rhetorical and scientific debates surrounding neurological difference. Given the great interest and importance of these disciplines we encourage future research projects that have the potential to produce further productive interchanges between these fields.

Acknowledgments

The authors thank Scott Huettel, Nico Boehler, Debra Hawhee, and Katie Rose Guest Pryal for their valuable comments on this article.

Notes

1 For a rhetorical-cultural analysis of brain-based lie detectors, see Littlefield.
2 The scientific evidence for these devices varies considerably. For instance, one 2006 study suggested that each hour of television or video viewing (regardless of type) was actually associated

with a 16.99-point *decrease* in MacArthur-Bates Communicative Development Inventory CDI score, an indicator of early language proficiency. See Zimmerman et al.

3 See, for instance, Mooney and Kirshenbaum; Specter.

4 Scholars hoping to work with fMRI research findings might wish to consult a textbook explaining basic methodological procedures, such as Scott A. Huettel, McCarthy, and Song's *Functional Magnetic Resonance Imaging*.

5 While this is typical, not all fMRI experimental designs test hypotheses about the specialization of localized regions of the brain. For example, a large number of recent papers have focused on decoding the information that is represented across the whole brain at a particular point in time to a particular class of stimuli.

6 At the time of writing, The American Psychiatric Association (APA) was considering proposed changes to the criteria for autism for the next edition of the *Diagnostic and Statistical Manual*, DSM-5. Previously, there were separate diagnostic categories for Asperger's Syndrome and Pervasive Developmental Disorder (PDD), two variants of autism. According to the APA, the new category would help to simplify diagnosis, since deciding where to draw the lines between sub-categories was akin to trying to "cleave meatloaf at the joints." See American Psychiatric Association.

7 Recent examples include *Mozart and the Whale* (2005), *Adam* (2009), and the HBO biopic *Temple Grandin* (2010).

8 Women can possess "male" brains, or men "female" brains, depending on how the individual scores on a test of systemizing versus empathizing, a fact that calls into question the use of the terms male and female to describe these brains in the first place.

9 For instance, the "intense world" hypothesis suggests that ASD stems from a hyperactive, hypersensitive brain, producing exaggerated (and confusing) reactions to sensory input (see Markram et al. 19). Autistic individuals often protest the "lack of empathy" or "mindblindness" characterization. One autistic person writes:

> sometimes doctors describe autistics as though they are emotionless automatons. This is far from the truth, especially as many autistics have parents or close relatives who have bipolar disorder. You can't get more emotional than bipolar disorder. I feel things very deeply. A lack of empathy isn't central to autism, it's just a feature of the social withdrawal.

See Alien Robot Girl.

10 See Feigenson for a discussion of the admissibility and persuasiveness of fMRI data as courtroom evidence.

References

Akitsuki, Yuko and Jean Decety. "Social Context and Perceived Agency Affects Empathy for Pain: An Event-Related fMRI Investigation." *NeuroImage* 47.2 (2009): 722–34.

Alien Robot Girl. Comment on "Do Supercharged Brains Give Rise to Autism?" *Plant Poisons and Rotten Stuff Blog* (2008). Web.

Arthos, John. "Locating the Instability of the Topic Places: Rhetoric, Phronesis and Neurobiology." *Communication Quarterly* 48.2 (2000): 272–92. Print.

Azim, Eiman, et al. "Sex Differences in Brain Activation Elicited by Humor." *Proceedings of the National Academy of Sciences of the United States of America* 102.45 (2005): 16496–501. Print.

Bandettini, Peter A. "Seven Topics in Functional Magnetic Resonance Imaging." *Journal of Integrative Neuroscience* 8.3 (2009): 371–403. Print.

Baron-Cohen, Simon. *The Essential Difference: The Truth About the Male and Female Brain.* New York: Basic Books, 2003. Print.

———. "The Extreme-Male-Brain Theory of Autism." *Trends in Cognitive Science* 6.6 (2002): 248–54. Print.

———. *Mindblindness: An Essay on Autism and Theory of Mind.* Cambridge: MIT P, 1997. Print.

Bazerman, Charles. *Shaping Written Knowledge.* Madison: U of Wisconsin P, 1988. Print.

Beaulieu, Anne. "From Brainbank to Database: The Informational Turn in the Study of the Brain." *Studies in History and Philosophy of Biology & Biomedical Science* 35 (2004): 367–90. Print.

———. "Images Are Not the (Only) Truth: Brain Mapping, Visual Knowledge, and Iconoclasm." *Science, Technology, & Human Values* 27 (2002): 53–86. Print.

Berkenkotter, Carol and Thomas N. Huckin. "You Are What You Cite: Novelty and Intertextuality in a Biologist's Experimental Article." *Professional Communication: The Social Perspective.* Ed. Nancy Roundy Blyler and Charlotte Thralls. Newbury Park: SAGE, 1993. 109–27. Print.

Burke, Kenneth. *A Rhetoric of Motives.* Berkeley: U of California P, 1969. Print.

Canessa, Nichola, et al. "The Effect of Social Content on Deductive Reasoning: An fMRI Study." *Human Brain Mapping* 26 (2005): 30–43. Print.

Carter, R. M., et al. "Activation in the VTA and Nucleus Accumbens Increases in Anticipation of Both Gains and Losses." *Frontiers in Behavioral Neuroscience* 3 (2009): 21. Print.

Condit, Celeste. "How Bad Science Stays That Way: Of Brain Sex, Demarcation, and the Status of Truth in the Rhetoric of Science." *Rhetoric Society Quarterly* 26 (1996): 83–109. Print.

Fahnestock, Jeanne. "Accommodating Science: The Rhetorical Life of Scientific Facts." *Written Communication* 15.3 (1998): 330–50. Print.

———. *Rhetorical Figures in Science.* New York: Oxford UP, 1999. Print.

Feigenson, Neil. "Brain Imaging and Courtroom Evidence: On the Admissibility and Persuasiveness of fMRI." *International Journal of Law in Context* 2.3 (2006): 233–55. Print.

Ferstl, Evelyn C. and D. Yves von Cramon. "Time, Space and Emotion: fMRI Reveals Content-Specific Activation During Text Comprehension." *Neuroscience Letters* 427 (2007): 159–64. Print.

Flower, Linda. "Cognition, Context, and Theory Building." *College Composition and Communication* 40.3 (1989): 282–311. Print.

Fox, Stuart. "New Brain Scan Quantifies the Formerly Subjective Feeling of Pain." *Popular Science* (2010). Web.

Friston, K. J. and R. Henson. "A Commentary on Divide and Conquer: A Defense of Functional Localisers." *NeuroImage* 30 (2006): 1097–99. Print.

Friston, K. J., et al. "A Critique of Functional Localisers." *NeuroImage* 30.4 (2006): 1077–87. Print.

Frith, U. and F Happé. "Autism: Beyond 'Theory of Mind.'" *Cognition* 50 (1994): 115–32. Print.

Greene, Joshua D., et al. "The Neural Bases of Cognitive Conflict and Control in Moral Judgment." *Neuron* 44.2 (2004): 389–400. Print.

Greimel, Ellen, et al. "Neural Mechanisms of Empathy in Adolescents with Autism Spectrum Disorder and Their Fathers." *NeuroImage* 49 (2010): 1055–65. Print.

Gross, Daniel M. *The Secret History of Emotion: From Aristotle's 'Rhetoric' to Modern Brain Science.* Chicago: The U of Chicago P, 2006. Print.

Happé, F. G. "An Advanced Test of Theory of Mind: Understanding of Story Characters' Thoughts and Feelings by Able Autistic, Mentally Handicapped, and Normal Children and Adults." *Journal of Autism and Developmental Disorders* 24.2 (1994): 129–54. Print.

Harris, Sam, Sameer A. Sheth, and Mark S. Cohen. "Functional Neuroimaging of Belief, Disbelief, and Uncertainty." *Annals of Neurology* 63 (2008): 141–47. Print.

Huettel, Scott A., Gregory McCarthy, and Allen W. Song, eds. *Functional Magnetic Resonance Imaging.* Sunderland: Sinauer Associates, 2004. Print.

Johnson, Davi. "How Do You Know Unless You Look?': Brain Imaging, Biopower and Practical Neuroscience." *Journal of Medical Humanities* 29 (2008): 147–61. Print.

Kane, Daniel. "How Your Brain Handles Love and Pain." *MSNBC* (8 February 2004). Web.

Kelland, Kate. "Vegetative Patient 'Talks' Using Brain Waves." *Reuters* (3 February 2010). Web.

Kennerley, S. W., et al. "Neurons in the Frontal Lobe Encode the Value of Multiple Decision Variables." *Journal of Cognitive Neuroscience* 21.6 (2009): 1162–78. Print.

Koch, K., et al. "Gender Differences in the Cognitive Control of Emotion: An fMRI Study." *Neuro-psychologia* 20 (2007): 2744–54. Print.

Koenig, Kathleen and Katherine D. Tsatsanis. "Pervasive Developmental Disorders in Girls." *Handbook of Behavioral and Emotional Problems in Girls.* Ed. Debora J. Bell, Sharon L. Foster, and Eric J. Mash. New York: Kluwer Academic/Plenum Publishers, 2005. Print.

Kompus, Kristiina, et al. "Distinct Control Networks for Cognition and Emotion in the Prefrontal Cortex." *Neuroscience Letters* 467.2 (2009): 76–80. Print.

Krämer, Ulrike M., et al. "Emotional and Cognitive Aspects of Empathy and Their Relation to Social Cognition—an fMRI-Study." *Brain Research* 1311 (2010): 110–20. Print.

Labar, K. S. "Beyond Fear Emotional Memory Mechanisms in the Human Brain." *Current Directions in Psychological Science* 16.4 (2007): 173–77. Print.

Lewiecki-Wilson, Cynthia. "Rethinking Rhetoric Through Mental Disabilities." *Rhetoric Review* 22.2 (2003): 156–67. Print.

Littlefield, Melissa. "Constructing the Organ of Deceit: The Rhetoric of fMRI and Brain Fingerprinting in Post-9/11 America." *Science, Technology, & Human Values* 34 (2009): 365–92. Print.

Logothetis, N. K., et al. "Neurophysiological Investigation of the Basis of the fMRI Signal." *Nature* 412.6843 (2001): 150–57. Print.

Logothetis, N. K. and B. A. Wandell. "Interpreting the Bold Signal." *Annual Review of Physiology* 66 (2004): 735–69. Print.

Lu, Shengfu, et al. "Recruitment of the Pre-Motor Area in Human Inductive Reasoning: An fMRI Study." *Cognitive Systems Research* 11.1 (2010): 74–80. Print.

Lynch, Dennis A. "Rhetorics of Proximity: Empathy in Temple Grandin and Cornel West." *Rhetoric Society Quarterly* 28.1 (1998): 5–23. Print.

Lynch, Michael E. "Science and the Transformation of the Animal Body into a Scientific Object: Laboratory Culture and Ritual Practice in the Neurosciences." *Social Studies of Science* 18.2 (1988): 265–89. Print.

Mak, Amanda K. Y., Zhi-guo Hu, John X. Zhang, Zhuang-wei Xiao, and Tatia M. C. Lee. "Neural Correlates of Regulation of Positive and Negative Emotions: An fMRI Study." *Neuroscience Letters* 457 (2009): 101–6. Print.

Markram, Henry, Tania Rinaldi, and Kamila Markram. "The Intense World Syndrome—an Alternative Hypothesis for Autism." *Frontiers in Neuroscience* 1 (2007): 19. Print.

McCabe, David P. and Alan D. Castel. "Seeing Is Believing: The Effect of Brain Images on Judgments of Scientific Reasoning." *Cognition* 107 (2008): 343–52. Print.

McRae, Kateri, et al. "Gender Differences in Emotion Regulation: An fMRI Study of Cognitive Reappraisal." *Group Processes & Intergroup Relations* 11.2 (2008): 143–62. Print.

Mooney, Chris and Sheril Kirshenbaum. *Unscientific America: How Scientific Illiteracy Threatens Our Future.* New York: Basic Books, 2009. Print.

Myers, Greg. *Writing Biology.* Madison: The U of Wisconsin P, 1990. Print.

Oakley, Todd V. "The Human Rhetorical Potential." *Written Communication* 16 (1999): 93–128. Print.

Ochsner, Kevin N., et al. "Reflecting Upon Feelings: An fMRI Study of Neural Systems Supporting the Attribution of Emotion to Self and Other." *Journal of Cognitive Neuroscience* 16.10 (2004): 1746–72. Print.

——. "Rethinking Feelings: An fMRI Study of the Cognitive Regulation of Emotion." *Journal of Cognitive Neuroscience* 14.8 (2002): 1215–29. Print.

O'Neil, Sara. "The Meaning of Autism: Beyond Disorder." *Disability & Society* 23.7 (2008): 787–99. Print.

Padoa-Schioppa, C. and J. A. Assad. "Neurons in the Orbitofrontal Cortex Encode Economic Value." *Nature* 441.7090 (2006): 223–26. Print.

Platt, M. L. and P. W. Glimcher. "Neural Correlates of Decision Variables in Parietal Cortex." *Nature* 400.6741 (1999): 233–38. Print.

Poldrack, Russell A. "Region of Interest Analysis for fMRI." *Social Cognitive and Affective Neuroscience* 2.1 (2007): 67–70. Print.

Poldrack, R. A., et al. "Guidelines for Reporting an fMRI Study." *Neuroimage* 40.2 (2008): 409–14. Print.

Prelli, Lawrence J. *A Rhetoric of Science: Inventing Scientific Discourse*. Columbia: U of South Carolina P, 1989. Print.

Quintilian. Trans. H. E. Butler. The Loeb Classical Library. *The Instituto Oratoria of Quintilian*. Ed. T. E. Page, E. Capps, and W. H. D. Rouse. Cambridge: Harvard UP, 1936. Print.

Racine, Eric, Ofek Bar-Ilan, and Judy Illes. "fMRI in the Public Eye." *Nature Reviews Neuroscience* 6 (2005): 159–64. Print.

Rangel, A. "The Computation and Comparison of Value in Goal-Directed Choice." *Neuroeconomics: Decision Making and the Brain*. Eds. P. W. Glimcher et al. New York: Academic P, 2009. 425–39. Print.

Reuter, M., et al. "Personality and Emotion: Test of Gray's Personality Theory by Means of an fMRI Study." *Behavioral Neuroscience* 118.3 (2004): 462–69. Print.

Sander, David, et al. "Emotion and Attention Interactions in Social Cognition: Brain Regions Involved in Processing Anger Prosody." *NeuroImage* 28.4 (2005): 848–58. Print.

Saxe, R., M. Brett, and N. Kanwisher. "Divide and Conquer: A Defense of Functional Localizers." *Neuroimage* 30.4 (2006): 1088–96; discussion 97–99. Print.

Schaich, Borg J., et al. "Consequences, Action, and Intention as Factors in Moral Judgments: An fMRI Investigation." *Journal of Cognitive Neuroscience* 18.5 (2006): 803–17. Print.

Schryer, Catherine F. "Genre Time/Space: Chronotopic Strategies in the Experimental Article." *JAC* 19 (1999): 81–89. Print.

Sinclair, Jim. "Don't Mourn for Us." *Autism Network International Newsletter* 1.3 (1993). Web.

Solomon, Andrew. "The Autism Rights Movement." *New York Magazine* (25 May 2008). Print.

Specter, Michael. *Denialism: How Irrational Thinking Hinders Scientific Progress, Harms the Planet, and Threatens Our Lives*. New York: Penguin, 2009. Print.

Swales, John. *Genre Analysis: English in Academic and Research Settings*. Cambridge: Cambridge UP, 1990. Print.

Tager-Flusberg, Helen. "Evaluating the Theory-of-Mind Hypothesis of Autism." *Current Directions in Psychological Science* 16.6 (2007): 311–15. Print.

Thomson, Helen. "Emotional Speech Leaves 'Signature' on the Brain." *New Scientist* (2009). Web.

Trautmann, Sina Alexa, Thorsten Fehr, and Manfred Herrmann. "Emotions in Motion: Dynamic Compared to Static Facial Expressions of Disgust and Happiness Reveal More Widespread Emotion-Specific Activations." *Brain Research* 1284 (2009): 100–15. Print.

Turner, Mark. "The Cognitive Study of Art, Language, and Literature." *Poetics Today* 23.1 (2002): 9–20. Print.

Weisberg, Deena Skolnick, et al. "The Seductive Allure of Neuroscience Explanations." *Journal of Cognitive Neuroscience* 20.3 (2008): 470–77. Print.

Zimmerman, Frederick J., Dimitri A. Christakis, and Andrew N. Meltzoff. "Associations Between Media Viewing and Language Development in Children under Age 2 Years." *The Journal of Pediatrics* 151.4 (2007): 364–68. Print.

Appendix 15.1

Article	Definition (y/n)	How defined?	How operationalized?
Kompus, Kristiina, et al.	No	n/a	Subjects presented with neutral or emotional faces; emotional faces were negative (fear or anger)
Krämer, Ulrike, et al.	Yes	Encyclopedia Britannica definition of empathy (p. 110) + Decety et al's list of components (3 of them)	Chose one of Decety et al's components to operationalize using faceless cartoons of "emotionally charged" vs. "emotionally neutral" situations that they had created
Mak, Amanda K.Y., et al.	No	Defines "emotion regulation" as dealing with "socially appropriate" behavior.	Used "emotional pictures" from the International Emotion Picture System plus extra pictures from popular media
Harris, Sam, et al.	No	Implicit—belief equated with truth, disbelief equated with falsity	Used fMRI to study the brains of 14 adults while they judged written statements to be "true" (belief), "false" (disbelief), or "undecidable" (uncertainty)
Ferstl, Evelyn C. and D. Yves von Cramon.	No	n/a	Twenty participants read two sentence stories half of which contained inconsistencies concerning emotional, temporal, or spatial information
Koch K., et al.	No	n/a	"Induced negative emotion by means of negative olfactory stimulation (with rotten yeast)" (2745), which is "an effective standardized and validated method of mood induction" (2745).

Continued

Appendix 15.1 Continued

Article	Definition (y/n)	How defined?	How operationalized?
Schaich Borg J., et al.	Yes	"For our purposes, 'emotions' are immediate valenced reactions that may or may not be conscious. We will focus on emotions in the form of negative affect. In contrast, 'reason' is neither valenced nor immediate insofar as reasoning need not incline us toward any specific feeling and combines prior information with new beliefs or conclusions and usually comes in the form of cognitive manipulations . . . that require working memory" (803).	Presented scenarios to subjects using both "dramatic (colorful)" and "muted (noncolorful)" language.
Azim, Eiman, et al.	No	(humor)	Showed cartoons that had previously been rated "funny" or "unfunny"
Sander, David, et al.	No	No, but emphasis here is on decoding/interpreting affective cues.	Voices—subjects listened to meaningless utterances read in angry vs. neutral prosody.
Canessa, Nichola, et al.	Yes	"Reasoning can be defined as a combination of cognitive processes that allows us to draw inferences from a given set of information and reach conclusions that are not explicitly available, providing new knowledge. Reasoning is the central nucleus of thinking and is essential in almost every aspect of mental activity, from text comprehension to problem solving and decision making" (930).	"In the present study, the effect of content on brain activation was investigated with functional magnetic resonance imaging (fMRI) while subjects were solving two versions of the Wason selection task, which previous behavioral studies have shown to elicit a significant content effect" (930).

Author			
Greene, Joshua D., et al.	Yes	"By 'reasoning,' we refer to relatively slow and deliberative processes involving abstraction and at least some introspectively accessible components" (389).	Subjects were asked to make various kinds of moral judgments (impersonal and personal) based on scenarios validated in an earlier study by Greene et al.
Reuter, M., et al.	No	n/a	"Subjects viewed pictures with sadomasochistic, erotic, disgusting, fear-inducing, and affectively neutral content. E.g. The disgusting pictures included unusual food, disgusting animals, poor hygiene, and body products such as excrement; fear-inducing pictures included scenes of animal threat, human threat, or disasters; erotic pictures contained either pictures of single naked subjects or pictures of couples in an intimate situation." (464)
Ochsner, Kevin N., et al. "Reflecting Upon Feelings"	No	n/a	"In this task, participants were presented with a series of blocks of photographic images and for each block were asked to judge either their own emotional response to each photo (pleasant, unpleasant or neutral), or to judge whether the image had been taken (indoors, outdoors, or not sure). The present study modified this paradigm through the inclusion of a third condition, which asked participants to judge the emotional response of the central character in each image (pleasant, unpleasant, or neutral)." (1748)

Continued

Appendix 15.1 Continued

Article	Definition (y/n)	How defined?	How operationalized?
Ochsner, Kevin N., et al. "Rethinking Feelings"	Maybe?	"The cognitive transformation of emotional experience has been termed 'reappraisal.'" (1215)	"We employed two conditions: On 'Attend trials,' participants were asked to let themselves respond emotionally to each photo by being aware of their feelings without trying to alter them. On 'Reappraise trials,' participants were asked to interpret photos so that they no longer felt negative in response to them.... Each trial began with a 4-sec presentation of a negative or neutral photo, during which participants were instructed simply to view the stimulus on the screen" (1217).
McRae, Kateri, et al.	Sort of	"Emotion regulation can be deliberate or habitual, conscious or unconscious, and can involve changes in the magnitude, duration, or quality of one or several components of an emotional response. Emotion regulation strategies can target one's own emotions or those of another individual, at a variety of time points in the emotion generation process (Gross, 2007). Because emotion regulation is an ongoing process, the overall trajectory of an emotional response can be characterized by the effects of regulation as much as the effects of 'pure' reactivity."	"At the start of each trial, an instruction word was presented in the middle of the screen ('decrease' or 'look'; 4 seconds), a picture was presented (negative [sic] if instruction was decrease (regulation instruction), negative or neutral if instruction was look (non-regulation instruction; 8 seconds) followed by a rating period (scale from 1–4; 4 seconds) and then the word 'relax' (4 seconds).... Following presentation of each picture, participants were prompted to answer the question 'How negative do you feel?' on a scale from 1 to 4 (where 1 was labeled 'weak' and 4 was labeled 'strong')" (147)

| Trautmann, Sina Alexa, Thorsten Fehr, and Manfred Herrmann. | No | n/a | "A set of emotional videos and video screen captures showing different facial expressions (see Fig. 4) was applied for the fMRI study. The stimuli were depicted from a stimulus data base of 40 female and 40 male non-professional actors displaying each of eight different emotional facial expressions (happiness (smiling and laughing), surprise, enjoying, fear, anger, sadness, and disgust) and neutral expressions. . . . Emotional expressions of actresses were triggered by a mood induction strategy (e.g., for disgust: 'imagine, you come home after two weeks of vacation but you forgot to take out the biowaste container' or happy: 'imagine you meet someone unexpectedly on the street who you really like and give him a smile because you are happy to see him'). For the purposes of the present study, only female dynamic and static emotional face stimuli (N = 40; see above for detailed explanation of gender differences) displaying positive (happiness), negative (disgust), and neutral expressions were used." (111) |

Continued

Appendix 15.1 Continued

Article	Definition (y/n)	How defined?	How operationalized?
Akitsuki, Yuko and Jean Decety.	Yes	"The perception of pain in others can be used as a window to investigate the neurophysiological mechanisms that underpin the experience of empathy, i.e., the capacity to share and appreciate others' emotional and affective states in relation to oneself (Decety, 2007; Goubert et al., 2009; Jackson et al., 2005). Empathy may be regarded as a proximate factor motivating prosocial behaviors and is crucial in the development of moral reasoning (Decety and Meyer, 2008)" (722).	"The task consisted of the successive presentation of animated visual images of hands and feet depicting painful and non-painful situations. Furthermore, these situations involved either an individual whose pain was caused by accident or an individual whose pain was inflicted on purpose by another person. A series of 144 stimuli were created and validated for this study. Validation of the material was conducted with a group of 222 participants (110, females) who were shown these dynamic stimuli and asked to estimate how painful these situations were and whether they believed that the pain was caused intentionally (Estabrook, 2007). Each animation consisted of three digital color pictures, which were edited to the same size (600 × 480 pixels). The durations of the first, second and third pictures were 1000 ms, 400 ms and 1000 ms respectively. These animated stimuli contained scenes of various types of painful and non-painful everyday situations" (723).

| Lu, Shengfu, et al. | Yes | "Inductive reasoning is defined as the process of inferring a general rule (conclusion) by observation and analysis of specific instances (premises). Inductive reasoning is used when generating hypotheses, formulating theories and discovering relationships, and is essential for scientific discovery" (74). | "The experimental tasks were adapted from a kind of intelligence test problems. The basal element of the task was a reverse triangle as shown in Figure 1. The three numbers located at three different positions may constitute a calculation rule, i.e., an equation like $Z = X + Y$. Figure 2 gave an example of the inductive reasoning task, which was assembled with three reverse triangles as mentioned above" (75). |

16

The Mock Rock *Topos*

MICHELE KENNERLY

Like the persona in Elton John's "Your Song," many ancient writers clearly felt their expressive talents lay with the manipulation of media other than stone. A representative example is Lucian, a perky member of the so-called Second Sophistic, who describes parental pressure to pick a pursuit and the subsequent dream that helped him settle on one. His family's meager economic circumstances necessitated he pick a banaustic *technê* that would bring in money quickly rather than a bombastic *technê* that might never pay dividends. Since Lucian's maternal uncle was a sculptor, and Lucian himself enjoyed scraping the wax out of his writing tablets and fashioning figures with it, his family arranged for an apprenticeship in sculpture. He gets off to a rocky start when he hammers a chisel too hard and breaks a plaque. His uncle beats him. After running home to mother and sniveling that his brutish uncle foresees and envies his superior talent, Lucian falls into a vivid dream.

In it, two female figures physically and verbally yank Lucian in their respective directions. They are Sculpture (*Hermogluphikê technê*)—"worker-like, man-like, with dusty hair, calloused hands, and garment bunched up; she was all powdery, like my uncle when he was smoothing stone by filing it"—and Culture (*Paideia*), who "had a beautiful face, fit figure, and well-ordered attire" ("The Dream, or Lucian's Career," §6).[1] Asking him not to balk at her unkempt appearance, Sculpture compares her look to that of famous sculptors like Pheidias, Polyclitus, and Praxiteles, rough and dirtied from their work. She promises Lucian a life of hard, honest labor that will sculpt his muscles and his character and during which he will be praised "not for his words" but for his works (§7). In her rejoinder, Culture concedes that Lucian may well turn out to be a Pheidias whose art all will admire, but that no one would aspire to be like him: "whatever your real qualities, you will always rank as a common craftsman (*banausos*) who makes his living with his hands" (§9). Under her tutelage, however, he will encounter the deeds and words of hallowed men, cultivate many virtues, and aspire to greatness. So

276

equipped, he will be able to aid his friends and his *polis* in times of need, and "at his speaking the many will listen open-mouthed, marveling at and counting you blessed in your power (*tês dunameôs*)" (§12). Upon losing the contest, Sculpture hardens into marble. Culture, meanwhile, becomes mobile, treating Lucian to a worldwide tour on her Pegasus-pulled chariot, after which she sets his father straight about the impoverished life of a sculptor.

A wandering envoy of *Paideia*, Lucian chose to produce vocal civic agents instead of mute aesthetic objects, but all the while he crafted discourses that blended the best of each effort. Although distinctive in its liveliness, Lucian's *agôn* between Sculpture and Culture is but one instance of a prominent strain of argument and assessment in ancient texts that places stones and words side by side for evaluation.[2] I propose a four-fold schema for organizing and understanding this strain, which I call "the mock rock *topos*," exploiting the ambiguity of mock (mimic/taunt) to capture a common ancient attitude toward verbal representations, written especially that they share certain qualities with stone and stonework but outperform them, too. Of course, sculptors often work in materials other than stone, and I do include references to bronze, ivory, and gold as well without laboring to invent other rhyming topical categories. Further, detractors of writers and writing often use lithic language in their criticisms.

The four-fold heuristic, hereafter designated "the m-heuristic," uses the sub-*topoi* of masterpiece, *mimêsis* (imitation, representation), movement, and memory to find and categorize dimensions of the mock rock *topos* that have the most to tell us about the competition between papyrus and stone, frequently matched rhetorical media in Antiquity. Those four areas are "places" to which ancient writers repeatedly (re)turn to build arguments, appeals, and analogies that affirm their choices.[3] Although individuated for analysis, the sub-*topoi* work in synthesis; in particular, because the overarching *topos* is *mock* rock, *mimêsis* threads through all four.

A marked material-mindedness drives ancient writers' articulations of the process of artistic objectification whereby ephemeral words become monumental— or just frozen stiff—texts. Accordingly, the next two sections focus on rhetoric, materiality, and criticism, the first by arguing for a more overt treatment of ancient texts as material objects moving through the world, and the second by considering the conditions that sometimes paired text and stone—resulting in their shared aesthetic and critical vocabulary—and other times pitted them against each other. Subsequently, the main sections organize Greek and Roman examples of each member of the m-heuristic, availing of discourses, dialogues, treatises, biographies, letters, and published speeches. To demonstrate the cultural complexity of ancient text-stone relations, the article concludes with a short venture into ancient libraries, wherein the representation competition between text and rock became more nuanced, and the two media complemented each other rather than competed with one another for representational supremacy.

Living in a Material World

Whether tightly rolled-up and stored, or slowly unrolled, fondled, and wound up again, the papyrus book-roll (Greek: *biblos/biblios*; Latin: *librum/libellus*) was, and in some cases scrappily remains, a material object. Although the primary medium of textual publication from the fifth century BCE through the first century CE, it competed with other material outlets of expression and persuasion, and many writers stake clear claims for their choice. The materiality of words struggling to earn a place on the page also holds considerable interest for ancient writers and critics. Whether graphic rhetors compare or contrast their methods, media, or products—both an orchestrated collection of words and a textual object—with those of stoneworkers, they frequently assert their superior status using elements of the m-heuristic.[4]

The mock rock *topos* highlights the thoroughgoing materiality of ancient textual composition and circulation. Materiality has lately been at the center of much scholarly activity in rhetoric. Bodies, brains, borders, and beasts, and also quilts, museums, statues, and cafés have become objects of rhetorical analysis (Selzer and Crowley; Gibbons; Cisneros; Hawhee "Toward a Bestial Rhetoric"; Morris; Dickinson, Blair, and Ott; Dunn; Dickinson).[5] Carole Blair marks it as curious that materiality "has rarely been taken as a starting point or basis for theorizing rhetoric, despite the frequent cues in our language about its material character," emphasizing that there are significant "similarities and differences among rhetorical media, because degrees, kinds, and consequences of materiality seem to differ significantly, but rather unpredictably, depending in part on whether the 'rhetoric' we describe is made of sound, script or stone" (17).

Rhetorical scholarship about Antiquity also participates in this move toward matter, finding in ancient ways of thinking, arguing, doing, and building resources for our contemporary conversations about materiality (see, e.g., Hawhee "Somatography"; Hawhee *Bodily Arts*). Some of this scholarship discounts the materiality of textuality despite the awareness ancient writers display about the distinctive physical assets and liabilities of their written words and fibrous medium. For instance, James Fredal has called for and provided examples of an "archeological rhetoric" that "begin[s] by looking rather at a cultural, social, bodily, topographic, and not merely textual domain," at "public spaces, lines of sight, and [the] sparkle" of marble (7, 9, 3). Although he does not, of course, exclude texts from his treatment of "persuasive artistry" in ancient Athens, he clearly excludes them from the category of ancient material culture (see the introduction, e.g., especially 7). Richard Enos, too, has urged a push beyond "the book" and into "nontraditional literary sources" and surfaces. His recent work has focused on epigraphy, that is, inscriptions (official or illicit, like graffiti) etched into the surfaces of "durable material such as marble, metal, or wood" ("Rhetorical Archaeology" 42; see also "Writing without Paper"). He also encourages historical work on "architecture, the plastic arts, and other aspects of archeology [that] could also expand our insights" into rhetoric's past

("Rhetorical Archaeology" 42). Somewhat incongruously, Enos argues for the importance of this "rhetorical archeology" by providing a pedagogical example that has more than a little to do with textual practices: he tells his classical rhetoric students that "most Greeks and Romans could not read silently" ("Rhetorical Archaeology" 43).[6] Such details, he posits, help students "reflect on the most fundamental of notions" about being a reader, writer, speaker, or listener in any given historical period ("Rhetorical Archaeology" 43). My analysis forwards this effort, but by taking another look at "the book" and how and why its users compare and contrast it to statues and reliefs.

Seeking out, feeling, and listening for the rhetorical dimensions of ancient materiality or the material dimensions of ancient rhetoric can be done in ways other than the polemically anti-textual. Robert Gaines's "corpus conception" (67) promotes an understanding of ancient rhetoric as "that body of information that contains all known texts, artifacts, and discourse venues that represent the theory, pedagogy, practice, criticism, and cultural apprehension of rhetoric in the ancient European discourse community" (65). Such an approach helps sustain the viability and continued theoretical applicability of ancient rhetoric without either restricting ourselves to or abandoning "the book." A collaborative digital humanities project currently underway is a prime if not altogether representative example (and enviably so) of this corpus conception in action. Richard Graff and Christopher Johnstone are pooling aural, visual, textual, and digital resources to produce the fullest picture, and to conjecture as to the sonic effects, of stony ancient discourse venues given our piecemeal, limited evidence. Further, Kathleen Lamp's attention to orators' strategic use of their built environments in their speeches and memory training offers a rock *topos* of another kind. Like mine, her arguments demonstrate that those working with written words incorporated elements of their material culture for persuasive purposes. Unlike Lucian, we rhetoricians do not have to choose between Sculpture and Culture, stone and text. By combining the two—as the mock rock *topos* does—we stand to learn more about what ancient writers who mocked (in both senses) rock professed to achieve or avoid. Analyses of recurring stone-text connections forged by assorted ancient writers also correct a recent trend toward excluding "traditional" writing processes and products from consideration as material rhetoric. As such, the m-heuristic contributes toward a greater refinement of our contemporary efforts to theorize and criticize the suasive contours of all manner of matter(s), whether classical or contemporary.

Graphic Language: A Lexicon of Textual-Sculptural Artistry

Scroll and stone became both analogous and agonistic due to an aesthetico-critical awakening in fifth-century BCE Greece whereby senses and sensibilities became attuned to materiality: not only to the way objects look, feel, and sound, but also to how they are constituted in the first place. That ancient arts—from song to architecture to sculpture to speech—"share so much descriptive and critical vocabulary" is one result of this "aesthetic materialism," as James I. Porter has named it (61, 482). Porter accounts for the terminological overlap between categories like the visual and the verbal by suggesting that, among other possibilities, "languages of description and analysis in different areas evolve[d] in coordinated ways, feeding off and into one another in a series of transformations, both together and essentially over time" (62). Andrew Ford's study of how the "textualization" of song and speech powered the rise of ancient literary criticism also aligns the objectification of discourse with its aesthetic valuation (*Origins* 155). The availability of the book-roll as a medium of discourse delivery materialized words in new ways. For ancient writers and readers, words came to have shapes, sizes, weights, and textures that could be measured, assessed, and compared. On the critical side, possessing a text or putting texts side by side enabled close analysis. On the creative side, once words were thought to have matter, they could be artistically, even masterfully, managed and manipulated (*manus* = hand and *pleno* = fill), like plastic media.

In his study of the criticism, history, and terminology of Greek art, J. J. Pollitt credits the third book of Aristotle's *Rhetoric* and its focus on the *aretai* (distinctive excellences) of style with jump-starting critical interest in and "an acute awareness of personal style as well as style in general" (60). Emergent from this attention were canonical lists of rhetors who exemplified particular styles. Some critic or another, Pollitt writes, "hit upon the idea of comparing specific orators with specific sculptors and painters thereby creating a comparative canon that included a description of the *aretai* of different artists" (60). As I show below, Cicero and Quintilian continued such comparisons to forward arguments about the development of rhetoric and the impossibility of seeking a singular model of oratorical perfection.

A major marker of the relationship between sculptural and textual processes, products, and qualities is the lexicon of artistry. Several ancient Greek and Latin words span the creative space between the plastic and verbal arts, connecting the respective activities and productions of stone- and word-workers and the qualities of those productions. This lexical kinship becomes, quite frequently, a contest. An inventory of the most striking shared terms is shown in Table 16.1.[7]

Graphic rhetors, rhetoricians, and critics readily used items from this lexicon for a range of reasons, as I show. In his treatment of formalism in Isocrates, Ford suggests that rhetors and rhetoricians used such terms to bolster their "claim to the status of artist, purveying a valuable product" ("Price" 33). Since a fixation on artistry can come at the expense of concern for argumentative merit, ethical soundness, and civic utility, users of this lexicon supplement it with grand appeals to those mainstays of rhetorical discourse, which we see clearly in the first sub-*topos*.

Table 16.1 Inventory of the Most Striking Terms

Term in Greek	Term in Latin	English translation	Process, product, quality
graphô	*scribo*	scratch, scrape, represent, draw, paint, write	process
technê	*ars*	craft; an explainable, teachable set of techniques or tactics for producing something	process
ergon	*factum*	deed, be it a symbolic activity or not	process and product
ponos	*labor/opus*	work	process and product
mimêsis	*imitatio*	representation, imitation, likeness	process and product
eikôn	*imago*	image, portrayal, likeness	product
schêma	*figura/forma*	figure or form	product
paradeigma	*exemplum*	model; precedent/ example; copy	product
mnêmeîon	*monumentum*	memorial, remembrance, record; monument	product
kosmos	*ornatus*	ornament, decoration, embellishment	quality
chrôma	*color*	color (some ancient statues were painted)	quality
glaphuros	*politum/ expolitum*	polished, finished, exact	quality
akribeia	*accuratio, diligentia*	exactitude, an etched or etched-like precision	quality

Sub-*Topos* 1: Masterpiece

Words!/Pens are too light./Take chisel to write.

(Basil Bunting, *Briggflatts* Part 1)

Isocrates's careful craftsmanship was and continues to be legendary. His writings contain the rhetorical tradition's first public defense of the defining burden of texts that challenge the beauty and obduracy of rock masterpieces: polish. He speaks not only for the *polis* but also for the polish that makes his *logos politikos* shine, and by implicating one with the best interests of the other. To put it in rhyming chiastic form, which befits the figure-loving Isocrates: political discourse without polish is all bluster whereas polished discourse without political import is all luster. They need one another, Isocrates proposes, to be at their best. His *polis*—polish link has two orientations in time. In his time, it provides the benefit of advisory words born of extensive reflection and revision. He laboriously produces thoughtful and actionable meditations on broad and significant cultural matters, asserting the superiority of his polished political discourse over the bang of inexperienced youngsters and the flash of the new sophists. In the long term, his tributes to Athens and certain esteemed members of the pan-Hellenic political community function as an enduring record of the kind of rhetorical artistry and civic virtue his *polis* inspired and honored.

His is not quick work. The rhetorical critic Dionysius of Halicarnassus, a Greek transplant to Augustan Rome, and Quintilian, among others, record ten years, at least, as the time Isocrates required to complete his *Panegyricus* (*On the Putting Together of Words* §25, *Institutio Oratoria* 10.4.4). Isocrates frequently and assertively professes to be a meticulous artisan of master works, never hiding his labor or denying how long he worked (cf., e.g., the last third of *Panathenaicus* and the opening passages of *Philip* [§1–30] and *Antidosis*). To craft a model discourse demands intensive scraping and scrapping, fitting and refitting of segments, and the final harmonizing and polishing of the whole. Plutarch later sneers that Pericles directed the construction of the Parthenon (which features the sculpture of Pheidias) in the same amount of time that Isocrates "sat at home, poring over his work [the *Panegyricus*], seeking out word choices" (*Moralia* 350e–351a). Cicero also deploys the comparative construction claim, but to rank "useless" beauty above useful banality. In his history of rhetoric's formal development, Cicero asserts that "it was more important to the Athenians to have a secure roof on their homes than the superlatively lovely ivory statue of Minerva; however, I should have preferred to be Phidias to the very best fabricator of roofs" (*Brutus* §257). Any orator with serviceable skills can reach out, roof-like, and protect a friend when troubles rain down, but few have what it takes to fashion Wisdom in words. Shortly after Cicero, Dionysius of Halicarnassus compares Isocrates's works to Pheidias's on the basis of their shared "solemnity, consummate technique, and reputation" (*to semnon kai megalotechnon kai axiômatikon*) (*Isocrates* §3).

Skillfully exploiting the homology between craftsmen emergent from the lexical ambiguities listed in the table above, Isocrates plainly situates himself among the finest craftsman of Hellas in the proem to his *Antidosis* (§2). He analogizes that to dismiss him as a dikographer (writer of law-speeches) is to call Pheidias a fashioner of mere figurines, or Zeuxis or Parrhasias, premiere painters, mere tablet daubers (*ta pinakia graphousin*; note the *graph-* verb). There is nothing "mere" about the way the four of them have perfected their respective art forms. Cheap logography, statuettes, and portraits might be hawked and haggled over in the agora, but a masterpiece is harder to come by. And more expensive by magnitudes. If we believe Plato's Socrates (always risky for us rhetoricians), then preeminent craftsmen of *logos* seem to have profited far more than other top creators: "I know of one man, Protagoras, who got more money from his skill than Pheidias, who wrought such celebrated works of art, or any ten other statue makers" (*Meno* 91d). Isocrates commanded huge sums for his commemorative *logoi* in particular, receiving 120,000 drachmas from Nicocles to eulogize Evagoras, his departed father (Plutarch, *Lives of the Ten Orators* 838a). The average Athenian laborer made about 1 for a hard day's work. Along with the aesthetic objectification of words came their commodification, giving words worth of another kind.

The two most famous critics of graphic rhetors in the early fourth century BCE were Alcidamas (*On Sophists* or *On the Writers of Written Discourses*) and Plato's Socrates (*Phaedrus*).[8] Among other points of criticism, they chide graphic rhetors for treating their writing like artistic masterpieces made of stone. Both Alcidamas and Socrates rib graphic rhetors for requiring a lot of time first to shape and then to polish their words (*Writers* §4, 10; *Phaedrus* 228a). They also describe the resultant constructions as *akribês*, painstakingly precise (*On Writers* §12, 16, 25, 33, 34; *Phaedrus* 234e). *Akribeia* (precision, exactitude) is a common term of critical analysis for both plastic and linguistic objects (Pollitt 122ff).

For his part, Alcidamas begins his chain of insults by calling any given writer not a rhetor but a *poiêtês*, "maker" (§2). Next, Alcidamas calls the products of graphic rhetors *tupoi*—meaning molds or figures wrought of stone or metal— with exactitude and flair that their extemporaneous speech could never match (§14). Then, using an architectural analogy, Alcidamas imagines each block of their meticulous "house of words" (*tês tôn onomatôn oikodomian*) toppling and crashing down when they try to insert spur-of-the-moment phrases and arguments (§25). Finally, Alcidamas returns to statuary, comparing carefully wrought discourses to bronze and stone statues and life drawings (*tôn chalkôn andriantôn kai lithinôn agalmatôn kai yegrammenon zôiôn*) that trump living bodies in beauty but not in utility (§27–28).

Socrates, who evidently thought that true communication could not be set in stone (literally or figuratively), wrote not one iota. In *Phaedrus*, Plato's version of him also compares writing to life drawing (*zôgraphia*), "for the creatures of drawing stand like living beings, but if one asks them a question, they preserve a solemn silence." Likewise, one might reckon that written words "spoke as if they had intelligence, but if you question them, wishing to know about their sayings, they always say one and the same thing" (275d–e). In Plato's *Protagoras*, Socrates likens all sophists to book-rolls, in that they repeat the same lines over and over, however arrestingly beautiful (329a).

The sub-*topos* of masterpiece comes to prominence in the burgeoning vocabulary of rhetorical criticism that Socrates applies to Lysias's written *logos* on love.

A fixation with control renders Lysias's *logos*, like the non-lover he champions within it, unfeeling and deadened. Structure-wise, Lysias reiterates the few points he sets forth in several different ways (235a), showing a reluctance to really warm to his subject. Structurally and stylistically, Socrates judges Lysias "to have thoroughly turned/chiseled" (*apotetorneutai*) his words in an effort to render them "clear and compact and precise" (*saphê kai stroggula, kai akribôs*) (234e). Plato's lexical choices here cast Lysias as an artisan of cold, hard objects. Again, *akribês* describes precision and exactitude in compositions of words or of stone. *Stroggula* describes the result of wearing down processes—like erosion—that polish rough, jagged edges of words or stones over time periods of near geological length. Socrates later compares Lysias's *logos* to an inscription on a bronze statue placed on the tombstone of Midas (264d–e). Devastatingly, he deems Lysias's book-roll to be a curious mix of the rock-solid and the easily deconstructed, the precise and the splattered (*beblêsthai*, 264b), the compact and the loose.

A mock rock moment in *Symposium* offers another example of rhetorical criticism. After the good-looking, prize-winning poet Agathon completes his speech on *erôs*, Socrates fusses about the unfairness of their seating arrangements such that he must follow someone whom, he puns, possesses the Gorgias/Gorgon head, whose eloquent emissions turn those within earshot to soundless stone (*lithon tei aphôniai*, 198c). Socrates chose that seat for his own amorous reasons and is, of course, being playful, but both he and Alcidamas use the language of shocked-stiff amazement to describe the effect polished prose has on those who encounter it (*On Writers* §27–8; *Phaedrus* 275d). Throughout Antiquity, Agathon was infamous for being finicky about the preparation of his written words. Aristophanes describes him as "smoothing words out in wax" before "casting them into a mold" (*kêprochutei goggullei kai choaneuei*) (Aristophanes, *Thesmophoriazusae* 52ff).[9] That Agathon works in wax initially seems a clear analogy to the sculptor's method of first modeling a figure in a cheap and pliable medium before moving to one expensive and unforgiving. But the wax could also refer analogically to a wax tablet, which was less costly than papyrus and more appropriate for the preliminary stages of writing.

Although Plato obviously wrote, he did not, like Isocrates, write about his extensive editing. But Diogenes Laertius reminds us that Plato once cared a great deal for drawing and writing poetry (*graphikês epimelêthênai kai poiêmata graphai*) (*Lives* 3.5; notice the double "*graph-*" verbs), both of which Plato abandoned after Socrates read one of Plato's plays and asked questions of it that Plato could not answer. Despite his disavowal of his artistry, Plato eventually joins not only Lysias but also Isocrates and Demosthenes in being described as spending a lot of time with his words. In *On the Putting Together of Words*, Dionysius of Halicarnassus cites Isocrates's at least decade-long preparation of the *Panegyricus* alongside a tale of Plato's editorial attachment to his dialogues:

> Plato did not cease, when eighty years old, to comb and curl his dialogues and reshape them in every way (*ktenizôn kai bostruchizôn, kai panta proton*

anaplekôn). Surely every scholar is acquainted with the stories of Plato's love of labor (*tês philoponias*), especially that of the tablet which they say was found after his death, with the beginning of the *Republic* ("I went down yesterday to the Piraeus together with Glaucon the son of Ariston") arranged in elaborately varying (*poikilôs*) orders.

(§25; see also Diogenes Laertius's Lives 3.37)

Because Isocrates and Plato "did not so much write words" (*ou grap-toîs . . . logous*) as "engrave" (*gluptois*) and "chisel" (*toreutois*) them, rhetors like Demosthenes worked to maintain the expected artistic standard of his time (§25; see also *Demosthenes* §51). In the last book of his *Institutio Oratoria*, Quintilian advises on how much written preparation an orator should do for different rhetorical situations. The ideal, he writes, is to follow this instruction he attributes to Demosthenes: that an orator will, "as far as possible, deliver only what he has sketched out (*scripta*), and, if circumstances permit, only what he has sculpted (*sculpta*)" (12.9.16). If he can help it, an orator will present to the public only that which he has artfully molded to the moment, but, of course, well ahead of the moment.

Sub-Topos 2: Mimêsis

Challenging Plato's indictments of *mimêsis* throughout the *Republic*, Aristotle stresses its centrality to human being, creating, and feeling (*Poetics* 1448b5ff). We craft likenesses for all manner of communicative and expressive purposes. For their part, graphic rhetors fashion likenesses for others to look upon and emulate, and their mimetic dimension is two-fold. Graphic rhetors offer to their readers model writings—one who (be)holds them is meant to marvel at and aspire to their internal architecture and artistry—and model subject matter; one is meant to marvel at and aspire to the thoughts, deeds, and words of exemplary represented people. According to those who prefer papyrus to stone or metal, writing on book-rolls affords a greater depth of representation and thus more mimetic potential.

The taunt side of the mock rock *topos* arises when graphic rhetors decry the difficulty of imitating a bronze body and, therefore, its comparative poverty as a character model. For instance, in his richly-wrought work *Evagoras*, a *logos* explicitly addressed to Nicocles, the bereaved son of the recently deceased Evagoras, Isocrates points out that "no one would be able to make their own bodily nature resemble (*homoiôseie*) a statue or a painting (*tois men peplasmenois kai tois gegramenois*), but it is easy for those who wish to take the trouble and are willing to be the best to imitate (*mimeîsthai*) the ways and thoughts (*tous tropous . . . kai tas dianoias*) of their fellows who are represented in speeches (*en tois legomenois*)" (§75). Even the most faithful representations of people's external forms do not showcase their *dianoia*, their complex inner-workings, their motivations, their judgment in context, all of which industrious readers could set themselves to modeling. It is for those reasons that Isocrates has "assembled [Evagoras's] virtues, arranged them in a speech, and passed them down to you to study and practice" (§76). Memorialized and materialized in papyrus, Evagoras's example lives on.

In Rome, Cicero renews this line of comparison and exhortation in his defense of the Greek-Syrian poet, Archias. His closing pleas to the jury highlight the mimetic prowess of writing poets like Archias, but we can safely presume that Cicero thought writing rhetors similarly capable: "Many superior men have been zealous to leave behind statues and images (*statuas et imagines*), *simulacra* not of their minds, but of their bodies, but shouldn't we much prefer to leave behind effigies (*effigiem*) of our wisdom and excellence, expressed and polished by the utmost talent (*summis ingeniis expressam et politam*)?" (Pro Archia §30). While it is possible to read in these examples an unfortunate trumping of mind over matter, of brain over body, I read them as instances of another sort of one-upmanship: graphic rhetors asserting their mimetic superiority to sculptors.

Being arguments for resemblance, analogies can be considered another facet of the *mimêsis* sub-*topos*. In the previous section, we saw Alcidamas's uncomplimentary comparison of carefully crafted speeches to beautiful stone or metal bodies. He contends that graphic rhetors produce "likenesses, forms, and imitations of the spoken word" (*eidôla kai schêmata kai mimêmata logôn*), just as artists issue forth "imitations of true bodies" (*mimêmata tôn alêthinôn sômatôn*, §27). Likewise, to Socrates's approval, Phaedrus calls writing an *eidôs* (likeness) of "the living and ensouled word," that is, the word spoken in thoughtful conversation (276a).

Graphic rhetors in Rome, on the other hand, commonly deploy elucidating comparisons of rock and recorded word as they wonder at the variety of rhetorical artistry and assess the development and increasing refinement of oratory, first in Athenian rhetorical culture and then in Roman. For example, in Cicero's *De Oratore* (3.26–31), Crassus opines that there is a single art of sculpture and a single art of painting, yet there are many "outstanding practitioners" whose statues or paintings differ widely from one another without departing from excellence; "and if this is surprising but still true in the case of these so-called mute arts (*mutis artibus*), it is certainly much more surprising in the case of speech (*oratione*), that is, language (*lingua*)." These comparisons between statues and written speeches reinforce speech's artistic objectification. And since the moment in which they originally intervened has passed, in some cases long passed, recorded speeches afford readers critical distance from which to examine form and construction.

In *Brutus*, a history of Roman rhetoric, and *Orator*, a treatment of the unattainable ideal of the *orator perfectus*, Cicero sets up comparisons between the development of oratory and that of other arts, such as sculpture (*Brutus* §70ff; *Orator* §5ff; see also Leen). As the fine sculpture of their predecessors did not "deter other sculptors to see what they could accomplish or what progress they could make" (*Orator* §5), so fine oratory should not cause "those who have devoted themselves to the study of eloquence" to "abandon hope or lessen their industry" (§6). Perfection might be unattainable and exceeding the excellence of earlier practitioners of one's art might be difficult, but they are worth striving for nonetheless. Further, in books two and twelve of his *Institutio Oratoria*, Quintilian also compares oratory's formal variety and progress with that of painting and sculpture (see Austin). The *orator perfectus*, he writes:

> has not yet been found, a statement which perhaps may be extended to all arts, not merely because some qualities are more evident in some artists than in others, but because one single form (*una forma*) will not satisfy all critics, a fact which is due in part to conditions of time and place, in part to the judgment (*iudicio*) and stance (*propositio*) of individuals.
>
> (12.10.2)

The comparisons of sculpture and oratory are back to back, and Quintilian transitions by asserting that, "[i]f we turn our attention to the various styles of oratory, we shall find almost as great variety of talents (*ingeniorum*) as of forms of bodies (*corporum formas*)" (12.10.10). Coming, as it does, on the heels of the sculpture section, "forms of bodies" likely refers to statues and their shapely varieties. These examples from Cicero and Quintilian's *rhetorica* classify as mock rock related to writing because, they both observe, superlative rhetors are those most known for treasuring the power of the pen as an aid to eloquence and for recording their speeches for posterity.

Earlier, Quintilian had divided his discussion of rhetoric into three parts: art (*ars*), artist (*artifex*), and the work resultant from them (*opus*) (2.14.5). This division allows for an easy reliance on other arts, artists, and their works to substantiate points about rhetoric. Quintilian refers often to sculpture when he turns to the question of rhetoric's material. If, as Plato's Socrates suggests, the material of rhetoric is speech, and "if this view be accepted in the sense that the word 'speech' is used of a discourse composed on any subject, then it is not the material but the work (*non materia sed opus*), like a statue is of a sculptor" (2.21.1; see also 2.19.3). Rhetoric's material must be something other than its product. Like Cicero, Quintilian "holds that the material of rhetoric is composed of everything that may be placed before it as a subject of speech" (2.21.4), although he concedes that this position exposes rhetoric to accusations that its scope is impossibly expansive and its material too multiple. Quintilian counters that rhetoric's multiplicity comes with limits and summons other, "lesser arts" (*artes minores*) to make his point: sculptors and makers of vessels might use the same materials—such as gold, silver, bronze, iron, wood, ivory, marble, glass, and precious stones—and "yet there is all the difference in the world between vessels and statues" (2.21.8–10). "So," Quintilian sums up, "that which is the material of rhetoric does not cease to be so if it is claimed by both it and other arts" (10).

Returning to fifth- and fourth-century Athens, we find that Socrates has mimetic affiliations with sculpture in both his dialogue appearances and biographical tradition. In several of Plato's dialogues about rhetoric, Socrates makes analogies to sculptors (and painters, cobblers, and doctors) as he tries to figure out whether rhetoric is a *technê*, what it produces, and what skills or character traits it relies upon or cultivates in its users (e.g., *Gorgias* 450d, 453c–d; *Protagoras* 311c).

Toward the end of Plato's *Symposium*, Alcibiades dares an extended comparison of the usually unwashed and unshod, always snub-nosed Socrates to statues of the satyr Silenus sold in the agora. They are both ugly, but their ugliness is only "an outward casting" (216d). Inside, they are masterpieces "golden and divine, perfectly fair and wondrous" (217a). Socrates's speech, above all, resembles Silenus statues, offering nothing attractive on the face of it:

> If you chose to listen to Socrates' discourses you would feel them at first to be quite ridiculous; on the outside they are clothed with such absurd words and phrases—all, of course, the gift of a mocking satyr. . . . But when these are opened, and you obtain a fresh view (*idôn*) of them by getting inside, first of all you will discover that they are the only speeches that have any sense in them; and secondly, that none are so divine, bearing so much virtue (*aretês*) in them, so largely—no, so completely—intent on all things proper for the study of such as would attain both the finest and the best.
>
> (221e–222a)

The vocabulary of internal/external has several layers. Not only Socrates's visage but also his spoken *logos* function like a cheap Silenus statue, with an outer surface that might appear simple and silly but with a deeper, richer significance that must be plumbed. That Socrates's students commemorate his words and ways in their book-rolls allows readers near and far to encounter him and learn that somatic shells and verbal forms matter less than core contents. Virtue stirs on the inside, rather than sits on the outside, and it is virtue and other features of internal character that graphic rhetors are best able to display with their tools, methods, and delivery medium.

Moving from the dialogical to the biographical in his account of Socrates, Diogenes Laertius reports that Socrates's mother practiced midwifery (*maieusis*); recall that Plato's Socrates calls his dialectical method "maieutic" in *Theaetetus* and *Symposium*. Socrates's father was a sculptor. Apparently, Socrates took after his father in a more literal sense. According to Laertius, one ancient writer called Socrates a stoneworker (*ergasasthai lithous*), and another "the sculptor, the enchanter of Greece, inventor of precise arguments (*akribologous*), the sneerer who mocked fine speeches, a somewhat Attic ironist" (§19). In Plato's *Euthyphro*, Socrates calls the famed sculptor Daedalus his "ancestor" (11c). Lucian's *Paideia*, in the aforementioned persuasive contest with Sculpture, also notes Socrates' sculpting lineage, which he abandoned for higher pursuits:

"Sculpture here had the breeding of Socrates himself, but as soon as he discerned the better part, he deserted her and enlisted with me. Since then, his name is on every tongue" (§12).

As Socrates's midwifery is figurative, perhaps the stoneworking he does in his advanced years becomes such, too. If Socrates's activities resemble his mother's in that he coaxes interlocutors to deliver, that is, to externalize, internal knowledge that accords with truth, beauty, and goodness, then perhaps they also resemble his father's: Socrates as sculptor finds the forms (*eidê*) of truth, beauty, and goodness inhering within himself and others, and he chips away in an effort to reveal them. Perhaps Socrates's philosophy is a forerunner of what Nietzsche would later call "philosophy with a hammer," only Socrates wields a chisel, too, shaping rather than destroying. Laertius notes that Socrates "used to express his astonishment that sculptors of stone images (*tas lithinas eikonas*) should fashion stone into a likeness (of a man) and should not take care lest they themselves appear to be mere blocks (and not men)" (§33). This was also a warning Lucian's *Paideia* gave him about choosing Sculpture: "all your care will be to proportion and fairly drape your works; to proportioning and adorning yourself you will give little heed, making yourself of less account than your marble" (§13). Self-crafting is an art of character—from the Greek *charaktêr*, meaning a distinctive mark pressed or stamped onto a surface—and one at which Socrates works tirelessly and mostly through the kind of extended conversational chiseling documented by Plato and Xenophon.

Sub-*Topos* 3: Movement

As its etymology clearly attests, a statue stands. In his aforementioned funerary work *Evagoras*, Isocrates elaborates on his point that not all artful and potentially enduring representations are created equal. He prefers his material and his method "because I know that noble men are not so much esteemed for their bodily beauty as honored for their deeds and intellect. Second, images stamped into metal or stone (*tous tupous*)[10] must necessarily remain solely among those who set them up, whereas images stamped into words (*tous logous*) can be circulated throughout Hellas" (§74). Written texts are mobile monuments. The words Isocrates provides in the face of death are not just epigraphs or epitaphs, which are written or spoken upon (*epi-*) a memorial; they are themselves a memorial. The mobility of book-rolls allows them to access, be passed around among, and dwelled on by those who think well (*diadothentas en taîs eû phronountôn diatribais*, §74), performing on behalf of the dead Evagoras (and eventually dead Isocrates) a textual *danse macabre* as they roll from reader to reader: he did this; what will *you* do while there's still time? *Graphô* sits at the root of "grave," and the written memorial highlights that connection.

The circulation of graphic rhetoric provides an advantage enjoyed by neither volatile vocalizations nor stationary epigrammatic objects, the former of which evaporate into, the latter of which sit unread in, the open air. Sit unread? In his book *The Scroll and the Marble*, Peter Bing examines relevant material evidence and holds "the un-read Muse"—punning on his earlier book, *The Well-Read Muse*—responsible for the "pervasive indifference" ancients seemed to have shown toward dedicatory writing on stone (127). Thus, even if a statue featured an epigrammatic caption detailing the *dianoia* of the depicted person, that caption was unlikely to be read; "[r]ooted to the spot, it has to wait, relying on the uncertain prospect of a literate person (not just any viewer) first of all seeing and then taking the trouble to read it" (Bing 122). Assessing processes by which Roman writers "turned paper into stone," Thomas Habinek explains that any solid epigraphic object "was difficult to move, or at least designed to remain in its original location; and it depended for its meaning on its relationship to a particular physical, social, and cultural context. . . . The standard verb for the situating of an inscription or its monument is *loco*, that is, to place" (109). Because they are not ground-bound, texts can circulate among the elite, enter into their conversations, and extend into yet more communicative circles. In turn, members of these circles may copy the text, extending its geographical and chronological reach and influence.

While Isocrates and other ancient graphic rhetors champion the peripatetic page, others indict the slow responsive speed of graphic rhetors and either the immobility or the hypermobility of their fussily fashioned words. This play of static and dynamic reminds us that words were fixed on a material surface that could circulate without the writer's wishes and beyond his control. (Or written words could be committed to memory—often compared to a traditional writing surface—whose mobility would be under the control of the memorizer.) As we saw above, Alcidamas mocked graphic rhetors by likening their methods and products to those of slow, meticulous "makers," especially sculptors. Graphic rhetors show overmuch "*meletê toû graphein*" (care for the written, §15 and §26), slowing if not outright stopping the situational responsiveness of their speech. Extemporaneous speakers are always on-call, ready to react at a moment's notice "whenever there is need to advise the mistaken, to console the unfortunate, to soothe the provoked, [or] to refute sudden allegations of blame" (§10). Their kairotic interventions speedily serve corrective and philanthropic functions, ones vital to sustaining communal order and sociality. Graphic rhetoric might be more beautiful, but it is fixed in place and cannot move (*akinêtos* §28), rendering it useless in pressing, fast-paced circumstances.

Just as Alcidamas gripes about graphic rhetoric's inflexibility during a live debate, Plato's Socrates, as we have seen, points to the incongruity between its seeming liveliness and silent stillness. Socrates also speaks to the graphic rhetor's struggle with looseness after letting a book-roll go out on the town. He reminds Phaedrus that "every word, once written down, is rolled around (*kulindeitai*) among both those who understand and those who have no interest in it" (275e). This rolling about smacks of textuality, of course, as readers roll, unroll, and re-roll papyrus sheets. Moving beyond Alcidamas's critique,

Socrates frames a text not as *akinêtos* but as superkinetic; once released from its writer, it really gets around.

In the *Phaedrus*, one word Socrates uses for an ingenious writer is "*logodaidalos*" (266e), a Daedalus—that is, a clever craftsman—of words and arguments. Daedalus's statues were famous for being able to move, a paradox of fixity and flux, just like writing on book-rolls. Socrates twice mentions these oddities in other dialogues. When conversing with Socrates about holiness, Euthyphro complains that every time they articulate a line of thought, it moves about and will not stay fixed in place. Socrates attributes this mobility to Euthyphro, joking that if it were Socrates's "works in words" (*ta en toîs logois erga*) that ran away, Euthyphro would blame it on Socrates's occupational kinship with Daedalus (*Euthyphro* 11c). Euthyphro, in turn, does blame Socrates, whereupon Socrates declares himself "more clever" (*deinoteros*) than Daedalus, since he can make both his own and Euthyphro's words move. Socrates then offers a serious programmatic statement about his words: "I would rather have my words stay still and sit unmoving (*tous logous menein kai akinêtôs idrûsthai*)[11]than possess the know-how of Daedalus and the wealth of Tantalus besides" (11e). In using the standard language of statues, Socrates emphasizes the steadfastness of his positions and reminds (Plato's) readers that he stands by his words and does not let them get away from him, wandering away on book-rolls, to be misinterpreted, maligned, or ignored.

The other instance appears when Socrates's discussion with Meno about virtue turns to the difference between true opinion (*orthês doxês*) and secure knowledge (*epistêmê*) (97dff). If we try merely to possess true opinion, it, like a captured statue of Daedalus, will soon pull free and continue to roam. "When fastened up," though, they are both worth a great deal: the statue for being "an altogether fine work" (*panu . . . kala ta erga*), and true opinion for being "a fine need/utility" (*kalon to chrêma*). If we bind true opinion with calculative reasoning (*logismôi*), it "will become knowledge and stay in place (*monimoi*)." It is through the give and take of conversation that Socrates affirms his epistemic fixity. Following Socrates's analogy in *Euthyphro* and *Meno*, his knowing words resemble a bound Daedalus statue. Amusingly, the fifth-century CE sophist Eunapius records that ancient Athenians called Socrates the "walking statue of wisdom" (*peripatoun agalma sophias*) (*Lives of Philosophers and Sophists* 462f), merging the fixity of the epistemic and the mobility of the peripatetic to capture a man set in his ways but ever moving about the city.

At least two of the cities Favorinus, a second-century sophist, visited found themselves mesmerized by his presence but unable to keep him and unable to do without him. They therefore erected statues—one of which he hails apostrophically as "O mute semblance of my *logos*" (*ô logôn emôn sigêlon eidôlon*) (Dio Chrysostom, *Corinthian Oration* §46)—to be ongoing calls to learning and culture for all those who looked upon them. After facing accusations of moral turpitude, Favorinus learns that his statue at Corinth has been pulled down out of sight. Trying to account for its absence, he wonders if the statue was one of Daedalus's roving creations but dismisses that possibility because:

> not since the death of Daedalus down to the present day has anyone made such progress in the art of sculpture as to impart to bronze the power of flight; no, even though they make statues of men with a fine and noble stride, and sometimes even riding on horseback, still these all maintain their pose and station and, unless someone moves them, so far as they are concerned bronze has no power to flee, not even if the statue has wings.
>
> (§10)

Bronze can mimic or suggest movement but cannot accomplish it without the assistance of, as in Favorinus's case, people eager to see it go. Athenians pull down his statue in their city as well, and, according to Philostratus, Favorinus declared that "Socrates himself would have been much better off if the Athenians had merely deprived him of a bronze statue (*tês eikona chalkên*), instead of making him drink hemlock" (*Lives of the Sophists* 490). In times good and bad for the represented person, his statue acts as a stand-in. During the former, reminding passersby of the traits for which he was fashioned in bronze, and during the latter, taking the early and maybe the only brunt of punishment for his indiscretions. While alive, Socrates had no statue. Perhaps Socratic book-rolls could have served the same punishment-taking purpose, had he had them. For example, from quite a chronological distance, Diogenes Laertius attests that Athenians publically burned Protagoras's book-rolls because of their atheistic content, while allowing him to undertake his mandated exile physically unscathed (*Life of Protagoras* §52). I return to Socratic and sophistic statues in the next section. For Favorinus—and Athenians and Corinthians for a time—his statues acted as immobile substitutes for his moving eloquence. In the discourse he publishes to redress its disappearance, he attempts to reassert control over his image, reputation, and fame through another medium, one proven to be far longer-lasting.

Sub-*Topos* 4: Memory

> *Sculpte, lime, cisèle;/que ton rêve flottant/se scelle/dans le bloc résistant!*
> Sculpt, file, chisel/let your floating dream/be sealed/in the resistant block.
> (Théophile Gautier, "L' ART" 187)

Most graphic rhetors consider written *logoi* the superior if not the superlative mimetic media, since they display the *dianoia* (thought) and *dunamis* (capacity/power) of the writer and the commemorated person, lend themselves readily to character modeling, and travel among many circles that can copy the text easily, begetting yet more mimetic cycles. Given that stone, bronze, gold, and other statue materials might seem more obdurate and enduring than a thin sheet of treated plant fiber, graphic rhetors make strange claims about the staying power of their texts. Yet it is the very material of statues—being expensive and designed for outdoor public places and spaces—that puts them at high risk of destruction. As J. E. G. Whitehorne writes, "even during periods of relative peace and stability one man's dreams of eternal recognition, for himself or his gods, had a habit of running foul of another's greed and ambition. Statues made of gold for the express purpose of ensuring their subjects' immortality disappear with almost indecent haste" (109–10).

Upon learning that his statue in Corinth had been pulled down, Favorinus enters into the record arguments on its behalf, as he might were it a sentient defendant on trial. In his defense, he mentions several destructive eventualities for statues: extreme weather, being melted down for the reuse of their raw material, sometimes for coin currency, and "though each statue is erected as if it will last forever, still they perish by this fate or by that, the most common and fitting fate and the one ordained for all things being the fate of time" (§37). Favorinus recalls the inscription borne by the bronze maiden placed at Midas's tomb—the very inscription that Socrates plays with as the *Phaedrus* turns to the topic of writing (264d–e)—and announces that seekers have found neither her nor the tomb (§38–9). Further, statues are often mislabeled and mistreated. Although Favorinus does not dispense with all forms of image-crafting, the vicissitudes of plastic media have become vices and no longer interest him. He concludes his discourse with an appeal to the goddess Fame. He pledges to place his image in her precinct so that no one and nothing can pull it down. "Forgetfulness," he claims, "has tripped up and cheated others, but judgment (*gnômê*) plays no tricks on any man of worth, and because of this, you stand upright for me like a man" (§47). The "you" is the new image of himself that Favorinus constructs with these words, one he credits not bronze or stone but fame and judgment with preserving from oblivion. Of course, fame is conferred by and judgment possessed by communities, in this case, readers of this and other published speeches.

The word Isocrates, Alcidamas, and other writers use for their own sort of artful supplements to memory is *mnêmeîon* (memorial, remembrance, record). In the *Phaedrus*, Plato's Socrates uses the word *hupomnêma* (reminder, 276d) to describe writing, which Isocrates sometimes uses as a synonym of *mnêmeîon*, and not disparagingly (*To Nicocles* §36). In Latin, those words become "*monumentum*," monument, literally, an object that teaches, warns, or advises the mind. Cicero refers to the collective papyrus pages of his Athenian predecessors as a looming "*monumentis litteris*" (literary monument, *Brutus* §26), emphasizing their physicality and instructional value and alluding to them as markers—and makers—of memory.

In the proem to his self-defense in *Antidosis*, Isocrates volunteers that he intends to "write a speech (*graphein logos*) that would be, as it were, an *eikôn* of my thoughts and my life as a whole. I hoped this would be the best way to make the facts about me known and to leave this behind as a memorial (*mnêmeîon*), much finer than dedicatory constructions of bronze (*polu kallion tôn chalkôn anathêmatôn*)" (§7). Within his discourse for Nicocles, in its famous hymn to *logos*, Isocrates calls speech "the *eikôn* of a good and faithful soul," in contrast to statues, which are likenesses of the body (*Nicocles* §5–9). We have seen before that Alcidamas unfavorably compares written speeches to statues. But, of course, Alcidamas also succumbs to writing's various seductions, boasting that with just a squeak of work (*mikra ponêsantes, Writers* §30) he can outdo graphic rhetors in their own medium (*logous graphein*, §32), explaining that not everyone has had a chance to hear him in person, adding that writing over time reflects growth in one's thinking and thus can be viewed as wholesomely diagnostic, and admitting his desire to leave behind "a memorial of myself" (*mnêmeîa . . . autôn*, §32). For all their supposed differences, he and Isocrates call their rhetorical projects by the exact same name.

The impulse to leave behind a trace of oneself or another after death is a major contributor to the sub-*topos* of memory, tying together immortality in memory and textual monumentality. Isocrates opens his written monument for Evagoras by emphasizing that "men of ambition and greatness of soul . . . do all that lies in their power to leave behind a memory of themselves that shall never die" (*athanaton . . . mnêmên*) (*Evagoras* §3). Whereas the lavish displays Nicocles held at this father's tomb are a thoughtful tribute (§1–4), Isocrates divines that Evagoras most longs for "a deserving account of his activities and the dangers he undertook" (§2). Isocrates insists that "a fine speech (*logos kalôs*) that recounts Evagoras' deeds would make his excellence/virtue (*aretê*) ever-remembered (*aeimnêston*) among all men" (§4). Tomb-side recitals of song and dance are momentarily impressive, but the monumentality of a written speech ensures the longevity of its celebrant. Isocrates claims that he has not needed to rely on rhetorical amplification to commemorate Evagoras, who, though mortal, "left an immortal memory (*athanaton . . . mnêmên*) of himself" through his deeds and character (§71). Isocrates's written *logos*, he wants readers to believe, merely prolongs Evagoras's unforgettable reputation.

Statues were made of or promised to several illustrious fifth- and fourth-century Greek rhetors and philosophers. Most notorious is the golden statue of Gorgias at Delphi. According to various traditions, he commissioned it himself, and it was either gilded[12] or solid gold. His nephew dedicated a statue to him at Olympia, whose inscribed black limestone base was uncovered in the nineteenth century and celebrates Gorgias's soul-training (see Morgan 378). Not once, but twice Phaedrus promises to erect a statue of Socrates if he outdoes Lysias's *logos* on *erôs* (*Phaedrus* 235d and 236b). Although Phaedrus never gets around to it—Diogenes Laertius reports that a contrite Athens erected a bronze statue to Socrates shortly after his state-mandated suicide (*Life of Socrates* §43)—Plato's Socratic dialogues themselves serve this function. He thus joins Isocrates, Alcidamas, and other graphic rhetors in using writing to preserve aspects of a person that spoken words, stone, and metal cannot. Isocrates was also memorialized with a statue, furnished by his grateful student Timotheus

(Plutarch, *Lives of the Orators* 838d), and it did not outlive the *eikôn* presented and preserved in *Antidosis*.

Isocrates, for one, prophesied that his memorializing self-defense in *Antidosis* would outclass and outlast a bronze statue. In his evaluation of Attic writers, Dionysius of Halicarnassus justifies their painstaking procedures similarly. Scoffers may call Demosthenes, for example, "so poor a creature that, whenever he was writing out his speeches (*hote graphoi tous logous*), he would work in meters and rhythms after the fashion of clay-modelers (*hoi plastai paratithemenos*), and would try to fit his clauses into these molds (*tupois*), twisting the words to and fro (*strephôn anô kai katô ta onomata*)" (On the Putting Together of Words §25).

His physical manipulation of words and sounds strikes them as paltry and passive. Dionysius rallies that Demosthenes wrote because he had a greater reputation (*doxa*) for clever/forceful speaking (*deinotêti logôn*) than his predecessors (§25) and wished to "leave behind an undying memory of his thoughts" (*mnêmaîa tês hautoû dianoias athanata katalipeîn*) (*Demosthenes* §51). Detractors of graphic rhetoric who compare it unfavorably to stonework are mistaken:

> for it is far more reasonable for a man who is composing public speeches (*logous politikous*), eternal memorials (*mnêmeîa . . . aiônia*) of his own powers (*dunameôs*), to attend even to the slightest details, than it is for the disciples of painters (*zôigraphôn*) and workers in relief (*toreutôn*), who display the dexterity and industry of their hands in a perishable material (*hulêi phthartêi*), to expend the finished resources of their art (*tês technes*) on veins and down and bloom and similar minutiae (*tên akribeian*).
>
> (*On the Putting Together of Words* §25)

The juxtaposition of the artistic media of writers and sculptors and the respective staying power of their products complicates an easy comparison of their methods. Dionysius even uses *akribeia* here in the negative sense of a trivial fussiness with minor details. He uses it elsewhere to compliment the "precision" of graphic rhetors, such as Lysias.

The memory sub-*topos* is sustained by both orality and textuality in at least two of Cicero's recorded speeches. In his third Catilinarian, he expresses a desire for a highly social *memoria* of himself rather than a quiet *monumenta* (§26). "Nothing mute delights me, nothing silent, nothing, really, of the kind that those less worthy can attain," he declares. He does allow that Romans might build him a monument, but one stored in and adored by their minds, extended by their conversations, and allowed to grow old and strong in the monuments of their letters (*litterarum monumentis*). His monumentalized memory relies on minds contemplating his achievements in talk or in text.

When agitating against Marcus Antonius years later, Cicero delivered to the senate what has come to be called the ninth Philippic. This speech abounds with the language of memorializing. In it, Cicero calls for the erection of a pedestrian (on-foot) bronze statue of dutiful Servius Sulpicus—who has died while undertaking an ambassadorial journey to Antonius's camp—on the speaking rostra. Cicero begins by establishing that such a dedication would be in keeping with the ways of their ancestors, who gave men who died for the sake of the republic a long-lasting memory (*diuturnam memoria*) in exchange for a short life (*pro brevi vita*) (§4), a *statua pro vita* (§5). What Cicero passes over is that the precedents he names were envoys to enemies, which Antonius is not, at least not formerly. Cicero wants to change that. Since the senate dispatched Sulpicius, thereby causing his death (*mortem*), they should grant him immortality (*immortalitatem*) by means of a statue (§10). The statue would diminish the sorrow of those mourning Sulpicius's death and demonstrate senatorial gratitude for his life-giving service, but, probably more significantly for Cicero, it would function as a very public announcement of Antonius's enemy status. It would be "an everlasting testament" (*testificatio sempiterna*) to his treachery against the Republic (§15). Strangely, Cicero points to the vulnerabilities of statues, pointing out their slow death by the turning of the seasons and aging of the material (§14). He likely makes this argument as a way of dismissing a competing proposal that Sulpicius be interred in a sepulcher, which, as nearly all tombs were, would be constructed outside of Rome rather than in the middle of the forum. Since a tomb outside of the city would not suit Cicero's purpose of hyperpublicizing Antonius's enmity, he deems it inappropriate for Sulpicius. But one could read Cicero's speech as operating as an epideictic public statue that at once praises and blames while avoiding the ravages of time, being first spoken into the air and then written on a page that brings about iterations of itself. At the emotional fulcrum of the speech, Cicero posits that "the life of the dead is set up (*est posita*) in the memory of the living" (§10). This verb, *pono*, can mean "erect or build" or "form or fashion," all possibilities that lie within the possibility of speech and its crafters to achieve, thanks to centuries of the mock rock *topos*.

Displaying Culture

The mock rock *topos*'s m-heuristic of masterpiece, *mimêsis*, movement, and memory demonstrates that graphic rhetors mimicked or taunted sculptors or sculpture to promote their own medium and methods, to explain the development of their art, and to manage how they would be remembered, among other reasons. Whether complimentary or critical, many ancient writers display sensitivity to the materiality of words plied for and applied to papyrus—also material—and released to readers. Their excessive matter-mindedness troubles the easy dichotomy between the symbolic and the material that undergirds some current work on material rhetoric, giving us reason to be cautious about excluding the creation and circulation of written words from that category. In 1982, in an early contribution to our understanding of rhetoric's materiality and in terms that fit this article uncannily well, Michael Calvin McGee stressed that "to say that we study rhetoric in a material way is not to claim that rhetoric is material because it is a sensible discourse I may handle and manipulate like rock" (32). Rather, it is to appreciate that a matrix of material conditions gives shape to "sensible discourse," both its production and its reproduction. In that spirit, I conclude with a larger, longer look at the mock rock *topos*.

Despite the frequent claims of graphic rhetors that it is their nested media—words written on book-rolls—that confer long life, it is actually successive generations of readers who do. Masterpieces require admirers, *exempla* require emulators, movement requires movers, and memory requires rememberers. The preservative role played by beautiful words is not to be discounted, for they arouse in readers an urge to copy, an urge all writers rely upon. But, being material objects, book-rolls were also display objects, emblems of education and culture that communicated learning and refinement. The symbolic value and actual cost of texts made them worth having and showing off, and private and public libraries were prime *loci* of exhibition.

Coincident with the development of the mock rock *topos*, proprietors of ancient libraries placed both book-rolls and portrait busts of particular authors in close proximity. Yun Lee Too traces this pairing practice back to the Hellenistic era, suggesting that author images in libraries "might stand as self-conscious gestures of textual origination" (195). The coordination of text and stone amplified the impact of a cultural and cultured experience for a reader-viewer in a library. Having translated Cicero under the stony glare of his bust in my undergraduate Latin course, I can attest to the rich imagined interactions it induces. The pairing of an image of an author's visage with a record of his (usually, although busts of Sappho survive) thoughts and talents brings an intimacy to the encounter that neither image nor text can achieve alone.

Statues located in libraries were a mute call to virtuosity in a number of publically esteemed areas. While it was still standing, Favorinus's Corinth statue was located in its library, its center of culture, what Favorinus calls "a front-row seat," where Corinthians "felt it would most effectively stimulate the youth to persevere in the same pursuits as myself" (§8). Presumably, his texts were also available in the library; those stirred by his visage or the very notion of being publically memorialized could seek out the source of his renown. Author images reinforced the cachet of contributing to culture through written words, acting as a visual who's who of the most celebrated or most cherished writers in a given collection.

As Too and others have emphasized recently, libraries were social sites where ideas were exchanged and imaginations engaged. Books brought people together, as they still occasionally manage to do. The mock rock *topos* promised readers that the labors of writing and the pleasures of reading were worthwhile. That ancient written works containing that pledge survive is a testament to its truth.

Notes

1 For ease of reader reference, I have adapted and adjusted translations from Loeb editions unless otherwise indicated in the Reference section.
2 Stone can, of course, be a writing surface, and writing on media other than papyrus, wax, or animal skin is known as epigraphy.
3 The four *topoi* I name are specific to a certain set of ancient writers who write about writing. Michael Leff, among others, traced the history of the *koinoi topoi* (common topics) from ancient to medieval rhetorical theory and also wrote about what an approach to rhetoric as action and performance entails for topical invention.
4 For a treasure trove of detail about ancient writing materials, see Frederic Kenyon.
5 This list pulls from recent articles and anthologies in rhetorical studies. Further, Greg Dickinson and Brian Ott led a workshop on "Rhetoric's Materiality" at the 2011 Rhetoric Society of America Summer Institute in Boulder, Colorado.
6 Actually, this view—and its uncritical linking of Greece and Rome as if there were not substantial differences in their literate and literary cultures—has been complicated by several classicists, the most recent being Holt Parker. One similarity in the literary cultures of ancient Greece and Rome hinges on genre: certain genres were made for ears, others for eyes. For a treatment of reading and writing in Aristotle's *Rhetoric*, see Richard Graff.
7 Table 16.1, populated by mock rock terms I frequently encountered while reading primary texts, offers a sliver of the possible terms one could include. For a more extensive but still not exhaustive collection of terms often shared by the visual and verbal arts, see the "Glossary" of terms and textual citations in Pollitt (113–449).
8 The latter portion of *Phaedrus* is the *locus classicus* of so-called Socratic views on writing, but see also Plato's *Seventh Letter* and the last third of *Protagoras*.
9 For space reasons, I will not include any other poets in my analyses, but all four sub-*topoi* of the mock rock *topos* appear with frequency in Roman poets, such as: Catullus, Horace, Ovid, Martial, and Statius. The sixth–fifth century BCE lyric poet Pindar also used the mock rock *topos* (see his Seventh Olympian and Fifth Nemean, for instance), perhaps starting the *topos* in the first place.
10 As highlighted above, *tupoi* is the word Alcidamas uses to describe a precisely written work.
11 The verb *idruô* means to sit down, settle, set up, and also to dedicate a statue.
12 Recall Alcibiades's description of Socrates as a common Silenus statue, ugly on the outside but golden on the inside.

References

Alcidamas. "*Peri Sophistôn.*" *Antiphontis Orationes et Fragmenta Adiunctis Gorgiae, Antisthenis Alcimantis.* Ed. Friedrich Blass. 1908. Google Books.

Aristotle. *De Arte Poetica Liber.* Ed. Rudolphus Kassel. New York: Oxford UP, 1965. Print.

Austin, R. G. "Quintilian on Painting and Statuary." *The Classical Quarterly* 38.1/2 (January–April 1944): 17–26. JSTOR (20 May 2012).

Bing, Peter. *The Scroll and the Marble: Studies in Reading and Reception in Hellenistic Poetry.* Ann Arbor: U of Michigan P, 2009. Print.

Blair, Carole. "Contemporary U.S. Memorial Sites as Exemplars of Rhetoric's Materiality." *Rhetorical Bodies.* Ed. Jack Selzer and Sharon Crowley. Madison: U of Wisconsin P, 1999. 16–57. Print.

Bunting, Basil. *Complete Poems.* Ed. Richard Caddel. New York: New Directions, 2000. 57ff. Print.

Cicero. *On the Ideal Orator.* Trans. James M. May and Jakob Wisse. New York: Oxford UP, 2001. Print.

———. *Rhetorica I: Libros de Oratore Tres.* Ed. A. S. Wikins. New York: Oxford UP, 1922. Print.

Cisneros, Josue David. "(Re)Bordering the Civic Imaginary: Rhetoric, Hybridity, and Citizenship in La Gran Marcha." *Quarterly Journal of Speech* 97.1 (2011): 26–49. Print.

Dickinson, Greg. "Joe's Rhetoric: Finding Authenticity at Starbucks." *Rhetoric Society Quarterly* 32.4 (Fall 2002): 5–27. JSTOR.

Dickinson, Greg, Carole Blair, and Brian L. Ott, eds. *Places of Public Memory: The Rhetoric of Museums and Memorials.* Tuscaloosa: U of Alabama P, 2010. Print.

Dunn, Thomas R. "Remembering 'A Great Fag': Visualizing Public Memory and the Construction of Queer Space." *Quarterly Journal of Speech* 97.4 (November 2011): 435–60. Print.

Enos, Richard Leo. "Rhetorical Archaeology: Established Resources, Methodological Tools, and Basic Research Methods." *The SAGE Handbook of Rhetorical Studies.* Ed. Andrea A. Lunsford, Kirt H. Wilson and Rosa A. Eberly. Thousand Oaks: SAGE Publications, 2009. 35–52. Print.

———. "Writing without Paper: A Study of Functional Rhetoric in Ancient Athens." *On the Blunt Edge: Technology in Composition's History and Pedagogy.* Ed. Shane Borrowman. Anderson: Parlor P, 2012. 3–13. Print.

Ford, Andrew. *The Origins of Criticism: Literary Culture and Poetic Theory in Classical Greece.* Princeton: Princeton UP, 2002. Print.

———. "The Price of Art in Isocrates: Formalism and the Escape from Politics." *Rethinking the History of Rhetoric.* Ed. Takis Poulakos. Boulder: Westview, 1993. 31–52. Print.

Fredal, James. *Rhetorical Action in Ancient Athens: Persuasive Artistry from Solon to Demosthenes.* Carbondale: Southern Illinois UP, 2006. Print.

Gaines, Robert. "De-Canonizing Ancient Rhetoric." *The Viability of the Rhetorical Tradition.* Eds. Richard Graff, Arthur Walzer, and Janet Atwill. Albany: SUNY P, 2005. Print.

Gautier, Théophile. *Émaux et Camée.* The Project Gutenberg E-book. 2011. Web. 23 June 2012. www.gutenberg.org/files/37733/37733-h/37733-h.htm.

Gibbons, Michelle. "Seeing the Mind in the Matter: Functional Brain Imaging as Framed Visual Argument." *Argumentation and Advocacy* 43 (Winter and Spring 2007): 175–88. Print.

Graff, Richard. "Reading and the 'Written Style' in Aristotle's *Rhetoric.*" *Rhetoric Society Quarterly* 31.4 (Autumn 2001): 19–44. JSTOR.

Graff, Richard and Christopher L. Johnstone. "Greek Rhetoric *in Situ*: Reconstructing Ancient Sites of Oratorical Performance." Joint keynote at the 2012 American Society for the History of Rhetoric Symposium, Philadelphia, PA, 25 May 2012.

Habinek, Thomas N. *The Politics of Latin Literature: Writing, Identity, and Empire in Ancient Rome.* Princeton: Princeton UP, 1998. Print.

Hawhee, Debra. *Bodily Arts: Rhetoric and Athletics in Ancient Greece.* Austin: U of Texas P, 2005. Print.

———. "Somatography." *Quarterly Journal of Speech* 93.3 (August 2007): 365–74. Print.

———. "Toward a Bestial Rhetoric." *Philosophy and Rhetoric* 44.1 (2011): 81–87. Print.

Isocrates. *Isocrates I.* Trans. David C. Mirhady and Yun Lee Too. Austin: U of Texas P, 2000. Print.

John, Elton. "Your Song." *Elton John.* Composed by Elton John with lyrics by Bernie Taupin. 1970.

Kenyon, Frederic. *Books and Readers in Ancient Greece and Rome.* Oxford: Clarendon P, 1932. Print.

Lamp, Kathleen. "'A City of Brick': Visual Rhetoric in Roman Rhetorical Theory and Practice." *Philosophy & Rhetoric* 44.2 (2011): 171–93. Print.

Leen, Ann. "Cicero and the Rhetoric of Art," *American Journal of Philology* 112.2 (Summer 1991): 229–45. JSTOR (9 November 2009).

Leff, Michael. "Up From Theory: Or I Fought the *Topoi* and the *Topoi* Won." *Rhetoric Society Quarterly* 36.2 (2006): 203–11. Print.

McGee, Michael Calvin. "A Materialist's Conception of Rhetoric." *Rhetoric, Materiality, & Politics.* Ed. Barbara A. Biesecker and John Louis Lucaites. New York: Peter Lang, 2009. 17–42. Print.

Morgan, Kathryn A. "Socrates and Gorgias at Delphi and Olympia: *Phaedrus* 235d6–236b4." *Classical Quarterly* 44.2 (1994): 375–86. JSTOR (21 May 2012).

Morris III, Charles E., ed. *Remembering the AIDS Quilt*. East Lansing: Michigan State UP, 2011. Print.

Parker, Holt N. "Books and Reading Latin Poetry." *Ancient Literacies: The Culture of Reading in Greece and Rome*. Ed. William A. Johnson & Holt N. Parker. New York: Oxford UP, 2009. 186–232. Print.

Pollitt, J. J. *The Ancient View of Greek Art: Criticism, History, and Terminology*. New Haven: Yale UP, 1974. Print.

Porter, James I. *The Origins of Aesthetic Thought in Ancient Greece*. New York: Cambridge UP, 2010. Print.

Selzer, Jack and Sharon Crowley, eds. *Rhetorical Bodies*. Madison: U of Wisconsin P, 1999. Print.

Too, Yun Lee. *The Idea of the Library in the Ancient World*. New York: Oxford UP, 2010. Print.

Whitehorne, J. E. G. "Golden Statues in Greek and Latin Literature." *Greece & Rome* 22.2 (Oct. 1975): 109–19. JSTOR (5 June 2012).

17

Parrēsia, Foucault, and the Classical Rhetorical Tradition

ARTHUR E. WALZER

Of Michel Foucault, Barbara Biesecker observed: "He rarely wrote or spoke about rhetoric per se" (352). This was an accurate description of Foucault's corpus through the publication of the third volume of *The History of Sexuality*, *The Care of the Self*, published just prior to his death in 1984. But as Biesecker also hinted, that neglect of rhetoric changed when Foucault took up *parrēsia* (fearless or frank speech) in the lectures he presented during the last three years of his life, 1981–1984.[1] Foucault examined *parrēsia* in both of its primary public manifestations: (1) an orator criticizing the *demos* in a democratic political context and (2) a counselor offering frank criticism of a prince in a monarchical context. Both have obvious relevance to the history of rhetoric, and in the lectures he offered on *parrēsia* as the holder of the chair of the History of Thought at the Collège de France, Foucault examined canonical rhetorical texts, including Pericles's three orations; Plato's *Gorgias*, *Phaedrus*, and *Epistles* 7 and 8; Isocrates's *On the Peace*, and *Areopagiticus*; Demosthenes's second and third *Philippics*; and Philodemus's *On Frank Criticism*. Foucault's lectures have inspired considerable work among scholars, especially classicists,[2] and his analysis of *parrēsia* is important and provocative for rhetoric scholars as well.

Historians of rhetoric are, however, likely to be disappointed in the genealogy of *parrēsia* that Foucault provides. Since claims to speak frankly always have rhetorical implication, *parrēsia* would seem to have an inherent rhetorical dimension; furthermore, *parrēsia* has a history within rhetoric. But, for his own legitimate reasons, Foucault programmatically conceives of *parrēsia* as conceptually opposed to rhetoric, and his genealogy ignores the treatment of *parrēsia* within the rhetorical tradition. My purpose in this essay is to offer an alternative analysis of *parrēsia* as well as a critique of Foucault's description of classical rhetoric. I cannot provide here a complete counter history of *parrēsia* within rhetoric—though such a history should be written. Rather, by rereading from a rhetorical perspective many of the texts that Foucault analyzes, as well as attending to the treatment of *parrēsia* within rhetoric that Foucault neglects, I hope to complicate the history of *parrēsia* he provided.

The difference in the history I will trace from Foucault's results from our different motivations and points of departure. Foucault examines *parrēsia* as a mode of truth telling: an orator or, more likely, a philosopher courageously tells truth to power, without regard to consequences. Foucault is interested in parrhesiastic speech activity in relation to the human subject, exploring the ontological implications of *parrēsia* for human subjectivity. He is also attracted to ancient instances of *parrēsia* as a possible additional starting point for a narrative of philosophy in the West. Foucault writes, "for a long time it was thought, and it is still thought, that basically the reality of philosophy is being able to tell the truth about truth, the truth of truth. But . . . there is a completely different way of . . . defining what philosophy's reality may be. . . . This [alternative] reality is marked by the fact that philosophy is the activity which consists in . . . practicing veridiction in relation to power. And it seems to me that this has definitely been one of the permanent principles of its reality for at least two and half millennia" (*Government of Self* 229–30). This interest in a "philosophical *ergon* . . . in relation to politics" (*Government of Self* 225) brings Plato's famous confrontations with the Sicilian tyrants, Dionysius I and II, as reported in Plato's *Epistles*, to the center of Foucault's analysis as a potential point of departure for a story of philosophy's origins in the West that emphasizes truth telling in the context of political engagement. Thus, as is true generally of Foucault's genealogies, in writing this history of *parrēsia*, intervening in the present is more important to him than describing the past (McGushin xxvi–xxviii; Nilson 69–70).

I read the history of *parrēsia* differently because my interest in it began from a different starting place and with a different motivation. My concern with *parrēsia* (and therefore with Foucault's last lectures) arose from an interest in how civic rhetoric has functioned in non-democratic political contexts—in Imperial Rome and Early Modern England, specifically. In these contexts, the "ideal counselor" replaces the "ideal orator" as the normative idea of the rhetor, since there is little opportunity under the principate or Renaissance monarchies for a speaker to empower a people or a senate. In this context, *parrēsia* is the counselor's obligation and opportunity: to speak frankly to a powerful prince is the best way for humanists to influence governing. But it is an opportunity accompanied by risk. If the risk is to be minimized, if the counselor is even to be heard, the focus of the counselor's internal negotiation will be how to offer frank, honest criticism without offense. Prudential reasoning and rhetoric are at the center of this negotiation, which needs to be grounded in ethos of friendship. My analysis proceeds from this context and from these pragmatic assumptions.

It is thus clear to me that valuable as Foucault's analysis of *parrēsia* is, it is not the only possible one, nor the most complete one. Foucault's paradigmatic instances of *parrēsia* are those in which an uncompromising orator or counselor states an unvarnished truth to a powerful person. This scene, constituted of a language of truth, is, however, only one parrhesiastic occasion. The author of the *Rhetorica Ad Herennium*, a text that Foucault does not cite, offers a more capacious, empirical analysis. When he reflects on how *parrēsia* has functioned and is functioning up to his time (circa 90–80 BCE), he acknowledges a feigned *parrēsia* as well as a sincere one and insists that an artful, rhetorical *parrēsia* that cultivates friendship is more effective than a bold, unvarnished one. In doing so, the author thus locates *parrēsia* within rhetoric and under the direction of prudential reasoning (*phronesis/prudentia*). In the course of this essay, I provide rereadings from this rhetorical perspective of many of the texts that Foucault cites in his analysis, arguing that what he sees as sincere can be read as feigned and what he sees as artless is often highly rhetorical. I will also show that over time as *parrēsia* becomes increasingly aligned with friendship, especially in the Hellenistic period, rhetoric and prudential reasoning become increasingly important to its practice.

Of the work written in the wake of Foucault's lectures on *parrēsia*, Carlos Lévy's is closest to mine in approach and conclusions. In a trenchant critique, Lévy faults Foucault for failing to appreciate the complexity in the Ancients' reception of *parrēsia*. But while I would characterize some of what Lévy hears in the Ancients' attitude toward *parrēsia* as a rhetorical turn, Lévy denies that *parrēsia* has a history within rhetoric, alleging a "refusal, or the incapacity, of rhetors to include *parrēsia* in their concepts" (324). Rhetoric is not, then, the basis for Lévy's critique, while it is mine.[3]

Foucault's Definition of *Parrēsia* in Relationship to Rhetoric

Foucault's genealogy traces *parrēsia*—the term and concept—from its first appearance in the fifth century BCE through the fifth century CE. Specifically, he characterizes the kind of genealogy he constructs as a "history of thought," that is, a genealogy that captures the ways an "unproblematic field of experience, or a set of practices . . . becomes a problem . . . incites new reactions and induces a crisis in the previously silent behavior, habits, practices, and institutions" (*Fearless Speech* 74; also *Government of Self and Others* 2–5). Foucault's genealogy of *parrēsia* in Antiquity begins with the term's appearance in Euripides's *Ion*, in which *parrēsia* is viewed as a precious right of citizenship (*Fearless Speech* 44). Under Athenian democracy, citizens were guaranteed a right of speech (*isegoria*), and citizens were free to speak all (*parrēsia*), to say whatever they wished (*Fearless Speech* 51–56). As Foucault shows, in the *Ion*, the parrhesiast is the person who exercises his right to speak and, the assumption is, speaks truthfully, courageously, and helpfully. *Parrēsia* has "only a positive sense of value" (*Fearless Speech* 71) at this point and is an unqualified good. But within ten years, the term and concept have become problematic. Foucault finds evidence of the problematic nature of *parrēsia* in a second Euripides's play, the *Orestes* in 408 BCE. In the play, critics of Athenian democracy complain that the Athenian citizen's right to speak (*isegoria*) and to speak freely (*parrēsia*) allowed, even encouraged, ignorant and pointless speech (*Fearless Speech* 57). Foucault notes that at this point *parrēsia* had a "pejorative sense" as well as a positive one (*Fearless Speech* 13, 57, 66).

Foucault's most complete *conceptual* analysis of *parrēsia* appears in his last lecture series, published as *The Courage of Truth*, when, in the first lecture, he summarizes the previous years' lectures on *parrēsia*. To paraphrase Foucault: *parrēsia* occurs when a speaker, at risk to himself or herself, speaks an unwelcome truth or gives unwelcome advice to a powerful person or group (9–11). After defining *parrēsia* thus, Foucault offers this detailed analysis:

> In short *parrhēsia*, the act of truth, requires: first, the manifestation of a fundamental bond between the truth spoken and the thought of the person who spoke it; [second], a challenge to the bond between the two interlocutors (the person who speaks the truth and the person to whom this truth is addressed). Hence this new feature of *parrhēsia*: it involves some form of courage, the minimal form of which consists in the parrhesiast taking the risk of breaking and ending the relationship to the other person which was precisely what made his discourse possible. In a way, the parrhesiast always risks undermining that relationship which is the condition of possibility for his discourse.
>
> (*Courage of Truth* 11; translator's interpolation)

Ideally, the parrhesiast has a primary commitment to state the truth as he or she understands it. This commitment is more important than maintaining or enhancing a relationship with a listener. In stating this truth, the parrhesiast knows there are risks: the risk of not being heard by the other party or parties or of being silenced entirely, though there is the possibility of each party to the parrhesiastic transaction agreeing to tolerate or even welcome a degree of frankness greater than either might ordinarily be ready to accept.

Since rhetoric ordinarily theorizes a relationship between speaker and listener or the audience as primary, there is necessarily tension between ideal *parrēsia* and ordinary rhetoric. Foucault turns this tension into a dichotomy and sets off the rhetorical transaction as foil to the parrhesiastic one. While the parrhesiast has an obligation to the truth and to forge a bond between self and speech, rhetoric, according to Foucault, "enables the person speaking to say something which may not be what he thinks at all, but whose effect will be to produce convictions, induce certain conducts, or instill certain beliefs in the person [to whom he speaks]" (*Courage of Truth* 13). The rhetor "is perfectly capable of saying, something completely different from what he knows, believes, and thinks. . . . You can see that from this point of view rhetoric is the exact opposite of *parrhēsia* [which entails on the contrary a] strong, manifest, evident foundation between the person speaking and what he says" (*Courage of Truth* 13; brackets are Foucault's editor's). In opposing rhetoric to *parrēsia* Foucault places rhetoric on the end of a spectrum opposite from it, in truth—falsehood, sincere—insincere dichotomies, aligning rhetoric with knowing falsehood and insincerity in contrast to *parrēsia*'s bond with truth and sincerity. These "two adversaries [of *parrēsia*], flattery and rhetoric, are profoundly connected to each other since the moral basis of rhetoric is always flattery in fact, and the privileged instrument of flattery is of course the technique, and possibly the tricks of rhetoric" (*Hermeneutics of the Subject* 373). Many readers of this journal would regard Foucault's description as a caricature—as if Socrates's attack in the *Gorgias* provided the first and final word about rhetoric in Greek and Roman settings.

Furthermore, even more problematic, Foucault characterizes rhetoric as a pseudo art of formulas that the parrhesiast must abjure. In the *Hermeneutics of the Subject*, Foucault reads Quintilian's claim that rhetoric is an art as evidence that for Quintilian rhetoric is merely a codification of generic conventions. According to Foucault, rhetoric is "not defined by a personal or individual relationship, let us say by the 'tactical situation' of the person speaking face to face with the person he is addressing," but is rather a collection of rhetorical rules derived from "the subject matter" or, in other words, generic conventions and formulas. *Parrēsia* by contrast is "defined by rules of prudence, skill, and the conditions that require one to say the truth at this moment, in this form, under these conditions" (*Hermeneutics of the Subject* 383–84). In the *Government of Self and Others*, Foucault reads the *Phaedrus* to support this characterization of rhetoric. He claims that in the *Phaedrus*, Socrates is not contrasting two types of rhetoric but opposing the pseudo art of rhetoric to a true philosophical art of discourse that is enacted by the parrhesiast. According to Foucault, Socrates compares rhetoric to medicine before it became a genuine art; at this time, medicine was "just the application of a recipe," not yet "an art of curing through knowledge of the body. So, in the same way . . . rhetorical *tekhnē*, the ability to persuade for which rhetoric still claims to be the *tekhnē*, is no more than a body of recipes" (*Government of Self* 334). The true art of discourse is embodied in philosophical discourse that combines dialectic with psychagogy (a guiding of the soul). The philosopher who has grasped and internalized the true connection between dialectic and psychagogy will have command of the true *tekhnē* of *logos*. That philosopher is "the parrhesiast, the only parrhesiast, which the rhetorician, the man of rhetoric cannot be or function as" (*Government of Self* 336).

At some points in these lectures Foucault seems more conflicted about the relationship between rhetoric and *parrēsia* than he does in the passages just quoted. At times, he seems prepared to acknowledge that *parrēsia* has a rhetorical dimension. For example, in the *Hermeneutics of the Subject*, Foucault states that, while *parrēsia* must be free from rhetoric's rules, the parrhesiast can use rhetoric "within strict, always tactically defined limits, where it is really necessary," referring to rhetoric as *parrēsia*'s "technical partner" (373). Similarly, in the *Government of Self and Others*, Foucault asks whether *parrēsia* is "a strategy of persuasion" that would "fall under . . . the art of rhetoric" (53). While he ultimately maintains that *parrēsia* does not fall within rhetoric, he notes that "between *parrēsia* and rhetoric there is a focal point of questions, a network of interactions, proximities, and intrications, etcetera, which we will try to disentangle" (53). Regrettably, however, when Foucault comes to disentangling the relationship between rhetoric and *parrēsia*, rhetoric becomes *parrēsia*'s antagonist, not its potential ally. My essay can be seen as an attempt to follow Foucault's initial suggestion, to tease out from the Ancients' reflections and performances the complex relationship of *parrēsia* to rhetoric—both in the less interesting instances where *parrēsia* is recognized as capable of being feigned and in the more interesting ones in which the Ancients acknowledge the importance of tact and strategy in offering frank criticism effectively and safely. Indeed, I will maintain that in Ancient Greece and Rome rhetoric is often *parrēsia*'s "technical partner."

Any rapprochement between rhetoric and *parrēsia* would begin with the acknowledgment that, contra Foucault, within Classical sources, rhetoric has been treated as a stochastic art, requiring prudential judgment in the face of complex situational variables that defy codification. For example, in a well-known passage contrasting his own true creative art of rhetoric from that taught by his rivals, Isocrates insists that rhetoric is not a matter of conventions, formulas and recipes:

> But I marvel when I observe these men setting themselves up as instructors of youth who cannot see that they are applying the analogy of an art with hard and fast rules to a creative process. For, excepting these teachers, who does not know that the art of using letters remains fixed and unchanged, so that we continually and invariably use the same letters for the same purposes while exactly the reverse is true of the art of discourse? For what has been said by one speaker is not equally useful for the speaker who comes after him; on the contrary he is accounted most skilled in this art who speaks in a manner worthy of his subject and yet is able to discover in it topics which are nowise the same as those used by others. But the greatest proof of the difference between these two arts is that oratory is good only if it has the qualities of fitness for the occasion, propriety of style and originality of treatment, while in the case of letters there is no such need whatsoever.
>
> (*Against the Sophists* 12–13)

There is, of course, an element of truth in Foucault's derogatory characterization: the handbooks are full of formulas. Since handbooks have been both commended and criticized throughout the history of rhetoric, it is fair to characterize the Ancients' understanding of rhetoric as both an art of conventions and a situational art requiring intuitive judgment, taste, and prudential reasoning. The two views have co-existed in a productive tension, at least since Aristotle's description of rhetoric as both a productive art (a means to producing speeches) and a practical art (requiring prudential reasoning in response to situational variables). While an art of rhetoric necessarily describes the generic conventions, whether to follow a convention or not and which convention to choose among the many codified is a matter of propriety, which, as Cicero notes, is most important and "is the one thing that cannot be taught by art" (*De Oratore* 1.132). Quintilian can be quoted to the same effect, calling propriety the "most essential" virtue of style: "unless [style] is adapted both to circumstances and to persons, it will not only fail to lend distinction to the oratory but will ruin it and make the facts work against us" (*Institutes* 11.1.2). Foucault's description of rhetoric, then, is at best incomplete. In the sections that follow, I offer rhetorical rereadings of many of the texts Foucault sites in support of his genealogy in effort to show that these texts often instantiate rhetorical means and norms.

Plato's *Gorgias*: Callicles as Parrhesiast?

Plato's *Gorgias* contains one of the earliest references to *parrēsia*, where it is mentioned twice. The first is interesting but unproblematic. Polus has objected to Socrates's stricture that he adhere to the conventions of Socratic dialectic and confine himself to answering and asking questions, without indulging in the "long-winded" speechifying that Socrates says characterizes Polus's earlier responses: "What? Won't you let me speak at any length I choose?" Polus objects. To which, Socrates responds, "Polus, it would certainly be dreadful for you to come here to Athens, where there's greater freedom of speech [*parrēsia*] than anywhere else in Greece, and then to be the only person denied that opportunity" (461d,e). Socrates suggests that the Athenian citizen's right of free speech [*isegoria*] can be used, especially by rhetoricians such as Polus, as a shield against just censure.

A second, more interesting, reference to *parrēsia* in the *Gorgias* occurs in the context of Socrates's exchange with Callicles, which Foucault analyzes at some length in *The Government of Self and Others* (357–74). Foucault focuses on the well-known exchange in which Socrates identifies Callicles as the touchstone on which Socrates can test the health of his own soul (*Gorgias* 386d). According to Socrates, Callicles possesses the three qualities of the ideal interlocutor for this purpose: he has knowledge, affection for Socrates, and candor (*parrēsia*) (487a). Because Callicles is this ideal, then if Socrates can bring him to agree that Socrates lives and teaches the truth, Socrates can be sure that he is living right. Foucault identifies this exchange as a "parrhesiastic pact of the test of souls" (*Government of Self* 365).

Foucault reads Socrates's identification of Callicles as the ideal interlocutor and parrhesiast as literal, not ironic. Some commentators agree (e.g., Plochmann and Robinson 127; Raalte). But most readers understand Socrates's description of Callicles as the touchstone and "godsend" (486e) as ironic or sarcastic (Jaeger 140, Michelini 56, and Stauffer 93–94). Socrates offers as evidence that Callicles has the requisite knowledge, that he has had "what many Athenians would call an adequate education" (487b), not Socrates's usual standard. Second, Socrates cites as proof that Callicles has affection for Socrates, that Callicles has advised, not only Socrates but also his own friends, that men of Socrates's age who continue to study philosophy deserve a "good thrashing" (485c). As a test of friendship, this seems obviously sarcastic. Finally, Socrates claims to accept Callicles as a man of candor, of frank speech (*parrēsia*), because Callicles is "not the kind of person to let any sense of propriety stand in the way of your speaking your mind" (487d). Socrates adds, in words that seem unmistakably sarcastic, "it's not just that you yourself have said you're not [a person who values propriety in speech], but also that your earlier words [that Socrates deserves a thrashing] confirm the truth of this claim" (487d). The passage seems ironic or sarcastic to me.

If Plato intends Socrates's discussion here as ironic, then there are already in the ancient world two understandings of *parrēsia* and the parrhesiast. One is the role that Socrates himself intends to play: as Jaeger notes, Plato intends Socrates to "appear as the image of true frankness, true kindness, and true *paideia*" (140). The other is the blusterer who conceals his intentions within the *ethos* of the parrhesiast. Lisa Michelini notes that Callicles's claim of frankness "may of course be another term for rudeness, a disregard for social restraints" (55). Moreover, if Socrates is ironic in stating that Callicles's disregard of propriety is proof that he is a parrhesiast (487d), then Socrates envisions an ideal of *parrēsia* and the parrhesiast that *honors propriety*—that preeminent rhetorical virtue. The key points are these: the irony in the exchange is possible only if *parrēsia* and the parrhesiast are already conventional, and two versions of *parrēsia*—a rhetorical one and a non-rhetorical one—are present in the fourth century.

Plato's *Epistles 7* and *8*: An Artful *Parrēsia*

Equally unsettling for the claim that *parrēsia* is not rhetorical in the sense of not artful are Plato's *Epistles 7* and *8*, which purport to be Plato's descriptions of his interactions with Dionysius I and II, the so-called tyrants of Sicily.[4] Briefly, the background is this: Plato was invited to Sicily by his former student, Dion, in order to influence the younger Dionysius—to transform him from tyrant to constitutional ruler. In this context Plato confronts Dionysius, interactions that are described in Plato's epistles.[5]

Foucault analyzes Plato's interaction with Dionysius, especially as reported in Plutarch and as presented in *Epistles 7* and *8*, at length in the *Government of Self and Others* (47–56; 214–43). In these pages, the importance of the confrontation to his analysis of *parrēsia* is clear: the interaction, Foucault asserts, is paradigmatic, the "matrix scene of *parrēsia*" (*Government of Self and Others* 50). The epistles, however, accommodate a reading that supports the conclusion that a prudential, rhetorical strategy is not incommensurate with legitimate *parrēsia*. Indeed, Plato's description of his encounter is thoroughly legible within rhetorical norms.

In *Epistle 7*, Plato and Dion hardly ignore rhetoric in their interactions with Dionysius. Plato writes that he and Dion undertook the challenge of "convincing" (*peisas*) Dionysius, of providing "arguments and persuasions" (*logôn kai peithous*) in a way that is virtually a model of rhetorical handbook advice on how to persuade in deliberative contexts. Plato's goal for his and Dion's interaction with Dionysius is to enable the emperor to acquire "harmony within himself, since in this he was surprisingly deficient" (332d). How did the two approach Dionysius the Younger? They do not fearlessly scold the emperor for his profligate ways. On the contrary: "Not that we expressed this [censure] openly, for it would not have been safe; but we put it in veiled terms and maintained by argument that this is how every man will save both himself and all those under his leadership, whereas if he does not adopt this course he will bring about entirely opposite results" (332d,e). And when it came to attempting to persuade Dionysius II to adopt a more virtuous path, Plato and Dion did what rhetoricians have long recommended: they sought a virtuous end by appealing to expediency, to their listener's self-interest: "And if he pursued the course we describe, and made himself right-minded and sober-minded, then, if he were to re-people the devastated cities of Sicily and bind them together by laws and constitutions so that they should be leagued both with himself and with one another against barbarian reinforcements, he would thus not merely double the empire of his father but actually multiply it many times over" (332e). As Quintilian writes: "It is very easy to commend an honourable course to honourable men; but if we try to ensure the right action from persons of bad character, we must take care not to seem to be criticizing their very different way of life, but must try to affect the hearer's attitude by appealing not to honour in itself, for which he has no regard, but to praise public opinion, and (if these vanities are ineffectual) the future advantages" (3.8. 38–39). Plato's strategy as parrhesiast conforms to this rhetorical norm; rhetoric here is the partner of *parrēsia*.

Rhetorical norms can similarly account for Plato's advice in *Epistle 8*. This letter, written following Dion's death, addresses both Dion's supporters (democratic reformers) and Dionysius's supporters. Plato argues for an end to the civil war between them on the grounds that Phoenicians will take advantage of this internal division to conquer Sicily. In his letter, Plato presents himself as a patriotic arbitrator, faulting both parties for their refusal to find common ground and end the civil war. In the terms of a rhetorical textbook such as Aphthonius's *Progymnasmata*, Plato's advice would be classed as an hypothesis— a specific argument concerning an action or policy that affects the city, specific in the sense that, unlike a generalized manifesto, it is attendant to the particular persons, actions, and cause (Aphthonius 94). This is what Plato does in advising the quarreling supporters of Dionysius and the democrats to create a constitution, with each side agreeing to subordinate their ambitions to the laws and to be ruled by a triumvirate comprised of the warring factions. The *Ad Herennium* maintains that political theses or hypotheses generally advance arguments from advantage, supported especially by arguments primarily from security, secondly from honor (3.2.3). The advice Plato offers conforms to these recommendations. How should the warring factions be advised not to pursue policies that seek to destroy each other? Not by arguing that it is morally wrong for Greeks to fight Greeks but because civil war will work to both parties' disadvantage: it is "by no means easy to do much harm to others without also suffering in turn much harm oneself," Plato states (*Epistle 8* 352d). The consequences of pursing the civil war is likely to be that Greek Sicily is a "province" of the Phoenicians or Opicians and the Greek tongue silenced forever in Sicily (353e). But following Plato's advice will also confer honor: creating a common constitution and subordinating partisan advantage to laws will make "those who obey [the constitution] blessed" (355c). Thus, the recommended course is "just *and* profitable" for both parties, Plato assures his audience (355d; my emphasis). With an introduction that expresses friendship and goodwill toward the Sicilians and a conclusion that, in calling on the dead Dion to speak, employs the rhetorical device of prosopopoeia, *Epistle 8* is not only the matrix scene of *parrēsia*, but also a textbook case of a specific deliberative hypothesis.

Parrēsia in Isocrates

Isocrates is important to any history of *parrēsia*. In his influential *To Nicocles*, written to Nicocles on his ascent to the throne of Salamis in Cyprus in 374 BCE, Isocrates offers counsel to the young prince. He warns Nicocles that, while ordinary subjects allow their friends, in a spirit of mutual goodwill, the freedom of speech (*parrēsia*) to point out faults, kings are denied the benefit of *parrēsia* because court counselors are prone to flatter, not to criticize (sections 3–4). Isocrates's gift to the prince will be frank advice, and he counsels Nicocles to "regard as your most faithful friends" his frankest critics and grant "freedom of speech" (*parrēsia*) to those "with good judgement" and the courage to "criticize your mistakes" (28). Thus, with Isocrates, political *parrēsia* not only moves from democratic contexts in Athens to non-democratic contexts, but also begins its transformation from a bold language of truth to a frank language of friendship. In his letter *To Antipater*, Isocrates underscores this point. He recommends a former pupil for a position at court for, among other qualities, his "frankness . . . not that outspokenness which is objectionable but that which would rightly be regarded as the surest indication of devotion to his friends," the type of frankness "which princes, if they have worthy and fitting greatness of soul, honour as being useful" (4–5).

But Isocrates also contributes to our understanding of *parrēsia* in democracy, albeit in a complex way. In his fictional oration *On the Peace*, the speaker both analyzes and performs *parrēsia* before an imagined Athenian Assembly.[6] The address is set in the period following the Social War (357–355 BCE) in which Athens fought against some of its former colonies who were now seeking independence. A peace treaty granting independence has been drawn up.

The speaker urges the Athenians to accept it and for Athens to forsake its "sea empire" entirely. In making his argument for peace, the speaker berates the audience. He attacks the Athenians for favoring speakers who pander to the audience's desires (sections 3, 4), for shouting down speakers who offer advice that challenges the audience's preconceptions (5), and for preferring flatterers to the wise (13). Under these conditions, the only orators who can practice *parrēsia* are "reckless orators" who care nothing for the genuine welfare of the state (14). The speaker insists that despite the implied risk, he will, nevertheless, speak "without reserve in complete frankness" (33). He then scolds the Athenians for hypocrisy in claiming to honor their ancestors, while not following the Ancestors' precedents (42) and for adopting policies inconsistent with Athens' deepest held principles (51–53).

In his analysis, Foucault focuses primarily on the content of the speaker's denunciation, not on his performance. The speaker's complaint that the Athenians shout down orators who present unpopular views is evidence of the abuse of *parrēsia* under the conditions of *isegoria* in Athenian democracy, that *parrēsia* has become possible only for those who pander to the *demos* (*Government of Self* 181–82). This pandering, permitted by *isegoria*, Foucault designates "bad" *parrēsia* (182). Under these conditions, "good" *parrēsia* will be silenced and in its place will be a false *parrēsia* (*Government of Self*, 301–02; see also *Fearless Speech*, 81–82).

While Foucault's interpretation is unexceptionable, a rhetorical reading of the speaker's performance in *On the Peace* is more complicated and equally credible. It is worth pointing out that while the speaker in *On the Peace* complains that orators who present unpopular views are routinely shouted down in the assembly, this speaker, claiming to present an unpopular view, is not interrupted. This raises the question: how much of a challenge is the speaker posing? Note that the speaker emphasizes that his proposal on behalf of signing a peace treaty does not demand sacrifice from his Athenian audience. Throughout the speech, he emphasizes that pursuing peace will not only ensure greater glory for Athens among its Greek allies and honor Athenian traditions but will also increase security and prosperity (18–19). And while the speaker certainly *is* critical of the Athenians, he also allows members of the audience to exempt themselves from his attacks by pointing out that he faults only some, not all: "I say these things, not with reference to all, but with reference to those only who are open to charges which I have made" (56).

So are Isocrates's speaker's attempts to ally himself with those orators who practice a "good" *parrēsia* merely a pose? If it is, the speaker would not be the first or the last political orator to claim to be confronting a harsh reality while actually telling an audience what it wants most to hear. My point is that it may not be so easy to distinguish "good *parrēsia*" from "bad *parrēsia*" when *parrēsia* is under the control of a morally neutral rhetoric. David Colclough captures well the interpretive challenge inherent in Isocrates's speaker's claim to speak frankly:

The whole speech, in its outspoken criticism of Isocrates' audience, is an example of *parrhesia* in action; it also, more significantly, continually draws attention to its own frankness. This explicit announcement of the intention to speak freely characterizes uses of *parrhesia*, ensuring that the audience or reader is aware of the speaker's valorisation of his or her words, and is forced to take a position in relation to this valorisation: is this true free speech or simply abuse? Is it appropriate or not? Such questions force the auditor or reader into an area of ethical consideration which immediately validates the notion of free speech even if what is being responded to is not accepted as such.

(22)

A few pages later, after considering Demosthenes's claims to frankness of speech, Colclough concludes that by the middle of the fourth century BCE, "one can discover a set of ideas about how to discuss speaking out which show that *parrhesia* is already considered to be an important part of the orator's armaments" (25). My point exactly.

Rhetorica Ad Herennium and Quintilian's Institutio Oratoria: A Rhetorical Parrēsia

Within the *Rhetorica Ad Herennium* (ca. 90–80 BCE), which Foucault does not reference, there is a complex understanding of *parrēsia*, one that would seem to unsettle Foucault's genealogy. His history of thought identifies an original idealized understanding of *parrēsia* ("good" *parrēsia*) and subsequently a "bad" *parrēsia*, the mindless chatter that the Athenian citizen's right to speak freely licensed. The *Ad Herennium* complicates this genealogy because it recognizes a feigned *parrēsia* and an artful one alongside of the sincere, direct one that Foucault emphasizes.

The initial definition of *licentia* in the *Ad Herennium* has the basic elements of Foucault's definition of *parrēsia*: *licentia* "is Frankness of Speech [*licentia*] when, talking before those to whom we owe reverence or fear, we yet exercise our right to speak out, because we seem justified in reprehending them, or persons dear to them, for some fault" (4.36.48). This definition thus emphasizes that the censure or criticism is justified, so *licentia* is truth telling, and it acknowledges the risk that Foucault emphasized, since it is spoken before those the speaker fears.

But in the examination of *licentia* that follows, the description departs from Foucault's parameters, for in the *Ad Herennium licentia* is not characterized by an absence of art or a willingness to disregard the auditor's response:

If Frank Speech of this sort seems too pungent, there will be many means of palliation, for one may immediately thereafter add something of this sort: "I here appeal to your virtue, I call on your wisdom, I bespeak your old habit," so that praise may quiet the feelings aroused by the frankness. As a result the praise frees the hearer from wrath and annoyance, and the frankness deters him from error. This precaution in speaking, as in friendship, if taken at the right place, is especially effective in keeping the hearers from error and in presenting us, the speakers, as friendly both to the hearers and to the truth.

(4.37.49)

While Foucault opposed *parrēsia* to flattery, the author of *Ad Herennium* insists that compliments do not undermine the speaker's commitment to the truth: praise can prevent the hearer from coming under the control of a counterproductive emotion and signal friendship (increasingly important in the history of *parrēsia*) on the part of the critic. Furthermore, while Foucault insisted that the bond between a speaker's words and thoughts must override the bond between speaker and listener, the *Ad Herennium*, on seemingly practical grounds, points out that unless that second bond is honored through a friendly tone the speaker's words will not be heeded. For the author, then, rhetorical propriety is typically a condition of successful *parrēsia*.

The *Ad Herennium* also acknowledges that *parrēsia/licentia* can be feigned:

There is also a certain kind of frankness in speaking which is achieved by a craftier device, when we remonstrate with the hearers as they wish us to remonstrate with them, or when we say "we fear how the audience may take" something which we know they will hear with acceptance, "yet the truth moves us to say it none the less." I shall add examples. . . . "Fellow citizens, you are of too simple and gentle a character: you have too much confidence in every one. You think that every one strives to perform what he has promised you. You are mistaken, and now for a long time you have been kept back by false and groundless hope, in your fatuity choosing to seek from others what lay in your power, rather than take it yourselves."

(4.37.49)

Perhaps we might dismiss the feigned frankness of statements like "I hesitate to criticize you but you are just too trusting and honest for your own good" as not *parrēsia* because the flatterer assumes no risk. Perhaps the *Ad Herennium's* acknowledgment of the duplicity in this feigned *parrēsia* would confirm Foucault's casting of rhetoric as the opposite of *parrēsia*. Nevertheless, within the context of a genealogy of *parrēsia* this acknowledgment of a counterfeit *parrēsia* suggests that *licentia/parrēsia* is at this point in its history conventional: legitimate conventions are put to a "crafty" purpose. The availability of conventional materials, whether used to deceive or not, indicates a degree of self-consciousness that complicates all claims of sincerity and spontaneity.

Foucault's interpretation of Quintilian's discussion of *parrēsia* (or *licentia*) in the *Institutes* similarly misses this rhetorical complexity. In *Fearless Speech*

(21) and in the *Government of Self and Others* (53), Foucault quotes Quintilian to support a view of *parrēsia* in Antiquity as the opposite of rhetoric. Foucault writes:

> In Quintillian's [*sic*] *Institutio Oratoria* for example (Book IX, Chapter II), Quintillian explains that some rhetorical figures are specifically adapted for intensifying the emotions of the audience; and such technical figures he calls by the name *exclamatio* (exclamation). Related to these exclamations is a kind of natural exclamation which Quintillian notes, is not "simulated or artfully designed." This type of natural exclamation he calls "free speech" (*libera oratione*) which, he tells us, was called "license" (*licentia*) by Cornificius, and "*parrhesia*" by the Greeks. *Parrhesia* is thus a sort of "figure" among rhetorical figures, but with this characteristic: that it is without any figure since it is completely natural. *Parrhesia* is the zero degree of those rhetorical figures which intensify the emotions of the audience.
>
> (*Fearless Speech* 21; parenthetical interpretations in the original)

But Foucault's analysis omits half of Quintilian's account. Quintilian classifies *parrēsia* with those figures that are "adapted to intensifying the emotions" and that "consist *chiefly in pretence*" (9.2.26; my emphasis). For Quintilian *parrēsia* is among the figures "chiefly" feigned. He continues on to write specifically of *parrēsia*: "The same may be said of Free Speech [*oratione libera*], which Cornificius calls Licence, and the Greeks *parrhesia*. For what is less 'figured' than true freedom? *Yet flattery is often concealed under this cover*" (*Institutes*, 9.2.27; my emphasis; my interpolation). Quintilian has thus identified a counterfeit *parrēsia* within the rhetorical tradition that complicates Foucault's genealogy.

Parrēsia as a "Language of Friendship" in Philodemus and Plutarch

In *On Frank Criticism* (*Peri Parrēsia*), Philodemus (110 BCE–40 BCE), an Epicurean philosopher from Hellenistic Gadara in Syria, analyzes *parrēsia* in the context of the philosophical schools, specifically in protreptic instruction in Epicurean schools. Frank criticism of students, both by their instructors (or guides) and by students offering helpful correction to each other, was central to the psychagogy (guidance of the soul) that was the purpose of formative education in the philosophical schools. *Parrēsia* is most important to spiritual discipline as a spiritual exercise (*askēsis*) practiced by the guide or teacher and student or seeker. Philodemus states that his text is an epitome of Zeno of Sidon's lectures on *parrēsia* delivered in Athens.[7]

On Frank Criticism explains the function of frank criticism and instructs on the way to deliver it in the process of psychagogy. Philodemus insists throughout that the guide's frank criticism be sensitive to situational (rhetorical?) variables. Instruction needs to be adapted to the disposition of the particular student. Guides must apply the art of *parrēsia* one way to students who are especially sensitive to criticism but employ a different way for those who are prone to bitterness (Fr. 7). While all students must be corrected when they err, the guide should proceed with moderation with the more vulnerable ones; more harshness is appropriate with the stronger students (Fr. 10). Praise should sometimes accompany criticism (Fr. 68). Tact is most important (Fr. 13). The guide may ascribe errors to others, including even himself, as a way to make criticism more palatable to those sensitive to it (Fr. 9). Philodemus characterizes *parrēsia* as a "subtle" art (Fr. 68), a conjectural art that must be adapted to the disposition of the particular student and to time and place. An analogy with the art of medicine pervades the treatise (e.g., Frs. 39, 63, 64, 69, 86). In their introductory essay to *On Frank Criticism*, Philodemus's editors comment that "there are no general rules that are valid for all instances" in Philodemus's art of *parrēsia*; in this quality, it is "like the art of the physician, the rhetor, or the pilot" ("Introduction" 23).

Foucault initially investigates psychagogy as a type of care of the self and the spiritual practice of *askēsis* as a means to that end (e.g., *Hermeneutics of the Subject*, 364–71). The seeker might be the powerful and privileged employer of the guide (as was Lucius Calpurnius Piso Caesoninus, whom Philodemus probably instructed). In his discussion of Philodemus in *Hermeneutics of the Self*, Foucault calls particular attention to the differences he sees between *parrēsia* as presented by Philodemus and rhetoric (381–86). In this discussion he notes that on moral grounds, rhetoric is an art capable of lying while *parrēsia* is "the naked transmission . . . of truth itself," adding later "without adornment" (382). Furthermore, rhetoric attempts to influence the listener to the advantage of the speaker, while in the parrhesiastic exchange, the teacher has the welfare of the student in mind (385). On technical grounds, the two arts of *parrēsia* and rhetoric also differ. As conceived by Cicero and Quintilian, rhetoric is not an art defined by "the tactical situation" of the parties to an exchange but an art defined "by subject matter," while what essentially defines the practice of *parrēsia* is appropriate timing (*kairos*) (383).

In his characterization of the rhetorical theories of Cicero and Quintilian, Foucault of course has it wrong: both understood rhetoric as a situational art in which success requires suiting what is said to the character of the particular audience, to the particular time and place, as well as to the forum in which the rhetor is speaking (see, e.g., Cicero, *De Oratore* 3.212 and *Orator* 71–72; Quintilian, *Institutes* 3.8.35, 4.1.52, and 11.1.1–7; also the collections edited by Sipiora and Baumlin and by Hariman). On technical grounds, Philodemus's instructions in the practice of *parrēsia* are similar to advice rhetoricians routinely give in other contexts. It would not, therefore, be inaccurate to describe rhetoric (to recall Foucault's phrase) as the "technical partner" of *parrēsia* in the context of the philosophical schools. On moral grounds, however, Epicureans were notoriously averse to rhetoric (Chandler, "Introduction" 1), and because of this, Philodemus would not describe *parrēsia* as a branch of rhetoric. But surprisingly, in his *On Rhetoric*, Philodemus does recognize epideictic rhetoric as an art, although he denies that status to judicial or political rhetoric (Philodemus, *On Rhetoric* Longo 21, 133, 135).[8] Clive Chandler has hypothesized that Philodemus conferred artistic status on epideictic rhetoric because he thought that the metrical and phonetic appeal of language in Sophistic epideictic (e.g., in Gorgias's speeches) did influence the soul in a way that met Epicureans' criteria for an art (Chandler, *Psychagogia* 147–67). This reference to the Sophists reminds us that psychagogy has a history in rhetoric—not only in Gorgias's speeches but also in a context far more relevant to Philodemus's analysis of *parrēsia*—Plato's *Phaedrus*. In the dialogue, Socrates initially acknowledges a psychagogic effect in Lysius's speech as read by Phaedrus, one that he regrets (234D). But later in the dialogue, he affirms a potential psychagogy for his reconstructed, idealized version of an art of rhetoric: the orator, trained in philosophy and therefore knowing the truth of what he presents, should classify his audience/students according to a taxonomy of souls and adapt his presentation to the particular disposition of his auditors (271A–278B). In the idealized theory of the *Phaedrus*, the art of rhetoric combines knowledge grounded in philosophy with soul science. I wonder if Philodemus would have accepted this theory of rhetoric as the art of *parrēsia* he describes in *On Frank Criticism*.

With Plutarch (46 CE–120 CE), writing in Greek but at Rome during the Second Sophistic, *parrēsia* is considerably tamed from the kind of blunt, heroic challenge to power that it sometimes had in its earlier incarnations. In his famous essay "How to Tell a Flatterer from a Friend," Plutarch understands *parrēsia* in the context of friendship: indeed, he refers to *parrēsia* as "the language of friendship" (51c). The paradigmatic case of *parrēsia* for him is offering moral correction to a friend or to a patron to whom one relates as a friend. His essay is in two parts, each sufficiently independent of the other that some scholars have speculated that Plutarch or an editor stitched the two into one (Engberg-Pederson 63). The first part of *How to Tell a Flatterer from a Friend* addresses directly the subject of the title, as Plutarch identifies for his patron the similarities between a genuine friend and a self-interested flattery that poses as one. Flatterers simulate the habits and language of friends most effectively, Plutarch warns, and among the most "unprincipled" of all of their devices is the flatterer's feigning of that "frankness of speech" (*parrēsia*), which we ordinarily take to be the very "language of friendship" (51c). Plutarch then advises Philopappos on the small *tells* that distinguish the genuine parrhesiast from the feigning flatterer.

Foucault's analysis of Plutarch's essay focuses on the first section—the duplicities of flatterers and the signs that reveal their duplicity. In *Fearless Speech* (135–38), he praises Plutarch for offering a "semiology" of the real parrhesiast (135–36). As Foucault acknowledges, however, the signs that function as discriminating ones are not linguistic since the speech conventions of feigned frankness are indistinguishable from the real thing; rather what is telling is a person's behavior—that his actions do not align well with his words and are not in themselves consistent over time.

The last section of "How to Tell a Flatterer from a Friend" (66e–74e) is devoted entirely to *parrēsia*. In recognizing the need for tact and strategy in the context of offering frank advice to a friend, Plutarch goes even further than Philodemus. He insists that "frankness has plenty of room for tact and urbanity if such urbanity does not impair the high office of frankness" (67f). If the advice that follows is not a rhetoric (and I think it would be seen as one by Cicero and Quintilian), it nevertheless is undeniably a case in which rhetoric serves as *parrēsia*'s "technical partner." With regard to the content of the frank criticism, Plutarch advises that we must avoid mockery or scurrility (67e); we should mix praise with blame (72c, 73e). If possible we should characterize the action we correct as inadvertent, not as a reflection of an ingrained character trait (73e, f). Plutarch further insists that occasion and timing are crucial to success. We should not criticize in the presence of a group, or criticize a man in the presence of his wife or children or a teacher in front of students (71c). Timing is all-important. Offer criticism while the person prospers, not in adversity because ill fortune is "admonition enough" (68d). Avoid faulting someone in the midst of hard drinking (68d). When others commit the fault you would criticize in your friend, point out that fault and condemn it in the hopes that the friend will see its application to him. Indeed, offering frank criticism is "an art," a medicine for the soul (74d).

With Philodemus and, even more, with Plutarch, genuine *parrēsia* is the language—the outward sign and sustaining means—of genuine friendship. In this parrhesiastic exchange between friends, the bond between speaker and listener must be equal to the sincerity bond that Foucault saw as *the* parrhesiastic bond. It is true that a rhetorical theory of *parrēsia* would have to acknowledge and honor the constraints normative to exchanges among friends—that the parties to the exchange have the best interests of the other exclusively in mind, for example. But a bond of friendship also requires the parties to an exchange to attempt to walk in the other's shoes, which is the paradigmatic rhetorical thought experiment, and to shape the presentation of advice prudently.

Conclusion

Foucault's important examination of *parrēsia* as a type of veridiction or mode of truth telling could have interesting implications for rhetoric, especially for a theory of a rhetoric of counsel. Nothing in this essay should discourage scholars in rhetoric from pursuing this productive line of inquiry. At the same time, because of his focus on human subjectivity within the conditions of truth telling (of which *parrēsia* is the featured example), Foucault bracketed off from his analysis rhetoric and the contributions to our understanding of *parrēsia* in classical theories of rhetoric. This essay attempts to right that imbalance by offering an analysis that draws on rhetorical theory and on rereadings of texts formative to Foucault's conclusions from a rhetorical perspective. It offers readings that show that from a rhetorical point of view what in Foucault is seen as sincere *parrēsia* might be feigned and what he reads as rhetorically artless is often highly rhetorical. Furthermore, it presents a genealogy of *parrēsia* that traces an evolution in the meaning of the term as *parrēsia* gradually moves away from situations of confrontations with power and becomes linked to exchanges among friends. Although having a rhetorical dimension throughout its history, at this point *parrēsia* takes on a thoroughly rhetorical character.

Notes

1 Rhetoric scholars have (productively) debated the question of whether the postmodern Foucault can be reconciled to a rhetorical tradition that operates within a classical, Aristotelian ontology and epistemology. In addition to Barbara Biesecker, see Carole Blair and Martha Cooper, Martha Cooper, Robert Danisch, Cheryl Geisler, Christian Lundburg and Joshua Gunn, Rayme McKerrow ("Critical Rhetoric"; "Critical Rhetoric in a Postmodern"), John Muckelbauer, and Bradford Vivian; Gae Lynn Henderson, Dave Tell, and Carlos Lévy bring Foucault's later lectures into the discussion.

2 Two collections published by Brill are evidence of this interest: *Friendship, Flattery, and Frankness of Speech: Studies on Friendship in the New Testament World*, ed. John T. Fitzgerald (Leiden: Brill, 1996) and *Free Speech in Classical Antiquity*, ed. Ineke Sluiter and Ralph M. Rosen (Leiden: Brill, 2004). See also the work by David Colclough, Christopher Gilbert, Matthew Landauer, Carlos Lévy, Edward F. McGushin, S. Sara Monoson, Herman Nilson, and Arlene W. Saxonhouse in References.

3 Lévy cites passages from Demetrius's *On Style* and from "Letter II" (attributed to Aeschines), in which a parrhesiast's claims of speaking only the truth and the whole truth are treated with suspicion; he thus offers a counter to Foucault's more univocal reading of the Ancients. And Lévy characterizes Socrates, who for Foucault is the foremost philosopher of *parrēsia*, as "full of defiance before a concept he began to reform without ever having integrated it into his own vocabulary" (321–22).

4 Plato's visits to Sicily are described in several ancient sources—including Plutarch's life of "Dion"; Diogenes Laertius's life of "Plato" and life of "Aristippus"; Diodorus's *Historical Library;* and perhaps most famously in Plato's letters, *Epistles 7* and *8*. Although the details in the several sources differ, the consensus is that Plato made three visits to Sicily—one while Dionysius I was ruler and two after his death when his son, Dionysius II, ruled. The visits were encouraged by Dion, the brother-in-law of Dionysius I and a former student of Plato's. Dion hoped that Plato would influence Dionysius II. But his efforts were resented by members of Dionysius's court, who saw Dion's intervention as an effort to turn Dionysius II toward constitutionalism and therefore as a threat to their power and positions. This put Dion and Plato in danger; Dion was eventually banished and killed. In Diogenes Laertius's account, although not in Plato's letters, Plato too was banished and sold into slavery by Dionysius, although he was subsequently "purchased" and released (Diogenes Laertius, "Plato," 3.18–19).

5 Plato's authorship of the letters attributed to him is a matter of scholarly controversy. According to R. G. Bury in his introduction to the Loeb edition, the seventh and eighth letters have the greatest claim to authenticity of the thirteen (391–92). Cicero assumed authenticity of *Epistle 7* (*Tusculan Disputations* 5.35) as did Plutarch. But Aristotle never mentions Plato's letters. Recent scholars are skeptical that any of the letters were written by Plato (George Boas, Ludwig Edelstein, Malcolm Schofield); Glenn R. Morrow is an exception, accepting the authenticity of at least *Epistle 7*. Foucault accepts *Epistles 7* and *8* as at least reflecting the general view of Plato and his school (*Government of Self and Others*, 210).

6 Isocrates likely wrote *On the Peace* as a companion piece to his *Archidamas*, another fictional speech, in this case put into the mouth of the Spartan king, Archidamas III, who, in contrast

to the speaker in *On the Peace*, exhorts the Spartan Assembly to fight to the death if necessary rather than accept the terms of a peace treaty with Corinth. See Phillip Harding; Arthur Walzer.

7 Col. VII B, p. 103. In the edition by David Konstan et al., *On Frank Criticism* is a collection of 93 fragments and 24 columns. "Col." indicates "column" and "Fr." "fragment" in this edition.

8 Philodemus's *On Rhetoric, Books I and 2* was translated by Clive Chandler (New York Routledge, 2006). Chandler based his translation on the text of the first two books created by Francesca Longo Auricchio; "Longo" indicates line numbers in this text. See Chandler, "Philodemus on Art and Rhetoric," 81–103.

References

Aphthonius. *Preliminary Exercises of Apthonius. Progymnasmata: Greek Textbooks of Prose Composition.* Trans. George A. Kennedy. Fort Collins: Chez l'auteur, 1999. Print.

Biesecker, Barbara. "Michel Foucault and the Question of Rhetoric." *Philosophy and Rhetoric* 25 (1992): 351–64. Print.

Blair, Carole and Martha Cooper. "The Humanist Turn in Foucault's Rhetoric of Inquiry." *Quarterly Journal of Speech* 73 (1987): 151–71. Print.

Boas, George. "Fact and Legend in the Biography of Plato." *Philosophical Review* 57 (1948): 439–57. Print.

Chandler, Clive. "Introduction." *Philodemus on Rhetoric: Translation and Exegitical Essays.* London: Routledge, 2005. 1–17. Print.

———. "Philodemus on Art and Rhetoric." *Philodemus on Rhetoric: Translation and Exegitical Essays.* London: Routledge, 2005. 81–103. Print.

———. "*Psychagogia* and Philodemus' *On Rhetoric*." *Philodemus on Rhetoric: Translation and Exegitical Essays.* London: Routledge, 2005. 147–67. Print.

Cicero. *De Oratore.* Trans. E. W. Sutton and H. Rackham. 2 vols. Cambridge: Harvard UP, 1967–1968. Print.

———. *Orator.* Trans. H. M. Hubbell. Cambridge: Harvard UP, 1939. Print.

———. *Tusculan Disputations, On the Nature of the Gods, and On the Commonwealth.* Trans. C. D. Yonge. New York: Harper Brothers, 1877. Print.

Colclough, David. *Freedom of Speech in Early Stuart England.* Cambridge: Cambridge UP, 2005. Print.

Cooper, Martha. "Rhetorical Criticism and Foucault's Philosophy of Discursive Events." *Central States Speech Journal* 39 (1988): 1–17. Print.

Danisch, Robert. "Power and the Celebration of the Self: Michel Foucault's Epideictic Rhetoric." *Southern Communication Journal* 71 (2006): 291–307. Print.

Demosthenes. *Orations I—XVII, XX: Olynthiacs, Philippics, Minor Orations.* Trans. J. H. Vince. Cambridge: Harvard UP, 1930. Print.

Diogenes, Laertius. *Lives of Eminent Philosophers. 2 vols.* Trans. R. D. Hicks. Cambridge: Harvard UP, 1930. Print.

Diodorus, Siculus. *The Historical Library of Diodorus of Sicily: Diodorus of Sicily.* Trans. H. Oldfather. 12 vols. Cambridge: Harvard UP, 1954. Print.

Edelstein, Ludwig. *Plato's Seventh Letter.* Leiden: Brill, 1966. Print.

Engberg-Pederson, Troels. "Plutarch to Prince Philopappus on How to Tell a Flatterer from a Friend." *Friendship, Flattery, and Frankness of Speech: Studies on Friendship in the New Testament World.* Ed. John T. Fitzgerald. Leiden: Brill, 1996. 61–82. Print.

Euripides. *Ion. The Bacchae and Other Plays.* Trans. Philip Vellacott. New York: Penguin, 1980. Print.

———. *Orestes. Orestes and Other Plays.* Trans. Philip Vellacott. New York: Penguin, 1980. Print.

Fitzgerald, John T., ed. *Friendship, Flattery, and Frankness of Speech: Studies on Friendship in the New Testament World.* Leiden: Brill, 1996. Print.

Foucault, Michel. *The Care of the Self*. Trans. Robert Hurley. New York: Vintage, 1988. Print.

———. *The Courage of Truth (The Government of Self and Others II): Lectures at the Collège De France 1983–84*. Trans. Graham Burchell. Ed. Frédéric Gros. New York: Palgrave McMillan. Print.

———. *Fearless Speech*. Los Angeles, CA: Semiotext(e), 2001. Print.

———. *The Government of Self and Others: Lectures at the Collège De France 1982–83*. Trans. Graham Burchell. Ed. Frédéric Gros. New York: Palgrave McMillan. Print.

———. *The Hermeneutics of the Subject: Lectures at the Collège de France, 1981–1982*. Trans. Graham Burchell. Ed. Frédéric Gros. New York: Palgrave McMillan. Print.

Geisler, Cheryl. "How We Ought to Understand the Concept of Rhetorical Agency. Report from ARS." *Rhetoric Society Quarterly* 34 (2004): 9–17. Print.

Gilbert, Christopher. "In *Dubiis Libertas*: A Diogenic Attitude for a Politics of Distrust." *Rhetoric Society Quarterly* 42 (2012): 1–25. Print.

Harding, Phillip. "The Purpose of Isokrates' *Archidamos* and *On the Peace*." *California Studies in Classical Antiquity* 6 (1973): 137–49. Print.

Hariman, Robert, ed. *Prudence: Classical Virtue, Postmodern Practice*. University Park: Penn State UP, 2003. Print.

Henderson, Gae Lynn. "The 'Parrhesiastic Game': Textual Self-Justification in Spiritual Narratives of Early Modern Women." *Rhetoric Society Quarterly* 37 (2007): 423–51. Print.

Isocrates. *Against the Sophists. Isocrates II*. Trans. George Norlin. Cambridge: Harvard UP, 1928–1929. Print.

———. *Areopagiticus. Isocrates II*. Trans. George Norlin. Cambridge: Harvard UP, 1928–1929. Print.

———. *On the Peace. Isocrates II*. Trans. George Norlin. Cambridge: Harvard UP, 1928–1929. Print.

———. *To Antipater. Isocrates III*. Trans. LaRue Van Hook. Cambridge: Harvard UP, 1928. Print.

———. *To Nicocles. Isocrates I*. Trans. George Norlin. Cambridge: Harvard UP, 1928–1929. Print.

Jaeger, Werner. *In Search of the Divine Centre*. Trans. Gilbert Highet. New York: Oxford UP, 1943. Print.

Landauer, Matthew. "*Parrhesia* and the *Demos Tyrannos*: Frank Speech, Flattery, and Accountability in Democratic Athens." *History of Political Thought* 33 (2012): 185–208. Print.

Lévy, Carlos. "Politics to Philosophy and Theology: Some Remarks about Foucault's Interpretation of *Parrêsia* in Two Recently Published Seminars." *Philosophy & Rhetoric*. 42 (2009): 313–25. Print.

Lundberg, Christian and Joshua Gunn. " 'Ouija Board, Are There Any Communications?' Agency, Ontotheology, and the Death of the Humanist Subject, or, Continuing the ARS Conversation." *Rhetoric Society Quarterly* 35 (2005): 83–105. Print.

McGushin, Edward F. *Foucault's Asēksis: An Introduction to the Philosophical Life*. Evanston: Northwestern U, 2007. Print.

McKerrow, Rayme. "Critical Rhetoric in a Postmodern World." *Quarterly Journal of Speech* 77 (1991): 75–78. Print.

———. "Critical Rhetoric: Theory and Praxis." *Communication Monographs* 56 (1989): 90–111. Print.

Michelini, Ann N. "*ΠΟΛΛΗ ΑΓΡΟΙΚΙΑ*: Rudeness and Irony in Plato's *Gorgias*." *Classical Philology* 93 (1998): 50–59. Print.

Monoson, S. Sara. *Plato's Democratic Entanglements*. Princeton: Princeton UP, 2000. Print.

Morrow, Glenn R. *Plato's Epistles*. Indianapolis: Bobbs-Merrill, 1962. Print.

Muckelbauer, John. "On Reading Differently: Through Foucault's Resistance." *College English* 63 (2000): 71–94. Print.

Nilson, Herman. *Michel Foucault and the Games of Truth*. Trans. Rachel Clark. New York: St. Martin's P, 1998. Print.

Philodemus. *On Frank Criticism*. Trans. David Konstan, Diskin Clay, Clarence E. Glad, Johan C. Thom, and James Ware. Atlanta, GA: Scholars P, 1998. Print.

———. *On Rhetoric, Books 1 and 2: Translation and Exegetical Essays*. Trans. Clive Chandler. New York: Routledge, 2006. Print.

Plato. *Gorgias*. Trans. Robin Waterfield. Oxford: Oxford UP, 1994. Print.

———. *Phaedrus*. Trans. Alexander Nehamas and Paul Woodruff. Indianapolis: Hackett, 1995. Print.

———. *Timeaeus, Critas, Cleitophon, Menexenus, Epistles*. Trans. R. G. Bury. Cambridge: Harvard UP, 1929. Print.

Plochmann, Kimball George and Franklin E. Robinson. *A Friendly Companion to Plato's Gorgias*. Carbondale: Southern Illinois UP, 1988. Print.

Plutarch. "Dion." *Plutarch's Lives*. Ed. Bernadotte Perrin. Cambridge: Harvard UP, 1970. Print.

———. "How to Tell a Flatterer from a Friend." *Morals*. Trans. Several Hands; Corrected; Rev. William W. Goodwin. Vol. 1. Boston: Little, Brown, and Co., 1878. Print.

Quintilian. *The Orator's Education [Institutio Oratoria]*. Trans. Donald A. Russell. 5 vols. Cambridge, MA: Harvard UP, 2001. Print.

Raalte, Marlein van. "Socratic *Parrhesia* and Its Afterlife in Plato's *Laws*." *Sluiter and Rosen*. 2004. 279–312. Print.

Saxonhouse, Arlene W. *Free Speech and Democracy in Ancient Athens*. New York: Cambridge UP, 2006. Print.

Schofield, Malcolm. "Plato and Practical Politics." *Cambridge History of Greek and Roman Political Thought*. Ed. Malcolm Schofield and Christopher Rowe. Cambridge: Cambridge UP, 2000. 293–302. Print.

Sipiora, Phillip and James Baumlin, eds. *Rhetoric and Kairos: Essays in History, Theory, and Praxis*. Albany: SUNY P, 2002. Print.

Sluiter, Ineke and Ralph M. Rosen, eds. *Free Speech in Classical Antiquity*. Leiden: Brill, 2004. Print.

Stauffer, Devin. *The Unity of Plato's Gorgias: Rhetoric, Justice, and the Philosophic Life*. Cambridge: Cambridge UP, 2006. Print.

Tell, Dave. "Rhetoric and Power: An Inquiry into Foucault's Critique of Confession." *Philosophy and Rhetoric* 43 (2010): 95–117. Print.

Vivian, Bradford. *Being Made Strange: Rhetoric Beyond Representation*. Albany: SUNY P, 2004. Print.

Walzer, Arthur. "Teaching 'Political Wisdom': Isocrates and the Tradition of *Dissoi Logoi*." *The Viability of the Rhetorical Tradition*. Ed. Richard Graff, Arthur E. Walzer, and Janet M. Atwill. Albany: SUNY P, 2005. 113–24. Print.

18

Deep Ambivalence and Wild Objects
Toward a Strange Environmental Rhetoric

NATHANIEL A. RIVERS

> If living in history means we cannot help leaving marks on a fallen world, then the dilemma we face is to decide what kinds of marks we want to leave.
> —William Cronon, "The Trouble with Wilderness" (23)

In his essay "Burning the Shelter," Louis Owens, environmentalist and one-time United States Forest Service ranger, reflects on his assignment to burn a shelter (the White Pass shelter in Washington's Glacier Peak Wilderness) as "part of a Forest Service plan to remove all human-made objects from wilderness areas" (211). It was a plan Owens "heartily approved." For five days, Owens "dismantled the shelter and burned the old logs, piling and burning and piling and burning until nothing remained" (211–12). "At the end of those five days," Owens writes, "I felt good, very smug in fact, about returning the White Pass meadow to its 'original' state" (212).

Returning from Glacier Peak, Owens encountered two old, Native American women hiking up the mountain. They were headed to the shelter Owens had just finished destroying. Their father built the cabin when he himself worked for the Forest Service. The old women were neither upset nor shocked by the cabin's destruction. As Owens describes it, taking the time to detail the two women's things ("thick wool caps," "small backpacks," and "staffs"), they were prepared with a plastic tarp, which they "would put inside the hemlock grove above the meadow, and the scaly hemlock branches would turn back the snow. They forgave me without saying it—my ignorance part of the long pattern of loss they knew so well" (212–13).

For Owens, this episode and his own actions and attitude performs the current environmental crisis: the assumption that humans are separate from nature and that our chief ethical, environmental task is to remove ourselves as much as possible. "Gradually, almost painfully," he writes, "I began to understand that what I called 'wilderness' was an absurdity" (213). He goes on, tracing the historical precedent of his smugness: "In embracing a philosophy that saw the White Pass shelter—and all traces of humanity—as a shameful stain upon the 'pure' Wilderness, I had succumbed to a 500-year-old pattern of deadly thinking that separates us from the natural world"—a pattern of thought deeply rooted in the Western tradition—"that sees humanity and 'wilderness' as mutually exclusive" (213). Owens argues that such thinking grounds "the global environmental crisis that sends species into extinction daily and threatens to destroy all life" (213).

Owens's story succinctly captures and critiques a troubling environmental rhetoric that places humans *outside* of nature. Owens concludes, "Our native ancestors all over this continent lived within a complex web of relations with the natural world, and in doing so they assumed responsibility for their world that contemporary Americans cannot even imagine" (213–14). Owens's insistence on complex relations gestures toward the kind of strange environmental rhetoric I want to mark. Its strangeness lies in the call for more relations and not less—not a removal of humans from the environment, which is the value underlying much contemporary environmentalism, but another way of comporting ourselves with environments. However, a call for renewed, complex relations may not be enough anymore. What might Owens mean by "assume responsibility" when the form of our response-ability is precisely what he is calling into question? For instance, the National Climate Assessment (NCA), released in 2014 by the US Global Change Research Program, summarized "the impacts of climate change on the United States, now and in the future" (iii). Drawing on an impressive array of sources and vetted by an extensive public review process, the ultimate aim of the report is to advance "understanding of [the challenge of climate change] and the need for the American people to prepare for and *respond to* its far-reaching implications" (3; emphasis added). We are in a moment when fully thinking through response-ability is a pressing national and international need. Recent theoretical work inside and around rhetorical theory pushes even further than Owens, intensifying the very idea of relations to a stranger place.

We need to think about rhetoric (and relations) more intensely both in the practice of rhetoric and in our study and theorizing of it. What is the place of rhetoric, who engages in rhetoric, and what exactly counts as rhetoric or as an effect or product of rhetoric? My argument is that environmentalism specifically needs a more intense rhetoric—one engaged not simply in human discourse, but in the nonhuman, in the object. As Bruce Foltz remarks in his Heideggerian analysis of the current environmental crisis, "it is . . . pertinent to speak of a genuine *krisis*: a deciding, a judgment, a sentence in which not only our future survival, but our comportment toward nature in general is called into question" (324). A crisis for Foltz is not a problem to be solved, but a kairotic opening through which we shape the world to come. We cannot decide once and for all what our responsibility is. Not everything we have built should stay; not everything we have done is wise and good. But the questions of what is done, what is not done, and what is undone require a more complex decision-making process.

Environmentalism and its concomitant rhetorics, however, frequently draw a bold line between humans and nonhuman nature: the animate and inanimate, and the animal, vegetable, and mineral. Nature, it is presumed, is that which is free from human contact and intervention. The way forward for environmentalism, then, is to lessen the impact and amount of human intervention: environments need to be preserved and/or conserved; wilderness areas need to be reclaimed or left apart from what humans have settled. We see this particular line of environmentalism at work in calls to reduce our footprint. Countering such environmentalisms, the environmental historian William Cronon, in his (in)famous "The Trouble with Wilderness," writes,

> the trouble with wilderness is that it quietly expresses and reproduces the very values its devotees seek to reject. The flight from history that is very nearly the core of wilderness represents the false hope of an escape from responsibility, the illusion that we can somehow wipe clean the slate of our past and return to the *tabula rasa* that supposedly existed before we began to leave our marks on the world.
>
> (16)

The flight from history Cronon describes echoes what Owen calls a troubling pattern of thought: the ontological fissuring of the human from the nonhuman.

However, Cronon's critique of "wilderness" is not full-throated. In the conclusion of the same piece, he notes that he is "forced to confront [his] own deep ambivalence about [wilderness's] meaning for modern environmentalism" (22). On the one hand, he argues, the notion of wilderness disconnects humans from their environment and thus often produces irresponsible behavior. The split between wilderness areas and settled areas works to activate all sorts of irresponsible behavior. For instance, we pick up after ourselves at Yosemite and then spray our sidewalks with Roundup. That is, we let ourselves off the hook when we imagine ourselves as out of nature. "On the other hand," Cronon writes,

> I also think it no less crucial for us to recognize and honor nonhuman nature as a world we did not create, a world with its own independent, non-human reasons for being as it is. The autonomy of nonhuman nature seems to me an indispensable corrective to human arrogance.
>
> (22)

Thomas Birch's treatment of wildness, which predates Cronon's ambivalence by a few years, resonates with Cronon.[1] Birch responds to the trouble with wilderness by stressing wildness. For Birch, wilderness areas become places where wildness is incarcerated. Birch aims, "to expose the bad faith that taints our mainstream justifications for wilderness preservation and to sting us out of it toward a more ethical relationship with wild nature, with wildness itself, and thereby with one another" (446). The move from wilderness to wildness and the chorus of calls for relations work to replace the human and the nonhuman on equal and agonistic footing.

Cronon's and Birch's critiques of wilderness are where I begin to trace a strange environmental rhetoric that gives wild objects their full due (in their withdrawn strangeness and vitality). Theirs is the beginning of the strange environmental rhetoric implicit in Owens's reflection on his own actions. I build from the assumption that much environmental rhetoric overemphasizes human agency. By giving ourselves the responsibility to save or fix the planet, we have over-invested in our own agency, enacting the same hubris that results in dispositions toward the nonhuman nature that environmentalists themselves might very well (and rightly) condemn. Drawing on work in new materialism and object-oriented ontology, I suggest that we can neither fully understand nor determine the environment and that we need a strange environmental rhetoric alive to this suggestion. Rethinking environmental rhetoric in terms of the nonhuman also requires a shift in how we think about rhetoric more generally.

Specifically, I hope to complicate environmental rhetorics that continue to reinscribe an unnecessary division between human and the nonhuman nature. To this end, I employ work in object-oriented ontology (OOO) and new materialism. In his review essay of philosopher Graham Harman (a key figure, along with Ian Bogost, Levi Bryant, and Timothy Morton, in OOO), Scot Barnett summarizes the OOO position:

> the project of object-oriented philosophy involves two key moves: first, the recognition of the ontology of individual objects or tool-beings and their perpetual withdrawal from other objects in the world; and second the attunement to the reality and implications of these objects coming into relation with one another and how those relations in turn produce new objects whose depths, like any other object, can never be fully known or expressed in language.

Object-oriented philosophy is part of a broader trend which seeks the reality of objects without reifying or reducing them. OOO walks the narrow path between scientific realism, which undermines objects into their component parts, and social construction, which overmines objects into their significance for humans—between equally untenable realism and idealism. Countering the philosophic project of criticism that reduces objects to either their features or to the human fetishists behind them, OOO invites wonder, which entails both astonishment and puzzlement.

New materialism is a project distinct from OOO. Describing her own brand of new materialism as "a kind of vitalism, an enchanted materialism" (447), the political theorist Jane Bennett articulates her own ontology this way: "I mean the ability of bodies [human, nonhuman, animate, inanimate] to become otherwise than they are, to press out of their current configuration and enter into new compositions of self as well as into new alliances and rivalries with others" (447). Bennett describes this ability as *thing-power*. Both OOO and new materialism posit a world full of vibrant objects with their own material-rhetorical agency that exceeds our particular abilities as humans to either describe or delimit.

Object-oriented ontology and new materialism can thus complicate and invigorate environmental rhetoric.[2] Individual objects, which I read broadly to include both the animate and inanimate, and the animal, vegetable, and mineral, perpetually withdraw from us and each other—they remain wild in never being fully known or controlled by us. And those *wild objects* relate with one another in ways unknown to us (as wild objects ourselves) and produce effects we cannot codify and might very well find threatening. Objects do not need to be kept wild; objects remain wild even in the midst of interaction. Wildness is inherent in them and is present even when we are. Such wildness is *everywhere*: Antarctica, Yellowstone, a city playground, the air ducts in my house, my desk drawer, and my large intestine. "Nature is wild, always wild," Birch argues, "in the sense that it is not subject to human control. . . . [H]umans are participants in a wildness that is far larger and more powerful than they can ever be, and to which human law bringing is so radically inappropriate as to be simply absurd" (460).

Extending object-oriented ontology and new materialism, I use Cronon's deep ambivalence toward "wilderness" and build on Birch's treatment of "wildness" to mark the strange environmentalism arrived at by Owens in the White Pass. Deep ambivalence names our agonistic entanglement with nonhuman nature that continually withdraws and resists human mastery. My argument necessarily traces a winding path. First, I explicate the environmental rhetoric I wish to complicate. Second, I articulate the OOO and new materialism I use to complicate this version of environmental rhetoric. Third, employing these ontological frameworks, I elaborate Cronon's deep ambivalence as an alternative, strange environmental rhetoric. Finally, I return to Owens's burning of the shelter asking how we might attend to the attitude Owens arrives at only after having burned the shelter and subsequently encountering the two Native American women. Owens's story is compelling, but toward what kinds of new rhetorics does it push us? Speculating upon what a strange environmental rhetoric might look like, I turn to the film *Trollhunter*, which performs deep ambivalence as a strange environmental rhetoric. Ultimately, deep ambivalence means only that we leave open as radically kairotic, as rhetorical, the question of our responsibility to the wild objects with whom we inhabit the earth. As such, deep ambivalence is applicable to rhetorical theory more generally. As Carl Herndl and Stuart Brown argue, "the field of environmental rhetoric is immense and remarkably varied, so varied in fact that we think it connects almost every part of our social and intellectual life, crossing boundaries between various academic disciplines and social institutions" (4). To think through environmentalism is to think through rhetoric.

Reading and Writing Contemporary Environmentalism

No one knows what an environment can do.
—Bruno Latour, *Politics of Nature* (80)

Environmentalism has always been heterogeneous, and the contours of our responsibility have been (re)defined many times.[3] Contention arises, then, in terms of how best to address the environment, to speak for or about it, to raise awareness, and to motivate action.[4] Considering the state of the planet, it should come as no surprise that achieving stasis is a problem for environmentalism. This section addresses the contemporary scene of both environmentalism and its rhetoric as well as scholarly discussions of environmental rhetoric—both rhetors and rhetoricians. This section sets the scene for the intervention of deep ambivalence. For some time there have been preservationists and conservationists, deep ecologists, and those calling for sustainability, efficiency, or sufficiency. Although spanning the globe, environmentalism is intensely local and personal, and so emerges movements like environmental justice that address not simply preservation or conservation of "wilderness," which are seen as preserving it only for a privileged few, but also urban environments where humans live as well. The concerns of environmentalism are present in all human agoras. Environmental rhetoric, then, addresses people and their relationships with both the humans and nonhumans who inhabit the global agora. It also concerns the future of that world and, by extension, everyone and everything in it. Given Herndl and Brown's observation, it is clear that I am not the first to contend that environmentalism is *the* issue for all time: no other issue could be more pressing. No issue could matter more.

If ever rhetoric were to work then surely it would be for the environment—its survival and thus our own. In traditional terms, environmental rhetoric attempts two things: convince an audience of the connection between human agency and efficacy and current environmental events or conditions. In other words, it hopes to demonstrate that humans have some definite effect through some concrete and identifiable means. Employing rhetoric, however, is never so clear cut. Debates and questions of strategy and tactics loom large, and it is on these questions that rhetoricians have largely focused. Should we call it global warming or climate change? Should we stress economic incentives? Should we privilege human concerns over the value of wildlife itself? It is a difficult challenge: just ask Al Gore on a good day. Second, such rhetoric must persuade the same audience that other human agencies must be employed to produce amelioratory effects. Much scholarship on environmental rhetoric explores how this is or can be done and how it is (frequently) countered or resisted. These are good questions in pursuit of a worthy goal, but they are not the only questions nor the only goals.

We can see these questions at work in discussions of science and technology relative to climate change. This resonance makes explicit some of the tacit assumptions in environmentalism. While arguing, "It would surely be irresponsible to question the reality of climate change, to vacillate at the point of action," sociologist Bronislaw Szerszynski writes, "it is the dominant technological framing of climate change that ultimately constitutes a more radical evasion of responsibility" (22). In other words, the problem's framing puts humans outside of the environment.

> To frame our predicament in this way is already to approach the weather with a very narrow set of questions. "Is it changing? How fast? Are we to blame? Can we alter it?" This way of reading propels us inexorably towards a calculative technological response of which the hubris of geoengineering is only the most blatant, emblematic form. We are also being drawn to forms of mitigation that presume to calculate the weather and promise to make it stable, and forms of adaptation which have at their heart a soteriological dream of security which can only ever be within the reach of the fortunate, and only then through its own forms of externalization.
>
> (Szerszynski 23)

This "framing of out predicament" Szerszynski refers to as reading and writing the weather, and "[i]t is too early to know if it is too late" (11). The idea that we are too late in reading our impact is troubling, but Szerszynski nevertheless describes it as "reassuring":

> first, we unknowingly marked the climate; then we learned to read those marks, to turn them into meaningful signs; through learning to read them we learned the laws governing our marking; and through learning to read the marks well, we are thereby learning to control our marking.
>
> (11)

While I am not dismissing such a course of action, I would like to suggest that there is a larger problem afoot here: the stress on and drive toward human mastery of the environment.

That detachment and alienation result from hubris is perhaps unsurprising—that such hubris pervades opposing sides of the debate about the environment perhaps is. "Fix" and "Save" resonate with "Slash and Burn"—both reduce environments to what we can say and do about them. "Our relation with the weather has been pulled towards a certain kind of reading that constitutes it as a code that can be mastered and controlled" (Szerszynski 19). The ideas of control and calculation built into our efforts to save the planet are the very same motives that move so-called exploiters of the environment. In much the same way that rhetoricians have drawn from critiques of technical reason (notably Andrew Feenberg), which is very much at play in the environmentalisms Szerszynski critiques, I am suggesting that rhetoricians should critically attend to environmentalisms that implicitly privilege human control. That is, rhetoricians focused on environmental matters should mark stranger environmental rhetorics that do not remake (even perhaps unwittingly) the sorts of ontological presuppositions that currently short-circuit environmentalism.

In Szerszynski's terms, the problem with something like Al Gore's *An Inconvenient Truth* is that it operates within the same logical parameters as its opposite. Gore suggests that with the right amount of data and the correct political will, humans can reverse the trend of global climate change and save the earth. Through our awesome technological might we have rewritten the face of the Earth. Through our awesome scientific might we can now, finally, read the earth and see the true effect of our awful agency. But, fear not, for it is that agency that will allow us to re-write (or right) the earth again. "Firstly," Szerszynski writes, "there are approaches which try to modulate the metabolism of the human-technology ensemble with its environment by reducing anthropogenic CO_2 emissions, typically by either reducing the amount of energy used or reducing its carbon-intensity" (17). Szerszynski continues:

> Secondly, a rather different set of climate technics work by intervening in the Earth's wider metabolic processes. They seek in a more direct way to make the weather an object of technological control, in an echo of the cold-war, military origins of climate change science. Such technocratic approaches, more favoured in the USA, are framed in terms of "geoengineering" or "global environmental management."
>
> (17)

This environmentalism is at work in *An Inconvenient Truth*. As Laura Johnson argues, *Truth* performs a "*tempered* apocalypticism, one that mixes apocalyptic appeals with scientific rationalism" (31; emphasis in the original). Such a mixture, however, leaves unchallenged the primacy, uniqueness, and universality of human agency. Gore's faith in human agency is a mirror image of the faith of the robber baron and the oil magnate.

In 2002 atmospheric chemist Paul Crutzen proposed that the current geological epoch be designated the "Anthropocene" to mark its status as "in many ways human-dominated" (23). Crutzen does so without obvious pride. He remarks: "A daunting task lies ahead for scientists and engineers to guide society towards environmentally sustainable management during the era of the Anthropocene" (23). This admonishment is built on an unsettling amount of hubris. Humans have overstepped their bounds and now dominate the environment; never fear, though, for this self-same domination is likewise the cure. It is telling that Crutzen sees the Anthropocene as daunting only for scientists and engineers who will lead the rest of us, we assume, to safety. If the environment is a code that can be read, mastered, and controlled, then the environmentalism suggested by this understanding will be anything but fully democratic or agonistic (much less object-oriented). And so we send Louis Owens up the mountain to remove our presence. Rather than acknowledging our place alongside other wild objects within an environment—which is ago-nistic by virtue of its contact and contingency—we see the maintenance of our disconnect from nature in order to save it: a failure to acknowledge not simply the limits of human agency, but that human agency emerges with, alongside, and sometimes against the agency of others.

There are, then, forms of environmentalism that, despite the best of inten-tions, nevertheless adopt positions that undermine their own goals. The pres-ence of such environmentalisms suggest that many views of the environment (at times seemingly at odds) are often different sides of the same coin: the coin that privileges the human, which almost always results in what Jimmie Killingsworth and Jacqueline Palmer describe as "humankind's 'alienation from nature'" (4). To return to Owens and the burning of the shelter, however, we see how such alienation can operate within environmentalism itself. Owens suggests that our efforts to save the wild are a kind of alienation. My response to such detachment and alienation is another kind of detachment altogether: Cronon's "deep ambiv-alence" or what is in object-oriented approaches called *withdrawal*. Not detach-ment but ambivalence: not alienation but the alien. The environment is finally not a problem to be identified and then solved, but a fundamental agonism (a *krisis*) that we must always work through—rhetoric's work is never done.

New Ontologies for a Strange Environmental Rhetoric

> Behind every apparently simple object is an infinite legion of further objects that
> "crush, depress, break, and enthrall one another."
>
> —Graham Harman, *Tool-Being*

While there are a range of thinkers I could employ in articulating the object-oriented and new materialist thought I am bringing to bear on contempo-rary environmental rhetoric, I highlight two particularly accomplished think-ers: Graham Harman, a philosopher, works on what he calls OOO, which is a primary strain of speculative realism, while Jane Bennett, a political theorist, works on what she calls vital materialism, which is a major strain of new mate-rialism. Harman admonishes us to consider objects in and of themselves—he articulates objects as wild even in the midst of relations—and Bennett's project maintains wild objects as vital while pulling them into relations (or what she, working from Gilles Deleuze and Félix Guattari, calls assemblages), arguing that it is only through such relations that any thing has agency. I should make it clear here that Bennett and Harman represent distinct projects that might very well be at odds: the relationship between speculative realisms such as OOO and new materialism has yet to be fully articulated. Harman, invested in the complete autonomy of objects, allows us to focus on them as strange. Bennett, focused on relations, allows us to place objects into assemblages that in turn produce unexpected outcomes. OOO attends to the strangeness of objects while new materialism increases the viscosity of their relations.

Both Bennett and Harman enunciate a response to the human-centrism of much contemporary philosophical and the political thought. Harman and his allies argue that philosophy (and its Kantian legacy) largely concerns itself with the problem of access (epistemology) rather than things in and of themselves (ontology). Bennett's new materialism (of which there are other flavors) advocates "the vitality of matter" on behalf of a more overtly political project. For example, Bennett examines the 2003 power blackout that affected large parts of North America. Calling the blackout a "cascade of effects" (37), she attributes the power outage not simply to human faults and failures but also to, for instance, electricity itself. "Electricity sometimes goes where we send it, and sometimes it chooses its path on the spot, in response to the other bodies it encounters and the surprising opportunities for actions interactions that they afford" (28). Whereas OOO privileges the autonomy of objects, new materialisms want to trace the work of all actors in assemblages. Despite their differences or, more accurately, because of them, both serve environmentalism in attending to *both* the irreducible wildness *and* fundamental entanglement of objects.

Harman's core argument is that *all* objects withdraw from *all* relations, and that human beings do not exist on some distinct ontological plain. Harman writes, "object-oriented philosophy holds that the relation of humans to pollen, oxygen, eagles, or windmills is no different in kind from the interaction of these objects with each other" (*Guerilla* 1). All objects attempt to reduce other objects but ever fail to fully capture or know them. Fire reduces cotton to its flammable features; humans reduce hammers to tools; hammers reduce nails to hammer-able objects. "The fact that humans seem to have more cognitive power than shale or cantaloupe," he argues, "does not justify grounding this difference in a basic ontological dualism" (83). For Harman everything is an object, and objects are not finally reducible, knowable, or exhaustible. All we ever know of objects are their surface features. Although, and lest we reinscribe Plato's allegory of the cave, these surface features are not to be gotten behind to find the real object underneath, even within the object there is wildness, as objects withdraw even from their own features. Inside objects there are only other objects just as withdrawn. There is for Harman an infinite regress of objects inside of other objects. Objects cannot be discovered in the traditional sense, not because of some practical limit that humans face, but because the object is in itself strange and withdrawn. "Objects," Harman argues elsewhere, "are units that both display and conceal a multitude of traits" (*Quadruple* 7). Withdrawal moves in both directions, and withdrawal is a feature of humans and nonhumans alike.

The structure of all relations that emerges from Harman is predicated on this withdrawal. We only ever glance off of other objects, which in turn only ever glance off of other objects. Objects know one another only by their exhaust: those parts of them that escape into our view. This is the speculation of speculative realism: objects are real not because they are fully present, but are real because they are constantly withdrawing. It is in light of withdrawal that Harman writes, "Contrary to the usual view, what we really want is to be *objects*—not as means to an end like paper or oil, but in the sense that we want to be like the Grand Canyon or a guitar hero or a piece of silver: distinct forces to be reckoned with" (*Guerilla* 140; emphasis in the original).

To flesh out what it might mean *to be reckoned with*, I turn to Bennett's work on "a political ecology of things," and her focus both on the philosophical project of countering "the idea of matter as passive stuff, as raw, brute, or inert" (viii) and the political project of encouraging "more intelligent and sustainable engagements with vibrant matter and lively things" (viii). Like Cronon, Bennett is concerned about our relations with other things, and she too wonders, "whether environmentalism remains the best way to frame the problems" (110). Also echoing Owens, Bennett notes that as she moved from standard environmentalism to what she calls vital materialism, "from a world of nature versus culture to a heterogeneous monism of vibrant bodies, I find the ground beneath my old ethical maxim, 'tread lightly on the earth' to be less solid" (121). The crumbling of this ground owes itself to a position not unlike Harman's. This is the vitalism of her vital materialism, which sees vitality as "the capacity of things—edibles, commodities, storms, metals—not only to impede or block the will and designs of humans but also to act as quasi agents or forces with trajectories, propensities, or tendencies of their own" (viii).[5] Bennett is after what she calls "a primordial swerve," which

> says that the world is not determined, that an element of chanciness resides at the heart of things, but it also affirms that so-called inanimate things have a life, that deep within is an inexplicable vitality or energy, a moment of independence from and resistance to us and other bodies: a kind of thing-power.
>
> (18)

An object is wild not only in its ability to resist but also in its ability to do its own thing.

But, unlike Harman, Bennett places things into constitutive relations: she removes them from the vacuum in which Harman places them. While OOO might portend inaction in the face of wildness, Bennett's new materialism emphasis interaction. She is fully concerned with relations between vital objects with their own ontological weight. As we move away from the warrants of environmentalism that Owens, Cronon, Birch, and Szerszynski critique, Bennett persuasively argues that we must "Give up the futile attempt to disentangle the human from the nonhuman. Seek instead to engage more civilly, strategically, and subtly with the nonhumans in the assemblages in which you, too, participate" (116). The thing-power of all bodies is precisely what constitutes the world as we know it. To imagine ourselves apart from this, or to see disentanglement as the ethical way forward, is to mistake not just some vague obligation to relate, but to a necessary participation in the agonistic assemblages that give life. We must also recognize that such assemblages are forever beyond our ability to name them, know them, control them, or correct them. Our obligation is shot through with risk, contingency, and strife: in short, agonism. With this recognition of thing-power as a constitutive force, we get closer to deep ambivalence.

Deep Ambivalence

> the feeling of affirming life despite its ambivalent incomprehensibility.
> —Rachel Greenwald Smith, "Materialism, Ecology, Aesthetics"

Vitality and withdrawal define wild objects in ways that allow us to reckon with them without reducing them. Deep ambivalence enacts the rhetoric of OOO and new materialism. "Ambivalence" derives from the German *ambivalenz*, which means equivalence or equivalency. In 1912, in the pages of *Lancet*, German psychologist Eugene Bleuler used *ambivalency* to name "a condition which gives to the same idea two contrary feeling-tones and invests the same thought simultaneously with both a positive and negative character" ("ambivalence"). Furthermore, the Latin root *ambi* means both or both sides, as in ambidextrous. In the oscillation of ambivalence, there is an attitude of equivalence. To feel ambivalent is to be equivalent. Deep ambivalence is thus an ontologically flavored rhetoric predicated on a kind of being in the world: being across a flat ontology in which all beings are equally emplaced. Deep ambivalence discloses the rhetoricity of all being in acknowledging the being otherwise of things in relations. Recall that the deep ambivalence I am describing here was born of an individual deeply committed to environmentalism. Cronon devoted considerable time to reflecting on the environment, about nature, and about "wilderness." That he arrived at "deep ambivalence," which he came to honestly, earnestly, and in light of the work he had done, is significant. A hard-earned and deep ambivalence is a worthy environmental rhetoric.

Like Harman and Bennett, in *Ecology without Nature*, Tim Morton helps us think through the implications of object-oriented and new materialist thought for environmental rhetoric, and does so through aesthetics. Whereas Harman is a philosopher and Bennett is a political theorist, Morton is a literary scholar concerned explicitly with environmental aesthetics. What I call wild objects Morton calls the strange stranger. Strangeness inheres even as we think of wild objects: "Life forms recede into strangeness the more we think about them, and whenever they encounter one another—the strangeness is irreducible" ("Here Comes Everything" 165). Morton argues, "ecological philosophy that does not attend to this strangeness is not thinking coexistence deeply enough" (165). The same is true for environmentalism, which often un-stranges the stranger in doing its work. Think again of how the rhetoric of *An Inconvenient Truth*—even in the title—is contingent on an accurate knowing of the environment in order to effect changes in behavior. As Szerszynski argues, "This story is one in which the diagnostic task of establishing the truth of anthropogenic climate change naturally gives way to the practical one of finding effective political and technical responses to it" (10). Is it possible to look into the eyes of a polar bear and see a strange stranger? A vital body with its own kind of thing-power? A wild object capable of making trouble, of biting back? A citizen-being who saunters into the agora making demands, making enemies, making friends? The reality of wild objects cannot be reduced, and it is in light of the irreducible strangeness of wild objects that we turn to deep ambivalence.

What Morton proposes with melancholia is a mode of engagement and intimacy predicated on strangeness. "Melancholia is precisely a mode of intimacy with strange objects that can't be digested by the subject" ("Here Comes Everything" 175). Melancholia is neither the resignation of depression nor the euphoria of mania: melancholia resonates strongly with Cronon's deep ambivalence, which is itself not resignation but recognition of and respect for strangeness. The consequences of shaking off our melancholia are dire, for it "starts to tell us the truth about the withdrawn quality of objects" (176). Read in concert with Morton, Szerszynski is confronting precisely those contemporary environmentalisms that attempt to shake off melancholia: "no decoding of [the weather] will tell us what we need to do, what level of emissions is safe, when we have 'done our bit,' when we have 'fixed the climate'" (Szerszynski 24). If objects withdraw, as Harman argues, then a decoding that leads to salvation is out as a viable environmentalism.

The project of decoding that Szerszynski describes can be countered by the melancholic mode of Cronon's deep ambivalence, which is neither the detachment of alienation nor the fantasy of decoding. Deep ambivalence, like melancholia, "is the default mode of [object-oriented] subjectivity: an object-like coexistence with other objects and the otherness of objects—touching them, touching the untouchable, dwelling on the dark side one can never know, living in endless twilight shadows" (Morton, "Here Comes Everything" 176). An inconvenient truth, we might say, that cannot be charted or fully digested. Deep ambivalence is wrapping your head, your hands, and your heart around that which you cannot completely wrap anything. Such ambivalence, as a feature of all objects and their relations, is already a style of engagement.

The basic ontological features described by Morton and others suggest a strange environmental rhetoric of wild objects. To speak of ambivalence everywhere—to speak of an ambivalent polar bear, for instance—is no doubt strange. But recall Bennett's claim that thing-power is both resistance and volition and Harman's critique of any ontological distinction between humans and nonhumans. To say that ambivalence is a feature of all objects is not to say that a polar bear's ambivalence is like mine. It is simply to acknowledge ontological equivalence. Wild objects are deeply ambivalent, but this does not mean disconnected. It means only that connections do not fully exhaust an object. Objects remain wild not in remaining untouched, but even in the midst of contact and of relations. In any relation there is excess, there is wildness unavoidably—a wildness we can neither preserve nor conserve, neither expend nor exhaust. Of course, this does not mean that there are not stakes or risks: a dead polar bear is wild, but it is still dead. The question, then, is what difference deep ambivalence makes in addressing the flight from history and evasion of responsibility that are at the heart of Owens's and Cronon's trouble with wilderness.

The challenge is thus operationalizing this ambivalence. How do we craft environmental rhetoric from this specific kind of ambivalence as an attitude? What sorts of agoras do we need? We must first recognize that ambivalence is not a solely human affair. "At some level," Morton argues, resonating with Folz's treatment of *krisis,*

> respecting other species and ecosystems involves a choice. This choice is saturated with contingency (it is our choice) and desire (we want something to be otherwise). There is no place outside the sphere of this contingent choice from which to stand and assess the situation—no "nature" outside the problem of global warming that will come and fill us in on how to work.
>
> ("Here Comes Everything" 167)

We are stuck here and we have to act everyday as we live alongside an innumerable and unknowable number of species. We have to build shelters, we have to eat, we have to live and survive. "Coming up with a new worldview means dealing with how humans experience their place in the world. *Aesthetics thus performs a crucial role,* establishing ways of feeling and perceiving this place" (*Ecology* 2; emphasis in the original). Morton thus asks, "What kinds of political and social thinking, making, and doing are possible?" (4). The aesthetic, rhetorical work we must always do is to find ways to relate through deep ambivalence. In this passage Morton echoes Kenneth Burke and the latter's treatment of literature as equipment for living. "One seeks to 'direct the larger movements and operations' in one's campaign of living," Burke writes. "One 'maneuvers,' and the maneuvering is an 'art'" (cited in Morton 298). This talk of maneuvering is agonistic: campaigns and maneuvers, if perhaps too militaristic, certainly point up the confrontational nature of living. They likewise attend to the emplaced nature of living: maneuvering takes place on the ground. And it is this grounded maneuvering toward which I now turn.

The Allegory of the Trollhunter

> Everyday has been a struggle with and for trolls.
>
> —Thomas, *Trollhunter*

A young Norwegian university student wearing a blue jacket is running into a forest. A camera and a boom microphone follow his footsteps. He has been brought here by a man claiming to be a trollhunter: someone who clandestinely manages trolls on behalf of the government. The young man and his friends, part of a crew filming a documentary on bear poaching, are running toward strange animal sounds and bright ultraviolet flashes of light. The trees and the underbrush slow them—there is confusion; there is darkness; there is noise. A man, the trollhunter, bursts into the frame of the documentary camera. He yells but one word: "TROLL!" It is equal parts surprising and hilarious.

The young man bolts, now following the footsteps of the trollhunter out of the forest. The young man, Thomas, is separated from the group, which hears him yell out in pain. Exhausted and terrified, the soon reunited group reaches the trollhunter's vehicle. Thomas has been bitten by what he suspects is a bear. However, seeing their own vehicle flipped over and gnawed on, the group eventually acknowledges the possibility that they have just encountered a troll. In a state of disbelief, Thomas considers the implications of being bitten by a creature in which he does not believe. Deeply ambivalent, perhaps, describes his attitude, which is both the state of his mind and the orientation of his body in an environment. The previously snarky and self-righteous university student has been bitten back into a reality far stranger than the one from which he thought himself apart. It is an attitude adjustment for our age, and, for the purposes of this essay, a strange environmental rhetoric worth examining.

Trollhunter—a tongue-in-cheek 2011 Norwegian film of the found footage variety (the title role is played by famed Norwegian comedian Otto Jespersen)— follows three Norwegian university students as they film a documentary about illegal bear hunting. The students are sure of themselves in their environmentalism and in their mission to protect bears, which is surely admirable. Following someone they believe to be responsible for a slew of poachings, the students discover that the individual is not hunting bears but hunting (or rather, managing) a population of trolls, which the government is keeping secret. It seems the trolls are moving beyond their traditional ranges: sheep are being killed, bridges are being damaged, and German tourists are being eaten. The trollhunter, an ex-solider named Hans, is attempting to discern what is driving the trolls so that they can be controlled. Is it habitat destruction? Is it climate change? Is the cause ultimately human? The way this strange film unfolds sheds new light on how we might answer these questions and whether or not they are the right questions after all.

Trollhunter can be viewed as the strange environmental rhetoric I am describing: it is a confrontation with our comportment toward the nonhuman, the wild. Deep ambivalence is performed in this mockumentary that begins as a student environmental exposé and quickly becomes a life-and-death crisis. The Norwegian government—via its Troll Security Service (TSS)—seeks to read and write the trolls. Throughout *Trollhunter*, we witness the trollhunter Han's describing trolls, reading newspapers for unknowing reports of troll activity, sharing the forms he uses to document each encounter, attending to troll tracks, and looking for other signs of their presence and movement. It will turn out that one troll is responsible for the trouble: he has escaped his territory. In *Trollhunter* we see wildness escape the bounds of wilderness. The "rogue" troll is infecting other trolls with an unidentified illness or virus.

A blood sample is secured—an incredibly dangerous job that involves Hans donning an almost medieval suit of armor—and taken to a veterinarian, from whom we learn about the physiology of trolls: their metabolism, their sensitivity to light, and so on. The team soon departs from the veterinary clinic and continues their journey, backtracking the trail of destruction to its presumed source. Along the way (and set amongst the beautiful landscapes of Norway), we learn that humans have been attempting to control—by measures, preserving and conserving—the troll population in Norway for many years. For instance, the trollhunter recounts a terrible story of when he had to exterminate families of trolls as part of this government cover-up. The movie is not at a loss to condemn human beings when it comes to their relationships with the environment and its other inhabitants. Within the context of the film, then, strangeness and withdrawal are neither invitations nor excuses for anything and everything the human can do. Giving up mastery and control by no means entails an anything-goes approach to environmental issues.

The film concludes with a series of intense events, starting with a phone call from the veterinarian who tested the blood sample Hans heroically obtained. The trolls are not responding to some direct, human intervention; the trolls have rabies. What the film suggests is that human beings are not the whole show—we are not the end all and be all of the earth. Trolls are not being driven by climate change or habitat destruction (these were, full disclosure, what I guessed, early in the film, as the cause of the trolls' troubles—this increased my surprise, and later, interest in the rabies twist). They were being driven by another, nonhuman agent. The blood work that "determines" the cause does little to reduce the trolls' status as wild objects; it simply reveals a whole wild and wide world of which we are only a small part. This strongly suggests a certain ambivalence built into the "nature of things" as wild objects. There is coexistence here, but it is not reducible to one kind of relation or one source of causation. As Morton writes, "The more we know about a strange stranger, the more she (he, it) withdraws" ("Here Comes Everything" 166). The wildness and strangeness of the troll are increased by the film's documentary, found footage style. Every move closer to the troll pushes the troll further and further away. "Bizarrely," Morton argues, "increased access (technically possible or not, hypothetical or not) does not decrease strangeness" ("Here Comes Everything" 166). Ambivalence and wildness persist despite and through our attempts to read and write the environment. Morton describes this as "doubt—the effect of things ceasing to be what you expect" (*Ecology* 200). The rabies virus becomes the wild object that reveals the wildness of all other objects.

Trolls resist this control, but not simply as a response to humans alone. It is not revenge but rabies—another wild object—that moves them and shapes their own dynamic. Ascribing revenge as the motive positions humans right back at the center of the universe. There is hubris hidden in guilt. As Bennett might argue, the agency of the trolls does not lie solely in their ability to resist us, but in their ability to do their own thing. Dead German tourists and a rabid Norwegian university student are but unintended consequences of the troll's own relation with rabies. We are not the only species with footprints. As Thomas remarks near the end of the film when he learns he too has rabies, "I don't have rabies. Hello. Dogs have rabies." "Humans encounter a world in which nonhuman materialities have power," Bennett reminds us, "a power that the 'bourgeois I,' with this pretensions of autonomy, denies" (16).

With the now panic-stricken students demanding immediate medical attention for Thomas, Hans sets out to confront and kill the largest troll there is: the troll who has somehow contracted rabies and is the source of its spread throughout Norway's population of trolls. Having previously heard from the vet about the pain experienced by trolls, there is more than an element of mercy when Hans kills the troll, but there is also an element of self-defense, of protection, and even of aggression. Like Thomas's biting earlier in the film, it is a deeply ambivalent act shot through with ethical ambiguity that cannot be resolved ahead of time by concepts like wilderness or a harsh and asymmetrical boundary between the human and the nonhuman. The decision to kill the troll is kairotic, and the justness of this act must be determined on the merits of the case rather than some ontological dualism that establishes principles such as preservation, conversation, exploitation, hierarchy, which in turn demand axiomatic responses.

But the film does not end with the troll's death. It concludes with Hans hiking off alone over the horizon and the documentary team running to escape the authorities who are desperate to get their hands on the footage. Hans, the last trollhunter, has done his final job, and the fantasy of control, of management, disappears over the horizon. We are told that no one has seen the students since, that the government continues to deny the existence of both trolls and the TSS, and viewers are then asked to contact authorities with any information about the students' whereabouts. The film's final scene depicts the prime minister's press conference after the cover-up has been achieved. During the conference, the prime minister lets it slip that trolls do in fact exist. The press corps misses the admission, and the credits roll. As Birch argues, wildness will always escape wilderness. The ambivalent conclusion of the film—the cover-up and the slip of the tongue—performs an attempt to exorcize wildness, which nevertheless escapes as exhaust in our anxiety about the environment.

"Han's entire life," Thomas remarks in a pause before the film's dramatic conclusion, "has revolved around trolls. Everyday has been a struggle with and for trolls. In many ways, he is a superhero here in Norway. What would we have done without him? That makes it all the more important for us to make this movie." A struggle *with* and *for* trolls. The trollhunter is positioned as largely ambivalent about his role. For example, he only begrudgingly allows the students to follow him because he is tired of keeping trolls a secret. He neither fully loves nor hates trolls, but he is at least equivalent with them. Trolls are not nature's wrath, but simply wild and powerful objects to be reckoned with. It is this deep ambivalence that Thomas celebrates.

Conclusion: Rhetoric's Footprint

Object-oriented ontology and new materialism are engagements (or reengagements) with matter outside normal subject–object, human–nonhuman, culture–nature relationships that lie at the heart of much contemporary, commonsense environmentalism. In suggesting alternate ways to relate to things, they are implicitly related to the concerns of environmental rhetoric. I began by outlining how contemporary environmental rhetoric follows the model we can see at work in something like *An Inconvenient Truth* and how this model is incomplete. To again borrow from Szerszynski, such a rhetoric "is one in which the diagnostic task of establishing the truth of anthropogenic climate change naturally gives way to the practical one of finding effective political and technical responses to it" (10). I applied new ontological frameworks to questions of the environment and linked them with arguments in and around environmentalism already leaning in such directions. I concluded with some tentative suggestions for how to develop and articulate a strange environmentalism built on Cronon's deep ambivalence.

In cultivating an attitude of deep ambivalence in humans, *Trollhunter* enacts the deep ambivalence of wildness itself. Deep ambivalence is an ontologically flavored rhetoric predicated upon a kind of being in the world—not so much a position we can actively adopt as an attitude that shapes activity. Deep ambivalence is a basic condition of being we must honestly face. We each act in time and each act participates in the agonistic composition of a world. There cannot, finally, be a path laid out ahead of us that allows us to save and fix the world (the notion of "wilderness" and the nature/culture binary are such paths). There is only ever a series of agonistic encounters between wild objects. This might at times look like any number of contemporary environmental strategies, or it might also look like a Norwegian calcifying a giant, rabid troll. It might be the building of shelter or a burning of one. Here is the frustrating thing for those with the will to read and write the weather: we cannot fully know what our responsibility will look like. As even Szerszynski argues, climate technics can play a role so long as they are "grounded in specific social projects that bind humanity together in new relations of interdependence" (25). Birch similarly argues that "even the preservation of wilderness as sacred space must be conceived and practiced as part of a larger strategy that aims to make all land into, or back into sacred space, and thereby to move humanity into a conscious reinhabitation of wildness" (464).

A strange environmental rhetoric troubles the means by which Cronon and Owens both argue we flee from history and escape responsibility. Far from advocating a hands-off or otherwise passive approach to nonhuman nature, a strange environmental rhetoric contends that all we ever do is interact with other, wild objects capable of acting back in strange, sometimes threatening ways. This is the agonism that constitutes environments over and over again. Deep ambivalence attends more earnestly to the environment as rhetorical in acknowledging its contingency and probability. A *krisis* demands deciding, which is conducted in conditions of uncertainty.

As rhetoricians complicate environmentalism, we might also introduce greater complexity to rhetoric more generally. Rhetoric has too long foregrounded epistemology at the expense of ontology. Deep ambivalence cannot be raised like awareness. Rhetoric has to be a comportment and not simply a call to action; there must be a clearing beforehand in which any such call can be voiced and heard. That clearing, however, will look different each time: the mechanisms of articulation will vary and evolve. For example, Lawrence Rosenfield helpfully points toward an epideictic rhetoric that, far from simply an act of reinforcing existing values, "suggests an exhibiting or making apparent (in the sense of showing or highlighting) what might otherwise remain unnoticed or invisible" (135). Epideictic rhetoric, to use the language of this essay, brings forth the strange. Summarizing Rosenfield's articulation of the epideictic, James Jasinski notes, "The true function of epideictic, therefore, is to reveal or disclose something—to bring new truths out into the open" (211). *Trollhunter*, then, provides a service to both environmentalism and to rhetorical theory. It performs a strange environmentalism and strange rhetoric—strange because it is an epideictic gesture in the name of ambivalence. Predicated on ambivalence, such a rhetoric falls outside the realm of simply praising and blaming already established values.

Within deep ambivalence as environmentalism, rhetoric itself will necessarily be stranger. Hence the appeal to the epideictic rhetoric disclosed by Rosenfield: a rhetoric of bringing forth the otherwise. So long as rhetoric remains wedded to the human and the human alone, environmental rhetoric will continue to miss the mark. Rhetoric, to repurpose a common environmental trope, must be the footprint: *all* the ways we mark and are ourselves marked, bitten, or stung. All footprints must be recognized as rhetorical, whether they are discursive or non-discursive, human or nonhuman. Avoiding footprints is both impossible and ethically suspect; ethics is about relations, and relations are about living in the world. The very nature of a response presumes that we cannot know in any given situation what our responsibility will be. To leave no footprint is to not have lived with others, and we have already had quite enough of that.

Acknowledgments

I thank the editor and the two anonymous reviews for their help in revising this essay: it is stronger for their thorough and insightful comments. My thanks as well to Paul Lynch, Rachel Greenwald Smith, Katie Dickman, and Matthew

Miller for their patient and generous readings of early drafts. Finally, thanks to Casey Boyle for his generous and productive feedback throughout the process of composing this essay.

Notes

1 The main forum for the "wilderness debate" takes place across two volumes edited by J. Baird Callicott and Michael P. Nelson: *The Great New Wilderness Debate* (1998) and *The Wilderness Debate Rages On* (2008). Cronon's essay is reprinted in the 1998 collection, which also houses Thomas Birch's essay. There is of course no way to here thoroughly engage the "wilderness debate." I focus on Cronon because of the terminology he uses to express his frustration and because, as the editors remark, "Cronon's essay, though largely unoriginal, is a forcefully written summary and crystallization of the case against the received wilderness ideas made piecemeal by" the other authors in the collection (*The Great New*, 12). Cronon's article was likewise the launching pad for a debate in the pages of *Environmental History* 1, no. 1.

2 Additional work in this area includes: Timothy Morton (*Hyberobects*), Joanna Zylinska, and Jeffrey Cohen.

3 So much so, that I cannot hope to provide a full accounting of it here. Even within environmental rhetoric there is much ground to cover. Stellar work includes: Tarla Rai Peterson, Craig Waddell, W. Michele Simmons, and Sidney I. Dobrin and Sean Morey. For a more comprehensive history of environmentalism, see Leslie Paul Thiele.

4 For instance, see the acrimonious debate in and around "The Death of Environmentalism," an essay (and now book) by Michael Shellenberger and Ted Nordhaus (http://grist.org/article/doe-intro).

5 Bruno Latour also contributes to the composition of what I am calling "wild objects":

> Actors are defined above all as obstacles, scandals, as what suspends mastery, as what gets in the way domination, as what interrupts the closure and the composition of the collective. To put it crudely, human and nonhuman actors appear first of all as troublemakers.
>
> (Politics 81, 17)

Latour's focus on environmental has only grown more pronounced in the last several years. Again resonating with Bennett's articulate of thing-power, Latour argues, "The point of living in the epoch of the anthropocene is that all agents share the same shape-changing destiny" ("Agency").

References

"Ambivalence." *OED Online*. Oxford: Oxford UP, 2012. Web.

Barnett, Scot. "Toward an Object-Oriented Rhetoric." *Enculturation* 7 (2011): n.p. Web.

Bennett, Jane. *Vibrant Matter: A Political Ecology of Things*. Durham: Duke UP, 2010. Print.

Birch, Thomas. "The Incarceration of Wildness." *The Great New Wilderness Debate*. Ed. J. Baird Callicott and Michael P. Nelson. Athens: U of Georgia P, 1998. 443–70. Print.

Callicott, J. Baird and Michael P. Nelson, eds. *The Great New Wilderness Debate*. Athens: U of Georgia P, 1998. Print.

———. *The Wilderness Debate Rages On*. Athens: U of Georgia P, 2008. Print.

Cohen, Jeffrey Jerome, ed. *Prismatic Ecology: Ecotheory beyond Green*. Minneapolis: U of Minnesota P, 2014. Print.

Cronon, William. "The Trouble with Wilderness, or Getting Back to the Wrong Nature." *Environmental History* 1.1 (1996): 7–28. Print.

Crutzen, Paul J. "Geology of Mankind." *Nature* 415.3 (2002): 23. Print.

Dobrin, Sidney I. and Sean Morey, eds. *Ecosee: Image, Rhetoric, Nature*. Albany: SUNY P, 2009. Print.

Feenberg, Andrew. "Subversive Rationalization: Technology, Power and Democracy." *Inquiry* 35 (1992): 301–22. Print.

Folz, Bruce. "On Heidegger and the Interpretation of Environmental Crisis." *Environmental Ethics* 6 (1984): 323–38. Print.

Harman, Graham. *Guerrilla Metaphysics: Phenomenology and the Carpentry of Things*. Chicago: Open Court, 2005. Print.

——. *The Quadruple Object*. Washington, DC: Zero Books, 2011. Print.

——. *Tool-Being: Heidegger and the Metaphysics of Objects*. Chicago: Open Court, 2002. Print.

Herndl, Carl G. and Stuart C. Brown, eds. *Green Culture: Environmental Rhetoric in Contemporary America*. Madison: U of Wisconsin P, 1996. Print.

An Inconvenient Truth. Dir. Davis Guggenheim. Perf. Al Gore. Paramount, 2006. DVD.

Jasinksi, James. *Sourcebook on Rhetoric: Key Concepts in Contemporary Rhetorical Theory*. Thousand Oaks CA: SAGE Publications, 2001. Print.

Johnson, Laura. "(Environmental) Rhetorics of Tempered Apocalypticism in *An Inconvenient Truth*." *Rhetoric Review* 28.1 (2009): 29–46. Print.

Killingsworth, M. Jimmie and Jacqueline S. Palmer. *Ecospeak: Rhetoric and Environmental Politics in America*. Carbondale: Southern Illinois UP, 1991. Print.

Latour, Bruno. "Agency at the Time of the Anthropocene." *New Literary History* 45 (2014): 1–18.

——. *Politics of Nature: How to Bring the Sciences into Democracy*. Cambridge, MA: Harvard UP, 2004. Print.

Morton, Timothy. *Ecology without Nature: Rethinking Environmental Aesthetics*. Cambridge, MA: Harvard UP, 2007. Print.

——. "Here Comes Everything: The Promise of Object-Oriented Ontology." *Qui Parle* 19.2 (2011): 163–90. Print.

——. *Hyberobects: Philosophy and Ecology after the End of the World*. Minneapolis, MN: U of Minnesota P, 2013. Print.

Owens, Louis. "Burning the Shelter." *The Colors of Nature: Culture, Identity, and the Natural World*. Ed. Alison H. Deming and Lauret E. Savoy. Minneapolis: Milkweed Editions, 2011. 211–15. Print.

Peterson, Tarla Rai. *Sharing the Earth: The Rhetoric of Sustainable Development*. Columbia: U of South Carolina P, 1997. Print.

Rosenfield, Lawrence. "The Practical Celebration of Epideictic Rhetoric." *Rhetoric in Transition: Studies in the Nature and Use of Rhetoric*. Ed. E. E. White. University Park: Penn State UP, 1980. 133–46. Print.

Shellenberger, Michael and Ted Nordhaus. "The Death of Environmentalism: Global Warming Politics in a Post-Environmental World." *Grist* (14 January 2005). Web.

Simmons, W. Michele. *Power and Participation: Civic Discourse in Environmental Policy Decisions*. Albany: SUNY P, 2008. Print.

Smith, Rachel Greenwald. "Materialism, Ecology, Aesthetics." *Mediations* 25.2 (2011): 61–78. Print.

Szerszynski, Bronislaw. "Reading and Writing the Weather: Climate Technics and the Moment of Responsibility." *Theory, Culture and Society* 27.2–3 (2010): 9–30. Print.

Thiele, Leslie Paul. *Environmentalism for a New Millennium*. New York: Oxford UP, 1999. Print.

Trollhunter. Dir. André Øvredal. Perf. Otto Jespersen. Magnolia Home Entertainment, 2011. DVD.

US Global Change Research Program. *National Climate Assessment*. Washington, DC, 2014. Web. 10 Aug. 2015.

Waddell, Craig, ed. *Landmark Essays on the Environment and Rhetoric*. Davis: Hermogoras P, 1998. Print.

Zylinska, Joanna. *Minimal Ethics for the Anthropocene*. Ann Arbor: Michigan Publishing, 2014. Print.

19
Exigencies for *RSQ*
An Afterword

RYAN SKINNELL AND MAUREEN DALY GOGGIN

Alone we can do so little; together we can do so much.

—Helen Keller

As historians—or what Maureen Goggin has termed "discipliniographers"[1]—of rhetoric and writing studies, we take up in this essay the question of exigencies that led to the founding of the Rhetoric Society of America (RSA) and *Rhetoric Society Quarterly* (*RSQ*). To tell this story—one marked by false starts and missed opportunities for those interested in rhetoric to come together to pool intellectual and material resources—we need to return to a time long before RSA and *RSQ* were established. Thus, this afterword operates paradoxically more as a *before*word. And so we circle back more than a century before *RSQ* to narrate the emergence of the intellectual context and material conditions for those who came to populate departments of English and of communication and to hold membership in relevant scholarly associations.

Carving out Intellectual and Material Spaces for Rhetoric

Some of this story will be familiar to readers because it has been told a number of times by a number of discipliniographers in both English and Communication. Nevertheless, it is worth telling again, in a slightly different way because of what it teaches us about how RSA and *RSQ* came to be.

In early pre-industrial, agrarian society, US higher education borrowed its model from Europe with a focus on Greek and Latin and with rhetoric, among other subjects, at the center. This classical education sought to serve pulpit, bar, and politics for those in upper classes—those who earned their class by birthright. The goal for its faculty was to instill knowledge, morality, values, and piety. The goal for its students was to demonstrate they had attained these ends. The term "class" did not reference subject matter, but rather referred to a group of students who moved through all topics together. The pedagogy was recitation—students recited what they had memorized to demonstrate they knew what they were supposed to know. The role of education, then, was to pass on but not to create knowledge. In the nineteenth century, in response to the seismic socio-economic shift to industrialization and the emergence of a middle- and upper-class based on accumulated wealth, there was a radical paradigm swing in higher education—making it look a lot more like it does today.

Modern higher education emerged in the mid to late nineteenth century in response to three distinct ideals: a Research Ideal with the goal to *create* knowledge, a Liberal Culture Ideal with a goal to spread cultivated taste and *preserve* knowledge, and a Utility Ideal—very much a US invention—with the goal to *use* knowledge.[2] Institutions of higher education (as well as other education institutions) developed accordingly. Thus, research universities were designed to uphold the Research Ideal, liberal arts colleges were intended to uphold the Liberal Culture Ideal, and a variety of schools—including agriculture and mechanical (A&M) universities, normal schools,[3] technical schools, and trade schools—emerged to meet the Utility Ideal.[4]

It might seem that the distinct missions of the different institutions would result in clear boundaries among schools, but this was not the case. The nineteenth-century American education scene was profoundly complex, in no small part because there was virtually no set of standards, nor any formal authority, to determine and enforce distinctions that differentiated one kind of school from another.[5] The United States Department of Education was founded in 1867, for instance, but its sole purpose was to assemble education statistics. As US Commissioner of Education John Eaton wrote in 1876, "[H]owever comprehensive [the Department of Education's] duty in regard to collecting and disseminating information, it provides for no exercise of authority and none should be expected from it."[6] Consequently, all sorts of education institutions—from Sunday schools to Ivy League colleges—taught overlapping curricula and competed for students.[7]

Notwithstanding the complexity of American education in the nineteenth century, there were some relatively common themes that emerged. Among them, writing took on increasing importance in secondary and postsecondary curricula, resulting in a pedagogical split between written English and spoken English and a concurrent bifurcation of rhetoric into Speech and English. Elective curricula also became increasingly popular, so colleges and universities could distinguish themselves from high schools and attract students interested in research, liberal culture, and utility.[8] As well, in attempts to forge a standardized education hierarchy, instruction in vernacular languages—especially English—progressively displaced Greek and Latin at the center of the postsecondary curriculum. And under industrialization, following a Fordist-model, higher education was further divided into disciplines (intellectual spaces) and academic departments (material spaces). Each of these developments had important consequences for the study of rhetoric.

The constellation of institutional, intellectual, and economic pressures and their effects on rhetoric is apparent in the shifts to what were considered "legitimate" areas of study in higher education. To claim disciplinary space for an academic subject, scholars had to demonstrate that their field was a *Wissenschaft*[9] (a science) rather than an art. A *Wissenschaft* created theory and knowing, whereas an art was understood as a practice and a doing. The struggle for resources to build departments—which remains with us today—was fierce. A subject had to be either a *Naturwissenschaft* (a natural science dealing with that made by nature) or a *Geisteswissenschaft* (a moral science dealing with that made by humans). Thus, each discipline began the arduous task of proving they were a science—something that created knowledge—and subjects began the struggle for material space as departments. Ironically, rhetoric, composition, forensics, and speech were considered by many people to be too broadly essential to be sheltered in discipline-based electives.[10] Which is to say, the essential arts of writing and speaking were considered by many teachers, administrators, and education commentators to be too important to be sciences. This perspective would eventually be damaging to rhetoric.

Speech and writing had been gradually separated from one another in many college curricula during the early nineteenth century, although vestiges of rhetoric remained in both. Speech and forensics were in some cases moved into oratory or elocution departments,[11] in other cases relegated to secondary schools, and in still other cases abandoned to extra-curricular debate societies and speech clubs.[12] Often they were focused primarily on delivery and declamation instead of the whole range of rhetorical canons, and as William Keith argues, speech education in the late nineteenth century was dispersed and weakened, "in a kind of limbo, important yet meaningless."[13] In any case, speech and writing teachers were increasingly distanced from each other by departmental/institutional structures, and rhetoric was pulled into multiple departments which were competing for the same resources—and none of which made rhetoric a central pursuit.

At the same time as speech and oratory were depriviling rhetoric, so too the discipline of English was developing away from rhetoric. The Modern Language Association (MLA), founded in 1883, emerged as the first professional scholarly organization for English studies amid vigorous arguments about the role, purpose, and viability of English studies as a discipline.[14] One goal that held the diverse, competing visions of English studies together was perhaps best expressed at the second MLA meeting in 1884 by then Secretary of MLA, A. Marshall Elliott, who argued "to move with all possible energy towards the establishment and legitimate maintenance of the claims of the Modern studies for the same rights and privileges as are now enjoyed by the classics."[15] To legitimize the study of English in the vernacular, nascent scholars in English studies had to demonstrate that their field was a rigorous pursuit—a *Wissenschaft*—worthy of a place in modern higher education. The struggle was not easy.

The battle is well illustrated in an argument by Th. W. Hunt addressing his profession in the first issue of *PMLA*. Hunt was writing in the context of his discipline's vigorous competition for resources, not only with departments in the natural and social sciences, but also with those in its own general area of ancient and modern language studies. He captured the nature of this internal territorial battle by protesting that "the English Department in our colleges has had to fight its way not only against illiteracy and ignorant prejudices but, also, against the persistent opposition of those from whom better things were expected."[16] Hunt excused "scientific men whose interests as instructors are in widely different lines" but indicted those in the humanities, especially in ancient languages, who ought "to have a just appreciation of" all that English studies entailed.[17] He ended with the impassioned plea for the relatively new field of English to be given "equal academic rank with any other department."[18]

Hunt included rhetoric as an area in his description of English studies as that which is concerned with the "historical, linguistics, legendary, poetic and rhetorical."[19] but a closer look at his argument reveals that his sights were more narrowly focused on literary studies. He was actually urging a "*marked increase of English Literary Culture in our colleges and in the country*."[20] He wanted to "insist that every American college should be instinct with English literary thought and life, so that faculty and students alike should feel it."[21] He went on to argue that the pressing question ought to be "what are our colleges doing specifically for English literature in America—for American Prose and Poetry?"[22] This narrow focus would have negative effects for the other subjects coalescing under the umbrella of English studies. In particular, as English studies became *hyperspecialized* in literature, the art of rhetoric—the art of speaking and the art of writing—was pushed aside as a "doing," treated as a set of basic skills that were important enough to be widespread requirements but basic enough that they could be appreciated by (and taught by) anyone.

Rhetoric did not disappear from English studies overnight. Until 1903, rhetoric had been a topic of the MLA Pedagogical section. Between 1901 and 1903, then president of the Pedagogical section, Fred Newton Scott, distributed three surveys regarding the viability of rhetoric: as a subject of graduate study, as a subject of undergraduate study, and as the preferred focus of composition classes. Responses were mixed. Those who perceived rhetoric as a science agreed that it belonged in the university; those who perceived it as an art thought it more viable in lower education. Rhetoric ultimately lost the day, at least in the MLA. Indeed, David Beard identifies this time as a "false start for rhetoric" in higher education.[23] In 1903, no longer interested in teaching or pedagogy, the MLA disbanded the pedagogical section and set its focus on cultivating interest in literature, erasing rhetoric altogether. That year, Scott formed a department of rhetoric outside of English at the University of Michigan that lasted until his retirement in 1930 when it was then absorbed by the English Department and reduced to composition. But Scott was virtually alone in his endeavor. As Beard points out:

The false start of rhetoric in the twentieth century, which centered around Fred Newton Scott, the Pedagogical Section of the MLA, and the University of Michigan, died not because Scott and his students were intellectually weak or unproductive, but because the institutional structures failed to support it.[24]

Of course rhetoric remained throughout this long period in many—probably most—postsecondary institutional structures.[25] As Robert J. Connors and others have demonstrated, first-year composition requirements were adopted in most colleges and universities by the turn of the twentieth century.[26] Ryan Skinnell argues that accreditation associations actively championed first-year composition requirements across American institutions, making it the most common requirement in higher education for more than 150 years.[27] And many of the materials and textbooks adopted in first-year composition classes were based on a truncated, formalized rhetorical theory that Connors has called "composition-rhetoric." Likewise, various forms of rhetorical instruction persisted in speech and forensics courses, debate societies, school newspapers, student publications, and literary societies. For the most part, rhetoric was significantly reduced as a disciplinary, intellectual priority in colleges and universities—even as speech and writing became increasingly sought after skills in American politics, business, and industry—but it never disappeared.

In 1911, the National Council of Teachers of English (NCTE) was founded to fill the void left by the dismantling of the MLA Pedagogical section and to fight against the threat of postsecondary English departments commandeering secondary English. Those in writing and speaking pinned their hopes for disciplinary space there. NCTE's J. F. Hosic, then head of the department of English at Chicago Normal College, founded the *English Journal* as an organ to explore the teaching of English from kindergarten through graduate school. However, the NCTE was created to deal with *all* issues in the teaching of English at *all* grade levels, and instructors of college writing and speaking had to compete with a diverse range of topics and instruction levels. They were, consequently, afforded very little space on convention programs and in the pages of the *English Journal*. As Beard notes,

> while the NCTE's (National Council of Teachers of English) *English Journal*, by virtue of serving as the publication not only of the researcher in rhetoric and composition but also the practitioner in secondary education, it could not support the research that Scott and his students did.[28]

Yet another false start for those in both oral and written rhetoric.

Eventually, the circumstances became untenable. In the throes of World War I, seventeen speech professors convened at a coffee shop during the 1914 NCTE convention to discuss their mutual interests and concerns. There they formed the National Association of Academic Teachers of Public Speaking and founded the *Quarterly Journal of Public Speaking*.[29] The move was not a snap decision but one that had been several years in the making. Since 1910, James M. O'Neill, first of Dartmouth and then University of Wisconsin, had been campaigning for speech departments independent from English and an independent speech association. Not everyone agreed. At the 1912 NCTE, some participants argued that the teaching of speech was best placed within departments of English. In response, O'Neill gave an impassioned keynote address at the 1913 NCTE arguing for a "dividing line between departments of Speech and English."[30]

We noted above the increasing pedagogical and institutional separation of rhetoric into written and spoken English in the late nineteenth century, and the 1910s marked a period of formalized *disciplinary* separations. Discouraged by poor treatment regarding tenure and promotion in departments of English and with little space or attention given at NCTE, O'Neill, Charles Woolbert, and C. D. Hardy formed a committee to look into creating a new association for teachers of public speaking. Hardy polled speech teachers to determine if they were interested in a new association. Replies from 116 teachers were returned and all but three were in favor. However, there was a split over whether the association should be founded separately or as an affiliation of NCTE. Only 41 of the 116 opted for an independent association while 42 voted for affiliation with NCTE. The remaining respondents argued for affiliation with other organizations. In response, a second ballot was sent with just two options: autonomy or affiliation with NCTE. The returned ballots were still mixed. By a slim margin, 57 voted for autonomy and 56 for affiliation with NCTE. O'Neill, Woolbert, and Hardy were not deterred. They set out to form a new association, and at the public speaking NCTE section meeting on Friday, December 4, 1914, a motion for the new association was put forward but tabled by a vote of 18 to 16. Dissatisfied with the tabling, O'Neill and sixteen others moved the next morning into the separate parlor at the Auditorium hotel.[31] Later O'Neill, who became the first President of the association, defended their actions that Saturday morning on the following grounds:

> First, that more than two of the people voting to table this motion were public readers—not teachers—or teachers in other departments than public speaking; secondly, this vote was taken at a time when the attendance was small—a number of strong supporters of the motion being absent at the time, and thirdly at least two (I think three) of the men who voted to take this motion were present at the conference the next morning and voted for all the motions passed at that meeting.[32]

Debates by nascent scholars in speech communication[33] emerged alongside those by nascent scholars in literary studies,[34] both presenting strong arguments for claiming that each was a *Wissenshaft*. Speech had to struggle to define itself as a respectable science, separate from shaman elocution; literary studies had to prove it focused on more than a leisure pastime. What distinguished the two from each other is the ways each organized in relation to the three ideals of modern higher education. Those in literature constructed the field along the lines of both research and liberal culture ideals, disdainfully rejecting the utility ideal. By contrast, early arguments to establish speech communication as a legitimate field centered on constructing an identity based on research and utility ideals. As Arthur Bochner and Eric Eisenberg point out, speech defined itself through a "combination of a utilitarian function and a scientific perspective" to break its bonds with English departments.[35]

Ironically, what connected literary studies to speech communication was that both rejected rhetoric at the time. Steven Mailloux notes, "Whereas the new discipline, Speech, viewed rhetoric as not scientific or modern enough, the older one, English, valued rhetorical traditions primarily as literary background, rhetoric not being in itself literary enough, and relegated its pedagogical practices to composition teachers."[36] Hence, yet again a missed opportunity for rhetoric.

In hindsight, it seems rather a shame that those interested in the teaching of writing didn't unite together with James O'Neill and the sixteen others who taught speaking.[37] Joining forces to teach and research speech and writing could have been quite powerful. Instead, those interested in writing remained in departments of English, still poorly treated in terms of professional advancement since writing was seen as a useful art but not a *Wissenschaft* and hence, not available for disciplinary status. Writing (capital "W" for literature and small "w" for composition) became the province of English studies and speaking became that of communication, and the two more or less went their separate ways.[38] Indeed it would take another World War before writing and speech (and rhetoric in both) really moved toward anything like rapprochement, and even that was characterized by fits and starts.

During the Second World War, a number of universities—famously, Iowa—were encouraged by the federal government to develop communication skills programs that brought speech and English teachers into closer connection to teach students reading, writing, speaking, and listening to serve the war effort. It was the first systemically meaningful, though ultimately unrealized, reconnection of writing and speech specialists in more than three decades. Another opportunity for a connection between speech and writing studies presented itself after the war. In 1947, NCTE and the Speech Association of America (SSA) held a joint conference on postsecondary teaching of reading, writing, and speech. The bonds between speech communication and rhetoric and composition might have been rewoven then. But as Diana George and John Trimbur discuss at length in "'The Communication Battle,' or Whatever Happened to the 4th C?", the alliance between speech and rhetoric and composition during this period ultimately failed, even despite what many speech and writing teachers recognized as a significant amount of shared interest.[39]

In the years between 1914, when speech communication teachers and scholars left NCTE to form their own group, and the early 1940s, speech communication developed in a number of significant research and practical directions, particularly in the growing popularity of debate teams and the burgeoning studies of mass communication and propaganda. Although not exactly a meteoric rise, as a consequence, rhetoric re-emerged in speech communication departments as an important, and ultimately valuable, component of study and teaching. English departments similarly grew and prospered, but not in ways that strengthened or recuperated rhetoric. As in earlier periods, rhetoric remained in the curriculum—mostly in first-year required writing courses—but it did not see the kind of revival in English that it did in speech in the early twentieth century. For all intents and purposes, rhetoric remained the handmaiden to literary studies into the 1940s. The inability of rhetoric and composition to extract itself from the literary studies shadow is at least part of the reason that English rhetoricians and speech rhetoricians had trouble reestablishing close ties. That began to change in the years after the war.

In 1948, an NCTE session titled "Three Views of Required English" stirred such an interest that it ran over time. Angered by the lack of time and space allotted first-year composition, participants from the session issued and were granted a formal request for a two-day spring conference. It was at this April 1949 conference held in Chicago that the first steps were taken to develop a permanent organization and a journal for college rhetoric and composition. Hailing the emergence of *College Composition and Communication* (*CCC*), Charles Roberts, its first editor, explained "we are no longer selling a pig in a poke; ours is an established organization, with annual meetings, and an official publication."[40] Hence an intellectual space was born. As the title of the organization, the Conference on College Composition and Communication (CCCC), hints, this new intellectual space, especially with its inclusion of communication with composition, might have forged a partnership between those in writing and those in speech. An alliance was formed as the journal *CCC* had a section devoted to the National Society for the Study of Communication (NSSC) news, and in turn, *The Journal of Communication* had a similar section for CCCC. But the alliance was short-lived and the NSSC section was abandoned in 1959. Alas it was yet another missed opportunity for those in writing and those in speech to join forces.

Despite the false starts, each attempt gave some strength to rhetoric as the basis of reconnection. Rhetoric, however, was not yet central to either composition or communication.[41] But in the decade of the long sixties, rhetoric appeared ripe for those interested in both oral and written texts. Speech rhetoricians were building on the rhetorical revival started in the early twentieth century by people like Charles Woolbert and Herbert A. Wichelns; English rhetoricians, like Richard Weaver and Porter Perrin, were recouping classical and pre-Enlightenment rhetoric; and both speech and English rhetoricians were beginning to take up the contemporary work of rhetorical theorists such as Kenneth Burke and I. A. Richards. Although reclaiming rhetoric had been a subject of some importance since at least the 1940s, the calls became louder and more frequent by the mid-1960s.[42] Pinpointing a precise date for the revival is debatable,[43] and perhaps not all that useful. What is clear and useful is that a full revival became possible under postmodernism, which values contingent truths—those that are at the center of rhetoric. This view comes in a moving call for the revival of rhetoric Wayne Booth gave at the 1964 MLA conference:

> My rhetorical point to a group of rhetoricians is two-fold: first, that in a rhetorical age rhetorical studies should have a major, respected place in the training of all teachers at all levels; and secondly, that in such an age, specialization in rhetorical studies of all kinds, narrow and broad, should carry at least as much professional respectability as literary history or as literary criticism in non-rhetorical modes. Whether we restore the old chairs of Rhetoric by name or not, chairs like my own Pullman Professorship ought to provide visible proof that to dirty one's hands in rhetorical studies is not a sure way to professional oblivion.[44]

The 1960s and early 1970s saw an explosion of publications revolutionizing and reviving rhetoric, such as:

> Edward P. J. Corbett, "The Usefulness of Classical Rhetoric" (1963)
> Edwin Black, *Rhetorical Criticism: A Study in Method* (1965)
> Wayne Booth, "The Revival of Rhetoric" (1965)
> James J. Murphy, "The Four Faces of Rhetoric" (1966)
> Robert L. Scott, "On Viewing Rhetoric as Epistemic" (1967)
> Lloyd Bitzer, "The Rhetorical Situation" (1968)
> Lloyd Bitzer and Edwin Black, *The Prospect of Rhetoric* (1971)[45]
> Chaïm Perelman and Lucie Olbrechts-Tyteca, *The New Rhetoric* (1971)[46]

Clearly, this was a powerhouse long decade for rhetorical studies. Here was the opportunity for those in speech and those in writing to join forces. They did so admirably with the founding of the Rhetoric Society of America (RSA).

Ending at the Beginning of RSA and *RSQ*

It has taken us some time to arrive at the founding of RSA, and we have necessarily oversimplified the history we tell above. But what this history attempts to make clear is that the founding of RSA represented a formal, disciplinary space where English and Communication rhetoricians could finally move together (if not without tensions) after years of deliberate separation and/or failed attempts to reconnect. RSA emerged from an invitational workshop on rhetoric organized by J. Carter Roland for the 1968 Conference on College Composition and Communication. Participants from several disciplines who shared a common interest in rhetoric gathered and defined the tripartite purpose of RSA: (1) to foster communication among those interested in rhetoric; (2) to distribute knowledge of rhetoric to the uninitiated; and (3) to encourage research, scholarship, and pedagogy in rhetoric. In December of 1968, the first *RSA Newsletter* (the forerunner of *Rhetoric Society Quarterly*) was published.

The fledgling society struggled initially—society meetings were held inconsistently and the newsletter appeared sporadically between 1968 and 1972. The struggle can be attributed in part to the members' desire for a vigorous scholarly forum that avoided simply reproducing other professional organizations, but it was also a function of continued points of disagreement among the various camps being brought together. The push and pull in the relationship between English and Communication rhetoricians that characterized early attempts were not suddenly relieved by the founding of RSA, and even many years on from that first workshop in 1968, disciplinary entrenchment is readily recognizable.[47] Nevertheless, RSA persisted. Intense commitment from the members helped to sustain RSA in the early years,[48] and the society was finally galvanized by the creation of a constitution drafted by Richard Larson and ratified by members in 1971, and by the appointment of an editor for the *Rhetoric Society Newsletter*. The constitution stipulated that the board must be comprised of two members from the field of English, two from speech communication, and at least one other member from yet a third field. Instructed by the newly formed board of directors to nominate someone from outside of English studies to edit the *Rhetoric Society Newsletter*, Larson enlisted George Yoos, a philosopher from St. Cloud University in Minnesota.

The subsequent intellectual story is more or less told in this volume. Under the skillful editorship of George Yoos (1972–1992), *RSN* was transformed from a practical tool for exchanging news items, descriptions of works-in-progress, and program descriptions to a sophisticated scholarly journal. The transformation was marked in 1976 when the journal was upgraded and renamed *Rhetoric Society Quarterly*. As the articles collected here demonstrate, *RSQ* has always been the site of significant, cutting-edge rhetorical research. It has always been one of the most important outlets for rhetorical scholarship that is engaged, critical, careful, and challenging. It still is, and all indications are that it will continue to be. *RSQ* is worth celebrating for that reason alone.

But the history we've told here suggests another reason to celebrate *RSQ* that the essays collected here offer a peek at but never quite address. As discipliniographers, we are interested in the stories we tell about ourselves, and one of the most persistent stories that rhetoricians tell themselves is about the challenges (and even the value) of working across disciplinary divides. Division is one of our earliest shared references, and we are still often unsure about how to feel about rapprochement.[49] We know we like each other, but we're still not sure if we're *in like* with each other. But *RSQ* gives us some cause for optimism.

In the fifty years since RSA was founded and the forty-two years since *RSQ* materialized, the journal has been a hinge point that has maintained the connections between English and Communication rhetoricians, even when other points of connection have been strained. In 2009, Roxanne Mountford argued in "A Century after the Divorce: Challenges to a Rapprochement Between Speech Communication and English" that the two camps are often woefully unaware of scholarship in the other camp, and that the long history of disciplinary estrangement has not, thus far, concluded.[50] Still, *RSQ* is a tenacious exception where English and Communication scholarship mingles and each observably influences the other. As Thomas Miller pointed out in an exchange with Steven Mailloux, Michael Leff, and Martin Nystrand about the disciplinary histories of rhetoric in English and Communication, *Rhetoric Society Quarterly* holds us intellectually together even in the event that we have trouble coming together in other ways. He writes, "Personally and professionally, I value *Rhetoric Society Quarterly* because it presents opportunities for me to participate in more specialized yet interdisciplinary discussions of rhetoric than composition journals offer."[51] There remains, and perhaps will always remain, strains on the rhetorical relationship that is meant to cross rhetoric's disciplinary homes. Nevertheless, as the essays in this collection so aptly demonstrate, we have much to teach each other, and lessons spoken/written across the pages of *RSQ* illustrate how exciting and generative our conversations are.

Although most of the credit for the survival and success of the RSA and *RSQ* belongs to the tenacity of its founding members and the able editorial leadership of Yoos, a death knell would surely have sounded for the organization if there had not been scholars, researchers, and teachers who could be uniquely served by, and in turn, contribute to, the society and its quarterly. This collection offers powerful proof of this robust dual role. And so we end where this collection begins, with the proof positive of a successful collaboration between those in English departments and those in communication.

Notes

1 Maureen Daly Goggin, *Authoring a Discipline: Scholarly Journals and the Post World War II Emergence of Rhetoric and Composition* (New York: Routledge, 2000), xxvii.

2 Laurence R. Veysey, *The Emergence of the American University* (Chicago: U of Chicago P, 1965).

3 Normal colleges were designed to educate and certify teachers, and departments of English in Normal colleges were the forerunners of English education. See Ryan Skinnell, "Institutionalizing Normal: Rethinking Composition's Precedence in Normal Schools," *Composition Studies* 41, no. 1 (2013): 10–26.

4 See, for example, Lawrence A. Cremin, *American Education: The National Experience, 1783–1876* (New York: Harper Colophon, 1982); Christopher J. Lucas, *American Higher Education, a History*, 2nd ed. (New York: Palgrave, 2006); Christine A. Ogren, *The American State Normal School: "An Instrument of Great Good"* (New York: Palgrave, 2005).

5 Cremin.

6 US Commissioner of Education, *Report of the Commissioner of Education, 1876–1877*, vol. 1 (Washington, DC: Office of Education, 1879), x.

7 Marc A. Van Overbeke, *The Standardization of American Schooling: Linking Secondary and Higher Education, 1870–1910* (New York: Palgrave, 2008).

8 Ryan Skinnell, "Harvard, Again: Considering Articulation and Accreditation in Rhetoric in Composition's History," *Rhetoric Review* 33, no. 2 (2014): 95–112.

9 The German root *"wissen"* means knowledge.

10 Skinnell, "Harvard," 100–01.

11 Ronald J. Matlon, "Jonathan Barber and the Elocutionary Movement," *The Speech Teacher* 14, no. 1 (1965): 38–43; Warren Guthrie, "The Development of Rhetorical Theory in America, 1635–1850, vol. 5, 'The Elocution Movement,'" *Speech Monographs* 15 (1948): 18–30.

12 David H. Grover, "Elocution at Harvard: The Saga of Jonathan Barber," *Quarterly Journal of Speech* 51, no. 1 (1965): 62–67.

13 William M. Keith, *Democracy as Discussion* (Lanham: Lexington Books, 2007), 33.

14 On the formation of the MLA, see William Riley Parker, "The MLA, 1883–1953," *PMLA* 68 (1953): 3–39; and Parker's landmark work, "Where Do English Departments Come From?" *College English* 28 (1967): 339–51; as well as Phyllis Franklin, "English Studies in America: Reflections on the Development of a Discipline," *American Quarterly* 30 (1978): 21–38.

15 A. Marshall Elliott, "Secretary's Report," *PMLA* 7 (1889): vii.

16 Th. W. Hunt, "The Place of English in the College Curriculum," *PMLA* 1 (1884): 120.

17 Ibid.

18 Hunt, 128.

19 Ibid.

20 Hunt; italics in the original, 128–29.

21 Hunt, 129.

22 Ibid.

23 David Beard, "Out of the Aerie Realm of the Intellectual Firmament," *Quarterly Journal of Speech* 93, no. 3 (2007): 349–51.

24 Beard, 350.

25 Gerald Nelms and Maureen Daly Goggin, "The Revival of Classical Rhetoric for Modern Composition Studies: A Survey," *Rhetoric Society Quarterly* 23 (1994): 11–26.

26 Robert J. Connors, *Composition-Rhetoric: Backgrounds, Theory, and Pedagogy* (Pittsburgh: U of Pittsburgh P, 1997).

27 Ryan Skinnell, *Conceding Composition: A Crooked History of Composition's Institutional Fortunes* (Logan: Utah State UP, 2016); Skinnell, "Harvard."

28 Beard, 350.

29 The founding 17 members were: I. M. Cochran (Carleton College), Loren Gates (Miami University), J. S. Gaylord (Winona Normal), H. B. Gislason (University of Minnesota), H. B. Gough (DePauw University), Binney Gunnison (Lombard College), C. D. Hardy (Northwestern University), J. L. Lardner (Northwestern University), G. N. Merry (University of Iowa), James M. O'Neill (University of Wisconsin), J. M. Phelps (University of Illinois), F. M. Rarig (University of Minnesota), L. Sarett (Northwestern University), J. A. Winans (Cornell University), I. L. Winter (Harvard University), B. C. van Wye (University of Cincinnati), and C. H. Woolbert (University of Illinois).

30 James M. O'Neill, "The National Association," *Quarterly Journal of Public Speaking* 1 (1915): 51–58.

31 This narrative bears striking similarity, as Goggin shows, to the narrative of the founding of the Conference on College Composition and Communication (CCCC) nearly forty years later (Goggin, *Authoring*).

32 O'Neill, 54.

33 Herman Cohen, *The History of Speech Communication: The Emergence of a Discipline, 1914–1945* (Annandale: Speech Communication Association, 1994).

34 Gerald Graff, *Professing Literature: An Institutional History* (Chicago: U of Chicago P, 1989); D. G. Myers, *The Elephants Teach: Creative Writing Since 1880* (Englewood Cliffs: Prentice Hall, 1996).

35 Arthur Bochner and Eric Eisenberg, "Legitimizing Speech Communication: An Examination of Coherence and Cohesion in the Development of the Discipline," *Speech Communication in the 20th Century*, ed. Thomas W. Benson (Carbondale: Southern Illinois UP, 1985), 303–04. For a comprehensive bibliography on the rise of English studies and its various disciplinary

spin-offs, see Maureen Daly Goggin, "The Tangled Roots of Literature, Speech Communication, Linguistics, Rhetoric/Composition, and Creative Writing: A Selected Bibliography on the History of English Studies," *Rhetoric Society Quarterly* 29.4 (1999): 63–87.

36 Steven Mailloux, "Disciplinary Identities: On the Rhetorical Paths between English and Communication Studies," *Rhetoric Society Quarterly* 30, no. 2 (2000): 10.

37 For a fuller history of communication, see Beard; Thomas W. Benson, ed. *Speech Communication in the 20th Century* (Carbondale: Southern Illinois UP, 1985); Cohen; William F. Eadie, "Stories We Tell: Fragmentation and Convergence in Communication Disciplinary History," *The Review of Communication* 11, no. 3 (2011): 161–76; Richard Leo Enos, "How Rhetoric Journals Are Shaping Our Community," *Philosophy and Rhetoric* 28 (1995): 431–36; Pat J. Gehrke and William M. Keith, "Introduction: A Brief History of the National Communication Association," *A Century of Communication Studies: The Unfinished Conversation*, ed. Pat J. Gehrke and William M. Keith (New York: Routledge, 2015), 1–25; Mailloux; Gerry Philipsen, "The Early Career Rise of 'Speech' in Some Disciplinary Discourse, 1914–1946," *Quarterly Journal of Speech* 93, no. 3 (2007): 352–54; Gerald M. Phillips and Julia T. Woods, eds., *Speech Communication: Essays to Commemorate the 75th Anniversary of the Speech Communication Association* (Carbondale: Southern Illinois UP, 1990); Karl R. Wallace, ed., *A History of Speech Education in America: Background Studies* (New York: Appleton-Century-Crofts, 1954); William Work and Robert C. Jeffrey, *The Past Is Prologue: A 75th Anniversary History of the Speech Communication Association* (Annandale: National Communication Association, 1989).

38 Beginning in 1914 until 1922 the organization was titled National Academic Teachers of Public Speaking. Then speech became the master term for communication. Between 1923 and 1945, the field renamed itself as the National Association of Teachers of Speech; between 1946 and 1969 the association again changed its name to the Speech Association of America; between 1970 and 1996 it was renamed the Speech Communication Association; then in 1997 amid debate it was yet again renamed the National Communication Association as interest in written rhetoric became stronger. For more details, see the National Communication Association website on its history www.natcom.org/about-nca/what-nca/nca-history/brief-history-nca.

39 Diana George and John Trimbur, "'The Communication Battle,' or Whatever Happened to the 4th C?" *College Composition and Communication* 50 (1999): 682–98.

40 Charles W. Roberts, "Editorial Comment," *College Composition and Communication* 1, no. 2 (1950): 22.

41 Carole Blair, "'We Are All Just Prisoners Here of Our Own Device': Rhetoric in Speech Communication After Wingspread," *Making and Unmaking the Prospects for Rhetoric: Selected Papers from the 1996 Rhetoric Society of America Conference*, ed. Theresa Enos, Richard McNabb, Carolyn Miller, and Roxanne Mountford (Mahwah: Lawrence Erlbaum, 1997), 29–36; Goggin, *Authoring*.

42 Blair; Nelms and Goggin; Richard Young and Maureen Daly Goggin, "Some Issues in Dating the Birth of the New Rhetoric in Departments of English: A Contribution to a Developing Historiography," *Defining the New Rhetorics*, ed. Theresa Enos and Stuart Brown (Newbury Park: SAGE Publication, 1993), 22–43.

43 Young and Goggin.

44 Wayne Booth, "The Revival of Rhetoric," *PMLA* 80 (1965): 12.

45 This was a collection of papers from two landmark conferences in 1970: The Wingspread Conference and the National Conference on Rhetoric.

46 Edward P. J. Corbett, "The Usefulness of Classical Rhetoric," *College Composition and Communication* 14 (1963): 162–64; Edwin Black, *Rhetorical Criticism: A Study in Method* (New York: Macmillan, 1965); Booth; James Murphy, "The Four Faces of Rhetoric," *College Composition and Communication* 17 (1966): 55–59; Robert L. Scott, "On Viewing Rhetoric as Epistemic," *Central States Speech Journal* 18 (1967): 9–17; Lloyd Bitzer, "The Rhetorical Situation," *Philosophy and Rhetoric* 1 (1968): 1–14; Lloyd Bitzer and Edwin Black, *The Prospect of Rhetoric: Report of the National Development Project* (Englewood Cliffs: Prentice Hall, 1971); Chaïm Perelman

and L. Olbrechts-Tyteca, *The New Rhetoric: A Treatise on Argumentation*, trans. John Wilkinson and Purcell Weaver (Notre Dame: U of Notre Dame P, 1971).

47 Roxanne Mountford, "A Century After the Divorce: Challenges to a Rapprochement between Speech Communication and English," *The Sage Handbook of Rhetorical Studies*, ed. Andrea A. Lunsford, Kirt H. Wilson, and Rosa A. Eberly (Thousand Oaks: SAGE, 2009), 408.

48 See correspondence among members in W. Ross Winterowd, "RSA: Genesis and Direction," *Newsletter of the Rhetoric Society of America* (September 1971): 3–6.

49 Sharon Crowley, "Communication Skills: A Brief Rapprochement between Speech and English Rhetoricians," *Rhetoric Society Quarterly* 34 (Winter 2004): 89–103; Andrea A. Lunsford, Kirt H. Wilson, and Rosa A. Eberly, "Introduction: Rhetorics and Roadmaps," *The Sage Handbook of Rhetorical Studies*; Andrea A. Lunsford, Kirt H. Wilson, and Rosa A. Eberly (Thousand Oaks: SAGE, 2009): xi–xxix; Mountford.

50 Mountford.

51 Thomas Miller, "Disciplinary Identification/Public Identities: A Response to Mailloux, Leff, and Keith," *Rhetoric Society Quarterly* 31 (2001): 107–08. See Mailloux; Michael Leff, "Rhetorical Disciplines and Rhetorical Disciplinarity: A Response to Mailloux," *Rhetoric Society Quarterly* 30 (2000): 83–94; Martin Nystrand, "Distinguishing Formative and Receptive Contexts Formation of Composition Studies: A Response to Mailloux," *Rhetoric Society Quarterly* 31 (2001): 92–104; Keith William, "Identity, Rhetoric and Myth: A Response to Mailloux and Leff," *Rhetoric Society Quarterly*, 30, no. 4 (2000): 95–106.

Index

ACCUPLACER 183
accuracy topos 248, 249, 250, 262
addressivity 191–3
aesthetics 46–7, 57, 64–9, 72–3, 335
affiliations 237n4
Agathon 284
agency 114–5, 131–64; agent and 188–9;
    attribution of 19507; automation and
    183–98; concept of 146; conditions for
    136; defined 145; doctrines of 143–4;
    human 329, 330; ideology of 132–4,
    140, 144–5, 159; illusion of 134–5,
    146, 148–9, 155n12, 196; interaction
    and 193–6; of machines 195; material
    195; moral 139; ontology of 148;
    ontotheology and 140–4; pedagogical
    concerns about 189; performance/
    performativity and 190–1; possession
    of 144–6; rhetorical studies and
    187–8, 189; significance of question
    of 132–4
agent function 194–5
agents *see* rhetorical agents
AIDS Memorial quilt 203
Alcidamas 283, 290
Aldington, Richard 59
alienation, from nature 330
Alliance for Rhetorical Societies (ARS)
    115–6, 137–8
Althorp, Charles 108
ambivalence 333–5, 339, 340
Amin, Ash 170–1, 173
amnesia 201, 206
anger 253
An Inconvenient Truth (Gore) 329,
    333–4, 339
Anthropocene 329–30
anxiety: about public speaking 193; birth
    event and 229
Appelbaum, L. Gregory 247–65
"Applications of the Terminology"
    (Burke) 72–3
Archias 286
archives 201–18
Aristotelian narrative of linearity 46–7,
    48, 49, 50
Aristotle 46–7, 49, 70, 195; on
    epideictic 94–109; on mimesis 285;

Nichomachean Ethics 101–3; Posterior
    Analytics 100; on rhetoric 306;
    Rhetoric 253, 280; *Rhetoric* 97–101
ARS *see* Alliance for Rhetorical Societies
art 69–71; emotion and 69–70, 78n12; of
    rhetoric 305–7, 315, 316; social nature
    of 68; society and 71–4
artists 56, 58, 65–6, 69–72, 286; society
    and 71–3
Asperger's syndrome 258–60, 265n5
assessment technologies 183–96
Astell, Mary 126
atheism 153, 156n17
Athenian democracy 95–7, 102–3, 303,
    310–1
audience 21, 69–70; agency and 133,
    190–1; camera-mediated 192–3;
    in communication models 167; in
    computer-mediated environments 83,
    86–7; emotions of 65; of epideictic
    performance 105–6; function of 101,
    104–5; imaginary 21; interaction/
    interactivity with 193–6; mechanized
    191–3; perceptions of 168; in public
    speaking 186, 191–6
Austin, J. L. 18
Austin, Texas 174–8, 180
authorship: collective 204–5; on Internet
    83, 88–9
autism 256–60, 265n5, 265n9
automation, of assessment 183–98
automatism 152
autonomous agent 132, 144, 146–8, 150,
    159, 163
AutoSpeech-Easy 184–93

Bakke, John 38
Ballif, Michelle 5, 45–53
Barnett, Scot 325
basic writing 31
Baudrillard, Jean 148
Beard, David 346–7
Bell, Clive 68–9, 78n12
Bellah, Robert 95
Bennett, Jane 325–6, 330–3
bias 249, 250, 251
Biesecker, Barbara 167, 225, 301
Bildungsroman 49

binaries 47, 50
Bing, Peter 290
Birch, Thomas 324–5
Bitzer, Lloyd F. 166–7
Bizzell, Patricia 119–30
Blair, Carole 278
Bleuler, Eugene 333
blogging 206
blood oxygenation level dependent
    (BOLD) activity 249–50, 258
Booth, Wayne 2–3, 351
Borch-Jacobsen, Mikkel 228, 230,
    232, 234
Bowling Green State University
    Conference on Rhetoric and the
    Modern World 32
Boyle, Casey 245
brain imaging 249–51, 261–3
Brooks, Van Wyck 78n14
Brown, Stuart 326, 327
Bryant, Donald C. 2, 38
Buber, Martin 37
Bundy, McGeorge 37
Burke, Kenneth 43, 196, 335; career of
    55–6; *Counter-Statement* 54–75; on
    courtship 236n3; on Flaubert 57–8,
    67–9; Freud and 221–2, 236n1; on
    Gide 66–8; on Gourmont 59–61; on
    identification 221–8, 235, 237n4, 255;
    on Mann 66–8; modernism and 54–6,
    61, 64–6, 72–4, 76n2; on nature of
    form 61–4, 68–70, 74; on Pater 58–9;
    on personality 238n9; on rhetoric
    222–3; on suggestibility 232–4
Bush, George 166, 168
Butler, Judith 189, 228

Callicles 307–8
camera-mediated communication 192–3
Campbell, Joseph 49
Campbell, Karlyn Kohrs 156n14
capitalism 94–5, 202
Caputo, John 151
Cesa, Kathie 114
Chauvin, Remy 173
Cicero 280, 282, 286–7, 295–7, 307, 315
cities 170–1, 173–8
civic engagement 150
civic participation 188
civic rhetoric 302
civic virtues 108
Cixous, Helene 49, 50, 51

Clark, Gregory 113–4
Clark, Lynne 145
classical education 343–4
classical rhetoric 301–19
climate change 323, 327–9
Clinton, Bill 107
CMC *see* computer-mediated
    communication
collective authorship 204–5
College Composition and
    Communication (CCC) 350
college students 32–3
Collins, Vicki Tolar 126
Commager, Henry Steele 36
commemoration 201–2, 216; *see also*
    memory
commercial culture 206
communication: camera-mediated
    192–3; computer-mediated 82–91;
    interpersonal 82; models of 165–6;
    public 165–6
communications course 1
community 169–70
composition: defined 24; ecological
    process of 172; process of 26–8;
    teaching of 24–31
computer-mediated communication
    (CMC) 82–91
Condit, Celeste 196
Conference on College Composition and
    Communication 1
Connors, Robert J. 347
conscience, voice of 234–6
constitutive rules 18–9
constraints 15–22
contagion 177, 232
conventions 15, 17–21
"cookies" 86
Corbett, Edward P. J. 4
counter-rhetorics 179
Counter-Statement (Burke) 54–75;
    aim of 56–7; "Applications of the
    Terminology" 72–3; "Lexicon
    Rhetoricae" 62–5, 68–71; "Mann and
    Gide" 66–8; "The Poetic Process"
    62–5, 68, 69, 77n11; "Program" 71–2;
    "Psychology and Form" 61–5, 69,
    70, 77n9, 77n11; "The Status of Art"
    72–3, 78n18; "Three Adepts of 'Pure'
    Literature" 57–61, 67–8
courtship 236n3
Cowley, Malcolm 65

credibility, on Internet 89
CriterionSM Online Writing
　Evaluation 184
Croce, Benedetto 56, 59, 64, 65m66, 76n6
Cronon, William 323–4, 326, 330, 333,
　334, 339–40
Crusius, Timothy 223, 224
Crutzen, Paul 329

Dadas 71, 72, 73
Davis, Diane 221–40
decision making 252–3
deep ambivalence 326, 330, 333–5,
　339, 340
Deleuze, Gilles 173
deliberative discourse 107
democracy 95–7, 102–3, 303, 310–1
Derrida, Jacques 46, 142–4, 147, 151
desire 232–4, 251–5
determinism 149
dialogue 15–6
Dialogues (Plato) 16
digital archives 201–18
digital technology 133
Dionysius of Halicarnassus 282, 295
disciplines 2
discourse 143; deliberative 107; epideictic
　94–109; Internet 82–93; objectification
　of 280; theories of 167–8
dissociation 235
dissociative method 60–1
dramatism 78n17
duBois, Page 49

Eberly, Rosa 114
ectoplasm 144–6
Edbauer, Jenny 165–81
editing process 22
educational mission 137
education system 343–4
ego 222, 228, 232, 238n17
Eliot, T. S. 59
Eliza effect 195
Elliott, A. Marshall 345
emotion 125–9, 252–5, 262
empathy 225, 227, 248, 253–60, 262,
　265n9
English studies 345–8
Enos, Richard 120–1, 278–9
environmental rhetoric 322–41
Epicureans 315–6
epideictic 94–109, 340

Epistles (Plato) 302, 308–10, 318n4,
　318n5
ethopoeia 195
ethos 89, 195
exigence 168
exigencies 343–53

False Memory Syndrome 239n19
Favorinus 291–3
feminism 188–9
feminist communities 124–5, 128
feminist historiography 45–53, 114,
　119–30
feminist research 119–30
Ferguson, Bruce 208
Ferreira-Buckley, Linda 121
First Great Awakening 150
flattery 305, 313, 316–7
Flaubert, Gustave 57–8, 60, 67–9
Folz, Bruce 323
Foote, Kenneth 212
Ford, Andrew 280
form, nature of 61–4, 68–70, 74
Foucault, Michel 142–4, 147, 153, 154n1,
　154n5, 155n13, 244; on parrēsia
　301–19; on Philodemus 315; on
　Plato 308; on Plutarch 316–7; on
　psychagogy 315; on Quintilian 313–4,
　315; on rhetoric 305–7
Fraser, Nancy 95
Fredla, James 278
Freud, Sigmund 65, 73, 78n14, 225,
　234; Burke and 221–2, 236n1;
　hypnosuggestive technique 230–2; on
　identification 221, 222, 228–32, 235,
　241n23; on melancholia 238n17; on
　voice of conscience 234–6
Freudian narrative of triangularity 46–50
Friedman, Ted 83
Friston, Karl 251
functional magnetic resonance imaging
　(fMRI) 247, 249–51, 255
functional regions-of-interest (fROI)
　approach 250–1
funeral orations 94

Gaines, Robert 279
Gale, Xin Liu 121–4, 127, 128
Garver, Eugene 13, 41
Geisler, Cheryl 131–8, 141–2, 144–51,
　158–64
gender differences, in online discourse 86

Gide, Andre 66–8
Gillis, John 202, 206
Glenn, Cheryl 121–5
Goffman, Erving 190–1
Goggin, Maureen Daly 4, 343–56
Gore, Al 329
Gorgias (Plato) 307–8
Gorgias at Delphi statue 294
Gorz, Andre 51n15
Gourmont, Remy de 57, 59–61, 77n6, 78n13
graduate students 32–3
Graff, Richard 279
graphic rhetors/rhetoric 278, 280, 283, 285–6, 288–97
Greene, Ronald Walter 150, 156n15, 187
Greenwich Village 54–5
Grice, H. P. 19
Grimaldi, William 100
Gross, Daniel 253
group formation 231–2
Guattari, Felix 50, 173, 330
Gunn, Joshua 139–56, 155n10, 155n12, 158–62
Gurak, Laura 83, 85–6, 88, 89, 90
Guth, Hans P. 12, 24–31

Habermas, Jurgen 94–5
Habinek, Thomas 290
habitus 135
Hamlyn, D. W. 100
Hardy, C. D. 348
Harman, Graham 325, 330–3
Haskins, Ekaterina 201–18
Hauser, Gerard A. 94–112, 115, 189
Hawhee, Debra 243
Heath, Robert 73
Heidegger, 140, 144, 147, 151
Henry, Madeleine 121–3, 142
Herndl, Carl 326, 327
Herzberg, Bruce 119
Hicks, Granville 65, 66, 73
higher education 343–4, 345–9
history: digital archives 201–18; feminist 45–53, 114, 119–30; oration and 36–8; revisionist 121; of rhetoric 119–30
homo dialecticus 225
hubris 328, 329
humanism 146–7, 154n1, 160–1
Hunt, Everett Lee 9n6, 12–3, 32–9

Hunt, Th. W. 346
Huyssen, Andreas 205–6
Hyde, Michael 197
hypertext 83–9, 204, 205
hypnosuggestive technique 230–2
hypotaxis 47
hysteria 231, 232–3

ideal counselor 302
idealism 325
identification 221–40, 255; dramatizing 222–8; failure of 235–6; primary 222, 228–30; rhetorical 223–4
identities, on Internet 87
identity 223–6
ideology 70, 76n4; of agency 132–4, 140, 144–5, 159; failure of 234–5
illocutionary acts 18
imaginary audiences 21
individual 225–6, 229–30, 237n8
inductive reasoning 254
Institutio Oratoria (Quintilian) 313–4
intellectual property rights 82
intellectuals 33
Intelligent Essay Assessor 184
"intense world" hypothesis 265n9
interaction/interactivity 193–6, 205–7
Internet: archives 201–18; authorship on 83, 88–9; growth of 82; identities on 87; user-generated content 206–7
Internet discourse: conformity in 90; credibility of 89; gender differences in 86; rhetorical criticism of 82–93; rhetorical patterns in 89–91
interpersonal communication 82
interruptions 16
Isocrates 280–6, 289, 290, 293–5, 306, 310–2, 318n6

Jack, Jordynn 247–65
Jameson, Fredric 225
Jardine, Alice 51n12
Jarratt, Susan 43, 121–5, 244–5
Jasinski, James 244
Jenniger, Philipp 107–8
Johnstone, Christopher 279
Johnstone, Henry, Jr. 2
judgment 101

Keith, Philip 41–2
Kennerly, Michele 244, 276–98
kinetic energy 191, 196

Kitto, H. D. F. 97
knowledge, genetic account of 100
krisis 101

Lacan, Jacques 142–4, 147, 152–3, 188
Lacoue-Labarthe, Philippe 227
Lamp, Kathleen 279
Landow, George 83, 88, 205
Lanham, Richard 83
Larson, Richard L. 3–4, 12
Latour, Bruno 327, 341n5
Leff, Michael C. 115, 148–9, 190, 193–4
Leitch, Vincent 76n2
Levinas, 240n21, 241n23
Lévy, Carlos 303
Lewiecki-Wilson, Cynthia 248
lexicon, of artistry 279–81
"Lexicon Rhetoricae" (Burke) 62–5,
    68–71
liberty 16–7
Liggett, Helen 179
Light, James 54
linearity 46–7, 49
linguistics, rules and conventions of 15,
    17–20
literary criticism 2, 32, 61, 129, 280, 351
literary studies 348–9
literature, society and 72–3
logic 46, 48, 50, 185, 248, 253
Loraux, Nicole 94
Lowell, Amy 59
Lowenthal, David 201–2
Lucian 276–7
Lundberg, Christian 139–56, 158–62
Lunsford, Andrea 190
Lybarger, Scott 166, 168
Lyotard, Jean-Francois 107
Lysias 283–4

machine scoring 183–90
MacLeish, Archibald 36–7
Mailloux, Steven 349
Mann, Thomas 66–8, 78n15
"Mann and Gide" (Burke) 66–8
Manovich, Lev 206, 218n5
Mantovani, Giuseppi 83
Marback, Richard 180
Massumi, Brian 179
masterpiece 281–5
mastery 277, 281–5
material agency 195
materiality 278–80, 296–7

melancholia 238n17, 334
memorials 202–4, 216, 289, 293
memory 277, 292–6; digital 204–17; false
    239n19; public 201–18
memory work 202, 205, 216
m-heuristic 277, 279, 296–7
Miller, Carolyn 183–200, 243, 244
Miller, Steven E. 90
mimesis 227, 277, 285–9
mindblindness 257, 265n9
mirror neurons 226–7
MLA *see* Modern Language Association
mock rock *topos* 276–98
modernism 54–6, 61, 64–6, 72–4, 76n2
Modern Language Association (MLA)
    345–7
monologue 15–7, 22
monomyth 49
monuments 202, 216, 293, 294
Moore, Barrington 96
moral agency 139
morality, public 103–6, 108
Morton, Tim 333–5, 337
Mountford, Roxanne 352–3
movement 277, 289–92
Munson, Gorham 55, 65, 66
Murphy, James J. 17
Museum of the City of New York
    208–9
museums 202, 203, 208–9, 216
MY Access! 184

NAMES project 203
narrative paradigms 46–51
National Association of Academic
    Teachers of Public Speaking 347–8
National Climate Assessment (NCA) 323
National Communication Association
    (NCA) 11
National Council of Teachers of English
    (NCTE) 1, 347–50
naturalistic fallacy 149
natural language processing 183
NCTE *see* National Council of Teachers
    of English
networks 169–70, 173
neuroeconomics 252–3
neuroessentialism 261, 263
neurological difference 256–60
neurons 226–7, 252–3
neuropolicy 261, 263
neurorealism 260–1, 263

neurorhetorics 244, 247–65; brain imaging 249–51; future directions 262–4; of reason and desire 251–5
neuroscience, in popular media 260–2, 264
New Criticism 56, 76n2
New Humanists 59, 64, 71, 73, 76n5
new materialism 325–6, 330–5, 339–40
Newsletter of the Rhetoric Society of America 3, 12
Ney, James W. 30
Nichomachean Ethics (Aristotle) 101–3
Nicols, Marie Hochmuth 37
Nietzsche, Friedrich 51n14
nobility 103–4
Nora, Pierre 202

object domain 2
object-oriented ontology (OOO) 325–6, 330–5, 339–40
obsolescence 205–6
Oedipal narrative 48–9, 222, 228, 230
O'Neill, James, M. 348
On Frank Criticism (Philodemus) 314–5
Ong, Walter 21, 123, 125
online communication 43, 82–91
On Rhetoric (Philodemus) 315–6
ontotheology 140–4
orators 35–6
Ouija Board metaphor 139–41, 158–63
Owens, Louis 322–6, 329–30, 339–40

panic-fear 232
papyrus 277, 278, 296
parrēsia 301–19; in Isocrates 310–2; Philodemus on 314–5, 317; Plato on 307–10; Plutarch on 316–7; Quintilian on 313–4; in relationship to rhetoric 303–7; in *Rhetorica Ad Herennium* 312–3
passivity 217n7
past: democratization of 205–6; remembrance of 201–2; *see also* history
Pater, Walter 57, 58–9, 73
pedagogy 145, 179–81, 343–4
perception, of audience 168
performance/performativity 190–1
performatives 18
personality 238n9
persuasion 222–4, 251–5
Phaedrus (Plato) 16, 46, 231, 283, 286, 290–1, 293, 294, 305, 316

phallogocentrism 49–50
Phelps, Louise Weatherbee 167–8
Philodemus 314–7
philosophical schools 314–5
philosophy 302, 331
phronêsis 101–3, 110n9
place 165, 169–71, 172
Plato 63–4, 283–93, 302; *Dialogues* 16; *Epistles* 7 and 8 308–10, 318n4, 318n5; *Gorgias* 307–8; *Phaedrus* 46, 231, 283, 286, 290–1, 293, 294, 305, 316
Plutarch 316–7
"The Poetic Process" (Burke) 62–5, 68, 69, 77n11
poetics 49
Poetics (Aristotle) 46
political relations 94–109
Porter, James I. 280
positron emission tomography (PET) 249
possession 144–6
Posterior Analytics (Aristotle) 100
posthumanism 7, 142, 143, 146–51, 154n4
postmodern agent 159–61
postmodern theory 122, 132, 142–4, 146–8, 154n8, 155n13, 159–63
potential energy 191
Pound, Ezra 59, 77n6
practical wisdom 101–3
Prelli, Lawrence 249
preparatory work 30–1
primary identification 222, 228–30
"Program" (Burke) 71–2
promises 18–9
Provincetown Players 54
prudence 101–3
psychagogy 314–6
psychoanalytical theory 47–9, 69, 153, 191
psychological universals 63–4
psychology 61–2, 65, 77n11
"Psychology and Form" (Burke) 61–5, 69, 70, 77n9, 77n11
public 165–6, 167
public communication 165–6
public discourse: in computer-mediated environments 82–91; epideictic 94–109
public memory 201–18
public morality 103–6, 108
public opinion 94–5

public speaking 17, 21; anxiety about 193;
    audience in 186, 191–6; automated
    assessment of 184–90; performativity
    of 190–1
public sphere 94–5, 106–9, 109n3

Q question 83
quantitative precision 249
Quarterly Journal of Public Speaking 348
Quarterly Journal of Speech 11–2
Quintilian 254–5, 280, 287, 305, 307,
    313–5

readers 22, 70
realism 166, 168, 325
reason 251–5, 262
recitation 344
Recovered Memory Therapy (RMT)
    239n19
re/dressing histories 45–53
regulative rules 18
remedial instruction 30–1
remembrance 201–4, 216
research: feminist 119–30; in
    neurorhetorics 247–65
responsibility 151–2
Reston, James 36
revision 22
revisionist history 121
Reynolds, Nedra 170
rhetoric: aim of 222–3; ancient 96–8,
    277–98; as art 305, 306–7, 315, 316;
    civic 302; classical tradition 301–19;
    concept of 167–8; counter-rhetorics
    179; distribution of 171–4, 178–81;
    environmental 322–41; feminist
    research in history of 119–30;
    field of 32–9; Foucault on 305–7;
    importance of 37–8; intellectual
    and material spaces for 343–51;
    parrēsia in relationship to 303–7;
    performance dimension of 190–1;
    political character of 94–109;
    production of 179–81; publicness 168;
    teaching of 148–9, 161–3, 189, 346–8;
    transdisciplinary nature of 244–5
Rhetoric (Aristotle) 97–101, 253, 280
Rhetorica Ad Herennium 312–3
rhetorical action 15
rhetorical agency *see* agency
rhetorical agent 135, 144–6, 152, 159–61,
    188–9, 194–5

rhetorical archeology 278–9
rhetorical criticism: ancient Greek 283–5;
    of Internet discourse 82–93
rhetorical ecologies 168–72, 177–81
rhetorical freedom 16–7
rhetorical materialism 244
rhetorical situations 166–81
rhetorical strategies 20, 22
rhetorical studies 2, 115–6, 131;
    agency in 187–8, 189; directions for
    future of 136–8; history of 344–51;
    neuroscience and 247–65; trends in
    244–5
rhetorical theory 20
Rhetoric Society Monthly (RSM) 245
Rhetoric Society of America (RSA) 3–4,
    11, 116, 343, 351–3
Rhetoric Society Quarterly (RSQ):
    in 1990s 41–4; in 2000s 113–7;
    2010-present 243–6; creation of
    1–4, 343, 351–3; early years of 11–3;
    professionalization of 41–3; special
    issues 243–4
Ricoeur, Paul 107
Rivers, Nathaniel A. 322–41
Rogers, Hester 126
Roosevelt, Franklin 37
Rosenberg, Harold 61–2
Rosenfield, Lawrence 340
Rowland, John Carter 2, 3
Royster, Jacqueline Jones 116, 121, 126–9
RSA *see* Rhetoric Society of America
RSM *see* Rhetorical Society Monthly
RSQ *see* Rhetoric Society Quarterly
Rueckert, William H. 74
rules 15, 17–20

SAA *see* Speech Association of America
Sappho 105
Schindler, G. 180
science 244; neuroscience 247–65
Scott, Fred Newton 347
sculpture 286–9, 291–7
séance 140–1, 147–8
Searle, John 18–9
Second Great Awakening 139, 140,
    150–1
Selzer, Jack 54–81, 221
sender-receiver models of
    communication 165–6
sentences 28–30
September 11, 2001 114–5

The September 11 Digital Archive 201, 207–17
sexuality 47–8
Shaughnessy, Mina P. 30–1
Shaviro, Steven 169–70
signification 142–3
situational contexts 166–81
situs 169–71, 173
Skinnell, Ryan 343–56
Smith, Craig 166, 168
Smith, Nelson J. 1–3, 12
Smith, Paul 50, 188–9
social justice 188
social theory 106
Socrates 16, 46, 283–4, 287–93, 305, 307–8, 316
Solon 96
speaking situations 21, 190–1
specialization 1–2, 9n6, 33
speech, vs. writing 21–2
speech acts 18, 20
speech act theory 15, 18
Speech Association of America (SAA) 1, 349
speech education 32–9, 345, 347–50
speeches 37–8
spiritualism 139, 140
Spivak, Gayatri 46, 50, 51n13
statues 285, 289–97
"The Status of Art" (Burke) 72–3, 78n18
Stein, Gertrude 69
Stevenson, Adlai 36
story telling 17
Strawson, P. F. 18
student writing 25–6
subjectivity 153, 154n5, 154n6
"suggect" 232–4
suggestion/suggestibility 230–4, 239n18, 239n19
Sutherland, Christine Mason 125–6
Swearingen, C. Jan 113
Symbolists 59, 60, 64–5, 66, 73, 78n12
sympathy 225, 227
Syverson, Margaret 172
Szerszynski, Bronislaw 328–9, 334, 339

Tauber, Lacey 175
teacher, role of 100
techno-liberal-arts 133
technological elitism 90–1
Tell, Dave 4–5
temporality 206
text-stone relations 277–98

"Three Adepts of 'Pure' Literature" (Burke) 57–61, 67–8
Thrift, Nigel 170–1, 173
Too, Yun Lee 297
transcendence 140, 156n15
Trollhunter 326, 335–9, 340
Turkle, Sherry 87
Twain, Mark 78n14

user-generated content 206–7

Valery, Paul 61
Vatz, Richard 166
Veeder, Rex 41, 42
vernacular commemoration 202–3, 207–8
video cameras 192–3
Vietnam Veterans Memorial 203–4
viral economy 173, 178
virtue 108, 109
vital materialism 330
voice of conscience 234–6

Walker, Jeffrey 41, 42, 113, 193
Walzer, Arthur E. 301–19
war 223
Warner, Michael 165
Warnick, Barbara 82–93, 204–5
Warren, Austin 79n19
Web: hypertext on 83–8; *see also* Internet
Welch, 133
Wells, Ida B. 126
Whitehorne, J. E. G. 293
wilderness 322–7, 333, 339
wild objects 326, 330, 334–5
Williams, Raymond 172
Winterowd, Ross 1–3
Wodiczko, Krzystof 203
women, feminist histiography and 45–53
Woolbert, Charles H. 9n6, 34–5, 348
WritePlacer Plus 183
writers 21–2
writing: automated assessment of 183–90; ecological process of 172; as performance 191; vs. speech 21–2; teaching of 12, 24–31, 349
writing assignments 27–8
written rhetoric 21–2

Xenophon 97

Yoos, George E. 4, 12, 15–23, 41, 352, 353
Young, Richard 9n12

Made in the USA
Columbia, SC
12 May 2021